THE DICTIONARY OF THE ESOTERIC

The DICTIONARY of the ESOTERIC

3000 Entries on the Mystical and Occult Traditions

NEVILL DRURY

MOTILAL BANARSIDASS PUBLISHERS
PRIVATE LIMITED • DELHI

First Indian Edition: Delhi, 2004

First Published in 2002 by Watkins Publishing, UK.

ISBN: 81-208-1989-6

Also available at:

MOTILAL BANARSIDASS

41 U.A. Bungalow Road, Jawahar Nagar, Delhi 110 007
8 Mahalaxmi Chamber, 22 Bhulabhai Desai Road, Mumbai 400 026
120 Royapettah High Road, Mylapore, Chennai 600 004
236, 9th Main III Block, Jayanagar, Bangalore 560 011
Sanas Plaza, 1302 Baji Rao Road, Pune 411 002
8 Camac Street, Kolkata 700 017
Ashok Rajpath, Patna 800 004
Chowk, Varanasi 221 001

FOR SALE IN SOUTH-EAST ASIA ONLY

Printed in India

BY JAINENDRA PRAKASH JAIN AT SHRI JAINENDRA PRESS,
A-45 NARAINA, PHASE-I, NEW DELHI 110 028
AND PUBLISHED BY NARENDRA PRAKASH JAIN FOR
MOTILAL BANARSIDASS PUBLISHERS PRIVATE LIMITED,
BUNGALOW ROAD, DELHI 110 007

ACKNOWLEDGEMENTS

I would like to acknowledge the pioneering work of Lewis Spence, who published the first major encyclopaedia of the occult in 1920. Without Lewis Spence, and the many other occult writers who have documented the world of magic and the paranormal since his time, the task of compiling a dictionary of this size would have been virtually impossible. I am also indebted to Annie Wilson of Watkins Books, for editing and proof-reading the revised text proofs.

This book is dedicated to the memory of the
Welsh mystic and author, Arthur Machen
(1863–1947)

PREFACE

When I began researching the Western "occult" philosophical traditions in the late 1960s it was difficult to obtain concise and up-to-date information on the various symbols, esoteric terminologies and personalities that made the world of mysticism and magic so intriguing. The principal sourcebook was a learned tome by Lewis Spence titled *An Encyclopaedia of Occultism*. This work, which was subtitled "A Compendium of Information on the Occult Sciences, Occult Personalities, Psychic Science, Magic, Demonology, Spiritism, Mysticism and Metaphysics" was an excellent compilation and remains so today. However it had first been published in London in 1920, and although it was reissued, unchanged, in 1960, it could hardly hope to offer information on the contemporary mystical and occult revival which was then well under way.

It was not until the late 1960s that the Human Potential Movement gathered momentum and terms like "transpersonal psychology" and "holistic health" became part of everyday usage. More recently there has been a resurgence of interest in Wicca and Goddess worship, and feminine aspects of esoteric spirituality. Clearly there has been substantial ground to make up since Lewis Spence's day.

The Dictionary of the Esoteric was compiled in order to provide a contemporary perspective on both the Western and Eastern esoteric traditions. Many of the entries – and there are over 3,000 of them – are cross-referenced: words in bold letters are explained in further detail elsewhere in the Dictionary.

This volume was first published by Harper & Row in 1985 under the title *Dictionary of Mysticism and the Occult* and republished in a revised edition in 1992 by ABC-Clio in the United States and Prism Press in Britain. This new edition has been revised throughout – especially in terms of updating the biographies of leading figures in the field who have died during the intervening period – and a number of corrections and new entries have also been included.

Nevill Drury
March 2002

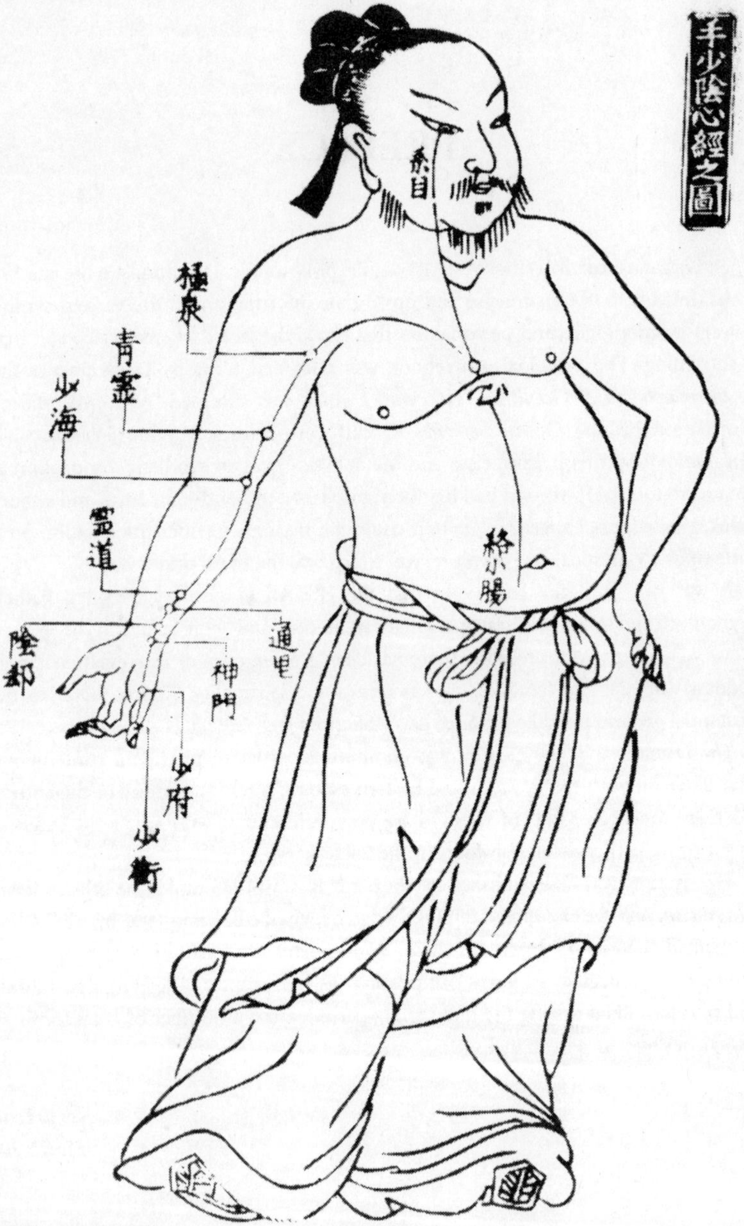

ACUPUNCTURE: A traditional Chinese drawing showing an acupuncture meridian, or ch'i *channel. The body is enlivened by the flow of* ch'i, *or life-force.*

A

A.·. A.·. The abbreviated form for Argenteum Astrum, or Silver Star, the magical order founded by **Aleister Crowley**. Crowley established this order in 1904 after leaving the **Hermetic Order of the Golden Dawn**.

Aah In ancient Egypt, one of the names of the **moon-god**.

Ab The ancient Egyptian term for the heart. It was regarded as the source of life and the seat of the conscience; hence it was crucial that the heart be preserved in the tomb.

Abaddon The name given by St. John in the Book of Revelation to the chief of the **demons** of the seventh hierarchy. Abaddon is also known as the "king of the grasshoppers" and the "destroying angel".

Abaris The Sethian high **priest** of **Apollo**. Abaris claimed to be able to ride through the air on a golden arrow given to him by his god. The priest foretold future events, banished disease, and produced the so-called Palladium **talisman**, which he sold to the Trojans to protect their town from assault.

Abayakora, Cyrus D.F. (1912–) The son of a Ceylonese hereditary chieftain, he learned to read **horoscopes** inscribed on palm leaves and believed he could divine the future. In 1940, before either Haile Selassie or General Charles de Gaulle had gained prominence, he predicted that they would achieve power later in life. He also claims to have predicted the assassinations of Gandhi, Mussolini, and John F. Kennedy.

Aben-Ragel Fifth-century Arabian astrologer. Born in Cordova, Aben-Ragel produced a book of **horoscopes** later published in Latin under the title *De judiciis seu fatis stellarum* (Venice, 1485).

Aberdeen Witches A group of **witches** in northeast Scotland who were persecuted at the Aberdeen Assizes during 1596–1597. The witches were organized in **covens** – groups of thirteen – and each member had a specific task in the magical arts. One of the accused, Helen Rogie, modelled figures of her victims in lead and wax; while another, Isobel Ogg, was said to be able to raise storms through **sorcery**. When the Assizes closed in April 1597, twenty-four people – twenty-three women and one man – were found guilty of **witchcraft** and executed.

Abiger A grand duke of **Hades** with a particular knowledge of matters pertaining to war. According to Wierius (**Johannes Wier**), he is a handsome, armoured knight with sixty of the "infernal regions" at his command.

Abominable Snowman A legendary creature who, according to local **folklore**, stalks the snow-covered slopes of the Himalayas. Regarded with horror by the Sherpas, the abominable snowman is said to be a half-animal and half-human creature with reddish hair. It is also referred to as the "yeti".

Aborigines, Australian Nomadic hunter-gatherers, many of whom now live in remote tribal reserves in northern and central Australia. Aborigines have a strong magical tradition, believing they can communicate with the sacred beings of the **Dreamtime**, including the rainbow serpent, the sky-gods, and the **spirits** of the dead. The Aboriginal sorcerer is called a "kaditcha man".

Abracadabra A magical chant or **incantation**. Quintus Serenus Sammonicus, the physician to Emperor Severus on the expedition to Britain in A.D. 208, used this formula to cure fevers and asthma. Rows of the word were written in a triangular formation on a piece of paper, which was then worn for nine days and thrown into a stream. As the word shrank on the paper, the ailment was supposed to diminish. The word itself may derive from the **Gnostic** deity **Abraxas.**

Abrahadabra A magical formula related to the medieval conjuration **Abracadabra.** Used in modern Crowleyian occultism as the magical name for "The Great Work of the Aeon of Horus". See also **Crowley, Aleister.**

Abraham the Jew (1362–1460) Abraham was probably born in Mayence, France, and travelled widely – through Austria, Hungary, and Greece, finally proceeding through Palestine to Egypt. At Arachi, on the banks of the Nile, he met a sage named Abra-Melin who initiated him into a range of magical secrets. Abraham returned to Wurzburg in Germany, undertook alchemical research, and endeavoured both to apply the magical arts in politics and to convert his children to his occult philosophy. He compiled his famous work *The Sacred Magic of Abra-Melin* when he was ninety-six years of age, as a legacy for his son Lamech. He gave details of the **invocation** of angelic forces and presented a series of magical **rituals** which took six months to perform. His magical system greatly influenced the occultist **Aleister Crowley**; and as recently as 1976 the pseudonymous "Georges Chevalier" published a diary based on his experience with the ceremonial invocations. See also **Magic.**

Abrams, Dr. Albert (1863–1922) See Radionics.

Abraxas **Gnostic** deity whose name in Greek letters had a numerical value of 365, thereby linking the god to the days of the year. An important deity in the **pantheon** of **Basilides**, Abraxas had historical links with the Greek **Aeon**; the Iranian god of time, **Zurvan**; and the Indian sky-god, **Varuna**. He was often represented on **talismans**. The symbolic concept of Abraxas as a deity of good and evil in one form has been put forward by **Carl Jung** in *Septem Sermones ad Mortuos*, and also by the novelist Hermann Hesse in *Demian*.

Absent Healing A form of **faith healing** that takes place without the healer being present. Absent healing usually involves the power of **prayer** or the "projection" of positive healing thoughts to the sick person.

Absolute, The A metaphysical term connoting the ground of all being, that which exists in and of itself. It is often used to describe the Great One **God**, or Creator, the Infinite and Eternal. As the supreme **transcendent** reality, it is the focus of many mystical traditions.

Abulafia, Abraham ben Samuel (1240–1291) A kabbalistic **mystic** born in Saragossa, who later represented himself as the Messiah, both to Christians and Jews. He decided to confront Pope Nicholas III; but when the Pope heard of this, an order was sent that the heretical mystic would be burned to death if he set foot in Rome. The Pope then died unexpectedly, just as Abulafia arrived at the city gate. The mystic was imprisoned, but was set free a month later, and he then travelled with a group of followers to Sicily.

Abulafia's approach to mysticism was purposeful and orderly, placing more emphasis on mental and spiritual integration than visionary flights of the **soul.** He believed in the divine symbolism of the Hebrew alphabet, and produced many mystical tracts, including *The Book of the Righteous* and *The Book of Life*.

Abyss In magical and kabbalistic terminology, the gulf between the Trinity (represented by **Kether**, **Chokmah**, and **Binah** on the **Tree of Life**) and the remaining **sephiroth** of manifested existence. Occultists believe that only **adepts** can bridge this gulf to higher spiritual consciousness. The Abyss is sometimes associated with the so-called "eleventh sephirah", **Daath.**

Acarya Hindu term for a spiritual teacher or **guru**. The term is usually associated with a south Indian group of theologians who succeeded the **Alvars** in the tenth century.

Achad, Frater (1886–1950) The magical name of Charles Stansfeld Jones, who was adopted by **Aleister Crowley** as his "magical son". Achad, who lived in Vancouver, gained occult respectability by interpreting the numerical keys to Crowley's *The Book of the Law*. He also produced highly original and sometimes confusing interpretations of the **Kabbalah** and the interconnecting **Tarot** paths on the **Tree of Life**, which are described in his books *QBL: The Bride's Reception* and *The Anatomy of the Body of God*. Achad began to lose his mental stability after taking the magical grade of **Ipsissimus**, which implied that his every action had **cosmic** significance. See also **QBL**.

Acheron In Greek **mythology**, one of the five rivers in **Hades**, specifically the river of woe. **Charon** ferried the **souls** of the dead across this river to the **Underworld**.

Acronymics Forming words from the initial letters of groups of words. For example, the word "laser" derives from "*L*ight *a*mplification by the *s*timulated *e*mission of *r*adiation". In the **Kabbalah**, acronyms were said to have related symbolic meanings. In Christian terminology, the acronym **Ichthus** (from the Greek, "fish") derives from the Greek phrase that translates as "Jesus Christ, Son of God, Saviour", and reflects Jesus' symbolic role as a "fisher of men".

Acupuncture A system of Chinese medicine. Its main technique involves the insertion of needles into specific points on the skin. Early accounts of acupuncture that date from the Han Dynasty (202 B.C.–A.D. 220) describe the needles as being made of stone. They were later fashioned from iron and silver, and these days are made of stainless steel. A contemporary acupuncturist requires a working knowledge of around one thousand acupuncture points on the human body, which lie along twelve lines known as **meridians**. Six of these lines are **yang** (positive) and six **yin** (negative), each of them relating to a particular organ or health process in the body. It is along these meridians that the life-force, **ch'i**, passes through the body, and the stimulation of specific acupuncture points is said to enhance the energy flow. There appears to be a high correlation between acupuncture channels and nervous reflexes, and some researchers now believe that acupuncture stimulation may trigger the brain's own painkillers – endorphins – thereby producing the well-known anaesthetizing effect associated with acupuncture.

Acuto-manzia A form of **divination** using pins. Thirteen tacking pins are used, ten of them straight and the remainder bent. They are shaken and allowed to fall on a table covered with a light film of talcum-powder dust. The reader studies the formation of the pins, and may predict future events from them.

Adam Kadmon Judaic concept of the archetypal man, the primordial human being formed in the creation of the universe. Every human being is said to reflect this archetypal form. Adam Kadmon is also, metaphorically, "the body of God".

Adams, Evangeline (1865–1932) The astrological nom de plume of Mrs. George Jordan, a descendant of President John Quincy Adams, who established an astrological practice in New York. Arrested in 1914 as a **fortune-teller**, she was acquitted by the judge after accurately diagnosing the **horoscope** of the judge's son in court. Her clients included Edward VII and Enrico Caruso, and at the peak of her fame she was attracting 300,000 letters a year from people seeking astrological advice. See also **Astrology**.

Adept An initiate or occult master; one who has gained profound magical powers and insights through **initiation**. In the theosophical system, adepts form part of the **Great White Lodge**, a group of mystical leaders who guide the world and its inhabitants through processes of spiritual evolution. The magical **Hermetic Order of the Golden Dawn** had four ceremonial grades of adept: Zelator Adeptus Minor, Theoricus Adeptus Minor, Adeptus Major, and Adeptus Exemptus, associated with grades of initiatory experience on the **Tree of Life**.

Adjuration A form of command made by an exorcist to an evil spirit. The exorcist may command the spirit to depart from the body of the possessed person. See also **Exorcism**.

Adonai The Hebrew word for "the Lord", used when speaking, reading about, or referring to Jehovah, God of Israel. The awesome and mysterious **Tetragrammaton** – or name of **God** – was held in such respect that Jews avoided pronouncing it and substituted **YHVH** in its place. In the magical ceremonies of the **Hermetic Order of the Golden Dawn**, it was used as a **god-name** in formulating the Pentagram of Earth.

Adoptive Masonry See **Co-Masonry**.

Advaita Hindu term for the doctrine of non-dualism, affirming the single, ultimate reality of **Brahman**. Advaita represents Hindu monism in its purest expression, and is associated with the teachings of the Vedantin **Sankara** (A.D. 750). See also **Vedanta**.

A.E. See **Russell, George**.

Aeon An enduring period of time. Sometimes aeons are linked to the procession of the **zodiac** – the Christian aeon being associated with the astrological cycle of **Pisces**. Some magical groups, especially those influenced by **Aleister Crowley**, refer to aeons in terms of characteristic patterns of mythic and ceremonial worship: the Aeon of Isis (worship of **lunar goddesses**); the Aeon of Osiris (worship of **solar gods**); and the Aeon of Horus (worship of the magical child who combines male and female forces in the **androgyne**). Aeons were also an important feature of **Gnostic** and Mithraic **cosmology**. The Greek god Aion is related to the Gnostic **Abraxas**, and was amalgamated into Mithraism in the second and third centuries A.D. See also **Mithra**.

Aeromancy **Divination** from the air and sky, using cloud shapes, comets, and other aerial formations.

Aesch Mezareph An expression meaning "purifying fire" and the name of a medieval treatise linking the **Kabbalah** and **alchemy**. In this process alchemical metals are linked to the **sephiroth** of the **Tree of Life** (e.g. **silver** with **Chesed**, tin with **Binah**, and **iron** with **Tiphareth**). The French magician **Eliphas Levi** believed *Aesch Mezareph* was one of the most important hermetic books. It was first translated into Latin by Knorr von Rosenroth and forms part of his *Kabbala Denudata*, published in 1714.

Aesir In Scandinavian **mythology**, a family of **gods** living in the stronghold **Asgard**, which was the equivalent of **Mount Olympus**. According to the writer Snorri Sturluson, **Odin** was the head of this community and **Thor** and the other gods were his "sons". The gods of the Aesir were locked in continual battles with another group of deities – the fertility gods of the **Vanir**, headed by Njord and Freyr.

Aetherius Society Occult society founded by **George King** in 1956. The group believes it is in contact with spiritual **masters** who live on various planets, including the Master Jesus, who is said to reside on **Venus**. These spiritual beings maintain a vigil over the earth by periodically visiting in **flying saucers**, which are said to radiate **cosmic** energy. Members of the Aetherius Society reciprocate this effect by spiritually "charging" certain mountains. The first such mountain to receive this treatment was Holdstone Down in Devonshire, England, where George King claimed the Master Jesus appeared before him.

Agaberte Daughter of the Scandinavian giant Vagnoste. A powerful enchantress with remarkable magical powers. Agaberte could transform her form, appearing sometimes as a wrinkled old woman hunched over with age, and on other occasions as a tall, vibrant woman who could touch the sky. She was said to be capable of overturning mountains, ripping up trees, and drying up rivers, with consummate ease.

Agapé A Greek word for "love", and the name given to early Christian love-feasts combining a common meal with **hymns** and **prayers**. Because the numerical value of agapé is 93, followers of **Aleister Crowley** regard it as one of the key magical words of the Aeon of Horus, typified by the deity **Aiwaz**, whose name adds to the same total.

Agent Term used in psychical research to connote a person who is a "transmitter" in telepathic experiments.

Agla A kabbalistic **magical formula** used to exorcise evil spirits. In modern **magic** it is one of the **god-names** of the **banishing ritual** of the Lesser Pentagram. It is made up of the initial letters of the Hebrew phrase *Athah gabor leolam, Adonai*, meaning, "Thou art powerful and eternal, Lord."

Aglaophotis An Arabian herb used in **sorcery** to evoke **demons**.

Agni Hindu term for fire, also personified as a **god**. Agni, a mediator between people and the gods, takes three forms; the **sun**, lightning, and fire. He devours or burns all in his path, but is greatly revered; among Vedic deities, Agni is the most important of all.

Agnishwattas A compound of two Sanskrit words: *agni*, "fire", and *shwatta*, "tastened" or "sweetened". In a literal sense, Agnishwattas are spiritual beings who are "sweetened" or purified by fire, and in theosophical usage they are among humankind's most important teachers, personifications of the spiritual quest.

Agnostic One who believes that we cannot have direct knowledge of **God**, and that it is impossible to prove whether or not God exists. In popular usage, the term sometimes refers to one who is unsure about the existence of the **soul**, **heaven** and **hell**, and **immortality**.

Agrippa, von Nettesheim, Heinrich Cornelius (1486–1535) Famous occult scholar and astrologer, born of noble parentage in Cologne. An attendant to Maximilian I, he entered the German secret service and spied on the French while attending Paris University. Here he encountered **mystics** and **Rosicrucians** and developed an interest in the **Kabbalah** and Hermetic philosophies. In 1531 he published his famous treatise, *De Occulta Philosophia*, which dealt with divine names, **natural magic**, and **cosmology**. He was rumoured to possess a magic mirror in which he could divine future events, and also dabbled in **necromancy**, believing he could conjure up the spirits of the dead. See also **Astrology**; **Hermetica**.

Ahad Islamic name of **Allah**, connoting his one-ness, or single nature.

Ahriman **Zoroastrian** personification of **evil**. The antagonist of "Wise Lord" **Ahura Mazdah**, Ahriman was committed to perpetuating lies against the Holy Spirit. In the **Gathas**, he is described as being locked in eternal conflict with the forces of Light and Truth.

Ahura Mazdah The Supreme God in **Zoroastrianism**. Aligned with the Holy Spirit, Ahura Mazdah – as the embodiment of Truth – was the sworn enemy of **Ahriman**, the personification of evil. In late Zoroastrianism, Ahura Mazdah became **Ohrmazd**, a fusion of the "Wise Lord" and the "Holy Spirit" in one being.

Aidoneus Greek form of the Lord of the **Underworld**, and the counterpart of the Roman **Hades**. Aidoneus raped **Persephone** and abducted her, snatching her down into the Underworld, where she became his Queen.

Ain Arabic word meaning "an eye", the "self", the "Divine Essence" of **Allah**.

Ain Soph Aur Hebrew expression meaning "**the Limitless Light**". In the **Kabbalah**, it represents the source from which all else comes forth.

Air One of the four alchemical **elements**, the others being **Fire**, **Water**, and **Earth**. The spirits of Air were known as **sylphs**. The three astrological signs linked to Air are **Gemini**, **Libra**, and **Aquarius**.

Aires, Enochian See **Thirty Aethyrs**.

Aiwaz Also Aiwass. The name of the **deity** from whom **Aleister Crowley** received his magical doctrine, *The Book of the Law*. Aiwaz communicated this doctrine to Crowley's wife, Rose, via **trance** state, while the couple were visiting Cairo in 1904.

Aix-en-Provence Nuns A classic example of the hysterical and tragic **witchcraft** delusion in France during the early years of the seventeenth century. The events of the Aix-en-Provence nuns focus on two women, Sister Madeleine de Demandolx de la Palud and Sister Louise Capeau, who were members of the small, exclusive Ursuline convent in Aix. Madeleine, who had entered the convent at the age of twelve, became very depressed with her environment and was sent back home to Marseilles. Here she was housed by a humorous and somewhat carefree family friend, Father Louis Gaufridi, with whom she subsequently fell in love. The relationship with an older man – Gaufridi was thirty-four – was frowned upon by the head of the Ursuline convent in Marseilles and Madeleine was taken into this convent as a novice. Here she confessed that she had been intimate with Gaufridi; and, undoubtedly to keep Madeleine's lover at a distance, the head of the convent, Mother Catherine, transferred the young novice back to Aix.

Madeleine soon began to develop dramatic shaking fits and severe cramps and had visions of **devils**. The hysteria soon spread to the five other nuns in the convent, one of whom – Louise Capeau – tried to rival Madeleine with the intensity of her visions. The Grand Inquisitor, Sebastian Michaelis, now became involved in the case and arranged for the two young women to be taken to the Royal Convent of St. Maximin to be treated by an exorcist. The demonic visions continued, with Louise claiming to be possessed by three devils and accusing Madeleine of being in league with **Beelzebub**, **Asmodeus**, **Ashtaroth**, and several thousand other evil spirits.

Later, Father Gaufridi was called in to attempt an **exorcism**. Madeleine mocked him with demonic condemnations and insults, and at first his part in the hysterical outbreak was unproven. However, when Madeleine continued with her visions, neighed like a horse, and told fantastic tales of sodomy and witch sabbats, Gaufridi was interrogated by the **Inquisition** in more depth. Finally, in April 1611, he was found guilty by the court of **magic**, **sorcery**, and fornication, and was sentenced to death. His execution was especially barbaric; he was humiliated, tortured, and finally publicly burned. His demise led to a sudden reverse in the fortunes of Madeleine who, the following day, seemed free of demonic **possession**. Louise Capeau, however, continued to have visions of witches and devils, and similar outbreaks of witchcraft hysteria were reported at St. Claire's convent in Aix, and at St. Bridget's in Lille.

In 1642, Madeleine was again accused of witchcraft. She was cleared of this charge, but a further attack against her ten years later resulted in the discovery of **witch's marks** on her body. She spent the rest of her life in prison.

Ajitz Among the Quiche Indians of Guatemala, a **sorcerer** who derives his power not from the **Devil**, but from "books of magic" described by some such sorcerers as "the books of the Jews".

Ajna Chakra The occult power centre known as the **third eye**, situated just above and between the two eyes.

Akasha From a Sanskrit word meaning "luminous", but referring to "essence" or "space", Akasha is one of the five Hindu elements: the black egg of **Spirit**.

Akashic Records Theosophical concept for an astral memory of all events, thoughts, and emotions that have arisen since the world began. **Psychics** are said to be able to tune into this dimension and receive authentic impressions of past ages. Some theosophical descriptions of Atlantis derive from apparent Akashic memories. See also **Theosophy**.

Aksakov, Alex N. (1832–1903) Russian statesman and psychical researcher who became Councillor of State to the Czar. His first contact with **spiritualism** was through the writings of **Emmanuel Swedenborg**, some of whose works he later translated. He brought several spiritualist **mediums** to Russia and was instrumental in establishing a scientific committee to investigate spiritualism in detail. Later, when spiritualism fell from official favour, he was compelled to publish his psychic research in other European countries. See also **Psychical Research**.

Al Hebrew term for **God**, the Most Ancient One. See also **El**; **Elohim**.

Alastor A cruel **demon** who, according to Wierius (**Johannes Wier**), was the chief executioner in **Hades**. The word "alastor" also has general usage, meaning an evil, avenging spirit.

Alaya Sanskrit term meaning "indissoluble" and referring to the basis or root of all things, including the **gods** and the universe.

Al Azif Said to be the original Arabic title for the legendary and probably fictitious work *The Necronomicon*, associated with **Howard Phillips Lovecraft**.

Albertus Magnus (1205–1280) Born in the town of Larvigen on the Danube, Albertus was regarded by his contemporaries as a major alchemist and theologian. Although he claimed inspiration from the Virgin Mary, and was one of the teachers of St. Thomas Aquinas, many suspected him of communication with the **Devil**. He did claim magical powers, including the ability to control the weather. Albertus is best known as an **adept** who claimed to have discovered the **Philosopher's Stone** and who conducted tests on gold produced through alchemical processes. See also **Alchemy**.

Albigenses Twelfth-century French sect named after one of its main centres, the town of Albi. Associated with the **Bogomils**, **Cathars**, and **Paulicians**, the Albigenses were strongly opposed to the Roman Catholic Church, which in turn branded them **heretics** and persecuted them severely during the **Inquisition**. The Albigenses believed that God had created as his firstborn **Lucifer**, who in turn escaped with a band of fallen angels to create the world and all its inhabitants. Jesus Christ was **God's** second son, and his role was to re-establish spiritual order in a totally evil world. This doctrine was quite unacceptable to the established Church, particularly with its implication that the Church, and humankind generally, was essentially demonic. The Inquisition dealt with the sect so savagely that after 1330 there were no more Albigenses left to persecute.

Alchemy The ancient science of transmuting base metals into **gold** and **silver**. The etymology of the word is uncertain, but it may derive from the Arabic *al kimiya*, meaning "the magical craft of the Black Country", a reference to northern Egypt and the Nile Delta (southern Egypt, by way of contrast, had red, sandy soil). The ancient Egyptians were master metalworkers and believed that magical powers existed in certain fluxes and alloys. When the Arabs conquered Egypt in the seventh century, they brought alchemy back with them to Morocco and Spain. From the ninth to the eleventh centuries, Seville, Cordova, and Granada were leading centres for alchemy; later, this **esoteric** science spread to France, England, and Germany.

The three main aims of alchemy were to attempt to make gold from base metals with the aid of the **Philosopher's Stone**; to search for an elixir that could prolong life indefinitely; and to acquire methods of creating life artificially. In the Middle Ages considerable fortunes were lost by wealthy patrons who financed alchemical experiments that came to nothing. **Nicholas Flamel** (1330–1418) claimed to have transformed **mercury** into silver and gold, but it is more likely that he acquired his wealth as the result of his moneylending business.

In some degree at least, alchemy was also a metaphor for spiritual transformation, a process quite divorced from laboratory experimentation. The imperfect person, leaden and dark, could become pure and golden through gradual processes leading to spiritual illumination. Basil Valentine, a celebrated alchemist and Benedictine monk, described alchemy as "the investigation of those natural secrets by which God has shadowed out eternal things" and **Jacob Boehme** regarded the Philosopher's Stone as the spirit of Christ, which would "tincture" the individual soul. In this sense, alchemy was both a precursor of modern chemistry and also a complex spiritual philosophy – one of the major sources of medieval esoteric thought.

Aldinach An Egyptian **demon** given to causing earthquakes, hailstorms, and tempests. He sometimes masqueraded in the form of a woman.

Alectorius Magical stone, normally crystal-clear, but sometimes with pink, flesh-like veins through it. It was believed to have many occult properties, including the power to bring fame and love to its owner.

Alectryomancy **Divination** through the actions of birds, often a black hen or a gamecock. In Africa, where this form of augury is practised, the diviner sprinkles grain on the ground and allows the birds to peck at it. When the bird has finished, the seer interprets the patterns that remain on the ground.

Aleuromancy **Divination** practised with flour. Among the ancient Greeks, the procedure was as follows: sentences were composed, written on small pieces of paper, and rolled up in balls of flour. The balls were then mixed up nine times and distributed to those who were eager for information on their destiny. **Apollo** presided over this form of divination. Aleuromancy is not widely practised today, but modern-day fortune cookies are a form of this type of fortune-telling.

Alexander of Abonotica Second-century **seer** and **oracle** who established a shrine on the southern shore of the Black Sea. Possessed of good looks and a fine voice, Alexander announced that both **Apollo** and the healing god **Asklepios** would manifest through his shrine and that he was their prophet. Alexander soon acquired a following and his fame spread as far as Rome; according to one tale, Emperor Aurelius consulted the seer of Abonotica before undertaking a military operation.

Alexander liked to appear before the crowds with a large but harmless Macedonian snake coiled around his neck. The actual head of the snake would be concealed under his arm and an artificial head – which was supposed to be that of Apollo – was allowed to protrude. Alexander, through sheer showmanship, managed to convince the crowds that the snake deity could give mystic oracles relating to the cause of disease, and could also divine the future. Alexander's shrine and cult survived for many years after his death.

Alfarabi (870–954) Common name of Abou-Nasr-Mohammed-Ibn-Tarkan, legendary Arabian musician, philosopher, and spiritual teacher. Born at Othrar in Asia Minor, Alfarabi was of Turkish origin. He studied the Greek and Neoplatonic philosophers, and was particularly influenced by Aristotle and **Plotinus**. He was also a noted musical composer, famous for his performances before the Sultan.

Alfheim In Scandinavian **mythology**, the home of **fairies, elves** and friendly **spirits**.

Algol A bright star in the constellation of Perseus. Known variously as the Demon's Head by the Arabs, Lilith by the Jews, and Medusa's Head by the Greeks, it was regarded as **evil**. This may be because a dark star that revolves around it periodically dims its radiance, giving the impression of an evil, winking eye.

Allah The **Supreme Being** in **Islam**, worshipped by the Arabs and proclaimed by **Mohammed** to be the only true god. According to this doctrine, God is One, there is no god but God. Moslems reject the trinitarian notion of the **Godhead** found in Christianity. Pictorial representation of Allah is forbidden, but Arabian artists are allowed to produce designs incorporating the letters of His name.

All Hallows' Eve Also known as Halloween, a **pagan** festival representing the change of season from autumn to winter, celebrated on October 31. It was also a time when the souls of the deceased revisited their former homes and once again enjoyed the company of their kinsfolk and friends around an open fire. Bonfires are one of the symbols of All Hallows' Eve, perhaps intended to retain something of the light and warmth of summer and early autumn by contrast with the onset of chilly winter winds. In the United States, Halloween has become a special occasion for children, who dress up as **ghosts** or **witches** and go from door to door seeking a "trick or treat".

Almadel In **ceremonial magic**, a **talisman**, fashioned with white wax, inscribed with the names of **angels** or **spirits**, and used in **ritual**.

Alomancy Divination by sprinkling salt. The diviner interprets future events by analyzing the patterns made by this action. Alomancy has probably given rise to the superstition that spilling salt is unlucky. Misfortune is averted by casting a small amount of the salt over the left shoulder.

Alpha A specific brain-rhythm pattern associated with relaxation and **meditation**. Measured as amplitudes of 8–13 cycles per second in an electroencephalograph (EEG) pattern.

Alphabet of Honorius See **Runes**.

Alphitomancy Divination by means of a leaf of barley, used to identify a culprit. Pieces of the leaf would be given to a group of accused persons. The innocent would suffer no ill effects, but the culprit would have an attack of indigestion and thereby identify himself.

Alpiel In the **Talmud**, the books of Jewish law, an **angel** who presides over fruit trees.

Alrunes In Norway, female **demons** and sorceresses capable of transforming into a variety of shapes. Statues of these sorceresses were clothed, served with food and drink, and highly respected. It was believed that the statues would cry out and bring catastrophe, if neglected.

Altered State of Consciousness A state of consciousness different from normal, everyday consciousness, the latter sometimes being referred to as the "consensus reality" on which normal patterns of communication are based. Altered states exclude or minimize the external world, allowing subconscious imagery to rise into consciousness. Altered states include some types of **dreams, trance** states, **out-of-the-body experiences, dissociation** experiences, mystical states, and **hallucinations** associated with **psychedelic** drugs.

Althanor A magical hill with a well, possessing the power to alleviate drought in the countryside.

Althotas A mysterious occultist whom **Count Alessandro di Cagliostro** claimed to meet in Messina. Althotas and Cagliostro allegedly travelled to Alexandria and Rhodes and then on to Malta, where they undertook a series of alchemical experiments under the sponsorship of Grand Master Pinto. The actual existence of Althotas has never been established, and some believe he was a fiction of Cagliostro's imagination.

Aludel In **alchemy**, the condensing receiver used to collect sublimates.

Alvars A group of saints who lived in southern India between the fifth and ninth centuries. The Alvars have influenced the devotional **bhakti** tradition of Indian mysticism, believing that the love of a devotee for **God** was the most sublime truth of all. The Alvars produced beautiful **prayers** and poetry that now form part of regular temple services.

Amandinus A coloured stone with mystical properties. Whoever wears the stone has the power to interpret **dreams** and **mysteries**.

Amanita muscaria Also known as fly agaric, the beautiful red-and-white-capped mushroom of fairy tales, usually found growing in forests beneath birch, fir, and larch trees. This mushroom, one of the oldest hallucinogens known to humanity, was until recent times the focus of shamanic rites among the Siberian and Uralic tribesmen. The ethnomycologist **R. Gordon Wasson** linked *Amanita muscaria* to the sacred plant called *soma* in the Indian ***Rig-Veda***.

Amaranth A flower symbolizing **immortality**. Amaranths often have colourful foliage and decorative flowers, and in occult tradition a crown of amaranths bestows **supernatural** gifts upon those who wear it.

Ambrosia In Greek **mythology**, the food or drink of the **gods**, which made them immortal. The gods were also able to use ambrosia to bestow the gift of **immortality** upon favoured human beings.

Amduscias According to Wierius (**Johannes Wier**), a grand duke of **Hades** who normally has the shape of a **unicorn** but appears to **magicians** in human form. Amduscias is best known for his ability to provide musical concerts in which the musicians are invisible to the onlooker, but the music is quite audible.

American Institute for Scientific Research Founded by **Dr. James Hyslop** in New York in 1906 to investigate **psychical research**. Hyslop was a pioneering parapsychologist who conducted a number of "clairvoyant experiments" into **extrasensory perception**. The American **Society for Psychical Research** emerged from this Institute.

American Psychical Institute and Laboratory Founded in 1920 in New York by **Dr. Hereward Carrington**, a psychic researcher best known for his interest in **spiritualism** and **astral projection**. Carrington was also assistant to **Dr. James Hyslop** in the American **Society for Psychical Research**.

American Society for Psychical Research See **Society for Psychical Research**.

Amesha Spentas In **Zoroastrianism**, a group of benevolent **spirits** under the command of **Ahura Mazdah**. They represented his noble attributes.

Amiante A type of fireproof stone recommended by Pliny as being useful to counteract magical **spells**.

Amida The Buddha of Infinite Light, symbolized by the **lotus** and the peacock. Amida Buddha reigns over the Western Paradise of Sukhavati. In Nepal, Tibet, and China this emanation of Buddha gained more importance than in India, and in Japan became the focus of a major cult. See also **Buddhism**.

Amnesia A state of temporary or prolonged loss of memory sometimes experienced by **mediums** when they go into **trance**. In such cases the possessed medium forgets any utterances or proclamations made during the trance session.

Amon Also Amen. Ancient Egyptian **deity** personifying the breath of life; also a **God** of fertility and agriculture. Worshipped mainly at Thebes, where he was part of a divine triad – the husband of Mut and the father of Khons. Sanctuaries were also dedicated to him at Luxor and Karnak.

Amoymon In **demonology**, the king of the eastern division of **Hades**. Also identified with Amaimon.

Am Tuat An important component of the ***Egyptian Book of the Dead*** describing the passage of the sun-god through the twelve dungeons of the **Underworld** (the twelve hours of night). Taking the form of the Ram, Afu-Ra travels by boat through the waters of darkness, vanquishing his opponents with **hekau**, or magical words of power. The sun-god gradually transforms, becoming **Khepera**, and is reborn from the thighs of the sky-goddess **Nut**, as his boat floats forth on the ocean of New Day.

Amulet A small object, worn or carried as a protection against misfortune or **evil**. Amulets vary considerably, ranging from a rabbit's foot or a coloured stone to an engraved and highly ornamented work in precious metal. The Egyptians had a wide variety of amulets, including motifs based on the eye of **Isis** and the backbone of **Osiris**. Among the **Gnostic** sects, amulets of **Abraxas** were popular. Today, astrological amulets are a continuing fashion. Perhaps the most common Christian amulet is that of St. Christopher, patron saint of travellers.

Anaesthesia State in which there is a loss of sensation in the body. Occultists believe that this effect can be brought about in trance **dissociation** where the "consciousness" is temporarily removed from the physical body.

Anahata Chakra In **Kundalini Yoga**, the occult power centre associated with the thymus gland and cardiac plexus. It is represented by the Tattva, or element, **Vayu**, symbol of water. See also **Yoga**.

Analgesia Insensibility to pain, sometimes associated with **yogis**, **psychic mediums**, and holy men who are able to enter an **altered state of consciousness** through their religious enthusiasm.

Ananda Hindu term for pure joy, unsullied by material considerations.

Ananse In Ashanti legends, the spider who gave rise to the material from which **Nyame** – the supreme sky-god – created the first human beings. Occultists in the **Ordo Templi Orientis** have adapted the mythology of Ananse, using the spider's web as a visual image for magically exploring the dark, reverse side of the **Tree of Life**.

Anathema An offering to a **deity**, usually hung up in a temple; also, the word used in the Roman Catholic Church as part of the formula in the excommunication of **heretics**.

Anatta Buddhist doctrine that there is no permanent human **soul** that reincarnates from one body to another. **Gautama Buddha** described the individual person not as a specific soul inhabiting a body, but as a collection of events, perceptions, and sensations within the spectrum of human consciousness, and which is constantly in a state of flux. Consequently, no "fixed" entity could survive death and pass to another realm. See also **Buddhism**; **Reincarnation**.

Ancestor Worship Worship of the **spirits** of deceased relatives, who are believed to witness and influence events on earth even after death. **Prayers**, supplications, and offerings are made by the descendants to appease the ancestor spirits and seek continuing goodwill.

Androgyne A hermaphrodite. In **alchemy** and **mysticism**, the androgyne is a sacred symbol because male and female polarities are united in one being, which therefore represents totality, unity, and oneness. See also **Dualism**.

Android An artificially created human being. The medieval magician **Albertus Magnus** was credited with having created such an entity, and there are many tales of the **golem** in Jewish mythology and legends. See also **Homunculus**.

Andvari Also Alberich. In Scandinavian **mythology**, a dwarf who jealously guarded the magic ring **Draupnir** and other precious belongings of the **gods**. When the ring was stolen by **Loki**, Andvari cursed the ring, causing grief and misfortune to befall all those who had anything to do with it.

Angel From a Greek word meaning "messenger". In Christianity, Judaism, and **Islam**, angels are immortal beings who serve as intermediaries between **God** and human beings. Angels are often arranged in a hierarchy, but their significance varies greatly. Enoch identified the top seven archangels as follows: **Uriel**, **Raphael**, Ragual, **Michael**, Zerachiel, **Gabriel**, and **Remiel**. For St. Ambrose, angels were comparatively low in the celestial scheme, which consisted of **Seraphim**, **Cherubim**, Dominations, Thrones, Principalities, Powers, Virtues, **Archangels**, and Angels. The months of the year, the astrological signs, and the planets all have angels assigned to them.

Angra Mainyu Alternative name for **Ahriman** who, in Zoroastrian **mythology**, personifies evil and darkness. He is locked in conflict with the god of light and goodness, **Ahura Mazdah**.

Angurvadel The magical sword inherited by Frithjof, a hero in Icelandic **mythology**.

Decorated with a golden hilt, the sword shone like the Northern Lights and glowed fiery red during times of battle.

Animal magnetism According to **Anton Mesmer**, the eighteenth-century hypnotist, animal magnetism was the vital force present in the human body and could be transmitted as a healing force from one person to another. Mesmer treated his patients by asking them to sit around a tub called a baquet that was filled with water and iron filings. A number of iron-rod conductors protruded from the tub, and the patients were asked to hold these while also being bound by cords to "close the force". Mesmer claimed that the positive magnetism could transfer to sick patients and restore their health.

Anima Mundi A cosmological concept of a **world soul** or governing force in the universe that allows divine thought to become manifested in laws affecting matter. According to the mystic **Marsilio Ficino**, the world soul is omnipresent, but cooperating star **daemons** assist in uniting spirit and matter. Ficino was influenced by **Plotinus** and other Neoplatonists who believed that the world soul established processes in the heavens that defined and influenced what occurred on earth. Philosophically, the world soul was midway between **spirit** and matter, a dimension of energy and vitality for the world below.

Animism The belief, common among many pre-literate societies, that trees, mountains, rivers, and other natural formations possess an animating power of **spirit**. In **spiritualism** the term also refers to the concept that inanimate objects as well as animate ones have a **life-force** or energy quite distinct from the physical form, and which is capable of existing without the physical "shell".

Ankh Egyptian symbol resembling a cross with a loop at the top. The ankh is a symbol of life, and every major Egyptian deity is depicted carrying it. It has been suggested by some that the symbol has a sexual origin, combining the penis and vagina in one motif; however, Egyptologist **Wallis Budge** regards this interpretation as "unlikely". The ankh is also known as the *crux ansata*.

Anselm de Parma (?–1440) Italian astrologer and author of *Astrological Institutions*. Wierius (**Johnnes Wier**) regarded him as a **sorcerer**, possibly because a sect known as the Anselmites claimed to be able to heal wounds and sores by the use of magic words. However, this sect probably derived its name from St. Anselm of Canterbury, who was known for spiritual healing. See also **Astrology**.

Antaskarana Sanskrit term comprising *antar*, "within", and *karana*, a "sensory organ". In theosophical usage, the link between the spiritual **ego** and the personal **soul**.

Anthony, St. Christian ascetic, born in Egypt around 250. He is best known for accounts of his demonic visions, which have inspired numerous artists. St. Anthony lived on a minimal diet, fasted frequently, and lived in isolation in conditions that may well have caused his **hallucinations**. He believed he was tormented by **devils** because they were "jealous of all mankind and particularly of the monks, for they cannot bear to see heavenly lives led upon the earth". It has been suggested that St. Anthony's visions may have also been caused by eating bread infected by **ergot** – the fungus from which **LSD** is synthesized.

Anthropomancy Barbaric form of **divination** using human entrails – usually those of virgins or young children. According to legend, the **magician** Julian the Apostate sacrificed a number of children during his ritual workings, in order to evaluate their entrails. Anthropomancy was also practised in ancient Egypt.

Anthroposophy Term associated with the German mystic and theosophist **Rudolf Steiner**, literally meaning "knowledge concerning man", and especially devoted to the study of the human spiritual nature. Steiner founded the Anthroposophical Society after breaking away from the **Theosophical Society**, and this new group eventually established many centres around the world.

Anti-Christ An **evil** Messiah who would work miracles, raise the dead, and walk on the water in imitation of Christ, but who in reality was his deadly antagonist. The concept of devil incarnate has recurred through Jewish and Christian history, being fuelled by such figures as the pagan Syrian King Antiochus IV; the mythic **Great Beast 666** in the Book of Revelation; and, in modern times, by Kaiser Wilhelm II and Adolf Hitler. Following his initiation with *The Book of the Law* – a mystical tract with distinctly blasphemous elements – the ritual magician **Aleister Crowley** also claimed to be the anti-Christ and Lord of the **New Aeon**.

Anubis Egyptian dog or jackal deity associated with the western desert, the home of the dead. A major figure in the Osirian **Underworld**, Anubis was the son of **Nephthys** and at times rivalled **Osiris** in importance. In the **Judgment Hall**, Anubis had the role of producing the heart of the deceased person for judgment. He also assisted in guiding the souls of the dead through the Underworld.

Anupapadaka In **Hinduism** and **Buddhism**, a term meaning "one who does not fall down as others do", and representing the source from which the Hierarchy of Buddhas comes forth in mystical emanation. Also used to mean the "inner god".

Apas In **Hinduism** and Western **magic**, the element **Water**, represented by a silver crescent.

Aphrodite Greek goddess of love and beauty, and one of the **Twelve Great Olympians**. According to some legends, she came forth from ocean foam near Cythera. She was described as fun-loving and beautiful, but was notoriously unfaithful. Her lovers included Adonis and Ares. The Romans identified Aphrodite with **Venus**.

Apocalypse An unveiling of hidden things, an **esoteric** or prophetic revelation. Often used to refer to the last book of the New Testament, the Revelation of St. John. There are also several examples of apocalypses in the **Gnostic** literature, including the *Apocalypse of Paul*, the *First and Second Apocalypses of James*, the *Apocalypse of Peter*, and the *Apocalypse of Adam*. These form part of the **Nag Hammadi Library**.

Apocrypha From a Greek compound root meaning "to hide away", secret teachings not available to the uninitiated. In Christian usage, the collective name of the fourteen books originally included in the Old Testament and still incorporated in the Vulgate of the Roman Catholic Church.

Apocryphal Of unknown origin. Sometimes used to mean "spurious".

Apollo Greek god of the **sun**, fertility, purity, and truth, and also a **deity** associated with healing, music, and poetry. He was the son of **Zeus** and Leto and the twin brother of **Artemis**, and was one of the **Twelve Great Olympians**. Among his other names are Helios, Hyperion, and Phoebus. Apollo had numerous shrines dedicated to him and was the chief deity of the **oracles** at Delphi, Delos, and Tenedos. His Colossus was one of the Seven Wonders of the Ancient World. Perhaps the most famous of the statues of Apollo that have survived is the marble "Apollo Belvedere" in the Vatican Museum. Because he epitomizes light and therefore mystical **illumination**, Apollo's influence in esoteric literature, as well as in the arts generally, has been enormous.

Apollonius of Tyana Greek philosopher and sage, credited with **supernatural** powers. Apollonius lived almost contemporaneously with Christ and was credited with performing a number of miracles, including raising a young noblewoman from death in Rome, saving a friend from marrrying a vampire, and witnessing the assassination of Domitian at Rome in his "spirit vision" while he was physically in Ephesus.

Apophis Also known as Apepi, a huge serpent that lived in the Nile and would attempt to prevent the sun-god **Ra** from travelling across the sky in his boat. Apophis represents the powers of darkness and is one of several images from Egyptian **mythology** that have been incorporated into the **magic** of the so-called **left-hand path**.

Apotheosis The act of raising a mortal to the rank of the **gods**. In ancient Egypt, the pharaohs were regarded as god-kings, and several Roman emperors were deified. See also **Deification**.

Apparition The "appearance" of someone living or dead in conditions that cannot be accounted for by a physical cause. Although apparitions are often thought of as **ghosts**, the term is also used in occult literature to describe human forms that appear to another person as the result of **astral projection** or **clairvoyance**. Here one person is "willing" his or her consciousness to appear to another person, for purposes either of observation or direct communication. Many accounts exist in parapsychological literature of a person "appearing" in spirit form at the time of **death**, as if wishing to communicate this fact to a friend or loved one some distance away.

Apport In **spiritualism**, a solid object like a flower or a piece of jewellery that allegedly manifests during a **seance**, not as a materialization from the **ether**, but by being "transported" to the seance room by non-physical means. It is highly likely that most, if not all, examples of claimed apportation are the result of sleight-of-hand deception.

Apsara In pre-Vedic Indian **mythology**, a water **nymph** who lived in a lotus pond or water tank. Sometimes associated with fertility rites, the apsaras also had some qualities in common with the classical **sirens**, who were also irresistibly beautiful and lured men to their deaths.

Apuleius, Lucius Roman philosopher and author who lived in the second century. Apuleius was initiated into the **mystery** traditions. After practising as an advocate in Rome, he retired to northern Africa where he devoted his life to literature. His writings incorporate many ancient legends. His best-known work is *Metamorphoses*, a novel that describes how a man was transformed into a monkey.

Aquarian Age Astronomical epoch beginning with the entry of the vernal **equinox** into the constellation of Aquarius around the year 2740. Each epoch lasts approximately 2000 years and, according to astrology, derives many of its dominant qualities from the **zodiac** sign associated with it. The present epoch is that of the constellation Pisces, identified symbolically with Jesus Christ – the "fisher of men". Many regard the Age of Aquarius as a new frontier in human spiritual evolution.

Aquarius In **astrology**, the sign of the **zodiac** for those born between January 21 and February 19. Aquarius is the Water Carrier, and the astrological motif is of a man pouring water into a stream from a flask. Aquarius is an **Air** sign and is ruled by **Saturn**. The "typical" Aquarius is quiet, shy, patient, intuitive, and confident that truth will prevail. He or she may at times seem lazy or distant, but this is really the cautious nature of Aquarius revealing itself.

Aquino, Michael See **Temple of Set**.

Arabi, Ibn al (1164–1240) Spanish **mystic** who lived in Seville for thirty years, devoting his time to law and Sufi poetry. While superficially his works often appeared as simple love poems, they concealed many complex **esoteric** ideas. He believed that essence and existence were one, and maintained that the task of the mystic was union with the Perfect Man, who was an emanation of **Allah** and personified by **Mohammed**. At the time of the mystic's union with **God**, the image of God became conscious of itself. In this sense, God needed man as much as man needed God. Many of Ibn al Arabi's contemporaries denounced him as a **heretic**. See also **Sufism**.

Arahat In Pali **Buddhism**, one who has reached the last stage of spiritual attainment, a "worthy one" who is enlightened.

Arallu In Babylonian **mythology**, the abode of the dead. Regarded as a dark, forbidding cave entered through a hole in the earth, this domain was ruled by **Ereshkigal** and her consort Nergal.

Ararita A divine name in the **Kabbalah** made up of a Hebrew sentence that translates as "One is his beginning. One is his individuality. His permutation is one." "Ararita" is used as an invocation in modern Western **magic**, for example in planetary **hexagram** rituals and in **Aleister Crowley**'s ceremony of the Star Sapphire.

Aratron According to the medieval **grimoire** *Arbatel of Magick*, an Olympian spirit that governs all aspects of the universe associated with **Saturn**. Aratron is said to have many attributes. He can make people invisible, is a master of **magic** and **alchemy**, and is able to convert plants into stone and stone into treasure. Beneath him he has 49 kings, 42 princes, 35 presidents, 28 dukes, 21 ministers, 14 familiars, and 36,000 legions of spirits.

Arbatel of Magick An important medieval work on ceremonial **magic** first published in Latin in Basle (1575) and subsequently translated into English by Robert Turner (London, 1655). The book names seven **angels** as spiritual beings for the aspiring magician to contact, and these angels are identified with celestial bodies. They are **Aratron** (**Saturn**); **Bether** (**Jupiter**); **Phalec** (**Mars**); **Och** (**sun**); **Hagith** (**Venus**); **Ophiel** (**Mercury**); and **Phul** (**moon**). The *Arbatel* provides the magical **sigils** for these entities, and also describes their special powers and virtues.

Arcana The plural form of *arcanum*, a Latin word meaning "something hidden in a box or chest". The meaning has widened to suggest a secret or a mystery. The **Tarot** cards are divided into **Major Arcana** (the twenty-two trump cards) and **Minor Arcana** (the fifty-six remaining cards divided into four suits: **cups**, **wands**, **swords**, and **pentacles**).

Arcane Anything hidden or mysterious, especially those things requiring a "key" to be understood. See also **Clavicle**.

Archangel In Christian **mythology**, seven archangels were assigned to the seven heavens. They were **Michael**, **Gabriel**, **Raphael**, **Uriel**, Jophiel, Zadkiel, and Samael. According to the Book of Revelation, because Samael (**Satan**) desired to be as great as **God**, there was a war in the heavens and "Satan, which deceiveth the whole world, was cast out into the earth, and his angels were cast out with him".

In the Jewish mystical tradition represented by the **Kabbalah**, the archangels attributed to the ten emanations on the **Tree of Life** are **Metatron** (**Kether**), Ratziel

(**Chokmah**), Tzaphqiel (**Binah**), Tzadqiel (**Chesed**), Kamael (**Geburah**), Raphael (**Tiphareth**), Haniel (**Netzach**), Michael (**Hod**), Gabriel (**Yesod**), and Sandalphon (**Malkuth**).

Islam also recognizes four archangels: Gabriel, Michael, Azrael, and Israfil. The Islamic equivalent of the "fallen angel" is the devil **Eblis**, who, as Azazil, was formerly close to God but fell into disgrace for neglecting God's command that he pay homage to Adam.

Archetype In the psychology of **Carl Jung**, a primordial image found in the **collective unconscious**. According to Jung, archetypes appear in mystical visions as sacred or mythic beings and have the power to "seize hold of the psyche with a kind of primeval force". Archetypes are often personifications of processes or events in Nature (e.g. the sun-hero or **lunar goddess**), or universal expressions of family roles (e.g. the Great Father and Great Mother).

Jung believed that mythic images have an "autonomous" existence in the **psyche**. This concept is important for religious and mystical thought because, historically, archetypal visions have often been regarded by mystics as personal revelations from an external divine source. For Jung, however, such experiences could be regarded as an expression of the most profound depths of the psyche. See also **Myth**; **Solar Gods**.

Archon In **Gnosticism**, planetary rulers who guarded the world collectively and who were assigned to certain "spheres". Some archons took their names from Old Testament designations of God (e.g. Sabaoth, **Adonai, Elohim, Iao**). When a person died, his or her **soul** would be barred from flying to God by archons who would not let the soul pass unless certain **magical formulae** were acknowledged. In this sense, Sacred Knowledge or **Gnosis** provided direct access to the higher spheres.

Aries In **astrology**, the sign of the **zodiac** for those born between March 21 and April 20. Aries the Ram is a symbol of aggression and dominance, especially as a result of its association with the Roman battering ram. It is often associated with politicians and military leaders. Arians are typically assertive, somewhat self-centred, and find it difficult to compromise their viewpoints. However, for the same reasons they are often idealistic, ambitious, and pioneering in their chosen pursuits. Aries is a **Fire** sign and is usually listed as the first figure in the zodiac.

Ariolists **Magicians** who used altars as part of their **divination** proceedings. They were said to conjure **demons** through the altar and observe any "trembling" or other manifestation of occult forces at work. Ariolists were usually regarded as demonologists and idolators.

Aristeas of Proconnesus (c. 675 B.C.) A mystic mentioned in the writings of Herodotus, **Pliny**, Suidas, and Maximus of Tyre, credited with remarkable occult powers. Pliny says that Aristeas was able to leave his body by taking the shape of a raven; and Maximus records that Aristeas claimed to be able to "fly" in a **trance** state, observing distant rivers, cities, and cultures that he had not visited in his normal day-to-day life. His poem *Arimaspea* records how he became possessed by **Apollo**, journeyed beyond Scythia to the Issedonians, and later had an encounter with the mythical **griffins**, who were sacred to Apollo and guardians of the precious gold. Aristeas may have been the classical Greek equivalent of a native **shaman**.

Arithmancy Greek and Chaldean method of **divination** by numbers. The Greeks would analyze the names of warring opponents, seeking their numerical value and predicting the outcome of the contest. The Chaldeans divided their alphabet into three sections of seven letters and linked these symbolically to the seven planets. Arithmancy is a precursor of **numerology**.

Arjuna In Hindu **mythology**, the son of **Indra** and Kunti and the boyhood friend of **Krishna**. He became a great warrior, but questioned his charioteer, Krishna, on the moral validity of war. Krishna indicated to him the nature of duty and the principles of life and death, and this interchange represents one of the main themes in the ***Bhagavad-Gita***.

Armomancy **Divination** by means of the shoulders. Subjects were inspected to see whether they were suitable candidates to be sacrificed to the **gods**.

Aromatherapy The use of essential oils that derive from flowers, plants, trees, and resins, for treating the skin, preventing infection, and fortifying the body against disease. The term was coined by the French chemist René Maurice Gattefossé. See also **Bach, Dr. Edward**.

Artemis The Greek goddess of the **moon** and of hunting, whose Roman equivalent was **Diana**. Always chaste, she protected young maidens from over-zealous youths and was quick to punish transgressors with her bow and arrows. The hind and the cypress tree were sacred to her. As a **lunar goddess** she has been an influential archetype for practitioners of **witchcraft** and the contemporary goddess-worship movement. Artemis became identified with Luna, **Hecate**, and Selene.

Arts, Black A general term, usually associated with **demonology** and **sorcery**, but sometimes extended to apply to the whole spectrum of occult subjects. Linked to the symbolic status of the **Devil** as a god of darkness, and antagonist of "light" and "truth". See also **Magic, Black; Satanism**.

Arundale, Dr. George S. (1878–1945) English theosophist and associate of **Dr. Annie Besant** and **Charles Leadbeater**. Arundale joined the **Theosophical Society** in 1895 and was invited by Annie Besant to go to India in 1903. He became professor of history and later principal of the Central Hindu College in Benares, which later became Benares University. He resigned from this post in 1913 to tutor **Krishnamurti** and later travelled and lectured internationally. He returned to India in 1917 and supported Dr. Besant in her campaign for Indian home rule. He succeeded Dr. Besant as president of the Theosophical Society in 1934.

Asanas Yogic postures associated with the practice of **meditation**. There are many different asanas, the most famous being the **lotus**, in which the meditator sits upright with the legs crossed, with the foot resting on the opposite thigh, and the hands resting palm upwards on the knees. Asanas are supposed to assist the process of meditation by allowing currents of psychic energy to flow more readily, for example causing the arousal of **kundalini** through the channel **sushumna**, which corresponds to the spinal cord. Other asanas include the "lion", the "serpent", and the "bow". See also **Yoga**.

Ascendant In **astrology**, the degree of the **zodiac** rising on the eastern horizon at the specific moment for which a **figure** is cast. The latter is also known as a **horoscope** and represents the 360-degree circle of the heavens. The ascendant at the point of birth is considered by many astrologers to be almost as important as the zodiac sign.

Ascending Arc In **Theosophy**, a "life-stream" of growing spiritual entities who pass upwards through a series of increasingly mystical planes of existence. May be contrasted with the so-called **descending arc**, where etheric beings descend towards the physical plane.

Ascetic One who takes the view that spiritual truth may be obtained by austere self-discipline and renunciation of wordly pleasures; a hermit.

Asgard In Scandinavian **mythology**, Odin's citadel in the sky and the dwelling place of the **Aesir**. Asgard, which could only be reached by crossing the rainbow bridge, included **Valhalla**, the hall of heroes killed in battle.

Ashcroft-Nowicki, Dolores (1929–) Successor to **W. E. Butler** and present director of the magical order known as **Servants of the Light** (SOL), which has its headquarters in St. Helier, Jersey, one of the English Channel Islands. Ashcroft-Nowicki is of Welsh ancestry and was born into a family with an extensive esoteric lineage. Her great-grandmother was a full-blooded **gypsy** and her grandmother practised gypsy magic. Both of her parents were also third-degree initiates. Ashcroft-Nowicki was tutored in the Fraternity of the Inner Light by C. C. Chichester and W. E. Butler and is the author of over a dozen books, including recent publications like *The Tree of Ecstasy*, *Daughters of Eve* and *Building a Temple*.

Ashipu Babylonian **priests** and **sorcerers** who performed magical ceremonies to counteract evil **spells** and control Nature. They also exorcised evil spirits, returning the sick to health.

Ashram The Hindu equivalent of a monastery. A place where a **sadhu** or **guru** is engaged in spiritual teaching with a group of devotees.

Ashtaroth Also Ashtoreth. A fallen angel and grand duke of **Hell**, the leader of forty legions of **devils**. He is described in the **Goetia** as riding on a **dragon** carrying a viper in his right hand. His breath is so offensive that the invoking **magician** must "defend his face with his magic ring".

Asklepios Greek **god** famed for his powers of spiritual healing. The son of **Apollo** by Coronis, Asklepios healed the sick through dreams and was also venerated at special shrines in his honour.

Asmodeus In **demonology**, the evil spirit who was king of the demons and who filled men's hearts with rage and lust. Asmodeus angered King **Solomon** by preying on one of his wives; and it was not until the **archangel Michael** intervened, offering King Solomon a magic ring, that this mighty demon could be conquered. Asmodeus was credited with a knowledge of geometry and astronomy and could also locate buried treasure. Asmodeus is sometimes identified with Samael.

Aspects In **astrology**, angular relationships between the Earth and any two celestial bodies. Some angles are believed to be "positive" and harmonious, others "negative" and unfavourable.

Asports The reverse of **apports**, asports are objects that disappear from **seance** rooms, allegedly passing through solid walls as if they were no barrier at all. These disappearing objects sometimes manifest elsewhere.

ASPR Initials of the American **Society for Psychical Research.**

Assagioli, Roberto (1888–1974) Italian psychotherapist who was interested in **psychic** phenomena, **telepathy**, **clairvoyance**, **precognition**, and **radiesthesia**. He was director of the Institute of Psychosynthesis in Rome between 1926 and 1938, and chairman of the Psychosynthesis Research Foundation in Greenville, Delaware, USA, from 1958 onwards. Psychosynthesis is a consciousness-expanding process that includes development of the **will** and active **imagination** and stresses the uniqueness of each individual. Its sympathy to **mysticism** aligns it, to some degree, with Jungian thought. Among

Assagioli's many books and articles, the best-known are *Psychosynthesis* (1965) and *The Act of Will* (1973).

Assiah In the **Kabbalah**, the "densest" of the four worlds of manifestation. Linked by occultists to the last of the four letters of the **Tetragrammaton**, YHVH.

Asson In **voodoo**, a sacred rattle filled with seeds and used in ceremonies, together with a small bell.

Astarte Phoenician fertility **deity**, worshipped at Tyre and Sidon. She was identified with the **moon** and depicted with crescent horns. The Greeks identified her with **Aphrodite**. See also **Lunar Goddesses**.

Astragalomancy **Divination** using knuckle bones, stones, or small pieces of wood marked with letters or symbols. The diviner asks a question and interprets these letters depending on how the objects lie on the ground. The use of dice for divination is a form of astragalomancy.

Astral Body The "double" of the human body, usually regarded by occultists as its animating force, providing the body with "consciousness". The astral body has a luminous, shining appearance, and is capable of passing through physical matter. The act of willed separation of the astral body from the physical is known as **astral travel**. Occultists believe that at death the astral body leaves its physical counterpart and finds a new existence on the **astral plane**. Some parapsychologists believe that ghostly **apparitions** are astral communications between persons who have just died and those who are dear to them. The astral body is often depicted as being joined to the physical body by a **silver cord** – an etheric umbilical cord – and some subjects who experience **out-of-the-body** dissociation report seeing this cord.

Astral Plane Occult concept of a plane of existence and perception paralleling the physical dimension, but one phase removed from it, and also containing imagery from the **unconscious** mind. Occultists believe it is the plane reached during **astral projection** and also the first of the spheres that the astral body reaches after **death**.

Astral Projection See **Astral Travel; Out-of-the-Body Experience.**

Astral Shell The personality in its phase of disintegration following the **death** of the physical body.

Astral Travel Sometimes known as the **out-of-the-body experience**. Astral travel is the conscious separation of the **astral body** from the physical body resulting in an **altered state of consciousness**, and sometimes in different qualities of perception. Astral travel is achieved by a variety of active **imagination** techniques or **trance**-inducing methods. Many people who experience astral travel, like **Robert Monroe**, author of *Journeys Out of The Body*, have reported conscious perception from a different vantage point (e.g. high up in the sky, enabling one to look down over a street or into rooms of another house at a distance). Professor **Charles Tart**, of the University of California at Davis, conducted a laboratory experiment in which a subject ("Miss Z") was asked to project her consciousness out of her body while it was monitored by electroencephalograph equipment. After four attempts Miss Z successfully read a five-digit random number located on a high shelf outside her normal range of vision and facing towards the ceiling. Tart believes it is his subject's ability to astral travel, rather than a facility for **telepathy** or **clairvoyance**, that enabled her to identify the number.

Astral travel has been reported by some subjects who experience the **near-death experience** (i.e. those who, as a result of an accident or operation, are declared clinically dead, but subsequently revive). Typically, near-death subjects may witness details of their operation or resuscitation, as if from a location several feet above their body. They may report details of conversations among hospital staff and other activities that are subsequently verified.

Sometimes astral travel also has a mythic dimension, where subjects report "**heaven** and **hell**" imagery during an out-of-the-body experience. This may indicate that subjects are engaged in a dissociative encounter with positive and negative **archetypal** imagery from the unconscious mind. See also **Bardo**.

Astrology A system based on the belief that celestial bodies influence the characters and lives of human beings. Astrologers claim that individuals are affected by the cosmic situation existing at the time of their births, and therefore plot a map of the heavens at the time of birth – a **horoscope**, or **figure** – for purposes of interpretation. Individuals fall under the influence of the twelve signs of the **zodiac**, and insights into the person's character and personality may also be interpreted from the **ascendant**. There are two main types of astrology; **mundane**, which deals with large-scale phenomena (e.g. wars, natural disasters, political trends, and the destiny of nations); and **horary**, which determines the implications of undertaking a particular action at a specific time. Astrology remains one of the most popular forms of **divination**.

Astrology, Electional Branch of **astrology** that calculates appropriate days for undertaking such important events as marriage, commencement of a business enterprise, purchase of a property or home, or the date for a major journey.

Astrology, Horary Because **astrology** deals with **aspects** governing the particular moment of time at which something comes into being, it is therefore possible to determine aspects governing the time a question is asked about future events. Horary astrology may thus be applied to gauge the appropriateness of taking a particular course of action at a particular time.

Astrology, Inceptional Branch of **astrology** that deals with the outcome of an event whose location, date, and time of occurrence are known.

Astrology, Medical Branch of **astrology** that correlates **signs** of the **zodiac** and planetary influences with diseases and malfunctions of bodily organs. Some of these traditional astrological correlations are as follows: **Aries**: diseases of the head and face, smallpox, epilepsy, apoplexy, headache, measles, convulsions. **Taurus**: diseases of the neck and throat, scrofula, tonsilitis, tumours. **Gemini**: diseases of the arms and shoulders, aneurisms, frenzy, and insanity. **Cancer**: diseases of the breast and stomach, cancers, consumption, asthma, and dropsy. **Leo**: diseases of the heart, the back and the vertebrae of the neck, fevers, plague, jaundice, and pleurisy. **Virgo**: diseases of the viscera or internal organs (e.g. the intestines). **Libra**: diseases of the kidneys. **Scorpio**: diseases of the sexual organs. **Sagittarius**: diseases of the hips and muscles, gout, and rheumatism. **Capricorn**: diseases of the knees and the surface of the skin. **Aquarius**: diseases of the legs and ankles, lameness, and cramps. **Pisces**: diseases of the feet.

Astrology, Mundane Astrology that concerns itself with large-scale phenomena like wars, national political and social trends, and disasters. Mundane astrology is based on the premise that cosmic influences affect large groups of people and also the physical structure of the Earth; but predictions made on this scale are necessarily less accurate than individual calculations based on the **natal horoscope**. In mundane astrology the **planets**

are said to relate to different roles in society: **sun** (executive heads and managers); **moon** (the working classes); **Mercury** (the intelligentsia); **Venus** (ambassadors of goodwill); **Mars** (military rulers); **Jupiter** (judges and other officers of the Law); **Saturn** (executives of state); **Uranus** (air, road, and rail transport); **Neptune** (social movements); and **Pluto** (organized labour groups). Compare with **Astrology, Natal**.

Astrology, Natal The branch of astrology that focuses on the natal horoscope. See also **Horoscope, Natal**.

Astrology, Predictive Branch of **astrology** that deals with predicting future events in one's life on the basis of the **natal horoscope**. Modern astrology has moved away from the traditional preoccupation with prediction, and is now more concerned with the analysis of character traits and the link between astrology and personal self-development.

Astromancy An ancient system of **divination** by the stars.

Astrometerology The application of **astrology** to forecasting future weather patterns and conditions, especially large-scale natural disasters like floods, earthquakes, and severe storms.

Asvamedha Hindu term for the ritual sacrifice of horses, associated with the Vedic period in India. Priests sacrificed horses on behalf of kings and chieftains to ensure an increased sense of power and also to renew fertility of crops and cattle.

Aswattha Sanskrit term for the mystical **Tree of Knowledge**, represented with its branches extending downwards and its roots upwards. The branches symbolize the visible, manifested universe, and the roots the invisible world of the spirit.

Atavism The concept that a primeval force related to an earlier phase of one's evolution can reappear after many generations. The English occult artist **Austin Osman Spare** practised atavistic resurgence, a technique combining magical visualization and **sexual magic**, in order to manifest animal aspects of his personality that he believed derived from his earlier incarnations.

Athame A ritual sword or dagger used by a **priestess** or **witch** in a magical ceremony. It has a black handle and magic symbols engraved on its blade.

Athena Also Pallas Athena. In ancient Greek **mythology**, the goddess of wisdom and one of the **Twelve Great Olympians**. She was born from the head of **Zeus**. Athena's Roman counterpart was Minerva.

Atlantean In theosophical **cosmology**, the **fourth root race** to emerge in human evolution (the present phase is that of the **fifth root race**).

Atlantis A lost continent said to have sunk beneath the sea after a natural cataclysm. Legendary accounts of Atlantis derive from **Plato**'s *Timaeus* and *Critias*, which describe conversations between Egyptian priests and the Athenian statesman Solon (c. 638–558 B.C.).

Some archaeologists believe that the legend of Atlantis may derive from the violent volcanic eruption that devastated the island of Thera (Santorini), seventy-five miles north of Crete, around 1470 B.C.

Atman Sanskrit term for the **self**, the essence of a human being. It also means the Universal Self, the state of pure consciousness that unites us with the **cosmos**.

Atonement To make amends for an offence, often by making a sacrifice to a **god**.

Attis Phrygian god of vegetation and fertility whose cult became popular in ancient Greece. Attis was the lover of **Cybele**, but deserted her for a **nymph**. Cybele became intensely jealous and aroused such a frenzy of madness in Attis that he castrated himself and died.

Atziluth In the **Kabbalah**, the purest of the four worlds of manifestation, sometimes called the archetypal world. Linked by occultists to the first of the four letters of the **Tetragrammaton, YHVH**.

Aufu In ancient Egypt, the term for the physical body, which was regarded as one of the five bodies of human beings. The other bodies were **Ka**, the double; **Haidit**, the shadow; **Khu**, the magical body; and **Sahu**, the spiritual body.

Augoeides Term used by the ceremonial magician **Aleister Crowley** to describe the **holy guardian angel** or higher self. Crowley devised several Augoeides **invocations**.

Augur In ancient Rome, a **magician**-priest who interpreted the flight of birds in order to prophesy future events. Signs on the augur's east side were favourable, those on the west unfavourable. The word "augury" is now used for all kinds of **divination**.

Augury See **Augur**.

Aum See **Om**.

Aura In occult terminology, the **psychic** energy field that surrounds both animate and inanimate bodies. The aura can be dull or brightly coloured, and psychics – those who claim to perceive the auric colours directly – interpret the quality of the person or object according to the energy vibrations. Bright red, for example, indicates anger; yellow, strong intellectual powers; and purple, spirituality. Occultists generally believe that the **halos** depicted around the head of Jesus Christ and the saints are examples of mystically pure auras. Theosophists distinguish five auras: the health aura, the vital aura, the karmic aura, the character aura, and the aura of spiritual nature. See also **Kirlian Photography**.

Aureole Circular or oblong **halo** said to surround the bodies of mystics and saints. The symbolism of the aureole is linked to that of the **sun** as a life-giving force, representative of spiritual energy. The oblong aureole was especially associated with Christ. See also **Aura**.

Auric Egg In theosophical terminology, the egg-shaped "source of the human **aura**" – the seat of spiritual, mental, intellectual, and emotional faculties.

Aurobindo, Sri (1872–1950) Indian **mystic**, philosopher, and poet whose given name was Aurobindo Ghose. Educated at King's College, Cambridge, where he studied classics, he returned to India and became active in the nationalist revolts. He was placed in prison and experienced a mystical transformation that totally changed his perspectives on life. On his release he went to Pondicherry, where he studied traditional forms of **Yoga**. He synthesized these into a new philosophy of purna (integral) yoga and founded a community of followers to put these new ideas into practice. After his death this group established a new city named Auroville on the Bay of Bengal, based on Aurobindo's spiritual teachings.

Austromancy **Divination** by means of interpreting the wind.

Automatic Painting and Drawing Artworks created during **mediumistic trance**. These artworks are sometimes produced at great speed and invariably without the conscious awareness of the seer. Among spiritualists, it is often thought that a **discarnate** entity or **spirit** is working through the body of the artist, while psychologists regard the phenomenon as a state of mental dissociation leading to manifestations from the unconscious mind. Examples in recent times include the automatic drawings of **Austin Osman Spare** and surrealist works by such artists as André Masson and Max Ernst.

Automatic Speaking Similar to **automatic painting and drawing**, except that the **medium** speaks without conscious awareness, usually in a **trance** state. In the case of **oracles**, it was assumed that a **god** was speaking through the medium.

Automatic Writing Similar to **automatic painting and drawing**, except that the **medium** writes without conscious awareness, usually in a **trance state**. The handwriting produced is often in an unfamiliar style, and often assumed to be that of a deceased person.

Automatism A general term in **spiritualism** and **parapsychology** for **automatic painting, drawing, writing**, and **speaking**, performed in **trance** without the conscious awareness of the **medium**.

Avalon, Arthur See **Woodroffe, Sir John George.**

Avatar In **Hinduism**, an **incarnation** of **Vishnu**. Used more generally by occultists and theosophists to denote any divine incarnation.

Avesta Sacred book of **Zoroastrianism**, said to have been written in gold ink on 12,000 ox hides. The work was destroyed by Alexander in 330 B.C., but one third of the text was memorized by the priests and later transcribed. This part consists of twenty-one books and includes a collection of hymns known as the **Gathas**, allegedly written by **Zarathustra** himself.

Avicenna Alchemical philosopher, born at Bacara in Persia, c. A.D. 980. Skilled in mathematics and medicine, he was appointed Grand Vizier by the Sultan Magdal Doulet, but fell from grace and died at the comparatively early age of fifty-six. According to rumours, Avicenna was served by elemental spirits known as **djinn**, and he had a knowledge of powerful **magical formulae** and **incantations**. Several treatises on Hermetic philosophy are ascribed to him, including *Porta Elementorum* and *Tractatulus de Alchimia*. The latter describes **mercury** as a universal spirit pervading Nature, and combines knowledge, borrowed from Geber, with metaphysical speculation.

Avidya Hindu term for ignorance. There are two main kinds: the absence of knowledge, and wrong knowledge. Ignorance obscures the personal quest for truth, but ends with the attainment of **illumination**.

Axis Mundi In mythology and **shamanism**, the axis of the world, often symbolized by the **World Tree**, which spans the different worlds and allows the **mystic** access from one plane of reality to another.

Azael In Hebrew **mysticism**, one of the **angels** who rebelled against **God**. He is said to be chained to sharp stones in the desert, awaiting the Final Judgment.

Azoth In **alchemy**, the Universal Medicine which, according to the *Book of the Wood of Life*, "contains within itself all other medicines, as well as the first principles of all other substances …". Symbolically analagous to **God** in Nature.

B

Ba In ancient Egyptian religion, the **soul**, represented as a bird with the head of a man. The ba would wing its way towards the **gods** after death, but could return to the body as long as the latter had not been destroyed.

Baal In Phoenician **mythology**, god of fertility and vegetation and associated particularly with the winter rains. Depicted as a warrior with a horned helmet and spear, he was second only to **El**. The word "Baal" itself means "lord", a title given by Semitic peoples to the ruling deity of each city.

Baalberith In **demonology**, keeper of the archives of **hell** and official of the second order.

Ba'al Shem Hebrew for "Master of the Divine Name", a term used from the Middle Ages onwards among Hasidists and Kabbalists to describe anyone who possessed secret knowledge of the **Tetragrammaton** and other sacred names. The most famous bearer of this title was Eliezer Ba'al Shem Tov (d. A.D. 1760), the founder of modern **Hasidism**. See also **Kabbalah**.

Baalzephon In **demonology**, captain of the guard and sentinels of **hell**.

Babau In French **folklore**, a mythic ogre who used to devour wicked children.

Babylon Capital of ancient Babylonia, built by King Nebuchadnezzar II. It was a magnificent city and the site of the famous Hanging Gardens. It has come to symbolize wordly existence at the opposite end of the spectrum from mystical **transcendence**. In mystical usage, therefore, its connotation has become, perhaps unfairly, negative.

Bacchanalia Roman festival in honour of Bacchus, god of wine. The rites were originally performed by women, but later included men. With time, the ceremonies became excessive and were finally banned by the Roman Senate in 186 B.C.

Bacchanals Worshippers of **Bacchus** who indulged in drunken orgies.

Bacchantes Women dedicated to the worship of **Bacchus**. Euripides described them in *Bacchae* as revellers who dressed themselves in furs and skins and wandered through forests and mountains filled with the divine spirit of their god.

Bacchus Roman god of wine, linked to the Greek deity **Dionysus**. He was the son of **Zeus** and Semele and the husband of Ariadne.

Bach, Dr. Edward (1886–1936) British physician who graduated from Birmingham University to University College Hospital, London, but subsequently discarded orthodox medicine for **homeopathy**. In 1930 he left his practice as a bacteriologist and pathologist at the London Homeopathic Hospital and began to search in the countryside for wild flowers with healing properties. Over seven years, Dr. Bach isolated thirty-eight flowers whose vital essence he believed could be used to treat such emotional afflictions as fear, loneliness, exhaustion, intolerance, and despondency. These treatments have become known as the Bach Flower Remedies, and include rock rose and aspen (for fear), water violet (for loneliness), and crab apple (for despondency).

Bacon, Roger (1214–1294) Medieval alchemist, born near Ilchester, Somerset, in England. He studied theology and science at Oxford and could write Latin, Greek, and Hebrew. He was credited with the discovery of gunpowder, probably as a result of his experiments with nitre. He also studied alchemy and came to believe in the **Philosopher's Stone**, by means of which it was thought that **gold** could be purified, base metals transformed, and the human body fortified against death. His works included *Opus Maius* and *The Mirror of Alchemy*.

Bad In Persian mythology, a **djinn** who had power over the winds and tempests and who could be summoned on the twenty-second day of the month.

Baha'i Religious faith and doctrine established in 1863 by Mirza Husayan Ali (Bahá'u'lláh), who was born in Tehran in 1817. He taught the unity of all races, creeds, and religions and believed in a process of continuous revelation. The Baha'i Faith has no formal clergy or ritual and regards members of the church as a vast single family. There are numerous Baha'i centres throughout the world.

Bahir More accurately, *Sefer Ha-Bahir*. One of the earliest works in kabbalistic literature, dating from the twelfth century A.D. This book is rich in symbolic language and describes the ten **sephiroth** of the **Tree of Life** in terms of divine attributes.

Baiame Among the Wiradjeri **Aborigines** of western New South Wales, a sky god who appears to men in their dreams and initiates them, helping them become great **shamans**. Baiame is described as a very old man with a long beard. Two great quartz crystals extend from his shoulders to the sky above him. When Baiame appears to Aborigines in their dreams, he causes a sacred waterfall of liquid quartz to engulf their bodies. They then grow wings and learn how to fly. Later, an inner flame and heavenly cord are incorporated into the bodies of the new shamans.

Bailey, Alice (1880–1949) English **mystic** who believed she was in contact with "Masters" on the inner planes, including **Koot Hoomi** and an entity called "the Tibetan". She founded the Arcane School and published a vast body of writings, some of which she said owed their direct inspiration to the Masters. Her books include *A Treatise on Cosmic Fire* and *Unfinished Autobiography*, published after her death.

Balam In the magical work known as the ***Key of Solomon***, a powerful king with three heads – the first that of a bull, the second a man, and the third a ram. He had the tail of a serpent, eyes of fire, and rode upon a bear. Balam had the power to make people invisible, and could predict future events.

Balder Also Baldur. In Scandinavian **mythology**, the **god** of the **sun** and the personification of wisdom, goodness, and beauty. He was the son of **Odin** and one of the **Aesir**.

Balfour, Arthur J. (1848–1930) British Conservative statesman who became Lord of the Treasury and succeeded Lord Salisbury as British Prime Minister. He was one of the early members of the **Society for Psychical Research**.

Bali In Indian **mythology**, a **demon** who became king of **Heaven** and Earth, but who was finally overcome by **Vishnu**, incarnating as a dwarf named Vamana. Vamana was granted a wish by Bali, and asked for as much land as could be obtained in three steps. Vamana covered the universe in two steps and with his third crushed Bali down into the **Underworld**.

Ballechin House A haunted house in Perthshire, Scotland, that was the subject of much controversy in the 1890s. Strange noises, including voices, footsteps, and knockings, were reported by two researchers, Colonel Lemesurier Taylor and Miss A. Goodrich-Freer, who conducted an investigation of the phenomena. Ballechin

House is regarded as one of the classic cases of haunted houses. See also **Hauntings**.

Bangs Sisters Chicago **mediums** Lizzie and May Bangs who produced spirit writings and drawings. They were investigated by Admiral William Usborne Moore and the noted parapsychologist **Dr. Hereward Carrington**, and exposed as frauds.

Banishing Ritual In **ceremonial magic**, a ritual designed to ward off negative or evil influences. The banishing ritual of the Lesser Pentagram is performed in a **magical circle** and commences in the East. The magician uses a sword to inscribe **pentagrams** in the air and invokes the **archangels Raphael, Gabriel, Michael**, and **Uriel** at the four quarters. The banishing also includes a ritual **prayer** known as the "Kabbalistic Cross".

Banisteriopsis Common ingredient in a number of **psychedelic** sacraments used by **shamans** in South America to contact the supernatural world. Yage, Caapi, and Ayahuasca all contain banisteriopsis and produce remarkable effects, including the separation of the "soul" from the body, visions of predatory animals and distant locations, the experience of **heaven** and **hell**, and explanatory visions of thefts and homicides. The active ingredients of banisteriopsis are the alkaloids harmine, harmaline, and d-tetrahydroharmine.

Banshee In Ireland and Scotland, a **nature-spirit** who takes the form of an old woman and wails mournfully under the windows of a house where a person will soon die.

Baphomet Demonic **deity** represented by **Eliphas Lévi** as a goat-headed god with wings, breasts, and an illuminated torch between his horns. The medieval **Order of the Knights Templar** was accused by Philip IV of France in 1307 of worshipping this god, but only a dozen of the 231 knights interrogated admitted to this practice. The name Baphomet may be a corruption of Mahomet (**Mohammed**). Eliphas Lévi identified Baphomet with the **Tarot** card ***The Devil***.

Baptism Ritual immersion in water, based on the ancient concept that water is the source of life. In Christianity, it symbolizes membership of the Church and the repentance of sins. It was parodied in medieval **witchcraft**, where children and toads were allegedly baptized on behalf of the **Devil** during the **witches' sabbath**.

Baquet See **Animal Magnetism**.

Barakah In **Islam**, a blessing bestowed by a holy person.

Barbanell, Maurice (1902–1981) Leading English authority on **psychic phenomena**. He founded the journal *Psychic News*, which he edited until 1946 and then again from 1960; he was also editor of the weekly newspaper *Two Worlds*. Barbanell was fascinated by **parapsychology** and **faith healing**, and gave **psychical research** considerable respectability. Among his many books are *The Case of Helen Duncan, Harry Edwards and His Healing*, and *This is Spiritualism*.

Bardo In Tibetan **Buddhism**, the state between **death** and **rebirth**. According to the ***Tibetan Book of the Dead***, the consciousness of deceased individuals passes through various Bardo visions, which are a symbolic manifestation of **karma** – good or evil deeds – and personality. The Tibetan lamas teach a technique of dying that enables the individual to pass through these Bardo visions, escaping from the karmic cycle of rebirth and entering **nirvana**.

Bardon, Franz (1909–1958) An influential modern **ritual magician**, Franz Bardon was born in Katherein, near Opava in the present-day Czech Republic. Bardon was the oldest of thirteen children and the only son of a devout Christian **mystic**, Viktor Bardon. According to a close friend of the family, Viktor prayed that his son might receive some form of spiritual **initiation** and he maintained that in 1924 the spirit of a high **Hermetic adept** entered the body of his fourteen-year old son in order to bring about this initiation.

In the 1920s and 1930s Bardon became a stage magician who gained fame in Germany under the stage name "Frabato". However he was also exploring authentic forms of **magic**, and in due course developed a model of the magical universe which drew in part on **Taoism** and **Hindu** cosmology as well as Hermetic concepts of the five **elements**. There is some evidence that Bardon was a member of the Fraternity of Saturn, an occult lodge which flourished in Germany in the early part of the 20th century.

Bardon's major work, *The Practice of Magical Evocation*, describes the 360 "spirits" of the **zodiac** and also provides their magical **sigils**. His other published works include *Initiation into Hermetics, The Key to the True Qabalah* and an "occult novel" titled *Frabato the Magician*, said to be based on true events.

During the last years of World War II Bardon spent nearly four years in a concentration camp. After the war, he practised as a naturopath and graphologist while also devoting himself to writing and research into the Hermetic traditions. However his career was interrupted when he was arrested during a Communist purge. He died in unusual circumstances in a prison hospital in Brno, Czechoslovakia, in July 1958.

Barren Signs In **astrology**, those signs which indicate a tendency towards barrenness, specifically **Gemini**, **Leo**, and **Virgo**.

Barrett, Francis Best known as the occult author of ***The Magus***, published in London in 1801. The work includes sections on magical herbs and stones, **alchemy**, **numerology**, and **ceremonial magic**, and includes portraits of such demons as Theulus and **Asmodeus**. He may have influenced the magical novels of **Bulwer-Lytton**, who regarded himself as an occult adept.

Barrett, Sir William F. (1844–1925) Pioneer of psychical research, Barrett was born in Jamaica and became professor of physics at Dublin University in 1873. He studied a range of paranormal phenomena, including **divination**, **telepathy**, and **spiritualism**, and believed telepathy to be an established fact. He helped found the **Society for Psychical Research** (SPR) in Britain with Edward Dawson, and later became its president. He was also instrumental in establishing the American Society for Psychical Research. Towards the end of his life, he abandoned the theory that all spiritual **mediums** were necessarily fraudulent. In a paper delivered to the SPR in 1924, he concluded that evidence existed for life after death and communication with the spirit world.

Bashir, Mir (1907–) Legendary Indian palmist, resident in Britain since 1948. He has worked with physicians and criminologists, describing diseases and personal characteristics useful for clinical identification, and has a library of hand prints that exceeds 50,000. Author of *The Art of Hand Analysis*. See also **Palmistry**.

Basilides Gnostic philosopher who lived and taught in Alexandria around A.D. 125–140. A disciple of Glaucias – who had known the apostle Peter – Basilides wrote twenty-four commentaries on the Gospels. He also developed a complex **cosmology** of his own, which involved 365 **heavens**, each with its own angelic population. Only the last of these heavens, embracing the earth, was immediately accessible to ordinary people. According to Basilides, the last heaven was headed by the "God of the Jews"; but the supreme principal over all 365 divisions was

Abraxas. Basilides was condemned by Bishop Irenaeus as a heretic.

Basilisk Also known as a cockatrice, this legendary beast was said to be a small, deadly serpent, born from a cock's egg and hatched by a toad on a bed of dung. It was often represented as having the head of a cock, a feathered back, and four pairs of legs. In legends, the basilisk had a deathly breath that made it much feared; and in the Middle Ages it was assumed that if a knight on horseback were to spear the creature with his lance, the basilisk's poison would pass up through the spear, killing both knight and horse. The only sure way to overcome the basilisk was to confront it with a mirror: the creature would die by gazing on its own reflection.

Bast Egyptian cat-headed **goddess**, daughter of **Isis**. She was worshipped at Bubastis in the Nile Delta and regarded as a goddess of fertility. As such, she is one of the most popular ancient Egyptian deities in contemporary **witchcraft** and **sexual magic** cults.

Bealing Bells A classic case of bells that allegedly rang without human intervention, as if through **poltergeist** activity. The incidents took place between February 2 and March 27 1834, and involved nine bells in the kitchen of Bealings House in Suffolk, England. At different times several members of the household observed the bells ringing spontaneously. No satisfactory explanation has ever been forthcoming.

Beatific Vision, The In Eastern and Western **mysticism**, the Union with God, or realization of oneself as **Brahman** – the supreme mystical attainment. It is sometimes called by the Hindus *Sat Chit Ananda*: "Being-Awareness-Bliss".

Bechard Described in the magical work *Grimorium Verum* as a spirit with power over winds, tempests, lightning, hail, and rain. **Magicians** could summon him with a magical charm bearing his **character**.

Beelzebub Traditionally, one of the most powerful demons – ranking in importance with **Lucifer**, **Ashtaroth**, **Satan**, and Beherit – Beelzebub was originally Baal-zebub, god of Ekron in the ninth century B.C., and is mentioned in 2 Kings 1:2. The Canaanites worshipped him in a temple unpolluted by flies; hence his popular designation as "Lord of the Flies". Flies were regarded as unclean creatures that thrived on corpses, and Beelzebub in this regard was thought of as a demon of decay. Luke 2:15 describes him as "chief of the devils".

Behemoth Described in the apocryphal *Book of Enoch* as a great monster and counterpart of **Leviathan**. In Hebrew **mythology**, the two beasts – the first of them masculine, the second feminine – slay each other on the final Day of Judgment.

Bel In Babylonian **mythology**, one of the supreme triad of the gods, the others being Anu, lord of the heavens, and **Ea**, lord of the waters. Bel was the chief god and founder of the Babylonian empire – his name literally means "King". The spelling "Bel" is the Akkadian form; its Semitic equivalent is **Baal**. Bel derives from the Sumerian god **Enlil**.

Belial Also Beliar, the demon of lies, described in the **Dead Sea Scrolls** as "an angel of hostility" whose "dominion is in darkness". He was one of the demons summoned by the notorious black **magician** and murderer **Gilles de Rais**. The name Belial possibly derives from the Hebrew expression *beli yaal*, meaning "without worth", generally applied to someone who was wicked and debased.

Bell, Book, and Candle Ceremonial excommunication whereby a **priest** reads a malediction from a book, tolls a bell for the dead, and extinguishes candles to indicate that the soul of the offending spirit has been cast forth from the vision of God.

Belomancy Divination by analyzing the path of arrows in flight.

Belphegor A **demon** who appears in the form of a woman, and whose name derives from a form of **Baal**, worshipped by the Moabites on Mount Phegor. Belphegor was a demon of discoveries and inventions.

Beltane A major **Wiccan** sabbat celebrated on April 30, Beltane is a **Celtic** fertility celebration. The name of this Sabbat may come from the Celtic deity Bel or Balor – god of light and fire – for in ancient times "bel-fires" were lit on the hilltops to celebrate the return of life and fertility to the world. Wiccans often celebrate Beltane by dancing the **maypole** and celebrating the love between men and women. Mythologically, Beltane honours the mating of the Sun God with the fertile Earth Goddess. Beltane is also known as May Eve.

Bender, Dr. Hans (1907–1991) German professor of psychology at the University of Freiburg who had a long association with **psychical research** and "borderline" psychology. Dr. Bender was a correspondent for the **Society for Psychical Research** in London and the author of several books and articles on **parapsychology**, **psychic mediums**, **poltergeists**, and **extrasensory perception**. His main books include *Mental Automatisms* (1936) and *Parapsychology: Results and Problems* (1953). Dr. Bender translated several English-language parapsychology classics into German, including G. N. M. Tyrrell's *Personality of Man.*

Bendit, Laurence Born in France, Bendit studied psychiatry at Cambridge University and gained the first doctorate in medicine ever awarded by a British university for a thesis on **parapsychology**. Deeply interested in psychic phenomena and the links between **extrasensory perception** and psychiatry, he joined the **Theosophical Society** and the **Society for Psychical Research** in London. Bendit published Paranormal Cognition in 1944 and co-authored the classic work *The Psychic Sense* with his wife Phoebe (published 1942, reissued 1957). The Bendits later moved from England to Ojai, California.

Bennett, Allan (1872–1923) A leading figure in the **Hermetic Order of the Golden Dawn**, he tutored **Aleister Crowley** and later became a worshipper of **Shiva** in Ceylon. Bennett's **magical name** was Frater Iehi Aour ("Let there be light"). He engaged himself in **ceremonial magic** with such vigour that he rivalled **Samuel MacGregor Mathers** as a dominant figure among the English occultists of his time. He wrote the powerful evocation of Taphthartharath, used for manifesting the spirit of **Mercury** to visible appearance. He also compiled part of the magical reference system known as 777, later published by Aleister Crowley. In 1900 he left England and became a Buddhist monk. He assumed the title Bhikku Ananda Metteya, and was influential in founding the British Buddhist Society in 1908.

Bennu In Egyptian **mythology**, a legendary bird believed to be the **reincarnation** of the soul of **Osiris**. Like the **phoenix**, the bennu bird rose to new life amidst the flames and was closely linked to the **sun**. At Heliopolis, where it was worshipped as a form of **Ra**, the bennu bird was said to fly forth from the Island of Fire in the **Underworld**, announcing the rebirth of the sun.

Bergson, Henri (1859–1941) French philosopher and author who became president of the **Society for Psychical Research** in 1914. Bergson believed that the human mind could operate and survive independently of the body, and he was impressed by the evidence for life after death

Bergson won the Nobel Prize for Literature in 1927. His sister, Moina, was married to **Samuel MacGregor Mathers**, a leading occultist and co-founder of the **Hermetic Order of the Golden Dawn**. See also **Mathers, Mrs. Moina.**

Berith In **demonology**, an evil duke, wearing red clothing and a golden crown, and riding a red horse. He is summoned by means of a magical ring. He claims to be able to turn all metals into gold, but is a notorious liar and not to be trusted.

Bermuda Triangle A term associated with the mystery surrounding **unidentified flying objects** (UFOs) and coined by Vincent Gaddis in the magazine *Argosy*. The triangle is an area defined by Bermuda, Florida, and Puerto Rico, where several ships and aircraft have disappeared without trace. While some **ufologists** associate these disappearances with extraterrestrial intervention, the more orthodox explanation is that atmospheric aberrations, including clear-air turbulence and electromagnetic gravitational disturbances, are responsible.

Bernadette, St. (1844–1879) Associated with Lourdes in France, St. Bernadette was Bernadette Soubirous, a shepherdess, who in 1858 claimed to have eighteen visions of the Virgin Mary. She later became a nun, and was canonized in 1933. Lourdes has become a famous healing site, and the Roman Catholic Church has established a bureau to authenticate **miracles** that occur there.

Bernard, Pierre Known as "Oom the Omnipotent", Bernard introduced Tantric **sexual magic** to the West when he began teaching **Hatha Yoga** at his New York Sanskrit College in 1909. His interests were not totally spiritual, however, and sexual charges were made against him by young girls under his tuition. Bernard subsequently married a vaudeville dancer, founded the Sacred Order of Tantriks, and established an occult college in New Jersey.

Besant, Dr. Annie (1847–1933) English theosophist and social reformer who became president of the **Theosophical Society** in 1891. During her life she was involved in many social movements, including the Fabian Society, the Indian Home Rule League, and the Boy Scouts. Originally an intellectual force rather than a spiritual one, she experienced a dramatic illumination by making contact with the Tibetan **mahatma** Master Moyra and became his disciple. In 1910 she and **Charles Leadbeater** began to sponsor **Jiddu Krishnamurti** as the new world teacher. The Order of the Star in the East was formed to promote this cause, but Krishnamurti later broke away, renouncing these spiritual claims. Dr. Besant was a leader in the Co-Masonic movement and a prolific author. Her best-known works include *The Ancient Wisdom, Evolution of Life and Form*, and an account of psychic experiments with Leadbeater titled *Man: Whence, How and Whither*. See also **Co-Masonry**.

Bestiary Medieval catalogue of tales about animals, real and mythical, portraying an allegorical or moral Christian theme. Bestiaries were often beautifully illustrated.

Bether According to the medieval **grimoire** the ***Arbatel of Magick***, an **Olympian** spirit that governs all aspects of the universe associated with **Jupiter**. Bether is said to be a "dignified" spirit who can produce miraculous medical cures and is capable of prolonging human life to seven hundred years. He also "reconcileth the spirits of the aire". Bether has beneath him 42 kings, 35 princes, 28 dukes, 21 counsellors, 24 ministers, 7 messengers, and 29,000 legions of spirits.

Bewitchment The act of gaining power over another person by means of **spells**, **incantations**, or **sorcery**.

Bhagavad-Gita "The Song of the Blessed", a major Hindu religious poem forming a part of the sixth book of the **Mahabharata**. It includes a dialogue between **Krishna** and **Arjuna** on moral questions arising from the tragic consequences of warfare. Krishna teaches Arjuna that positive action in the world is necessary, and that one must follow the calling of one's inner nature, recognizing that the **self** is eternal.

Bhakti Hindu term for total devotion to, and love for, **God**. In **yoga**, a distinction is drawn between the path of devotion and that of knowledge (Jnana). Bhakti Yoga is one of the major paths of yoga (the others include Mantra Yoga, Matha Yoga, **Raja Yoga**, and **Laya Yoga**). Among the deities most revered by followers of Bhakti Yoga are **Shiva**, **Shakti**, and **Vishnu**.

Bhikku Pali term for a Buddhist monk, or lay follower of **Gautama Buddha**. Bhikkus follow a monastic lifestyle, are celibate, and seek to overcome all worldly attachments. They wear yellow or saffron robes and are supported by alms. Much of the bhikku's day is spent in **meditation**, **prayer**, and chanting.

Bible Collection of books comprising the scriptures of the Old and New Testament, and the **Apocrypha**. The Old Testament includes those works recognized as authentic by the Jews, including the books of the Law, the Prophets, and the Sacred Writings. The Apocrypha includes the books of the Greek Septuagint, which were not included in the Hebrew canon, but are included in the Vulgate. However, the Apocrypha are often omitted from the authorized versions of the Bible. The New Testament includes those books recognized by the Church in the fourth century as canonical. These may be divided under three headings: history (Matthew to Acts), epistles (Romans to Jude), and prophecy (Revelation). The discovery of the **Dead Sea Scrolls** and the **Nag Hammadi Library** has brought to light further works of vital significance to Christianity. However, their scriptural relevance has yet to be fully determined.

Bibliomancy **Divination** by means of a book, often the Bible. The book is opened at random and the person points to a line or passage while keeping the eyes closed. **Moslems** use the **Qur'an** for this purpose; in the Middle Ages, Virgil's *Aeneid* and Homer's *Iliad* were popular.

Bicorporeal Astrological term for signs that include two symbolic figures. See also **Astrology**; **Double-bodied Signs**.

Bilocation The ability to appear in two places, far apart, at the same time. Compare with **Apparitions**; **Astral Travel**.

Binah In the **Kabbalah**, the third mystical emanation of the **Tree of Life**, following **Kether** and **Chokmah**. Occultists identify Binah with the Great Mother in all her forms. She is the womb of forthcoming, the source of all the great images and forms that manifest in the universe as **archetypes**. She is also the supreme female principal in the process of creation and, via the process of **mythological correspondences**, is associated with such deities as the Virgin Mary, **Rhea**, **Isis**, and **Demeter** in other pantheons.

Bioenergy Expression used by therapist Wilhelm Reich to describe the life energy in the body. According to Reich, this life-force can become trapped in muscle groups when they contract in spasm, following emotional shocks or repression of sexual instincts.

Biofeedback Literally, feedback from the body, "procedures which allow us to tune in to our bodily functions and, eventually, to control them". Biofeedback was pioneered in the United States by Dr. Joe Kamiya in San Francisco, California. He monitored **alpha**

brain waves with an electroencephalograph (EEG) device that produced a pleasant sound only at certain levels of alpha. He discovered that subjects could learn to generate or suppress alpha waves, and that when alpha was enhanced it led to feelings of inner well-being. Biofeedback is now used in hospitals to control abnormal body functions (e.g. migraines). It also has applications in controlling so-called involuntary or "autonomic" body functions such as heart rate and blood pressure.

Bioplasma Term proposed in 1966 by the Russian scientist V. S. Grischenko to describe the "fifth state of matter", in addition to the established categories: solids liquids, gases, and plasma. According to Grischenko, bioplasma – or biological plasma – is present in all living organisms and to this extent equates with what is elsewhere described as the universal **life-force**. The energy field or corona depicted in **Kirlian photography** is regarded by several Russian parapsychologists as evidence for the existence of bioplasma. See also **Ch'i**; **Prana**.

Bioplasmic Body Among Soviet parapsychologists, a term used as a synonym for the **astral body**.

Biorhythms The theory, based on research by Dr. Hermann Swoboda, Dr. Wilhelm Fliess, and Dr. Alfred Teltscher, that everyone is affected, throughout life, by three internal cycles – physical, emotional, and intellectual. The physical cycle, which affects resistance to disease, strength, co-ordination, and other body functions, takes twenty-three days to complete. The emotional cycle, which includes such factors as sensitivity, mood, perceptions, and mental well-being, passes through twenty-eight days. The intellectual cycle, which includes memory, alertness, and the logical aspects of intelligence, takes thirty-three days.

The cycles begin at the time of birth and from "zero", rise into a high, positive phase, after which they begin to decline or become negative. Biorhythms have a predictive quality because they relate to cyclic behaviour patterns. Knowledge of likely "up" and "down" days is a way of anticipating a potential period of positive activity or warning against a particularly negative phase. One would not want to make important decisions or place oneself at risk in an especially negative phase. By contrast, "up" days are times of high performance and creativity.

Birch In Scandinavian **mythology**, a tree sacred to **Thor**, and a symbol of spring. The **witch's broomstick** was traditionally made of birch.

Birthstone In **astrology**, gems ascribed to particular signs of the **zodiac**. They are Diamond (**Aries**); Emerald (**Taurus**); Agate (**Gemini**); Ruby (**Cancer**); Sardonyx (**Leo**); Sapphire (**Virgo**); Opal (**Libra**); Topaz (**Scorpio**); Turquoise (**Sagittarius**); Garnet (**Capricorn**); Amethyst (**Aquarius**); and Bloodstone (**Pisces**).

Bittul Ha-Yesh In the eighteenth-century Jewish charismatic movement, **Hasidism**, the term for the self-annihilation of the **ego** – a process believed to lead to spiritual knowledge and mystical states of consciousness.

Black Arts See **Arts, Black**.

Black Box See **Radionics**.

Black Magic See **Magic, Black**.

Black Mass Satanic practice, deliberately parodying the central ritual of Roman Catholicism, in which the **host** (representing the Body of Christ) is stolen from a church, consecrated by an unfrocked priest, and desecrated. The ceremony includes activities forbidden by the Church, including the alleged sacrifice of unbaptized infants and the recitation of the Lord's Prayer backwards. In the Middle Ages, the threat of satanism was greatly exaggerated by the **Inquisition**, although undoubtedly small groups of **heretics** and **satanists** did exist (see **Albigenses, Knights Templar, Witches**). In modern times there have been spasmodic outbreaks of satanism, the most visible of which was represented by Anton La Vey's **Church of Satan** in San Francisco, California, in the late 1960s.

Blackwood, Algernon (1869–1951) One of England's most famous occult novelists, Blackwood grew up in the Black Forest and later attended Edinburgh University. A one-time member of the **Hermetic Order of the Golden Dawn**, he was a journalist with *The New York Times* and a prolific writer of mystical and supernatural tales. His works include *John Silence, The Bright Messenger*, and *Pan's Garden*.

Blake, William (1757–1827) English visionary artist, poet, and mystic who, like his father, was profoundly influenced by **Emmanuel Swedenborg**. Blake was apprenticed to an engraver, began to exhibit at the Royal Academy in 1780, and devised new methods of printing. However, his inner world was populated by **spirits** and visions. As a child he communicated with angelic beings and later, as an engraver, he claimed that the spirit of his deceased brother Robert had shown him new printing techniques. Blake's poetry and art are profound and richly symbolic, and he was very much a myth-maker. His **cosmology**, while unique in many respects, in some degree resembles that of the **Kabbalah**. Blake's works include *Songs of Innocence, The Marriage of Heaven and Hell, Songs of Experience*, and *The Book of Urizen*.

Blavatsky, Madame Helena Petrovna (1831–1891) Russian **mystic** and adventurer who founded the **Theosophical Society** in 1875. As a child, she claimed to converse with invisible friends and was often frightened by phantoms. After an unsuccessful marriage at the age of seventeen, she travelled widely through Europe, America, and Asia; and, after journeying in India and Tibet, claimed that she had been initiated by **mahatmas** or **Masters** into the secrets of esoteric **mysticism**. She believed that these Masters helped her to write many of her major works, which in turn provided the foundation for modern Theosophy. Her first book was *Isis Unveiled*, and this was followed by *The Secret Doctrine, The Key to Theosophy*, and *The Voice of Silence*, among many others. Madame Blavatsky was a powerful **medium**, but it is likely that many of the psychic powers she claimed were given to her by the Masters were clever deceptions. Her main contribution to mystical thought was the manner in which she sought to synthesize Eastern and Western philosophy and religion, thereby providing a framework for understanding universal occult teachings.

"Blessed Be" Phrase used by **witches** both as a greeting and as a farewell.

Bletonism **Divination** by analyzing currents of water.

Blood Synonymous in **magic** with **life-force**, blood is used by some **sorcerers** and black magicians to inscribe magical **names of power**, and to sign magical pacts with spirits; it is also consumed as a power-bestowing sacrament.

Blue A colour with varying symbolic ascriptions in **mysticism** and naturopathy. Bishop **C. W. Leadbeater** believed that blue, as a component of the human **aura**, indicated religious sensitivity and devotion, while some other mystics associate it with the throat **chakra**. Some naturopaths and spiritual healers believe that blue light may be used to treat burns, dysentery, colic, respiratory problems, and rheumatism.

Bodhi Sanskrit term meaning "to awaken". Wisdom or enlightenment is achieved only by emptying the mind and realizing pure and eternal Truth.

Bodhidharma (470–543) Indian monk who brought traditional forms of Indian **meditation** to China, and who is credited with introducing **Ch'an Buddhism** – the form that would later give rise to **Zen**.

Bodhisattva In **Buddhism**, one who aspires to be like the Buddha, but who has not quite attained complete enlightenment. In theosophical usage it refers to one who has become aware of his own divinity and has attained the sense of immortality while still on earth. In their next **incarnation**, such a person may become a fully realized Buddha and have no further need of **rebirth**.

Bodhi Tree The tree under which **Gautama Buddha** sat when he became enlightened. The tree was located at Gaya, Bihar, and belonged to a species related to the fig tree.

Body of Light Occult term for the **astral body**. Magicians believe that the body of light takes the form conjured in the **imagination** and that they can transfer their consciousness to this form, bringing it to life on the **astral plane**.

Boehme, Jacob (1575–1624) German shoemaker who, at the age of twenty-five, experienced a mystical transformation that had a profound and lasting effect on his life. A devout Lutheran, Boehme believed literally that **God** was far away, in the distant reaches of the universe – although mystical visions brought this presence nearer. Nevertheless, life on earth was a constant struggle between good and **evil**. In many instances, Boehme felt, evil seemed to have the upper hand. He therefore felt constrained to "wrestle with the love and the mercy of God" in order to break through "the gates of Hell". Like a true **mystic**, Boehme came to the view that the human will had to subjugate itself to God's will because the latter represented true Reality. Interested in astronomy and **cosmology**, Boehme equated God the Father with the sky, and Jesus Christ with the **sun**. The light from the stars represented the Holy Spirit. To achieve true union with God, a person had to go through a process of "spiritual birth", recognizing the divine essence that lies within. Like the Kabbalists, who were an influence on his thought, Boehme believed in the concept of the **macrocosm and microcosm** – that people mirror the universe and are a reflection of God. Thus the mystic way is essentially a path to self-realization.

Boggart Mischievous spirit, fond of **poltergeist** activities. The boggart had a semi-human appearance, with certain animal characteristics such as fur or a tail. Legends concerning boggarts abound in Yorkshire, England.

Bogie In Scottish **mythology**, **goblins** or phantoms that were harmful and had a frightening appearance. Variants on this theme can be found elsewhere (e.g. the Yorkshire "bug-a-boo"). The modern equivalent, which has a more colloquial and less supernatural connotation, is "bogeyman".

Bogomils Tenth-century Bulgarian sect, which maintained that there are two creative forces in the universe, good and **evil**. They believed that the world was intrinsically evil and that the **Devil** had assisted in creating Adam. They also claimed that Christ's resurrection was illusory and that the Holy Cross was a demonic symbol, detestable to **God**.

Bokor Also, Bocor. In **voodoo**, a practitioner of **magic** who is not necessarily an initiate and is therefore distinguished from the **houngan** or priest.

Bolen, Jean Shinoda Best known for her popular books *Goddesses in Everywoman* and *Gods in Everyman*, Bolen is a Jungian analyst and also Clinical Professor of Psychiatry at the University of California. Intrigued by what she has called "the global return of the Goddess in different forms", Bolen has identified herself with a spiritual perspective which discards the dominance of the old patriarchal forms of religion. Bolen supports the concept that both men and women should live their lives archetypally, and believes that **myth** has a major role to play in this process. According to Bolen, myth is a form of metaphor and allows us to see our ordinary lives from a different perspective.

Bone, Eleanor A noted modern **witch**, and a spokesperson for the **modern witchcraft** movement. Together with **Patricia Crowther** and Monique Wilson, she was one of the heirs to the estate of the warlock **Gerald Gardner**.

Bonewits, Isaac (1949–) Allegedly the world's "first academically accredited **magician**", Bonewits was born in Royal Oak, Michigan. He graduated with a bachelor's degree in **magic** from the University of California in Los Angeles and went on to found the Aquarian Anti-defamation League. He was associate editor of the now defunct *Gnostica* journal and is the author of *Real Magic*.

Book of Changes See ***I Ching***.

Book of Splendour Literal translation of the title of the ***Zohar***, the main work of the medieval **Kabbalah**, written by the Spanish mystic **Moses de Léon** around 1280.

Book of the Dead Title for a work that describes the after-death condition and provides guidance for the passage of the deceased soul through **heaven** and **hell** states. There are also descriptions of deities one might expect to encounter on the after-death visionary journey. The best-known examples are the ***Egyptian Book of the Dead*** and the ***Tibetan Book of the Dead*** (see **Bardo**). Other examples include the Egyptian texts known as the ***Am Tuat*** and *Book of Gates*, and the *Ethiopian Book of the Dead* (*Lefefa Sedek*), which combines Christian and Gnostic thought.

Book of Thoth A modern term for the **Tarot**, based on the mistaken assumption that the Tarot had an Egyptian origin. It derives largely from the theories of French occultist **Antoine Court de Gébelin**, who believed that the Tarot was part of an initiatory procedure in the **Great Pyramid**; and **Aleister Crowley**, who used this title for his own work on the Tarot.

Borley Rectory Popularly regarded as the "most haunted house in England", Borley Rectory stood opposite Borley Church in Essex until it was gutted by fire in 1939. Reverend H. D. E. Bull was rector at Borley from 1862 to 1892, and several members of his family reported seeing, at different times, a phantom nun and also a phantom coach and horses that would appear and then suddenly vanish mysteriously. Strange footsteps, ringing bells, whisperings, and unexplained lights were also reported, and comparable events occurred after Reverend Lionel Foyster became rector in 1930. Borley Rectory was investigated by the famous "ghost hunter" **Harry Price**, and a number of reputable impartial witnesses, including members of the BBC, the Royal Air Force, and the diplomatic corps; but the results were inconclusive and were challenged by the **Society for Psychical Research**. Criticisms levelled at Price by other parapsychologists were later withdrawn, and **hauntings** seem to have continued on the rectory site. No satisfactory explanation has yet been produced.

Boucan Ritual bonfires lit by practitioners of **voodoo** just prior to the New Year, to "re-fire" the **sun**.

Boullan, Joseph-Antoine (1824–1893) Defrocked Roman Catholic priest who became leader of the eccentric Church of Carmel in Lyons after the death of its founder, Pierre Vintras. Boullan and his followers believed that since the Fall of Adam and Eve people could only be redeemed by sexual intercourse with superior celestial beings such as **angels**, **archangels**, and **saints**. How this was achieved is not immediately obvious, but on some occasions attractive young women took the place of archangels. Boullan came under attack from four rival occultists, **Stanislas de Guaita**, **Oswald Wirth**, **Edward Dubus**, and **Sar Josephin Peladan**, whom he believed had cursed him to die as a result of **black magic**. The French novelist **Joris-Karl Huysmans** became involved with Boullan and represented his side of the magical battle in the French newspapers. Huysmans became convinced of the reality of the magical confrontation when he began to experience astral attacks himself – "fluidic fisticuffs", which would strike his face at night. The skirmishes became more intense on both sides. Huysmans wrote that Boullan would "jump about like a tiger … He invokes the aid of St. Michael and the eternal justiciaries then, standing at his altar, he cries out: 'Strike down Peladan, strike down Peladan …'" As it happened, it was Boullan who succumbed first, dying suddenly in January 1893. Huysmans was convinced that Boullan had died of supernatural causes. "It is indisputable that Guaita and Peladan practise black magic every day," he said in an interview. "Poor Boullan was engaged in perpetual conflict with the evil spirits they continually sent him from Paris … . It is quite possible that my poor friend Boullan has succumbed to a supremely powerful spell." Boullan's magical activities are described in Huysman's novel *Là Bas*. See also **Magical Attack**.

Brahma Hindu creator god in the trinity that also includes **Vishnu** (the preserver) and **Shiva** (the destroyer). He was born from **Narayana**, the primeval egg. Brahma is depicted as having four faces and four arms (representing the Vedas) and is seated on a lotus throne. The world creates and destroys itself in the long cyclic process known as the "days and nights of Brahma".

Brahman In **Hinduism**, the Supreme Reality, the eternal and ineffable Truth which transcends all boundaries. Brahman is more than **God**, more than Spirit, totally beyond definition; the Absolute.

Braid, Dr. James (c. 1795–1860) Scottish surgeon who invented the term "hypnotism" and investigated **Anton Mesmer**'s theories of **animal magnetism** in 1841. He disagreed with Mesmer's idea that a practitioner could transmit magnetic force to a patient, and believed that the hypnotist's role was to assist the process of self-induced trance by encouraging the act of mental concentration. Despite his later influence on modern neurology and physiology, Braid was interested in a number of unorthodox medical pursuits, including **phrenology**. He also wrote a number of semi-occult books, including *Observations on Trance* (1850) and *Magic, Witchcraft, Animal Magnetism and Electro-Biology* (1852). His book *Hypnotic Therapeutics*, published in 1853, included an appendix titled "Table-Moving and Spirit-Rapping", popular topics in **spiritualism**. See also **Hypnosis**.

Breath A vital constituent of life, associated with the element **Air** and also with the **soul**. Many cultures believe that the last breath of the dying person releases the soul from the body. In **Hinduism**, the breath or life-current is known as **prana**.

Briah In the **Kabbalah**, the second of the four worlds of manifestation, associated with the spiritual level of the **archangels**. Linked by occultists to the second of the four letters of the **Tetragrammaton**, **YHVH**.

Britten, Emily Hardinge (1823–1899) English **psychic medium** who founded the spiritualist newspaper *Two Worlds*. She wrote many books, including the *History of Modern American Spiritualism* and a work on comparative **spiritualism** titled *Nineteenth Century Miracles.*

Broceliande Mystic forest in Brittany, in France, where the legendary **wizard Merlin** courted the beautiful siren-maiden Vivian.

Brocken Spectre An effect caused when a person standing on a mountain peak causes a giant shadow to reflect on clouds or in fog. Named after Mount Brocken in the Herz range in east Germany, a site traditionally associated with witches' revelry on **Walpurgis Night**.

Broomstick, Witch's According to tradition, **witches** rode through the air with broomsticks between their legs, en route to the **witches' sabbath**. It is now believed that the witches' flight was a hallucinogenic dissociation effect brought on by such psychotropic **flying ointments** as **henbane** and belladonna that were rubbed into the skin, and that the broomstick is a euphemism for the male penis, in much the same way that the **maypole** is also a symbol of fertility.

Brothers of the Shadow In **Theosophy**, a term given to those who follow the illusory path of **black magic**. Compare with **Left-hand Path**.

Brown, Rosemary English psychic, who in 1970 claimed to make contact with the **spirits** of several famous musical composers who subsequently used her as a "channel" for their compositions. Among the composers were Beethoven, Debussy, Chopin, Schubert, and Stravinsky. The Philips Company has issued a recording of Rosemary Brown's spirit-classics, but the general consensus is that the new compositions do not reflect the standard of excellence that might have been expected.

Brujo, Bruja In Peru and Mexico, a **witch** or **sorcerer**. The term has become more familiar as a result of the **Carlos Castaneda**'s descriptions of the shaman **Don Juan Matus**.

Budapest, Zsuzsanna Emese (1940–) One of the most influential practitioners of Goddess worship in the United States, Z. Budapest (as she is now generally known) was born in Hungary in 1940, the daughter of a **psychic medium**. Zsuzsanna's mother, Masika Szilagyi, composed poems and invocations while in trance, claimed an impeccable pedigree as a **shamaness**, and could trace her mystical lineage back to the fourteenth century. At the age of nineteen, Budapest emigrated to Illinois from Vienna, where she had been studying languages, and renewed her interest in German literature at the University of Chicago. Later she worked in theatre in New York, studying techniques of improvisa-tion, before moving to Los Angeles in 1970.

Soon after arriving in Los Angeles she opened what became a legendary occult shop, the Feminist Wicca, on Lincoln Boulevard in Venice Beach. This store served as a "matriarchal spiritual centre", dispensing candles, oil, incense, herbs, jewellery, Tarot cards and other paraphernalia, and also emerged as a meeting place for women wishing to perform **rituals** together. Soon there were groups of neopagan women meeting for ceremonies on the **equinoxes** and solstices and Budapest proclaimed that "feminist spirituality had been born again".

Budapest's form of magical worship, which she calls Dianic witchcraft, excludes men altogether. She acknowledges that there are men who wish to discover the "inner woman" within themselves but maintains that there are other occult groups that cater for this need. According to Budapest, women's mysteries must be kept pure and strong, and men have no place in them. As she once explained during an interview: "We have *women*'s circles. You don't put men in women's circles – they wouldn't be women's circles any more. Our Goddess is Life, and women should be free to worship from their ovaries."

Budapest now favours an equal mix of lesbian and heterosexual women in her circles to "balance the polarities" in her rituals. She is a practising lesbian herself although she has not always been so inclined. Formerly married, with two sons – one a physicist, the other a fighter pilot in the marines – she has since adopted a strongly feminist position and has chosen to deliberately avoid what she calls the "duality" of man and woman. Her emphasis on *women*'s mysteries allows the different phases of womanhood to be honoured in their own right: the young, the mature and the older woman each have much to offer, and in Budapest's group ceremonies are performed for each of these phases of life. Z. Budapest is a noted **Wiccan** author and has produced several publications, the most important of which is *The Holy Book of Women's Mysteries* (revised edition 1989).

Buddhism One of the world's great religions, founded by Siddhartha **Gautama**, the Buddha (or "enlightened one") who was born in Nepal around 563 B.C., the son of a king of the Sakyas tribe. Gautama was raised in luxury, but at the age of twenty-nine renounced worldly attachments and left his wife and home to seek **enlightenment**. After six years of austere living, he meditated beneath the **Bodhi Tree** and became enlightened. According to Buddha, enlightenment consists of recognizing four Truths: (1) that individual existence is painful; (2) that pain stems from the attachment to worldly things, which are ephemeral; (3) that happiness can be achieved by detaching oneself from material things; and (4) that **nirvana**, or egoless bliss, can be achieved by following the Noble Eightfold Way (right views, right intention, right speech, right action, right livelihood, right effort, right mindfulness, and right concentration).

Buddha's teaching and philosophy gave rise to two main schools: **Theraveda** or **Hinayana**, the form found in southern Asia (Sri Lanka, Burma, Thailand); and **Mahayana**, the form found in northern Asia (China, Tibet, Korea, Japan).

Buddhism does not recognize a God and denies the existence of a permanent **self**. It advocates **karma**, whereby all deeds have a positive or negative consequence in this or in future lives, and that **rebirth** is the outcome of this. The task of those who follow the Noble Eightfold Way is to break the chain of karma, with its endless cycles of rebirths, and thereby attain the dissolution of consciousness in nirvana.

Budge, Sir E. A. Wallis (1857–1934) A leading translator of ancient Egyptian texts, including the *Book of the Dead*, Budge was Keeper of Egyptian Antiquities in the British Museum from 1892-1924. He is believed to have been associated with the so-called "Egyptian Temple" of the **Hermetic Order of the Golden Dawn**.

Bull-roarer Piece of wood attached to a string, which, when spun around in the air, produces a loud humming noise. It is used in the ceremonial rites of the Australian **Aborigines**.

Bulwer-Lytton, Sir Edward (1803–1873) English novelist, best known for *The Last Days of Pompeii*. He regarded himself as a occult adept and considered his magical novels like *Zanoni* and *A Strange Story* to be his main work, despite their less popular appeal. Bulwer-Lytton studied at Cambridge, and on several occasions entertained the French occultist **Eliphas Lévi** at Knebworth, his family residence. He was at one time the honorary Grand Patron of the *Societas Rosicruciana in Anglia*, a predecessor of the **Hermetic Order of the Golden Dawn**.

Bunyip In Aboriginal **mythology**, an imaginary creature said to haunt rushy swamps and billabongs. It was fond of eating men and was greatly feared by the **Aborigines**.

Burt, Sir Cyril (1883–1971) Distinguished English psychologist who became interested in **extrasensory perception**, **clairvoyance**, **telepathy**, and **psychic mediums**. Some of his most original work included his experimental research on mental telepathy among schoolchilden.

Butler, W. E. (1898–1978) English occultist and author who trained as a member of **Dion Fortune's Fraternity of the Inner Light**, and was also a protégé of the psychic Robert King. Butler established a magical order, **Servants of the Light** (SOL). The SOL has continued to develop modern techniques of visionary magic known as **pathworkings**.

C

Cabala Alternative spelling for **Kabbalah**, **Qabalah**.

Caballi According to occult writer L. W. de Laurence, the **astral bodies** of people who die by violence, prior to their natural terms of life. They wander the earth until that time span has elapsed.

Cabinet In **spiritualism**, a small space, usually enclosed by curtains, in which **mediums** claim to "condense" the psychic energy required for spirit-manifestations in a **seance**. Some mediums sit inside the cabinet, others outside it.

Cabiri Also Kabiri. Agricultural deities of Phrygian origin worshipped in Greek religion, especially in Samothrace, Lemnos, Thebes, and Macedonia. The mystery rites were second only to those of **Eleusis**. The main deities worshipped were **Zeus** and **Dionysus**.

Caboclo In the Brazilian Christian-magical sect **Macumba**, **spirits** who "work" in the forest and know the secrets of plants and herbs.

Cacodemon An evil **spirit** capable of changing its shape so rapidly that it could not be identified. In medieval **magic** it was sometimes identified with the "evil **genius**" inside each person, and in **astrology** it was linked to the twelfth **house**, the **sun**.

Caduceus The staff carried by the Greek god **Hermes** and the Roman Mercury, represented as having two snakes curling around it, and wings at the top. Occultists sometimes compare the staff with the symbolism of the psychic energy currents **ida** and **pingala**, which are said to encircle the central nervous system in **Kundalini Yoga**.

Caecus In Greek mythology, a fire-breathing monster, half-beast, half-human, who lived deep in a cave, away from the sun. He slaughtered people and kept their skulls as an adornment in his cave. Caecus was finally overcome by **Heracles**.

Cagliostro, Count Alessandro di (1743–1795) Regarded by Thomas Carlyle as the "Prince of Quacks", Cagliostro was a traveller, self-claimed alchemist, and occult opportunist. Born in Palermo, his real name was Guiseppe Balsamo. After misleading a goldsmith named Marano into believing that hidden treasures could be located by **ceremonial magic**, he escaped to Messina, where he made contact with an alleged alchemical adept named **Althotas**. They travelled together to Alexandria and Rhodes and later conducted alchemical experiments with Grand Master Pinto on Malta. Pinto's sponsorship allowed Count Cagliostro, as he now styled himself, to live in great wealth and style. Cagliostro married Lorenza Feliciani in Italy and became a well-known figure in many European courts, charming princes, kings, and queens, and assuring them that his alchemical secrets could help them swell the royal coffers. He also became deeply interested in **Freemasonry**, and acquired a reputation as a **medium** and **faith healer**.

Cagliostro also became involved in the famous Diamond Necklace affair, and was charged by Madame de Lamotte of stealing the valuable jewellery. This was later dismissed in court, but a more serious charge was forthcoming. The Holy Office ordered his arrest in 1789 on the grounds that Freemasonry was a heresy, and he spent the rest of his years in the Castle of San Leo near Montefeltro. See also **Alchemy**; **Egyptian Masonic Rite**.

Caliburnus The magical sword of King Arthur. See also **Excalibur**.

Camelot The name of King Arthur's legendary court. Various sites have been suggested for Camelot, including Exeter and the pre-Roman earthwork known as Cadbury Castle, near Glastonbury.

Campbell, Joseph (1904–1987) Internationally renowned as a scholar of comparative **mythology**, Campbell taught at Sarah Lawrence College in Bronxville, New York for thirty-eight years. He was strongly influenced by Jung's concept of the Collective Unconscious and believed there were universal parallels between myths, **dreams** and art. In his four-volume series, *The Masks of God*, he presented his study of world mythologies, classifying them as primitive, oriental, occidental and creative. Campbell gained widespread popular recognition following his broadcast interview series *The Power of Myth*, conducted in 1985–86 with Bill Moyers. In addition to his *Masks of God* series, Campbell also wrote *The Hero with a Thousand Faces*, *Myths to Live By* and *The Inner Reaches of Outer Space*, as well as editing *A Portable Jung*. Campbell has been a major influence on the personal growth movement, particularly among those seeking to explore the mythic and archetypal aspects of daily life.

Cancer In **astrology**, the **sign** of the **zodiac** for those born between June 22 and July 22. A **Water** sign, ruled by the **moon**, cancer is symbolized by the crab and is the fourth sign of the zodiac. Those born under this sign are supposed to be sensitive, sentimental, and impressionable. True to the symbol, they "float with the tide". Cancer is also said to be the most "maternal" sign.

Candlemas A major **Wiccan** sabbat, also known as **Imbolc** and celebrated on February 2, Candlemas has been described as "the quickening of the year, the first stirrings of spring within the womb of Mother Earth". *Imbolc* means "in the belly" and this sabbat is very much a fertility celebration. The focus is on light and new life, as opposed to the darkness of winter which has now receded. Candlemas is sometimes known as the Feast of Lights.

Candomblé Afro-Brazilian cult, associated with the magical **Macumba** religion and native to the state of Bahia.

Cannibalism The act of eating human flesh, sometimes with a view to acquiring the special qualities and characteristics of the deceased. In some pre-literate societies cannibalism is linked to "eating the god" and is a feature of magical **initiations**. The term apparently derives from the West Indian man-eating Caribs, but cannibalism has occurred in many cultures, worldwide. It is also known as anthropophagy.

Cannon, Alexander Highly qualified physician and psychiatrist who developed an interest in **magic** and **psychic** phenomena while travelling in India and Tibet. He claimed to have met the "Great Ones" and had his baggage levitated across a precarious chasm. This claim brought him widespread disrepute, and for a time his career as a doctor was in jeopardy. After he retired he employed two **mediums** to help him with medical diagnosis, and he continued his researches into **hypnosis** and "nervous diseases". Cannon was also the inventor of a number of eccentric machines, including a 400,000-volt static electricity device for "de-possessing" people, and a piece of equipment that could allegedly read human thoughts. His books include *The Invisible Influence* and *Powers that Be.*

Canon, The Title of a mystical book written by William Stirling and first published in London in 1897. *The Canon* describes the **esoteric** laws that governed the arts, sciences, politics, music, and astronomy in ancient cultures. The links between ancient **gods** and numerical values, and the symbolic proportions of sacred temples, are also evaluated. Stirling believed that in classical ancient societies (Greece, Rome, Egypt), the **priests** regulated the lives of people by interpreting cosmic cycles and laws, and that this metaphysical vision of society has since been lost.

Canonization Recognition by the Church that a man or woman is a **saint**. In Roman Catholicism the Pope is the final arbiter.

Capnomancy **Divination** by means of interpreting patterns in smoke, often associated with sacrificial offerings and incense thrown onto hot coals.

Capricorn In **astrology**, the **sign** of the **zodiac** for those born between December 22 and January 20. An **Earth** sign, ruled by **Saturn**, Capricorn is symbolized by a goat with the tail of a fish (a sea-goat). The source of this sign is the Babylonian god **Ea**, a deity associated with rivers and seas; but the characteristics ascribed by astrologers to this sign owe more to the goat than to the fish. A typical Capricorn is "sure-footed" and clear-headed – possibly too serious – and sets high personal standards. There is also an economy of style in the actions and pursuits of Capricorns, which sometimes makes them appear self-centered.

Cardinal Signs In **astrology**, the **zodiac** signs **Aries**, **Cancer**, **Libra**, and **Capricorn**, whose cusps coincide with the four cardinal points as follows: Aries (east); Cancer (north); Libra (west); and Capricorn (south).

Cardinal Virtues Those personal qualities regarded as important by a particular nation or society. For example, the ancient Greek "wisdom, courage, temperance, and justice" and the Christian "faith, hope, and charity".

Cargo Cults Belief among native islanders, especially the Melanesians, that cargo ships and aeroplanes can be summoned magically to provide goods and money. The practice seems to be based on the native perception of the "white man's" power, and its belief that ideally roles should be reversed allowing Western wealth and material possessions to be redistributed. For example, inhabitants of an island in the New Hebrides (Vanuatu) believe that a white leader named Jon Frum will arrive, bringing "cargo" in a huge scarlet aeroplane, and that he will drive all other white people from the island, helping the native inhabitants regain control. They also believe an army is waiting in the crater of a volcano to help him. In the magical **rituals** designed to summon him, Jon Frum is carved in wood and painted red, alongside a representation of his aircraft.

Carpocratians **Gnostic** sect, founded in the second century by Carpocrates. According to Irenaeus, Carpocrates advocated that a person could only find salvation by experiencing "every sinful and infamous deed" – a libertine philosophy that some Gnostic scholars believe reflects the essentially rebellious nature of many of the Gnostic sects.

Carrel, Dr. Alexis (1873–1944) French biologist and surgeon who emigrated to the United States and joined the Rockefeller Institute for Medical Research in 1906. He received the Nobel Prize for medicine in 1912. He wrote many medical and scientific works, but is best known for his popular book *Man, the Unknown* (1935). Carrel believed in **spiritual healing** and the **laying-on-of-hands**, and experimented with **hypnosis** and **telepathy**.

Carrington, Dr. Hereward (1880–1958) Psychical researcher, born on the English island of Jersey, who went to the United States in 1899 and worked with Professor **James Hyslop** at the American **Society for Psychical Research**. He investigated several **mediums**, including **Eusapia Palladino** and **Mrs. Eileen Garrett**, and was also a pioneering researcher of **astral travel** and the **out-of-the-body experience**. He corresponded with **Sylvan Muldoon** and contributed a long introduction to his classic work, *The Projection of the Astral Body*. Carrington also authored several books on **psychical research** and spiritual growth, including *Modern Psychical Phenomena, Higher Psychical Development*, and *Essays in the Occult*.

Cartomancy Divination by means of cards, for example **Tarot** cards or the **Zener cards** used by Professor **J. B. Rhine** in testing precognition.

Cartopedy Occult technique, Persian in origin, of assessing personal characteristics by examining the soles of the feet. Cartopedy was sometimes used to predict the future.

Case, Paul Foster (1884–1954) American occultist who made a detailed study of the **Tarot** and founded an occult centre known as the Builders of the Adytum (BOTA) in Los Angeles. Case claimed to be the American head of the **Hermetic Order of the Golden Dawn** and to have received "inner plane" teachings from the spiritual Masters of that order. Case also believed in the rather fanciful idea that the Tarot had originated around 1200, when a group of scholars from around the world met in Fez, Morocco, and synthesized the universal **mystery** teaching into the pictorial form of the Tarot. This eccentric viewpoint notwithstanding, Case produced one of the best books on the symbolism of the cards, *The Tarot, A Key to the Wisdom of the Ages*, and also a book of Tarot meditations titled *The Book of Tokens*. He was succeeded at BOTA by Dr. Ann Davies.

Castaneda, Carlos (1925–98) Peruvian-born anthropologist and author, whose real name was thought to be Carlos Arana.

Castaneda studied at the University of California at Los Angeles, and claimed to have made the acquaintance of an old Yaqui Indian named **don Juan Matus**, who allowed him to become his apprentice in **sorcery** and **magic**. Castaneda experienced new types of perception after ingesting datura and **psychedelic** mushrooms, had visionary encounters with the peyote god Mescalito, and underwent astral transformations into the form of a crow. Castaneda's first book, *The Teachings of don Juan*, was published by University of California Press in 1968 and became a counterculture classic. It was followed by a number of volumes detailing Castaneda's magical experiences with don Juan and other sorcerers, such as don Genero and La Catalina. Castaneda's third book, *Journey to Ixtlan*, earned him a Ph.D.

Castaneda was not without his critics, including the eminent anthropologist Weston La Barre, who described Castaneda's writings as "pseudo-profound, deeply vulgar pseudo-ethnography"; and the psychologist Richard de Mille, who believes don Juan is a fiction. Some critics claim that Castaneda amalgamated tales of other Indian **shamans** into his accounts. For example, there is a strong resemblance between magical attributes ascribed to the Huichol shaman Ramon Medina Silva and those of don Genero in *A Separate Reality*. Castaneda, however, kept a low public profile; and, while maintaining that his magical writings were factually based, did not become part of the debate surrounding their authenticity.

Caste The hierarchical system of dividing Hindu society into four sections, or varnas. These are the **brahmans** (priests); ksatriyas (warriors); vaisyas (businessmen and landowners); and sudras (serfs and labourers). The division has religious implications, for members of the first three varnas are believed to be twice-born, whereas sudras are not.

Casting a Horoscope In **astrology**, the act of making a **horoscope** by incorporating basic data of time, date of birth, location, and so forth. Horoscopes can be cast for the day (when the sun is above the horizon), or for the night (when the sun is below the horizon).

Castle of the Interior Man Mystical term for the seven stages of spiritual growth through which the **soul** ascends towards the Divinity. These are (1) **prayer** and concentration on **God**; (2) prayer directed at obtaining knowledge of the mystical significance of manifested reality; (3) self-renunciation, or the so-called "dark night of the soul"; (4) surrender to the will of God; (5) a state of union with the Divinity so that one's will and the will of God become one; (6) a state of ecstasy where the soul is filled with love and joy; and (7) the mystic marriage with God in which the inner being enters **heaven**.

Cat Animal with strong occult associations. In ancient Egypt, there were cat-headed goddesses (e.g. **Bast** and **Sekhmet**) associated with fertility and sexual power. In the Middle Ages, black cats were regarded as incarnations of the **Devil** and gave rise to much popular **superstition**. Cats are also said to be popular **familiars** of **witches**: the modern witch **Rosaleen Norton** believed that cats had more integrity and sensitivity than human beings, and she claimed a special psychic rapport with them.

Catacomb Subterranean cemeteries in which martyrs were buried. Most Christian catacombs date from the third and fourth centuries, and the term was first applied to vaults located beneath the basilica of St. Sebastian in Rome. The tombs of the martyrs became sites for pilgrimages and were also places where Christians hid when fearing persecution. The latter situation eased with Constantine's Edict of Milan (A.D. 313), when

Christianity became an officially recognized religion in the Holy Roman Empire.

Catalepsy In medicine, an abnormal condition whereby a person is unconscious and does not respond to stimuli. The breathing and heart rate are slow, and the limbs are rigid. This condition sometimes occurs in cases of schizophrenia and hysteria and can also be caused by **hypnosis**. Some occultists regard it as an example of **astral projection**, in which the **astral body** is some distance removed from the physical organism.

Cathars See **Albigenses**.

Catherine of Siena (1347–1380) Catholic **saint** and **mystic** who was born in Siena, Italy. She joined the Dominican Order at the age of sixteen, and in due course became a noted Church reformer, seeking to reconcile the Florentines and the Pope, and persuading Gregory XI to return to Rome from Avignon in 1376. Although she could not write, she dictated numerous letters and also a fine inspirational work, which has become known as *The Dialogue of St. Catherine of Siena*. In 1375 she received on her body the **stigmata** of Christ's wounds. She was canonized in 1461.

Catoblepas A bizarre, mythic creature that inhabited Ethiopia. According to **Pliny**, its head was so heavy that it was usually bent down towards the ground. If it ever raised its eyes towards a person, however, that person would fall down dead on the spot.

Catoptromancy **Divination** by means of a mirror. The ancient Greeks placed mirrors under water, or held them in a fountain, and would carefully observe and interpret the reflections.

Cauldron Ancient magical symbol connoting transformation and germination. It is an image signifying new life, and has a strong association, like the **cup**, with the element **Water**. Medieval **witches** were said to stir their magical concoctions in a cauldron, and it is also found as a symbol on the important **Tarot** card ***Temperance*** in the Crowley-Harris pack. Here it represents the fusion of opposites, harmony, and synthesis.

Causal Body In theosophical usage, one's "personal god", the principal force in one's inner being. Also known by the Sanskrit term *Karana-sarira*. Sometimes associated with the immortal **soul**.

Cavendish, Richard (1930–) A leading contemporary authority on **magic** and **witchcraft**, he was educated at Oxford University and has lectured widely. He was the editor of the encyclopedic series *Man, Myth and Magic* (1970–1971), which brought many international authorities on magic and **mythology** together for the first time. Among his best-known books are *The Black Arts, Visions of Heaven and Hell*, and *Encyclopedia of the Unexplained*.

Cayce, Edgar (1877–1945) American **psychic** and healer. Born in Kentucky, the son of a farmer, Cayce received a limited education. However, he found later in life that he could enter **trance** states, diagnose other people's illnesses, and prescribe remedies. He also claimed to be able to describe previous incarnations and was therefore forced to adopt a religious belief in **reincarnation**, which had not been part of his Christian upbringing. His readings, given while in trance, have been recorded and preserved, and in 1931 the Association for Research and Enlightenment was formed to collate and document them. Numerous books have been written about him and he remains one of America's most famous and popular psychic writers.

Cecrops Legendary being in Greek mythology, who was half-man and half-**dragon**. The earliest king of Attica, he founded Athens and brought political stability and religious observances to Attica.

Celestial From the Latin *caelum*, "heaven", anything divine, blessed, or "heavenly". Sometimes used to describe the "higher spheres" of consciousness and intelligence.

Celestial Magic See **Magic, Celestial.**

Celts An ancient people who spread through western Europe, settling in Brittany, south-western England, Wales, Scotland, and Ireland prior to the seventh century B.C. Their religion was a fertility cult in which certain animals – the pig, horse, bull, and bear – and certain trees and rivers were sacred. Worship took place in open groves. The scholars among the Celts were **Druids**, and this class produced the chieftains, judges, and **magicians**. After the Roman conquests, Celtic religious practice fell into abeyance and was replaced by Christianity. However, Celtic influences remain in certain languages – Gaelic, Manx, and Welsh – and in many folklore customs.

Census of Hallucinations Nineteenth century survey undertaken by the **Society for Psychical Research**. Seventeen thousand people who claimed to see **apparitions** were questioned in detail and a large number of responses describing **hauntings**, **premonitions**, and claimed cases of **telepathy** were reported in the PSR *Proceedings* (Vol. 10. 1894).

Centaurs Hostile creatures, half-man and half-horse, who dwelt in Thessaly and worshipped **Dionysus**. The most famous (and peaceful) centaur was Chiron. He taught people how to use medicinal plants and herbs and also gave instruction to many of the Greek heroes, including Achilles, Aeneas, and Jason.

Cerberus In Greek **mythology**, an awesome three-headed dog who guarded the entrance to **Hades**, in order to prevent anyone still living from entering. In Greek legends the heroes Aeneas, **Orpheus**, and **Odysseus** succeeded in passing him and visiting the **Underworld**. Cerberus was the offspring of **Typhon** and **Echidna**.

Ceremonial Magic See **Magic, Ceremonial.**

Ceres Roman equivalent of **Demeter** and mother of Proserpina (**Persephone**). Ceres/Demeter was goddess of agriculture – the grain, harvest, and fertility of the earth – and was a central figure in the mystery teachings at **Eleusis**.

Cernunnos Name by which some modern **witches** refer to the **Horned God**. Cernunnos was a Celtic god depicted as having the head of a bull, a man's torso, the legs of serpents, and the tail of a fish. He was lord of wild animals.

Ceromancy **Divination** by means of inspecting melted wax. In the Middle Ages, the **magician** would melt wax in a brass vessel and then pour it onto cold water in another container. The congealed wax globules would then be symbolically interpreted.

Cetiya In India, an earthen mound venerated as the tomb of a **saint**. The cetiya evolved into the **stupa**, an often elaborate domed roof characteristic of Buddhist architecture.

Chabad Mystical.system developed by Rabbi Schneur Zalman (1747–1812) which influenced Hasidic thought. The term itself derives from the first letters of three emanations on the kabbalistic **Tree of Life: Chokmah** (wisdom), **Binah** (understanding), and **Daath** (knowledge). See also **Hasidism**.

Cha-cha In **voodoo**, a gourd rattle filled with seeds, used for percussion during dances.

Chakras In **Kundalini Yoga** the spiritual nerve centres that align with the central nervous column, **sushumna**. The yogi learns to arouse the kundalini energy through the chakras from the base of the spine to the crown of the head. The chakras, from lowest to highest, are **Muladhara** (located near the genitals); **Svadhisthana** (sacral region); **Manipura** (solar plexus); **Anahata** (chest); **Visuddha** (neck); **Ajna** (between the eyebrows); and **Sahasrara** (crown of the head). The meaning of the Hindu word *chakra* is "wheel", but the symbolism implies a spiritual centre in the human body; the chakras do not correspond literally to any organ, and are mystical rather than biological in nature. See also **Yoga**.

Chaldean Oracles Oracles and mystical sayings allegedly deriving from the Chaldean **Magi** and **Zoroaster**, but transcribed and translated by the Neoplatonists.

Commentaries on the Oracles were written by Psellus, Pletho, **Iamblichus**, and **Porphyry**. The Oracles have much in common with **Gnosticism**. See also **Neoplatonism**.

Chalices See Cups.

Chams Indochinese group in Thailand and Kampuchea famous for their **sorceresses**. The magical **initiation** rites involve cutting a cockerel into two halves and dancing with it, while uttering magical **incantations**. The Chams believe that the magical **spells** can transform the dead bird into a live crow, confirming that the initiation is successful. Cham sorceresses have an extensive knowledge of ritual spells for propitiating evil spirits. They also interpret omens favourable to harvesting the rice crop and other agricultural produce.

Ch'an Buddhism One of the major forms of **Mahayana Buddhism**; in Japan, it gave rise to **Zen**. Ch'an Buddhism avoids the rational labelling of concepts and takes the view that reality can only be experienced by over coming the duality of objective and subjective perception. As in Zen, **enlightenment** is sudden rather than gradual. Ch'an Buddhism was introduced to China by the Indian monk **Bodhidharma**.

Changeling A deformed or ugly child said to have been left by the **fairies** as a substitute for a healthy, attractive one. According to legend, the fairies could only snatch a baby away before it was christened. Changelings were often thought to be senile fairies disguised as infants; in comparatively recent times, both children and adults have been accused of being changelings and put to death. In 1894, a young woman living near Clonmel in Ireland was accused by her husband and family of being a changeling and was burned alive.

Changing Woman Favoured **deity** among the Navajo Indians. She was the consort of the **sun** and the mother of twin offspring, Monster Slayer and Child of the Water, who slew the monsters that threatened humanity.

Channelling Spiritual practice in which a person opens their awareness to inner-plane communications from a discarnate being, spirit-helper or guide. The person who is channelling serves as an intermediary during this process and is temporarily possessed by the other being or entity. Messages may be transmitted to others present, but here the voice heard will be that of the possessing entity. The channeller is unaware of the messages that are being communicated and only learns of them from others, after returning to a state of full waking consciousness. See also **Oracle**; **Medium**.

Chaos The amorphous mass that existed prior to the creation of the universe. Because there was no light, it could not be perceived. In Greek mythology, Chaos was a **deity**, one of the oldest of the **gods** and father of Erebus, god of darkness.

Character See Sigil.

Charioteer, The In the **Tarot**, the card of the **Major Arcana** that depicts the Charioteer riding through his kingdom and surveying the positive and negative aspects of the world around him. Occultists regard *The Charioteer* as the warrior-like aspect of the Male **archetype** and the destructive face of the Great Father. He is the antithesis of the peaceful qualities symbolized by ***The Emperor***. In Western **magic**, which combines the Tarot paths of the Major Arcana with the ten **sephiroth** on the **Tree of Life**, the path of *The Charioteer* connects **Geburah** and **Binah**.

Charm In **magic**, an **incantation** or object believed to have special supernatural power. The word derives from the Latin *carmen*, meaning "a song". Compare with **Talisman**.

Charon In Greek **Mythology**, the boatman who ferried the souls of the dead across the Rivers of Death (**Acheron**, the **Styx**). It was customary for the living to pay for Charon's services by placing a silver coin beneath the tongue of the corpse at the time of burial. The Greeks believed that a proper funeral was necessary before a spirit could be ferried across to the infernal regions. However, some of the Greek heroes managed to deceive Charon. **Orpheus**, for example, charmed him with his lute, and Aeneas bribed him with the Golden Bough. **Odysseus** also passed by him and was able to converse with the ghosts of dead heroes in the **Underworld**.

Chayot Hebrew term for the "lightning flash" described by Ezekiel. It is commonly used by the **Merkabah** mystics to describe states of spiritual ecstasy. See also **Hayyoth**.

Cheiro Pseudonym of Count Louis Hamon (1866–1939), a famous palmist and occultist. A descendant of an Irish Huguenot family, Hamon went to India, where he learned the *hastirika* technique of interpreting the lines of the hand; he later studied **astrology** in the Vatican library. Hamon became famous for his predictions and had many notable clients including King Edward VII, King Leopold of Belgium, the Czar of Russia, Pope Leo XIII, Lord Kitchener, and Mark Twain. He predicted when both Edward VII and Lord Kitchener would die and advised Mark Twain, who at the time was facing bankruptcy, that he would become rich again. In 1931, five years before Edward VII abdicated, he wrote in *Cheiro's World Predictions* that the monarch would "fall a victim of a devastating love affair. If he does, I predict that the Prince will give up everything, even the chance of being crowned, rather than lose the object of his affection." Cheiro did not live to witness the abdication. He had moved to California, and died there at the exact time and place he had predicted. Cheiro is remembered for his numerous books on **palmistry** and prediction, including *Confessions of a Modern Seer*, *Cheiro's Guide to the Hand*, *The Language of the Hand*, and *Cheiro's Book of Numbers*. See also **Palmistry**.

Chela Hindu term for the pupil of a spiritual teacher, or **guru**.

Chelidonius A magical stone, said to be taken from the body of a swallow. A cure for melancholy and fever.

Chenrezig National deity of Tibet, known as the Lord of Mercy. He is often depicted as a herdsman with four arms, or as a composite being with eleven heads, a thousand arms, and an eye in the palm of his hand. Ever compassionate, he comes speedily to help those in distress. The **Dalai Lama** has traditionally been regarded as an **incarnation** of Chenrezig.

Cherub A winged **angel** with a human head, descended from creatures with animal bodies. In Western art the cherub is represented as a beautiful child. See also **Cherubim**.

Cherubim **Angels** of light, who, according to the Book of Revelation, sing eternally "Holy, Holy, Holy, Lord God Almighty who was, and is, and is to come". There are four of them around the heavenly throne: one like a man, one like a lion, one like an eagle, and one like an ox, and each has six wings.

Chesed In the **Kabbalah**, the fourth mystical emanation on the **Tree of Life**. Occultists identify Chesed as the ruler (but not creator) of the manifested universe; and he is characterized as stable, wise, and merciful by contrast with his more dynamic and destructive opposite, **Geburah**. By the process of **magical correspondences**, Chesed is associated with the Greek god **Zeus** and the Roman **Jupiter**.

Cheval In **voodoo**, the horse, and, by extension, the person "mounted" by the spirit-deities for the journey into **trance**. The term therefore symbolizes voodoo **possession**.

Ch'i In Taoist **mysticism** and traditional Chinese medicine, the flow of energy in the body; also, "the breath of life". Practitioners of **acupuncture** believe that ch'i flows through channels of the body known as **meridians** and that an imbalance of ch'i leads to disease. Stimulation of acupuncture points along these meridians helps to rectify this imbalance. In Japan, ch'i is designated "ki". See also **Taoism**.

Child Guides In **spiritualism**, the **spirits** of children who present themselves as **controls** for the **medium**. Spiritualists believe that although these child-spirits often show playful characteristics, they offer mature and adult revelations concerning the hereafter.

Chimera Mythic fire-breathing monster combining the front of a lion, the body and head of a goat, and the head and tail of a serpent. The chimera was slain by Bellerophon riding on the winged horse **Pegasus**.

Chirognomy **Divination** and prediction based on the shape of the hand as distinct from the lines of the palm. The position of the thumb, the shape of the fingers, the fingernails, and the texture of the skin, are all taken into consideration.

Chirographology The study of hands and handwriting. Compare with **Graphology**.

Chirology Alternative name for **chirognomy**.

Chiromancy **Divination** by interpreting the lines and markings of the palm. The major lines of the palm include the lines of life, the head, the heart, and destiny, and other minor lines include those of intuition and marriage. A palmist analyzes whether the lines are distinct or faint, straight or branched, and looks also for other symbolic indicators, like cross and star formations. See also **Palmistry**.

Chirosophy Alternative name for **Chiromancy**.

Chokmah In the **Kabbalah**, the second mystical emanation on the **Tree of Life** following **Kether**. Occultists identify Chokmah with the Great Father, the giver of the seminal spark of life which is potent only until it enters the womb of the Great Mother, **Binah**. From the union of the Great Father and the Great Mother come forth all the images of creation. By the process of **magical correspondences**, Chokmah is associated with such deities as **Kronos**, **Saturn**, **Thoth**, Atum-Ra, and **Ptah**, in other pantheons.

Chopra, Deepak (1947–) Born In New Delhi, the son of a cardiologist, Chopra studied medicine, graduating from the All India Institute of Medical Sciences in 1968 before emigrating to the United States. Drawn to alternative medicine in the 1970s, Chopra used transcendental meditation to help himself stop smoking and then became an adherent of ayurvedic medicine. He has since blended holistic health, **New Age** philosophy, metaphysics and a self-help orientation into a series of highly successful publications. Chopra's books include *Ageless Body, Timeless Mind; Perfect Health, How to Know God* and *The Seven Spiritual Laws of Success.*

Choronzon In Western **magic**, the Demon of **Chaos** and Guardian of the **Abyss. Aleister Crowley** described him as "the first and deadliest of all the powers of evil". This point notwithstanding, Crowley nevertheless invoked Choronzon while experimenting with the so-called **Thirty Aethyrs** in a magical ritual on the top of an Algerian mountain in December 1909.

Christian, Paul (1811–1877) Pseudonym of J-B Pitois, a French occultist whose writings blend **astrology, Kabbalah, Tarot,** and **spiritualism.** His best-known work is *A History of Magic* (1870).

Christian Science Religion founded by **Mary Baker Eddy,** which reinterprets aspects of orthodox Christianity. Christian Scientists believe that **God** and **Spirit** are good, and that matter and **evil** are not truly real. The healing of disease – which itself is usually caused by fear – occurs by virtue of the presence of Truth in a person. One who lives life in accordance with the Divine Spirit has no place for evil, sin, or disease. Members of the Church do not smoke, drink, or consume drugs, and they do not discuss illness because "sick thoughts make sick bodies". The Mother Church is situated in Boston, but there are branches in most parts of the world. The key text of Christian Science is Mary Baker Eddy's *Science and Health,* first published in 1875.

Chromotherapy Also known as Colour Therapy, the analysis and use of colours in spiritual healing. One of the most common applications is to apply coloured light to the body to heal imbalance. There were healing temples of light and colour at Heliopolis, the Egyptian centre for the worship of Atum-Ra; and in more recent times such occult figures as **Rudolph Steiner** and **C. W. Leadbeater** have paid much attention to the symbolic analysis of colour as part of the human **aura.** The healer Dinshah Ghadiali, who compiled a work on colour vibrations titled *The Spectro-Chromometry Encyclopedia,* used to treat his patients by shining light on them through coloured glass or by asking them to drink pigmented fluids.

Chthonian From the Greek *chthon,* "earth", deities or spirits from the earth or **Underworld,** often associated with the souls of the dead.

Chuang Tzu (c. 399–295 B.C.) Notable Chinese philosopher who ranks next to **Lao Tzu** as a major Taoist thinker. Chuang Tzu was opposed to the doctrinaire Confucianists, believing in freedom and peace and exploring the mystical realm of "Nothing Whatever". His major work, *Chuang Tzu,* is one of the classics of Chinese literature.

Church of Satan Headed by occultist **Anton La Vey,** the Church of Satan was located on California Street in San Francisco, and claimed an affiliated membership of seven thousand supporters. It encouraged the development of the animal instincts, self-indulgence, and free sexuality, and included in its rituals a satanic "mass". Male and female participants in the ritual wore black robes, with the exception of a naked woman who volunteered to be the "altar" during the ceremony. La Vey made invocations to **Lucifer, Belial,** and **Leviathan;** drank from a chalice which was then placed on the "altar"; and encouraged the congregation to focus their mental energies on achieving their secret desires. The **ritual** ended with satanic **hymns** accompanied by an electric organ. The Church was effectively superseded in 1975 by the **Temple of Set**, which until recent times was headed by Dr. Michael Aquino.

Churingas Among the **Australian Aborigines**, oval stones or pieces of wood bearing sacred inscriptions. They were not to be seen by women or uninitiated men, and were linked to animal **totems**.

Cicatrization Literally, the act of producing a scar on the body (Latin: *cicatrix*); but in many pre-literate societies a form of decorative embellishment on the skin associated with magical and religious beliefs.

Circadian Rhythms Biological and physiological functions which occur approximately once a day (Latin: *circa diem*). These include sleep patterns and fluctuations in urine and blood pressure. The existence of these rhythms lends some credibility to the theory of **biorhythms**.

Circe In Greek **mythology**, a **sorceress** banished to the island of Aeaea after poisoning her husband. She lived in a palace surrounded by woods and had magical **spells** that enabled her to transform men into wild beasts. Circe would attract men to her domain by beautiful singing. When **Odysseus** and his men landed on her island some of the band, headed by Eurylochus, were invited to dine with her. Eurylochus feared a trap, but many of the men accepted the invitation and dined with her, drinking wine that was drugged. Circe used her magic to turn them into hogs and Eurylochus hastily reported to Odysseus what had happened. **Hermes** gave him a herb called moly to counteract Circe's **magic**, and Odysseus was able to force the sorceress to change the hogs back into their original human form. In due course, Circe became an important ally to Odysseus and gave him valuable advice on how to descend into **Hades**, encounter **ghosts**, and avoid the snare of the **sirens**. See also *Odyssey*.

Circle In **mythology**, a symbol of totality and wholeness; and in Western **magic**, an important symbol used in ceremonial workings within the Temple. In the **Hermetic Order of the Golden Dawn**, the circle is inscribed on the floor of the Temple and represents the Infinite **Godhead** and Divine Self-Knowledge that the **magician** aspires to. **God-names** are inscribed around the periphery and the magician traces the circle with a ritual sword as part of the ceremonial procedure. The circle may be circumscribed by an equal-sided geometrical figure whose number of sides corresponds with the **sephirah** associated with the god (e.g. a **hexagram** in a **Tiphareth** ritual invoking **Osiris** – Tiphareth is the sixth sephirah on the **Tree of Life** and is linked to gods of the sun).

Circumambulation In ritual **magic** procedure, walking around an object or person three times in succession.

Circumcision For a man, removal of all or part of the foreskin. The practice often has an initiatory purpose, introducing the person to the adult phase of life.

Cit Hindu term for the Pure Consciousness that transcends the human mind and the manifested universe. It is the Real **Self**.

Clairaudience In **spiritualism**, the psychic ability to hear voices and sounds attributed to the deceased. The most famous example in history is perhaps that of Joan of Arc (c. 1412–1431), the French heroine who claimed to hear supernatural voices urging her to aid the Dauphin in the struggle against the English army. Clairaudient perception is usually claimed only by **psychic mediums** and **sensitives**.

Clairsentience In **spiritualism**, the psychic sense that something significant is about to happen. Popularly known as a "hunch".

Clairvoyance In **spiritualism**, the psychic ability to see **discarnate** beings and **spirits.** Sometimes the term is also used to describe the visionary perception of future events. Clairvoyance may be related to **astral travel** and also bears resemblance to some types of dream states. Clairvoyants believe that for accurate perceptions of the spirit world to "come through", the environment should be receptive and positive. Harsh light and hostile influences work against clairvoyant communication.

Clavicle From the latin *clavis* meaning "a key", the mystical key to "unlocking" an occult secret. Examples from occult literature include the medieval **grimoire** known as the *Key of Solomon* (*Clavicula Solomonis*) and **Eliphas Lévi**'s *Key of the Mysteries* (*La Cléf des Grandes Mystères*).

Clear In **Scientology**, one who has attained a state of enlightenment and has total control over their own mind. The first person to attain this status, other than founder **L. Ron Hubbard** himself, was John McMaster, who resigned from the Scientology movement in November 1969 after a disagreement over ethics.

Cledonomancy **Divination** by heeding chance remarks or events.

Cleromancy **Divination** using objects with distinguishing marks to identify them. In Rome these objects were sacred to **Mercury** and consisted of black and white beans or dice.

Cloud of Unknowing Famous mystical work, dating from the late fourteenth century, whose author is unknown. The book says that the "cloud of unknowing" that separates us from **God** can be penetrated not by intellect, but by love. Sometimes God bestows mystical inspiration – "a beam of ghostly light" – allowing devotees to glimpse some of God's secrets.

Cloven Foot Also cloven hoof. The mark of the **Devil**, based on the superstition that the Devil, as an imperfect being, always exhibits a sign of his bestiality as a distinguishing mark.

Clover In its three-leafed form, a symbol of the Trinity and a protection against **witchcraft** and the forces of **evil**.

Clymer, Reuben Swinburne American occultist who claimed to succeed **Pascal B. Randolph** as a magical **adept** and who headed a number of allegedly **Rosicrucian** organizations in the United States. These included the Sons of Isis and Osiris, the College of the Holy Grail, the Church of the Illumination, and the Rosicrucian Fraternity. Among Clymer's main books are *A Compendium of Occult Laws*, *The Rosicrucian Fraternity in America*, and *Mysteries of Osiris*.

Coagulation In **alchemy**, the act of converting or "crystallizing" a liquid into a solid form.

Cochinada In Peru, **witchcraft** potions made from the offal of vultures and river snakes. They are used to inflict bad luck or illness upon one's enemies.

Cock Lane Ghost Famous case of alleged **haunting** and **poltergeist** activity at a house in Cock Lane, Smithfield, London, in 1762. Rappings were heard in the house and were said to be those of the **ghost** of Mrs. Kent, a former occupant, who stated she had been murdered by her husband. The incident attracted large crowds and widespread attention and was investigated by many notable figures of the day, including Dr. Samuel Johnson, Oliver Goldsmith, and Horace Walpole. The tenant of the house at the time was a man named Parsons, and it seemed possible to the investigators that he had invented the ghost in order to blackmail the deceased woman's husband. The cause of the mysterious rappings was eventually traced to Parson's eleven-year-old daughter Elizabeth, and Parsons was prosecuted.

Coelus In Roman **mythology**, the personification of the "overhanging heavens" and the equivalent of the Greek **Uranus**.

Coffin Texts In ancient Egypt, inscriptions on the sides of coffins assuring the deceased that they would be sustained with good food and drink and confirming the **immortality** of the **soul**. The Coffin Texts were the successors of the earlier Pyramid Texts, which included **spells** and **incantations** for the safe passage of the pharaohs to the next world. The Coffin Texts extended these benefits beyond the exclusive domain of the pharaohs, to the Egyptian nobility.

Cohoba Hallucinogenic snuff, made from the beans of *Anadenanthera colubrina* and *peregrina* (also known as *yopo*, *vilca*, and *huilca*). It was used by the precolonial Incas to obtain a visionary hypnotic state and remains in use among the Mashco Indians of northern Argentina. Its use in the West Indies has died out. See also **Hallucination**.

Coincidence An event, or two or more events occurring at one time, which happen without any apparent cause. Occultists incline to the view that no events are coincidental, but form part of a universal plan or "cycle". All predictive occult sciences (e.g. **astrology** and the many other forms of **divination**) take this view; and in the East the law of **karma** states that every action has a consequence – in this or in future lives.

Collective Unconscious Concept of psychologist **Carl Jung**, who believed that certain primordial images in the unconscious mind were not individual in origin, but "collective" – being symbolic expressions of the "constantly repeated experiences of humanity". In Jung's view, these collective images were mostly religious motifs, acknowledged almost universally as significant. An example would be the mythic image of the **sun**, represented in numerous legends as the sun-hero and worshipped in Greece as **Apollo**, in Egypt as **Osiris**, and in ancient Persia as **Ohrmazd**.

College of Psychic Studies Organization founded in 1884 by the Reverend **Stainton Moses** and **Alfred Russel Wallace**, and originally known as the London Spiritualist Alliance. It encourages free enquiry into **psychical research** and does not tie its members to specific opinions or beliefs. Membership of the college is worldwide and it has attracted many well-known supporters, including **Sir Oliver Lodge**, the fantasy writer **Algernon Blackwood**, and Sir George Trevelyan. The College has a library containing eleven thousand volumes on all matters pertaining to **extrasensory perception**, and publishes a quarterly journal called ***Light***.

Co-Masonry Also adoptive Masonry. Term used in **Freemasonry**, allowing for the admission and initiation of women. Traditionally, women were not allowed into the Order of Freemasons; but historically there have been certain exceptions. **Count Cagliostro** admitted women in the so-called Egyptian rite and the Duchess of Bourbon presided as Grand Mistress in the Grand Orient of France (1775); the Rite of Mizraim established Masonic lodges for both men and women as early as 1819. In authentic Co-Masonic orders, the rites have the same structure as in orthodox Freemasonry and men and women hold corresponding ranks.

Commanding Signs In **astrology**, the signs **Aries**, **Taurus**, **Gemini**, **Cancer**, **Leo**, and **Virgo**, which are said to be "powerful" because of their proximity to the **zenith**.

Communicograph In **spiritualism**, a device used for contacting the **spirits** of the dead. It consists of a small table whose surface has letters of the alphabet that can be illuminated electrically. Beneath the table is a small pendulum that sways freely. When spirits are summoned and the pendulum begins to swing, the electric circuit is closed and letters light up on the table – allowing a spirit-message to be spelt out.

Compact In **satanism**, an agreement by which a person renounces Christ, the apostles, the **saints**, and all Christian values, in order to follow **Lucifer**. In return, Lucifer bestows upon his followers worldly possessions or special powers. In an example that survives from the events associated with the **Aix-en-Provence nuns**, Father Louis Gaufridi offered himself to the **Devil** and received the following benefit: "I, Lucifer, bind myself to give you, Louis Gaufridi, priest, the faculty and power of bewitching by blowing with the mouth, all and any of the women and girls you may desire..." Unfortunately, the compact was short-lived. Gaufridi was accused of **sorcery** and publicly burned at Aix in 1611.

Compacts, Death In **spiritualism**, an agreement between two people that the first one to die would endeavour to communicate psychically from the "other side", as proof of survival.

Concentration The act of focusing one's attention on a particular point, image, or thought. It is a common feature of meditative disciplines requiring mind control (e.g. magical visualization and **yoga**).

Cone of Power In **witchcraft**, the ritual act of visualizing a "cone of energy" and directing it towards whatever goal or task is at hand. Witches with psychic vision claim it is perceived as a silver-blue light that rises from the magic **circle** in a spiral.

Conjunction In **astrology**, the situation when two planets occupy the same degree position on a **horoscope**.

Conjunction In Neoplatonic **magic**, the act of invoking a number of gods collectively, or "in conjunction". According to Psellus, Julian the Chaldean summoned Aion, **Apollo**, and **Hecate** simultaneously in certain magical rites. See also **Neoplatonism**.

Conjuration The act of evoking **spirits** by means of ritual formulae or **words of power**. In **ceremonial magic**, these spirits are urged to manifest within a **triangle** inscribed on the floor of the Temple (the triangle being a symbol of manifestation). Usually incense, or smoke, or some other "manifesting medium" is provided so that the spirits can be conjured to visible appearance rather than remain unmanifested on the **astral plane**.

Conjuring Lodge Tent or hut used by North American Indians for conducting mediumistic activities. It has a parallel in the **cabinet** of spiritualists.

Consciousness From the Latin *conscire*, "to know", the faculty of being aware, of feeling and perceiving. Often equated with **Mind**. The conscious mind, which functions in the everyday world and determines what, for each of us, is our operative reality, is often distinguished from the unconscious mind of **dreams**, repressed memories, unfulfilled fantasies, delusions, and **hallucinations**, which are only experienced in an **altered state of consciousness**. Many mystical traditions teach that true **enlightenment** is not experienced unless the mind is transcended.

Constant, Alphonse Louis See **Lévi, Eliphas**.

Contact Healing Spiritual healing by means of **laying-on-of-hands**, as distinct from **absent healing**, where the subject and healer are located at a distance from each other.

Contagious Magic See Magic, Contagious.

Contemplation The ability to hold an idea or image in the mind without being distracted by outside influences. A common characteristic of **mysticism**. The "contemplative life" associated with ascetics and mystics is characterized by **prayer** and **meditation**.

Control In **spiritualism**, the term used for the "personality" that presents itself through the **medium** at a **seance**. Sometimes the control is also referred to as a **guide**.

Conversion The act of adopting a new religious belief that profoundly alters one's perspective on the world, and brings with it new values and sometimes a change in personality.

Cook, Florence (1856–1904) English **medium** who, under the sponsorship of a wealthy patron, held numerous **seances** at her own home. She claimed to have heard **spirit** voices since she was a young child, and as a teenager gave psychic demonstrations at tea parties. During seances she became possessed by a spirit-control named Katie King, the daughter of a buccaneer. On occasion, Katie "materialized" and was allegedly photographed. Florence Cook was extensively investigated by **Sir William Crookes**, who maintained that she was authentic; but his affections towards her may have made him biased in her favour. Florence was denounced by other investigators as a clever trickster who masqueraded as a spirit by modifying her appearance in the dim light of the seance room.

Cooper, David A. A leading teacher of Jewish meditation, Rabbi Cooper studied mystical Judaism in the Old City of Jerusalem and has been a student of the mystical traditions for more than thirty years. Although his work also encompasses **Sufism**, Vipassana and **Zen**, he is best known for his illuminating study of the **Kabbalah**, *God is a Verb*, published in 1997. Along with his wife Shoshana, he now directs the Heart of Stillness Hermitage near Boulder, Colorado.

Cord, Silver Impression of an umbilical cord linking the physical and astral bodies, perceived by subjects during an **out-of-the-body experience**. Although pioneer research into **astral projection** suggested this was a common effect, it seems to be quite rare. According to the British parapsychologist **Celia Green**, only 3.5 per cent of subjects report seeing the silver cord, while Australian psychic researcher Peter Bicknell maintains that only 2 per cent of his subjects report it.

Cordovero, Moses (1522–1570) Spanish Kabbalist who lived in Safed and was a teacher of **Isaac Luria**. Drawing on the **Zohar**, Cordovero maintained that **God** was the transcendent First Cause and that the **sephiroth** of the **Tree of Life** were the instruments by which he gave life to the world. Cordovero's interpretation of the **Kabbalah** tends towards pantheism. His two main books are *Pardes Rimmonium* (Cracow, 1592) and *Elimah Rabbati* (Lvov, 1881).

Corn Dolly In England, Scotland, and Germany, a human figure or animal shape fashioned from the last sheaf of corn from the harvest. It is kept to ensure that the next year's harvest will be bountiful, and undoubtedly represents a **folklore** custom based on fertility worship.

Cornucopia The horn of plenty, a horn overflowing with flowers, fruit, and produce, symbolizing prosperity and abundance. It is named after one of the horns of the goat Amalthea, which suckled the infant **Zeus**.

Corona Discharge Term used by investigators of **Kirlian photography** to describe the vibrant energy field that surrounds all living things.

Corpora Supercoelestia In **spiritualism**, super-heavenly bodies visible only through psychic perception on the **astral plane**.

Corybantes Priests of the goddess **Cybele**, who performed Phrygian mysteries. The rites were characterized by orgies and self-mutilation. The cult spread to Greece, Rome, and Crete.

Cosmic From the Greek *kosmos*, qualities or characteristics pertaining to the universe. The **Rosicrucians** define cosmos as "the Divine, Infinite Intelligence of the Supreme Being permeating everything, the creative forces of God".

Cosmic Consciousness Expression used by Richard Maurice Bucke (1837–1902) in his book of the same name (1901). Bucke described how, on one occasion, a "momentary lightning-flash of the Brahmic Splendor" gave him the experience of "cosmic consciousness". He argued that one could evolve from "simple consciousness" to "self consciousness" and finally reach the state of "cosmic consciousness" already attained by spiritual leaders like **Gautama Buddha**, Jesus Christ, and **Mohammed**.

Cosmic Egg Hindu symbol for the universe. In some Indian epics the universe is born from the Cosmic Egg, in others it is contained within it. See also **Egg**.

Cosmic Epochs In **astrology**, the division of time into periods of approximately two thousand years represented by different signs of the **zodiac**. The Age of Pisces is symbolically linked to Christ, the fish being a well-known motif of the early Christians; and the next epoch will be the **Aquarian Age**. Astrologers differ on when this epoch will commence. Some maintain that it began in 1948, others that it will not begin until around A.D. 2400. The epoch takes its name from the constellation in which the sun appears at the spring **equinox**.

Cosmic Ice Cosmological theory proposed by Austrian engineer **Hans Horbiger** (1860–1931), who speculated on whether a comet that appeared in 1882 was made of ice. Ten years later, Horbiger had a vision that gave him insights into the nature of the universe, and with Philipp Fauth – an amateur astronomer – he set about writing *Glazialcosmogonie* in order to attract recognition for his theories. Horbiger believed that the universe was filled with hot metallic stars and "cosmic ice" and that, whenever the two collided, an enormous explosion took place, giving birth to a stellar system. Horbiger believed that the Earth's moon had been "captured" thirteen thousand years ago and would eventually spiral down onto the Earth's surface, causing havoc and destruction.

Occultists drawn to Horbiger's theories found in his speculation a possible explanation for the destruction of **Atlantis**. His **cosmology** was also adopted by several members of the Nazi hierarchy, including Heinrich Himmler who, like many other followers of Horbiger, linked the original Aryan master race to a group that had arisen "in Atlantis", somewhere in northern Europe. Adolf Hitler shared Himmler's admiration for Hans Horbiger, declaring him one of the greatest cosmologists who had ever lived.

Cosmic Mind Occult and mystical term for "Universal Mind", or **God**. Sometimes equated with **cosmic consciousness**.

Cosmic Picture Gallery Colloquial term for the so-called **Akashic records**, the astral memory of all events that have taken place in the world.

Cosmogony From the Greek *kosmos*, "the

universe", a theory describing the origin and creation of the universe and its inhabitants.

Cosmology From the Greek *kosmos*, "the universe", the study of the universe and its perceived attributes, including space, time, change, and eternity. In mystical and esoteric literature, it is often used to denote the study of **gods** and goddesses, the process of Creation, and the nature of Reality. See also **Cosmogony; Magical Correspondences; Myth.**

Cottingley Fairies Alleged case of fairy sightings at Cottingley, near Bradford, England. In 1917, two girls – aged sixteen and nine – claimed that fairies played with them in the garden, and photographs were produced in support of this claim. **Sir Arthur Conan Doyle** and L. Gardner investigated the case and asserted that the case was true. Gardner wrote a book titled *Fairies* as a result. However, one of the girls, when an elderly woman, confessed that the photographs and claims were fraudulent.

Coué, Emile (1857–1926) French psychotherapist and hypnotist who studied under H. Bernheim and A. A. Leibault. He believed strongly in using hypnotic instructions to the subconscious mind to eliminate disease and imbalance. An advocate of self-healing, he became famous for the saying "Every day, and in every way, I am becoming better and better". This phrase, and other short, fixed phrases repeated frequently in order to make a mental impression, comprise the practice of Couéism. See also **Hypnosis; Mantra.**

Couéism See **Coué, Emile.**

Council of American Witches Witchcraft group based in St. Paul, Minnesota, which practises rites celebrating the rhythms of life and Nature, marked by the phases of the **moon** and the four seasons. Members value the symbolic power of sexuality and the special role of witchcraft in interpreting the laws of Nature. The Council has as its chairman Carl Weschke, an occult publisher and practitioner, who was initiated by the witch Lady Sheba.

Counter-charm A **charm** used to negate the effect of another charm.

Court de Géblin, Antoine (1725–1784) French theologian and linguist who believed that the **Tarot** originated in ancient Egypt and formed part of an initiatory procedure associated with the worship of **Thoth**. Knowledge of these esoteric symbols was acquired by the **gypsies** and disseminated throughout Europe. Court de Geblin's view expressed in his mammoth nine-volume work *Le Monde Primitif* (1775–1784), was typical of the romantic obsession with lost cultures prevalent in the eighteenth century.

Coven A group of **witches** who gather together to perform ceremonies at **esbats** and sabbaths. Traditionally, the number of members in a coven has been assumed to total thirteen. The earliest reference to this is the claim of **Isobel Gowdie** in 1662 that the Auldearne witches had "thirteen persons in each coven". The famous scholar of witchcraft, **Margaret Murray**, reinforced the idea that a coven consists of twelve members plus a leader masquerading as the **Horned God**; but it now seems that covens do not necessarily have a specific numerical membership and that groups of witches gather in various numbers according to the nature of the rituals to be performed. See also **Witches' Sabbath.**

Crab Creature depicted on the fourth **sign** of the **zodiac, Cancer**. The crab is often regarded as a dualistic symbol, because it is equally at home in sea and on land. It is also shown in an "evolutionary" capacity on the **Tarot** trump of ***The Moon***.

Creative visualization Technique of visualization which utilizes mental imagery in order to achieve specific goals or outcomes. Creative visualization is a central aspect of practical magic, where specific outcomes are sought in a ceremonial or ritual setting.

Creed A system of belief, especially in Christianity, where the Apostles' Creed represents a major statement of Christian doctrine.

Cremation Disposal of the body of the dead by burning, rather than by burying. Cremation was practised from an early date among the Hindus in India, and was also a custom in Rome in the first century A.D. Cremation was unpopular for many years with the Christian Church because it seemed to run counter to the belief in resurrection. Since the nineteenth century, however, it has become commonplace.

Crescent The shape of the waxing **moon**, symbolic of fertility and abundant growth. It is often depicted as an emblem on the heads of lunar deities. See also **Lunar Goddesses**.

Crisis Apparitions Ghostly **apparition** of a person who, at the time, is undergoing some sort of crisis (e.g. dying). Examples are given in the psychic classic *Phantasms of the Living*, compiled by Gurney, Myers, and Podmore.

Critical Day In **astrology** and the study of **biorhythms**, a day associated with negative energy or unfavourable aspects that are likely to produce bad luck or an unpropitious outcome.

Croiset, Gerard (1909–1980) Dutch **clairvoyant** – popularly known as "the man with the X-ray mind" – who worked with police in Britain, Holland, and the United States to locate missing persons and solve murder mysteries. Croiset had an occult faculty for linking objects to people, but did not enter **trance** states or use any occult devices to obtain his results. He worked for over twenty years with Professor W. H. C. Tenhaeff at Utrecht University, investigating paranormal phenomena.

Cromaat A **Rosicrucian** salutation, used in **rituals**, deriving from the Egyptian word *maat*, "truth". In the Hall of Maati, in the Egyptian **Underworld**, the soul of the deceased was weighed against the "**feather** of truth" and the goddess **Maat** presided over this judgment.

Cromlech A circle of large, vertical stones associated with Celtic sun-worship. Sometimes the circle surrounds one or more **dolmens**.

Cromlech Temple Occult group founded in Britain around 1900, whose members were interested in **esoteric** interpretations of Christianity. The group did not practise **ceremonial magic** and insisted that all members proceeding beyond the first grade of **initiation** believe in the Christian faith. It encouraged those seeking practical magical techniques to join the **Hermetic Order of the Golden Dawn**, but remained in itself sufficiently Christian to attract a number of Anglo-Catholic clergymen.

Cronus See **Kronos**.

Crookall, Robert (1890–1981) British geologist, who, in the last years of his life, devoted much of his time to compiling cases of **astral projection** and **out-of-the-body experiences** (OBE). Crookall compared cases of subjects in a good state of health with those who had nearly died during their experiences, and came to the conclusion that the OBE resembles information received through **psychic mediums**. In Crookall's view the **astral body** separates from its physical counterpart after **death** and continues on another plane of existence.

Crookall was a member of both the British and American **Societies for Psychical Research**, and a prolific author. His books include *The Study and Practice of Astral Projection* (1961), *More Astral Projections* (1964), *The Techniques of Astral Projection* (1964), *The Interpretation of Cosmic and Mystical Experiences* (1969), *Out-of-the-Body Experiences* (1970), and *What Happens When You Die?* (1978).

Crookes, Sir William (1832–1919) Prominent physicist who discovered thallium and invented the radiometer, but also had a strong interest in paranormal phenomena, becoming a founder member of the **Society for Psychic Research**. Crookes investigated **Daniel Dunglas Home**, Kate Fox, and **Florence Cook**, attending possibly more **seances** than anyone before or since. He was convinced of the reality of mediumistic "materializations" and also believed he had witnessed the **levitation** of both objects and human beings. His best-known book is *Researches in the Phenomena of Spiritualism* (1874).

Croslet Alchemical term for a crucible. See also **Alchemy**.

Cross Ancient pre-Christian symbol interpreted by some occultists as uniting the male phallus (vertical bar) and the female vagina (horizontal bar). It is also a symbol of the four directions and a powerful weapon against **evil**.

Cross-correspondences A term invented by a practitioner of **automatic writing**, Mrs. Verrall, to describe parallels between the automatic scripts or **trance** utterances of any two **mediums** operating separately and independently. Examples of cross-related mediumistic scripts were compiled by members of the **Society for Psychical Research** and published in its *Proceedings*.

Crossroads In **witchcraft**, a traditional meeting place. Probably as a result of the fear of persecution, crossroads were popular as places where witches could scatter quickly if apprehended.

Crowley, Aleister (1875–1947) Probably the most famous – and notorious – occultist of the twentieth century, Aleister Crowley was raised in a strict Plymouth Brethren home and initially took up interests appropriate for an enterprising young man: he studied at Cambridge, acquired a passion for mountain climbing and rowing, and became a very fine chess player. Only after becoming friendly with **Allan Bennett** did he embroil himself in ritual **magic** and the struggle for personal power.

Crowley was initiated as a Neophyte in the **Hermetic Order of the Golden Dawn** in November 1898, and rose to the grade of Practicus within two months. He aspired to lead the Order, but failed to dislodge its leader, poet **W. B. Yeats**. After quarrelling with **MacGregor Mathers**, Crowley decided to seek his mystical fortunes elsewhere. He and his wife Rose travelled through Ceylon and India, arriving in Cairo in March 1904, where they took quarters near the Boulak Museum. It was here that the magical breakthrough occurred.

Crowley performed a magical ceremony invoking **Thoth**, the Egyptian god of Wisdom, and Rose meanwhile appeared to be entering a state of reverie. After announcing later that "Horus was waiting", she led her husband to the museum and showed him exhibit 666, a statue of **Horus** in the form of **Ra-Hoor-Khuit**. Crowley was impressed that the number of the exhibit tallied with the number of the **Great Beast** in the Book of Revelation, and he subsequently came to believe that he was the **Anti-Christ**. Rose meanwhile fell into **trance** back at the hotel and began to dictate a blasphemous work known as *The Book of the Law*, which confirmed Crowley as Lord of the **New Aeon**.

It was profoundly disrespectful to other spiritual leaders and included such lines as "With my Hawk's head [i.e. Horus] I peck at the eyes of Jesus … I flap my wings in the face of Mohammed." However, it convinced Crowley that he had received a major initiation, perhaps of a magnitude only occurring every two thousand years.

Crowley founded a new Order, the **Argenteum Astrum**, and claimed exclusive contact with magical Egyptian forces, specifically through an entity called **Aiwaz**. In due course this Order initiated around one hundred people, including **Austin Spare**, Pamela Hansford-Johnson, and **Victor Neuberg**. Crowley's new Order in turn inspired others, including **Louis T. Culling**'s Great Brotherhood of God, the Californian branch of the **Ordo Templi Orientis**, and a group calling itself the Fellowship of Ma Ion.

Aleister Crowley died a confused man in 1947, but he did leave behind an enormous outpouring of magical writing. His most important occult books include *Magick in Theory and Practice*, *The Book of Thoth*, *Book Four*, *The Vision and the Voice*, *The Confessions*, and the *Qabalah of Aleister Crowley*.

Crowley, Vivienne Senior Lecturer in the Psychology of Religion at King's College, University of London, Dr. Crowley is also an initiated **Wiccan** priestess and a practising **Kabbalist**. Her many books include *Wicca: the Old Religion in the New Age* and *A Woman's Kabbalah* and several publications on the work of **Carl Jung**.

Crowther, Patricia (1927–) English **witch** who, with **Eleanor Bone** and Monique Wilson, was heir to the estate of **Gerald Gardner**. She describes herself as High Priestess of the Sheffield **coven** and Queen of the Sabbat, and continues to attract attention for her views on magical **initiation**, pagan folklore, and cosmic symbolism. Her books include her autobiography *Witchblood* (1974) and *Lid off the Cauldron* (1981), a guide to witchcraft, planetary rituals, and magical **spells**.

Crumbine, Dr. Camual (1860–1959) American physician who undertook extensive research into **hypnosis**. Subjects in trance were asked to identify people and events at a distance, and the results were verified by telephone. Many believe Crumbine successfully demonstrated that under hypnosis subjects may become telepathic.

Crux Ansata The Egyptian **ankh**, a cross with an oval loop replacing the upper vertical bar. Important in ancient Egyptian religion as the symbol of life.

Cryptesthesia General term for psychic perception, including **clairvoyance**, premonition, and **telepathy**. Coined by **Dr. Charles Richet**.

Cryptomnesia Capacity to activate the memory while in a state of **trance**, drawing forth otherwise unconscious information.

Crystal Mystical symbol of the **Spirit**. Its associations derive from the fact that crystal, though solid and tangible, is also transparent. Among many shamanic groups, natural crystals are regarded as power-objects.

Crystal Ball Ball made of crystal or glass, used by clairvoyants for **skrying**. In this technique, the **clairvoyant** uses the ball to focus the gaze and enter a state of **trance** reverie. Paranormal visions may then arise, which form the basis of the **divination**.

Crystal-gazing Popularly associated with fortune-telling, crystal-gazing is a form of **skrying** in which a **medium** stares fixedly into a **crystal ball**. The first impressions may be hazy, but according to many mediumistic accounts this effect clears away and specific visionary scenes then present themselves.

Occultists believe that the crystal ball is a focus for the medium's psychic perception and that the crystal ball does not, in itself, cause the visions to appear.

Crystalomancy **Divination** by means of a crystal ball or a mirror-like pool of water. See **Crystal-gazing**.

Cthulhu A mythic **cosmology** described by **H. P. Lovecraft**. Cthulhu is the "Great Old One" who lies sleeping beneath the sea in the sunken city of R'lyeh.

Cube Symbol of the four **elements** and identified with solidity and endurance. In occult symbolism, the thrones of sacred deities are often depicted as cubes (for example, the Ancient of Days, as depicted in ***The Emperor*** card in the **Tarot**, sits on a cubic throne inscribed with the motifs of **Aries**). In **Hermetic Order of the Golden Dawn** ritual, the magical altar consists of a double cube of wood and has ten exposed faces, representing the ten **sephiroth** on the **Tree of Life**.

Culling, Louis T. American occultist and member of the Great Brotherhood of God, who practised a form of ritual magic based largely on the teachings of **Aleister Crowley** and the **Ordo Templi Orientis**. He published a number of occult works, including *The Complete Magickal Curriculum of the Secret Order G.B.G.*, *The Incredible I Ching*, and *A Manual of Sex Magick*.

Cult A system of religious or magical beliefs. The term is used to describe practitioners of those beliefs, the ceremonies, and the patterns of worship.

Culture Hero A historical figure whose accomplishments become idealized in the form of a myth and who then serves as an **archetype** for that culture or society. See also **Deification**.

Cummins, Geraldine (1890-1969) Noted Irish **medium** who claimed contact with the spirits of Phillip the Evangelist and the psychic researcher **F. W. H. Myers**, among others. Despite the fact that she had never visited the Middle East, Geraldine Cummins applied her mediumship to obtain remarkably specific details of the early history of Christianity and the work of the Apostles. She later claimed to communicate with the spirit of Myers concerning the progress of the human soul on the spiritual planes. She wrote at a prodigious speed, and her scripts had a coherent, legible quality that impressed many psychical investigators, including **Dr. R. H. Thouless** and Professor C. D. Broad – both of whom were at different times presidents of the **Society for Psychical Research**. Geraldine Cummins became known as the "medium with integrity". Her many books include *The Scripts of Cleophas*, *The Road to Immortality*, *They Survive*, *Unseen Adventures*, and *Mind in Life and Death*.

Cunningham, Scott (1956–1993) Well-known American-born authority on **natural magic**, **Wicca** and **herbalism**, Cunningham was introduced to the Craft in 1971. In 1974, following in the footsteps of his father – who was also a prolific author – he enrolled in a course in creative writing at San Diego State University and decided to become a professional writer. His many works included *Magical Herbalism*, *Techniques of Natural Magic*, *Wicca: A Guide for the Solitary Practitioner* and *The Truth About Witchcraft Today*.

Cupel In **alchemy**, a clay or bone-ash crucible used for testing and refining **silver** and **gold**.

Cupid Roman god of love, associated with the Greek god **Eros**. Cupid was often depicted as a beautiful winged boy who would fire arrows from his bow. The arrows would bring love to those whom they struck.

Cups Also known as Chalices, one of the four suits of the **Tarot**, ascribed to the element **Water**.

Curandero, Curandera In Mexico and Peru, a folk-healer or **shaman** skilled in summoning spirits to heal the sick. One of the most famous contemporary healers in Peru is Eduardo Calderon, a shaman who uses San Pedro cactus in an all-night curing ceremony that combines Indian and Christian rituals and features a selection of **power-objects**. The anthropologist **R. Gordon Wasson** documented in several books the healing vigil, or **velada**, of the Mexican Mazatec shaman Maria Sabina, who made use of sacred mushrooms as a healing sacrament.

Current 93 Term used by the followers of **Aleister Crowley** to describe the magical energies associated with the Aeon of Horus, which Crowley is said to have initiated in 1904 when *The Book of the Law* was revealed to him. One of Crowley's main magical dicta was "love under will", and the Greek words **agape** (love) and **thelema** (will) both had a numerical value of 93. So too did the mystical Egyptian entity **Aiwaz**, who was credited by Crowley as inspiring *The Book of the Law*.

Curse Invocation or oath made with evil intent. Curses are associated with **black magic** or **sorcery** and are intended to harm or destroy opponents or property. Cursing is probably based on the idea that sound vibrations have a causal result; in many religions the sounds uttered by the beneficent gods are said to give rise to the universe or sustain it. Sounds uttered in the name of evil forces have an opposite, destructive effect. Curses therefore often require the evocation of evil spirits. See **Demonology**, **Spells**.

Curupira Brazilian dwarf-like creature represented in folklore as being bald, one-eyed, and having large ears and a hairy body. He always rode on a pig, often with his feet turned backwards.

Cusp In **astrology**, the imaginary line that separates one **sign** or **house** of the **zodiac** from another.

Cybele Phrygian fertility goddess who was linked symbolically to mountains and wild animals, and who was represented in myth travelling in a chariot drawn by lions. Cybele was linked by the Greeks to the **mother-goddess Rhea** as the cult of Cybele spread from Phrygia and Lydia to Greece. The priests of Cybele were known as **Corybantes**. Her worshippers offered her passionate and intense homage, bewailing the death of her lover Attis with solemn ceremonies, chanting, and prayers, and then indulging in frenzy, jubilation, and song to herald his spiritual **rebirth**.

Cyclops Hideous creatures described in ***The Odyssey*** as monsters with a single eye in the centre of their foreheads. **Odysseus** was captured by the strongest of the Cyclops, Polyphemus, but escaped by making him drunk and striking him in the eye with a fiery brand.

D

Daath In the **Kabbalah**, "knowledge", the child of **Chokmah** and **Binah** on the **Tree of Life**. It is sometimes referred to as the "false" eleventh **sephirah**, because it is the seat of conceptual rather than absolute knowledge.

Dactylomancy **Divination** by means of rings. Sometimes the ring is held on a string and allowed to swing unassisted against the side of a glass, thereby indicating yes or no to questions asked. A ring may also be suspended over a round table inscribed with letters of the alphabet and used as a type of **pendulum** to produce a mediumistic "message". The use of wedding rings is popular in this divinatory art.

Dactyls Phrygian **soothsayers**, **sorcerers**, and exorcists who brought their magical skills to Italy, Greece, and Crete. They are credited with discovering minerals at Ephesus and bringing musical instruments to Greece.

Dadouchos Greek term meaning "torch-bearer". He was a celebrant in the **Mysteries of Eleusis**. There was also a role for the Dadouchos in some of the rituals of the **Hermetic Order of the Golden Dawn**, especially the Neophyte and Zelator grades.

Daedalus In Greek **mythology**, the architect of both the **labyrinth** and the legendary Palace of Minos. It was he who gave Ariadne the clue to guide Theseus through the passages of the labyrinth using a thread. Minos imprisoned him, but Daedalus and his son Icarus made themselves wings from feathers and wax and escaped. However, Icarus was lost when he flew too close to the sun, causing the wax to melt.

Daemon From the Greek *daimon*, a spirit, an evil spirit or **demon**. Also used as a term for beings at an intermediate level between **God** and humanity. The word *daemon* therefore becomes identified with the concept of an inspiring intelligence or **genius**.

Dagda Chief **deity** of the **pagan** Irish tribes, among whom he was god of fertility and the earth. Known as "The Lord of Great Knowledge", he controlled life and death with a great club and had a **cauldron** with magical powers. An able craftsman and a legendary player of the harp, he was also a fine warrior and defeated the powerful Fomorians in a mighty battle.

Dagoba A Buddhist shrine or mound, containing relics of the Buddha or a saint. Typical relics would include teeth, pieces of bone, or fragments from the **bodhi tree**. Examples of dagobas may be found in India, Sri Lanka, and Burma. In some respects dagobas resemble **stupas** but the latter do not always contain relics. See also **Buddhism**.

Dagon Phoenician god of the earth, and later of the sea. He also had the title **Baal**.

Dakini In Tibet, a **witch** or terrifying female **demon** that appears to the **magician** during his rituals. Sometimes used in India as a general term for earth-mother deities.

Dakmah In **Zoroastrianism**, the so-called "Tower of Silence" where the bodies of the dead are left to be devoured by preying vultures.

Dalai Lama The leading **lama** or high monk of Tibet, usually referred to as Gyalwa Rinpoche. The Tibetans believe that the Dalai Lama is a reincarnation of the four-armed deity **Chenrezig**, and that the present Dalai Lama is the fourteenth such incarnation. When the Dalai Lama dies, a great search is undertaken by the lamas to identify the newborn child who has received the noble soul of the spiritual leader. The Dalai Lama has traditionally been regarded as the spiritual leader of Tibet.

Dana Also Danu. **Mother-goddess** in the Irish Celtic **pantheon**. Dana represented fertility and abundance and was said to be the mother of the later deities, the **Tuatha De Danaan**, also known as the **Sidhe**, or fairy folk of Irish folklore and legend.

Dance Rhythmic bodily movements, often accompanied by music, chanting and clapping, which – from an occult point of view – may result in an **altered state of consciousness** or **trance** state, especially when performed in a ritual setting. Dance has this function in many forms of primitive worship, and is a characteristic of fertility rites, and the ceremonies of the **dervishes**, **voodoo**, and **witchcraft**.

Dance of Death Popular theme in the Middle Ages, in which a skeleton led men and women to the grave – the final stage of life's journey. In the Spanish *danza macabra*, skeletons are shown carrying a scythe, a clock, and a banner; while in the medieval **Tarot**, the card *Death* shows a skeleton wielding his scythe through a field of bodies, levelling king and commoner alike.

Dano In Peruvian **magic**, harm inflicted through **sorcery**, resulting in different kinds of illness.

Danse de Rejuissance In **voodoo**, a religious dance of celebration, often following a ceremony.

Dante Alighieri (1265–1321) Italian poet who was born in Florence and spent much of his life in political exile in northern Italy. Although he wrote works on politics and the nature of Italian dialects, he is perhaps best remembered for his remarkable poem *Divina Commedia* (1300–1321), which describes a visionary journey through **hell**, purgatory, and paradise.

Dante described the ten divisions of hell as regions where the unbaptized, the lustful, the gluttonous, the spendthrifts, the heretics, the violent, the fraudulent, and the malicious spent their days in torment. **Lucifer** was depicted as an icy monster among followers devoid of feelings. Dante also described the journey through the ten spheres of **heaven**, spanning from St. Peter's Gate to the highest revolving spheres and the **Primum Mobile**, and thence to the Empyrean domain where human **will** and God's will became as one.

Daphnomancy **Divination** using the laurel plant. A branch of laurel was thrown into a fire and, if it crackled in the flames, the tidings were favourable; if it burned quietly, the omen was negative.

Dark Night of the Soul Evocative phrase used by St. John of the Cross to describe the experience of **mystics** who feel depressed and isolated, alienated from the world, and even from God – prior to the attainment of mystical **transcendence**. See also **Juan de la Cruz**.

D'Arpentigny, Casimir Stanislaus (1798– ?) French **mystic** who had such beautiful hands that he frequently compared them with the courtiers of Louis XVIII. He believed that the thumb was an index of talent and genius and developed the concept of **chirognomy**. His works include *La Chirognomonie* and *La Science de la Main*.

Darshan Sanskrit term meaning "sight" or "vision". Many Hindus believe that the act of seeing a **saint** or **guru** confers a spiritual blessing, and that when the spiritual leader makes eye contact with a **chela**, an important psychic link is established.

Dashwood, Sir Francis (1708–1781) Wealthy English aristocrat who combined a life of privilege with a taste for the bizarre.

He worked for Frederick, Prince of Wales, and met many leading figures of the day. His contacts allowed him the opportunity of numerous liaisons with aristocratic mistresses and an outlet for his promiscuous and voracious tendencies. Despite his marriage to the somewhat pious widow of Sir Richard Ellis, Sarah, he continued to gather like-minded friends around him and decided to form a group of **initiates** who would hold sexual orgies to worship the **Great Goddess.** He called his brotherhood The Knights of St. Francis – naming it after himself, not the saint – and attracted a membership of thirteen, including the Marquis of Queensberry, the Earl of Sandwich, and the Prince of Wales himself. Meetings were held at Medmenham Abbey near Marlow on the Thames, and they employed the services of whores who were transported from London by coach. These sexual practices at the Abbey continued for around fifteen years, and it became known as the Hell-fire Club after acquiring a reputation as a place of devil-worship. Sir Francis Dashwood later moved the premises to a location at West Wycombe, where he had underground tunnels and a central chamber excavated, allowing his group to continue to meet in secret.

Datura **Psychedelic** plant with magical associations, especially among **shamans** in Mexico and South America. Pulverized seeds of datura are dropped into native beers and the intoxication that follows is accompanied by vivid **hallucinations** – which may last up to three days. Jivaro shamans use the experience to diagnose disease and divine theft. Datura can also produce auditory hallucinations and may result in conversations with imaginary beings.

Davenport Brothers Ira and William Davenport were American-born **psychic mediums** who became well known for their seances in both Britain and the United States between 1860 and 1870. Taking their seats in a **cabinet** with their hands firmly bound, and after the lights had been dimmed, they would manifest "spirit hands" that were able to play musical instruments that had been provided for the experiments. While many were impressed at the time, it is now felt that the Davenports were clever conjurors.

David-Neel, Alexandra (1868–1969) French writer and explorer who made an early study of **mysticism** and magical practices in Tibet. She described life with the **lamas** in the monasteries and also various ceremonial techniques, like the *rolang* ritual of bringing a corpse to life by animating it with magical formulae. She is best remembered for her classic work *With Mystics and Magicians in Tibet* (1931), but was the author of several other works, including *My Journey to Lhasa*, *Tibetan Journey*, and *Initiation and Initiates in Tibet.*

Davis, Andrew Jackson (1826–1910) American **mystic**, clairvoyant, and psychic healer who became known as the "Poughkeepsie Seer". Interested in **clairvoyance** and **trance**, he was heavily influenced by both **Swedenborg** and **Mesmer** and wrote extensively on the basis of his own clairvoyant visions. In due course he became a leading figure in the American spiritualist movement. His main work was *The Principles of Nature*, published in 1847. See also **Spiritualism**.

Day of Creation According to Genesis, God created the world and its inhabitants in six days and rested on the seventh. In the **Kabbalah**, which interprets Genesis symbolically, the "seven days of Creation" are equated with the seven **sephiroth**, or emanations from God, depicted on the **Tree of Life** beneath the Trinity of **Kether**, **Chokmah**, and **Binah**.

Day of Yahweh In Jewish mysticism and the **Kabbalah**, the Day of Judgment. According to some kabbalists there were two judgments affecting human fate; one after death, the other after the resurrection of the dead.

Dead Sea Scrolls Collection of ancient Jewish religious writings, in the form of scrolls. Most of the documents were written in Hebrew, some in Aramaic and a few in Greek. They were found in caves at **Qumran** on the west side of Jordan, at the northern end of the Dead Sea, not far from Jericho, between 1947 and 1956. The scrolls date from c. 150 B.C. to A.D. 68, when the community of **Essenes** who owned them were routed by the Romans. Among the scrolls are very early scripts on various Old Testament books. They also mention a pre-Christian "Teacher of Righteousness" who was a member of the sect. Compare with **Nag Hammadi Library**.

Death The end of life, described in a popular psychedelic graffiti as "the highest 'high' of all: that's why they leave it till last..." Occultists regard death as a transitory stage characterized by the departure of the **astral body** and its journey to higher spheres. Advocates of **spiritualism** believe it is possible to communicate with earthbound spirits of the dead at **seances**, and that apparitions of those close to death may appear to their loved ones. See also **Apparition, Banshee, Reincarnation.**

Death In the **Tarot**, the card of the **Major Arcana** that depicts a skeleton figure wielding a scythe over a field of human bodies. A river flows through this macabre landscape and leads towards the **sun**. Occultists believe that death precedes **rebirth**, that the lower instincts need to "die" before spiritual **illumination** can be attained. In Western **magic**, which combines the Tarot paths of the Major Arcana with the ten **sephiroth** on the **Tree of Life**, the path of *Death* connects **Netzach** and **Tiphareth.**

Death Coach A medieval **superstition** common in many parts of England and Wales, that death travels in a horse-drawn coach, collecting the souls of the dying. Both horse and coach are black, and sometimes the driver is depicted without a head.

Death Posture Term used by the English occultist and artist **Austin Osman Spare** to describe a state of self-induced **trance** in which he would "open" his mind psychically to the formation of magical images. Spare would meditate on his reflection in a mirror until his body went rigid, while at the same time concentrating on a magical **sigil**. Once he had reached a state of "oblivion", Spare found that marvellous magical images would well up from his subconscious mind, some of which he linked to earlier personal incarnations. He produced automatic drawings using this technique. See also, **Automatic Painting and Drawing.**

Debility In **astrology**, a term applied to a planet whose position in the **horoscope** weakens its influence. .

Decad In **numerology**, the number **ten.**

Dee, Dr. John (1527–1608) Classical scholar, philosopher, mathematician, and astrologer who began his career as an academic at Cambridge University and then travelled widely in Europe. Following a meeting with Jerome Cardan in England in 1552, he became interested in the **conjuration** of spirits. When Elizabeth I came to the throne, Dee was invited to calculate the most beneficial astrological date of her coronation.

Dee's excursion into **magic** began in earnest when he met **Edward Kelley**, who was both a **medium** and a **skryer**, and who claimed to communicate with **angels** in his spirit-vision. Dee and Kelley made use of a **crystal ball** and wax tablets, or **almadels,** engraved with magical symbols and the sacred names of God. The tablet for a given invocation was laid between four candles and **angels** summoned as Kelley stared into the crystal. In 1582 Kelley began to receive messages in a new angelic language called "Enochian". Dee was amazed by these events and wrote in his diary: "Now the fire shot oute of E. K., his eyes, into the stone agayne. And by and by he understode nothing of all, neyther could reade any thing, nor remember what he had sayde …" On occasions Kelley seemed to become possessed by spirits, some of which – according to Dee – manifested to visible appearance: "… at his side appeared three of fowr spirituall creatures like labouring men, having spades in their hands and theyr haires hanging about theyr eares …" The spirits wished to know why they had been summoned, and Dee bade them depart. They desisted, nipping Kelley on the arm. Dee writes: "Still they cam gaping or gryning at him. Then I axed him where they were, and he poynted to the place, and in the name of Jesus commaunded those Baggagis to avoyde, and smitt a cross stroke at them, and presently they avoyded …"

The eighteen "Enochian Calls" received by Edward Kelley and John Dee were later used as conjurations by the contemporary English occultist **Aleister Crowley** while on an expedition in the Algerian desert with the poet **Victor Neuburg**. A dictionary of the Enochian language, edited by the Australian linguist Dr. Donald Laycock, was published in London in 1978. See also **Magic, Enochian.**

Defensive Magic See **Magic, Defensive.**

Deggial General term in **Islam** for an imposter or liar, but also used to denote the **Anti-Christ**. He is described as having one eye and eyebrow, and the symbols of the infidel impressed upon his forehead. According to tradition he will first appear in Iraq or Syria mounted on an ass, and 70,000 Jews are expected to follow him. He will destroy the world and its cities with the exception of **Mecca** and **Medina**, which will be protected by the **angels**.

Dehar Among the non-Islamic Kalash Kafirs of Pakistan, the dehar is a **shaman** who is skilled in entering a state of **trance**. The dehar invokes **supernatural** beings, kills a sacrificial animal, and sprinkles its blood upon an altar and then onto a fire. He then rivets his attention upon the altar and becomes physically rigid. Soon a shivering sensation passes through his body, his muscles begin to tremble, and his jaw jerks violently. The dehar often begins to sway, and foam pours from his mouth. He gradually sinks into a deep trance and his soul goes on a **spirit-journey**. It is shamans of this type who have led some anthropologists to link **shamanism** with epilepsy and to identify the shaman as one who "can rescue himself from his own affliction".

Deicide The act of killing a **god**. In pre-literate societies this occurs with the slaying of a totemic animal identified with a deity, or a **priest** who incarnates the god. In Christianity the crucifixion of Jesus represents an example of deicide.

Deification The act of elevating a human being or mortal to the status of an immortal **god**. Among the best examples are the ancient Egyptian **Imhotep**, and the Greek **Asklepios**, both of whom became healing divinities.

Deity From the Latin *deus*, a **god**, or supreme being. In polytheistic religions there are many gods who rule the world collectively and preside over different aspects of life affecting people and Nature; in monotheistic religions there is one supreme deity who reveals different aspects of his being to the world, but is nevertheless One. In general terms, there are deities who create the world, deities who maintain or govern it, and lesser deities who serve the rule of humankind and usually have specified functions. The magical and occult traditions draw on both polytheistic religions (ancient Greek, Roman, Egyptian, Celtic, and Scandinavian) and monotheistic religions (Judaism, Christianity). Within the **monotheistic** tradition most occultists lean towards the **esoteric** schools of thought associated with the **Kabbalah** and **Gnosticism**. See also **Monotheism; Polytheism.**

Déjà Vu From the French meaning "already seen", the sensation of having visited a place "before", often taken to be evidence of **reincarnation**. It is normally regarded as a symptom of a psychological process whereby the unconscious mind is stimulated to "remember" events that have previously occurred elsewhere and which are somehow associated by the person with the new location.

De la Warr, George (1904–1969) English practitioner of **radiesthesia** and **radionics** who was a follower of **Dr. Albert Abrams**. With his wife Marjorie, George de la Warr produced more refined models of Abrams's celebrated black box, amalgamating features proposed by Abrams's main American disciple **Dr. Ruth Drown**. De la Warr endeavoured to correlate various parts of the body and the diseases to which they were prone, and eventually arrived at four thousand such correlations. His instrument included a series of cards identifying the diseases in this way, but also required that the operator of the machine tune in mentally to the disease and its location. The standard instrument, which is still used by practitioners of radionics, has nine dials on a panel, a magnet set at 90 degrees to the dials, and a plate for a sample of the patient's blood – the latter being used as a focus for the patient's health condition. De la Warr was probably quite sincere in his development of black boxes and other types of quasi-medical equipment, but there seems little ground for supposing that his devices had any valid electronic function.

Delphic Oracle Influential **oracle** who made pronouncements at the Temple of Apollo at Delphi, beneath Mount Parnassus. Apollo's priestess was named the Pythia, a reference to the Python or giant serpent that **Apollo** had slain when he first came to Delphi. After sacrificing a goat, the Pythia would mount a tripod and squat there, breathing in intoxicating smoke – possibly from **henbane** seeds – and awaiting divine inspiration. As she entered a state of **trance**, priests would interpret the oracles from the Pythia, and relay her answers to the inquirers.

Deluge In Greek **mythology**, the flood sent by **Zeus**, which was so severe that only the tip of Mount Parnassus could be seen. The Deluge has been identified by some **mystics** and occultists with the destruction of **Atlantis**, although this legend is now believed to have its source in the volcanic eruption on the island of Thera c. 1470 B.C.

Dematerialization In **spiritualism**, materializations are said to occur when the **medium** exudes **ectoplasm** through a natural orifice (often the mouth), and this "astral matter" takes the form of a spiritual manifestation. When the ectoplasm returns to the medium it is said to be "dematerialized".

Demeter In Greek **mythology**, the goddess of corn and agriculture. As Mother Earth she sustained everyone and in turn was revered at festivals held in her honour, with the different agricultural activities such as ploughing, sowing, and harvesting. In the same way that the passage of seasons brought forth new produce, the cycles of life were seen as an omen for people and a promise of "new life". Accordingly, Demeter was an important **deity** in the **Mysteries of Eleusis**. She was the mother of **Persephone**.

Demi-god Especially in ancient Greece, a classical hero, half-human, half-divine.

Demiurge From the Greek *demiurgos*, a "fashioner" or "architect", the creator of the world. For the **Gnostics** he was not the supreme Reality, but a middle-ranking deity who proposed laws for the world that the initiated could transcend.

Demogorgon In Roman **mythology**, an **Underworld** deity who lived at the centre of the earth. An awesome, frightening god, he was associated with **Chaos** and Eternity. In the late Roman Empire (fifth century), he was often invoked in magical rites.

Demon From the Greek *daimon*, a **devil** or evil spirit. See **Demonology**.

Demoniac One possessed of a **demon** or evil spirit.

Demonology The study of **demons** and evil spirits, and the rites and superstitions associated with them. Many **deities** associated with Middle Eastern and Egyptian religions (e.g. **Baal**, **Ashtaroth**, **Bel**, **Apophis**, and **Set**) have become associated either with demonology or the gods of **black magic** and the **left-hand path**.

Demonomancy **Divination** by means of evoking **demons**. The magician would seek prophecies from the evil spirits summoned in ritual. See also **Magic, Black**; **Magic, Ceremonial**.

Dense Body Theosophical concept, also present in some forms of **Gnosticism**, which regards matter as the densest emanation from the **Spirit**. In mystical and occult belief, people have several bodies – for example, a spiritual, etheric, mental, or **astral body** – as well as a physical body. The last of these is regarded as the "densest" and the furthest removed from **god** and **Spirit**. See also **Etheric Body**; **Mental Body**; **Theosophy**.

Deosil In **witchcraft**, the ritual act of moving around a **circle** in a counterclockwise direction. The witch faces the circle and then moves to the right: this is said to produce positive magic. If the witch moves to the left, negative magic is obtained and this direction is termed **widdershins**.

Dermatoglyphics The scientific study of the grooves of the skin, especially those leading to correlations with a person's mental and medical condition. Some occultists believe that **palmistry** may be scientifically validated through this method. An example of this technique is fingerprint analysis.

Dervishes, Whirling Sufi mystics who whirl or dance in order to enter a state of **ecstasy**. They believe that in this state communication with **Allah** is made easier. Other dervishes enter an **altered state of consciousness** by repeating mantric verses from the **Qur'an** or through rhythmic chanting. See also **Sufism**.

Descendant In **astrology**, the degree of the ecliptic which is setting. In the same way that the **sun** rises on the eastern horizon, identifying the **ascendant**, the sun sets in the evening on the western horizon producing the descendant. The first **house** begins at the ascendant, the seventh house at the descendant.

Descending Arc In **Theosophy**, the descent of a procession of spiritual beings from ethereal and spiritual realms of being towards the physical plane of existence. See also **Ascending Arc**.

Descent into Hell In many mythologies, demi-gods and heroes have had the ability to descend into the **Underworld**, to glimpse the hereafter and return with sacred knowledge in order to guide and inspire mankind. Aeneas used the Golden Bough as his passport to **Hades**, and **Odysseus** visited the Underworld in order to hold discourse with the ghosts of dead heroes. Christ is said to have descended into hell for three days before "rising from the dead". Similarly, in Egyptian **mythology**, as represented in the ***Am Tuat***, the sun-god Afu-Ra would descend each night into the Underworld – the twelve dungeons representing the twelve hours of the night – and would be reborn with the new day.

Desire Body Alternative term for the "astral" or "soul" bodies of man. See **Astral Body**.

D'Esperance, Madame Elizabeth (1855–1919) Pseudonym of the **psychic medium** Elizabeth Reed (née Hope) who lived at Newcastle-upon-Tyne, England. She drew pictures of departed **souls**, engaged in **automatic writing**, and allegedly materialized the spirit of a young Arab girl while in trance. On different occasions onlookers seized this **spirit**, whose name was Yolande, and more than once found her to be none other than Madame D'Esperance herself. However, the medium does seem to have experienced a degree of psychic **dissociation** because she felt considerable pain when her alter ego was handled in this way. Madame D'Esperance was credited at one **seance** with dematerializing her body from the waist down. She remains one of the most spectacular examples of psychic mediums in the history of spiritualism, See also **Dematerialization**.

Destiny One's fate or foreordained future. In Greek **mythology**, Destiny was a **god** beyond **Zeus**'s control, and, together with the three **Fates** dared to oppose his will.

Destructive Magic See Magic, Destructive.

Devachan In **Theosophy**, a state of existence between **incarnations**, the abode where the soul finds spiritual fulfilment not attained in the previous incarnation. It is regarded as a state of "blissful imagination", where the ego can reflect peacefully on the possibilities and potentialities of life.

Devadasi In India, a temple prostitute. Traditionally, these women were well educated, skilled in dance and music, and often possessed knowledge of sacred art forms.

Devas From the Sanskrit term meaning "celestial beings". In **Theosophy**, a hierarchy of spirits who help to rule the universe. Some of these devas belong to the "higher mental world", others to the **astral plane**. Members of the semi-Arctic **Findhorn** community in Scotland attribute the abundance of their crops to the presence of nature-devas sustaining the growth.

Devas In **Zoroastrianism**, evil **genii** or malevolent spirits ruled by **Angra Mainyu**, the god of darkness.

Devil, The The personification of **evil** called **Lucifer** or **Satan** in Christianity, **Eblis** in **Islam**, and **Ahriman** in **Zoroastrianism**. Many religious devotees, especially **fundamentalists**, believe that the Devil is still active in the world, luring people away from **God** and spiritual salvation. Those who approach mysticism and religious belief from a psychological viewpoint are more inclined to view the Devil as a negative **archetype** of the mind, personifying adverse and destructive human characteristics.

Devil, The In the **Tarot**, the card of the **Major Arcana** that depicts the Devil, illuminated by a torch, with a naked man and woman bound in chains to his throne. The Devil's goat-like form is a reminder of his bestiality and the inverted pentagram on his brow represents retrograde evolution. Occultists believe that the card of *The Devil* demonstrates that individuals should acknowledge and transcend their animal nature. In Western **magic**, which combines the Tarot paths of the Major Arcana with the ten **sephiroth** on the **Tree of Life**, the path of *The Devil* connects **Hod** and **Tiphareth**.

DEVIL: A Tarot card of the Major Arcana showing the Devil and his subjects (Marseilles Pack).

Devil's Bridge According to legend, an old woman from Aberystwyth, Wales, was searching for her cow and found it stranded, inaccessibly, on the opposite side of a chasm. The **Devil** appeared to her in the form of a monk and agreed to conjure a bridge crossing the chasm, if she would surrender to him the first living thing that would pass across it. She agreed and was about to step onto the bridge when she noticed the monk's cloven hoof beneath his robes. Taking a crust of bread from her pocket she threw it in front of her, bidding her dog to go and retrieve it. The dog leaped forward, thereby saving the old woman from an unintended pact with the Devil.

Devil's Chain French tradition that the **Devil** is chained to rocks near the Abbey of Clairvaux. Farmers in the district strike a hammer on an anvil each Monday morning before work, symbolically strengthening the chain so he cannot escape and wreak havoc on their crops.

Devil's Dandy Dogs A pack of supernatural black hounds who, according to a Cornish legend, followed the **Devil** across lonely hillsides on stormy nights. They had bright, effulgent eyes and fire coursing from their nostrils. If ever the dandy dogs captured human beings, they would tear them to shreds. The only protection against these fearsome creatures was **prayer**.

Devil's Girdle Allegedly worn by **witches** in the Middle Ages as a token of their allegiance to the **Devil**.

Devil's Hoofmarks The popular name given to a series of inexplicable "hoofmarks" seen in untrodden snow in Devon on February 8 1855. The marks, which were in a single line, stretched for a hundred miles around Exmouth, Lymphstone, and Teignmouth and were imprinted on haystacks, in open fields, on rooftops, and up the side of walls. The incident was originally reported in *The Times* (February 16 1855) and described in *The Book of the Damned* by **Charles Fort**. It was further investigated by Rupert Gould (*Oddities*, 1928).

Devil's Mark In **witchcraft**, a mark on the body said to be an initiation motif given by the **Devil**, and which is insensitive to pain. In the Middle Ages, Inquisitors searched victims accused of witchcraft in order to locate any such marks and thereby prove their guilt. The practice of searching for the Devil's mark became illegal in England in 1662.

Devil's Pillar Three stones, preserved in Prague, which – according to legend – are the remains of a pillar with which the **Devil** intended to slay a priest who had signed a diabolic **pact**. St. Peter cast the Devil into the sea, the priest repented, and the Devil broke the pillar in rage.

De Wohl, Louis (1902–1961) Austrian astrologer of Hungarian descent, who at one time advised Adolf Hitler but later worked for the British Intelligence. De Wohl believed that all of Hitler's major coups were related to planetary aspects provided by his astrologers, most notably **Karl Ernest Krafft**. After escaping to Britain, De Wohl was introduced to Lord Winterton, Viscount Horne, and Lord Halifax – at the time Secretary of State for Foreign Affairs. De Wohl claimed that he could anticipate many of Hilter's military manoeuvres by making the same astrological calculations as Hitler's astrologers, and he was taken on as a captain in the British army with the covert purpose of providing astrological data to the British War Office.

De Wohl also visited the United States during the war years, and made contact with the American Federation of Scientific Astrologers. He maintained that Hitler would only attack a country when the two major **malefics**, **Saturn** and **Uranus**, were in the zodiacal sign that ruled the nation in question. De Wohl anticipated Wavell's military successes in North Africa and also predicted that Montgomery would triumph over Rommel. After the war he went to Switzerland, where he died in Lucerne in 1961. His books included *I Follow My Stars*, *Common-sense Astrology*, and *Secret Service of the Sky*. See also **Astrology**.

Dexter In **astrology**, a right-handed aspect – the exact opposite of a **sinister aspect**. The concept derives from Ptolemaic astronomy, which assumed that the Earth was at the centre of the universe, with the sun, moon, and stars revolving around it. The terms "dexter" and "sinister" are not used extensively in modern astrology, which nowadays follows the scientific system of astronomy.

Dhamma The Pali spelling of **Dharma**.

Dhammapada, The Major Buddhist work, which contains many teachings of **Gautama** in the form of verse. It is thought that the book dates from the First Buddhist Council (477 B.C.). *The Dhammapada* includes a statement of the so-called **Four Noble Truths** and the **Eightfold path**. See also **Buddhism**.

Dharana In **yoga**, the act of concentration. In **meditation**, this skill includes the ability to focus on an object or image without becoming distracted.

Dharma Sanskrit term for duty, virtue, and law; ethical rules of conduct transmitted from one generation to the next. The three traditional enemies of dharma are lust, greed, and anger. In its occult application, the term means the laws of Nature that maintain order in the universe, uplifting the soul and providing for spiritual growth.

Dharmakaya Sanskrit term meaning the "Body of the Law" and relating to bodies, or vehicles, of higher consciousness. In central Asian **Buddhism**, dharmakaya is the third of the so-called trikayas. In the state of dharmakaya the mystic is about to enter **nirvana**.

Dhyana In the system advocated by **Patanjali**, the seventh of the eight limbs of **Raja Yoga**. Dhyana is a meditative state where the yogi surrenders to the emptiness of space, and transcends awareness of time. It is often thought of as "pure experiencing", without relating to any specific experiences. Dhyana is an important step towards **samadhi**.

Dhyan-Chohans Tibetan planetary spirits who are believed to guide the spiritual evolution of the planet. The term derives from a Sanskrit-Tibetan root meaning "Lords of Meditation".

Diablero Term used in Mexico to describe a black magician or **sorcerer**, especially one who has the magical ability to transform into the shape of animals. The term is virtually synonymous with **Brujo**. Compare with **Lycanthropy**; **Nagual**.

Diabolism Acts, rituals, and worship associated with the **Devil**. See also **Magic, Black**; **Sorcery**.

Diakka A term coined by American spiritualist **Andrew Jackson Davis** to describe troublesome or evil **spirits** who tried to harass and interfere with those still alive on Earth.

Diana The Roman moon goddess. See **Artemis**.

Dianetics A branch of **Scientology** described by its founder, **L. Ron Hubbard**, as a form of "psychotherapy". Scientology proposes eight "dynamics". Of these, Dianetics covers the first four; *dynamic one*: the urge towards the expression of one's individuality;

dynamic two: the urge towards survival through sexuality and the rearing of children; *dynamic three*: the urge towards survival in groups (e.g. in schools, societies, and nations); and *dynamic four*: the urge towards the survival of humankind.

Diasia In ancient Greece, a ritual offering to the **gods** of the **Underworld**.

Dice Small cubes whose six faces have spots representing the numbers 1 through 6. Dice may be cast randomly as a form of **divination**, and are sometimes used by parapsychologists in **ESP** experiments to test whether psychics can predict the fall of the dice with better-than-chance results.

Dicyanin Screen Device invented by **Dr. Walter Kilner** to enable the human eye to view the **aura**. According to Kilner, these screens induce fatigue in the eye and thereby make it more sensitive to subtle or etheric forms. When a screen is placed across each eye they constitute **Kilner-screen goggles**.

Dignity In **astrology**, a situation where the position of a planet strengthens its influence in a **horoscope**. The exact opposite of **debility**.

Diksa In **Hinduism**, the spiritual **initiation** of a novice, by a **guru**. Sometimes the guru offers **prayers** and stimulates the development of spiritual consciousness in the region of the **third eye**. Usually, the ceremony involves providing the novice with a special **mantra** as a focus for **meditation**. This mantra is secret and should never be revealed.

Dingwall, Dr. Eric J. (d. 1986) Leading British occult author who at one time was honorary assistant keeper of printed books at the British Museum. He became a director of the American **Society for Psychical Research** in 1921 and was later a research officer with the Society for Psychical Research in London. He investigated several **psychic mediums** and wrote a number of books. His best-known works include *Revelations of a Spirit Medium*, co-authored with Harry Price (1922); *Some Human Oddities* (1947); and *Very Peculiar People* (1950). He also contributed to a book on the famous haunting of **Borley Rectory**.

Dionysia Festivals characterized by orgies and revelry, held in Athens in honour of **Dionysus**.

Dionysus Greek god of wine, fertility, and revelry who was worshipped in frenzied orgies, the most famous of which was held at Athens in the spring. Dionysus symbolized freedom and spontaneous impulses, and encouraged a distinct lack of reverence for the other gods. Dance, music, and wine were regarded by his followers as a release, a real surrender to the pure, unfettered joy of being alive.

Directions, Four In Western **magic**, the four directions are symbolized in ritual by the four **archangels**: **Raphael** (east), **Michael** (south), **Gabriel** (west), and **Uriel** (north); representing the elements **Air**, **Fire**, **Water**, and **Earth** respectively. According to the *Grimoire of Honorius*, the four directions also have four demons associated with them: Magoa (east), Egym (south), Baymon (west), and Amaymon (north).

Direct Painting and Drawing In **spiritualism**, a situation at a **seance** where a **discarnate** entity appears to use and direct the faculties of a psychic artist – in this case producing paintings and drawings by "guiding" the pen or brush.

Direct Voice In **spiritualism**, a phenomenon whereby a "spirit" or **discarnate** entity appears to speak through the **medium** at a **seance**. Often the voice, both in tone and style, is remarkably similar to that of the deceased person, and such occurrences are regarded by spiritualists as examples of temporary spirit-**possession**.

Direct Writing In **spiritualism**, a situation at a **seance** where a **discarnate** entity appears to use and direct the faculties of the **psychic medium** – in this case communicating written messages by "guiding the pen".

Dis Roman name of **Hades**, ruler of the **Underworld**.

Discarnate Not living; without a physical form or body. See also **Spirits**.

Disciple One who follows, or is a student of, a spiritual teacher or doctrine.

Discs See **Pentacles**.

Disease In pre-literate societies, illness is thought to be caused by the loss of one's soul or spirit, often as the result of **sorcery**. The **shaman** may undertake a **spirit-journey** to recover the soul and restore good health to the patient.

Disembodied Existing without a physical body. Often used to describe **discarnate** entities and **spirits**, or the mind in a state of **dissociation**.

Dismemberment In **mysticism**, the act of dismemberment may be symbolic of a death and renewal process leading to visionary **rebirth**. In some shamanic societies, the act of initiation includes **dreams** or **trance** journeys where the person involved is devoured by hostile adversaries or wild animals, but is restructured by the gods and given new spiritual powers. Several ancient mythologies refer to a similar process. **Dionysus** was formed from the heart of the dismembered Zagreus, and **Isis** restored the fragmented body of **Osiris** after he had been slain by **Set**.

Displacement In **psychical research**, a situation that arises when a subject is trying to predict the fall of **dice** or a card in an experiment, but consistently achieves a "hit" with the target immediately before or after it.

Dispositor In **astrology**, when a planet is located in a certain **house**, the ruler of the sign on the **cusp** is known as the dispositor of that planet.

Dissociation The act of separation. Used in occult terminology to describe the separation of the **astral body** from the physical. Compare with **Out-of-the-body Experience**.

Distillation The act of boiling a liquid to produce a vapour and then converting the vapour back into a liquid by cooling it. In **alchemy**, this vapour was considered to be the **spirit** of the substance concerned. Distillation helped purify it, and condensation allowed these pure qualities to be amalgamated.

Dittany of Crete Aromatic plant found on Mount Ida in Crete. It was sacred to the **lunar goddess** and was said to cure somnambulism. Dittany was used in magical ceremonies as a sedative.

Divination The act of foretelling the future, often by interpreting omens. Among the many forms of divination are predictions based on the symbols of the **Tarot** cards; the fall of **dice**, yarrow sticks, or coloured beans; and the configuration of such natural phenomena as clouds or the wind. See also **Augur**; ***I Ching***.

Divine Pertaining to, or having the nature of, **God**. Something or someone who is sacred or holy. See also **Priest**.

Divine Light Mission Organization established by **Guru Maharaj Ji**, which teaches **meditation** upon the **life-force**.

This meditation focuses on four types of mystical energy, known as the experiences of Light, Harmony, Nectar, and the Word; these allow the practitioner to develop a deep and spiritual self-knowledge. There are an estimated eight million followers of Guru Maharaj Ji around the world, and numerous international branches of the Divine Light Mission.

Divine Nothingness The nothingness which transcends existence, known in the **Kabbalah** as **Ain Soph Aur**, the "Limitless Light" which has not yet become specific, or manifest.

Divine Right Concept that **God** bestows authority to rule upon the King, thereby raising the monarch above the will of the common people. Possibly related to the Roman practice of worshipping emperors, the idea of the divine right of kings was taken up by Louis XIV in France and by the monarchs of the House of Stuart in England.

Divine Soul In **Theosophy**, incarnation or manifestation of divinity as represented by the "inner Christ" ("Christ-Man") or "inner Buddha" (Manushya-Buddha) within a highly evolved spiritual person.

Divining Alternative term for dowsing. See also **Dowser**.

Divining Rod See **Dowser**.

Divis A variant on **devas**. In Persian mythology, they were cat-headed **devils** with horns and hooves.

Dixon, Jeane (1918–1997) Contemporary American **psychic** who attracted widespread attention in the media for her predictions. She claimed to have foretold the assassinations of President John Kennedy, his brother Senator Robert Kennedy, and Martin Luther King, Jr., as well as many other events affecting American and world history. Many of her predictions did not come to pass but, perhaps inevitably, she was remembered for her successes. Jeane Dixon used cards, a **crystal ball**, **astrology**, and **numerology** as methods of **divination**, but often simply "felt" that certain things were going to happen. She produced an autobiographical work, *My Life and Prophecies* (1970), and was the subject of a biography titled *A Gift of Prophecy* (1966), written by Ruth Montgomery.

Djinn See Genii.

Dogma A religious belief or teaching said by an institutional church, sect, or group to be true. The Christian belief in the Virgin Birth and Christ's resurrection are examples of this; but the concept of a "true doctrine" can apply to any religious, mystical, or occult teaching supported as a literal truth by a group of practitioners or devotees.

Dogon Pagan Sudanese tribe who dwell in the Republic of Mali and whose magical practices include rainmaking ceremonies and masked dances.

Dolmen From a Breton expression meaning "table of stone", a Celtic megalith consisting of a large, unhewn stone resting on two or more uprights.

Don Juan Matus Yaqui Indian **brujo** from Sonora, Mexico, who allegedly initiated the anthropologist **Carlos Castaneda** into **shamanism** and primitive **magic**. The teachings and philosophy of don Juan Matus are documented in Castaneda's popular books. Several critics, among them Richard de Mille and **Weston La Barre**, have doubted whether don Juan ever existed; others believe don Juan to be a fictitious composite of several **shamans**. Castaneda himself always maintained that don Juan Matus was a real and authentic shaman and other members of Castaneda's magical group, including

Florinda Donner, have also confirmed his existence.

Donnelly, Ignatius J. (1831–1901) American lawyer and publisher who for six years (1863–1869) was a Republican congressman. He is remembered in occult literature as the author of *Atlantis: The Antediluvian World* (1882) and *Ragnarok: The Age of Fire and Gravel.* Donnelly, above all others, first generated serious interest in the origins of **Atlantis.** The British Prime Minister William Gladstone was so impressed by Donnelly's theories that he sought treasury funds in order to locate the lost continent in the Atlantic ocean. Gladstone, however, did not succeed in convincing his political colleagues to undertake the task. In 1894 a German-language edition of *Atlantis* was published in Leipzig, giving rise to a whole school of Atlantean **cosmology** that influenced **Hans Horbiger** and, in turn, several members of the Nazi regime, including Adolf Hitler and Heinrich Himmler. Horbiger believed that Atlantis was engulfed by a satellite of moon-like proportions. His theories of cosmic cycles helped give rise to the German Master Race concept, which held that some races and nations (most notably the Aryans) had evolved during "favourable" evolutionary epochs, while others (Jews and Negroes) had come into existence during an "unfavourable" cosmic cycle.

Certainly, Ignatius Donnelly could not have foreseen the misinterpretations that would arise from his work. However, he was not without a degree of eccentricity himself. In 1885 he turned his attention away from Atlantis and diverted his energies into identifying the "true" author of Shakespeare's plays. In *The Great Cryptogram*, Donnelly confirmed the view, first postulated by Reverend James Wilmot in 1785, that the mysterious originator of Shakespeare's works was none other than Francis Bacon, Viscount of St. Albans and one-time Lord Chancellor of England. While *The Great Cryptogram* has since faded into obscurity, Donnelly's *Atlantis* remains in print and has been revised and updated by Egerton Sykes.

Doppelgänger From a German expression meaning "double walker", the human double or **astral body**. The doppelgänger may be projected in an **out-of-the-body state** and can then appear to another person as an **apparition.**

Double Term used in traditional occultism to describe the **astral body** or **doppelgänger.**

Double-bodied Signs In **astrology**, signs whose symbols incorporate two figures: **Sagittarius** (half-man, half-horse); **Gemini** (twins) and **Pisces** (two fish).

Doukhobors Nonconformist religious sect which originated in Russia in the late eighteenth century and which now has representation in Canada. The Doukhobors reject Christian ritual and the doctrine of the Trinity and believe in the sanctity of people and the Holy Spirit. Many members of the sect are firm pacifists and attend protest rallies in the nude. Around twenty thousand members of the Doukhobor sect reside in Alberta, British Columbia, and Saskatchewan, and there have been periodic clashes with the Royal Canadian Mounted Police.

Dove Mystical symbol of peace, love, and tranquillity. The Old Testament story of Noah describes how, during the Great Flood, a dove returned to the Ark with an olive leaf in its beak. The Syrian goddess Atargatis was associated with a golden dove, and doves were also sacred to the Greek goddess of love, **Aphrodite.** Doves guided Aeneas on his quest for the Golden Bough; and in Roman mythology **Venus** was depicted as riding in a chariot drawn by doves. According to Slavic belief, the soul turns into the form of a dove at the point of **death.**

Dowden, Hester Psychic medium and pianist; the daughter of Professor Edward Dowden of Trinity College, Dublin. She was investigated by the noted psychical researcher **Sir William Barrett**, and is best remembered for her **ouija board** message that Sir Hugh Lane, the art authority, had drowned with the sinking of the S.S. *Lusitania* in May 1915.

Dowding, Lord H. T. C. (1882–1970) Distinguished Air Chief Marshal in the Royal Air Force who, after his retirement, investigated **spiritual mediums** and became involved in systematic **psychical research**. Convinced of the evidence for life after death, he wrote several books, including *Lychgate* and *Dark Star*.

Dowser A person skilled in locating underground sources of water by means of a divining rod. The dowser uses a Y-shaped rod that is generally made of hazel, but is sometimes made of metal or substitute woods like rowan or ash. As the dowser walks above the location of the underground water, the rod jerks in an involuntary and spontaneous manner, indicating to the dowser both the location and depth of the supply.

Dowsing See **Dowser**.

Doyle, Sir Arthur Conan (1859–1930) Scottish doctor who is best known as the author of the Sherlock Holmes adventure stories, but who also spent many years of his life investigating **spiritualism** and **extrasensory perception**. He believed in mental **telepathy** and became a member of the **Society for Psychical Research**. In 1902 he met **Sir Oliver Lodge** at Buckingham Palace when they were receiving their knighthoods, and the two men found they had a common interest in mystical and spiritualist beliefs. Following the death of his son, Kingsley, shortly after the end of World War I, Conan Doyle became increasingly interested in contacting the spirits of the dead at **seances**; on one occasion he claimed to have heard his son's voice speaking to him through a Welsh **medium**. Conan Doyle later became president of the London Spiritualist Alliance, the British **College of Psychic Science**, and the Spiritualist Community. His many books on the subject include *The Vital Message*, *The History of Modern Spiritualism*, and *The Edge of the Unknown*.

Draci Evil water **spirits** that like to prey on women. According to a twelfth-century legend, the draci take the form of wooden plates floating on a stream. As women reach out to receive the plates they are dragged down to the bottom of the stream to care for, and nurse, the demonic offspring of the water spirits.

Draconian Current According to the magical system developed by the Tantric occultist **Kenneth Grant**, the Draconian Current is an ancient Egyptian magical tradition named after Draco, the son of **Typhon** – the Primeval mother. See **Tantra**.

Dracula Character in a famous novel by the Irish writer Bram Stoker (1847–1912). Here Dracula is depicted as a seductive **vampire** who drinks the blood of beautiful women. The fictional Count Dracula is thought to have his origin in fifteenth-century Romania. Prince Vlad V tortured not only the Turkish invaders in his country, but his own subjects as well, and his father was known as Vlad Drakul – the Devil. Castle Dracula, located north of Bucharest in the Carpathian mountains, has become a tourist attraction, and there are now Dracula societies in both the United States and Britain.

Dragon A mythical creature that has appeared universally in **legends** and folktales and whose symbolism is very diverse. In Western and Middle-Eastern **mythology**, dragons were originally associated with the water deities. Often they were said to dwell at the bottom of the sea where they guarded precious treasure; they could also breathe thunder and lightning, causing rain to fall. In Western cultures the dragon has usually been regarded as hostile to people, and is associated with dark and **evil forces**. Medieval sages tell of numerous battles between virtuous knights and hostile dragons, and in the Book of Revelation St. Michael casts a fearful and monstrous dragon out of heaven: it had "ten horns and seven heads, with ten diadems upon its horns and a blasphemous name upon its heads …"

In the East, the symbolism of the dragon was more positive. It was usually benevolent, was especially friendly towards monarchs, and often guarded the royal treasures. In China, it became the symbol of imperial power; and, according to **Chuang Tzu**, it represented the cosmic vibrancy of life itself.

The colour of dragons varies considerably. In China, they could be red (associated with science) or white (representing the moon). The multi-headed dragon in the Book of Revelation was also red, but in Christian mythology it symbolized gross evil and the forces of **chaos** and destruction. In ancient Greek literature, the earliest mention of dragons occurs in the *Iliad*, where Agamemnon is described as having a blue dragon motif on his swordbelt and a three-headed dragon emblem on his breastplate. In other cultures, dragons can also be yellow, brown, or black.

Different societies tend to draw on familiar animals in formulating their dragons and, as a result, they are often composite creatures. In ancient Babylon, one particular dragon had the head and horns of a ram, the forelegs of a lion, a reptilean body, and the hind legs of an eagle. A dragon described by the ancient Chinese writer Wang Fu had the head of a camel, the horns of a stag, the eyes of a demon, the ears of a bull, the neck of a snake, the belly of a clam, the scales of a carp, the claws of an eagle, the soles of a tiger, and long whiskers on its face. Medieval dragons often had huge jaws, luminous eyes, a forked tongue, eagle's feet, and bat's wings. The dragon-chimera described by Homer combined a lion, a serpent, and a goat.

Wherever it is found, the dragon represents awesome power on a scale to be reckoned with. As a personification of primeval force, it may be hostile or friendly to people, but its **supernatural** and cosmic presence is universally acknowledged.

Draupnir In Scandinavian **mythology**, the magical ring made by the dwarfs for **Odin**, king of the **gods**. When Odin's son **Balder** was slain, Odin placed the magical ring on the funeral pyre.

Dream Occurrence during the period of sleep associated with rapid eye movements (REM). Sigmund Freud regarded dreams as an expression of the wish-fulfillment of repressed desires and an amalgamation of memories and associations based on recent events. However, dreams sometimes also have mysterious and inexplicable contents that have led them to be linked with **extrasensory perception**. Mark Twain had a vivid dream in which he "saw" his brother's corpse resting in a metal coffin with a bouquet of crimson flowers on his chest. A few weeks later, Twain's brother was fatally injured when the boiler of a boat exploded. A metal coffin was donated by friends, and when Twain arrived at the funeral service the scene was as he had dreamed it – except the flowers were a different colour.

Prophetic dreams seem to be comparatively rare, however, and most dreams appear to derive from a familiar external stimulus that triggers patterns of association. The nineteenth-century researcher Alfred Maury described how, when eau de Cologne was placed near his nostrils, he dreamed he was in an exotic Egyptian bazaar; and how, when a section of his bed fell across his neck, he dreamed that he was being guillotined in the French Revolution.

While most Freudian psychologists believe that the contents of dreams usually reflect wish-fulfillment or image-association, **Carl Jung** proposed that sometimes dreams also reveal sacred **archetypes** – profound mythic symbols that are central to religious and mystical experience. According to Jung, these archetypes are symbols not from one's personal unconscious, but from the **collective unconscious** – universal psychic motifs representing the "constantly repeated experiences of humanity". Dreams that include visionary archetypes and symbolic revelations of this type are sometimes known as **high dreams**.

Dream, High A dream in which sacred or **transcendental** images appear and which invariably has a profound effect on the dreamer. Compare with **Dream, Lucid; Peak Experience.**

Dream, Lucid Term used by **Celia Green** of the Institute of Psychophysical Research in Oxford to describe the situation where the dreamer is aware that he or she is dreaming and therefore is conscious within the dream state. There are close parallels between the lucid dream, the **out-of-the-body experience,** and the paranormal phenomenon popularly known as **astral travel.** The definitive study is Celia Green's *Lucid Dreams* (1968).

Dream Body Theosophical and mystical term for the **astral body**, so named because many occultists believe that **dreams** are images that have a reality of their own on the **astral plane**. See also **Theosophy**.

Dreaming True The capacity for controlling and bringing consciousness to one's **dreams**. See also **Dreams, Lucid.**

Dreamtime In Australian Aboriginal **mythology**, the period during the creation of the world when heroes and totemic animals roamed the earth, establishing links with sites now regarded as sacred. For tribal **Aborigines,** the Dreamtime still continues as an ongoing sacred reality, and provides a sense of mythic identification and purpose. See also **Totem.**

Drown, Dr. Ruth American chiropractor and pioneer of **radionics,** who developed the famous black box of **Dr. Albert Abrams.** Dr. Drown also believed that she could diagnose disease and treat a patient from a distance, using a sample of the patient's blood as a "link". However, she was not able to substantiate her claims scientifically. Tests conducted on her modified black box at the University of Chicago in 1950 were also very discouraging. Dr. Drown was harassed by the American Medical Association, convicted of medical quackery, and died in a California prison. However, her belief that there is "a resonance between the whole human body and each of its parts" is now accepted as a philosophical viewpoint by many adherents of **holistic health.**

Druids Celtic **priests** in pre-Christian Britain and Gaul. The Druids were skilled in astronomy and medicine, and worshipped the **sun**, making use of much earlier Neolithic cromlechs and stone circles that had already been erected. They believed in the **immortality** of the soul and in **reincarnation,** and regarded the **oak** tree and **mistletoe** as sacred. The centre of Druidism was at Anglesey, but the Druids also raised monoliths at Aldborough and York and made use of Stonehenge as an observatory-temple. The Celtic religion was eliminated in Gaul and England after the Roman conquests, but lingered on in Scotland and Ireland until the coming of the Christian missionaries.

Druses Religious sect in Syria and Lebanon whose origin dates from the eleventh century. The Druses combine the Christian gospels, the Pentateuch, the **Qur'an**, and **Sufi** allegories in their doctrines, and also believe in **reincarnation.**

Dryads Also Dryades. In Greek **mythology**, **nymphs** who presided over woods and trees. The nymph living in a tree would die at the same time as her tree. Dryads often took the form of a huntress or shepherdess, and the **oak** tree was sacred to them.

Dualism In **mysticism** and religious **cosmology**, the doctrine that two opposing forces, one good and the other **evil**, are forever counterposed against each other. The classical example of dualism in world religion is traditional **Zoroastrianism.** In later Zoroastrianism, good (personified by **Ahura Mazdah**) eventually triumphed over evil (**Ahriman**).

Dual Signs See **Double-bodied Signs.**

Ducasse, Dr. Curt J. French-born American philosopher who became interested in **psychic mediums** and **extrasensory perception.** An active member of the American **Society for Psyschical Research**, he wrote widely on the philosophical issues associated with **death** and personal survival. His main books include *A Critical Examination of the Belief in a Life After Death* and *Nature, Mind and Death.*

Dukes, Sir Paul (1889–1967) Leading British exponent of **yoga** who was knighted for his work in the secret service. He worked with Nadine Nicolaeva-Legat and also with Diana Fitzgerald, who later became his wife and established a leading yoga school in South Africa.

Dumb Signs In **astrology**, the so-called "mute" symbols of the **zodiac**, **Cancer**, **Scorpio**, and **Pisces**.

Dunne, John William (1875–1949) Irish mathematician and aeroplane designer who built the first British military aircraft in 1906–1907. Since the age of nineteen, despite his scientific background, he had also been interested in **spiritualism** and **psychic** phenomena. In his early twenties Dunne noticed that his **dreams** were often predictive, so he began to keep a record of their contents. Many of these dreams related to distant events. One such dream appeared to foretell a major volcanic disaster in Martinique. In his dream Dunne saw the inhabitants being engulfed in lava, and got only one detail wrong in predicting the event: he said four thousand people would perish, when in fact the death-toll later proved to be forty thousand. Dunne published two important books, *An Experiment with Time* and *The Serial Universe*, which described his dreams and put forward the "serial" concept of time, in which events occur on one plane of existence and become subsequently "real" on another. Dunne believed that the quality of time experienced by the unconscious mind (where extrasensory faculties come into play) was somehow different from the normal perception of time experienced in waking reality; and that by tapping the Universal Mind, one could travel in the mind's eye to the past or the future.

Dunninger, Joseph American conjuror who claims to be able to replicate, through trickery, all psychical and spiritualist phenomena. He is the author of a standard work on conjuring, *Dunninger's Complete Encyclopedia of Magic* (1971).

Dunsany, Lord (1878–1957) Irish dramatist and novelist whose full name was Edward John Morton Drax Plunkett, the eighteenth Baron Dunsany. Gifted with a superb facility for portraying **myths** and **legends**, Dunsany helped establish the fantasy genre made popular by later writers like **J. R. R. Tolkien.** Among his most enchanting books are *The Gods of Pegana* (1905) and *Time and the Gods* (1906).

Duppy In West Indian folk-belief, the part of a person that survives **death.** Ghostlike and

evil, duppies can be awakened from the grave by their relatives and bribed to perform certain things – however, they are obliged to return to their graves by daylight. Compare with **Zombies**.

Durva In Indian **mythology**, a manifestation of Parvati, the wife of **Shiva**. Durva took the form of a destructive goddess with a weapon in each of her ten arms, and successfully overcame a fierce demon.

Dwarfs Small, hairy men who, according to Scandinavian folk-legend, lived beneath the earth, were expert steelsmiths, and were skilled in fashioning precious jewellery. The dwarfs made **Odin**'s magical sword and **Freya**'s beautiful necklace, and have a major part in Richard Wagner's *The Ring of the Nibelung*. The English fantasy-book illustrator **Arthur Rackham** provided memorable depictions of dwarfs in the two-volume adaptation of Wagner's work, *The Rhinegold and the Valkyrie* and *The Twilight of the Gods*.

Dweller on the Threshold Concept of a hostile **spirit** entity representing the accumulated bad **karma** of an occultist and appearing to such a person on the **astral plane** as a force to be overcome. The concept of the Dweller on the Threshold is thought to derive from the mystical novel *Zanoni* by **Sir Edward Bulwer-Lytton**.

Dyad In **numerology**, the number **two**.

Dyaus In Indian mythology, the Aryan sky-god who was the husband of the earth-goddess Prithivi and father of **Indra**.

Dzyan, Book of According to **Madame Helena Blavatsky**, a volume of commentaries on the seven secret volumes known as the *Books of Kiu-te*. The latter, taken as a whole, constituted what Madame Blavatsky called "a digest of all the occult sciences", and could be termed *The Book of the Secret Wisdom of the World*. These teachings, said to be the work of "initiated teachers" in Tibet, formed the underlying basis for her own theosophical masterwork, *The Secret Doctrine*. See also **Theosophy**.

E

Ea In Babylon, the god of water who was also "Lord of Wisdom", the patron of **magic**, arts and crafts, and the creator of people. He had the gifts of prophecy and **divination**, and was often represented as having the body of a goat and the tail of a fish. It is thought that the symbolism of the **zodiac** sign **Capricorn** derives from him.

Eagle Bird with many occult associations. The eagle is linked in **astrology** to **Scorpio**, which with **Taurus**, **Leo** and **Aquarius** is one of the "fixed" signs of the **zodiac**. Occultists also identify these signs with the four letters of the sacred **Tetragrammaton YHVH**, the eagle being associated with the first H. In general terms, the eagle symbolizes height (and therefore **transcendence**), light, spirit, and the powers of the **imagination**.

Ear of Corn Mystical symbol of fertility and growth, also linked to the **sun** because of its golden colour.

Earth One of the four alchemical **elements**, the others being **Fire**, **Water**, and **Air**. The spirits of the Earth are gnomes and **goblins**. The three astrological signs linked to Earth are **Taurus**, **Virgo**, and **Capricorn**. See also **Alchemy**.

Earthbound Term used in **spiritualism** to describe **discarnate** beings, or **spirits**, who remain close to the domain where they lived in real life. They are often accused of **hauntings**, but can be dispelled by **exorcism**. See **Apparitions**; **Ghosts**.

Earth Plane The physical domain of everyday reality, as distinct from the **astral plane**, the **ether**, the spirit dimension, or the higher worlds. In the **Kabbalah** this place of existence is called **Malkuth**, the Kingdom.

East The direction of the rising **sun**, and therefore associated with new life, light, spiritual **illumination**, and **initiation**. All **white magic** rituals commence with salutations to the eastern quarter, and in kabbalistic magic this direction is ruled by the archangel **Raphael**, symbolizing the element **Air**.

East-West Foundation Organization established by Michio and Aveline Kushi in Boston to study oriental **mysticism**, religious beliefs, and health practices. Michio Kushi is the author of several books on oriental healing and macrobiotics.

Ebionites Descendants of the original Jerusalem Church, which ceased to exist as a body after the destruction of Jerusalem in the year 70. The term comes from the Hebrew *ebionim*, meaning "poor", and reflects the fact that members of the original Christian community sold all their possessions and shared common property. They believed that Jesus was human, but was nevertheless the Messiah of Israel, and rejected Paul's vision of Christianity as a universal religion of salvation. After the establishment of orthodox Christianity, the Ebionites were regarded as **heretics** and were denounced by the influential Church Father Irenaeus with the same hostility that he directed against the **Gnostics**.

Eblis The **Devil** in **Islam**. The **Qur'an** describes Eblis as an **angel** who originally dwelt in heaven and was once close to **God**. However, he fell from grace for disobeying a command. Eblis is composed of the elements of **Fire** and, according to Moslem belief, roams the world until the Last Judgment.

Echidna In Greek mythology, the fearsome daughter of **Tartarus** and **Gaea**. Half-human and half-serpent, she was the mother of the three-headed dog **Cerberus**, who guarded the entrance of **Hades**. Echidna was finally slain by Argus, the monster with a hundred eyes.

Eckankar See Twitchell, Paul.

Eckhart von Hochheim (Meister Eckhart) (c. 1260–1328) German mystic who entered the Dominican friary at Erfurt and was strongly influenced by St. Augustine. Eckhart sought to understand the way in which the Word of God (**logos**) influenced the world and believed that in order to experience "the immensity and the supreme excellence of the divine light" one had to renounce wealth and possessions and transform oneself into a receptacle for **God**'s wisdom. Eckhart's view that God was both being and essence and that creatures other than human beings could, in a limited degree, also participate in God's essence, aroused the suspicions of the papal authorities. In March 1329, a papal bull condemned twenty-eight "articles" from Meister Eckhart's works as potentially heretical and his propositions were closely examined, even though Eckhart's religious commitment was not in question. Allegedly, Eckhart refuted the twenty-eight dangerous propositions and at the end of his life professed the Catholic faith.

Eclipse In astronomy, the interception of light as one heavenly body passes in front of another. For hundreds of years astrologers have tended to regard eclipses of the **sun** and **moon** as omens of disaster, although **oracles** in Alexander the Great's army interpreted the event of a lunar eclipse to predict a Macedonian victory over the Persians.

Ecsomatic Experience Term used by the British parapsychologist **Celia Green** to describe the **out-of-the-body experience**, especially when it occurs involuntarily. When it is "willed" to occur it is known as **astral projection**.

Ecstasy A state of joy, rapture, or spiritual **enlightenment** in which a person feels lifted up into a state of visionary **transcendence**. Ecstasy is a profound **altered state of consciousness** and is often associated with **trance**. See also **Out-of-the-body Experience**; **Shamanism**.

Ectenic Force In **spiritualism**, the mysterious psychic force that allegedly causes objects to move supernaturally, without physical intervention. This force is said to emanate from **psychics** and is believed by some occultists to explain the phenomenon of **table-turning** and spirit-rappings.

Ectoplasm From the Greek words *ektos*, "exteriorized", and *plasma*, "substance", a term coined by Professor **Charles Richet**, one-time president of the **Society for Psychical Research**, to describe the mysterious substance said to issue forth from the bodies of **psychic mediums** during their **seances**. Described variously as being gelatinous or jelly-like, and viscous, it is usually white in colour and characteristically oozes from the mouth of the medium. Spiritualists believe it to be the materialization of the **astral body**. While some mediums seem to have experienced pain when the ectoplasm was touched or exposed to light, there are other cases where the ectoplasm was clearly a fabrication, made of such substances as egg white, cheesecloth, or wood pulp.

Eddas Medieval Icelandic sagas that are the main source of Scandinavian **mythology** and traditional religious beliefs. The so-called *Elder Edda*, which is in the form of poetry, dates from around the twelfth century, and its authorship is unknown. The *Younger Edda*, which is in prose, was written by Snorri Sturluson around 1230.

Eddy, Mary Baker (1821–1910) Founder of **Christian Science**. Mary Baker Eddy was born at Bow, New Hampshire, and was the youngest of six children. Raised as a Congregationalist, Mary was a sick child and suffered from a spinal disease. Although her education was inadequate, she read widely, wrote poetry, and studied **homeopathy**. She married three times, and her third husband, Asa G. Eddy, was originally one of her students: she married him in 1877 after her second husband, Dr. Daniel Patterson, deserted her.

While she was still married to Patterson, she made contact with **Phineas P. Quimby**, a mental healer from Portland, Maine, who believed that good thoughts could banish disease from the body and maintained that this healing technique had been used by Jesus. A month after Quimby's death in 1866, Mary Patterson (as she then was) had a bad fall on some ice and it was thought she might never walk again. She prayed and read the New Testament in order to recover. This event is usually regarded as the birth of Christian Science and the date of Mary Patterson's emergence as a spiritual leader in her own right. She believed that **God** had worked through her, and began to align herself with spiritualists who had similar metaphysical views of healing and spiritual awareness. Her book *Science and Health*, published in 1875, became the bible of the Christian Science movement.

Edwards, Harry (1893–1976) Famous psychic healer who was renowned throughout England for his spiritual healing technique of **laying-on-of-hands** at mass gatherings. Edwards claimed that he discovered his healing powers while serving as an officer in Persia during World War I. One day, while passing through the city of Kermanshah, he heard screams from a harem and discovered that a woman had been savagely stung by a scorpion. He promptly pressed his hand over the wounded area and apparently saved her life.

As his fame as a spiritual healer grew, Edwards began to draw large crowds. At Kings Hall, Manchester, he attracted a gathering of seven thousand people. Those in need of healing would come forward for laying-on-of-hands. The complaints he was best able to treat were those that have also been cured in Christian healing services – arthritis, spinal lesions, paralysis, and sometimes blindness and deafness. However, Edwards claimed that he was not guided by God so much as by deceased spirits, especially those of Pasteur and Lord Lister. Edwards later established a spiritual healing sanctuary at Shere in Surrey, and consulted with many leading politicians and members of the royal family. See also **Psychic Healing**.

Effigy Image or representation of a person, often used in magical ceremonies or **spells**. Sorcerers and black magicians may burn or stick pins into an effigy of a particular person in order to bring harm to that individual. See also **Magic, Black**.

Efreet Also afreet, ifrit, yfrit. A type of **genii** or djinn in Islamic **mythology**.

Egg In many religious and mystical cosmologies, both the universe itself and also major deities are said to have been born from an egg. The Hindu world-egg was known as Hiranya-garbha and, when it hatched, **Brahma**, the sun-god, came forth. The Egyptian solar deity **Ra** was also born from an egg, as were the twins of Greek mythology, Castor and Pollux. According to the teachings of the **Orphic Cults**, "God, the uncreated, created all things ... [and] the unshapen mass was formed in the shape of an egg, from which all things have proceeded".

Eglinton, William Nineteenth-century English **psychic** who demonstrated a form of spirit-writing at **seances**. Eglinton would sit with a subject in a darkened room and together they would hold a slate beneath a table. A small piece of chalk or graphite would be held between the table and the slate to allow "spirit messages" to be inscribed on the slate. At a successful seance a spirit would manifest, inscribe a message, and complete the communication with three noisy "raps".

The slate, covered with spirit messages, would then be shown to those present at the seance. Eglinton attracted considerable attention for his psychic performances and convinced several conjurors of his authenticity. However, on at least one occasion he was seen to write the spirit messages by himself and in earlier years had been caught faking spiritualist **manifestations**. His reputation rests in the balance.

Ego One's personal identity. **Mystics** and **occultists** tend to regard the ego as essentially illusory and believe that the **self** may assume many personalities in different lifetimes, as part of the spiritual quest towards **self-realization**. See also **Reincarnation**.

Egrigor A **thought-form** created in psychic groups or magical ceremonies by the combined "will" or visualization powers of the participants. According to the psychic **Ted Serios**, if thought-forms are projected forcibly enough, they can leave an image on photographic film. Magicians believe it is often more effective to work ceremonially with an egrigor since this provides a cumulative effect in terms of magical visualization and one can benefit from magical workings which have taken place at an earlier time.

Egums In the **Macumba** spiritist religion, the **souls** or **spirits** of the dead.

Egyptian Book of the Dead Ancient Egyptian account of the afterlife, including details of burial procedures and the passage of the deceased through the **Judgment Hall** en route to the other world. See also **Book of the Dead**.

Egyptian Masonic Rite Magical **ritual** devised by **Count Alessandro di Cagliostro**. Cagliostro claimed that Egyptian Masonry held the key to the **Philosopher's Stone** and that participants could discover their "primitive innocence". Cagliostro admitted both men and women to his lodge, his wife assisting with the **initiation** of the female neophytes. She would breathe upon the faces of her neophytes and say, "I breathe upon you this breath to cause to germinate in you and grow in your heart the truth we possess; I breathe it into you to strengthen in you good intentions, and to confirm you in the faith of your brothers and sisters ... "

The women later donned white robes and took part in a ceremony where they were encouraged to cast off the "shameful bonds" imposed on them by their male masters. They were subsequently led into a garden and later to a temple, where they had an "initiatory" encounter with Cagliostro himself. Naked, he would descend on a golden sphere through the roof of the temple and order his neophytes to discard their clothing in the name of Truth and Innocence. He then explained to them the symbolic nature of their quest for **self-realization** before once again mounting the golden ball and rising up through the temple vault. The intentions of Cagliostro and his wife in bestowing these gifts were not purely altruistic, for it seems that the ladies who were initiated paid large sums in order to participate. However, many of his clients came from the Parisian aristocracy and could no doubt afford it.

Ehrenwald, Dr. Jan Czechoslovakian psychiatrist who became interested in the links between **telepathy** and psychoanalysis. A member of both the British and American **Societies for Psychical Research**, he became a leading authority on the scientific investigation of **extrasensory perception** and maintained that so-called **psi** phenomena were neither occult nor **supernatural**, but could be explained by scientific processes. His many books include *Telepathy and Medical Psychology* (1948), *From Magic Healing to Encounter* (1976), and *The ESP Experience* (1978).

Eidetic General System Adaptation of **biofeedback** developed by Henry Evering and Dr. Terry Burrows in Toronto, Canada, to monitor both internal and external (or environmental) factors affecting human consciousness. Practitioners monitor electrical skin resistance, skin temperature, heart rate, muscle tension, and brainwave rhythms and learn how to adapt the "eidetic imagery patterns" indicated by biofeedback to the personal decision-making process. In essence, the Eidetic General System is a form of personal growth involving pattern-recognition.

Eidolism The belief in **ghosts**, **souls**, and disembodied **spirits**.

Eidolon From the Greek term meaning "an image", the **double**, **astral body**, or phantom.

Eight In **numerology**, a number indicating strength of character and individuality of purpose. People whose birth dates reduce to eight are said to demonstrate independence of thought and a sense of coolness at home, and often find it difficult to let go of their inhibitions. **Hod**, the eighth **sephirah** on the kabbalistic **Tree of Life**, is associated with the rational intellect.

Eightfold Path In **Buddhism**, the eight attributes or qualities presented by **Gautama Buddha** as the means of attaining **nirvana**. They are Right Understanding, Right Thoughts, Right Speech, Right Actions, Right Livelihood, Right Effort, Right Mindfulness, and Right Concentration. These eight attributes may be divided as follows: the first two represent wisdom, the next three mortality, and the last three concentration.

Eighth Sphere Theosophical term used synonymously with the **Planet of Death** to describe the place where very evil **lost souls** are finally destroyed. It is said by some to be a literal location somewhere in the **cosmos**, and by others to be a symbolic "condition of being". See also **Theosophy**.

Eisai (1141–1215) Japanese monk who introduced **Zen Buddhism** to Japan from mainland China. Eisai also introduced the practice of drinking tea; he considered this beverage to be an excellent contributor to health and long life.

Eisenbud, Dr. Jule (1908–) American psychiatrist who investigated famous psychics **Ted Serios** and **Gerard Croiset**. Dr. Eisenbud's main contribution to **parapsychology** has been in research experiments where subjects are stimulated to produce **psi** phenomena through subliminal perception.

Ekagrata Sanskrit term meaning "one-pointedness", used in reference to **meditation** to describe the act of concentrating the mind on a single thought or image.

Ekisha In Japan, a **fortune-teller** who combines **astrology** and **palmistry**. This is a popular method, and ekishas may be found at streetside stalls practising their divinatory art.

Ek Oankar In Sikh religious practice and belief, the sacred name of the **Supreme Being**. Sikhs believe in a monotheistic **God** whom they describe as "the One Indivisible Being". See also **Monotheism**.

El Hebrew term for **God**. Used as a **god-name** in modern magical ceremonies, specifically in formulating the Pentagram of Water. See also **Hermetic Order of the Golden Dawn**.

El Supreme **deity** among the Phoenicians, and specifically god of rivers and streams. El was the father of the other gods and was usually depicted as a very old man with a flowing beard.

EVOCATION: magicians use magical spells to evoke spirits. This line drawing – 'Of a Neophyte and How the Black Art was Revealed to Him by the Fiend Asomuel' – was produced by Aubrey Beardsley in 1893.

Elder Brother Theosophical term for an occult initiate. Synonymous with **adept**, **master**, **rishi**, or master of wisdom. See also **Theosophy**.

Electional Astrology See **Astrology, Electional**.

Electronic Recording Phenomenon See **Electronic Voice Phenomenon**.

Electronic Voice Phenomenon In 1971 the electronic engineer Konstantin Raudive (1909–1974) published a book titled *Breakthrough*, which claimed that unidentified and possibly **supernatural** voices appear on electronic recording tapes when other material is being recorded. The voices usually require high amplification and often the language patterns are broken and confused. However, Raudive succeeded in isolating many examples of speech that seem to emanate from people who are no longer living on the planet. The voices speak in many different languages, but always in a tongue familiar to those people making the recording. Raudive's experiments have led to speculation that the recorded voices are communications from the **spirit**-world and **discarnate** spirits. Others believe that the tapes are recording impressions from the so-called **Akashic records** or astral memory of the planet.

Elementals Spirit-creatures said by **magicians** to personify the qualities of the four **elements**. These creatures are **salamanders** (**Fire**); **mermaids** and **undines** (**Water**); **sylphs** (**Air**); and **gnomes** and **goblins** (**Earth**).

Elementary In **Theosophy**, the disembodied **soul** of a wicked or depraved person. The **astral bodies** of good people are believed to decompose quickly as their spirits move onto a new evolutionary path, but the elementaries of the less evolved tend to cling to the **earth plane** for a longer time. In this situation they appear as **apparitions** or **ghosts**.

Elementary Spirit See **Elementals**.

Eleusis, Mysteries of Famous religious and mystical ceremonies held at Eleusis, near Athens. The ceremonies, which were founded by Eumpolus, included purifications and fasts, and were sacred to the fertility goddesses **Demeter** and **Persephone**. The mystery revealed to participants concerned **immortality** and spiritual **rebirth**. Until recently, it was assumed that the **rituals** at Eleusis were of a theatrical nature, although the archaeological remains in the initiation temple do not suggest this. According to the ethnomycologist **R. Gordon Wasson**, the mysteries at Eleusis were of a **psychedelic** nature, induced by the **ergot** that grew on the cereal crops in the nearby fields. According to Wasson, participants in the mysteries consumed a drink that contained barley water, mint, and ergot, and were immediately transported into a spirit-world. "What was witnessed there," he notes, "was no play by actors, but *phasmata*, ghostly apparitions, in particular the spirit of Persephone herself." Wasson's belief has been supported by Albert Hofmann, who synthesized **LSD** from **ergot**. The psychedelic explanation also appears to find support in the *Homeric Hymn to Demeter*, which describes how participants felt a "fear and a trembling in the limbs, vertigo, nausea and a cold sweat" before the vision dawned in the darkened chamber.

Eleven In Christianity, eleven disciples remained loyal to Jesus and therefore the number has come to symbolize spiritual strength, idealism, and moral virtue. As the first number after **ten**, it represents "revelations" and visionary insight. However, to the extent that it falls short of **twelve**, a number that denotes completeness, eleven is a transitional number. In the **Kabbalah**, which features ten **emanations** on the **Tree of Life**, the so-called "eleventh sephirah", **Daath** (knowledge), is not normally ranked with the other ten, and represents an intermediary stage bridging the **Abyss** between the three **sephiroth** of the Trinity and the Seven "Days" of creation. To this extent the number eleven has an element of danger about it. It is sometimes associated with martyrdom. See also **Numerology**.

Elf See **Elves**.

Elfin Elf-like. Having similar qualities to **elves**.

Eliade, Mircea (1907–1986) Romanian-born authority on comparative religion and **mysticism** who was professor of the history of religions at the University of Chicago. A remarkably prolific author, Eliade produced a number of scholarly works on a wide range of subjects. *Yoga: Immortality and Freedom*, *Shamanism*, and *A History of Religious Ideas* were among his major books; but he wrote widely on the nature of religious experience, the symbolism of the sacred, and patterns of initiatory experiences.

Elixir of Life In **alchemy**, a drink said to restore youth or grant **immortality**. It was associated with the **Philosopher's Stone**, from which these life-giving properties derived.

Elliott, Reverend Graeme Maurice (1883–1959) English clergyman who investigated **psychic** phenomena and was interested in the relevance of paranormal events in the study of Christianity. Following a meeting with **Sir William Barrett** and **Sir Oliver Lodge**, he lectured widely on **spiritualism** and helped establish the Churches' Fellowship for Psychical Study. Elliott was secretary of this organization from 1954 until his death, and also wrote several books. These include *The Psychic Life of Jesus* (1938), *Spiritualism in the Old Testament* (1940), and *The Bible as Psychic History* (1959).

Elohim One of the sacred names of **God** in Hebrew scriptures and the **Kabbalah**, and used by magicians as a **god-name** in magical ceremonies. It is the plural form of **El**, meaning "God".

Elongation In **spiritualism**, the lengthening of the human body – a phenomenon said to be associated with certain **physical mediums**. Daniel Dunglas Home, a medium otherwise renowned for his claimed art of **levitation**, was reported to elongate by up to one foot during a **seance**. Other mediums whose legs and arms are said to have stretched include **Florence Cook**, her sister Katie, and **Eusapia Palladino**.

Elves Spirit-creatures said to be descended from the children of Eve. They were hidden from the sight of **God** because they were unclean. In German and Scandinavian **mythology**, there were elves of light and elves of darkness. Black elves were comparable to **dwarfs**, but white elves resembled **angels**. In folk-legend, elves are often depicted as small **fairies** who dance around flowers in the garden, leaving elf-rings and elf-mounds as tokens of their presence, and occasionally firing elf-arrows at people to cause them harm.

Elysian Fields In Greek **mythology**, "the fields of the blessed". See **Elysium**.

Elysium In Greek **mythology**, the place where deceased heroes and virtuous people lived in eternal life. Originally, Elysium was located in the West, on the shores of Oceanus. Other classical writers located Elysium in the **Underworld**.

Emanation A **vibration** that issues forth from a single source. In **mysticism**, the world is sometimes considered to be the most physical, dense, or "gross" emanation of the **Godhead**. The mystical cosmologies of the **Kabbalah**, **Gnosticism**, and **Neoplatonism** conceived the Creation process in this way. In the Kabbalah, for example, there are ten emanations, or **sephiroth**, which issue forth from **Air Soph Aur**, the limitless light. These emanations manifest through Four Worlds, which are successively more dense. They are named **Atziluth**, **Briah**, **Yetzirah**, and **Assiah**, respectively.

Emerald Precious stone with magical associations. The emerald is sacred to **Venus** and is also identified with the **zodiac** sign **Taurus**. The alchemical tablet of **Hermes Trismegistus** was said to be fashioned of emerald, and the Egyptian **Eye of Horus** was often of emerald colour.

Emerald Tablet The tablet of emerald (*Tabula Smaragdina*) was allegedly found clasped between the hands of the corpse of **Hermes Trismegistus**, the mythic founder of the Hermetic tradition. The tablet included a text upon which the principles of medieval **alchemy** are based. See also **Hermetica**.

E-meter In **Scientology**, a device used in auditing sessions. The E-meter is based on the so-called "Wheatstone bridge", which measures the resistance of a body to a small electrical charge. The E-meter is a refinement of this device and is said to measure "the impingement of an individual himself (the spirit) upon the body, by the direct action of thought". In essence, it is claimed that the E-meter is a "truth device", and it is used to audit "pre-clears" (those who have not yet attained **enlightenment**). See also **Clear**.

Emotional Body Alternative term for the **astral body** or **desire body**.

Emperor, The In the **Tarot**, the card of the **Major Arcana** that depicts a benign and peaceful ruler seated on his throne and looking out over the mountains of his kingdom. **Occultists** regard *The Emperor* as a form of "the Ancient of Days", a wise and loving ruler who has compassion for the inhabitants of the universe and sustains them. He is the antithesis of the destructive qualities symbolized by ***The Charioteer***. In Western **magic**, which combines the Tarot paths of the Major Arcana with the ten **sephiroth** on the **Tree of Life**, the path of *The Emperor* connects **Tiphareth** and **Chokmah**.

Empress, The In the **Tarot**, the card of the **Major Arcana** that depicts the Great Mother seated on a throne in a field of wheat with the River of Life flowing beside her. **Occultists** regard *The Empress* as a representation of **Hathor**, the Mother of the Universe. She also resembles **Demeter**, goddess of the grain. In Western **magic**, which combines the Tarot paths of the Major Arcana with the ten **sephiroth** on the **Tree of Life**, the path of *The Empress* connects **Binah** and **Chokmah**.

Encausse, Dr. Gérard See **Papus**.

Enchanted One who is bewitched or caught in a magic spell. See also **bewitchment**.

Enchiridion of Pope Leo Non-Christian collection of **charms** and **prayers** said to be effective against poison, fire, wild beasts, and tempests. The charms were first printed in Rome in 1523 and were said to have been favourably regarded by Emperor Charlemagne.

Engram In **Scientology**, a recording in one's memory of events associated with pain. The engram is not accessible to the analytical mind in the form of normal recall or experience, but can be stimulated into consciousness by "mental image pictures".

Enki Sumerian counterpart of the Babylonian god **Ea**.

Enlightenment In mysticism, the achievement of self-realization through awakening the "inner light" of spiritual knowledge. See also **Nibbana; Nirvana; Satori.**

Enlil Sumerian god of the air, wind, and storms. He was worshipped at Nippur, the sacred city of Sumer, and was later regarded as Lord of the Earth. He was adopted by the Babylonians as the deity **Bel**.

Ennead In **numerology** and **mythology**, the number **nine**. In ancient Egypt there were cycles of nine gods, of which the Ennead of Heliopolis is one example.

Enoch, Book of Apocryphal Jewish book that has influenced the kabbalistic tradition and is considered part of the **Merkabah** mystical literature. There are three versions of *The Book of Enoch*. The Ethiopian version was first discovered by the Scottish explorer James Bruce in 1773 and is the text most commonly republished. The second version, titled *The Book of the Secrets of Enoch*, is a Slavonic text and was found in the Belgrade public library by Professor Sokolov in 1886; an English translation was issued in 1896. The Hebrew *Enoch*, identified as *Enoch III*, was translated by Hugo Odeberg in 1928. Some versions of *Enoch III* include lists of the **magical names** and **magical formulae** ascribed to the important archangel **Metratron**, who is regarded by contemporary **occultists** as the ruler of **Kether**, the first **sephirah** on the kabbalistic **Tree of Life**. See also **Kabbalah**.

Enochian Magic See **Magic, Enochian**.

Ensalmo In Peru, a **spell, enchantment**, or **charm** believed to have been brought to that country by the Spanish conquerors.

Entered Apprentice In **Freemasonry**, a person who has been given the first degree of **initiation**.

Enthusiasm Psychic state of being possessed by **God**. Mystical inspiration of this sort is often accompanied by prophetic pronouncements and revelations.

Entity A **discarnate** or disembodied **spirit**, or "presence". See also **Apparition; Ghost**.

Enuma Elish Babylonian Creation saga recorded in a cuneiform text in the seventh century B.C. It describes how Apsu, the sea god, and his wife **Tiamat** gave birth to the worlds and the other gods. Apsu was seized by **Ea**, and Tiamat sent a horde of monsters to reclaim him. Ea then summoned **Marduk**, god of the grain, to fight Tiamut, and he finally killed her in a bloody battle. Tiamut's body was severed into two halves, creating the heavens and the earth. Marduk became ruler of the gods after this victory.

Ephemeris Reference work, used by astrologers, which lists the positions of the **sun** and **planets** on each day of the year, including details of longitude, latitude, and declination. It is used in constructing a **horoscope**. See also **Astrology**.

Epopt "One who is instructed in a secret system of mystical knowledge." Epopt is the Fourth Degree in the magical system recognized by the magical **Fellowship of Kouretes** in California.

Epstein, Perle Born in New York, Perle Epstein is a leading contemporary writer on the **Kabbalah**. A descendant of the eighteenth-century kabbalist **Ba'al Shem Tov**, she is the author of several works on mysticism, including *Kabbalah: The Way of the Jewish Mystic, Oriental Mystics and Magicians*, and *The Way of Witches*.

Epworth Poltergeist Classic case of **poltergeist** activity, which began in December 1716 at the Parsonage in Epworth, Lincolnshire. Loud rappings and noises were heard by all members of the Wesley family over a period of two months. Sometimes the noises were quite specific in character. Mrs. Wesley notes in her account that as she and her husband descended the stairs one day there was a loud noise similar to someone emptying a large bag of coins at their feet. This was then followed by the sound of glass bottles being "dashed into a thousand pieces". On other occasions running footsteps and groans were heard and a doorlatch lifted several times. The Epworth poltergeist case is regarded as one of the best-documented in the annals of British psychical research, but no satisfactory explanation has been forthcoming.

Equilibrium A state of rest produced when equal and opposite forces are counter-balanced. The term is also used to describe inner balance and harmony. Compare with **Individuation.**

Equinox The time at which the sun crosses the equator. This takes place on March 21 and September 22 each year, and on these days the length of day and of night are equal.

Equinox, The Series of occult books compiled by **Aleister Crowley**, which he decided to publish twice a year, coinciding with the vernal and autumnal **equinoxes**. Ten issues appeared between 1909 and 1913. The so-called *Blue Equinox* was published in Detroit in 1919. Several of Crowley's most important writings, such as *The Vision and the Voice*, first appeared in *The Equinox*.

Ereshkigal Sumerian Queen of the **Underworld**, sometimes linked to **Hecate**. She had a bizarre appearance, with a sharp horn extending from her forehead, the ears of a sheep, the body of a fish, and scales like a serpent.

Ergot Parasitic fungus, *Claviceps purpurea*, which attacks barley, wheat, and rye. **R. Gordon Wasson** has suggested that the visionary experiences of neophytes in the **Mysteries of Eleusis** may have been caused by the presence of ergot in the sacred barley-water drink; and Linda Caporael has similarly proposed that ergot poisoning at Salem village may have caused convulsions and **hallucinations** wrongly associated with "witchcraft". **LSD**, one of the most powerful **psychedelics** known, was first synthesized from ergot by Dr. Alfred Hofmann in 1943. See also **Flying Ointments; Salem Witches.**

Erinyes The so-called Three Furies of Greek **mythology**. Tisiphone, Alecto, and Megaera were fearsome to behold and looked like old hags with snakes for hair, bat's wings, and bloodshot eyes. They killed their victims with scourges. The role of the Erinyes was to avenge wrongdoings and breaches of social custom. Each of the Three Furies had a different function. Alecto maintained Justice, Megaera punished jealousy, and Tisiphone avenged evil. They were also known by the placatory term Eumenides, or "Kindly Ones".

Eros The Greek god of love, equivalent of the Roman **Cupid**. The birth of Eros is obscure. Some say he was the son of **Aphrodite** and **Zeus**, others maintained that Ares or **Hermes** was his father. However, it is probable that he actually predated Aphrodite as the personification of universal passion – the force that brought the cosmic gods together in order to create the universe in the first place.

Esalen Institute Famous "growth" institute founded by Michael Murphy and Dick Price, located on a cliff edge at Big Sur, California. Esalen Institute offers workshops that specialize in different consciousness-expanding modalities, including t'ai chi, **meditation**, gestalt therapy, and **shamanism.** Esalen Institute is closely associated with the international **transpersonal psychology** movement, a philosophical school that emerged from humanistic psychology and which is dedicated to studying visionary and **peak experiences**, **mysticism**, and **altered state of consciousness**.

Esbats In **Wicca**, the so-called "lesser" celebrations (by way of comparison with the four **Greater Sabbaths**). There are thirteen months in the lunar calendar, and therefore there are usually thirteen esbats each year. Wiccans believe that esbats are marked by a sense of heightened psychic awareness resulting from the **lunar** energy of full moon, and many Wiccans like to perform their specific magical workings at this time. Esbats are a time for **invocations**, love magic, and healing ceremonies but they are also a time for dancing, drinking and feasting – the word "esbat" itself is thought to derive from the Old French word *s'esbattre*, meaning "to frolic and amuse oneself". Traditionally, the esbat lasts from midnight till cock-crow.

Each of the esbats has its own name and this is linked symbolically to the time of the year in which it occurs. The first occurs in October just before the festival of **Samhain** (All Hallows' Eve, or Halloween) and is called *Blood Moon*. It is traditionally associated with the slaughter of animals for food prior to the onset of winter and is therefore represented by the colour red. *Snow Moon* rises in November and is associated with the first falls of snow. *Oak Moon* is the full moon in December. It is linked to the colour black and also to the **oak** – sacred symbol of the Dark Lord aspect of **Cernunnos** – since it is his wood which is burnt at Yule. *Ice Moon*, represented by the colour purple, comes in January, followed by *Storm Moon* in February – a time when the ice and sleet may turn to rain. This full moon is linked to the element **Water**, and to the colour blue. March brings the *Chaste Moon*, the return of spring from the depths of winter, and is represented by the colour white. In April, *Seed Moon* is a time when the seeds in the earth bring forth new life, and this esbat is represented by the colour green. *Hare Moon* rises in May and is dedicated both to the **Goddess** and to fertility. Its colour is pink, symbolic of love. June brings the *Dyad Moon* and, as American neopagan author Gwydion O'Hare has noted, this name alludes to "the visible presence of the God and Goddess reflected in the bright sun and green fields". The associated colour is orange, "the colour of the summer sun". The *Mead Moon* comes in July and is a time for dancing and revelry. Traditionally this is the time when honey mead was made for the ensuing harvest celebrations and accordingly its symbolic colour is yellow. August brings the *Wort Moon* – a reference to the dark green abundance of harvest time – and September is the month of the *Barley Moon*. This is the season when grain is harvested: brown is the symbolic colour for this esbat. Finally, *Wine Moon* is the esbat which arises as a consequence of the difference between the solar and lunar calendars. Unlike the twelve-month cycle of the solar calendar there are usually thirteen full moons in any given year, and this esbat is the thirteenth. It honours the sacrament of wine and its colour is burgundy red. *Wine Moon* precedes *Blood Moon*, and so the lunar cycle continues. As mentioned earlier, esbats are sometimes referred to as "lesser" Wiccan celebrations. As **Doreen Valiente** has noted, "the esbat is a smaller and less solemn occasion than the sabbat". The major sabbats, on the other hand, are celebrations which link contemporary Wicca directly with festivals honoured by the **Celts** and **Druids**. See also **Witches' Sabbath**.

Eschatology Doctrines relating to "the last things": **death**, **heaven**, **hell**, purgatory, and the final judgment.

Esdaile, James (1808–1859) Scottish surgeon who, through 1847, conducted experimental tests in a Calcutta hospital where patients were anaesthetized using hypnotic techniques. A government report commented that Esdaile and his Indian staff had successfully induced in the patients complete insensibility to pain, even in cases requiring complex operations. With **James Braid**, Esdaile was one of the pioneers of **hypnosis**. He wrote several books, including *Mesmeric Facts* (1845) and *Natural and Mesmeric Clairvoyance* (1852).

Esoteric Term applied to teachings that are secret, and only for initiates of a group; mysterious, occult, "hidden".

ESP See **Extrasensory Perception**.

Essence The distinctive or intrinsic qualities of a person or thing. From an occult viewpoint, one's essence is not the **ego**, but the **self**; and for many **mystics** this essence, in reality, is part of **God**.

Essene Pre-Christian group of Jewish **ascetics** who lived a monastic life, held goods in common, and were associated with the settlement at **Qumran**, the site of the **Dead Sea Scrolls**. They rejected the rituals of the Temple, were predominantly pacifist, and believed in the **immortality** of the **soul**.

Eternal Something that lasts forever or that is true beyond all time. **Mystics** and **occultists** sometimes refer to "eternal truth", "eternal joy", and "eternal beauty".

Eternity From the Latin *aeternitas*, an immeasurable length of time; time without beginning or end.

Ether According to occult belief, the fluidic substance that fills all space, pervades all matter, and is active in all processes of life.

Etheric Body In **occultism**, the matrix that holds the physical body together and which, at **death**, separates completely. The etheric body is affected by the nature of the **astral body** and the **mental body**, and ensures that the physical body is a reflection of the type of being inhabiting that form. In occult belief, therefore, the physical form is a reflection of more "subtle" internal bodies, and the etheric body is midway between the physical and astral forms.

Etheric Projection After projecting the **astral body** in an act of willed **dissociation**, the **occultist** may wish to draw forth the etheric body. According to occult belief this is a white, cloud-like replica of the physical body and resembles a **ghost** or **apparition**. When the etheric body is projected, the physical body lapses into a state of deep trance, resembling death. At this stage the occultist is breathing, and maintaining life, through his or her projected astral body. See also **Astral Projection**.

Etteilla Follower of **Court de Géblin**, whose real name was Alliette. In true esoteric tradition, he felt that his name had more mystique if reversed. Etteilla maintained that the **Tarot** had been conceived by seventeen **magi** and written down one hundred and seventy-one years after the Great Flood. Despite these unlikely claims, which were popular in France at the time, Etteilla produced one of the most beautiful Tarot packs – which he called "The Grand Etteilla". These cards have since been published in facsimile form.

Eva C (c. 1890–1943) French materialization **medium**, also known as Marthe Béraud. She claimed to materialize the spirit of "Bien Boa" at the home of General Noel in Algiers. Eva C and General Noel's Arab coachman – who posed as the ghost – both subsequently admitted to deception, but several psychical researchers were convinced of the medium's authenticity.

Evans-Wentz, W. Y. (1878–1965) American scholar whose first fieldwork was in the areas of Britain and Europe associated with Celtic folk-legends. Evans-Wentz discussed the legends of the **fairies** with peasants and rural dwellers who still clung to the old beliefs, and he brought these accounts together in his first book, *The Fairy-Faith in Celtic Countries* (1911). In this book Evans-Wentz noted that fairies and similar supernatural beings are perceived in an **altered state of consciousness.** His book thus broke new ground in presenting a psychological framework for mystical and religious beliefs and also took full account of the research into psychic phenomena being undertaken by **Sir William Crookes** and **Sir Oliver Lodge** at that time. Evans-Wentz later travelled to India and explored the Kashmir. He subsequently received training in **yoga** and became the **chela** of Lama Kazi Dawa-Samdruop in Sikkim. As a result of his contact with this Lama, Evans-Wentz was able to edit and translate several important works of Tibetan **mysticism**, including *The Bardo Thodol* (better known as the ***Tibetan Book of the Dead***), *Tibetan Yoga and Secret Doctrines*, and *The Tibetan Book of the Great Liberation.* Evans-Wentz also produced a book on **Milarepa.** See also **Bardo.**

Eve According to Genesis, the first woman, formed by **God** from one of Adam's ribs. The Hebrew name for Eve, *Hawwah*, means "the mother of all living things". To this extent Eve is one of the great female mythic **archetypes.**

Evil That which is debased, wicked, and opposed to the principles of spirituality and goodness. Associated with darkness and personified in the form of **devils, demons,** monsters, and other images of depravity, bestiality, and vice. See also **Satan.**

Evil-eye The occult belief that certain people can inflict harm or cause **bewitchment** by glancing at their victims. This **superstition** was noted by many classical writers, including Herodotus, Horace, Ovid, Virgil, Plutarch, and **Pliny**, although the definition of which eyes are "evil" varies from place to place. People with a squint are often accused of possessing the evil-eye, as are dwarfs and hunchbacks. Certain popes – including Pius IX and Leo XIII – were both accused of it, as were King Louis XIV of France and Emperor Wilhelm II of Germany. In Mediterranean countries it has been more common to accuse people with blue eyes, while in northern Europe dark-eyed people are more suspect. The various protections against the evil-eye include bright ornaments designed to divert attention and **charms** said to counteract the evil influence. The symbol of Mercury's **caduceus**, church bells, horseshoes, crescent symbols, silver rings, and knotted cords are also said to be powerful antidotes to the effects of the evil-eye.

Evocation In **ceremonial magic**, the calling forth of a **spirit** using **spells** or **words of power.** In modern magical **rituals**, a triangle is used to contain the power of the spirit. The magician places a **talisman** in the centre of the triangle before summoning the spirit in ritual and then stands outside the area of evocation. Without these symbolic restraints, occultists believe they can lose control over the manifestations and become possessed. See also **Possession.**

Evola, Julius (1898–1974) Highly regarded Italian metaphysician who, together with other leading esotericists like Arturo Reghini, Giulio Parese and Pietro Negri, founded the mysterious UR Group in Rome in 1927. The purpose of this magical group was to bring their individual identities into such a state of superhuman power and awareness that they would be able to exert a magical influence on the world. To do this they employed techniques derived from ancient **Tantric** and **Buddhist** rituals as well as rare **Hermetic** texts. Evola's works published in English include *The Yoga of Power, The Hermetic Tradition, Eros and the Mysteries of Love* and *The Mystery of the Grail.* An anthology of major writings by Evola and other members of the UR Group, *Introduction to Magic*, was published in the United States in 2001.

Evolution, spiritual In **mysticism** and **occultism**, the spiritual development and growth of the **self** through different forms. In some systems evolution may be through plant, animal, human, and superhuman forms; others emphasize uniqueness. Many mystical groups believe in spiritual evolution through a number of different lifetimes. See also **Reincarnation**.

Excalibur In the Arthurian legends, the magical sword of King Arthur. It was the sword drawn forth from the anvil in the castle of King Pendragon, which identified Arthur as heir to the throne, and in other accounts was the sword kept by the Lady of the Lake. Also known as **Caliburnus**, it is possibly linked to the magical sword Calabolg, which belonged to the Irish folk-hero Fergus.

Excommunication Penalty inflicted by the Christian Church in which a believer is cast forth from the Christian community following a charge of **heresy**. The sinner is prevented from taking the sacraments of communion and, in the Church's view, is cut off from God.

Exegesis The interpretation and elucidation of sacred texts and holy scriptures, including the identification of sections of the texts which are prophetic or allegorical. The term also applies to the literary commentary on those texts.

Exorcism Ceremony at which **evil** or satanic forces are banished – either from a location or from within a possessed person. Many cases are cited in the New Testament where Jesus cast forth devils from afflicted people and urged his disciples to do likewise in his name.

Modern Christian exorcism follows the same principle. The priest recites the Lord's Prayer, makes the sign of the cross with holy water upon the forehead of the possessed person, places his hands upon him, and orders the evil spirit to depart in Christ's name.

Occultists also have their own type of exorcism, although it is more intended as a protective psychic barrier against harmful influences sent by a rival occult group. Different forms of **banishing rituals** are believed to ward off evil or demonic influences and are used in **white magic** to ensure that all rituals performed within the **magic circle** are of an untainted nature. See also **Possession; Psychic Attack**.

Exoteric The opposite of **esoteric**. Teachings which are not reserved for initiates or occult groups, but which are available to the public at large.

Exteriorization Occult term used to describe **astral projection** and the **out-of-the-body experience**.

Externalization The act of making internal mental or spiritual events visible in the external world. In spiritualist **seances** this is said to occur when images from the **astral plane** manifest in **ectoplasm**. In ritual **magic**, normally invisible spirits are summoned to manifest in the smoke of burning incense. See also **Evocation**.

Extra In **spiritualism**, a **supernatural** image that appears on a normal photograph and which is often said to constitute proof of the spirit-world. Usually, this image is the face of a deceased person whose spirit is said to be present at a **seance**; at other times it may be the image of a **ghost** at the site of a **haunting**. See also **Psychic Photography**.

Extrasensory Beyond the normal range of the senses.

Extrasensory Perception (ESP) General term used to describe phenomena that cannot be perceived through the normal senses. These events and data are often referred to collectively as **psi** phenomena. ESP includes **mental telepathy**, **clairvoyance**, **automatism**, **clairaudience**, **psychometry**, **precognition**, and certain forms of **divination**. It may also involve using supernormal faculties inaccessible to most people, such as the ability to project the **astral body**; the ability to enter states of **dissociation**, mediumism, or **trance**; or the use of what British occult author Colin Wilson terms **Faculty X**.

Extratemporal Perception (ETP) Virtually synonymous with **extrasensory perception**, except that ETP provides for the possibility of the paranormal transcendence of time. A person with ETP can travel in an **altered state of consciousness** to both the past and the future.

Extraterrestrial A being from another planet or dimension. The term is commonly used in accounts of **unidentified flying objects** where the inhabitants of **flying saucers** and "mother ships" are said to have come to earth from elsewhere in space. This trend was started by amateur astronomer George Adamski who, in the mid-1950s, described how he had made contact with Venusian space-beings. His book, *Inside the Space-Ships*, included photographs of extraterrestrial spacecraft that closely resembled lampshades and hubcaps, and are not taken seriously by most ufologists.

Exu **Macumba** god of **magic** and chief intermediary between human beings and the gods.

Eye-biting Inflicting harm by using the **evil-eye**.

Eyeless Vision The psychic ability to see without the eyes, often by perception through the skin. Psychical researchers believe that different colours may radiate different temperatures, allowing highly sensitive persons to perceive these differences through their fingertips as colour variables. The case of Frederick Marion was investigated by **Harry Price** and **Professor R. H. Thouless**, among others, and tests have also been carried out by Dr. Abram Novomeisky of the Nizhniy Tagil Pedagogical Institute in Russia. Perception through the skin is sometimes known as paroptic vision or dermoptical perception.

Eye of Horus Popular ancient Egyptian **amulet**, which could face right or left, depicting the eyes of the god **Horus**. According to the Egyptologist **Wallis Budge**, it represented both the **sun** and **moon**. The amulets were usually made of gold, silver, granite, lapis lazuli, or porcelain.

F

Fachan Evil Irish spirit who, like the **Cyclops**, had one eye in the centre of its forehead. A hand protruded from its chest and a leg from its haunch. Its body was covered with ruffled feathers. The fachan would leap out at unwary travellers and kill them.

Facsimile Writing In **spiritualism**, the ability of certain **mediums** to replicate the writing styles and signatures of deceased people.

Faculty According to **Plato**, there is a division of the **soul** into three faculties: the appetitive, the spirited, and the rational. When these faculties are in harmony, the individual experiences inner peace. When they are not, the result is disorder and conflict. The term also has a general application in the study of mind and consciousness and refers to specific talents and abilities. In **parapsychology**, for example, psychics are credited with possessing a "faculty" for **psi phenomena**.

Faculty X Term used by British occult author **Colin Wilson** to describe the paranormal potential of the human mind. Wilson defines it in his book *The Occult* as "that latent power that human beings possess to reach beyond the present" and believes it "is the key to all poetic and mystical experience". Wilson does not believe that Faculty X is an occult faculty. He thinks of it rather as "the power to grasp reality ... it unites the two halves of man's mind, conscious and unconscious". Wilson first conceived of Faculty X in 1966 and based the novel *The Philosopher's Stone* on the issues associated with it. He believes that all human beings require Faculty X for the next stage of evolution.

Fafnir In Scandinavian **mythology**, the son of Hreidmar who changed himself into a **dragon** and slew his father in order to gain the treasure **Loki** had stolen from the dwarf **Andvari**. Fafnir was later killed by Sigurd, who roasted his heart.

Fagail In Celtic **folklore**, the "parting gift" of the **fairies**. It could be lucky or unlucky, depending on the circumstances.

Fairies Spirit creatures with magical powers who could bring good luck or evil to mankind through their **spells** and **enchantments**. In Ireland, the fairy-folk were traditionally known as the Sidhe – pronounced "shee" – or **Tuatha de Danaan**, and inhabited the hills and slopes. They were aristocratic, and lived in a beautiful, eternal land called the Land of the Ever Young. They also had monarchs. For example, in County Galway, Fin Bheara and Nuala were king and queen of the Connacht fairies. In Wales, the king and queen of the fairies – known there as the Tylwyth Teg – were Gwydion ab Don and Gwendhidw, while Shakespeare records the fairy-rulers in *A Midsummer Night's Dream* as Oberon and Titania. Wherever they were found, the fairies had their own domain, or "fairy-land", and lived in small groups beneath trees or under the fairy knolls. Some fairies have been regarded as spirits of the streams, rivers, lakes, and woods, and to this degree resemble **elementals** and **devas**. See also **Dryads**.

Fairyland The domain of the **fairies**.

Fairy ring Circle of grass whose colour or texture differentiates it from grass elsewhere in the field. **Fairies** held their nocturnal dances on these locations, especially on **All Hallows' Eve** and May Eve.

Faith Belief or trust in a spiritual or occult teaching.

Faith Healing Ancient healing tradition in which an appeal is made to a spiritual source – usually a **god** or **spirit** – to participate in healing the sick. Sometimes the god is believed to manifest as a divine presence; on other occasions the healing "energy" is transmitted through a **medium** to the patient and the cure effected. The technique of **laying-on-of-hands** is a common form of faith healing.

Christianity has a strong healing tradition and has its very foundations in Jesus Christ's spiritual powers. During his lifetime around forty healing miracles were recorded. In the Middles Ages, the Church encouraged recognition of the shrines of **saints** and claimed that their relics could also transmit a healing power. Several denominations of the Christian Church today hold regular healing services where the sick can receive laying-on-of-hands, anointing with oil, and prayer.

Faith healing is not confined to the Christian tradition. The ancient Egyptians believed that the body could be divided into thirty-six parts, each associated with a god who could be invoked to cure a specific disease. The Babylonian priests of **Ea** would sprinkle water from a sacred stream over the body of a person suffering from illness, and in ancient Greece, according to Suidas, **Asklepios** healed the writer Theopompos with laying-on-of-hands.

Fakir Indian **mystic** or holy man skilled in performing allegedly miraculous or paranormal acts. These include sitting on beds of nails without feeling pain, enduring self-mutilation, charming snakes, or performing the legendary Indian rope-trick. The term is also used to describe Islamic **dervishes** and beggars seeking alms, and comes from the Arabic word *faqir*, meaning "a poor person".

Falin Scottish **demon** said to haunt the highest crags of the mountains near Glen Aven. His head was twice the size of his body and he only appeared before daybreak. To cross his path before the sun had risen on it led to certain death.

Fall In the Old Testament, the fall from grace of Adam and Eve, who were separated from **God** and expelled from the **Garden of Eden** after disobeying his command and eating the fruit of the Tree of Knowledge of Good and Evil. In kabbalistic magical **cosmology**, the Fall is symbolized by the **Abyss** on the **Tree of Life** and is traversed during the visionary experience of the sephirah **Daath** (knowledge).

Fallen Angel An **Angel** cast forth from **heaven** for disobeying the commands of **God**. Fallen angels are associated with the powers of darkness and become known as **demons**. **Lucifer**, the "light-bearer", is the classic example.

Familiar In medieval **witchcraft**, a **spirit** or **demon**, usually in the form of an animal, that accompanied the witch or warlock and provided magical powers. Sometimes a drop of blood from the witch was included in the animal's food, allegedly forming a psychic bond between the witch and the familiar. According to a seventeenth-century account, dogs, cats, foals, chickens, hares, rats, and toads were common familiars. Witches sometimes consulted their familiars when making predictions or seeking omens.

Fana In **Sufism**, a term meaning "becoming absorbed in God". This may involve three stages: the act of seeking forgiveness from **God**; the request for blessings from the prophet **Mohammed**; and finally, the act of merging with the Divine Oneness. The Islamic mystic **Abu Hamid Ghazali** wrote: "When the worshipper no longer thinks of his worship or himself but is altogether absorbed in Him whom he worships, that state is called fana."

Fang-Shih Taoist term for **magicians** who were skilled in producing magical spells and summoning spirits. In ancient China, such magic predated **Taoism** itself. The best-known Fang-Shih magician was Li Shao-chun (second century B.C.), who evoked the "demon" of a cooking stove in order to conjure up the spirit of a dead woman for the emperor.

Fang-Shu The Taoist term for **magic**, **occultism**, and **divination**. See also **Taoism**.

Far-memory Expression used by English novelist **Joan Grant** to describe the psychic recall of earlier incarnations. The writer incorporated her very detailed impressions of past lives into her books. Joan Grant was married to psychiatrist Dennis Kelsey, and together they developed a technique for diagnosing symptoms of mental illness caused by traumas they believed originated in earlier incarnations. These methods are described in their jointly authored book *Many Lifetimes* (1968). See also **Past-life Regression**; **Reincarnation**.

Farr, Florence (1860–1917) Actress and one-time mistress of George Bernard Shaw, Florence Farr was introduced to modern **ceremonial magic** by **W. B. Yeats** and joined the Isis-Urania Temple of the **Hermetic Order of the Golden Dawn**. Tiring of **MacGregor Mathers**'s autocratic tendencies, she left the Golden Dawn to form her own group, the Sphere. In 1896 she published a work titled *Egyptian Magic* (republished in 1982), which included extracts from the **Gnostic** Bruce Codex. In this text Jesus Christ is portrayed as an initiator as well as a teacher, and provides his disciples with an understanding of the **archons** and **aeons**. Sacred names of power are also included in the text.

Farrar, Stewart (1916–2000) and **Janet** (1950–) Among the most influential practitioners of contemporary witchcraft in the 1980s and '90s, the Farrars had already assumed a leadership role in London's neopagan community a decade earlier. Janet Farrar (née Owen) was born in 1950 and was raised in East London in a strictly Christian family: her grandfather was a church councillor in their Anglican parish. However she began to drift away from Christianity during her adolescent years and later became briefly involved in **Transcendental Meditation**. She worked for a while as a model and then became a secretary in the Beatles' London office. Around this time Janet visited Alex and Maxine Sanders' coven in Notting Hill Gate. She was impressed by **Wicca** as a spiritual path and decided to join the circle. It was here that she met her husband Stewart Farrar. Stewart had been raised as a Christian Scientist but later became an agnostic – a position he maintained until becoming a devotee of **witchcraft**. He studied journalism at University College, London, during the 1930s, served as an anti-aircraft gunnery instructor during the Second World War, and later worked for several years as an editor for Reuters. He also produced several radio drama scripts for the BBC before becoming a feature writer for the weekly magazine *Reveille* in 1969. It was in his capacity as a journalist that Stewart Farrar had been invited to the Sanders' coven – he had come simply to write an account of a Wiccan initiation. He did not realize at the time that he himself would become a dedicated convert to neopaganism.

Despite the substantial difference in their ages – thirty-four years – Janet Owen and Stewart Farrar were drawn together as magical partners and in December 1970 , a few months after taking their initiations, they left Sanders' group to form a coven of their own. They married five years later in a traditional Wiccan handfasting ceremony and in 1976 moved to Ireland, where Stewart was able to gain tax-relief as an author of science fiction novels, his other major interest. For a time the Farrars ran a coven in a secluded farmhouse near Drogheda, north of Dublin, before returning to Britain in 1988.

Like **Gerald Gardner** and Alex Sanders before them, the Farrars always emphasized that they were supporting an authentic Celtic tradition. They co-authored several major works on neopaganism, including *Eight Sabbats for Witches*, *The Witches' Way*, *The Witches' Goddess* and *The Witches' God* – all of which were published both in Britain and the United States – and through their writings and advocacy strongly influenced neopagan thought and practice on both sides of the Atlantic. Following Stewart Farrar's death in 2000, Janet Farrar has continued to promote neopaganism internationally together with her new partner Gavin Bone. See also **Sanders, Alex.**

Fascination The act of using the **evil-eye** to cause harm, or to induce a state of **trance** in victims so that one can cause illness or impotence to befall them. See also **Witch Ball.**

Fasting Practice in which the normal intake of food is greatly reduced and the practitioner subsists for a period of time on water or fruit juice, or nothing at all. Fasting may produce an **altered state of consciousness** resembling a **psychedelic** state, and throughout history many visionaries have fasted in order to obtain mystical revelations. Jesus Christ fasted for forty days in the desert, and many Christians fast during Lent – the forty-day period leading up to Easter. All devout Jews fast on Yom Kippur, the Day of Atonement; and Moslems fast during Ramadan, a one-month period in which they abstain from food or sex between the hours of dawn and dusk.

Fat, Sorcerers' In the Middle Ages, **sorcerers** and black magicians were accused of using human fat in their **spells** and **rituals,** a reference to the popular superstition that **black magic** involved human sacrifice.

Fatalism The belief that all occurrences and events in one's life are predetermined by a **supernatural** power – for example, **God**, one's **horoscope**, the numerological symbolism of one's name, and so on … and that one's free will is powerless to effect any changes to this destiny. See also **Fate.**

Fatal Look Belief that one's gaze can inflict death. A variant on the **evil-eye.**

Fate One's destiny, or preordained future. Those who trust in fate believe that the pattern of their lives is fixed at birth and cannot be altered. See also **Fatalism; Fates, Three.**

Fates, Three Known in ancient Greece as the Moerae, and in ancient Rome as the Parcae, the three Fates were the daughters of **Zeus** and Themis, and determined the destiny of all mortal beings. Clotho presided at birth and spun the thread of life; Lachesis was responsible for allocating the length of one's life; and Atropos cut the thread of life with her shears.

Father, God the In many cosmologies, the father of the **gods** is not the creator of the universe, but its overseer or ruler. The fate of humankind rests with him. Such deities include **Zeus** (Greek); **Jupiter** (Roman); **Ra** (Egyptian); **Odin** (Scandinavian); and **Yahweh/Jehovah** (Hebrew). In the **Tarot**, the symbolism of the father-god is personified in two trumps, ***The Emperor*** (passive/merciful) and ***The Charioteer*** (active/destructive). See also **Demiurge.**

Fauns Creatures who had bodies that were half-goat, half-human and who attended **Pan,** the Greek god of Nature. They were younger than **satyrs,** but somewhat similar.

Faust Legendary figure who is said to have made a pact with the demon **Mephistopheles** in return for worldly goods and magical powers. Faust seems to be a composite persona, based in part on historical figures. **Johannes Wierius** believed that Faust was a drunken **occultist** who lived in Cracow and Germany and was regarded as a deceitful trickster, but there are other figures on whom the accounts may be based. Dr. George Faust was a necromancer and astrologer who worked as a schoolmaster in Kreuznach in 1507. He may be the same as the Dr. George Faust of Heidelberg who, in 1528, was banished from the town of Ingolstadt for soothsaying. A Johann Faust, meanwhile, obtained a theology degree from Heidelberg University in 1509. The occult authority E. M. Butler inclines to the view that the two Fausts may have been brothers or twins. Whichever is the case, it seems that they helped give rise to the legend of Faust's pact with the Devil.

Fay Possibly derived from the Latin word *fata*, meaning "one's individual fate". The English expression "fay" means "enchanted" or "bewitched".

Feather In ancient Egyptian religion, the personification of truth, represented by the goddess **Maat**. In the **Judgment Hall**, presided over by **Osiris**, the heart of the deceased was weighed against a feather and his or her fate decided accordingly.

Feilding, Francis Henry Everard (1867–1936) English barrister who joined the **Society for Psychical Research** in London and became its secretary from 1903 to 1920. He investigated the materialization medium **Florence Cook** and also the Italian medium **Eusapia Palladino**, whom he was convinced was genuine.

Fellow of the Craft In **Freemasonry**, one who has attained the second degree of **initiation.**

Fellowship of Kouretes Magical order in Tujunga, California, which combines ancient Greek **mythology**, **modern witchcraft**, and magical **rituals**. It recognizes six degrees: Hieros, which includes instruction in the Greek alphabet and trance magic techniques; Daduchos, which involves "inner plane" **astral projection** and communication with **god-forms**; Mystes, which features astral projection, divination, and **sexual magic**; Epopt, which teaches communication with the **holy guardian angel**; Hierodule, which includes initiation as a **priest** or **priestess**; and Harcharios, an honorary degree in which the priest or priestess is reminded that there are still many **esoteric** secrets to learn.

Feminine Planets In **astrology**, the **moon** (associated with **lunar goddesses** of fertility); **Venus** (associated with goddesses of love and beauty); and **Neptune** (associated, like the moon, with the element **Water**).

Feminine Polarity See **Feminine Principle.**

Feminine Principle In mystical cosmologies there is often a specific relationship between masculine and feminine forces. The feminine principle is usually regarded as receptive (symbolizing the womb from which the universe is born); lunar (reflecting light rather than providing it); and intuitive rather than intellectual. In patriarchal cosmologies it is often also regarded as negative. See also **Binah; Chokmah; Lunar Goddesses; Male Principle; Yin.**

Feminine Signs In **astrology**, the even-numbered signs of the **zodiac**: **Taurus, Cancer, Virgo, Scorpio, Capricorn,** and **Pisces.**

Feng-Hwang Mystical Chinese bird, sometimes said to be the "Chinese **Phoenix**". Symbolic of fire, it was regarded as a personification of virtue and was considered an omen favourable to the emperor. It first appeared during the reign of Ch'eng Wang and disappeared after the death of Hung Wu.

Fenris Wolf Also Fenrir. In Scandinavian **mythology**, the monstrous and ferocious wolf that was the offspring of **Loki** and Angerboda. Always hostile to the gods, it was set free during the awful holocaust of **Ragnarok** and swallowed both **Odin** and the sun. It in turn was slain by Odin's son **Vidar**, who survived Ragnarok and heralded the **New Age**.

Fertility Deities Gods and goddesses who symbolize the cycles of fertility in Nature. Because of the cyclic passage of the seasons, they are often associated with myths of **rebirth**. In ancient Greece, among the most famous fertility goddesses were **Demeter** and **Persephone**, in whose honour the rites of **Eleusis** were celebrated. The goddesses **Aphrodite** and **Venus** and the gods **Hermes**, **Dionysus**, and **Osiris** were all deities associated with fertility; other examples can be found in most of the world's cosmologies.

Fetch In Irish **folklore**, the **apparition** or **double** of a living person, which was said to appear as an **omen** of that person's imminent death, especially if seen in the evening. The fetch usually had a ghostly appearance.

Fetish Symbolic object or **talisman** regarded by an individual as having the magical power to ward off **evil**. Some fetish objects are believed to house protective spirits. Fetish objects are common in primitive western African religion.

Fetishism Especially in pre-literate African religion, the belief in, and worship of, guardian spirits that reside in **fetishes**.

Ficino, Marsilio (1433–1499) Florentine philosopher and **mystic** who translated the works of **Plato**, **Plotinus**, and Proclus and also the tracts ascribed to the legendary **Hermes Trismegistus**. He believed that the universe was an emanation of God, and that one could attract celestial influences by meditating on the symbols of the planets. His works include *Theologica Platonica de Immortalitate Animarum* and *Libri de Vita*.

Fields of Mourning In Greek **mythology**, that section of the **Underworld** inhabited by the spirits of lovers who had committed suicide. Phaedra, Dido, and Laodamia, among others, resided there.

Fifth Root Race According to **Theosophy**, the human species as it stands in its current phase of evolution. Theosophists believe that we are midway through the fifth root race at present, and that two **root races** – the sixth and seventh – will follow, making human spiritual evolution complete.

Figu In the **Macumba** spiritist religion, an **amulet** worn to ward off **evil**. It took the form of an ornamental fist with the thumb inserted between the middle and index fingers.

Figure In **astrology**, the map of the heavens more popularly known as the **horoscope**.

Findhorn Spiritual community located in north-east Scotland. The Findhorn foundation was founded in 1962 by Peter and Eileen Caddy on the site of a derelict caravan park. At the time the land was overgrown with gorse and nettles, and the soil was very poor. However, the Caddys developed the land and began to grow crops there. Eileen Caddy maintains that she was guided by a spirit-entity known as "Elixir" – God's voice – who spoke to her and provided details of how the community should develop. Findhorn now has a large vegetable garden, which supports a community of around two hundred, and is based very much on the principle of co-operating with Nature. Some members of the Findhorn Foundation believe that Nature spirits, or **devas**, have helped to make the crops grow under difficult environmental conditions.

Findlay, J. Arthur (1883–1964) English spiritualist, author, and founder of the Glasgow Society for Psychical Research (1920). He also co-founded Psychic Press Ltd., which publishes *Psychic News*. He spent many years investigating spiritual phenomena and wrote widely on the subject. His best-known book, *On the Edge of the Etheric*, has gone through sixty editions and has been translated into nineteen languages. See also **Spiritualism**.

Fir Pine tree with many magical and mythic associations. In Phrygia it was sacred to **Cybele**, and in ancient Roman mythology, **Rhea** turned **Attis** into a pine tree to prevent his death. The Romans regarded unopened pine cones as symbols of virginity and these were accordingly sacred to **Diana**. The pine was also sacred to **Dionysus**, whose devotees often wore foliage from the fir tree.

Sometimes the fir symbolizes the "axis of the world" and for **shamans** serves as a bridge between the everyday world and the **supernatural** dimension. For these shamans the fir is the "Universal Tree" that grows at the "Centre of the World". One Yakut legend mentions that the souls of the shamans were born in a fir tree on Mount Dzokuo; another that the great shamans are found in the highest branches of the fir tree and the lesser shamans lower down. See also **Nature Worship**.

Fire One of the four alchemical elements, the others being **Earth**, **Water**, and **Air**. The spirits of Fire are known as **salamanders** (a mythic variety not related to the small, newt-like amphibian that is an actual species). The three astrological signs linked to Fire are **Aries**, **Leo**, and **Sagittarius**. See also **Alchemy**.

Firedrake In comparative **mythology**, a fire-breathing **dragon** who lives in a cave and guards buried treasure. Firedrakes are often associated with the spirits of the dead and in some mythologies personify the immortal **life-force** of the deceased person.

Fire Temple In **Zoroastrianism**, a temple for worship that includes a "fire sanctuary" that is sometimes accessible only to the priest. The fire, which personifies **Ahura Mazda**, is never allowed to go out.

Fire-walking The ability to walk through fire without being burned or harmed in any way. Practitioners are often in a state of **trance** when they perform this act. Fire-walking has been practised in many different regions of the world including India, Hong Kong, Fiji, Natal, Malaysia, Hawaii and the West Indies.

Fire-worshippers Term sometimes used to refer to the devotees of **Zoroastrianism**.

Firmament In ancient **cosmology**, the "vault of the heavens" invariably associated with sky-gods. **Nut**, the Egyptian goddess of the sky, is a characteristic example: she was often represented with an elongated body that arched across the sky so that only her fingertips and toes touched the earth.

First Cause The mysterious force – often called **God** – that gave rise to the universe and sustains all living things.

First Church of Christ, Scientist The official title of the organization founded by **Mary Baker Eddy** in 1879 and popularly known as **Christian Science**.

First Matter In **alchemy**, the first manifestation of the **Godhead**, perceived as a fusion of **Spirit** and Matter. The First Matter was essentially formless, and constituted the darkness from which the universe was subsequently born. The alchemist **Thomas Vaughan** describes it in his work *Anthroposphia Theomagica*: "I conceive it (to be) the effect of the Divine Imagination, acting beyond itself in contemplation of that which was to come, and producing this passive darkness…" Vaughan goes on to say that the "splendour of the Word" cast the darkness down into an abyss of formless night and eventually the Divine Spirit produced light and life from that darkness.

First Order In the **Hermetic Order of the Golden Dawn**, the five grades of **initiation** preceding **Tiphareth** at the centre of the **Tree of Life**. These grades were Neophyte (a grade not ascribed to the Tree of Life); Zelator (**Malkuth**); Theoricus (**Yesod**); Practicus (**Hod**); and Philosophus (**Netzach**).

Firth, Violet See **Fortune, Dion**.

Fisher King In the Arthurian legends, the lord of the Castle of the **Holy Grail** and keeper of the bleeding lance (a symbol linking the Grail legend to Christianity). The Fisher King was so named because fishing was his only pastime. He was a cripple and could only be restored to health by a question put to him by the Grail hero.

Five In **numerology**, the number associated with versatility, restlessness, and adventure. People whose names "reduce" to five (when mathematical ascriptions are given to each of the letters) are said to love speculation and risks, and a varied environment. They are fond of travel and resist responsibility or any other factors in their lives that would tend to tie them down.

Five Stupid Vices In **Buddhism**: desire, anger, foolishness, arrogance, and doubt.

Five Violations In **Buddhism**, crimes that prevent an individual from attaining **enlightenment**: patricide; matricide; murder of an **arahat** (a "worthy one", or monk); causing disorder in a monastic community; or striking a Buddha and making him bleed.

Flagae Spirits or **familiars** that appear to the **witch** or **magician** in a mirror and reveal **esoteric** truths or obscure information.

Flagellation The act of whipping or scourging the body. Some ascetics inflict this punishment upon themselves to atone for their sins. Certain occultists, among them **Aleister Crowley**, have practised self-flagellation to strengthen the **will**.

Flamel, Nicholas (1330–1417) French alchemist born of poor parents who subsequently attained great wealth, allegedly by discovering the **Philosopher's Stone**, which could transmute base metals into **gold**. He claimed guidance from an **angel** named Bath-Kol who showed him a book bound in copper with leaves of bark and characters inscribed in gold. Although this book was not bequeathed to him, Flamel maintained in an account written in 1399 that a comparable work – bound in brass and "graven all over with a strange kind of letters" – came his way for the modest price of two florins. The book contained symbolic statements relating to **alchemy** and contained hints on how the **Great Work** might be attained. Flamel says he sought guidance on how to interpret the book from one "Anselm, a practicer of physic", but disagreed with his views. He travelled to Spain in search of other opinions, but returned to France, where he resorted to prayer in order to gain the insights he required. Flamel writes that on January 17 1382, with his wife Perrenelle, he successfully performed an experiment in which he transmuted a pound and a half of mercury into "pure silver" and that in the following April he transmuted mercury into gold.

Historians have regarded Flamel's account with rather less enthusiasm, however, and believe his claim to be totally spurious. It is more likely that the wealth he did obtain resulted from his business as a scrivener and moneylender. The issue is complicated by the fact that many of the works ascribed to Flamel are of dubious authorship, so we cannot be sure of the authenticity of his claims.

Flamen In ancient Rome, the rank of sacrificial **priest**. There were fifteen such priests, each ascribed to a different god. Those serving **Jupiter**, **Mars** and Quirinus (the name of Romulus after he became a god of war) were regarded as the most important.

Flammarion, Camille (1842–1919) French astronomer and founder of the French Astronomical Society (1887) who became interested in psychic phenomena and became president of the **Society for Psychical Research** (London) in 1923. Flammarion was particularly interested in **psychic mediums** and issues associated with **death**. He investigated the famous medium **Eusapia Palladino** who wrote a number of books on **parapsychology**, including *The Unknown Forces of Nature* (1909), *Death and its Mystery* (3 vols., 1923), and *Haunted Houses* (1923).

Flexed signs In **astrology**, the **mutable** or **double-bodied signs**.

Floromancy Belief that flowers radiate vibrations and have curative properties in healing disease. According to practitioners of floromancy, flowers are said to respond to a sympathetic or hostile environment and are affected by electrical shocks. Professor Jagadish Chandra Bose of Calcutta's Presidency College experimented with the effects of electrical currents on plants around the turn of the century and was convinced that plants possess a **life-force** or soul.

The most recent proponent of floromancy is American lie-detector specialist Cleve Backster, who wired three philodendrons to galvanometers on different occasions to see how the plants would respond to a nearby trauma. Backster monitored the plants as he placed a brine shrimp in boiling water nearby, resulting in its instant death. According to Backster and three corroborating investigators, Backster's galvanometer readings showed significantly higher electrical resistance when the brine shrimps were being killed, than on other occasions – suggesting that the plants were responding "emotionally" to the traumas occurring nearby. Unfortunately, attempts to replicate Backster's experimental results have so far proved unsuccessful.

Flournoy, Theodore (1854–1920) Swiss professor of psychology who studied the **psychic medium** Helene Smith. Smith's paranormal abilities included **automatic writing** and speaking in tongues (**xenoglossy**). She also claimed to be a **reincarnation** of both a Hindu princess and Marie Antoinette, and maintained that the son of one of her spiritualist colleagues had been "transported" in spirit form to Mars and was able to provide details of the inhabitants of the planet. Flournoy documented these claims in his book *From India to the Planet Mars* (1900), and came to the view that many components of Helene Smith's revelations resulted from "repressed" and potentially familiar information. Flournoy rejected the idea that spirits were involved in Smith's mediumistic pronouncements, but believed that she may have possessed **mental telepathy**, which enabled her to obtain obscure information used in building her fantasy personas.

Fludd, Robert (1574–1637) Elizabethan **mystic**, musician, astrologer, and occult artist who studied **Hermetica** and **Rosicrucian** philosophy. Fludd believed in the kabbalistic cosmology in which the Absolute God or **YHVH** transcends good and **evil**. He was interested in the notion of cosmic harmony, **emanations**, and mystical hierarchies of spirit-beings, and portrayed the **Hermetic axiom**, "as above, so below", in many of his symbolic compositions. Fludd's works, many of which included detailed cosmological diagrams and "occult **mandalas**", were interpreted by many of the best engravers in Europe.

Fluid Body In **occultism** and **Theosophy**, a synonym for the **astral body**.

Flux Fluidity and change; the act of flowing. According to **Taoism**, nothing in the universe is fixed; all phenomena ebb and flow according to the vibrant interplay of **yin** and **yang** energies.

Flying Ointments Lotions rubbed on the skin and used by medieval **witches** to produce states of **dissociation**, **trance**, and the perception of having flown to the **witches' sabbath**. According to American anthropologist **Michael Harner**, European witches rubbed their bodies with hallucinogenic ointments made from such plants as deadly nightshade (Atropa belladonna), **mandrake** (Mandragora) and **henbane** (Hyoscyamus); the **psychedelic** constituent, atropine, was absorbed through the skin. This produced the visionary sensation of going on a "trip" on a broomstick and meeting with other witches and demons at the Sabbath. In 1966 the German scholar professor Will-Erich Peukert of Göttingen mixed a witches' brew consisting of belladonna, henbane, and **datura** and rubbed it on his forehead. He also invited his colleagues to do the same. According to a report of the experiment, "they fell into twenty-four hour sleep in which they dreamed of wild rides, frenzied dancing, and other weird adventures of the type connected with medieval orgies".

Flying Saucers Popular term for **unidentified flying objects** coined by the American businessman Kenneth Arnold. Arnold claimed that on June 24 1947, when he was flying his private aeroplane solo near Mount Rainier in Washington, he saw nine unidentified discs travelling near the mountain at a speed of approximately one thousand miles per hour. Arnold described the discs as resembling a "kind of saucer" made of metal and glittering in the sun. Investigators of unidentified flying objects now prefer the all-encompassing term **UFO** because, since Arnold's sighting, there have been many claimed sightings of irregular-shaped objects including cigar-like UFO's that have become known as "mother ships".

Fo In Chinese **Buddhism**, a term for a saintly person who is about to attain **nirvana**. It is also used to describe the Buddhas generally, especially **Gautama**.

Fodor, Nandor (1895–1964) Hungarian-born psychoanalyst who was a member of many international psychical research bodies and was London correspondent for the journal of the American **Society for Psychical Research** (1936–1939). He wrote widely on **parapsychology**, **psychical research**, and the **poltergeist** phenomenon. Among his many books were the *Encyclopaedia of Psychic Science* (1934), *On the Trail of the Poltergeist* (1958), *The Haunted Mind* (1960), and *Mind Over Space* (1962).

Fohat Tibetan term, used in **Theosophy**, meaning "Divine Nature" or "Primordial Light". Fohat has been described as "the presence of cosmic electricity" and was regarded by **Madame Helena Blavatsky** as the vital and mystical force underlying thought and consciousness.

Folklore **Superstitions** and beliefs that develop into a tradition of legends and stories ascribed to **gods**, **spirits**, **demons**, and other supernatural beings. Oral folklore traditions are often passed from one generation to the next as a collection of tales and anecdotes.

Fontenay, Guillaume de (1861–1914) French cavalry officer who specialized in the analysis of **psychic photography**. He was critical of many photographs that purported to show etheric emanations from the bodies of **psychic mediums**, but produced photographs himself which allegedly showed levitation in **seances** with **Eusapia Palladino**. He was awarded the Fanny Endem prize by the French Academy of Science for his research into **parapsychology**.

Fool, The In the **Tarot**, the supreme card, which symbolizes "he-who-knows-nothing" – the person who therefore has knowledge of **No-Thing**, "that which is unmanifest or **transcendent**". This realm lies beyond the created universe and no qualities or attributes may be ascribed to it. In Western **magic**, which combines the Tarot paths of the **Major Arcana** with the ten **sephiroth** on the **Tree of Life**, the path of *The Fool* connects **Kether** and **Chokmah**.

Forau In **demonology**, one of the attendants to **Sargatanas**, a Brigadier of **hell** knowledgeable in the magical art of attaining invisibility.

Forcas In **demonology**, a grand prince of **hell** who commands twenty-nine legions of devils.

Ford, Arthur (1897–1971) Well-known American spiritualist and **psychic medium** who became a member of the American **Society for Psychical Research**. He began his career after meeting **Sir Arthur Conan Doyle**, but gained international fame following his association with the Episcopalian clergyman **Bishop James Pike**. Pike consulted Ford after the death of his son Jim, and believed that Ford had made contact with his **spirit**. Ford also maintained that since 1929 he had been in contact with the deceased spirit of Houdini and claimed, as a result, that he had the keys to break the code which Houdini had left to test proofs of survival. Ford did not emerge from these claims unscathed, however, and several charges of fraud were laid against him. Ill health forced him to retire, and he died in 1971.

Foreknowledge Knowledge of future events. See also **Clairvoyance; Divination; Extrasensory perception; Precognition.**

Fort, Charles Hoy (1874–1932) American eccentric and author whose researches into mysterious and unexplained phenomena made him a forerunner with regard to modern interest in **UFOs** and the paranormal. Fort was a prodigious collector of newspaper clippings and, on the basis of 100,000 press cuttings, compiled four books: *The Book of the Damned* (1919), *New Lands* (1923), *Lo!* (1931), and *Wild Talents* (1932). These works were subsequently brought together as *The Books of Charles Fort* and published through the auspices of the **Fortean Society** in 1941. Fort was interested in unexplained showers of frogs, snails, snakes, and fish that fell from the sky; in the appearance of **supernatural** or inexplicable lights; in **ghosts** and **poltergeists**; and in such events as the case of the **Devil's Hoofmarks**. A biography of Fort, titled *Charles Fort, Prophet of the Unexplained*, was written by Damon Knight and published in 1971.

Fortean Society Organization founded in New York in 1931 to promote the books of **Charles Hoy Fort** and to continue his investigatory work into unexplained phenomena.

Fortified sign In **astrology**, a **sign** that is well positioned or well aspected in a **horoscope**.

Fortuna Roman goddess of happiness and good fortune and the counterpart of the Greek goddess Tyche. She bestowed wealth on some lucky mortals, but poverty on those who had fallen from favour. Notoriously fickle, she was also regarded as the goddess of chance.

Fortune, Dion (1891–1946) Leading English occultist and author. Fortune, whose real name was Violet Firth, grew up in a household where the teachings of **Christian Science** were rigorously practised. When she was twenty she suffered a serious nervous breakdown and, as she recovered, she found herself motivated to study psychology and the occult. She joined the **Theosophical Society** and also took courses in psychoanalysis at London University. In 1919 she became a member of the **Hermetic Order of the Golden Dawn** and began to write occult fiction based on her understanding of **magic** and **astral travel**. Dion Fortune came into conflict with **Moina Mathers**, wife of one of the co-founders of the order, and claimed that she was being subjected to **magical attacks**. In 1922 she established the **Fraternity of the Inner Light** with her husband Penry Evans, who was also an occultist. This society in turn gave rise to the contemporary occult group **Servants of the Light**, at present headed by **Dolores Ashcroft-Nowicki**. Dion Fortune wrote a number of important occult works, but her best known is *The Mystical Qabalah*, which is regarded by many occultists as one of the best textbooks on magic ever written. See also **Occultism**.

Fortunes In **astrology**, two planets – **Jupiter** (associated with wisdom, wealth, and generosity) and **Venus** (associated with love) – are said to determine one's "fortune". Jupiter is sometimes termed the "Greater Fortune" and Venus the "Lesser Fortune". The other particularly favourable bodies are the **sun**, the **moon**, and **Mercury**.

Fortune-teller One who claims to predict the future through **divination**. Fortune-telling may take different forms, but the most popular contemporary forms are **astrology**, **Tarot**, and, to a lesser extent, **numerology**.

Four In **numerology**, the number associated with hard work, practicality, and also unhappiness and defect. People whose names "reduce" to four (when mathematical ascriptions are given to each of the letters) are said to be stolid and uninspiring, but often very methodical in routine work situations. They are plodding and unadventurous and do not attain success easily.

Four Directions See **Directions, Four**.

Four Elements See **Elements**.

Four-footed Signs In **astrology**, the signs of the **zodiac** that represent quadrupeds: **Aries**, **Taurus**, **Leo**, **Sagittarius**, and **Capricorn**.

Four Noble Truths In **Buddhism**, recognition that all individual or selfish existence is founded in misery; that individuals attach themselves to worldly objects, which are ephemeral and illusory; that happiness and **enlightenment** can only be obtained by detaching oneself from the material world; and that **nirvana** can be found by pursuing the **Eightfold Path**.

Fourth Dimension Following the formulation by Albert Einstein (1879–1955) of the principles of relativity, it has now become popular to regard time as the "fourth dimension" of space. Some occult writers refer to the "fourth dimension" as a mysterious domain where paranormal events occur, but this concept has no practical application in scientific **parapsychology**.

Fourth Root Race According to **Theosophy**, the "Atlantean" Race that succeeded the Lemurians and preceded the present era. The Fourth Root Race ended with a cataclysm when **Atlantis** sank beneath the waves. See also **Atlantis**; **Lemuria**; **Root Race**.

Four Universals In **Buddhism**: kindness, pity, joy, and indifference. They are also known as the Four Immeasurables and the Four Infinite Minds.

FREEMASONRY: The different schools of Freemasonry are united by the belief that God is "The Great Architect of the Universe". Man has always been a builder, but for the Freemason the most noble task is to reflect spiritual realities in worldly activity. Temples are of the earth, but they point upwards to the heavens.

Fox, George (1624–1691) Spiritual healer and **psychic** who was also founder of the Society of Friends, or Quakers. Fox, who lived at the time of Oliver Cromwell, claimed to "see" the restoration of the monarchy three years before it happened and was also credited with several "miracle" cures, which he performed by **laying-on-of-hands.**

Fox, Matthew (1940–) : Author, priest and proponent of Creation Spirituality, Fox grew up in Madison, Wisconsin, and joined a Dominican order when he was nineteen. Fox maintains that he always sought to focus more on spirituality than on religion and his particular emphasis was not only on the contemplative experience but on justice in the wider world. Fox believes in the divinity of the earth and maintains that Jesus was a pantheist. In rejecting the more orthodox concept of theism – of a God separate from the world – Fox has adopted a perspective that takes him to the very edge of Christian orthodoxy, if not beyond it altogether. For Fox, Christianity should be experiential rather than constricted by doctrine. "Our job", he says, "is to keep our hearts open and learn the new names for divinity ... everything is in God and God is in everything." Fox is a prolific author and lecturer. Among his many books are *The Coming of the Cosmic Christ, Original Blessing: A Primer in Creation Spirituality* and *Illuminations of Hildegard of Bingen.*

Fox, Oliver One of the first pioneers of **astral projection**. Fox considered one of the best projection techniques to be the "Dream of Knowledge", by which he meant acquiring consciousness in the **dream** state. His personal account of these practices was published in the *English Occult Review* (1920) and in his book *Astral Projection* (republished in 1962). Leading psychical researcher **Dr. Hereward Carrington** regarded Fox's account to be "the only detailed, scientific and first-hand account of a series of conscious and voluntarily controlled astral projections which I have ever come across".

Fox's work has done much to shape the current research on **out-of-the-body experience** by parapsychologists like **Dr. Charles Tart** of the University of California at Davis, and **Celia Green** of the Institute of Psychophysical Research, Oxford. Fox's account remains one of the three pioneering sources on astral travel, the other two being *The Projection of the Astral Body* by Sylvan Muldoon and Dr. Hereward Carrington, and *Journeys out of the Body* by Robert Monroe.

Fox Sisters Sisters Kate (1841–1892) and Margaretta (1838–1893) are credited with giving rise to modern **spiritualism**. The Fox family lived at Hydesville in Arcadia, New York. Their wooden house already had a reputation for "mysterious noises" prior to their arrival, and in March 1848, so the story went, inexplicable rappings began to disturb the two girls who were then aged seven and ten. Kate noticed that, when she clapped, the rappings seemed to stop, and the girls devised a code to enable them to communicate with the unseen agency that was producing the noises. One rap meant "no", two raps "yes", and three "uncertain". In due course the entire Fox family became convinced that they had contacted the spirit of a man who had been murdered by a former resident of the house for financial gain. In April 1848 Mr. Fox and his family dug in the cellar of their home and uncovered human remains – including fragments of hair, teeth, and bones – which they claimed were those of the murdered man, but the evidence was certainly rather slight.

In later years Mrs. Fox and her daughters began to tour America, discussing the rappings and talking about the spirit world. From time to time accusations of fraud were levelled at the Fox family, and finally both Kate and Margaretta confessed that the rappings were fraudulent. Margaretta later withdrew her confession and, as a result, the case of the Fox family rappings remains in some doubt. However there is no doubt that the precedent for contacting spirits through rappings was established by these events and the impact of the Fox family on later spiritualism has been considerable.

Franck, Adolphe (1809–1893) Orientalist and Hebraist who was professor of natural philosophy at the Collège de France and produced one of the earliest general works on the **Kabbalah**. Franck's *La Kabbale: ou la philosophie religieuse des Hébreux* was first published in Paris in 1843 and translated into English by I. Sossnitz for its American publication in 1926. Franck's interpretation of the Kabbalah focused especially on the system of **emanations** from the **Godhead** and, according to the modern kabbalistic authority Gershom Scholem, placed too much emphasis on **pantheism**. This criticism notwithstanding, Franck's work did much to pave the way for later research into Jewish **esoteric** thought.

Fransisters and Brothers Interdenominational mystical order founded by Laurel Elizabeth Keyes, in Denver, Colorado, in 1963. Keyes spent many years studying the mystical connotations of sound and its application in **meditation** and health care. In her system, known as Toning, practitioners learn to build up **vibrations** within the body that manifest the rhythms of life, and visualize colours as they chant and hum. They believe that, in a psychic sense, they are attracting magnetic currents into the body through the feet. The organization of Fransisters and Brothers, which studies the connections between Toning and **meditation**, is a non-profit group that maintains it is working towards universal peace and overcoming religious differences.

Fraternity of the Inner Light Occult group formed by **Dion Fortune** in 1922. She had joined the **Hermetic Order of the Golden Dawn** two years earlier, but felt that the London Lodge, to which she belonged, consisted "mainly of widows and grey-bearded ancients" and needed a new spark of life. The Fraternity of the Inner Light was established to interest the general public in the magical tradition through lectures and publications, and to recruit people interested in more **esoteric** work. For a time the society was known as the Christian Mystic Lodge of the Theosophical Society, but this title was soon discarded.

Fravashis In Persian **mythology**, guardian spirits, or **genii**, who defended all living creatures in the eternal battle between good and **evil**. See also **Magi**; **Zoroastrianism**.

Freemasonry This international institution now has the nature of a benevolent, friendly society, but was originally an **esoteric** organization. It still has elaborate secret rites and ceremonies and a code of morals, and requires that its members believe in "the Great Architect of the Universe". Freemasonry is descended from a guild of stonemasons that existed in fourteenth-century England; but modern Masonry dates from the establishment of the Grand Lodge of London (1717). Freemasonry later spread to the United States and Europe. In some countries Freemasonry is suppressed by the state. Traditionally, it has aroused hostility from the Roman Catholic Church, although in recent years this antagonism has subsided. See also **Co-masonry**.

Freud, Sigmund (1856–1939) The founder of psychoanalysis and a pioneer in the study of **dreams**, Freud was one of the pioneering thinkers of the twentieth century. From the perspective of transpersonal psychology, Freud's model of the unconscious mind is now considered limited but his great contribution to the study of human perception was in his scientific exploration of the unconscious mind and his analysis of dreams. Freud derived many of his most creative inspirations from biology and emphasized sexual repression and infantile sexual trauma as the roots of neurosis. This alienated him from many of his colleagues, and some of his most notable students, including **Carl Jung** and Alfred Adler, broke away to establish their own schools of psychology. Nevertheless, Freudian perspectives continue to underpin Western medical psychiatry. Among Freud's most influential books are *The Interpretation of Dreams, The Psychopathology of Everyday Life* and *Three Contributions to the Theory of Sexuality.*

Frustration In **astrology**, a situation where three planets present themselves in conflict and one of the planets frustrates the **aspects** arising from the other two.

Fuath Evil water-**spirit**, described in Scottish folklore. It had yellow hair, a tail and mane, webbed feet, and lacked a nose. The term *fuath* is sometimes used to describe Nature spirits generally, without implying an evil connotation.

Fulcanelli Mysterious and semi-legendary alchemist who is said to be one of the only serious researchers to have pursued the **Philosopher's Stone** in the twentieth century. In the early 1920s, a French student of **alchemy** named Eugène Canseliet was given a manuscript by Fulcanelli called *The Mystery of the Cathedrals.* It created a sensation when it was published in Paris in 1926, and included descriptions of the heretical, **pagan**, and alchemical motifs that embellished the masonry of Gothic cathedrals in Bourges, Amiens, and Paris. Fulcanelli then disappeared and for many years was seen by no one. However, Canseliet claims that when he saw him briefly many years later – when Fulcanelli should have been around 110 years old – "he looked not older than I was myself" (around fifty). Fulcanelli is regarded as a modern **Comte de Saint Germain**, who similarly claimed to have discovered the alchemical secret of eternal youth.

Fuller, Curtis (1912–) American journalist who, in 1948, founded *Fate* magazine, a popular occult journal that became the most widely read magazine of its type in the world. See also **Occultism**.

Fuller, John Frederick Charles (1878–1966) British military historian and soldier who became a disciple of **Aleister Crowley** and produced a volume titled *The Star in the West* (1907), which praised his magical philosophy. Fuller contributed to Crowley's journal ***The Equinox*** and is thought to have originated the term "Crowleyanity" to describe the teachings of the Aeon of Horus, outlined in *The Book of the Law* (1904).

Fundamentalist One who clings to the fundamental teachings or beliefs of a religious or mystical creed and interprets all facets of this belief as being literally true. Fundamentalists resist theological speculation or symbolic interpretations of their beliefs. The term is often used to describe Christians who insist that the Bible contains the absolute truth and the complete revelation of **God**.

Furfur In **demonology**, a count from **hell**, often depicted as a winged stag.

Furies, Three See **Erinyes**.

Future That which is still to come. Some **occultists**, among them traditional astrologers, believe that **destiny** or **fate** is preordained and that methods of **divination** reveal what lies ahead. However, in humanistic **astrology** and those forms of modern **occultism** that accommodate modern findings in psychology, interest in the future has diminished and been replaced by methods that interpret one's "potential" rather than one's "destiny".

Fylfot Cross Symbol used in modern ceremonial magic. Resembling a swastika whose arms point to the left, the Fylfot Cross is divided into squares bearing the twelve signs of the zodiac and the signs of the four elements, with the motif of the sun in the centre.

Fylgja In Scandinavian mythology, a guardian spirit that appeared to a person in dreams and took a symbolic form appropriate to the characteristics of that person. In some respects the fylgja resembles the human double or doppelgänger.

G

Gabriel Archangel who, in the biblical narrative, explained the meaning of certain visions to Daniel and informed Zacharias that John the Baptist had been born. In modern Western magic Gabriel is considered to be the archangel of the element Water and is invoked in the West.

Gaea In Greek mythology, the earth-goddess who was born after Chaos. She united with her son Uranus to produce the twelve Titans and was also the mother of the Cyclops.

Galactides Magical stone, resembling an emerald, which is said to make ghosts visible and magical formulae audible. It also bestows love and friendship.

Galvanic Mirror Magnetized disc, consisting of a concave copper section and a convex zinc section joined together. It is used for the visionary activity of skrying and is a modern variant on the crystal ball.

Gandareva In Sumerian mythology, a dragon-like demon known as the "Master of the Abyss" who provided assistance to an evil dragon intent on devouring the world. After several hostile encounters, the dragon and the demon were slain by Keresaspa.

Gandharvas Hindu gods of the atmosphere who resembled centaurs in form, and were the lovers of the beautiful apsaras, or water nymphs. The apsaras loved to sing and dance, and the Gandharvas were regarded as the genii of music.

Ganesha Also Ganpati. In Indian mythology, the god of wisdom and literature. Depicted as half-man, half-elephant, Ganesha was fat and jolly and bestowed good fortune. The son of Parvati, he was created from dust combined with mist from her body. He is a popular figure in the Hindu pantheon.

Ganges Sacred river in India that originates in the Himalayas and flows over 2,500 kilometers to the Bay of Bengal. In the Indian Tantric tradition, the Ganges is compared to **ida**, the feminine psychic energy channel through which the mystical **kundalini** is aroused. The Ganges is sometimes also regarded as the semen which flows from **Shiva**'s phallus. See also **Tantra.**

Ganpati See **Ganesha.**

Gardner, Gerald Brousseau (1884–1964) English **warlock** credited with providing the impetus behind the revival of **modern witchcraft**. Gardner spent much of his life in the Far East, where he worked as a rubber planter and customs official. Interested in nature-worship, he contacted a witchcraft **coven** in the New Forest after returning to England, and subsequently became an initiated member. Gardner later produced a novel about witchcraft titled *High Magick's Aid* (1949). He followed this with two works of non-fiction, *Witchcraft Today* (1954) and *The Meaning of Witchcraft* (1959), in which he revealed many of the teachings of traditional witchcraft. Gardner's personal tastes extended to **sexual magic**, sadomasochism, and voyeurism, and these characteristics tend to be present in witchcraft groups which derive from him. Gardner had some contact with the ceremonial magician **Aleister Crowley** and was also involved at one time with the Tantric magical group **Ordo Templi Orientis.**

Garland, Hamlin (1860–1940) American novelist and psychical researcher who grew up as a farmer in Wisconsin. He began to investigate **spiritualism** in 1891 after learning that the evolutionist **Alfred Russel Wallace** was interested in **psychic phenomena**. Garland turned to fiction for a living and won the Pulitzer Prize for his book *Daughter of the Middle Border*. He also wrote two novels with psychic themes and became a member of the American **Society for Psychical Research**. Garland was an enthusiastic investigator of **psi phenomena** and reported his own findings in *Forty Years of Psychic Research* (1936) and *The Mystery of the Buried Crosses* (1939). See also *Psychical Research.*

Garrett, Eileen (1893–1970) Irish **psychic medium** who first developed her **psi** abilities under the guidance of the spiritualist **James H. McKenzie** at the British College of Psychic Science (1924–1928). She was later invited to participate in parapsychology experiments with **Dr. J. B. Rhine** at Duke University and also took part in other tests involving **automatic writing** and long-distance **telepathy**. Mrs. Garrett later worked with several leading psychical researchers, including **Dr. Hereward Carrington**, **Dr. Alexis Carrel**, and **Dr. Nandor Fodor**; and in 1951 she helped establish the Parapsychology Foundation to encourage the scientific investigation of psi phenomena. Mrs. Garrett believed that psychic mediums may tap forces in the unconscious mind during their seances, and did not believe that mediumism necessarily demonstrates personal survival of **death**. See also **Psychical Research.**

Garters Thongs or strings tied around the leg above the knee and regarded by **witches** as a symbol of rank.

Garuda Bird In Hindu **mythology**, the Bird of Life who was capable of creating and destroying all things. He was regarded as the deadly enemy of the **nagas** or serpents, who lived beneath the earth in magnificent temples and palaces. Buddhist myths describe how, when the nagas came to listen to **Gautama Buddha**, they had to be protected from Garuda demons.

Gate of Horn In Greek **mythology**, the gate through which authentic dream-oracles relating to future events came forth from the **Underworld.**

Gate of Ivory In Greek **mythology**, the gate through which misleading and deceitful **dreams** were sent to people from the cave of **Hypnos**, god of sleep.

Gates of Dreams Two sets of gates in the classical Greek **Underworld.** One was fashioned of horn, the other of ivory. See **Hades, Gate of Horn, Gate of Ivory.**

Gatha In **Buddhism**, a poem or chant. The term is also used to describe each of the twelve divisions of the Mahayana canon.

Gatha In **Zoroastrianism**, a song or **hymn** in the sacred writings collectively known as the **Avesta**, which includes many of the myths and religious beliefs of ancient Persia.

Gaufridi, Louis See **Aix-en-Provence Nuns.**

Gautama Buddha Also Gotama Buddha. The historical founder of **Buddhism**, as distinct from the many **buddhas** in the history of Eastern **mysticism** who are "enlightened ones".

Geburah Hebrew word for "Judgment", "power", the fifth **emanation** of **sephirah** on the kabbalistic **Tree of Life.** In Western **magic**, Geburah is associated with **Mars**, the Roman god of war, and represents severity and justice. The destructive forces of the sphere of Geburah are intended to have a purging, cleansing effect in the Universe. Geburah represents the creator-god, who applies discipline and precision in governing the cosmos and removes unwanted or unnecessary elements after their usefulness has passed. The symbolism of Geburah is reflected in the **Tarot** card *The Charioteer*. See also **Kabbalah.**

Geh In **Zoroastrianism** and also among the **Parsis**, prayers recited five times a day, commencing sunrise. Devotees face the sun as they pray and each geh is believed to have an **archangel** associated with it.

Gehenna The Jewish **hell**, derived from the Hebrew *Ge Hinnom* – the Valley of Hinnom. This was the valley in Palestine where the Israelites sacrificed their children to Moloch, god of the Ammonites. Gehenna came to be regarded as a place of torment and abomination, and the hell-fire imagery reflects the fact that the Valley of Hinnom was a place where refuse was discarded and fires lit to avoid the spread of deadly disease. All of these factors were subsequently compounded into the "bottomless pit of eternal fire" where the wicked are said to be punished when they die.

Geller, Uri (1946–) Israeli **psychic** who has become internationally famous for his alleged ability to use his mental powers to bend metal keys and cutlery without touching them. Geller has performed before large gatherings of people and submitted himself for experimental tests at the Stanford Research Institute. However, he declined to be investigated by a *New Scientist* panel of experts and the British **Society for Psychical Research.** Despite the controversy that surrounds him, and the claims by some stage magicians that the so-called "Geller effect" of bending cutlery by mind-power can be achieved by conjuring, Geller has impressed many scientists with his alleged **psi** abilities.

Geller Effect Term used to describe the paranormal ability to bend metal objects, apparently through mind-power. See **Geller, Uri.**

Geloscopy The act of **divination** by means of analyzing a person's laughter.

Gem Precious or semi-precious stone, often with magical associations. Some gems are linked to different **sun signs** in **astrology**, while others are said to emit vibrations of coloured light which have mystical significance. Compare with **Crystal**. See also **Birthstones**.

Gematria Occult method, used by practitioners of the **Kabbalah** for turning Hebrew words or phrases into a numerical equivalent. Words or phrases with the same numerical total are said to be symbolically related. For example, the word Messiah (*MShICh*) totals 358, as does the word Nachash (*NChSh*), which means "the serpent of Moses". Some Christian Kabbalists in the Middle Ages believed that the image of the brass serpent was a prefiguration of Christ on the cross and, as a result, in medieval iconography Christ is sometimes depicted as a serpent entwined around a crucifix. See also **Notarikon**; **Temurah**.

Gemini Sign of the **zodiac** for those born between May 21 and June 21, and symbolized by the Twins. Geminis are said to be imaginative but materialistic, and their intellectual attainments are often superficial. They can be rash, unstable, and "two-faced", but are outgoing people and like to express themselves. They make good actors and politicians. An **Air** sign, Gemini is ruled by **Mercury**. See also **Astrology**.

Genethlialogy Branch of **astrology** that specializes in the study of personal characteristics associated with the moment of birth. It is synonymous with **natal astrology**, in which a **horoscope** is cast for the precise date, time, and place of birth.

Genii Also known as djinn, genn, or ginn in Arabic, a **daemon** or **genius** of a higher order than human beings, and formed of "more subtle" matter. According to Islamic belief, the genii ruled the earth before the creation of Adam and were regarded as an intermediate race of spirit-beings between **angels** and people. They were believed to have special architectural skills and, according to the **Qur'an**, were employed by Solomon to assist in erecting his magnificent temple.

Genios In Peruvian **magic** and **witchcraft**, magical spirit-allies that the witch can control for good or evil purposes. See also **Familiars**.

Geniture In **astrology**, the **aspects** and configurations of a person's nativity or **natal horoscope**.

Genius In Roman **mythology**, a spirit said to be present at one's birth and who guides and protects a person throughout their life. The Roman genius resembles the Greek **daemon**. In occult belief, a person of genius is one who is in tune with one's true **will** and who holds conversations with the **holy guardian angel**. To this extent one of the basic aims of modern Western **magic** is the discovery of one's inner genius.

Geomancy Form of **divination** by interpreting the pattern of objects thrown on the ground. Gravel, small stones, sticks, seeds, or even jewels may be used. The practitioner holds the objects in cupped hands, concentrates on the divinatory request, and then allows the seeds or stones to drop. Interpretations are made intuitively on the basis of the patterns on the ground.

Germer, Karl (1885–1962) German occultist who became head of the **sexual magic** group **Ordo Templi Orientis** after the death of **Aleister Crowley** in 1947. Germer was a dedicated follower of Crowley and assisted in the publication of some of Crowley's more obscure writings, such as *Magick Without Tears*. His magical name in the Ordo Templi Orientis was Frater Saturnus. See also **Occultism**.

Gharb i Mutlaq Arabic expression, used in Islamic **mysticism**, meaning "the Absolute Void", the plane beyond manifestation.

Ghazali, Abu Hamid (1059–1111) Islamic **mystic** who received instruction in **Sufism** at Tus, where he was born, and also at Nishapur. After lecturing in law and theology at Baghdad, he began to become more absorbed in mysticism. He travelled to Damascus where he spent two years in **meditation**; undertook a pilgrimage to Mecca; and returned to Tus, where he wrote his classical work *The Revival of the Religious Sciences*. Convinced that the principles of Islamic spirituality could be applied to all aspects of life, he came to view Sufism as the supreme path to enlightenment and believed **God** to be the sole and total Reality. God, he wrote in his *Confessions*, had brought light into his own heart: "the light which illuminates the threshold of all knowledge."

Ghost General occult term for a **spirit** or **apparition**, often said to be the disembodied **astral body** of a person who has died. Ghosts are said to haunt locations that they were fond of when they were alive on earth.

Ghost Club Organization formed in London around 1862 to investigate psychic phenomena and detect cases of fraud. The club was initially small and exclusive, but was expanded in 1938 by **Harry Price**. It attracted several notable members, including the poet and novelist Sir Osbert Sitwell and the biologist Sir Julian Huxley. After World War II the Ghost Club declined for a time; but in recent years it has again revived under the leadership of English occult researcher **Peter Underwood**.

Ghost Dance, Great Among certain Native Americans, a type of ceremony whereby dancers communicated in **trance** with the spirits, or **ghosts**, of the dead. The dance began after the visionary Paiute Indian, Wovoka (also known as Jack Wilson), became sick with a fever in 1899 at the same time that the **sun** was in eclipse. He was taken to see **God** in trance, and communicated with the people in heaven. God taught Wovoka a dance ceremony to hasten the reunion with the dead, encourage goodness, and abolish war. God also gave him songs to control the weather and advised him that Jesus was back on earth. Wovoka became known among a wide range of Indian tribes as a direct messenger of the Great Spirit. His influence on the Arapaho, the Cheyenne, the Shoshone, the Kiowa, and even the warlike Sioux, was considerable.

Ghost-seer One who has the **psychic** ability to see and converse with the **spirits** and **ghosts** of the dead. See also **Apparition**; **Astral Body**.

Ghoul A **spirit** or **demon** that feeds on the bodies of dead human beings. See also **Ghul**.

Ghul Arabic term for a terrifying being or entity which drives one insane. It is also used to describe the monsters and evil spirits said to haunt forests, cemeteries, and lonely places, which terrorize and kill the living and also dig up and devour the bodies of the dead.

Giants In Greek **mythology**, a group of monsters with serpentine bodies and the heads of men who made war on the **gods** of **Olympus**, hurling rocks and trees at their adversaries. The giants were finally defeated by **Heracles**. Giants are also featured in Scandinavian mythology as large, somewhat cumbersome creatures often given to evil and mischievous deeds.

Giger, Hans Ruedi (1940–) Swiss occult fantasy artist who created the space entity known as "the Alien" for the Oscar-winning film of the same name. Giger's paintings feature Medusa-like women with ghostly-pale skin and snakes in their hair, and draw strongly on the left-hand path of Western **magic** as well as on fantasy and horror fictions like *The Necronomicon*. Claws, needles, machine-guns and barbs also feature strongly in his works. For many people the works themselves are both disturbing and fascinating at the same time and often exhibit a macabre beauty. However his nightmare fusions of the human and the mechanical also evoke a sense of *no escape* – a sense that we are all trapped in a hell of our own making. Selections of Giger's work are now on permanent display at his museum in Castle St. Germain in Gruyère, Switzerland, which opened in June 1998. The Limelight nightclub on West 20th Street in New York recently inaugurated its H. R. Giger room, featuring exhibits of several of his most surreal and visionary artworks. See also **Left-hand path; Medusa.**

Gilbert, R. A. A leading British scholar of the Western esoteric tradition, Gilbert read philosophy and psychology at the University of Bristol and now works as an antiquarian bookdealer. His works include *The Golden Dawn: Twilight of the Magicians, Revelations of the Golden Dawn*, and an authoritative biography of Arthur Edward Waite titled *A. E. Waite: Magician of Many Parts.*

Gilgulim In the **Kabbalah**, the "cycles" or **incarnations** that one's **soul** goes through on the path to enlightenment.

Girdles Employed by **witches** to fasten their robes and also to measure the radius of the **magical circle** within which **invocations** and other magical acts are performed. The girdle is knotted at different intervals to indicate the lengths required.

Girtabili In the Babylonian creation-myth, a fearsome **dragon** in league with the sea-goddess **Tiamat**, who took the form of half-man, half-scorpion.

Glastig In Scottish **folklore**, a spirit-creature who was half-woman, half-goat and was generally kind to elderly people, helping them with their housework and other menial tasks. On occasion, however she was known to be mischievous and was fond of leading unwary travellers astray.

Glossolalia See **Xenoglossy.**

Glyph A magical symbol that represents a person's name and birthdate. It is regarded as having strong magical powers and has a comparable role to a **talisman** or **amulet**. Some occultists believe that glyphs can be worn as **charms** to ward off misfortune or disease. See also **Sigil.**

Gnome Mythic elf-like creature, said in folk-legend to live under the earth. Gnomes are similar to **goblins** and are often associated with buried treasure. In the symbolism of Western **magic**, gnomes are regarded as the spirits of the element **Earth**. See also **Elements.**

Gnosis Greek term for "knowledge". The term applies to certain religious sects that emerged during the formative years of early Christianity, and which believed in "hidden spiritual knowledge". Gnosis, from their viewpoint, consisted of the **esoteric** truths underlying religious teachings and represented the initiatory pathway to illumination and wisdom. Although the Gnostic sects varied considerably – some of them specializing in **astrology** and **cosmology**, others offering **esoteric** interpretations of the teachings of Jesus Christ – the main factor that differentiated them from mainstream Christianity was their emphasis on knowledge rather than faith.

It seems clear that **Zoroastrianism** exerted a considerable influence on Gnosticism. As in Zoroastrian dualism, the Gnostics were inclined to reject the world – and matter – as **evil**, and focus their visionary techniques on attaining the world of spirit. One of the main Gnostic deities, **Abraxas**, also had a Persian antecedent in **Zurvan**, the Zoroastrian god of time. The extensive Gnostic library discovered at Nag Hammadi in Egypt in 1947 represents the most complete source of Gnostic scriptures available. See also **Nag Hammadi Library**.

Gnostic One who believes in a "higher spiritual knowledge". The term is also used to describe **esoteric** sects that emerged in the early Christian centuries and which were regarded by orthodox Church fathers like Irenaeus as heretical. See also **Gnosis**.

Gnostic Aquarian Society Organization established by American publisher Carl L. Weschke with a view to bringing together **occultists** from different traditions. Weschke has established annual festivals in Minneapolis that offer lectures and workshops on such topics as **astrology**, **magic**, and **palmistry**; and leading exponents of these occult techniques are invited to attend. The festivals coincide with the autumnal **equinox**.

Gnosticism See Gnosis; Gnostic.

Goat Animal with occult associations. The **Devil**, or **Horned God**, was said to take the form of a goat when he presided over the **witches'** sabbath, although this demonstrates some confusion between the Devil and the horned goat-god **Pan**, who was the Lord of Nature. The goat is also featured in the **zodiac** as the sign **Capricorn**, which has as its motif a composite creature that combines a goat with a fish.

Goblin Mischievous and ugly fairy-creature, similar to a **gnome**. In Western **magic**, both gnomes and goblins are regarded as the spirits of the element **Earth**. See **Elements**.

God The **Supreme Being**, and Ruler of the Universe. In Judaism, his name is **Yahweh** or **Jehovah** (**YHVH**); among the ancient Greeks, he was called **Zeus**; the Romans knew him as **Jupiter**; the Egyptians as **Ra**; and the Scandinavians as **Odin**.

God, High An omniscient deity or ruler-god, invariably associated in world mythologies with the sky. High gods may be distinguished from lower-ranking **gods**, **angels**, **devils**, and **elementals**. The term was coined by Scottish anthropologist **Andrew Lang**.

Goddess, Great See **Great Goddess**.

God-form The image of a **god**. Ritual **magicians** use the expression "taking the god-form" when they visualize themselves as **gods** (e.g. **Thoth**, **Isis**) in a ceremonial context.

Godhead The essential nature of **God**. See also **Deity**.

God-name A magical word of sacred power. According to **esoteric** tradition, knowledge of the secret names of **God** bestows special benefits upon the **occultist** because, in uttering the formula, the **magician** becomes that god by virtue of imitation. In kabbalistic magic, the various names of God (**Adonai**, **Shaddai**, **El**, **Elohim**, **Jehovah**, and so on) are regarded as powerful god-names, and are used in ritual **invocations**. See also **Hekau**; **Kabbalah**; **Magic, Imitative**; **Words of Power**.

Gods, Goddesses In polytheistic religions, where a multiplicity of deities are believed to hold sway over the universe, magical powers are vested in a **pantheon** of gods. Each of the gods has different attributes, and each requires different rites of appeasement, veneration, and invocation. In contemporary Western **magic**, Egyptian – and to a lesser extent Greek – **polytheism** has had a pronounced influence on the structuring of ceremonial **rituals**. Occultists often choose to focus their magical activities on acquiring specific attributes (e.g. love, wealth, peace, wisdom), and gods are selected to personify these qualities in ritual.

GNOSIS: Spiritual knowledge. Gnostic adherents believe that religious beliefs should be based on experiential self-knowledge and not on inherited doctrine or dogma. This illustration depicts the Gnostic deity Abraxas.

Goetia Tradition of **black magic**, including **incantations**, **ceremonies**, and techniques of **sorcery**, often associated with medieval **grimoires**, which provided practical instructions for contacting demonic spirits. The classical work on Goetia is *The Book of Ceremonial Magic* by A. E. Waite (1898), which includes selections from several of the main grimoires.

Gold Metal associated with the **sun**. Gold also represents the "inner light" of mystical **illumination** and to this extent is the supreme "spiritual" metal. See also **Alchemy**.

Golden Age The mythical first age of humankind, where all was perfect and innocent. In Greek **mythology**, it was portrayed as eternal spring. Some **occultists** have also identified it with **Atlantis** and **Lemuria**, mythic lost continents said by some to be the "font of civilizations" and the source of true **esoteric** knowledge.

Golem In Jewish **folklore**, a creature – usually a human being – made artificially by means of **magic** and sacred names. In the **Kabbalah**, there are many references to the creative power of the letters of the Name of God; the idea emerged that through the use of holy names the magician could simulate God's act of creation and produce a subservient, robot-like being. According to the Kabbalist **Moses Cordovero**, people had the ability to give "vitality" to the golem, but not "soul" or "spirit". In seventeenth-century Europe the golem was recognized as a creature that could assist people in daily tasks, but it was feared that the creature could grow day by day and present a threat to its masters. To avert this danger it was considered that periodically the golem should be reduced to dust by removing the letter *aleph* (symbolic of creation) from its forehead. See also **Simulacrum**.

Good, Sarah Member of a **coven** in Salem, Massachusetts, who was arrested after being accused of **witchcraft** by two young children, one of whom was the nine-year-old daughter of a church minister. Sarah became a leading figure in the Salem witchcraft trials and was taken to Gallows Hill on July 19 1692. Here, the Reverend Nicholas Noyes urged her to confess her heresy; but in return she is alleged to have put a curse on him, saying, "If you take away my life, God will give you blood to drink". Sarah Good was hanged shortly afterwards. See also **Salem Witches**.

Gorgons In Greek **mythology**, three winged monsters who had serpents for hair, fierce claws, and a stare that could turn men into stone. Their bodies were covered by scales and, according to Aeschylus, they had only one tooth and eye among them. The Gorgons – Euryale, Stheno, and Medusa – were the daughters of Ceto and Phorcys. The first two sisters were immortal, but Medusa was mortal. Perseus cut off Medusa's head and placed it on the shield of **Athena**. Medusa's terrifying eye had the same power even after her death.

Gowdie, Isobel Scottish farmer's wife who became celebrated for her spontaneous **witchcraft** confession in 1662. Isobel, who lived with her husband at Auldearne, near Inverness, claimed that many years earlier she had been initiated into a **coven** under the sponsorship of one Margaret Brodie. During the ceremony the master of the coven had bared her shoulder, cut it, and drawn forth some blood, which he then mixed with spittle in order to make a mark on her forehead. He then "baptized" her as a member of the coven. Isobel began attending coven meetings, learned certain "mating dances", acquired the magical knowledge to change into a hare and other animals, and described how she had sexual intercourse with **demons** and the **Devil**. She also confirmed that a coven normally consisted of thirteen people. Apparently, Isobel's husband had no knowledge of Isobel's involvement with witchcraft until, fifteen years after her **initiation**, she came forward to confess to the elders of the church at Auldearne. Isobel named several other members of the coven and they were arrested shortly afterwards. Although Isobel repented her crimes, she was hanged and her body later burned – the traditional fate of a witch in Britain at that time.

Gracchi The **souls** of Roman heroes who had not yet been born. They were seen in the **Underworld** by Anchises and Aeneas, and are mentioned in Book Six of Virgil's *Aeneid*.

Grad, Dr. Bernard (1920–) Canadian professor of psychiatry at McGill University, Montreal, who has been involved in unusual experiments in spiritual healing. Grad established an experimental setting in which a psychic healer was asked to place his hands on mice located in the compartments of a galvanized iron box for fifteen minutes, twice daily for six weeks.

In one test with two control groups, the mice were subjected to a deficiency of iodine resulting in the induced enlargement of the thyroid gland. Grad found that the LH group of mice (those that had received **laying-on-of-hands**) did not register the iodine deficiency to the same extent as the control group of mice. In another experiment designed to test the healing of wounds on the bodies of the mice, there were three separate groups of mice: a control group, the LH mice, and a group given electro-thermal treatment. Each animal was temporarily put to sleep, and a coin-sized section of skin removed from its back. The wound area in each case was traced and recorded. After fourteen days it was evident to Professor Grad that the LH mice were healing faster than the other groups. Grad believe that the act of laying-on-of-hands transferred a healing energy to the subject and, in the case of the mice, resulted in a speedier recovery. Grad's tests are among the most impressive scientific studies of spiritual healing practices. See also **Faith Healing; Psychic Healing.**

Grandier, Urbain (1590–1634) Priest at Loudun in France, who was accused unfairly in 1633 of practising **magic** and causing nuns to be possessed by **demons**. Several nuns at the Ursuline convent at Loudun had conspired to discredit Grandier after he had fathered an illegitimate child and taken a mistress. In order to claim that Grandier had "bewitched" them, they began exhibiting signs of hysteria that included exaggerated erotic behaviour, gasping fits, and convulsions. The Mother Superior, Sister Jeanne, named Grandier and the demons **Asmodeus** and Zabulon as the cause of "spirit-possession" at the convent. A commission was subsequently established by Cardinal Richelieu to investigate the bizarre happenings at Loudun, and Grandier was consequently sent for trial. A highly suspect document, purporting to be a pact between Grandier and the **Devil**, was brought forward as evidence. The document had a damaging effect and at the conclusion of the trial, in an appalling travesty of justice, Grandier was found guilty of practising magic and was condemned to be burned alive for his "crimes".

Grant, Joan (1907–1990) English author who incorporated what she claimed were impressions of previous incarnations into her novels. Drawing on a psychic ability she termed "far memory", Joan Grant recounted previous lives in Egypt, the Holy Land, and pre-Columbian America. Her best-known books are *Winged Pharoah, Lord of the Horizon*, *Return to Elysium*, and her autobiographical *Time Out of Mind* and *A Lot to Remember*. See also **Reincarnation.**

Grant, Kenneth (1924–) English **occultist** who, after the death of **Aleister Crowley** in 1947, continued as one of his followers and established his own Isis Lodge in 1955. Grant claims to be the world head of the **Ordo Templi Orientis** (OTO), although this claim is disputed by another branch of the OTO that currently operates from Berkeley,

California. Grant has collaborated with **John Symonds** in editing and annotating several of Crowley's works, including *The Confessions* and *The Magical Record of the Beast 666*. He is also the author of several important works on modern Western **magic**, including *The Magical Review*, *Cults of the Shadow*, *Nightside of Eden*, and *Outside the Circles of Time*. He has also produced two definitive works on the English trance artist and occultist **Austin Osman Spare**, *Zos Speaks* and *Images and Oracles of Austin Osman Spare*.

Granthi Hindu term meaning "a knot". According to the Bengali **mystic** Anandamayi Ma (Most Blissful Mother), the aim of **meditation** is to "unravel the knots that constitute the **ego**" and overcome the bonds that tie down the **soul**.

Graphology The analysis of handwriting, in which aspects of one's character and personality are inferred. Details of the height of each letter, inclination, spacing, and general presentation are taken into consideration. Some graphologists divide each letter of the alphabet so that the top third of the letter represents the spiritual aspects of a person's make-up, the middle third the emotions, and the lower third the physical and sexual qualities. Graphology is not generally used in a predictive capacity.

Graveyard Ghost A **ghost** or **apparition** seen near a grave in a cemetery. According to various reports they are ethereal and nebulous in appearance and often emit a "glow".

Gray, William G. British ceremonial **magician** whose mother was an astrologer and whose father had links with **Theosophy**. Gray was the British delegate to the Spiritual Symposium held in Dallas, Texas, in 1970 under the auspices of the Sangreal Foundation, and was regarded by magical authority **Israel Regardie** as one of the foremost contemporary writers on the Western magical tradition. Gray's many books on **magic** and the **Kabbalah** include *The Ladder of Lights* (1968), *Magical Ritual Methods* (1969), *Inner Traditions of Magic* (1971), and *The Talking Tree* (1975).

Great Beast, The The name for the **Anti-Christ** in the Book of Revelation, and the name popularly associated with the magician **Aleister Crowley**, especially after he asserted himself as Lord of the **New Aeon** in 1904. Crowley was convinced that he was incarnating a new magical era that would supersede Christianity, and accordingly he often styled himself the "Great Beast 666". Crowley spent much of his later life seeking the Whore of Babylon, who could be an ideal magical partner, and his notorious sex life attracted considerable attention in the press during the 1930s.

Greater Hekhaloth Jewish visionary text of the **Hekhaloth** school dating from the early Talmudic phase of Jewish **mysticism** (first century A.D.). The Hekhaloth were different "chambers" or "halls", through which the **mystic** ascended in **meditation**. During this meditative journey, divine **God-names** would be repeated in a **mantra** and the mystic would project his consciousness into a spirit-vehicle that would journey to each hall in turn, presenting a sacred "seal" to the **archangel** guarding the chamber. Just prior to the seventh chamber the mystic entered a chariot and was then lifted up into a profound state of mystical **ecstasy**. This experience was called the journey of the **Merkabah**. See also **Rising on the Planes**.

Great Goddess The personification of fertility and the regenerative powers of Nature. She took many different forms in classical **mythology**. For example, she was **Cybele** in Phrygia, **Astarte** in Phoenicia, **Isis** in Egypt, **Demeter** in the Greek mystery religion, and **Dana** among the Celts.

Great Pyramid See **Pyramid, Great.**

Greatrakes, Valentine English magistrate who lived in Ireland and discovered that he had **spiritual healing** powers, particularly in treating the "King's Evil" (scrofula). Between 1662 and 1667, Greatrakes acquired a reputation as a healer by gently stroking the limbs of his patients "in order to squeeze the illness out of them". Greatrakes claimed that his powers came from God, and he impressed the noted chemist Robert Boyle. He later performed several acts of spiritual healing among a multitude gathered at Ragley, in Warwickshire, and had similar success in Lincoln's Inn Fields, London. Greatrakes finally gave up spiritual healing when he felt his powers were waning.

Great White Lodge In **Theosophy**, the hierarchy of spiritual **masters** or **adepts** who are said to constitute the "inner government" of the world.

Great Work, The Referred to in **alchemy** as the *summum bonum*, the Great Work represented mastery of the secrets of alchemical transmutation, especially the power to transform base metal into **gold**. In the **Hermetic Order of the Golden Dawn** tradition of modern Western **magic**, it is regarded as a metaphor for self-initiation. It is associated with the rituals of spiritual rebirth that focus on **Tiphareth** (the sun sphere at the centre of the **Tree of Life**), and with knowledge of the **Holy Guardian Angel**.

Green, Celia (1935–) English parapsychologist who has undertaken extensive experimental research on the **out-of-the-body experience**, popularly known as **astral projection**. In 1961, together with two other graduates of Oxford University, she established the Institute of Psychophysical Research at Oxford to continue the scientific study of paranormal phenomena. The Institute publishes its proceedings from time to time, and these have included two pioneering works by Celia Green herself: *Out-of-the-Body Experiences* (1968) and *Lucid Dreams* (1968).

Gremlin Imaginary creature responsible for causing mischief and pranks affecting aircraft. The origin of the name is disputed. According to one account, a British bomb squadron stationed in India just prior to World War II coined the term by combining *Grimm's Fairy Tales* with "Fremlin's Elephant Ales". Another version is that an RAF pilot called for a weather report from Le Bourget in 1922 and was told, "Gremlins sur la Manche" ("Gremlins over the English Channel"). At this exact moment his radio died. The gremlin was generally said to resemble a jack-rabbit crossed with a bull terrier, invariably wore green breeches and a red jacket, and had a top hat and spats. Gremlins were fond of drinking petrol, distracting the pilot, interfering with radio communications, and even causing the pattern of stars in the heavens to distort – thereby making accurate navigation impossible. These days gremlins have presumably been superseded by computers that make their pranks impossible.

Grenier, Jean (1589–1610) Often dubbed "the wolf-boy", Grenier lived in seventeenth-century France and was said to be a **werewolf**. He was discovered by some village girls disturbing a flock of sheep and related to them how he sometimes wore a wolf-skin and attacked sheep, dogs, and even human beings. Grenier claimed that his powers of bestial transformation were given to him after he signed a **pact** with the **Devil**. The boy was imprisoned in the Franciscan friary of St. Michael Archangel at Bordeaux, and convinced onlookers of his werewolf characteristics when he consumed a quantity of raw offal and ran around on all fours. He died after seven years of imprisonment. See also **Lycanthropy**.

Griffin A mythical creature with the head and wings of an eagle and the legs of a lion, the griffin was said to be the largest of all birds. When it spread its wings, it was capable of obscuring the rays of the **sun.** It was also the sun's guardian and was sacred to **Apollo.** The Greek epic poem *The Arimaspea* tells of battles between the griffins and the one-eyed Arimaspi tribesmen for ownership of the sacred gold. See also **Aristeas of Proconnesus.**

Grimoires Medieval collections of magical **spells, rituals,** and **incantations,** which invariably claimed authorship from classical Hebrew or Egyptian sources. Among the best known are *The Sacred Magic of Abra-Melin the Mage, The Lemegeton* (or *Lesser Key of Solomon*), *Clavicula Salmonis* (or *Greater Key of Solomon*), *The Sworn Book of Honorius,* and the *Grimoire of Armadel.* See also **Goetia;** ***Key of Solomon.***

Gris-Gris **Amulets** worn by African tribesmen to protect them from **sorcery** and **evil** forces. The term is also used to describe the **witch-doctors** and **magicians** who send forth evil **spells** and **bewitchment.**

Grof, Dr. Stanislav (1931–) Czechoslovakian psychiatrist, now resident in the United States, who is a leading authority on **LSD,** visionary experiences, and **altered states of consciousness.** Grof believes that **psychedelics,** if used in a careful and intelligent manner, allow access to mythic levels of consciousness and have profound applications in psychotherapy. Grof has also put forward the view that images of **heaven** and **hell** may be related to the foetal experience of union with the mother in the womb, and the traumatic passage through the birth canal. His books include *Realms of the Human Unconscious, The Human Encounter With Death* (co-authored with Joan Halifax), *LSD Psychotherapy, Beyond Death* (co-authored with Christina Grof) and *The Adventure of Self-Discovery.* Dr. Grof was formerly a scholar-in-residence at **Esalen Institute** in Big Sur, California, and is a leading figure in the **transpersonal psychology** movement.

Group-Soul In **Theosophy** and **spiritualism,** the concept that a single spirit governs a number of **souls,** who incarnate at different times and build up a collective **karma.** The group-soul thus guides individual souls on the upward path of spiritual evolution through the cyclic process of **reincarnation.**

Gryphon See **Griffin.**

Guaita, Stanislas de (1861–1897) French Marquis who established a **Rosicrucian** lodge in Paris as a meeting place for **occultists.** Among his many magical associates were **Gérard Encausse, Sar Peladan,** and Oswald Wirth. Guaita learned from Wirth that a magical **coven** had been established by **Joseph-Antoine Boullan** at Lyons; and, for reasons which are not quite clear, Guaita decided that he would firmly oppose it. Guaita wrote to Boullan condemning his occult practices, and subsequently urged his Rosicrucian cohorts to curse Boullan with all the magical power they could muster. Over several years a "psychic battle" raged between Guaita in Paris and Boullan in Lyons, culminating in Boullan's death. Guaita was accused in the Paris press of causing Boullan's death "by black magic", and the matter was finally settled in a duel between the journalist who had made the charges – Jules Bois – and Guaita. Fortunately, neither man was killed but both were slightly wounded, and honour was restored. See also **Magic, Black; Magical Attack; Occultism.**

Guardian Spirit Belief in a personal, protective **spirit** that overviews one's day-to-day activities and provides warning of impending danger. For the Romans, the idea of the **genius** – as the protective spirit of a person or place – had this connotation.

In **spiritualism**, the discarnate **guide** that communicates through a **psychic medium** has much the same role.

Guide In **spiritualism** and **channelling**, a protective **spirit** that is able to offer advice and guidance through a **psychic medium** at a **seance**. Sometimes the medium takes on the visual or verbal characteristics of the guide when entering a state of **trance**. Red Indians, Hindu masters, Egyptian priests, and Chinese sages seem to be among the most common types of guides in modern spiritualism, possibly because they personify eternal wisdom.

Guide Meditation See **Steinbrecher, Edwin**.

Guided Imagery Technique used in psychotherapy and also in magical **pathworkings**, whereby a subject is asked to visualize specific images in sequence. In magical procedure, the subject is led along pathways of the **Tree of Life** into archetypal areas of consciousness. The **Major Arcana** of the **Tarot** provides an ideal framework for guided imagery work. Examples of Tarot visualizations for use in guided imagery are provided in Nevill Drury's *Everyday Magic* (2002) and *Sacred Encounters* (2002), Ted Andrews' *More Simplified Magic* (1998) and Dolores Ashcroft-Nowicki's *The Shining Paths* (1983).

Guiley, Rosemary Ellen Contemporary American metaphysical author currently based in Arnold, Maryland. Guiley specializes in works on dreams, intuition and visionary experience. Among her best-known books are *Breakthrough Intuition*, *Dreamwork for the Soul*, *The Encyclopedia of Dreams* and *The Encyclopedia of Witches and Witchcraft*.

Guirdham, Arthur (1905–) Former Chief Psychiatrist at Bath Hospital in England who in 1961 began to explore what appeared to be powerful reincarnational dreams experienced by one of his patients. This patient, whom Dr. Guirdham referred to as "Mrs. Smith" to conceal her identity, had been suffering from frightening dreams of murder and massacre since the age of twelve – dreams so intense that she would shriek loudly during her sleep. Mrs. Smith told Dr. Guirdham that she had written down her dreams when she was still a thirteen-year-old schoolgirl, and because these notes contained details about people and names she had never heard of – things which continued to puzzle her – she allowed Dr. Guirdham to read them. Mrs Smith's notes contained verses of songs written in medieval French, a subject that his patient had never studied at school. The notes also contained drawings of old French coins and jewellery as well as specific references to individual people and the layout of particular buildings.

Mrs. Smith believed that her dreams seemed to refer back to the thirteenth century and the region around Toulouse. This had been a stronghold of the **Cathars**, a group of Christians who believed in catharsis, or purification, but who also believed in reincarnation and the **Gnostic** concept of the spiritual transcendence of the soul. Catharism was so strong in southern and western Europe that the Roman Catholic Church came to regard it as a serious threat to religious orthodoxy. It was branded a heretical movement and a crusade was led against it.

Mrs. Smith believed that she had been a member of the Cathar community in Toulouse in a previous life. During her terrifying nightmares she experienced being burned at the stake, recalling vividly such details as the hissing of the flames and the intense bleeding from her body. She also described a crypt where prisoners had been held, prior to their execution.

Dr. Guirdham contacted Professor Pere Nelli, a specialist medieval scholar at Toulouse University, who confirmed that details from Mrs. Smith's dream records seemed to provide an accurate account of the Cathars of

Toulouse, and in 1967 Dr. Guirdham visited this region of southern France himself. Here he was able to gain access to additional Cathar documents available only to specialist scholars. Dr. Guirdham found that all of the details in Mrs. Smith's nightmares were accurate and that even the songs which she had written down as a child were correct. Other details were impressively specific as well. For example, Mrs. Smith's dream notes indicated that Cathar priests did not always wear black garments but sometimes wore garments that were blue or green. This fact was not known to medieval scholars when Mrs. Smith first recorded her dreams in 1944, and was not officially documented until details relating to a local Inquisition were published by Professor Duvernoy of Toulouse University in 1966.

Dr. Guirdham subsequently discovered similar reincarnational memories in other patients and presented his exploration of the Cathars and reincarnational memories in his books *The Cathars and Reincarnation* and *We Are One Another*. See also **Reincarnation**.

Gunas, Three Hindu term for the three qualities of primordial matter, or **prakriti**, which co-exist in a state of equilibrium. These are **sattva** (harmony), **rajas** (motion), and **tamas** (inertia and heaviness). One of the aims of **yoga** is to transcend the limitations of the three gunas. See also **Tattvas**.

Gunzolus, Dr. Charles H. American **mystic psychic medium**, and spiritual healer, who specializes in analyzing the biblical healing tradition and conducting **seances**. He is the force behind the Gunzolus University of Spiritualism located in Indianapolis. See also **Psychic Healing**.

Guppy, Mrs. Samuel (c. 1860–1917) Controversial **psychic medium** who was discovered by **Alfred Russel Wallace**. She was credited with producing **apports** at **seances**, including butterflies, ducks, and a white cat; she also developed the concept of the spiritualist's **cabinet**, in which materializations could occur. She is best known for her remarkable claims of "psychic transportation" and **levitation**. According to one account, on June 3 1871, she was "transported" from her home in Highbury in London to a **seance** taking place several miles away; and on another occasion she manifested to onlookers in a well-lit drawing room after a similar act of psychic flight. Mrs. Guppy's claims are regarded somewhat sceptically, but there is no evidence that she gained financially from her claims of psychic powers.

Gurdjieff, George Ivanovitch

(1872–1949) Mystical teacher of Greek and Armenian parentage, Gurdjieff was born at Kars, on the Russo-Turkish border, and was interested in paranormal phenomena from an early age. He was fascinated by people who could enter **trance** states and was absorbed by tales of miracle healings. Finally, he set off with a friend named Pogossian to find the "secret knowledge" in the monasteries of central Asia. After many travels he arrived in Moscow, but left Russia when the communists came to power in 1917 – not because of their materialistic ideology, but because of the crudeness of their vision of humanity. By now Gurdjieff was convinced that most forms of politics trapped people rather than set them free. In Gurdjieff's view, people had to learn to emerge from their routine existence and rediscover a sense of alertness and vitality.

Gurdjieff went to Finland, then to Turkey, and finally established his Institute for the Harmonious Development of Man at Fontainebleau, south of Paris. It was here that Gurdjieff put into practice what his travels and inquiries had taught him to believe. Gurdjieff's followers were encouraged at the Institute to work hard, to maintain secrecy, and to work towards valuing life. He pushed his followers to the edge of their endurance, often handing out tasks at the Institute that taxed them to the limit. Only through this type of effort, he argued, could one overcome the slavery of robot-like existence that most people confuse with real life.

Gurdjieff was supremely practical and was inclined to downplay knowledge obtained from books. Instead, he emphasized the lessons learned from life itself, and often reminded his pupils that "man must live until he dies". Gurdjieff did, nevertheless, produce books of his own. They include an account of his early life, *Meetings With Remarkable Men*, and a rather more obscure volume titled *Beelzebub's Tales to his Grandson* – in which he outlined, in the form of a cosmological legend, how one can awaken to a new type of consciousness and find one's path in the universal scheme.

Gurdjieff had many admirers. One of these, the British physician Kenneth Walker, said of him: "No one who came into personal contact with Gurdjieff ever failed to be impressed by him, and by the range of his knowledge. There is no doubt that he has an important message for humanity in this critical period of its history."

Gurney, Edmund (1847–1888) English psychologist who, together with **Sir William Barrett, Henry Sidgwick**, and **F. W. H, Myers**, founded the **Society for Psychical Research** in London in 1882. Gurney began attending **seances** in 1874 and was also interested in **mental telepathy** and **hypnotism**. He was one of the first researchers to recognize that **psychic mediums** tap unconscious thought processes while in a state of **trance**. His most important book was the parapsychology classic *Phantasms of the Living* (1886), co-authored with F. W. H. Myers and **Frank Podmore**.

Guru Hindu term for a spiritual teacher or leader who guides a pupil, or **chela**, towards self-knowledge and enlightenment. Some gurus give their chelas individual **mantras** upon which to meditate. The interaction between teacher and pupil can be quite complex and may involve a process whereby the guru challenges the concepts and self-image of the chela in order to reduce the pupil's ego, thus allowing a new spiritual awareness to dawn. The chela is required to submit totally to the spiritual leader despite the difficulties and obstacles faced on the path to self-knowledge.

Guru-parampara Sanskrit term meaning "a succession of teachers". It is used in modern **Theosophy** to denote a succession of spiritual **masters** who pass on **esoteric** knowledge and ensure that the mystery teachings continue in an unbroken tradition.

Gwragedd Annwn In Welsh folk-legend, beautiful female water-spirits, resembling **mermaids**, and found in lakes. They were said to sometimes marry mortals and live normal, happy lives.

Gypsies Wandering nomadic groups said to be of Indian origin who travelled through Egypt in the fourteenth century and entered western Europe through the region of Bohemia. Their name derives from the word "Egypt", and the expression "bohemian" now has the connotation of one who is eccentric and unconventional. The gypsies spread through the Balkan peninsula and later travelled to Germany, France, and Italy before arriving in Britain around 1500. Gypsies have been traditionally associated with **fortune-telling**, especially **palmistry** and **Tarot** card **divination**. Some gypsies, especially those who call themselves Romanies, claim to be able to forecast the weather by interpreting the flight of birds and also maintain that they have the psychic power to predict events far off into the future.

Gyromancy Form of **divination** whereby one walks around a circle until one collapses. The diviner's position relative to the circle determines the outcome of future events.

H

Hades The **Underworld** of classical Greek **mythology**. Hades (or Aidoneus) was also the god of the Underworld, and the brother of **Zeus**. He snatched **Persephone** away from the Nysian plain where she was picking flowers, and made her queen of the Underworld. In Roman mythology, Hades was called **Pluto** and the Underworld was called **Dis**.

Hadit Chaldean form of the Egyptian god of darkness, **Set**. **Aleister Crowley** and his magical disciple **Kenneth Grant** have identified Hadit with **Satan**; however, they regard him not so much as an adversary of people, but as the master of magical **initiation**. In Crowleyian **cosmology** there is a link between Hadit and the entity **Aiwass** that inspired *The Book of the Law*.

Hag An old woman or **witch**, or someone who is deformed and ugly. The term derives from the Old English *haegtesse*, "a witch".

Hagith According to the ***Arbatel of Magick***, there are seven different **spirits** of **Olympus**, appointed by **God** to rule the world. Hagith is the spirit of **Venus** and governs all aspects of beauty. He is said to be able to convert copper into gold and has 36,536 legions of lesser spirits at his command.

Hag of the Dribble In Welsh **folklore**, a **banshee** who carried stones in her apron and then let them shower down, making a "dribble". She flapped her raven wings against the windows of houses where people would soon die, and howled mournfully in the twilight.

Hag-ridden One who is troubled by nightmares and is "ridden" like a horse in the night by frightening and evil **witches**. See also **Hag**.

Hag-seed The child of a **witch**. See also **Hag**.

Haidit In ancient Egypt, the term for the "shadow", one of the five human bodies. The Haidit equated approximately with what we know as the **unconscious mind** and was capable of taking an **astral** form. See also **Aufu; Ka; Kuh; Sahu**.

Hakata Pieces of wood, bone, or ivory used for **divination** by African **witch-doctors**. The objects are inscribed with symbols resembling signs of the **zodiac** and are cast upon the ground where they are then interpreted. See also **Geomancy**.

Halifax, Dr. Joan (1942–) American anthropologist and director of the Ojai Foundation in California, who has worked with **spiritual healers** and **shamans** around the world. Her book *Shamanic Voices* (1979) presents visionary shamanic narratives from many cultures, including the Tavgi Samoyed of Siberia, the Wiradjuri of Australia, the North American Sioux, the Eskimos of Greenland, and the Huichol and Mazatec Indians of Mexico. Dr. Halifax's other books include *The Human Encounter with Death* (1977) and *Shaman: The Wounded Healer* (1982). See also **Shamanism**.

Hall, Manly Palmer (1901–1990) American author and student of the Western **mystery** tradition who founded the Philosophical Research Society in Los Angeles in 1936. A prolific and highly regarded author, his best-known books include *The Secret Teachings of All Ages, Man, the Grand Symbol of the Mysteries, Sages and Seers*, and *Codex Rosae Crucis*.

Halloween See **All Hallows' Eve**.

Hallucination A visual illusion or state of perception that is not compatible with familiar, everyday reality. Hallucinations are often brought on by the action of **psychedelic** drugs or by conditions of **sensory deprivation**. In some cultures hallucinogens are thought to provide access to a **magical reality**. For example, among the Jivaro Indians of eastern Ecuador, **shamans** take a hallucinogenic beverage made from the **banisteriopsis** vine in order to gain access to the **spirit** world. In their visions they often report giant, mythic jaguars and writhing snakes, which they interpret in an initiatory way. The Cashinahua Indians of Peru similarly use hallucinogens to contact the **nixi pae** spirit beings who are accompanied by brightly coloured snakes, armadillos, and singing frogs.

It has been suggested that the magical flight of **witches** to the **witches' sabbath** resulted from hallucinatory ointments rubbed into the skin. Here atropine was the ingredient causing the aerial sensation and the visionary experience of dissociation. See also **Altered State of Consciousness; Flying Ointments.**

Halo Circle of light, often depicted in art as a golden ring around the head of a saint. Indicative of high spirituality, it is said by some **occultists** to be associated with the **aura** and is possibly connected with the electromagnetic energies depicted in **Kirlian photography**. The halo is also known as a **nimbus.**

Halomancy Also alomancy. **Divination** by throwing grains of salt onto a flat surface and interpreting the forms and shapes that result.

Hamadryads In Greek **mythology**, the spirit-nymphs of woods and trees. See also **Dryads.**

Hambaruan Among the Dayaks of Borneo, the **soul** or **spirit** of a person, which may leave the body when it wishes and undertake a journey. It then becomes vulnerable to **sorcery** and the clutches of evil spirits. Compare with **Astral Body**.

Handedness The distinction between left-handed and right-handed people has a magical connotation. Left-handed people are often thought to be "sinister" (the Latin word meaning "left"); or are regarded as having unusual characteristics, such as the ability to cast the **evil-eye**. In modern **occultism**, the spiritual path of **white magic** is said to be that of the **right-hand path**, whereas the path of **black magic** is referred to as the **left-hand path.**

Hand of Glory In **witchcraft**, a lighted candle positioned between the fingers of a dead person's hand – usually that of a criminal condemned to death. The Hand of Glory was supposed to have the magical power to freeze people in their footsteps.

Hands, Divination by See **Palmistry.**

Hands of Spirits In **spiritualism**, a situation at a **seance** where only the hands of a **spirit**, and not its whole body, manifest. The American medium **Daniel Dunglas Home** was said to produce this phenomenon.

Handwriting Analysis See **Graphology.**

Hanged Man, The In the **Tarot**, the card that at one time was regarded as a parody of Christ's crucifixion, but in fact represents a figure who reflects a greater spiritual wisdom in the world and is therefore shown upside down. His head is sometimes depicted as a beacon, with **light** streaming forth to the world below. The source of his inspiration is the Great Ocean of Spirit, **Binah**, higher up on the **Tree of Life**. In Western **magic**, *The Hanged Man* is ruled by the element **Water**, which makes the symbolism of his "reflective" nature more apparent. *The Hanged Man* is ascribed to the path between **Hod** and **Geburah** on the Tree of Life.

Hanon-Tramp German expression for a

type of nightmare in which a **demon** is thought to suffocate people as they sleep.

Hansel, Charles E. M. (1917–) English psychologist who holds the Chair of Psychology at the University College of Swansea, and who has written extensively on **parapsychology** and **extrasensory perception**. Hansel is generally critical of most claims made on behalf of **telepathy**, **clairvoyance**, and **precognition**, and his book *ESP: A Scientific Evaluation* was described by his publisher as "an important book in an area marked by misinformation, misguided enthusiasm, and prejudice". Hansel does bring to parapsychology the required degree of scientific rigour, but his approach to paranormal powers is mostly negative.

Haoma In ancient Persia, a sacramental drink that was supposed to confer **immortality**. Prepared from the haoma plant and mixed with milk and water, it represented a type of **ambrosia**. Haoma was also personified as a **deity**.

Harakhtes The Greek name of the Egyptian god **Horus**, especially with regard to the sun's path across the sky. As **Ra** became increasingly identified with Horus, the Greeks referred to the deity as **Ra-Horakte**. The occultist **Aleister Crowley** identified with this aspect of **Horus**, regarding himself as "the Crowned and Conquering Child, Lord of the New Aeon". Crowley spelled the name Ra-Hoor Khuit. See also **New Aeon**.

Hardy, Sir Alister Clavering (1896–1985) British zoologist who became interested in paranormal phenomena and in the potential effect the findings of psychical research might have on biology and science. He was president of the **Society for Psychical Research** between 1965 and 1969. His special interests were **mental telepathy** and research into children's **invisible playmates**. Hardy's books include *The Open Sea* and *The Divine Flame*.

Hare Krishna Movement Sect dedicated to **bhakti**, or devotional **Hinduism**. This form of Hindu belief focuses on love for **Krishna**, who is regarded as the Supreme **Godhead**. Devotees of the Hare Krishna Movement regard the sixteenth-century Indian saint, Sri Chaitanya Mahaprabu as their founder. He encouraged the public singing and chanting of the holy names of Krishna to the accompaniment of brass cymbals and drums; following this example, the saffron robes and mantric chanting of the Hare Krishnas have become internationally famous. The figurehead of the modern Hare Krishna Movement, until his recent death, was His Divine Grace A. C. Bhaktivedanta Swami Prabhupad, who brought the message of Krishna-bhakti to the West when he arrived in New York in 1965. The movement has since spread to most major Western countries. See also **ISKCON**.

Harmakhis See **Hor-m-akhet**.

Harmony A state of accord, balance, and agreement. It is often used in **mysticism** to denote inner balance and well-being. In the kabbalistic tradition of Western **magic**, the sphere of harmony is **Tiphareth**, located at the centre – or heart – of the **Tree of Life**. See also **Kabbalah**.

Harmony of Opposites Mystical and occult concept that **cosmic consciousness** may only be attained by transcending duality when such distinctions as "male" and "female" or "object" and "subject" cease to be real. Many cosmologies portray a dynamic interplay between opposites: the Chinese **yin** and **yang**; the yogic **ida** and **pingala**; and the distinction, in Jewish **mysticism**, between thrones (static) and chariots (mobile) as vehicles of **God**. In the **Kabbalah** there are three vertical columns on the **Tree of Life**. The outer two, located beneath **Chokmah** (male) and **Binah** (female), represent archetypal polar opposites; and these opposites are resolved, or harmonized, by virtue of the **Middle Pillar**, which stands between them and joins **Kether** and **Malkuth** – the first and last spheres on the Tree. See also **Androgyne; Dualism; Individuation; Tiphareth.**

Harner, Michael J. (1929–) American anthropologist who spent many years of field research in the Upper Amazon, Mexico, and western North America learning techniques of **shamanism** from native Indians. Harner has now adapted the traditional shamanic techniques for western practitioners, using a method that combines drumming and visualization to allow people to enter "the magical reality". This "journey" entails visualizing the cosmic tree, entering its root system, and travelling through to the lower world, where one may make contact with a **power animal** or **magical ally**. A variant on this is to ascend to the upper world through a tunnel of smoke.

Harner has been visiting professor at Columbia, Yale, and the University of California, Berkeley, and is at present Chairman of the Foundation for Shamanic Studies in Mill Valley, California. He is the author of a practical book on shamanism titled *The Way of the Shaman* (1980), and has also published two academic books on the subject: *The Jivaro* (1972), and *Hallucinogens and Shamanism* (1973). See also **Journey of the Soul.**

Harpies In Greek **mythology**, horrible winged creatures with the bodies of vultures and the heads of women. They contaminated food, gave off a disgusting odour, and snatched away the souls of the dead.

Harpokrates One of the Greek names for **Horus**, Harpokrates was regarded as the God of Silence and was depicted as a child with his finger on his mouth. In the form of **Hoor-paar-Kraat**, Harpokrates was considered special by occultist **Aleister Crowley**, who regarded himself as the "child of the gods".

Harsiesis In ancient Egyptian **mythology**, "Horus, the son of **Isis**" who, as a child, was protected from his evil uncle **Set** and grew up skilled in the techniques of warfare. He hoped to avenge **Osiris**'s death by decapitating the serpent Set and bringing his head to his mother Isis. However, Set recovered from his wounds and continued to be his sworn enemy until, after a lengthy confrontation, Horus was confirmed by the **gods** as "Lord of the Two Lands". See **Horus.**

Hart, Dr. Hornell (1888–1967) Leading American parapsychologist and sociologist who was a member of both the American and British **Society for Psychical Research**. He was interested in the nature of **apparitions** and also wrote on **astral projection**. His best-known book is *The Enigma of Survival: The Case for and against an After-Life* (1959).

Hartmann, Franz (1838–1912) German occultist and theosophist who for many years resided in the United States. He was the founder of the Order of the Esoteric Rose Croix and was also affiliated with a magical group that eventually became the **Ordo Templi Orientis**. His best-known books are *Magic, Black and White* and *In the Pronaos of the Temple of Wisdom*. See also **Occultism; Theosophy.**

Haruspex In ancient Rome, a priestly office connected with **divination**. The Haruspex inspected the liver, heart, and entrails of animals and also interpreted the movements of the flames in the altar-fire during ritual sacrifice. See also **Augur.**

Hashish Hallucinogenic resin made from the flowers of Indian **hemp**. It has powerful visionary qualities and can produce a euphoric **altered state of consciousness** when smoked or eaten. It is regarded as sacred in Tibet and is widely used as a sacrament in Central America. The Cuna Indians of Panama and the Cora Indians of Mexico both use it in their religious ceremonies. See also **Hallucination**.

Hasid Plural is Hasidim. From the Hebrew word meaning "pious". One who is a devotee of the mystical movement known as **Hasidism**.

Hasidism Jewish mystical movement founded in Poland by Israeli-born Eliezer **Ba'al Shem** Tov (c. 1700–1760). A **Hasid** is one who places total faith and trust in God and who interprets the "inner meaning" of the Law. Ba'al Shem believed in "serving God with joy" and his services were accompanied by wild, enthusiastic singing, frenzied dancing, and potent drink. The body of Ba'al Shem was said to tremble as he recited his prayers, and this type of **ecstasy** was transmitted charismatically to the congregation who would shout and cry out in joyful communion with God. Hasidism draws heavily on the kabbalistic teachings of **Isaac Luria**, and still continues as a movement within Judaism. The main centres of Hasidism today are New York and Israel. See also **Kabbalah**.

Hatha Yoga Form of **yoga** that teaches techniques relating to the physical control of the body. It makes use of special postures known as **asanas** and rhythmic breathing methods known as **pranayama**. Yoga recognizes the interrelatedness of mind and body, and the word *hatha* itself consists of two polar opposites: *ha*, meaning "sun" (masculine), and *tha*, meaning "moon" (feminine). Hatha Yoga is the best-known and most popular form of yoga.

Hathor In ancient Egyptian **mythology**, the queen of heaven. As a mother-goddess and cosmic **deity**, she personified love, beauty, and joy and was depicted in the form of a cow with the sun-disc between her horns. Her sanctuary was located at Dendera.

Hathors In ancient Egypt, a group of women, usually numbering seven, who had the **psychic** gift of predicting the future of a newborn child.

Hauntings Occasions and locations where **ghosts** or other discarnate entities present themselves, either as **apparitions** or through disturbances and noises associated with **poltergeist** phenomena. Such locations often include churches, graveyards, castles, rectories, hotels, and, occasionally, open spaces. The English **Ghost Club** investigates alleged hauntings.

Hayyoth In the **Kabbalah**, the four angelic beings of Ezekiel's vision who carry the Throne of Glory. They are also described as being like spiritual flashes of lightning that burst in four directions from the **Merkabah** (the throne in motion, when it becomes a "chariot") and in turn give rise to whirlwinds. The hayyoth are the source of the four cardinal **directions** and the four **elements**.

Hazel Tree with strong mythic associations. In Roman **mythology**, Apollo was said to have given a hazel rod to **Mercury** to enhance human "virtues", and the rods of Moses and Aaron were also made of hazel. In the Middle Ages hazel rods were thought to be effective against mischievous **fairies** and **demons** and, as a result, white magicians have traditionally fashioned their wands from hazel. Forked hazel twigs are also used by **dowsers**. See also **Magic, White**.

Healing by Touch See **Faith Healing**; **Laying-on-of-hands**; **Psychic Healing**.

Health Aura In **spiritualism** and **faith healing**, an **emanation** from the **etheric body**, which is perceived psychically as a pattern of straight lines (good health) or wavering lines (poor health). See also **Aura**.

Heathen From the Old English, *haethen*, one who has not been converted to Christianity. It particularly applies to cultures that worship a multiplicity of **gods** rather than one, and for whom ancestor spirits and **idols** also have special significance. It is virtually synonymous with **pagan**.

Heaven A mental construct of sacred archetypal images, which the disembodied human consciousness enters after its final separation from the physical body. Heaven is thus a mirror image of the most attractive and positive aspects of a culture or society, and epitomizes the spiritual "rewards" earned while on earth.

Heavenly Man In the **Kabbalah**, the archetypal spiritual being associated with **Kether**, the first sphere of the **Tree of Life**, which allows **God** to take a human form. Without the concept of the Heavenly Man, no attributes could ever be ascribed to God, for he transcends all limitations. The Heavenly Man is also known as **Adam Kadmon**.

Hecate In Greek **mythology**, a goddess with magical powers who took different forms. As a **lunar goddess** she was identified with **Artemis**, and as a goddess of the **Underworld** she was closely associated with **Persephone**. She had a frightening appearance, with snakes in her hair, and was attended by howling dogs. Annual festivals were held in her honour on the island of Aegina; there sacrifices were made and **magicians** and **witches** sought her aid.

Hedonism The belief that the pursuit of pleasure is the most important activity in life. **Pagan** worshipers who idolize sensuality and indulge in orgies personify the cult of hedonism. See also **Corybantes; Dionysus**.

Hegemon In the **Hermetic Order of the Golden Dawn**, a ceremonial role representing the Goddess of Truth and Justice. The Hegemon presides over the admittance of new candidates for the grade of **Neophyte**.

Heindel, Max (1862–1919) Pseudonym of theosophical writer Max Grashof. Heindel was influenced by **Rudolf Steiner** and claimed to be an authentic **Rosicrucian**. He founded the Rosicrucian Fellowship in California, which is unrelated to the ongoing AMORC Rosicrucian organization situated in San Jose. Heindel's main work was *The Rosicrucian Cosmoconception*. He died in 1919, but his wife Augusta continued the Rosicrucian Fellowship and was a strong advocate of his teachings until her own death in 1938.

Hekau In Egyptian **magic** and **mythology**, sacred **words of power** used to dispel **evil** and darkness. In the Egyptian **Books of the Dead**, specifically in the texts known as the ***Am Tuat*** and *The Book of Gates*, the Sun-god proceeds through the dungeons of the **Underworld** (the twelve hours of night) by uttering hekau that cast aside hostile forces. These include abysses of darkness, streams of boiling water, appalling smells and stenches, demonic serpents, and monsters of all shapes and sizes.

Hekhaloth The "heavenly halls" of **God**'s palace, glimpsed in visions by Jewish **mystics** as they ascended from one sphere to the next. The main text associated with this visionary activity is the ***Greater Hekhaloth***, which dates from the first century A.D.

Hel In Norse **mythology**, an earth-goddess who became the queen of the dead. She ruled over those who died of natural causes – for example, old age and disease – as distinct from those who were killed in battle and whose souls went to **Valhalla**.

Hell The domain of the wicked, after **death**. It is conceived variously as a ghostly **Underworld** (the Greek **Hades**); as a pit of fire and damnation (the Jewish **Gehenna**); or as a large communal grave (as in the

Mesopotamian afterworld). The Christian hell appears to derive from the Jewish vision of eternal fire and torment, and the Islamic vision of hell similarly resembles it. Hell typically personifies the most negative and destructive images projected by a culture and is regarded by **occultists** as an accumulation of negative **thought-forms**, or images, within the mythic realms of the unconscious mind.

Hell Fire Club Eighteenth-century satanic club, founded by **Sir Francis Dashwood,** whose members gathered at Medmenham on the Thames. The group sang blasphemous hymns and conducted orgies in chambers excavated beneath a hill, and within the ruins of a disused abbey.

Helpers, Spirit In **spiritualism, discarnate** entities who are anxious to assist the living. They are often thought to have departed recently from an earthly existence themselves, and therefore still have bonds to the **earth plane** of existence.

Hemp, Indian Popular name for the hallucinogenic plant *cannabis*. It has been associated by some authorities with the mystical Indian sacrament **soma**, although the ethnomycologist **R. Gordon Wasson** believes that soma is in fact ***Amanita muscaria***. According to Mahayana Buddhist tradition, **Gautama Buddha** lived on one Indian hemp seed a day as he progressed towards spiritual **enlightenment**. He is sometimes depicted with "soma leaves" in his begging bowl. See also **Hallucination; Hashish.**

Henbane *Hyoscyamus niger*, a poisonous, narcotic plant associated with **witchcraft** and **sorcery**. Henbane contains alkaloids which can cause the illusion that one has transformed into an animal, and it has traditionally been regarded as the active component of **Circe**'s magical potion. It is also possible that the **Delphic Oracle** made her prophecies after inhaling smoke from burning henbane seeds. See also **Flying Ointments; Hallucination; Lycanthropy.**

Hepatoscopy Form of **divination** in which the liver of a sacrificed sheep was inspected and diagnosed by **augurs**. This was a common practice among the Etruscans, Hittites, and Babylonians.

Heptad In **numerology**, the number **seven.**

Hera In Greek **mythology**, the queen of the **gods** and **heaven**. Hera was both the sister and wife of **Zeus** and the daughter of **Kronos** and **Rhea**. Hera was a jealous wife and was hostile to Zeus's many mistresses and illegitimate offspring. She was, nevertheless, perceived as the goddess of women and childbirth, and especially of marriage.

Heracles Also Hercules. In Greco-Roman **mythology**, a legendary hero who achieved great fame for his bravery and strength. The son of **Zeus**, Heracles had a mortal mother – Alcmene – and as a result attracted the jealous wrath of Zeus's wife Hera, who sent two serpents to destroy him when he was still an infant. Heracles survived by strangling them. Hera nevertheless persisted with her interference and one day, when Heracles had grown up and become a married man, she filled him with madness and rage, causing him to murder his children. Heracles consulted the **Delphic Oracle** and was told to go into service with King Eurystheus to atone for this wicked deed. As a result, he performed the twelve labours of Heracles, which included slaying the dreaded monster, **Hydra.**

Herbalism See **Herbal Medicine.**

Herbal Medicine Tradition of medicine linked at different stages of its development to **witchcraft, astrology**, and **alchemy**. Herbal medicine dates back at least as far as

3000 B.C., when the Chinese Emperor Shenung compiled a major work on herbs, titled *Pen Tsao*. In it he praised the healing properties of ginseng, cinnamon, and the bark of the mulberry tree. The ancient Egyptians valued olive oil, cloves, myrrh, and castor oil, and developed a wide knowledge of "essential oils" for curative and embalming purposes. The ancient Greeks also valued herbal medicines, and Pliny's *Natural History* records that herbalism was endorsed by the great physician Hippocrates.

Possibly because of its **pagan** associations and frequent references to the healing deities **Apollo** and **Asklepios**, much of the herbal knowledge that filtered through to the Middle Ages from ancient Greece was discarded as non-Christian and linked to witchcraft and **magic**. In England, Nicholas Culpeper (1616–1654) combined astrology, magic, and herbalism in his work *The English Physician Enlarged* (1653); while the Swiss herbalist and alchemist **Paracelsus** (1493–1541) classified plants according to the colour symbolism of the flowers. Paracelsus also believed in the curative properties of such metals as **mercury** and antimony.

One of the most curious aspects of herbs in the Middle Ages, however, is that some herbal concoctions were supposed to bestow magic powers. One herbal recipe dating from around 1600 describes how olive oil, rose water, and marigolds could be mixed together and used to obtain a glimpse of the **fairies**: "The roses and the marigolds are to be gathered towards the east, and the water thereof to be made of pure spring water. Put the washed oil into a vial glass and add hollyhock buds, marigold flowers, wild thyme tops and flowers, young hazel buds, and the grass of a fairy throne. The thyme must be gathered near the side of a hill where fairies used to be. Set the glass in the sun for three days so that the ingredients can become incorporated. Then put away for use ..."

Modern herbalism has since become a systematic branch of naturopathy, and quaint folk-recipes like this one no longer form part of herbal medicine. However, some contemporary herbalists believe that modern doctors are unjustly predjudiced against their traditional remedies, and periodic accusations of "witchcraft" and "superstition" are still made against herbal practitioners.

Hercules See **Heracles.**

Heresy From the Greek *hairesis*, meaning "choice", a heresy is a religious teaching regarded as contrary to, or deviating from, the accepted and established form of doctrine. It is most frequently associated with the Christian religion, especially in regard to the Church's persecution of unorthodox groups of believers (**Albigenses, Cathars, witches**, et al.) during the Middle Ages. It also applies to the condemnation of **Gnostic** sects by orthodox Church Fathers such as Irenaeus. However, heresy has arisen in other religions as well. In ancient Egypt, the pharaoh Akhenaten sought to suppress the established cult of Amun – thus making himself a heretic – and in **Islam** the Sufi mystic Mansur al-Hallaj was crucified in Baghdad in 922 for linking himself with **God.** See also **Inquisition.**

Heretic See **Heresy.**

Hermaphrodite A bisexual human being or animal. In **mysticism** and **occultism**, the symbol of the human hermaphrodite or **androgyne** has special significance because it represents the fusion of opposite polarities, and therefore characterizes a major development on the spiritual path to transcending duality. The **Tarot** card of ***The Fool*** shows a hermaphroditic figure walking over a cliff-edge – the cliff representing manifested reality – and embracing universal "space". The card thus symbolizes the mystical act of surrendering one's individuality, or **self**, in transcendental union with the **Godhead.** See also **Dualism; Harmony of Opposites.**

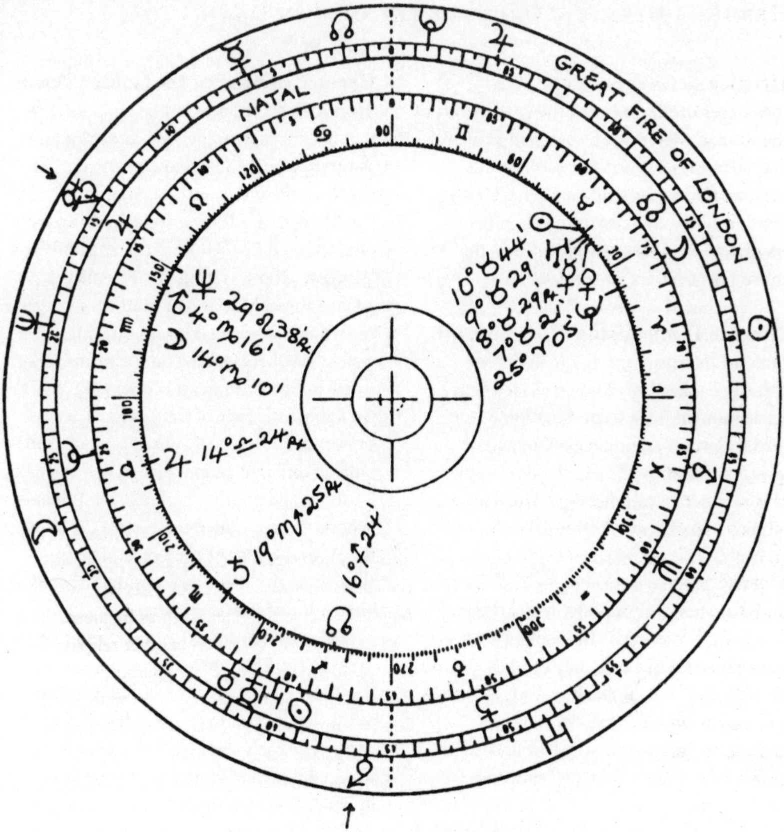

WILLIAM LILLY
May 1, 1602

HOROSCOPE: The horoscope of astrologer William Lilly, who is said to have successfully predicted the Great Fire of London. Lilly's horoscope reveals an aptitude for psychic intuition. On the day of the Fire, Lilly's Mars/Pluto aspect was placed in the midpoint of his Sun/Uranus/Mercury/Venus conjunction and Saturn.

Hermes In Greek **mythology**, the messenger of the **gods** and the counterpart of the Roman **Mercury**. Hermes had many roles and attributes. He was god of the wind, oratory, trade affairs, and athletics. He also conducted the souls of the dead on their passage to the **Underworld**, and was the protector of sacrificial animals.

Hermes Trismegistus "Thrice-greatest Hermes", the principal figure in the mystical literature collectively known as **Hermetica**. He is thought to be a combination of the Greek **Hermes** and the Egyptian god of wisdom, **Thoth**; and takes the role, in the Hermetica, of a prophet or spiritual leader who can save the world from **evil**.

Hermetica Collection of mystical tracts and dialogues – primarily Greek in origin – including references to the healing gods **Asklepios** and **Imhotep** and also **Isis, Osiris**, and **Thoth** (or Tat). The literature as it exists today consists collectively of fourteen sermons by **Poimandres** or Pymander ("the shepherd of men", and their "spiritual leader"), the so-called "Perfect Sermon" of Asklepios, twenty-seven excerpts from the collection of the fifth-century writer Stobaeus, and a selection of fragments from the Church Fathers relating to the **mystery** tradition. There are several translations of the **Hermetica** in English, including those of John Everard (1650), J. D. Chambers (1882), and G. R. S. Mead (1906).

Hermetic Axiom Axiom ascribed to **Hermes Trismegistus**, which describes the relationship between **macrocosm and microcosm**. It is expressed, "As above, so below."

Hermetic Chain In **Theosophy**, a succession of spiritual teachers who have maintained the **mystery** tradition and kept the **esoteric** teachings accessible for those trained to receive them.

Hermetic Order of the Golden Dawn Magical order founded in England in 1888 that has strongly influenced contemporary Western magical beliefs and practices. The rituals of the order were based originally on five Masonic grades discovered in the papers of a deceased English **Rosicrucian. Dr. Wynn Westcott**, who was himself a **Freemason**, asked **Samuel MacGregor Mathers** to expand the material to form a more complete occult system. Mathers worked on the formation of a new body of rituals and chose as his basis the kabbalistic **Tree of Life**, using its ten **sephiroth** (or levels of consciousness) as the basis of different ceremonial grades. Westcott, Mathers, and another occultist, **Dr. William Woodman**, appointed themselves the heads of the Second Order of the Golden Dawn (known as the "Red Rose and the Cross of Gold": ***Rosae Rubae et Aurea Crucis***), which in effect governed the first seven grades on the Tree of Life. The other three, representing the Third Order, were symbolically linked to the Trinity and were said to be the domain of **Secret Chiefs** – spiritual masters who would guide the Order and provide Mathers, in particular, with magical inspiration.

The first Golden Dawn Temple, that of Isis-Urania, was opened in London in 1888. By 1896 there was a Temple of Osiris in Weston-Super-Mare, a Temple of Horus in Bradford, a Temple of Amen-Ra in Edinburgh, and a Temple sacred to Ahathoor in Paris. The names of these temples indicate the strong influence of Egyptian mythology which, along with Rosicrucian, Greek, Celtic, Enochian, and some Hindu elements, characterized the rituals.

The Golden Dawn attracted many notable occultists, including poet **William Butler Yeats; A. E. Waite**, originator of a popular **Tarot** pack and the leading occult scholar of his day; and **Aleister Crowley**, the famous, and later notorious, "Great Beast 666". As Mathers became increasingly autocratic, the order began to fragment; with Mather's death in 1918, the original Golden Dawn splintered completely. However, other derivative groups emerged, including the Stella Matutina. Between 1937 and 1941, **Israel Regardie**, a one-time secretary to Aleister Crowley, published the complete rituals of the Stella Matutina in four volumes under the title *The Golden Dawn*. These books constitute the most complete magical system produced in modern times. See also **Magic, Enochian**.

Hermetic Teachings The doctrines of the **Hermetica**. The term is also applied to the Western **mystery tradition** in a general and non-specific way.

Hermit, The In the **Tarot**, the card representing the lonely ascent of the **mystic**, who climbs the cosmic mountain following the lamp of his own inner light. **Occultists** regard *The Hermit* as a form of the "Ancient of Days", the wise, patriarchal figure who shuns outward appearances (he wears a dark cloak) in favour of the sacred, mystical reality. In Western **magic**, which combines the Tarot paths of the **Major Arcana** with the ten **sephiroth** on the **Tree of Life**, the path of *The Hermit* connects **Tiphareth** and **Chesed**.

Hesperus The name given to the planet **Venus** after sunset. It is also known as the Evening Star.

Hex In **witchcraft**, a **spell** or **curse** inflicted upon a person or property. The term derives from the German *Hexse*, "a wizard". In Pennsylvania, where the art of hexing became popular, there are still **hexters** who make **amulets** and **talismans** to ward off evil influences.

Hexagram In the *I Ching*, one of sixty-four patterns of long and short lines (decided by throwing yarrow stalks) that have different divinatory interpretations. A long or "firm" line is said to be **yang**, or masculine; and a short or "yielding" line is **yin**, or feminine. The four main Hexagrams are called *Ch'ien* (consisting of six yang lines); *K'un* (consisting of six yin lines); *T'ai* (three yin lines above three yang lines); and *P'i* (three yang lines above three yin lines). See also **Divination**.

Hexagram In Western **magic** and **mysticism**, a symbol known as "the Star of David". It consists of two superimposed triangles, one whose apex faces up, the other down. The hexagram thus embodies the **Hermetic Axiom**, "As above, so below". The triangle that points upward is regarded as masculine, that which points down as feminine. In Western magic many **rituals** involve the inscription of the hexagram with the magical sword. Hexagram rituals may be used to "invoke" or "banish" each of the planetary forces, and are regarded by **occultists** as having considerable magical power. The six points of the hexagram are sometimes shown surmounting the kabbalistic **Tree of Life**, with the uppermost point in **Daath** and the lowest in **Yesod**. The sacred **god-name Ararita** is often used in hexagram rituals.

Hexter A "hex-doctor": one who has magical antidotes for **spells** and **curses**. See also **Hex**.

Heywood, Rosalind (1895–1980) Author and broadcaster with a longstanding interest in **psychical research**. In 1938 she became a member of the **Society for Psychical Research** in London, and also put herself forward as a subject for medical tests on the **psychedelic** effects of **mescaline**. Her best-known book is *The Sixth Sense* (1959), published in the United States under the title *Beyond the Reach of Sense*.

Hierarchy of Adepts In many mystical and occult groups, the idea of a hierarchy of spiritual **masters** has been popular. In **Theosophy** these adepts are often thought to be discarnate lamas or Tibetan priests, skilled in **esoteric** lore. In Western **magic**, some

occultists, especially **MacGregor Mathers** and **Aleister Crowley**, have claimed privileged contact with "masters" or **Secret Chiefs**. Invariably, recourse to an occult hierarchy is made when a particular mystical teaching is given to followers and requires endorsement from a "higher source". See also **Mysticism**; **Occultism**.

Hieratic That which is consecrated by **priests** for a sacred ritual use. The term also applies to the cursive writing employed by the priests of ancient Egypt.

Hiereus Ceremonial role within the **Hermetic Order of the Golden Dawn**, personifying the dark aspects of the ancient Egyptian god **Horus**. Hiereus is described in the order's rituals as representing "the Terrible and Avenging God at the Confines of Matter, on the borders of the **Qlippoth**". He guards the sacred mysteries from **evil** but is himself "enthroned upon matter and robed in Darkness". Hiereus thus defines the border between good and evil in magical rituals. See also **Magic, Ceremonial**.

Hieroglyphics Sacred inscriptions in the form of pictorial motifs. In ancient Egyptian **mythology** hieroglyphics were regarded as "the speech of the gods" and decorated the walls of tombs and temples.

Hieroglyphs In **spiritualism**, writings or scrawled expressions attributed to a **discarnate** entity and produced at a **seance** by a **psychic medium** while that person is in a state of **trance**. See also **Direct Writing**.

Hierology The study of sacred writings. The term is commonly used with reference to the ancient Egyptian texts.

Hierophant From the Greek *hieros*, meaning "holy", one who serves as a **priest** and interprets the sacred and divine mysteries. In the **Hermetic Order of the Golden Dawn**, the Hierophant is a member of the Second Order.

Hierophant, The In the **Tarot**, a card representing the divine authority of the **priest**, who personifies wisdom and mercy and acquires these qualities from mystical inspiration. In Western **magic**, which combines the Tarot paths of the **Major Arcana** with the ten **sephiroth** of the kabbalistic **Tree of Life**, the path of *The Hierophant* connects **Chesed** and **Chokmah**.

High Dream See **Dream, High**.

Higher Self One's spiritual **self**, realized fully through **meditation** as the divine essence that links each human being to God. See also **Cosmic Consciousness**.

High God See **God, High**.

High Magic See **Magic, High**.

High Priestess, The In the **Tarot**, a card representing the virginal lunar priestess who has had no union with a male deity. In a mystical sense, she has the potential for motherhood (manifestation and form), but has not yet realized the possibility of giving birth to myriad forms within the **cosmos**. Her virginity and innocence symbolize her purity and place her mythologically above the **Abyss**, which separates the Trinity and the manifested universe. In Western **magic**, which combines the Tarot paths of the **Major Arcana** with the ten **sephiroth** of the **Tree of Life**, the path of *The High Priestess* connects **Tiphareth** and **Kether**. *The High Priestess* is a transcendental aspect of the Roman goddess **Diana**. See also **Lunar Goddesses**.

High-scoring Subject In experimental studies of **extrasensory perception**, a subject who succeeds in scoring above the laws of chance and who is therefore credited with **paranormal abilities**.

Hill, Arthur (1872–1951) British writer and psychical researcher who assisted **Sir Oliver Lodge** in researching spirit **mediums.** He was a member of the Council for Psychical Research in London between 1927 and 1935, until ill health forced him to resign. Among his many books on the paranormal are *New Evidences in Psychical Research* (1911), *Spiritualism, Its History, Phenomena and Doctrine* (1918), and *Psychical Science and Religious Belief* (1928). See also **Psychical Research.**

Hilton, Walter (d. 1396) Fourteenth-century English **mystic** who was a member of an important group of mystical thinkers that also included **Julian of Norwich** and Richard Rolle. Hilton produced a tract titled *Epistle to a Devout Man in a Temporal Estate*, which offered principles of spiritual guidance to those who were affluent; and for a time he was wrongly regarded as the author of the *Imitation of Christ*. He wrote sensitively on contemplation, love, and grace, but was also very practical, offering guidance for spiritual transformation through contemplation and **prayer.**

Hinayana Buddhism There are two major forms of **Buddhism**, Hinayana (the so-called "Lesser Way") and **Mahayana** (the "Greater Way"). The division derives from a council of Buddhists at Patna during the reign of the Indian King Asoka (c. 264–228 B.C.) and represents the distinction between doctrinal and esoteric Buddhism, respectively. Hinayana Buddhism stresses close adherence to the text of the **Pali** Canon and is more concerned with the moral precepts of **Gautama Buddha** than with the concept of **bodhisattvas** found in the Mahayana tradition. Hinayana Buddhism is prevalent in Burma, Thailand, Vietnam, Laos and Cambodia.

Hinduism One of the great world religions, practised mainly in India but also with large numbers of devotees in the West. Hinduism identifies **Brahma** as the absolute creator **deity** who is the supreme reality behind manifested forms. The other two chief deities making up the triad (known as the trimurti) are **Vishnu**, the preserver, and **Shiva**, the destroyer. Vishnu is believed to incarnate through different **avatars**, one of whom was **Krishna.**

Two of the main teachings of Hinduism are that people earn **karma** as a result of positive or negative actions in the world, and that these actions determine consequent incarnations as the soul transmigrates. These doctrines notwithstanding, the manifested world is regarded as **maya**, or illusion, and the essential aim of Hinduism is mystical **transcendence.** The various paths of **yoga** have been developed for this purpose.

Hinduism is an extremely complex religion and involves many minor deities as well as the major ones, in addition to a host of **devils, demons, spirits,** and **ghosts.** Both **Jainism** and **Buddhism** were reform movements that originated within Hinduism. See also **Transmigration.**

Hippomancy Form of **divination,** practised among the Celts, in which the gait of white horses was symbolically interpreted.

Hob-goblin A mischievous **imp** or **goblin** who produces fear and apprehension, especially in children.

Hocus-pocus A derogatory term used to describe erroneous beliefs, also used with reference to sleight-of-hand deception. It is thought to derive from the Eucharistic phrase *Hoc est corpus*, "This is my body".

Hod The eighth **emanation** or **sephirah** on the kabbalistic **Tree of Life.** In Western **magic** Hod is associated with the planet **Mercury** and represents intellect and rational thought. It also represents the structuring and measuring capacities of the mind as opposed to the emotional and intuitional aspects, which are ascribed to **Netzach**. Hod has no exact parallel in the **Tarot**, but is closely linked to the card ***Judgment***, ascribed to the path between Hod and **Malkuth**. See also **Kabbalah; Sephiroth.**

Hodgson, Richard (1855–1905) Australian-born psychical researcher and psychologist who worked closely with **William James, James Hyslop,** and **Henry Sidgwick** in pioneering **parapsychology**. He was sent to India by the British **Society for Psychical Research** to investigate **Madame Helena Blavatsky**, and concluded that her mediumistic claims were fraudulent. However, he later endorsed **Mrs. Leonore Piper** as an authentic **medium**, and believed that she was indeed in touch with **discarnate** spirits. See also **Psychical Research.**

Hogmanay Scottish name for New Year's Eve, an occasion celebrated with drinking and merriment. Hogmanay is a reminder of the cycles of the seasons; ushering out the past year and welcoming the new one which lies ahead.

Holistic Health Branch of medicine which holds that health stems from the balance of body, mind, and spirit, and that emotional and stress-related factors account for a large proportion of disease. A holistic doctor therefore evaluates the whole person, not merely the physical symptoms of disease, in guiding the patient back to health. Holistic medicine often draws on principles of oriental medicine, for example **acupuncture**, shiatsu, and **meditation.**

Holle Also Holda. In German **folklore**, the queen of the **elves** and **witches** who was also a goddess of the sky. She caused showers of snow by shaking her feather bed, and rain would fall when she washed her veil. Holle was often depicted as a wrinkled **hag** who rode in the sky during thunderstorms.

Holt, Henry (1840–1926) Publisher and author who became an authority on **psychical research**. In 1914 he produced a book titled *The Cosmic Relations*, which brought together many of the diverse strands of research into **paranormal** phenomena, especially those previously scattered through the annals of the British **Society for Psychical Research**. Holt later expanded this work and retitled it *The Cosmic Relations and Immortality*. His company published the *Books of Charles Fort* in 1941 but has since become a major general publishing house, without a paranormal focus. See also **Fort, Charles.**

Holy That which is sacred or divine, originates in **God** or a **pantheon** of **deities**, or is put aside for worship. It also has the connotation of being awe-inspiring and **transcendent**.

Holy Grail The **cup** used by Jesus Christ at the Last Supper and which, according to legend, was brought to Britain by Joseph of Arimathea. The quest for the Holy Grail was central to the legendary exploits of the knights of King Arthur, although in this capacity is seems to have been a symbol of perfection and virtue.

Holy Guardian Angel In Western **magic**, the spark of **God** that is the essence of every man and woman. Knowledge of the holy guardian angel is synonymous with **cosmic consciousness.**

Holy Seal The scar left on the body after the act of complete castration. In initiatory rites of **sexual magic** the Holy Seal may be accorded special significance.

Holzer, Hans (1920–) Austrian-born American author and psychical researcher who has written extensively on occult and paranormal phenomena. He has worked as a freelance writer and drama critic and holds degrees from Vienna and Columbia

Universities. Best known for his investigative studies of **ghosts**, **apparitions**, and **psychic photography**, he has narrated several film documentaries and is research director on the New York Committee for the Investigation of Paranormal Occurrences. Among his best-known books are *ESP and You, The Truth About Witchcraft*, and *Psychic Photography: Threshold of a New Science*. See also **Psychical Research**.

Home, Daniel Dunglas (1833–1886) Remarkable spiritualist and **psychic medium** who claimed that he possessed the power to **levitate** at will. Home was born in Scotland but went to Connecticut with his aunt when he was nine. As a young boy he was believed to be possessed by **devils** because of **poltergeist** activities that occurred in his presence after his mother's death; attempts to exorcise him failed. Later, as his reputation as a psychic medium grew, he held **seances** in full light and allegedly caused tables and chairs to move without any visible cause. He was also said to materialize spirit-hands and play musical instruments without touching them.

In 1855 he went to England, where he received a mixed reception. William Thackeray and John Ruskin admired him, but Robert Browning was unimpressed and wrote a scathing poem titled *Mr Sludge, the Medium* after watching him perform. Home later demonstrated his talents before the Czar of Russia and the German Kaiser, but the Roman Catholic Church saw fit to expel him in 1864 as a "sorcerer". Home's most remarkable psychic feat occurred in 1868 when, at the home of Lord Adare in Buckingham Gate, London, he is said to have levitated out of a third-floor window and then entered through another. This event had three witnesses: Lord Lindsey, Captain Charles Wynne, and Lord Adare himself.

Home was later "tested" experimentally by the psychical researcher **Sir William Crookes** who, in 1871, announced that he was convinced of Home's authenticity. Home has an almost unique reputation among mediums in that, throughout his career, he was never caught cheating or using his powers to deceive. He accepted gifts, but desisted from charging fees. As such he remains one of the most impressive figures in the history of **psychical research**. He wrote two books: *My Life* (1863) and *Lights and Shadows of Spiritualism* (1877).

Homeopathy Philosophy of natural health developed by the German doctor and scholar Samuel Hahnemann (1755–1843). The word derives from the Greek *homoion pathos*, "treating disease with the same substance". In general, homeopathic medical care is characterized by the belief that "like can be used to treat like" and that a medicine which produces disease symptoms in a healthy body can also produce a curative effect in an ailing one. Hahnemann experimented with aconite, strychnine, and belladonna and came to the view that potent poisons could be used in small doses to ward off disease by stimulating the body's natural self-healing processes. Hahnemann also believed that disease was a result of imbalance in the body, not a cause of it; and he did not differentiate between mind and body in classifying symptoms. For this reason he can be regarded as a pioneer of psychosomatic medicine. His major writings are included in *The Organon of Medicine* (1810) and *Chronic Diseases* (1828).

Homunculus In **Alchemy**, a creature comparable to the **golem**, which was artificially created by magical means. Sperm was placed in a sealed vessel together with other obscure ingredients and incubated by being buried in horse manure for forty days. At the end of this period the embryo would begin to appear. Medieval **magicians** believed one could obtain a child in this way, but at the most it would only attain twelve inches in height. It was advisable to keep the homunculus in a glass jar, for this was its familiar environment. The alchemist **Paracelsus** claimed that he was successful in creating a homunculus.

Hoodoo Form of cult-magic, which originated in Africa and bears some similarities to **voodoo**. In Hoodoo magic, which was popular among blacks on the plantations in the southern United States, **charms** were worn to bring good luck. They could also be used to direct misfortune against an enemy.

Hoor-paar-Kraat Form of **Horus** accorded special significance by the occultist **Aleister Crowley** in his assumed role as Lord of the **New Aeon**. Crowley identified this form of Horus, the twin of **Ra-Hoor-Khuit**, as symbolic of the "solar sexual energies" that were part of his own idiosyncratic form of **sexual magic**.

Hope, William (1863–1933) **Psychic medium** who claimed to have developed a technique for photographing **spirits** and **discarnate** entities. Although he was exposed by **Harry Price** as a fraud, many spiritualists continued to believe that he possessed genuine psychic powers.

Hopkins, Matthew (d. 1647) Notorious self-styled "**witch**-finder" who was the son of a Puritan minister and mounted witch-hunts in Suffolk, Norfolk, Essex, and Huntingdonshire. His career began when he discovered members of a local **coven**, searched their bodies for the **Devil's mark**, and realized that he could earn a living by reporting witches to the local authorities. Hopkins subsequently decided to purge the whole of East Anglia of witchcraft and went from village to village seeking those accused of "bewitching" their fellows. Hopkins employed the notorious technique of floating witches in a pond. Because water was associated with Christian baptism, it was assumed that the pond would reject a witch and make her float. A person innocent of witchcraft would sink – possibly drowning in the process. Hopkins was at his peak of activity between 1644 and 1646, but was finally forced by public pressure to desist from his brutal campaign. It is thought that he caused the deaths of at least two hundred people.

Hor The name by which the ancient Egyptians referred to the **god** better known by his Latin name, **Horus**.

Horary Astrology See **Astrology, Horary**.

Horbiger, Hans See **Cosmic Ice**.

Hor-m-akhet The ancient Egyptian name for the famous Great Sphinx at El Gizeh in Egypt; the Greek name is **Harmakhis**. The sphinx, which combined a lion's body with a man's head, represented the mystical power of the Pharaoh. The Great Sphinx is fashioned in stone, dates from c. 2900 B.C., and measures 58 meters (189 feet) in length. See also **Sphinx**.

Horned God Symbol of male sexuality in **witchcraft**. The Horned God is usually identified as the Greek **god** of Nature, **Pan**, who presided over woods and forests and played his magical pipes. Part man, part goat, Pan was fond of lechery and frolicked with the wood-nymphs. The Horned God is also identified by some witches as **Cernunnos**, a Celtic deity combining the attributes of a bull, a man, a serpent, and a fish.

Horoscope In **astrology**, a **figure** or map of the heavens, encompassing 360 degrees which, for a specific moment in time, identifies the positions of the **planets** and the **sun** in different **signs** of the **zodiac**. Astrologers interpret the relationships or **aspects** between the planets and Earth as favourable or unfavourable influences pertaining to the specific moment for which the horoscope is cast. While the most significant moment in a person's life is the time when he or she first draws breath, horoscopes may also be cast for occasions other than one's time and date of birth. Horoscopes may be drawn up to ascertain favourable conditions for important future events – a marriage, birth of a new company, travel overseas – and may even be cast to determine the likely political future of a nation. In this instance the date of birth of the nation dates from its independence or date of constitution.

Horoscope, Natal In **astrology**, a **horoscope** of the heavens for the precise moment when the person first drew breath. It is also known as a **nativity** or **geniture**.

Horoscope, Progressed In **astrology**, a **horoscope** cast on the basis of "one day for one year", so that it is drawn up for a date that is as many days after the person's date of birth as that person's age in years.

Horoscope, Solar Revolution In **astrology**, a **horoscope** cast for the moment in any year when the **sun** reaches the exact longitude it occupies in the **radix**.

Horse Brasses Amulets attached to the harness and trappings of a horse in order to ward off evil influences. Because they were shiny, they were said to deflect the hostile power of the **evil-eye**.

Horse-shoe, Lucky Good-luck **charm**, often nailed above doorways to ward off **evil** forces. It is made of **iron**, traditionally regarded as a powerful protection against **witchcraft**. Its crescent shape is reminiscent of lunar worship.

Horse-whisperer In British **witchcraft**, a person thought to possess the magical ability to communicate with horses and make them do one's bidding. The **words of power** and magical **charms** used to bring about these results were jealously guarded secrets.

Horus Latinized form of the Egyptian god **Hor**, who originally was a falcon-headed **deity** with the **sun** and **moon** for his eyes. As the pharaohs came to identify themselves with **Ra**, Horus became associated with the sun. At different times, Horus was considered to be the son of **Atum**, **Ra**, and **Osiris**. He is best known for his role in Osirian mythology, where he avenged the death of his father by finally overcoming **Set**.

Host In Christianity, the sacred bread regarded as the "body" of Christ in a Communion service. It symbolizes Christ's personal sacrifice on behalf of humankind (from the Latin *hostia*, meaning "a sacrificial victim"). In various accounts of **black magic** and the **satanic mass**, the host is desecrated.

Houdini, Harry (1874–1926) American escape artist and conjuror who attained fame by escaping from ropes and handcuffs. He was highly critical of **spiritualism** and replicated several alleged "phenomena" by mechanical means. Before his death he made a pact with his wife that he would try to communicate with her by code, and she attended a number of **seances** in order to receive messages from him. The **psychic medium** Arthur Ford claimed to have contacted Houdini's spirit, but charges of fraud were made and the matter was never satisfactorily resolved. Houdini was fond of exposing spiritualists, as his book *Miracle Mongers and their Methods* (1920) demonstrates.

Houngan In **voodoo**, a **priest**. The word derives from *gan*, "chief", and *houn*, "of the spirits", in the language of the Fons people of western Africa.

Houris In **Islam**, dark-eyed virgins who dwell in **Paradise**. The **Qur'an** mentions that each deceased person who enters **heaven** is allowed seventy-two houris to attend to their needs.

Hours In **astrology**, each hour is important because planetary positions vary as the earth rotates on its axis and moves around the sun. In a **horoscope**, each two-hour period of the day is known as a different **house** and attracts different **aspects**. See **Astrology, Horary**.

House In **astrology**, one twelfth of the total circle of the heavens. This section – or arc – of the **horoscope** spans thirty degrees and covers two hours in time as the earth rotates on its axis. The term "house" is differentiated from **sign**, which refers to the specific twelvefold division of the **zodiac** commencing with **Aries** and culminating with **Pisces**.

Houston, Jean For over thirty years American psychologist and philosopher Dr. Jean Houston has lectured and conducted seminars around the world. Renowned for her work in exploring myth and transformation, her approach also encompasses music, meditation, visualisation, movement and dance. A past-president of the Association for Humanistic Psychology, Houston is the author of numerous books, articles and instructional audio tapes. Her principal publications include *The Possible Human*, *The Search for the Beloved* and *The Hero and the Goddess*. She also co-authored *Mind Games and Listening to the Body* with her husband, Robert Masters.

Hsiang-ming shih In Taoism, a **soothsayer** or **fortune-teller** who divines the future by means of the hexagrams of the *I Ching*.

Hsin In **Taoism**, the intuitive or spiritual mind. *Hsin Chai*, meaning "the fasting of the mind", represents the transcendence of mind and the attainment of **cosmic consciousness**.

Hubbard, Lafayette Ronald (1911–1986) The founder of **Scientology** and **Dianetics**, Hubbard claimed extrasensory powers, including knowledge of past incarnations, and appears to have derived many of his Scientology principles from **occultism** and science fiction. In the late 1930s and early 1940s he wrote a succession of serials for the pulp magazine *Astounding Science Fiction* under both his own name and as "René Lafayette". He was also involved with the occult group **Ordo Templi Orientis** and worked with one of **Aleister Crowley**'s followers, Jack Parsons, in 1945. Hubbard's best-known book is *Dianetics: The Modern Science of Mental Health*. See also **Clear**; **Engram**.

Huebner, Louise American witch who claims to be the "Official Witch of Los Angeles County" and once cast a **spell** to increase the sexual vitality of the region. She is a regular newspaper columnist, casts **horoscopes**, and gives psychic readings. She has published a book, *Power Through Witchcraft*, and has recorded a record album, *Seduction Through Witchcraft*.

Huldra In Norse **mythology**, a wood-nymph or **fairy** who appeared in the form of a beautiful woman, but had a concealed tail. Huldras were said to play enchanting music that had an air of melancholy.

Human Potential Movement Term given to the movement that arose in the late 1960s and early 1970s as humanistic psychologists and other social thinkers began systematically to explore the potential of human consciousness. This included research into the mind/body relationship, the study of left- and right-brain hemisphere functions, **peak experiences**, and mystical states of consciousness. To some extent, the movement combines elements of the aftermath of the **psychedelic** era of the 1960s with the revival of interest in Eastern philosophies and **holistic health**. It has strong links with

transpersonal psychology and with the activities of the **Esalen Institute** in California.

Human Signs In **astrology**, those signs of the **zodiac** whose motifs have a human form: **Gemini**, **Virgo**, and **Aquarius** (**Sagittarius** is sometimes included).

Hun In **Taoism**, the "heavenly" part of the soul. This is distinguished from the earthly part, **p'o**. Hun and p'o were deemed to be positive and negative, respectively.

Hun-tun In ancient Chinese **cosmology**, the force of **chaos** – personified as an emperor-god – who presided in the universe before the orderly and dynamic forces of **yin** and **yang** came into being.

Hurkos, Peter (1911–1988) Dutch seaman and manual worker who developed psychic powers following an accident. In 1943, while he was engaged in painting the walls of a school, Hurkos fell from a ladder and was unconscious in a hospital for three days. As he lay in bed with a fractured skull, he spontaneously accused the patient next to him of being a "bad man" who had sold a gold watch bequeathed to him by his deceased father. These events turned out to be correct, and Hurkos sensed that he had mysteriously acquired paranormal faculties. He later collaborated with police in Britain and the United States to try to solve murder cases, and to trace the location of missing persons through **extrasensory perception**.

Hutin, Serge (1929–) French occult author, born in Paris, who has written widely on **alchemy**, secret societies, **Gnosticism**, **Freemasonry**, **reincarnation**, and **astrology**. One of his best-known books is *Astrology: Science or Superstition?* published in Belgium in 1970 and translated into English in 1972.

Hutton, Ronald Currently Professor of History at the University of Bristol, Dr. Hutton is a leading authority on the history of **witchcraft** and **pagan** traditions in Britain. His publications include *The Pagan Religions of the Ancient British Isles* and his widely acclaimed *Triumph of the Moon* – the definitive history of modern witchcraft.

Huxley, Aldous (1894–1963) English novelist and essayist who, in the latter part of his life, became interested in **altered states of consciousness**, Eastern philosophies, **parapsychology**, and unusual health-care treatments. He wrote *The Devils of Loudun* (1952), describing alleged satanic **possession** of nuns in a seventeenth-century Ursuline convent (see **Grandier, Urbain**); and in *The Doors of Perception* (1954) and *Heaven and Hell* (1956) Huxley described his mystical experiences with **mescaline**. Huxley also published articles defending **extrasensory perception** and **psi** phenomena. A volume bringing together his writings on psychedelics and the visionary experience was published under the title *Moksha* in 1977. See also **Psychedelic**.

Huysmans, Joris-Karl (1848–1907) French novelist, of Dutch ancestry, who wrote a number of decadent novels including *A Rebours* and *Là-bas*, which includes a description of a **black mass**. He was fascinated by the satanic crimes of **Gilles de Rais**, and also became involved in the magical feud between **Joseph-Antoine Boullan** and **Stanislas de Guaita**. Boulan features in *Là-bas* as the character Dr. Johannes.

Hydesville Hamlet in New York state where **spiritualism** was born, with the mysterious rappings of the **Fox sisters**.

Hydra In Greek **mythology**, a monster born of **Typhon** and **Echidna**. It took the form of a water snake with nine heads, one of which was immortal. The Hydra caused widespread havoc and destruction around Lerna, and **Heracles** was sent on his second "labour" to destroy it. Heracles and his assistant Iolaus succeeded in this task by burning the heads of the Hydra as Heracles struck them off with his club. The immortal head was buried beneath a rock-pile.

Hydromancy Form of **divination** in which the colour and patterns of flowing water are studied and interpreted. Sometimes ripples are counted as stones are dropped in a stream.

Hyle In **alchemy**, the so-called **First Matter** from which all material in the universe was born. Hyle encompasses the four **elements** and is synonymous with the **Philosopher's Stone**. The alchemist **Raymond Lully** regarded it as a "fusion of natural principles".

Hymn A song of praise or adoration, usually offered in an act of worship. In Christianity, hymns are sung in praise of **God**. Hymns were also part of the religious ceremonies in ancient Greece (e.g. *The Homeric Hymn to Demeter*), as well as in Egypt , India, and China. Hymns are also sung in some occult ceremonies. For example, they were part of the Mass performed in Anton La Vey's **Satanic Church**.

Hypnagogic State State of consciousness between waking and sleep in which hallucinatory images often appear. They arise in a state of drowsiness characterized physiologically by the presence of **alpha** rhythms and the slowing of eye movements.

Hypnopedia The ability to memorize information supplied during **hypnosis**. Suggestions are made by the hypnotist directly, or through tape-recorded instructions.

Hypnopompic State State of consciousness between consciousness and unconsciousness. See **Hypnagogic State**.

Hypnos In Greek **mythology**, the god of sleep. He was the father of **Morpheus**, god of **dreams**, and the twin brother of **Thanatos**, god of **death**. The Roman counterpart of Hypnos was Somnus.

Hypnosis A form of **trance** in which the subject's powers of concentration are mobilized and subconscious memories and perceptions brought to the surface. The **hypnotherapist** provides the subject with cues which allow the individual to overcome personal barriers and emotional blockages, and bring into consciousness abilities and memories formerly neglected. The term "hypnotism" was coined by the Scottish surgeon **Dr. James Braid**, who rejected the theory of **Anton Mesmer** that magnetic force could be transmitted from one person to another. Braid believed that mesmerism produced a state of consciousness combining relaxation and enhanced awareness. He derived the name "hypnotism" from the Greek god of sleep, **Hypnos**, although in coining this expression he clearly misnamed the process in question.

Hypnotherapist A therapist who employs **hypnosis** in treating patients.

Hypnotist One who practises **hypnosis**.

Hypocephalus In ancient Egypt, a disc of bronze, inscribed with **magical formulae** or **words of power**. It was placed beneath the heads of mummies, apparently to ensure warmth for the corpse.

Hyslop, Dr. James (1854–1920) American psychologist and philosopher who became an active member of the American **Society for Psychical Research** and investigated several **spiritual mediums**, including **Mrs. Leonore Piper**. Dr. Hyslop worked with **Hereward Carrington** and **Richard Hodgson**, and also with fellow psychologist **William James** in investigating psychic and mystical phenomena. After his retirement as Professor of logic and ethics at Columbia University in 1902, Hyslop lectured and researched widely in the field of paranormal phenomena and produced a number of books on the subject. These included *Enigmas of Psychic Research* (1906), *Life After Death* (1918), and *Contact with the Other World* (1919). See also **Psychical Research.**

Hysteria, Witchcraft Medieval phenomenon associated with **witchcraft** persecutions and cases of alleged satanic **possession.** The classic cases of hysteria include those of the **Aix-en-Provence Nuns** and the so-called incident of the "**Devils of Loudun**", in which **Urbain Grandier** was unjustly condemned to death. **Isobel Gowdie** is an example of a witch whose magical fantasies and decadent activities led to her execution. Many modern authorities on medieval witchcraft hysteria interpret it as symptomatic of mental illness and sexual repression. Some outbreaks of witchcraft hysteria may also have been caused by ergot poisoning in the local bread, leading to unsettling and misunderstood visionary states comparable to those experienced under LSD.

I

Ialdabaoth According to the Gnostic text *The Apocryphon of John*, an **archon** or spiritual ruler created from the "shadow" of **Chaos** by **Sophia.** Ialdabaoth then created the heavens and the earth. According to various tracts, Ialdabaoth was arrogant and androgynous, and took the form of a boastful lion. See also **Androgyne; Gnosis.**

Iamblichus (250–325) Neoplatonic **mystic** and philosopher who, together with Julian the Theurgist and Julian the Chaldean, was one of the authors of the spiritual tracts known collectively as the **Chaldean Oracles.** Iamblichus was a practitioner of **theurgy**, or sacred magic, and believed that the **soul** could be lifted up to the domain of the **gods** through **incantations** and **prayer.** Iamblichus wrote the classic mystical work *On the Mysteries* (translated into English by Thomas Taylor in 1821), and was regarded by the Emperor **Julian the Apostate** as a finer intellect than **Plato.** See also **Neoplatonism.**

Iao A **god-name** equivalent to the **Tetragrammaton** among certain **Gnostic** groups (e.g. the followers of the Valentinian teacher Marcus, who lived in Gaul in the latter part of the second century). It is also the sacred name which, according to Clement of Alexandria, was worn by initiates of the mysteries of **Serapis.** The modern magician **Aleister Crowley** ascribed special significance to the name, regarding it as the "formula of the Dying God", and relating it to sacrificed male deities – **Dionysus, Osiris, Balder,** Adonis, and Jesus Christ. See also **Gnosis; Valentinus.**

Iblis See **Eblis.**

IC See **Imum Coeli.**

Icaros In Peruvian folk-belief, **witchcraft** or healing orations, **exorcisms**, and songs. They are sometimes performed to ward off **evil** influences.

I Ching Also known as *The Book of Changes*, Chinese book of **divination** dating from at least 1000 B.C. Confucius and the Taoist sages valued it highly, and in recent times it has again become popular as a method of divination. The *I Ching* is said to gauge the flow of **yin** and **yang** energies and offers the seeker an appropriate course of future action based on the interplay of positive and negative forces that shape our destinies. Usually, a heap of fifty yarrow sticks is used – some short and the others long. The stalks are divided in heaps until a combination of stalks provides an arrangement that can be identified as one of the lines in a **Hexagram**. The lines are built up from the bottom to the top (i.e. from "earth" to "heaven"), and the Hexagram is formed from six lines. When the Hexagram is completed, the meanings are read in the *I Ching* itself. A system of divination by coins can also be used. In modern times, the noted psychoanalyst **Carl Jung** and the translator of Buddhist and Taoist texts, John Blofeld, have both expressed their belief that the *I Ching* seems to work infallibly. See also **Taoism**.

Ichthus One of the mystical and symbolic titles of Jesus Christ. *Ichthus* is the ancient Greek word for "fish", but it is also an acronym derived from the Greek phrase that translates as "Jesus Christ, Son of God, Saviour". Some astrologers associate the present Christian epoch with the Age of Pisces, and maintain it will eventually be superseded by the **Aquarian Age** in the year 2740.

Ichthyomancy Form of **divination** in which the entrails of fish are inspected and interpretations offered as a consequence.

Icon From the Greek *eikon*, "an image", a pictorial image of Christ, the Virgin Mary, or a saint. Icons are associated with the Eastern Orthodox Church. However, the term is also used generally to mean a sign or symbol, especially in regard to a sacred image.

Ida In **Kundalini Yoga**, the negatively charged lunar current that circles around the central axis of the nervous system, **sushumna**. It counterbalances the positively charged solar current known as **pingala**.

Idol An object or image representing a **god** or **spirit**, and regarded as possessing divine or magical powers. Idols often form part of ceremonial worship and are characterized as belonging to **heathen** or **pagan** ritual practice. One who worships idols is known as an idolater.

Ifreet See **Efreet**.

Ignis Fatuus From the Latin, "foolish fire", the flickering, ethereal light sometimes seen over graveyards. Scientifically, it is thought to be associated with the combustion of gases from matter in a state of physical decay, but it has a **folklore** association with **ghosts**, **spirits**, and **discarnate** entities. It is sometimes known as the **will-o'-the-wisp**.

IHVH See **Tetragrammaton**.

Illuminati Term used by occultists from the late fifteenth century onwards to describe spiritual **adepts** who had received mystical insights or "illumination" from a **transcendent** source. The Order of the Illuminati was founded by the Bavarian professor of law **Adam Weishaupt** in 1776, but this was hardly **esoteric** in any mystical sense and based most of its "secrets" on the work of Voltaire and the French Encyclopedists. Weishaupt and another enthusiast, Baron Adolph Knigge, later adapted the order's teachings in order to infiltrate **Freemasonry**. A decree in Bavaria in 1784 banned all secret societies – including

Freemasonry – and the order declined. However, it was revived around the turn of the century by the occultists Leopold Engel and **Theodor Reuss.** In recent times the idea of a secret brotherhood of adepts or Illuminati has been popularized by fantasy occult writer **Robert Anton Wilson** and New Age guru Stuart Wilde. See also **Occultism.**

Illumination Mystical or spiritual **enlightenment.** When this level of consciousness is attained, one is said variously to be an **adept,** a **Master,** a **Buddha,** or a **saint.** See also **Illuminati.**

Illusion A false impression or delusion, or a misinterpreted perception of an actual form or object. Many critics of **spiritualism** believe that alleged "psychic materializations" are sleight-of-hand illusions involving physical objects that have no supernatural origin whatever. The perception of **ghosts, spirits,** or **witches** in the branches of a tree on a dark and stormy night, or in the flickering flames of a fire, may similarly be illusory, and the product of one's **imagination.**

Image Magic See **Magic, Image.**

Image-taking Term used by modern trance occultists to describe a situation where a hostile or paradoxical image presents itself during a magical **pathworking.** After the pathworking is complete, the occultist then "takes the form" of the paradoxical image by re-conjuring it into consciousness while other members of the group ask questions to try to discover its source or meaning. See also **Occultism.**

Imagination The image-making faculty of human consciousness. The ability to summon a mental image and retain it at will is central to many mystical and occult practices. In Eastern **meditation,** sacred images known as **yantras** may be used as a mental discipline; while in Western **magic** occultists learn to use images of the four **elements** as doorways to the **astral plane.** In this instance, visions arise that characterize the element chosen as an entry-point, and may involve supernatural encounters with **elementals** or **spirits.** The magical act of assuming the **god-form** also depends on the powers of the imagination, because here the magician is imagining himself to be the **god** invoked in ritual. Eastern mysticism assumes that the mental imagery produced by the imagination is essentially illusory. It is known in **Hinduism** as **maya.**

Imaging The act of producing mental images and retaining them in consciousness. The technique is a form of mental concentration used in **guided imagery** work and in magical **pathworkings.**

Imam Title given to **Moslem** spiritual leaders. It was originally a title of **Mohammed** and his four immediate successors.

Imbalance Condition lacking balance. In **occultism** it is used to describe disorderly psychic or mental states. Ritual magicians warn **neophytes** that a state of imbalance or unpreparedness can lead to psychic **possession** as one particular image or "force" becomes predominant in one's consciousness. Meditative work on the so-called **Middle Pillar,** and the **Tarot** cards associated with it, may help to rectify psychic imbalance.

Imbolc A **witches' sabbath** held on February 1, and corresponding to the first signs of Spring.

Imhotep Egyptian architect and healer who lived during the reign of Pharaoh Zozer (c. 2778–2723 B.C.). He once sought the cause of a terrible famine by consulting sacred texts, and advised Zozer accordingly. Imhotep is also credited with several miraculous cures, and healing temples were erected in his honour. It is thought that by around 525 B.C.

Imhotep had acquired the status of a **god**. As such, he represents the first documented example of **deification**.

Imitative Magic See Magic, Imitative.

Immanent Term used in **mysticism** to describe the idea that the essence of **God** pervades the universe in all its manifested forms. It is the opposite of **transcendent**, in which God is regarded as having an existence beyond the confines of material creation.

Immortal One who will live forever. The term is especially used with reference to the **gods** of Greek and Roman **mythology**, but also arises as a claim among certain occult **adepts**. The **Comte de Saint Germain** claimed to his followers that he would live forever, and his true dates of birth and death have never been ascertained.

Immortality The state of eternal life or unending existence.

Immutable In **astrology**, the "fixed" quality ascribed to certain **signs** of the **zodiac**. These signs, which are said to be "acted upon" rather than to "instigate action" in the cosmos, include **Aquarius** (fixed **Air**); **Scorpio** (fixed **Water**); **Taurus** (fixed **Earth**); and **Leo** (fixed **Fire**).

Imp A small **demon**, often retained in a bottle by a **magician**. The French eighteenth-century **grimoire** *Secret des Secrets* describes how an imp can be trapped in a bottle by appealing to the Holy Trinity and then reciting the sacred words of Moses; Io, Zati, Zata, Abata. The alchemist **Paracelsus** is said to have trapped an imp in the pommel of his sword; and the nineteenth-century Frenchman Alexis Berbiguier allegedly devised a variety of methods for trapping the imps he believed were persecuting him. Berbiguier concocted "anti-demonic" soups, stupefied imps with tobacco, and trapped them inside bottles. Others he "pinned" to his clothes and bed and kept captive. The term "imp" is sometimes used to refer to a witch's **familiar**.

Impersonation In **spiritualism**, the belief that one spirit can mimic and impersonate another, thus confusing and deluding the **psychic medium** receiving messages at a **seance**. Such spirits are often described as "naughty" or "mischievous".

Imum Coeli In **astrology**, the lowest heaven – the lowest point of the ecliptic. It is the cusp of the fourth **house**, and is often abbreviated to **IC**.

Inanna In Sumerian **mythology**, a war goddess who was associated with the sky. She also personified the power of love and in due course became closely identified with the Babylonian goddess **Ishtar**.

Incantation From the Latin *cantare*, "to sing", magical **words of power** recited in a ceremony or **ritual**. In many mythologies, the utterances of **God** are said to have given rise to the universe and provide a sacred vibration that sustains it. In **ceremonial magic**, the magician – by assuming a cosmic role through ritual – uses sacred formulae or incantations in order to obtain the supernatural power ascribed to God (or the **gods**). This power may be used by the magician for his or her own spiritual growth and development (**white magic**) or to bring harm to enemies (**black magic**).

Incarnate That which has a physical, bodily existence. In **mysticism** and **occultism** it is assumed that a **spirit** or **soul** animates the physical body, bringing it to life. See also **Incarnation**.

Incarnation One's present life. Many **mystics** and **occultists** believe that the spiritual evolution of the **soul** occurs as the

self passes through many incarnations, acquiring self-knowledge and insights from each successive lifetime. When mystical **enlightenment** and true **self-realization** are attained, further incarnations become unnecessary. Within Eastern mystical terminology, the **wheel of life and death** is then broken. See also **Reincarnation.**

Incarnations, Divine In **mysticism** and comparative religion, the concept that the **Godhead** incarnates in the form of an **avatar** or spiritual leader who subsequently gives rise to a new religious expression. In Christianity, Jesus Christ is regarded as a divine incarnation of **God** (God the Father and God the Son being "one"); while in **Hinduism**, **Krishna** is considered to be an incarnation of **Vishnu.** In Tibet, the **Dalai Lama** is thought to be an incarnation of **Chrenrezig**; while in ancient Egypt the pharaohs incarnated **Ra.**

Incarnations, Satanic Term sometimes applied to political tyrants and dictators who have inflicted such terror, misery, and bloodshed upon the world that they are assumed to be incarnations of **Satan** or the **Devil.** Examples from world history include Attila the Hun, Adolph Hitler, and Joseph Stalin.

Incense From the Latin *incendere*, "to set on fire", a substance used in ceremonial worship which, when burned, gives off a pleasant aroma. The fumes of incense are believed by some to please the **gods** and ward off **demons.** Occultists, however, believe that the smoke of incense may be used to manifest **spirits** and **elementals** generally and, in this regard, the magical entity summoned to visible appearance may be either good or **evil.** See **Magic, Ceremonial.**

Inceptional Astrology See **Astrology, Inceptional.**

Incommunicable Axiom See **Ineffable Name.**

Inconjunct In **astrology**, term used to describe a **planet** that does not present an **aspect** with another planet. See also **Horoscope.**

Incubus A male **spirit** or **demon** believed to visit women during the night and subject them to sexual depravity, lust, and terrifying nightmares. This "demon lover" invariably appeared to a woman in the form of her normal partner or lover, but the act of lovemaking was always unpleasant. During the medieval **witch** trials, it was often maintained that a demon or devil had an ice-cold penis or an organ made of steel. The female equivalent of the incubus is the **succubus.**

Independent Voice Communication In **spiritualism**, a phenomenon where the voice of a **spirit** or **discarnate** entity does not manifest through a **medium** but is heard from a separate location. Sceptics have interpreted this as an act of ventriloquism on the part of the medium, but spiritualists regard it as a type of **direct voice** communication.

Individuality In occult and mystical belief, one's persona or **ego.** It is essentially illusory and transient, disappearing at **death.** Most **occultists** believe it should be distinguished from the **self** which survives death and reincarnates. See also **Reincarnation.**

Individuation In the analytical psychology of **Carl Jung**, the concept of "making the self whole". For Jung, this process included harmonizing the forces of one's external life with the events of both the **human unconscious** and the **collective unconscious.** Jung was interested in mystical systems that could lead people towards spiritual transformation. See also **Harmony of Opposites.**

Indra In Indian **mythology**, the main Vedic god. He was lord of thunder, warfare, and storms, and was also associated with fertility because of the rain he brought to the parched earth. Indra was often depicted carrying a bow in one hand and a thunderbolt in the other.

Inductor In **psychometry**, an object that is handled by the practitioner in order to receive "psychic impressions". This object is often a piece of jewellery or some comparable personal possession.

Inedia The apparent ability of certain **mystics**, **fakirs**, and **saints** to survive without food.

Ineffable Name In Jewish **mysticism**, the sacred name of **God** deemed too sacred to be pronounced. See also **Tetragrammaton**.

Inferior Planets In **astrology**, those **planets** whose orbits are within that of the Earth: **Venus** and **Mercury**. Sometimes the hypothetical planet Vulcan, said by some astrologers to orbit between Mercury and the **Sun**, is also included.

Infernal Court Dignitaries and officers forming a hierarchy within the kingdom of **Satan**, or the **Devil**. Within the **infernal regions**, there are said to be dukes, ambassadors, ministers, and so forth, who promulgate **evil** in the world.

Infernal Regions The **Underworld**. See also **Hades; Hell**.

Infinite That which has no boundaries or limitations. The word is often used to describe the qualities of wisdom and knowledge ascribed to ruling **deities** or to **God**. In many mystical systems God is referred to as **Infinite Light**.

Infinite Light Mystical term for the **Godhead**. It is the name given to the "Source of All Being" in the **Kabbalah**, where it is known as **Ain Soph Aur** – the supreme **cosmic** reality which transcends all attributes and limitations.

Influenced Writing Phenomenon associated with **extrasensory perception** in which a subject's handwriting is affected by thought impressions from another person. See **Mental telepathy**.

Initiate One who has successfully passed through a ritual of **initiation**. In **occultism**, an initiate is regarded as one who possesses superior **esoteric** knowledge.

Initiation Magical ceremony involving a sense of transition or self-transformation. The subject may be shown new symbolic mysteries, given a secret name or **words of power**, or granted a higher ceremonial rank. In the **Hermetic Order of the Golden Dawn**'s system of **magic**, from which most forms of modern Western **occultism** have evolved, there were different grades of initiation for each level of the **Tree of Life** leading up to **Tiphareth**. A candidate attaining Tiphareth would then proceed to membership of the Second Order. Magicians sometimes take a new **magical name** or motto, depending on their stage of attainment. Magical initiation may not be formally acknowledged unless the candidate has a particular visionary experience that confirms his or her new magical status.

Inner Chiefs In the **Hermetic Order of the Golden Dawn**, transcendental beings on the inner planes who were presumed to provide spiritual guidance. The occult counterpart of the Theosophical "Masters" or "Mahatmas", the Inner Chiefs were considered by **MacGregor Mathers** to be the source of his authority. The poet **William Butler Yeats**, also a leading member of the Order, doubted their existence. See **Magical Attack; Master**.

Inner guide A helper-figure from the inner realm who can be contacted via a state of visionary consciousness. Meditators and those who practise **channelling** or **shamanic visualization** often make contact with inner guides. See also **Spirit-helper**.

Inner Light In **mysticism** and **occultism**, the light of **God** within. The experience of the "inner light" is equated with **cosmic consciousness** and represents a profound level of mystical attainment. Sometimes the expression is used to indicate that every person is potentially **divine**, and contains the spark of **Godhead**. This view, sometimes characterized as the microcosm within the macrocosm, reflects the **Hermetic** axiom: "As above, so below" – God is in us, we are in God. See also **Macrocosm and Mircocosm**.

Inner Light, Fraternity of the
See **Fraternity of the Inner Light**.

Inquisition Roman Catholic tribunal instituted by Pope Gregory IX in 1233 to suppress heretical movements deemed to be hostile to Christianity. This was expanded in 1320 to deal with cases of **witchcraft** where heretical beliefs and practices were involved. The Spanish Inquisition was especially cruel and malicious towards heretics and dissidents.

Insanity State of mental imbalance. Among **occultists**, the symptoms of insanity sometimes manifest as demonic or satanic **possession**, where the subject feels tormented and dominated by **devils**. In this instance, the subject is unable to distinguish objective and subjective reality and may suffer extensive **delusions** and **hysteria**. Negative images derived from the subject's belief system appear within the field of consciousness as hostile and powerful forces and usually can only be removed or "banished" by means of a ritual of **exorcism**. A ceremony of this kind similarly draws on the subject's belief system, but replaces evil and negative images with positive and reassuring ones. See also **Banishing Ritual**.

Inspiration In Western **magic**, the act of allowing one's personal **daemon** or guiding **genius** to direct one's thoughts and intentions. One can also be inspired by opening oneself to channels of sacred knowledge through communication with **angels**, **archangels**, and **God**. See also **Cosmic Consciousness**; **Magic, High**; **Theurgy**.

Inspirational Writing and Drawing
In **spiritualism**, inspirational ideas and impressions received from a **supernatural** or **transcendent** source and incorporated into writings and works of art. In such cases the inspiring spirit does not directly control the hand of the writer or artist. Compare with **Automatic Painting and Drawing**; **Automatic Writing**.

Institut Métapsychique International
Organization founded in Paris in 1918 by Jean Meyer in order to investigate paranormal phenomena. Its members included **Sir Oliver Lodge**, **Dr. Charles Richet**, and **Camille Flammarion**. One of the **psychic mediums** investigated by the institute was the controversial **Eva C.**

Instrument In **spiritualism**, a term sometimes ascribed to a **control** with reference to the **psychic medium**, who is the channel for communications. In this respect, the medium is the "instrument" through whom **paranormal** phenomena are manifest.

Insufflation According to the French occultist **Eliphas Lévi**, an important practice in the occult application of medicine. Insufflation is the act of breathing on another person and, in certain circumstances, it restores life. Warm insufflation, according to Lévi, aids the circulation of the blood and eliminates gout and rheumatism; cold insufflation soothes pain. Lévi considered that the two methods should be used alternately, and seems to have believed that the healing technique activated magnetic forces. To this extent it can be compared with the theories of **Anton Mesmer**. Candidates in **Count Alessandro di Cagliostro's Egyptian Masonic Rite** were also breathed upon as part of their initiation.

Intellect The cognitive and rational powers of the mind. In Western **magic**, the human intellect is symbolized by the eighth **sephirah** on the **Tree of Life**, **Hod**, which is characterized as masculine. Compare with **Netzach**.

Intelligence In **occultism**, a force or power – usually regarded as **discarnate** – which serves as an inspirational force for an individual magician or a ritual order. The mysterious entity **Aiwaz** (who, according to the ritual magician **Aleister Crowley**, inspired the *Book of the Law*) is an example of a supernatural "intelligence". See also **Egrigor**.

International Spiritualist Federation Spiritualist organization, founded in London in 1923 to maintain communications between other international spiritualist groups, especially those concerned with afterlife beliefs and contact within **spirits**. See also **Spiritualism**.

Intuition Subjective faculty of the mind that often produces insights and perceptions that cannot be attained by the rational intellect. In Western **magic**, human intuition is symbolized by the seventh **sephirah** on the **Tree of Life**, **Netzach**, and is characterized as feminine.

Invisible Playmates Concept developed by **Sir Alister Hardy**, that young children often communicate spontaneously with invisible, and apparently imaginary, friends. Whether these communications are sometimes of a mystical or **paranormal** nature or simply involve fictitious playmates created as substitutes for real friends is a point of debate that has not been satisfactorily resolved.

Invocation In **ceremonial magic**, the act of summoning an **angel** or **god** for a positive or beneficial purpose using sacred **god-names** or **words of power**. In Western magic, the formulae of invocation usually involve Hebrew names ascribed to **God** (e.g. **El**, **Jehovah**, **Adonai**, **Shaddai**) or the names of **archangels** – especially those associated with the four **elements**: **Raphael** (**Air**); **Michael** (**Fire**); **Gabriel** (**water**); and **Uriel** (**Earth**). Magical invocations take place within the **magical circle**, which is regarded within the ritual as a sacred space, distinct from the profane, unsanctified territory which lies outside it. Compare with **Evocation**.

Involution See **Descending Arc**.

Ipsissimus In the **Hermetic Order of the Golden Dawn**'s system of Western **magic**, the supreme ritual grade of the Third Order, indicating that the magician had attained the state of consciousness symbolized by **Kether** on the kabbalistic **Tree of Life**. In specific terms, the Golden Dawn grades covered the first four spheres of the Tree of Life, and the *Rosae Rubae et Aurae Crucis* grades the next three. The Third Order grades comprised **Magister Templi** (**Binah**), **Magus** (**Chokmah**), and Ipsissmus (**Kether**).

Iron A metal with magical associations. In the Middle Ages, iron was regarded as a powerful protection against **witches** and the damaging influence of the **evil-eye**. A **horseshoe** is considered lucky because it is made of iron, and is believed to ward off **evil** forces.

Isagoge The only published volume in the projected nine-volume series known as the *Arbatel of Magick*, first issued in English translation in 1655. The *Isagoge* is an introductory volume, or beginner's text, consisting mostly of magical aphorisms.

ISF The initials of the **International Spiritualist Federation**, founded in London in 1923.

Ishtar In Babylonian **mythology**, a fertility- and mother-goddess who personified the planet **Venus**. She had two aspects: one was warlike and aggressive, the other gentle and loving. Ishtar is associated with the Sumerian goddess **Inanna** and the Phoenician **Astarte**.

Isis In Egyptian **mythology**, the wife of the fertility-god **Osiris** and the mother of **Horus**. Isis was a great goddess of **magic** and enchantment and succeeded in piecing together the fragments of Osiris's body after he had been murdered by **Set**. She also tricked **Ra** into revealing his secret, magical name. Isis was also a fertility-goddess and at times was identified with **Hathor**.

ISKCON Acronym for the International Society for Krishna Consciousness, the organization founded by A. C. Bhaktivedanta Prabhupad, who, until his recent death, was world head of the **Hare Krishna movement**.

Islam Religion founded by **Mohammed**. The word *Islam* in Arabic means "submission" and a **Moslem**, or devotee of Islam, is one who submits to **God**. There are said to be "five pillars" in Islam: the profession of faith that "there is no God but Allah, and Mohammed is his prophet"; the act of praying five times a day in the direction of **Mecca**; the payment of taxes; the fast of Ramadan; and the pilgrimage to Mecca, which should be undertaken by every Moslem at least once during their lifetime. Moslems worship God, but not Mohammed. They believe in **Paradise** and **hell**, and follow the principles of religious law outlined in their holy book, the **Qur'an**. The mystical branch of Islam is **Sufism**.

Isolation Tank Mechanical device developed by neurophysiologist **Dr. John Lilly** for exploring meditative states and "inner space". Lilly constructed the tank to eliminate external stimuli (light, sound, spatial awareness) and to stimulate the unconscious mind to compensate for the loss of external input. In such a way, the belief systems of the mind would present themselves in visions, intuitive insights, and **trance** experiences. Lilly designed the tank to hold water at 93 degrees F, the temperature at which the human body is neither hot nor cold. In his book *The Centre of the Cyclone* (1972), Lilly describes how on several occasions he floated naked in total darkness and silence, experiencing heightened inner awareness. During one of these sessions, Lilly writes, "I became a bright luminous point of consciousness, radiating light, warmth and knowledge. I moved into a space of astonishing brightness, a space filled with golden light, with warmth, and with knowledge." Since Lilly's pioneering research, isolation tanks have been modified and refined, and are now available for commercial hire. They are generally known as **samadhi tanks**.

Ithyphallic Expression meaning "with erect phallus", used in reference to **fertility cults** and **phallic worship**. Many prehistoric cave paintings depict ithyphallic figures and are believed to represent the regenerative powers of Nature.

Iynx Chaldean symbol of universal being comparable to the **archon** of the **Gnostics**. The Iynx-beings were described as "free intelligences" that transmitted **cosmic** energy from one plane of existence to another and were depicted as living spheres or winged globes.

J

Jabberwock Mythic, imaginary creature, invented by Lewis Carroll, which had "eyes of flame" and which "came miffling through the tulgey wood and burbled as it came …"

Jacobi, Jolande Hungarian psychotherapist who trained with **Carl Jung** and was strongly influenced by him. She wrote numerous articles on Jungian topics, including **archetypes**, **dream** symbolism, and **synchronicity**, and is perhaps best known for her overview work, *The Psychology of C. G. Jung* (1942).

Jacob's Ladder A ladder that appeared to Jacob in a dream. The ladder spanned **heaven** and earth, and **angels** would use it to descend from heaven. Medieval hermeticists interpreted the ladder as a symbol of the alchemical process of transformation and compared Jacob's ladder to a rainbow incorporating all the "colours" spanning Spirit and Matter. See also **Alchemy; Hermetica.**

Jade Stone with occult and magical significance, especially in China. Jade is said to possess the quality of **immortality**, and as such played an important role in traditional burial rites where it was often placed beside the orifices of a corpse to prevent bodily decay. Jade is also associated with Chinese **necromancy** and is normally associated with the masculine principle, **yang**, in Chinese cosmology.

Jaffé, Aniela German psychologist who worked at the C. G. Jung Institute in Zurich between 1947 and 1955 and was personal secretary to **Carl Jung** from 1955 till his death in 1961. She wrote several articles on Jungian thought, including "The Creative Phases in Jung's Life", and was responsible for recording and editing Jung's major autobiographical work, *Memories, Dreams, Reflections* (1963).

Jagrat Sanskrit term for the state of consciousness when one is awake; the exact opposite of swapna, or sleep. Because the waking world is regarded by the Hindus as essentially illusory, this state of consciousness is considered to be the lowest level of perception. See also **Hinduism; Turiya.**

Jaguar Animal with magical significance, especially in South American **shamanism.** In Brazil, the jaguar is thought to be the form that the **sun** takes during the night; and among the Jivaro Indians of Ecuador – as with other South American tribes – the jaguar has an initiatory function. When the Jivaro take **Datura** near the sacred waterfall, it is often reported that a pair a giant jaguars appear, fighting with each other and rolling towards the **shaman.** The latter has to prove his courage by reaching forward to touch the visionary creatures. This act of bravery bestows strength and supernatural power upon the shaman. See also **Initiation.**

Jaina Cross Symbol of the Jains which resembles a **swastika.** See also **Jainism.**

Jainism Indian religion that takes its name from the word *jina*, "the conqueror", a title given to **Mahavira** – a saviour-figure who was a contemporary of **Gautama Buddha.** Mahavira was not the founder of the Jains, but one of twenty-four "saviours" who represent the archetypal models for religious devotion. Jains place great emphasis on not harming any living creatures and carefully avoid stepping on insects. They also practise non-violence and believe, like Hindus, in the laws of **karma.** Jainism is largely confined to India and has approximately two million adherents.

Jambudvipa According to both Hindu and Buddhist traditions, one of the secret names of India; the name literally means "Rose-apple Tree Island".

James, William (1842–1910) American psychologist and philosopher whose writings on religion and mystical experience have strongly influenced the **human potential movement.** While James was not especially interested in such notions as "God" or "Absolute Truth", he stressed personal growth and self-improvement, and valued the mystical or **transcendental** experience as a means to that end. For him, **cosmic consciousness** was a continuum "into which our several minds plunge as into a mother-sea or reservoir".

James helped to found the American **Society for Psychical Research** in 1884 and was a pioneer of **psychedelic** research. He experimented with nitrous oxide, which he believed offered access to mystical states of consciousness. "The keynote of the experience", he wrote, "was the tremendously exciting sense of an intense metaphysical illumination." James also conducted experiments with the **psychic medium Mrs. Leonore Piper**, and stated that she possessed "a power as yet unexplained". He came to believe that **hauntings, phantasms**, and **trance** experiences were essentially natural phenom-ena that would eventually be explained scientifically. James was the author of several books, including *Principles of Psychology* (1890), *The Varieties of Religious Experience* (1902), and *The Meaning of Truth* (1909).

Janus Distinctive Roman **deity** who had two faces, each looking in opposite directions. Janus was god of doorways and he has given his name to January, the first month of the year. In this respect, Janus looks forward to the events of the new year, and back upon the old.

Japa In **yoga**, the repeated utterance of a **mantra**. Sometimes the japa is dedicated to the person's **guru**. In **Tantrism** it is considered to be the manifestation of **Shiva** and **Shakti**, personified by the two lips of the devotee (male and female, respectively). The term japa is also used to mean "invocation".

Jaquin, Noel (1893–1974) A follower of the nineteenth-century palmist W. G. Benham, Jacquin was one of the first researchers who endeavoured to put **palmistry** on a scientific basis. Jaquin believed that the lines on the palm, the shape of the hands, and the texture of the skin all offered clues to an individual's personality traits, including any latent criminal tendencies. Jaquin worked with Scotland Yard on different criminal cases and wrote several standard books on palmistry, including *The Human Hand* and *The Hand Speaks*.

Jataka In **Buddhism**, an entertaining story relating to the birth of a **buddha** in present or past times. Usually the buddha incarnates as a human being, but occasionally there are tales of existences in the form of a **spirit** or animal.

Jehovah A form of **Yahweh**, the personal name of **God** among the Jews. Traditionally, the name was sacred and never written down. See also **Tetragrammaton**; **YHVH**.

Jehudah of Worms (d. 1217) German **mystic** whose teachings influenced medieval **Hasidism**. Jehudah believed in a "two-fold glory". The inner inspirational glory came from the Holy Spirit, but there was also the visible glory present in the lives and visions of the prophets.

Jettatura Italian term for casting the **evil-eye** upon a victim. See also **Bewitchment**; **Spell**.

JHVH See **Tetragrammaton**.

Jibrill In **Islam**, the name for **Gabriel**, the **archangel** who appeared to **Mohammed** in a cave and showed him a silken cloth bearing certain inscriptions. Mohammed was told that "Thy Lord hath created all things, and hath created man of congealed blood."

Jihad Arabic word meaning "striving", used in **Islam** to describe a crusade against the infidels. A jihad is thus a "holy war". It can also be used to describe the inner war with one's lower, or less evolved, personal nature.

Jinn See **Genii.**

Jinnistan Mythic country believed in Persian folk-legend to be the home of the **genii** or djinn who served King Solomon.

Jiriki Japanese term meaning one's inner, mystical strength. It is distinguished from tariki, the strength of another person.

Jiva Sanskrit term for a "living being", the individual or egoic consciousness. According to yogic tradition, when jnana, or knowledge, overcomes **maya**, or illusion, the notion of jiva ceases to exist. See also **Jnana Yoga.**

Jivanmukta In **yoga**, a "liberated soul", a yogi who has attained this state of self-knowledge in his present **incarnation** has no further need to reincarnate and, after death, his soul merges with the Absolute. See also **Reincarnation.**

Jivatman Sanskrit term, similar to **jiva** in meaning but emphasizing that the **atman**, or true **self**, is the most significant aspect of one's individual consciousness.

Jnana Yoga Form of **yoga** that maintains Supreme Reality may be attained through intellect and reason, and by pursuing "higher knowledge". In this tradition, the intellect is employed to distinguish eternal and "real" phenomena from those events which are transitory and illusory. Jnana Yoga stresses the importance of self-discipline in attaining knowledge of the real **self.**

Jnana-marga Sanskrit term meaning "the path of knowledge". See also **Jnana Yoga.**

Jnani From the Sanskrit *jnana*, "knowledge", jnani is "one who knows", a wise man.

John of the Cross See **Juan de la Cruz.**

Johnson, Dr. Raynor C. (d.1987) English-born Australian physicist who wrote widely on **paranormal** phenomena and mystical experiences. Johnson described the **mystic** as "the scientist of ultimate things". In his important book *Watcher on the Hills* (1959), Johnson wrote that it was the mystic "who has verified in his experience that the *basic* data of religion are trustworthy; that God *is*, that he is infinitely beyond us and yet infinitely near, that he is Love and Beauty, Wisdom and Goodness – Perfection's own unutterable Self". Johnson's other well-known books are *The Imprisoned Splendour* (1953) and *Nurslings of Immortality* (1957).

Joint Colloquial expression for a cigarette containing **hashish** or **marijuana.**

Jones, Charles Stansfeld See **Achad, Frater.**

Joseph of Arimathea The wealthy Jew who, according to the biblical narrative, removed the body of Christ from the cross. According to medieval legend, Joseph caught the blood of Christ in the cup known as the **Holy Grail** and later brought it to Glastonbury in England.

Joss stick In traditional Chinese religious practice, a fragrant stick burnt in ritual offerings to placate the **gods** and drive away evil spirits.

Journey of the Soul In **shamanism**, the "journey" undertaken by a **medicine-man** or healer in order to recover the **soul** of a person who is bewitched or inflicted with disease; or, alternatively, to communicate with the **gods**. The journey occurs in a state of trance-dissociation and often employs the use of drum rhythms and the ingestion of **psychedelic** sacramental plants. See also **Trance, Shamanic.**

Jove A Roman name for **Zeus.** Jove was normally referred to as **Jupiter.**

Joy In **astrology**, a term used to describe the harmonious situation where planets have a strong affinity with the **signs** of the **zodiac** in which they are located. The **sun** in **Leo** is a classic example.

Juan de la Cruz (1542–1591) Spanish monk of the Carmelite Order who practised fasting and self-denial as part of his mystical discipline. He met Teresa de Jesus (Teresa of Avila) and supported her Carmelite reforms, which resulted in his being imprisoned in Toledo in 1575. He escaped to southern Spain nine months later and spent much of his remaining life as a confessor to the nuns of the reform movement.

Juan de la Cruz is best known for his mystical works *The Dark Night of the Soul* and *The Ascent of Mount Carmel*, which describe the relationship of people to God based on Juan's personal experience. According to his belief, one approaches **God** by removing selfish desires and other obstacles during the "Night of Senses". This period of self-denial and ascetism is not uncommon in the mystical tradition. The second phase of spiritual **enlightenment** Juan calls the "Night of the Soul"; and the **mystic**, as the receptacle of God's grace, finds that the environment becomes increasingly unfamiliar as finite memory is replaced with infinite knowledge and understanding. The mystic has to expand consciousness beyond its normal confines in order to glimpse God and, in so doing, radically changes his or her perception of the normal everyday world in a transformation process that is at the same time both terrifying and illuminating.

Judge, William Quan (1851–1896) Irish-born American Theosophist and follower of **Madame Helena Blavatsky**, who helped found the **Theosophical Society** in 1875 and become president of the American **Society for Psychical Research** in 1895. He was the founder of *The Path* and *The Theosophical Forum* and the author of *The Ocean of Theosophy*, first published in the United States in 1893. This book, for which Judge is best known, has been described as a condensation of the essential principles contained in Blavatsky's *The Secret Doctrine*, and is considered one of the best general introductions to **Theosophy**.

Judgment In the **Tarot**, the card that shows naked figures rising out of their coffins and embracing the "light" of new life. Their upstretched arms make the shape of LVX (Latin: "light") as the archangel **Gabriel** revives them, and a trumpet sounds in triumph. *Judgment* is regarded by occultists as one of the early paths on the inner magical journey (the others being ***The World*** and ***The Moon***), and its path links **Hod** and **Malkuth** at the base of the **Tree of Life.**

Judgment Hall In Egyptian **mythology**, the hall in the **Underworld** where **Osiris** and forty-two other **deities** presided over the judgment of the dead. Osiris sat beneath a canopy and a balance was placed before him. The heart of the deceased was now weighed against a **feather** – the symbol of truth – and the subject's fate decided accordingly. **Anubis**, the jackal-headed god, stood nearby, as did a number of other deities, including **Bast**, Kenemti, Neba and Khemi. A devouring snake was also present, ready to consume the wicked. However, those who were judged to be virtuous subsequently spent their days enjoying the blessings of Osiris and reaping grain in the **Elysian fields.**

Ju-Ju Name given to African magical rites which involve secret societies, **witch-doctors**, magical **amulets**, **curses**, and **exorcisms**. Ju-Ju men are able to cast out **demons** and rid the client of disease or the effects of a **curse**. They are also said to have telepathic powers, which enable them to identify the source of the

bewitchment and overcome the **sorcery** of evil **spells**. See also **Mental Telepathy**.

Julian of Norwich (c. 1342–1420) Benedictine nun who believed that **God** manifested to the world through life, love, and light. In May 1373, she experienced a number of visions of the Passion of Christ followed by a revelation concerning God's goodness and the hostility of the **Devil**. Julian's only known book, *The Revelation of Divine Love*, was written in two versions, the longer of which was not completed until twenty years after her visionary experiences. Julian of Norwich ranks with **Richard Rolle** and **Walter Hilton** as one of the most notable medieval English mystics.

Julian the Apostate (331–363) Roman emperor who was a nephew of Constantine the Great and was raised as a Christian. However, in his youth he converted to **pagan** beliefs. After a period as governor of Gaul he succeeded Constantius as emperor in 361 and began reviving pagan worship. Julian had been introduced earlier to initiatory rites sacred to **Mithra** and after his succession he began to introduce the Persian cult to Constantinople and Athens. It is thought that Julian had a desire to conquer Persia in the belief that Mithra would protect him, but this proved not to be the case. He was slain in battle during the Persian expedition.

Jumala In traditional Finnish **mythology**, the name of the supreme God. The **oak** tree was sacred to him, and he was often depicted holding a cup of **gold** filled with precious coins.

Jumar Imaginary creature described in Giovanni Battista Porta's book *Natural Magick* (1589) as the offspring of a bull and an ass.

Jung, Dr. Carl (1875–1961) Founder of analytic psychology and a pioneer of the exploration of mythic symbolism as a function of human consciousness. Jung was born at Kesswil, in Thurgau, Switzerland, and studied medicine in Basle and Paris. He later worked with Sigmund Freud for a number of years, but began to differ in his interpretation of the functions of the unconscious mind. Freud believed that the unconscious contained infantile tendencies that had been repressed because the maturing adult found them "incompatible"; but Jung believed that there was a stratum in the unconscious that included a vast source of images and symbols which transcended the individual experience. The study of these images led Jung to formulate the concept of the **collective unconscious** and the theory of **archetypes** – profound, primordial images that presented themselves in the **myths**, **folk-lore**, and **legends** of different cultures and which symbolized universal, **cosmic** processes.

Jung also differed from Freud in his interpretation of **dreams**, which he believed to be a "specific expression of the unconscious" that compensated for aspects of the personality that were unbalanced. By heeding the messages presented symbolically by dreams, one could heal imbalance and work towards the goal of **individuation** – the attainment of inner wholeness.

In his later years, Jung became absorbed with ancient cosmologies and spent a considerable time analysing **Gnostic**, alchemical, and mystical systems of thought. He provided commentaries for Richard Wilhelm's translations of the ***I Ching*** and *The Secret of the Golden Flower*, and wrote many major works on spiritual dimensions in psychology. Among his most important books are *Aion* (1951), *Symbols of Transformation* (1952), *Mysterium Coniunctionis* (1955), and *The Archetypes and the Collective Unconscious* (1959). Jung's autobiography, *Memories, Dreams, Reflections*, was published posthumously in 1963. See also **Alchemy**; **Mysticism**.

Juno In Roman **mythology**, the sister and wife of **Jupiter**. She reigned as queen of the **gods** and was the equivalent of the Greek Hera.

Jupiter In Roman **mythology**, the brother and husband of **Juno**, and the father of the **gods**. Jupiter was regarded as wise, all-knowing, and merciful, but was also god of thunder and lightning. In **astrology**, the planet Jupiter inspires optimism, happiness, and abundance.

Jurupari Among the Tupi and Guarani Indians of Brazil, a demonic **spirit**, hostile to women, who resides in the woods and guards animals. He is the principal **deity** of these tribes.

Justice In the **Tarot**, the card that depicts a female **deity** seated on a throne, holding a pair of scales and a large, fearsome sword. **Occultists** regard *Justice* as the path on the **Tree of Life** where one faces one's accumulated **karma** and learns to overcome the negative and hostile visions of one's own wrongdoings. *Justice* thus demands balance, adjustment, and total impartiality in assessing one's true spiritual direction. The card is ruled by **Venus**, but owes much of its symbolism to the Egyptian concept of the **Judgment Hall**, and the goddess depicted has the same role as **Maat**, goddess of Truth. *Justice* is the path linking **Tiphareth** and **Geburah** on the **Tree of Life**.

Juturna In Roman **mythology**, a **nymph** with whom Jupiter fell in love. She became a goddess of lakes and springs and had a fountain in the Roman Forum dedicated to her.

K

Ka In Egyptian **mythology** and **magic**, the human **double**. Occultists compare the Ka to the **astral body**, which can be projected into a mental or imaginal realm and act as a vehicle for exploring the more subtle planes of consciousness.

Ka'ba In **Islam**, the location in **Mecca** towards which **Moslems** are required to pray. The Ka'ba is a sacred temple containing the mystical Black Stone and is situated in a square at the centre of Mecca.

Kabbalah Also Qabalah, Cabala. From the Hebrew word QBL meaning "an oral tradition", the **esoteric** and mystical division of Judaism. The Kabbalah presents a symbolic explanation of the origin of the universe, the relationship of human beings to the **Godhead**, and an emanationist approach to Creation whereby the Infinite Light (**Ain Soph Aur**) manifests through different **sephiroth** on the **Tree of Life**. Although the central book of the Kabbalah, ***The Zohar***, was not written down until around 1280 – probably by **Moses de León** – the Kabbalah has spiritual links with **Gnosticism** and other early mystical cosmologies.

In the Kabbalah, all manifestations are said to have their origin in Ain Soph Aur and the successive **emanations** of the Godhead reveal aspects of his divine nature. The system is thus monotheistic in essence, but allows for the tenfold structure of the sephiroth upon the Tree of Life. The emanations, as they proceed from the Godhead to the manifested world, are: **Kether** (the Crown); **Chokmah** (Wisdom); **Binah** (Understanding); **Chesed** (Mercy); **Geburah** (Power); **Tiphareth** (Beauty and Harmony); **Netzach** (Victory); **Hod** (Splendour); **Yesod** (Foundation); and **Malkuth** (the Kingdom).

Occultists in the **Hermetic Order of the Golden Dawn** used the kabbalistic Tree of

Life as a matrix or grid for comparing the archetypal images of different mythologies that could be employed in ceremonial magic. For example, the merciful father (Chesed) has parallels in other pantheons, namely **Odin** (Scandinavia); **Zeus** (Greece); **Jupiter** (Rome); and **Ra** (Egypt). This system of comparisons became known as **mythological correspondences**. It has also become common in the occult tradition to link the ten sephiroth of the Tree of Life with the twenty-two cards of the **Major Arcana** of the **Tarot**, a concept first proposed by the magician **Eliphas Lévi**. See also **QBL**.

Kabbalist A practitioner of the **Kabbalah**. The term is also used generally to mean an **occultist** or a follower of **esoteric** traditions.

Kabir (1440–1518) Indian mystic, born in Benares, whose philosophy combined **Hinduism** and **Sufism**. Kabir rejected the caste system and believed that mystical truths were for the common people, not just for the elite. Venerated by both **Moslems** and Hindus alike, he was a strong influence on his contemporary, **Guru Nanak**, founder of the **Sikhs**. Kabir's writings, which include songs and wise sayings, are known collectively as the *Bijak*.

Kachina Among the Hopi Indians, ancestral spirits and gods of the clouds who are impersonated by masked dancers in **ritual** ceremonies. The principal Kachina dances are held in February and relate to the fertility of crops. Beans and corn are given to the people to show that the gods and spirits of the Kachina cult can sustain the supply of food though the winter months.

Kachina Dolls Hopi figurines, ornately carved and coloured, that represent the ancestor **spirits** in the **Kachina** cult.

Kadaitja Among the Central **Australian Aborigines**, **sorcerers** or **medicine-men** who can see **spirits**, heal the sick, and perform acts of **magic**. The kadaitja is said to be able to fly through the air in the form of an eagle-hawk and dig his claws into his victim. See also **Shamanism**.

Kakodemon Gnostic term used to describe an evil inspirational **genius**. See also **Daemon**.

Kala Circle In **sexual magic**, the **yoni** of **Kali**, venerated as a "circle of flowers and essences" and identified as the focal **chakra** in Tantric ritual. See also **Tantra**.

Kalevala Traditional Finnish epic, which includes **legends**, poems, and folk songs and describes the creation of the world and the adventures of mythic heroes. The name is also applied to Finland itself.

Kali Fearsome Hindu goddess personifying the dark and terrifying forces of Nature. The word kali means "black", and the goddess had a dark skin, bulging bloodshot eyes, and protruding fangs. She wore a string of human skulls around her neck and was often depicted mutilating her victims. Kali is said to be the cause of disease and fevers, and blood sacrifices are still made to her to appease her wrath.

Kali-yuga Sanskrit term denoting the present epoch, the so-called fourth, or "iron" age. The Kali-yuga, which will last for 432,000 years, commenced with the death of **Krishna**, which some authorities date from 3120 B.C. See also **Yuga**.

Kalki In **Hinduism**, the final **avatar** of **Vishnu**, a **deity** who previously incarnated as **Krishna** and **Rama**. When he appears, Kalki will destroy the wicked aspects of the world and herald a new era, or maha-yuga. Kalki will appear as a horse-headed giant, brandishing a sword and riding a white horse in the sky.

Kalpa Sanskrit term for a vast cycle in time, equivalent to one thousand **yugas**. A kalpa represents one "Day of Brahma" in Hindu **cosmology**, and is 4320 million years in duration.

Kalwah In **Sufism**, the act of isolating oneself in a retreat or cave for the purpose of **meditation**, **prayer**, **fasting**, or chanting.

Kama Hindu personification of love and desire. Kama was the son of **Vishnu** and **Lakshmi** and was depicted as an attractive young man riding on the back of a large bird or elephant. The term is also used generally to describe human desires and sometimes has the same connotation as Christian "sin". See also **Hinduism**.

Kamaloka From two Sanskrit words *kama*, "desire", and *loka*, "place" – the after-death plane where the **astral** forms of deceased persons gradually disintegrate. Kamaloka resembles the Greek **Hades**.

Kamarupa From two Sanskrit words *kama*, "desire", and *rupa*, "form" – an **astral shell** or **apparition** that survives **death**, but which owes its existence solely to mental and physical desires. Some **occultists** believe that kamarupas are responsible for the "phenomena" that manifest in spiritualist **seances**.

Kamea See **Magic Number Square**.

Kami In **Shinto**, a **spirit** or **god**. The term is used to describe both **high gods** and Nature spirits. According to Shinto belief, after death a person's **soul** becomes a kami.

Kamma The **Pali** spelling for **karma**.

Kapila Indian mystic and member of the Samkhaya school, who lived around the seventh century B.C. He is described in the *Bhagavata Purana* as the fifth incarnation of **Vishnu**, and is identified in both the *Ramayana* and the ***Mahabharata*** as a form of **Agni**, god of **Fire**.

Kaplan, Aryeh (d. 1983) Leading contemporary author on the **Kabbalah**. His major work, *Meditation and Kabbalah*, was the first text in English to provide a coherent translation of important visionary texts of the **Hekhaloth** tradition. His other works include *Meditation and the Bible* and *Jewish Meditation*.

Kappa In Japanese folk-legend, a river-goblin that had scaly limbs, the body of a tortoise, and a head like an ape. Hostile to humans, it could be overcome by acts of politeness because a life-sustaining substance would drain from its head if it bent over to return a bow. See also **Goblin**.

Kardec, Allan (1804-1869) The pen-name of French spiritualist Denizard Rivail who studied animal magnetism and later worked extensively with **psychic mediums**. He was a strong supporter of the doctrine of **reincarnation** and derived his assumed name from beings whom he claimed were his former incarnations. Kardec became the editor of *La Revue Spirite* and founded the Parisian Society for Spiritualistic Studies. Largely uninfluential in Britain and the United States, his biggest following has been in France and Brazil. Kardec's books include *The Spirits' Book*, *The Medium's Book*, and *Spiritualist Initiation*.

Karezza **Sexual magic** technique advocated by Thomas Lake Harris (1823–1906), who derived it from tantric yoga. Energy is aroused through erotic stimulation, but the semen is not discharged. The energy instead is said to give birth to magical forms which may be directed for an occult purpose. See also **Tantra**.

Karma Hindu concept of actions followed by consequences. A person who lives a virtuous life builds up good karma, while a person committed to wrongdoing accumulates bad karma. According to Hindu belief, the circumstances of one's present incarnation are a consequence of karma established in a former life, so it follows that the development of good karma is central to the process of spiritual growth. See also **Reincarnation**.

Karma Yoga Path of yoga in which the devotee performs selfless actions in service to the **Godhead**.

Katcina See Kachina.

Kauravas In the Indian classic the *Mahabharata*, the cousins of the **Pandavas** – the family of **Arjuna**. The Pandavas and the Kauravas were enemies.

Kavvanah Hebrew term meaning "mental concentration". Among the **Hasidim** it was used to mean the "one-pointedness" used in **meditation**.

Kavvanoth Hebrew term for meditative exercises developed in sixteenth-century kabbalism. These were essentially visualisations based on the ten **sephiroth** of the **Tree of Life**. See also **Kabbalah**.

Kelipoth See Qlippoth.

Kelley, Edward (1555–1595) Alchemist, **magician**, and **skryer** who worked with **Dr. John Dee**, summoning angelic spirits in **trance**. Together they evolved **Enochian magic**. See also **Alchemy**.

Kellner, Karl (d. 1935) German **occultist** who claimed to make contact with three **adepts** – two of them Arabs, the other a Hindu – while travelling through India and the Middle East in 1896. Kellner was given certain sexual **yoga** secrets and decided to form an **esoteric** society. In a reference to the **Knights Templar**, whom he believed possessed comparable knowledge, Kellner named his new institution the **Ordo Templi Orientis** (OTO), or Order of Oriental Templars. The journal of the OTO, *Oriflamme*, proclaimed in 1912 that the Order possessed "the key which opens up all Masonic and Hermetic secrets, namely, the teaching of sexual magic ... " Kellner was succeeded by **Theodor Reuss** who, in 1912, invited the English ceremonial magician **Aleister Crowley** to join the Order. Crowley became head of the organization in 1922. See also **Grant, Kenneth; Magic, Ceremonial; Magic, Sexual.**

Kelpie In Scottish **folklore**, a water-spirit that took the form of a horse. Usually grey or black, its hooves pointed backwards and it had a mischievous nature. Kelpies would lead travellers astray as they mounted to cross a river or stream, and sometimes they would devour them as well.

Kensho In **Zen Buddhism**, the first experience of **satori**.

Kephalonomancy Bizarre method of **divination** among the Lombards in which lighted carbon would be poured on the baked head of a goat, and the names of those accused of crimes would be called out. If crackling occurred, it was assumed that the person whose name had been called was guilty as accused. This form of divination was also practised using the head of an ass.

Keres In ancient Greek **mythology**, evil **spirits** associated with violent death. They were the offspring of **Nyx**, and were sometimes connected with the **Furies**.

Kerux In the magical system practised in the **Hermetic Order of the Golden Dawn**, a ceremonial role in the probationary grade admitting new candidates. Kerux personified the "reasoning faculties" – i.e. mental intelligence.

Kether In the **Kabbalah**, the first mystical **emanation** on the **Tree of Life**. Occultists identify Kether as the state of consciousness where creation merges with the veils of non-existence associated with (**Ain Soph Aur**, the limitless light). Kether lies on the **Middle Pillar** and transcends the duality of **Chokmah** (Male) and **Binah** (Female), which lie immediately below on the Tree. It is therefore symbolized in the mystical tradition by the heavenly **androgyne**, and represents a state of mystical **transcendence** and union with the supreme One Reality. It may be compared to **satori** and **nirvana** in **Zen Buddhism** and **yoga**, respectively.

Key In **occultism**, a symbol indicating access to a secret or **mystery**: something normally "hidden". The medieval **grimoire** known as the *Key of Solomon* and **Eliphas Lévi**'s *Key of the Mysteries* are examples of magical books employing this symbolism. See also **Clavicle**.

Keyes, Laurel Elizabeth See **Fransisters and Brothers**.

Key of Solomon Title of a famous medieval **grimoire** published in two forms: *The Greater Key of Solomon* and *The Lesser Key*, or **Goetia**. *The Greater Key* contains magical instructions, **prayers**, **conjurations**, and **pentacles** for each of the **planets**. *The Lesser Key* contains detailed commentaries on the nature of the **spirits** summoned in **ceremonial magic**, including those used in medieval **witchcraft** and **necromancy**.

Keys of the Tarot Term used to describe the twenty-two cards of the **Major Arcana** of the **Tarot**, which reveal an initiatory function when viewed as a sequence of meditative **archetypes**. See also **Initiation**.

Khabs Am Pekht In the **Hermetic Order of the Golden Dawn**, a magical phrase derived from ancient Egypt and used as a magical proclamation and statement of spiritual purpose. It translates as "Light in Extension".

Khaibit In ancient Egyptian **magic** and **mythology**, "the shadow". See **Haidit**.

Khalif Arabic term meaning "successor". It was originally used to denote the first four spiritual leaders who succeeded **Mohammed**, although it is now used to describe any senior leader in **Islam**.

Khandas Buddhist term for the five distinguishing human attributes: *rupa* (form); *vedona* (name, feeling); *sanna* (perception); *sankhara* (memory); and *vinnana* (consciousness). In Sanskrit they are called **skandhas**. See also **Buddhism**.

Khechari Mudra In **Siddha Yoga**, a yogic **mudra** in which the tip of the tongue is curled back into the throat and upward into the nasal pharynx. According to **Swami Muktananda**, this mudra breaks the so-called "knot of Rudra" in the **sushumna** and allows the **kundalini** to rise to the spiritual centre or **chakra** known as **Sahasrara**.

Khepera In ancient Egyptian **magic** and **mythology**, the **sun**-god in his form as a **rebirth deity**. Khepera emerges from the final dungeon of the **Tuat**, or **Underworld**, and prepares to float forth on the ocean of the sky. He takes the form of a scarab-beetle and is received by **Nut**, the sky-goddess.

Khu In Egyptian **mythology** and ritual, the "magical body". **Occultists** believe that the Khu can be awakened once a person has learned to distinguish physical sensations and conscious and unconscious thought processes. The use of ritual **mantras** or **magical formulae**, sacred postures and gestures, and the internal activation of inner spiritual centres or **chakras**, are all ways of developing the Khu.

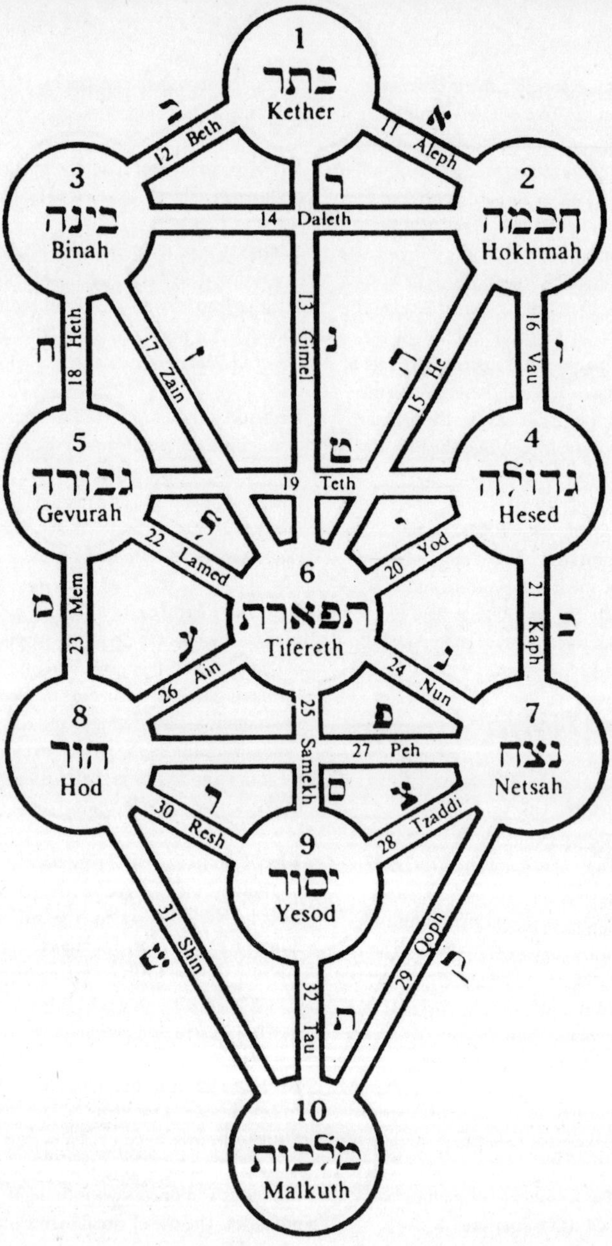

KABBALAH: The mystical tradition in Judaism. The Tree of Life reveals the pathways to the Godhead.

Khubilgan In traditional Buryat **shamanism**, a soul-animal, or **familiar**, which guarded the **shaman** and was essential to his healthy life. Loss of the Khubilgan would invariably lead to the shaman's death.

Khunrath, Henry (1560–1601) German alchemist who studied medicine at the University of Basle and later practised in Hamburg and Dresden. A follower of **Paracelsus**, he composed a mystical tract that described the seven steps leading to **enlightenment**. This book, which was titled *Amphitheatrum Sapientae Aeternae Solius Verae, Christiano Kabbalisticum Divino Magicum* (*Christian-Kabbalistic, Divine-Magical Amphitheatre of the Eternal*), was published after his death, in 1609. It identified Christ as the means of attaining perfection, and described the *Ruach Elohim* – the spirit on the face of the waters of Creation – as the **Philosopher's Stone**, the very source of life.

Ki The Japanese term for **Ch'i**.

Kilas The Buddhist term for **Klesas**.

Kilner, Dr. Walter J. (1847–1920) British doctor who developed special screens which he believed made the human **aura** visible to normal sight. The screens consisted of two pieces of glass with dicyanin solution sealed hermetically between them. Kilner maintained that the eyes could be psychically "sensitized" by looking through the screen. Two such screens are called Kilner-screen goggles. Kilner's theory is explained in his book *The Human Atmosphere, or the Aura Made Visible by the Aid of Chemical Screens* (London, 1911; republished New York, 1965).

Kilner-screen Goggles See **Kilner, Dr. Walter J.**

King, Francis X English occult historian who was one of the first writers to document the contemporary magical revival. His principal books include *Ritual Magic in England* (1970), *Sexuality, Magic and Perversion* (1971), and *The Secret Rituals of the O.T.O.* (1973). He also co-authored an important introductory text on Western **magic**, *Techniques of High Magic* (1976), with **Stephen Skinner**, and produced a sequel to *Ritual Magic* titled *The Rebirth of Magic* (1982) with Isabel Sutherland. Francis King is credited, with **Israel Regardie**, as one of the main occult writers to revive interest in the **Hermetic Order of the Golden Dawn**.

King, George (1919–1997) English **psychic healer** and **occultist** who founded the **Aetherius Society**. Raised as a Christian, King studied **yoga**, **meditation**, and **metaphysics**, and in 1954 began to explore techniques of spiritual healing. King claimed that the deceased **spirits** of several notable figures – including **Sir Oliver Lodge** – guided him in this work. He also maintained that in May 1954 he was visited in his London flat by a "great Yogi **adept**" who was able to pass through solid walls and doors as if they were no barrier. The adept told him that he had been selected by the Great **Masters** to represent the spiritual cause in the coming conflict with materialistic science. King established the Aetherius Society soon afterwards and believed that periodically the Great Masters – including Jesus Christ – visited Earth in flying saucers. King spent much of his time engaged in spiritual healing, and wrote a book describing his methods, *You Too Can Heal*, which was first published in 1976. See also **Occultism**.

King, Katie Trance personality who manifested through **psychic medium** Florence Cook at **seances**. Katie was allegedly the daughter of Henry Morgan, the buccaneer, but had a remarkable resemblance to Florence herself. **Sir William Crookes** investigated the phenomenon of Katie King and Florence Cook and maintained that the manifestations were authentic, although some critics have suggested that Crookes had an emotional attachment to Florence and may have been biased in her favour.

King of the Wood In ancient Rome, the **priest** who overviewed the outdoor sanctuary of **Diana** at Nemi. This shrine was in a sacred grove and the priest was regarded as Diana's representative on Earth.

King's Evil Superstition that the touch of a king could heal scrofula. Edward the Confessor (1004–1066) and Charles II (1630–1685) are English monarchs who performed the ceremony.

Kingsford, Anna Bonus (1846–1888) English **mystic** and **occultist** who was interested in dreams and "**esoteric** Christianity". With Edward Maitland she formed the Hermetic Society, an organization contemporaneous with the **Hermetic Order of the Golden Dawn**. She also was friendly with **Macgregor Mathers** and **Madame Helena Blavatsky**. Anna Kingsford's best-known work is *The Perfect Way*, first published in 1882.

Kirlian Photography Process discovered accidentally by Soviet electrician Semyon Kirlian. While repairing an instrument in a research institute, he noticed an unusual effect occurring with a subject undergoing electrotherapy. Tiny flashes of light passed between the electrodes and the person's skin, and Kirlian thought he would try to photograph the discharge. After a period of experimentation, he succeeded in photographing a luminous "corona" around his fingers; over the next ten years he worked with his wife Valentina refining his instruments. Kirlian believes that his corona-photographs reveal energy levels in living objects (hands, leaves, fingers) and some subsequent Kirlian researchers have compared the vivid colours in Kirlian photographs with the colour variations in the **aura** allegedly perceived by psychics. The present status of Kirlian photography is controversial. Dr. William Tiller of Stanford University believes that Kirlian photography merely monitors changes in the skin's surface chemistry and dismisses the colour variations as irrelevant; parapsychologist **Dr. Thelma Moss**, on the other hand, believes that Kirlian energy patterns have profound implications for the study of health and may even have applications in cancer research.

Kiss of Shame In **satanism**, the act of ritually kissing the **Devil** on the buttocks.

Klesas In **yoga**, the causes of human pain and suffering. They are *avidya* (ignorance); *asmita* (ego-centredness and identification with the physical body); *raga* (attraction to pleasure); *dvesa* (aversion to that which gives pain); and *abhinivesa* (the desire to cling to life).

Knight, Gareth (1930–) Pseudonym of Basil Wilby, a leading contemporary authority on the magical applications of the **Kabbalah**. Knight was born in Colchester, England, in 1930 and in 1953 enrolled in the study course of the Society of the Inner Light, a group founded by **Dion Fortune**. In 1962 he began editing the occult magazine *New Dimensions* and three years later co-founded the publishing company Helios Books. Knight later founded his own esoteric school based on the principles of the Society of the Inner Light and this has since given rise to two further splinter offshoots, the Avalon Group and the Companions of the Inner Abbey. Knight's main books include *A Practical Guide to Qabalistic Symbolism*, *The Experience of Inner Worlds*, *A History of White Magic* and *The Magical World of the Tarot*. Knight is currently working on a series of books based on Dion Fortune's archive material.

Knights Templar Order of medieval knights founded in 1118, initially to protect pilgrims travelling to the Holy Land. Originally the knights were very poor and two knights had to ride on one horse. However, they became a rich order of knights after King Alfonso of Aragon and Navarre bestowed wealth upon them, and by the end of the twelfth century they had 30,000 members – most of them French. During the reign of Pope Clement V, the Order of Templars suffered a major setback. The knights were accused of **heresy**, and in particular of denying Christ, the Virgin, and the Saints. They were described as worshipping the **Devil** in the form of **Baphomet**, roasting the bodies of dead Templars, spitting on the crucifix, and engaging in unnatural sexual acts. Many confessions were extracted under torture and a number of knights were slowly burned to death in horrible executions. While the true nature of the Knights Templar may never be known with certainty, it is likely that many knights in the Order were influenced by the **esoteric** traditions of **Manicheism**, the **Albigenses**, and the **Cathars**. To this extent they were continuing the mystical **Gnostic** philosophy, which the orthodox Church, since earliest times, had sought to eradicate.

Koan In **Zen Buddhism**, a paradoxical riddle in the form of a short poem. Koans are often considered to provide the very quintessence of profound truths.

Kobold In German folk-belief, a **gnome** or **spirit** that haunts houses or underground mines.

Koch, Dr. Walter German astrologer who has also made an extensive study of colour symbolism, **parapsychology**, and **divination**. His books include *Astrological Science of Colours* (1930), *Your Colour – Your Character* (1953), and *Prophecy and Astrological Prediction* (1954). See also **Astrology**.

Kodashim From the Hebrew, meaning "holy things", a division of the Jewish **Mishna**, or oral teaching relating to the Law. The Kodashim is one of the six divisions of the Mishna and includes eleven tractates relating to different forms of temple service.

Koot Hoomi Visionary **adept** and **Master** who allegedly appeared to English theosophist **Alice Bailey** on several occasions. Bailey noted that he wore a turban during his first visit in 1895 and she took him to be Jesus Christ. She discovered later that this was not so, but felt nevertheless that he was a "Master who is very close to Christ … and an exponent of the love-wisdom of which Christ is the full expression". Bailey regarded the "Master K. H." as a spiritual inspiration even though she remained a staunch, fundamentalist Christian throughout her life. See also **Theosophy**.

Koran See **Qur'an**.

Kosmon Bible Remarkable book produced by **Dr. John Ballou Newbrough** through "automatic typewriting". The bible, which is some nine hundred pages in length, contains details of the spiritual rulers of earth in different periods of its history and condemns many of the world's leading religions as the inspiration of "false **deities**". The Kosmon Bible is better known as **Oahspe** and was first published anonymously in New York in 1882.

Kosmos The ancient Greek word for "order", applied by **Pythagoras** to describe the universe. See also **Cosmos**.

Krafft, Karl Ernst (1900–1945) Swiss astrologer and cosmologist who was employed by the Nazis for propaganda purposes. The Austrian astrologer **Louis De Wohl** believed that many of Hitler's major coups were related to planetary aspects calculated by Krafft, and De Wohl was taken on by the British War Office to forecast the moves likely to be taken by Hitler on the basis of **astrology**. Krafft's career with the Nazis was erratic and for a time he was imprisoned. He once had the temerity to suggest that General Montgomery's astrology chart was stronger than Field-Marshal Rommel's. Krafft was arrested in 1943 and died en route to Buchenwald in 1945.

Kraken Semi-mythical monster that bears some relation to a giant squid. According to various accounts by fishermen working the sea around Norway, England, and Newfoundland, krakens have found their way into the fishing nets; but these have invariably been found to be squid. The mythic kraken is altogether more fearsome, and in Norwegian accounts was described as a monster over a mile in length, with horns like ship-masts, and a flair for destroying fishing boats in one fell swoop.

Kramer, Heinrich (1430–1505)
Co-author, with **Jacobus Sprenger**, of the notorious ***Malleus Maleficarum***, a work that fuelled the Holy **Inquisition**'s campaign against **witchcraft** and **heretics**. Kramer was an experienced Dominican Inquisitor and first aroused fear and hostility in the region of the Tyrol. He had a major ally in Archduke Sigismund, who rewarded him for his efforts, and is regarded as the major contributor to the *Malleus*. He died while on an apostolic mission to Bohemia.

Krippner, Stanley (1932–) Noted American parapsychologist who was formerly a director of the Dream Laboratory at the Maimonides Medical Center in New York. Krippner has spent many years researching the subject of telepathic communications in the **dream** state under controlled conditions. He is also interested in **Kirlian photography** and the links between technology and life-energy, and in recent years he has been conducting experiential workshops in "personal" mythology with Dr. David Feinstein. Dr. Krippner's books include *Dream Telepathy* (1973), co-authored with **Montague Ullman** and Alan Vaughan, *Future Science* (1977), co-edited with John White, and *Personal Mythology*, co-authored with Dr. David Feinstein (1988). See also **Mental Telepathy; Parapsychology.**

Krishna The eighth **avatar** of **Vishnu** and a major figure in the ***Bhagavad-Gita***, where he is **Arjuna**'s charioteer. In the war between the **Kauravas** and **Pandavas**, Krishna took the side of the latter. He survived the war, but was later killed when the arrow of a hunter struck him in the heel – his one vulnerable point. The **Kali Yuga** dates from his death.

Krishna-Consciousness Term sometimes associated with the Hare Krishna sect. See **Hare Krishna Movement; ISKCON.**

Krishnamurti, Jiddu (1895–1986) Indian **mystic** who lived at Adyar, Madras, as a young boy and was noticed by the theosophist **Rev. Charles W. Leadbeater**, because he had a remarkable **aura**. Leadbeater and **Dr. Annie Besant**, both leading figures in the **Theosophical Society**, later proclaimed Krishnamurti to be a World Teacher, a claim Krishnamurti subsequently denied. While Krishnamurti rejected the role of **guru**, he established himself as a leading yogic philosopher and spent much of his time lecturing internationally. His many books include *Commentaries on Living, The First and Last Freedom, The Impossible Question*, and *The Urgency of Change*.

Kriya In **yoga**, a physical or mental response to the awakening of **kundalini**. Kriyas are regarded as "purifying" movements, which allow the yogic practitioner to adapt to the energies of higher consciousness.

Kriyashakti From the Sanskrit. Meaning "power of action", the **paranormal** ability of "mind over matter". Regarded as one of the **siddhis**, or **psychic powers**, it can be compared to the force said to produce **psychokinesis**.

Kronos Also Cronus. In ancient Greek **mythology**, the god of time, who existed before the creation of the world. In other versions he was one of the **Titans** – the youngest son of **Uranus** and **Gaea** and the husband of **Rhea**. Kronos swallowed each of his children, but **Zeus** was saved and later rescued the others. After a fight with the Titans, Zeus then deposed Kronos and gained supremacy over the world. In Roman mythology, Kronos is identified with **Saturn**.

Krsna Sanskrit spelling of **Krishna**.

Kshanti Sanskrit term for "patience", "serenity", and "peace".

Kübler-Ross, Elisabeth (1926–) A world-renowned authority on **death** and dying, Kübler-Ross received her M.D. degree from the University of Zurich in 1957. After conducting seminars on death she moved into the field of working therapeutically with the terminally ill. Over the last twenty years Dr. Kübler-Ross has studied more than twenty thousand people who have had near-death experiences. She now considers it important that death be considered as a transitionary state of consciousness leading to another kind of existence, rather than as a decline into oblivion. Kübler-Ross has given workshops and lectures on the dying process in many countries. Her many books include *On Death and Dying*, *Death – the Final Stage of Growth* and *On Life After Death*.

Kuei The Chinese term for the **lingam**, or phallus. It is symbolized as an oblong section of jade, terminating in a triangle, and is often embellished with the seven stars of the Great Bear, representing the seven days of the week.

Kulabel Among the Djerag and Djaru Aboriginal tribes of the East Kimberleys in Australia, the name of the Rainbow Serpent. The **medicine-man** is "killed" by the serpent at a water-hole and the serpent enters his body, making him "sick and mad" and then bestowing magical powers upon him. See also **Aborigines, Australian**.

Kumara In **Hinduism**, a virginal or celibate boy. The first kumaras were the seven sons of **Brahma**.

Kumari In **Hinduism**, a virginal maiden. In Nepal and Bengal, kumaris are often worshipped as personifications of the divine goddess **Shakti**, mother of the universe.

Kumbhaka In **Hatha Yoga**, a technique performed during **pranayama**. The breath is held after inhalation, stabilizing the inward and outward flow of **prana**, or life-energy. This has a profound effect on the meditator, allowing him to calm the mind and focus on the true **self**.

Kundalini From a Sanskrit term meaning "coil" or "spiral", spiritual and psychical energy that may be aroused systematically by techniques of **yoga** and which can be channelled through the **chakras** from the base of the spine to the crown of the head. Kundalini is often symbolized as a coiled serpent and is sometimes associated with the goddess **Kali**. See also **Ida**; **Pingala**; **Sushumna**; **Tantra**..

Kundalini Yoga See **Kundalini**; **Tantra**; **Yoga**.

Kyteler, Dame Alice Fourteenth-century Irish aristocrat accused of **witchcraft** and **demonology**. Dame Alice lived in Kilkenny in south-east Ireland and practised fertility rituals with Sir Arnold le Poer, a relative of her fourth husband. Alice would sacrifice red cockerels at different times of the year, and Sir Arnold participated in ceremonies wearing a horned mask. These strange practices came to the attention of the Bishop of Ossory, Richard de Landrede, who was determined to stamp out witchcraft in

Ireland and earn favour with the Pope. Dame Alice escaped to Dublin and later travelled to England, where she lived for the rest of her life. Others in Alice's circle were not so lucky. Her friend and servant Petronilla de Meath was cast into a dungeon and later burned alive before the Bishop in November 1324.

L

Labyrinth Legendary complex of passages and mazes built by the master builder Daedalus at the palace of Minos in Crete. King Minos confined the **Minotaur** in the labyrinth and it was fed on human sacrifices – seven boys and seven girls sent each year from Athens.

Ladder of Life Mystical symbol of ascending stages of consciousness. The ladder appears in Jacob's dream as the bridge between **heaven** and earth and in the **Kabbalah** as the **Tree of Life** or "Ladder of Lights". The rungs of the ladder represent different **emanations**, or levels of existence in the Cosmos. Theosophists use the term interchangeably with **hermetic chain** and **golden chain**.

Lakshmi In Hindu **mythology**, the goddess of fortune and beauty. Lakshmi was originally a sea-goddess, and is best known as the wife of **Vishnu**. She is also associated with the sacred plant **tulasi**.

Lama In Tibet, a high-ranking monk, especially one who heads a monastery.

Lamaism Term used to describe **esoteric** Tibetan **Buddhism**, which belongs to the **Mahayana** tradition. This form of Buddhism was introduced to Tibet during the seventh century and includes shamanic, Bon, and Tantric components. Lamaism is characterized by **mantras**, **exorcisms**, elaborate ritual ceremonies, and belief in the idea that the Dalai Lama incarnates a **bodhisattva**. The best-known Lamaist tract is the *Tibetan Book of the Dead*, a guide to post-mortem states of consciousness. See also Bardo; Evans-Wentz, W. Y.

Lamia In ancient Greek **mythology**, Lamia was the daughter of **Poseidon** and a mistress of **Zeus. Hera** was so jealous of her she destroyed Lamia's children and deformed her appearance so that she now took the hybrid form of a woman with the body of a serpent. Lamia lured victims to her domain and devoured them, and in ancient Rome became identified as a blood-sucking witch.

Lamias Also Lamiae. General term for female **demons** who could take many forms. As **mermaids**, they could lure boats to destruction; but on other occasions they resembled goats, with horses' hooves. Lamias were said to hiss like serpents and feed on the flesh of corpses. Compare with **Ghoul; Siren.**

Lammas A major **Wiccan** sabbat celebrated on August 1. The word "Lammas" is thought to mean "loaf-mass" and this is the time of year when the first corn is harvested. Known to the **Druids** as *Lughnassadh*, this Sabbat marks the season of autumn and was traditionally a celebration to Lugh, the Celtic sun god. *Lughnassadh* is associated with the waning power of the sun – in mythic terms the God has begun to die – but it is also a season in which one can reflect upon the fruits of the earth. **Wiccans** gather at Lammas to celebrate the gifts of abundance which have come forth from the womb of the Goddess. Mythologically, *Lughnassadh* represents fulfilment – the reaping of all that has been sown. See also **Witches' Sabbath.**

Lampadomancy Form of **divination** using the flame of a lamp or torch. The actions and movements of the flame are interpreted as an **oracle**. See also **Pyromancy.**

Lang, Andrew (1844–1912) Scottish folklorist, parapsychologist, poet, and author who edited collections of fairy tales for young children and had a deep interest in comparative mythology. He became interested in psychical research after reading a paper on the **Cock Lane Ghost** and joined the **Society for Psychical Research** in 1906 – becoming its president in 1911. Awarded a Doctor of Letters degree by Oxford University, Lang was a prolific author. His books include *Custom and Myth* (1884), *Myths, Literature and Religion* (1887), *The Book of Dreams and Ghosts* (1897), and *Magic and Religion* (1898). See also **Folklore.**

Lao Tzu (604–531 B.C.) Legendary Chinese sage credited as being the founder of **Taoism** and author of the famous spiritual classic the *Tao Te Ching*. Very little is known about Lao Tzu, and many scholars have doubted his historical existence. He is said to have served in the imperial archives at Lo and, according to one account, lived for two hundred years. He had a meeting with Confucius, who is supposed to have said: "I know that a bird can fly, a fish can swim, and an animal can run. But the dragon's ascent to heaven on the wind and the clouds is something which is beyond my knowledge. Today I have seen Lao-Tzu, who is rather like a dragon."

Lapis Exilis Mythic stone that enabled the **phoenix** to regain its youth. This stone is regarded by some authorities as synonymous with the **Holy Grail.**

Lapis Judaicus Identified in some degree with the **Lapis Exilis**, this mystical stone is said to have fallen from the crown of **Lucifer** and was retained by the angels of the air. It is also called Theolithos.

Lapis Philosophorum Latin for **Philosopher's Stone.**

La-place In **voodoo**, the apprentice or assistant to the **houngan**, or priest.

Lares Roman household **gods** and **spirits** that protected the family, property, and servants. They also guarded the farmlands and sometimes whole cities. Shrines to the lares would be found in most Roman homes and also at various crossroads.

Larvae In Roman **mythology**, the **souls** of deceased persons that were unceasingly restless because of crimes or violence committed while alive on earth. The Larvae were similar to **ghosts**, and the Romans believed they were a cause of madness in the living. They were sometimes referred to as **lemures**.

Latifa Term in Islamic **mysticism** usually translated as "subtlety". It refers to the inner spiritual faculties that can be aroused by a **Master**. The seven latifa may be compared with the **chakras**, although they do not correspond exactly. See also **Islam**.

Laurel Tree with magical and mythic associations. The Greek **nymph** Daphne was pursued by **Apollo** and prayed to be changed into another form. **Athena** transformed her into a laurel and this tree thereafter became sacred to Apollo. The leaves of the laurel were also chewed by the **Delphic Oracle** to induce visionary powers of prophecy, and were hung over doorways to send **ghosts** away.

La Vey, Anton Szandor (1930–1997) American satanist of Romanian-German-gypsy parentage, who was the founder and head of the **Church of Satan** in San Francisco, California. Earlier in his career, La Vey played oboe in the San Francisco Ballet Orchestra, worked as a lion-trainer, assisted in hypnotism shows, and became a police photographer. He began holding an occult studies group, which included film-maker Kenneth Anger; and in 1966 he shaved his head and proclaimed himself high **priest** of the Church of Satan. La Vey claimed an affiliated membership of nine thousand members in the United States, France, Italy, Germany, Britain, and South America, and was an advisor on several occult feature films, including *The Mephisto Waltz* and *Rosemary's Baby* – where he appeared on screen as the **Devil**. La Vey's books include *The Satanic Bible* (1969) and *The Satanic Rituals* (1972).

Law of Retribution Popular term for the law of **karma**.

Laya From the Sanskrit root *li*, meaning "to disintegrate", the mystical point between manifest and unmanifest in the cosmos – the calm state of equilibrium.

Laya Yoga School of **yoga**, in which the practitioner learns to attain **samadhi** through meditative practices that absorb the mind into the **self**.

Laying-on-of-hands A form of **spiritual healing** in which the healer lays hands on the body of the subject and thereby acts as an intermediary channel for divine force, or healing power. When this power is transmitted through the healer to the diseased or injured person, that person may be restored to health and well-being. See also **Contact Healing; Edwards, Harry; Life-force; Miracles.**

Leadbeater, Reverend Charles Webster (1847–1934) Curate in the Church of England who had a longstanding interest in **occultism** and joined the **Theosophical Society** in 1884. In due course he became a major figure in the Theosophical movement, alongside **Madame Helena Blavatsky** and **Annie Besant**. Leadbeater discovered **Krishnamurti** in Adyar, Madras, and he and Annie Besant believed he was a World Teacher, a claim Krishnamurti denied. Eager in his pursuit of **paranormal** and mystical knowledge, Leadbeater travelled widely – to the United States, Ceylon, and Australia – and founded a commune of Theosophists in Sydney. He also helped to establish the Liberal Catholic Church and became its second presiding bishop.

From time to time Leadbeater was charged with engaging in homosexual activities involving his young students, and he acquired a reputation as a pederast. Despite the attacks on Leadbeater's credibility, however, it is clear that he possessed a genuine **psychic** ability. He was a remarkably prolific author, whose works include *The Masters and the Path, The Chakras, Clairvoyance, The Hidden Side of Things, Man Visible and Invisible, The Science of the Sacraments,* and *A Textbook of Theosophy*. An authoritative biography of Leadbeater, *The Elder Brother*, written by Dr. Gregory Tillett, was published in London in 1982.

Leader, Circle In **spiritualism**, a person other than the **medium** who is entrusted to lead the circle, administer, and overview the procedures and help in any emergency.

Leading Houses In **astrology**, the cardinal **signs** – **Aries**, **Cancer**, **Libra**, and **Capricorn** – that are assigned to the first, fourth, seventh, and tenth houses respectively. See also **House**.

Leary, Dr. Timothy (1920–1996) Controversial American psychologist who became a figurehead of the 1960s counter-culture and an advocate of **psychedelic** drugs as a tool to transform popular consciousness. A colleague of Baba **Ram Dass** (Richard Alpert) at Harvard University, Leary was evicted from his academic post because of controversy surrounding his experimental use of psychedelics. He subsequently established a private research centre in a Gothic mansion set in lavish grounds at Millbrook, New York. This became the scene of many extraordinary psychedelic escapades, including an encounter with Ken Kesey's "merry pranksters". Leary advocated the use of **LSD** in conjunction with the ***Tibetan Book of the Dead*** and wrote his book *The Psychedelic Experience* (co-authored with Richard Alpert and Ralph Metzner) as a practical guide to experiencing the **Bardo** visions. He later became interested in cyberspace technology, and towards the end of his life advocated what he called "designer death" – consciously planning your own transition through death. His many books include *The Politics of Ecstasy, High Priest, Psychedelic Prayers, Chaos and Cyberculture,* and his autobiography, *Flashbacks*.

Lecanomancy Form of **divination** in which a stone or similar object is thrown into a basin of water. The image of the object in the rippling water, and the sound it makes dropping to the bottom, are interpreted as having divinatory significance. An alternative method is to drop oil on the surface of the water and interpret the shapes that form there. See also **Hydromancy**.

Lecour, Paul (1871–1954) French civil servant who had a strong interest in **mysticism** and Christianity and founded the Society for Atlantean Studies at the Sorbonne in 1926. He photographed **Eva C**'s "ectoplasm experiments" and produced several books on mystical topics, including *The Seventh Sense* (*Le Septième Sens*) and *St Paul and the Christian Mysteries* (*Saint Paul et les Mystères Chrétiens*).

Lee, Ann (1736–1784) English mystic who was an influential figure in the religious movement known as the Shakers. After hearing a sermon from Jane Wardley, who claimed Christ would return to earth in the form of a woman, Lee joined the movement. She was later imprisoned for disturbing the peace and, while in prison, had a vision of herself as the "Bride of the Lamb". Thereafter she became known as "Mother Ann" and "Ann the Word". In 1774, with a handful of followers, she emigrated to the United States and settled at Watervliet, near Albany, New York. The community she established was pacifist and communistic and dedicated to celibacy and chastity.

Leek, Sybil (1923–1983) English-born witch who went to live in the United States in 1964 and began to attract widespread media coverage for her **pagan** beliefs and practices. Sybil Leek claimed to trace her witchcraft ancestry back to the twelfth century. Well known for her radio programmes on witchcraft, she opened an occult restaurant ("Sybil Leek's Cauldron") and wrote several books, including *Diary of a Witch, The Sybil Leek Book of Fortune-telling* and *Cast Your Own Spell.*

Leffas Occult term for the **astral bodies** of plants. See also **Floromancy**.

Left-hand Path From the Latin *sinister*, "left", the path of **black magic** and **sorcery**. Practitioners in this tradition seek to use magic to acquire personal power, rather than for the purpose of spiritual transcendence. See also **Brothers of the Shadow**.

Legend Fables and romantic tales ascribed to heroes and heroines and also the lives of the **saints**. Legends (from the Latin *legendus*, "to be read") were usually read aloud at gatherings or at matins.

Lei-kung In Chinese **mythology**, the god of thunder, who was depicted as a gruesome man with a blue body, claws, and wings. He carried a hammer and would punish guilty people whose crimes had not been discovered by the processes of law.

Leland, Charles Godfrey (1824–1903) American folklorist and authority on **witchcraft**. Leland went to college in the United States and later studied at the Universities of Heidelberg and Munich and at the Sorbonne in Paris. After fighting on the side of the rebels in the 1848 revolution, he returned from Paris to the United States and took up a career as a journalist. A few years after marrying he was again involved in a military campaign, this time the American Civil War.

After fighting at the Battle of Gettysburg, Leland left with his family for London to begin a new life and acquire new interests. He began to study **folklore** and **gypsy** legends, taught himself Romany – the language of the gypsies – and after ten years in England moved to Florence, Italy. There Leland became friendly with a young woman called Maddalena, who told him that the old gods were still being worshipped in secret, and Leland discovered to his surprise that there was still a cult of **Diana** in the guise of Aradia, Diana's daughter. Leland described in his book *Aradia*, the Gospel of the Witches how ritual offerings were made to Diana each month when the moon was full, and he provided a detailed description of a **coven** meeting. Leland's writings influenced **Gerald Gardner** and have had a strong effect on **modern witchcraft**.

Lemegeton Title given to the medieval work of **black magic** or **goetia** known as *The Lesser Key of Solomon*. It was translated from French, Latin, and Hebrew manuscript copies by the occultist **MacGregor Mathers**. According to **A. E. Waite**, the most complete extant copy is in French and dates from the seventeenth century; however, the medieval demonologist **Johannes Wier** refers to it, so other versions must have existed at an earlier date. See also ***Key of Solomon***.

Lemuralia Also Lemuria. Roman festival held each May to exorcise the **lemures** from the home. The lemures were distracted by throwing black beans in their direction.

Lemures Term used variously to describe hungry **ghosts** (ancient Rome); the **elementals** of **Air**; or the elementary spirits of deceased persons that manifest during spiritualist **seances** causing rappings and other "phenomena".

Lemuria Mythic lost continent said by some theorists to have existed in the Indian Ocean, or in the Pacific. Lemuria is often compared to **Atlantis**, except its inhabitants were said to be not so highly evolved. Theosophists believe that the human species has evolved through different **root races**, and describe the Lemurians as the third root race, preceding both the Atlanteans and the present human species. Lemuria is sometimes referred to as "Mu".

Le Normand, Marie (1772–1843) Famous occult diviner, known as "the Sybil of the Faubourg Saint Germain", who was acclaimed for predicting the futures of the French revolutionary Jean Paul Marat and the Jacobin statesman Maximilien Robespierre. Drawn into the exclusive circle of Josephine Beauharnais, she read Napoleon's **horoscope** and later established a salon in Paris where she read fortunes in the cards for wealthy clients. After the fall of Napoleon she went to Belgium and read the fortune of the Prince of Orange. However, a dispute with the Belgium customs department resulted in her imprisonment, and she finally died a forgotten and neglected figure. See also **Divination**.

Leo In **astrology**, the **sign** of the **zodiac** for those born between July 23 and August 22. A **fire** sign, ruled by the **sun**, Leo is symbolized by a lion and is the fifth sign of the zodiac. Those born under this sign are said to be proud, ambitious, generous, friendly, and practical; they can also be obstinate and boastful. Leos are supposed to be good managers and organizers.

Leo, Alan (1860–1917) British astrologer, generally considered to be the father-figure of modern **astrology**. Leo became a member of the **Theosophical Society** in 1890, and in the same year produced a monthly journal entitled *Astrologer's Magazine* (later retitled *Modern Astrology*). In 1915, Leo also founded the Astrological Lodge of the Theosophical Society. One of Leo's principal aims was to promote astrology to a wide general market. He did this through his "shilling" **horoscopes** and his prolific writings. Leo's published works include *Astrology for All, How to Judge a Nativity, The Progressed Horoscope*, and *Esoteric Astrology*.

León, Moses ben Shem Tov de (c. 1240–1305) Spanish Jewish mystic who was born at León near Castile. He became a member of the local community of Kabbalists and was influenced by Todros Abulafia and Joseph Gikatilla. By about 1286 he had compiled a major work in Aramaic, which he called a "Mystical Midrash"; this forms a major part of the ***Zohar***, one of the principal works of the **Kabbalah**. Moses de León lived for some time in Guadalajara and later in Avila, although in the 1290s he also spent much of his life wandering and meeting other **mystics**. He was the author of over twenty works, many of which survive only as fragments. Moses de León died in Arevalo.

Leonard, Gladys Osborne (1882–1968) British **trance** medium who claimed to have a **control** named "Feda" – an Indian girl who had died around 1800. Feda allegedly guided Mrs. Leonard to become a professional **psychic medium** and warned of an impending world catastrophe (World War I). In 1915, Mrs. Leonard had several meetings with **Sir Oliver Lodge**, whose son Raymond had been killed in action. Lodge wrote an account of the **seances** at which Raymond revealed his post-mortem survival, and Mrs. Leonard achieved widespread fame as a result. She was later tested by psychical researcher Whately Carington, who came to the conclusion that "Feda" was not merely a projection of Mrs. Leonard's personality but showed distinct and separate characteristics. Mrs. Leonard published her autobiography, *My Life in Two Worlds*, in 1931.

Leprechauns In Irish **folklore**, small **dwarfs** or **elves** who were said to haunt wine-cellars and guard mounds of hidden treasure. See also **Dwarf; Elves; Fairies**.

Leshy Also Lesiy. In the traditional **mythology** of the Slavic peoples, a wood spirit or **satyr** with both human and animal characteristics. Traditionally, the Leshy was said to have a green beard and a blue skin. The Leshy inhabited the forests and lured unwary travellers into caves, but was fortunately alive only during the spring and summer months.

Levater, Johann Kaspar (1741–1801) Swiss poet, **mystic**, and theologian who is remembered as the founder of the system of **physiognomy**, whereby a person's character is inferred from aspects of physical appearance. The philosopher Johann Goethe (1749–1832), who was a personal friend, helped Levater compile his four-volume magnum opus, *Physiognomical Fragments for the Promotion of the Knowledge and Love of Man*, which was published in 1775–1778. Levater was also a supporter of the Freemason and occultist **Count Alessandro di Cagliostro**.

Lévi, Eliphas (1810–1875) The magical name of Alphonse-Louis Constant, the son of a poor Parisian shoemaker. Lévi studied for the priesthood, but was asked to leave on account of his sexual permissiveness. He worked for a time as a political caricaturist and then turned to magical and hermetic philosophy. He produced a number of books that have since become occult classics, despite their shoddy scholarship. Lévi's best work is contained in *The Mysteries of Magic*, an anthology of his writings edited by **A. E. Waite**. His other books include *Le Dogme et Ritual de la Haute Magie*, *Histoire de la Magie*, and *La Clef des Grandes Mystères*, which are available in a variety of English-language editions. From an occult viewpoint, Lévi is remembered mainly for two things: he made the important observation that the twenty-two cards of the **Major Arcana** of the **Tarot** appear to correlate symbolically with the kabbalistic **Tree of Life**; and the fact that the magician **Aleister Crowley** claimed to be Lévi's **reincarnation** and occult successor. See also **Hermetica**.

Leviathan According to the biblical narrative, a monstrous fish or sea-serpent formed on the fifth day of Creation. For the Jews, Leviathan was a symbol of **God**'s awesome power and as such he also features in the Day of Judgment. As a symbol of **chaos** and destruction, he was incorporated into medieval **demonology**. Leviathan is regarded by occultist **Kenneth Grant** as the negative or Qlippothic equivalent of the **Tarot** image ***The Hanged Man***, which is ruled by the element **Water**. See also **Qlippoth**.

Levitation The act of raising the human body, or any other physical object, into the air without visible means. It has been claimed that levitation may be caused by mental concentration and will power. It is also a paranormal ability ascribed to certain **psychics**, **trance mediums**, and **fakirs**. The best-documented case in modern times has been that of **Daniel Dunglas Home**, who is said to have levitated out of a third-floor window at the residence of Lord Adare in London in 1868.

Leys Alignments of ancient megaliths, **dolmens**, and stone circles, whose patterns are said to constitute grids of "power", or ley lines. The amateur archaeologist Alfred Watkins first brought attention to these alignments in 1921, and psychical researchers and **mediums** have since claimed that patterns of psychic energy emanate from the leys. Some **ufologists** believe that the ley lines are power-grids used to guide extraterrestrial visitors who have allegedly contacted human civilization since earliest times and who have profoundly influenced various **myths** and **legends** relating to the origin and cultural development of the human species.

Libation The ceremonial act of pouring wine in honour of a god. In ancient Rome libations were poured over the **lares** or household deities.

Libellus Merlini The *Little Book of Merlin*, a Latin tract ascribed to Geoffrey of Monmouth, which described the supernatural prophecies of "Ambrosius Merlin" relating to the symbolic vision of the battle of the white and red dragons (said to represent the Saxons and Britons respectively).

Liber Lapidum Medieval book on precious stones, dating from about 1123. Written by Bishop Marbod of Rennes, it ascribes symbolic values to several stones. For example, onyx is supposed to induce nightmares, a sapphire may be used to protect oneself from fear, and the sardonyx represents the inner mystical **self.**

Libra In **astrology**, the **sign** of the zodiac for those born between September 23 and October 22. An **Air** sign, ruled by **Venus**, Libra is symbolized by a pair of scales and is the seventh sign of the **zodiac**. Those born under this sign are said to be intuitive, artistic, and charming. They are given to making comparisons and can therefore become quarrelsome; they may also be moody and whimsical. Librans are said to be ideally suited to careers in the arts, antiques, and theatre.

Licking a Charm Phrase used to describe a remedy for counteracting a **spell** inflicted on a child. The method was to lick the child's forehead in an upward vertical direction, then across, and up again. The taste of salt on the tongue was taken as a sure sign of enchantment.

Lien In ancient China, the sacred eight-petalled **Lotus.**

Life, Tree of See **Tree of Life.**

Life-atom Theosophical concept of the monad. See also **Life-wave.**

Life-flow See **Life-force.**

Life-force Term for the universal life energy that sustains all living things in the universe. It is known variously as **prana** (Sanskrit), **ch'i** (Chinese **Taoism**), and **ki** (Japanese **Buddhism**); and in animistic religions it is worshipped as god-in-Nature. Compare with **Pantheism.**

Life-wave In **Theosophy**, a host of **monads** or "spiritual **life-atoms**" that exercise a profound creative influence on all levels of manifestation, including the **physical plane.** Different Theosophic systems maintain variously that there are three, seven, or ten such "life-waves".

Ligature of the Faculties From the Latin *ligare*, "to bind", a term used in **mysticism** to confirm that physical activity (e.g. verbal **prayer** or **mantras**), is impossible in a state of **transcendent** consciousness.

Light Universal symbol of illumination and **transcendence**, equated with the **Spirit** and with the **Godhead**. In the **Kabbalah** the supreme Reality is **Ain Soph Aur**, "the limitless Light", and mystics universally describe light filling their souls, or sweeping their minds into a state of transcendent bliss. White light contains all colours and also all "virtues". It therefore symbolizes Totality and One-ness. Many cosmologies, especially those from ancient Persia and Egypt, describe illumination and initiation in terms of the forces of Light conquering the forces of Darkness.

Light English spiritualist journal, founded by **Stainton Moses** and Dawson Rogers in 1881 under the auspices of the **London Spiritualist Alliance**. The journal still exists and is now published quarterly by the **College of Psychic Studies** in London.

Light, Collector of Term used in **astrology** to describe a situation where a planet receives aspects from two other **significators** which are in a position of **dignity**. The collector of light is then seen as a mediating influence and is said to bring a harmonious outcome to quarrels, disagreements, and lawsuits.

Lightness Quality ascribed to the element **Air**, also associated with spontaneous dance and the urge to rise above oneself. It is thus linked to **ecstasy**, and is a quality described by those who have the **out-of-the-body experience** or claim the **paranormal** faculty of **levitation**.

Light Planets In **astrology**, a reference to those bodies that are swift in motion and have a "light" gravity (the **moon**, **Venus**, and **Mercury**).

Lights Term applied in **astrology** to differentiate the **sun** and **moon** from the other **planets** in the **horoscope**.

Lila Hindu term referring to the divine "play" or "sport" of the **gods**, whether in love or in Nature.

Lilith According to Hebrew tradition, the first wife of Adam. Lilith is a "dark" form of the goddess, identified as being vengeful, hostile to childbirth, and demanding of human sacrifice. Lilith's name means "night monster" and she was sometimes characterized as a night-demon or **phantom** who, like **Hecate** and **Lamia**, personified **evil** and darkness. In the magical tradition of the **Hermetic Order of the Golden Dawn**, Lilith is described as "Queen of the Night and of Demons" and is one of the **Qlippoth**, the negative form of **Malkuth**.

Lilly, Dr. John (1915–2001) American neurophysiologist who was a major pioneer in the study of **altered states of consciousness** and was also well known for his work on communication with dolphins. In his book *The Centre of the Cyclone* (1972), Lilly described his theories of the operations of the human mind on the basis of his personal exploration of sensory deprivation states. Lilly found that visionary experiences could arise during extended periods of confinement in an **isolation tank**, and that these experiences related directly to the "programming" patterns in the mind produced by religious beliefs and doctrine. In a later work, *Simulations of God* (1976), Lilly put forth his view that religious beliefs often inhibit mystical illumination and impose a limit or constriction on the experience of **transcendental** reality. Dr. Lilly's other books include *Programming and Metaprogramming in the Human Biocomputer* (1972); *The Dyadic Cyclone*, co-authored with Antoinetta Lilly, (1976); *The Deep Self* (1977); and *The Scientist* (1978).

Lilly, William (1602–1681) English astrologer who lived during the reign of Oliver Cromwell and was patronized by him during the dispute between the Royalists and Roundheads. Lilly is said to have predicted the death of Charles I, the Great Fire of London, and the Restoration, and wrote many works relating to **astrology** and prediction. His most famous almanac was *Merlinus Anglicanus* (1641).

Lines of Power See **Leys**.

Lingam Hindu symbol of the phallus, representing the life-giving powers of the universe. It correlates with the Chinese **yang** force. The term lingam, in its literal form, is Sanskrit for a "sign" or "form". The lingam is sacred to **Shiva**.

Linga Sharira From the Sanskrit, "body pattern", the etheric counterpart of the physical body. It may thus be used to describe the **astral body**.

Lion Animal with mythic and magical associations. The lion symbolizes **gold** and the **sun** and was sacred to the followers of the cult of **Mithra**. In ancient Egypt devotees of **Sekhmet** worshipped her in the form of a lion-headed goddess. The lion, as **Leo**, is the fifth sign of the **zodiac** and is identified in this capacity as one of the three **Fire** signs (the other two being **Sagittarius** and **Aries**). The lion is also featured in the symbolism of the **Major Arcana** of the **Tarot**. On the card of ***Temperance***, the lion symbolizes Fire and is counterbalanced by the Eagle (**Air**). On the card ***Strength***, however, it represents brute force that yields to intuition with the evolution of spiritual consciousness. In **alchemy**, the lion is a symbol of **sulphur**, and in different contexts may be a symbol of both Fire and **Earth**. The emblem of the lion is also a common motif in heraldry.

Lion Posture Position adopted by **Gautama Buddha** as he prepared to enter **nirvana**. Gautama lay stretched out on his right side, his head supported by his right arm.

Lipikas In Hindu **mythology**, the "Lords of Karma" who embody the law. Although some consider the lipikas to be **gods** or high **devas** who judge humankind, it is probably more accurate to think of them as self-regulating abstract forces that exist in Nature and maintain order.

Lithomancy **Divination** by means of precious stones. One method is to take stones, each of which have planetary or symbolic significance, and scatter them on a dark surface. The stone that reflects the most light provides the **omen** in divination. See also **Birthstones**.

Little People Affectionate term for **fairies**, used as an alternative to naming them directly.

Loa In Haitian **voodoo**, deities that possess the practitioner while the latter is in a state of **trance**. There are two main groups – the rada gods, of Dahomean origin, and the petro gods, of Caribbean origin. Loas are invoked at ceremonies by **vevers**, sigil designs which are drawn on the ground.

Lobsang Rampa Pseudonym of Cyril Henry Hoskin (1910–1981), author of the famous international best-seller ***The Third Eye***, which described the initiatory experiences of a Tibetan high priest. After being discovered living in Dublin, Hoskin maintained that he was possessed by the spirit of a genuine **lama** and that his writings were authentic. Despite the controversy that surrounds *The Third Eye* and its sequels, there is no doubt that the writings of Lobsang Rampa have had an enormous influence in the popular mystical market and have often stimulated readers to pursue a more detailed study of **yoga**, **meditation**, and other spiritual disciplines. See also **Initiation**.

Loch Ness Monster Mysterious underwater creature, which in recent years has been the subject of spasmodic "sightings" on Loch Ness in Scotland. During the early 1970s the Loch Ness Investigation Bureau – which included scientists, technicians and volunteers – made a concerted, though unsuccessful, effort to photograph the monster; there have been periodic research excursions to the Loch since then to monitor underwater sonic echoes and take photographs from mini-submarines. The Loch is 22 miles long, 1 mile wide, and 750 feet deep, so extensive surveillance is required. The current theory is that the Loch Ness Monster may be a species of plesiosaurus – an aquatic reptile otherwise thought to be extinct. According to marine biologist Jacques Cousteau, there would need to be fourteen such creatures in the Loch to enable them to breed and survive as a species.

Lodge, Sir Oliver (1851–1940) Noted British Psychical researcher and physicist who was Principal of Birmingham University

(1900–1919) and was knighted in 1902 for his services to science. Lodge researched electricity and thermal conductivity and was a pioneer of radio technology. In 1884 he became interested in the possibility of thought transference and subsequently began to research **psychic mediums** and **trance states**. He investigated the mediumship of **Mrs. Leonore Piper** and **Eusapia Palladino**, and then engaged in seances with **Mrs. Gladys Leonard** in an effort to contact his son Raymond, who had died in World War I. Lodge was impressed by the evidence he received and subsequently championed the belief in life after death. Lodge was president of the **Society for Psychical Research** (1901–1903) and was also a prolific author. Among his many books are *Man and the Universe* (1908), *Survival of Man* (1909), *Raymond: Or Life After Death* (1916), *Ether and Reality* (1925), and *Why I believe in Personal Immortality* (1928).

Logos Greek term meaning "word" or "thought", used in **Gnostic** terminology to mean a **deity** in the manifested universe. In both **magic** and religion, the vibrational quality of sound and the power of the utterance have been regarded as most important. In the Book of John (1:1) it is written, "In the beginning was the Word, and the Word was with God, and the Word was God … all things were made through Him and without Him was not anything made that was made." Similarly, in the **Kabbalah**, the world is said to have been formed by the utterance of the sacred Name of God – a forty-two letter extension of **Tetragrammaton**. A similar emphasis pertains in ritual **magic**. In his book *The Key of the Mysteries*, the noted occultist **Eliphas Lévi** writes: "All magic is in a word, and that word pronounced kabbalistically is stronger than all the powers of Heaven, Earth and Hell." See also **God-names, Hekau, Words of Powers.**

Lohan Chinese Buddhist term for one who has attained **enlightenment**. It is identical to the **Pali** Buddhist term **arahant**. See also **Buddhism**.

Lokapalas In Hindu **cosmology**, Vedic protector-spirits who guarded the eight quarters of the world.

Lokas In **Hinduism**, "places" or "locations" that can be either material or spiritual spheres, and which indicate the different "densities" of matter. In **Buddhism**, the lokas are the six worlds of **illusion: heaven**, the human world, the world of the asura demons, the animal world, the world of hungry **ghosts**, and **hell**. One incarnates in a different loka according to the quality of one's **karma.**

Loki In Scandinavian **mythology**, the god of fire, who was originally a member of the **Aesir**. Loki guided the mistletoe that killed the sun-god **Balder**, and as a consequence the other gods bound Loki to a rock, with a snake dripping poisonous venom over him. Loki was saved by his wife and joined the evil monsters and giants as the sworn enemy of the Aesir.

London Spiritualist Alliance Founded in 1884 by **Stainton Moses** and **Alfred Russel Wallace**, this organization encouraged unbiased research into **psychic** and **paranormal** phenomena. It became the **College of Psychic Studies**, which still exists today and publishes the quarterly journal *Light*.

Lord Term used in **astrology** as a synonym for **ruler**. It is customary to use the expressions "ruler of a **sign**" and "lord of a **house**".

Lord of the Flies Title given in medieval **demonology** to **Beelzebub**, whose name is a combination of **Baal** (a Phoenician **deity**) and *zebub* (a fly). Beelzebub claimed to be the first

angel in the first heaven, but he had wings because he was a fly, not because he was a "fallen angel".

Lord of the Year In **astrology**, an expression most commonly used to describe the **planet** that has the most **dignities**, or strongly favourable aspects, in a solar revolution **horoscope**.

Lorelei In German folk-legend, a beautiful maiden who sat on a steep rock near St. Goar on the Rhine, luring boatmen to crash their vessels on the dangerous rocks. The Lorelei would sit combing her hair and singing beautiful songs, and in many respects resembled the **sirens** of classical Greek **mythology**.

Lost Soul In **Theosophy**, a being devoid of any possibility of spiritual redemption who has sunk to the level of the eighth sphere or the so-called **Planet of Death**. At this level "lost souls" disintegrate and pass out of existence.

Lotus Plant sacred in many different cultures. In ancient Egypt it was dedicated to the sun-god **Horus**, who had come forth from the lotus blossom, thereby gaining eternal youth. In ancient Persia it was similarly regarded as a symbol of the **sun**. The lotus plant is sacred among the Hindus because **Brahma** was born from it, and it also heralded the birth of **Gautama Buddha**. In Chinese **Buddhism**, the Western Heaven is the location of the Sacred Lake of Lotuses and it is here that the souls of the virtuous rest in lotus buds until they are admitted to **Paradise**. In Japan, the eight-petalled lotus is a symbol of the past, present, and future.

Lotus, Full Alternative name for the **lotus posture**.

Lotus, Half Term used to describe a variant on the **full lotus**, where the legs are crossed but only one foot is pulled up to rest on the opposite thigh. Western devotees of **yoga** sometimes find this posture easier to maintain without discomfort.

Lotus-eaters From the Greek, *Lotophagi*. In Greek **mythology**, the inhabitants of a region in north-west Africa who lived on the sweet **lotus-fruit**, which was said to cause forgetfulness. **Odysseus** visited the lotus-eaters on his journey home from the Trojan War.

Lotus Posture A classical **asana** in **yoga**. The yogi sits on a mat with the left foot over the right thigh and the right foot over the left thigh. The hands may be placed either in the lap or over the knees, palm upwards. This posture is used during **meditation**: the yogi concentrates his attention on the region of the **third eye** and seeks spiritual self-knowledge.

Lotus Sutra Popular name for a **Mahayana Buddhist** text whose full name is *Saddharma-Pundarika Sutra* (the *Lotus of the True Doctrine*). Dating from the second century, the text emphasizes **Buddha** the Eternal, Omniscient, Omnipotent – the creator/destroyer of the world. The Lotus Sutra proclaims that each person has the potential for buddhahood. The text has been especially influential in the Orient, and remains the main scripture in Chinese **Buddhism**.

Loudun See **Grandier, Urbain**.

Loup Garou Voodoo term for a **werewolf**.

Lourdes Sacred healing site at the foot of the Central Pyrenees in France, where many people have claimed miraculous cures and remissions from disease. It was here in 1858 that a young shepherdess, Bernadette Soubirous, had eighteen visions of the Virgin Mary and was instructed to bathe in a spring near the River Gave. Bernadette herself suffered from asthma, and this continued to recur, even after her visions of the Virgin. She also had rheumatism and a tumour, and died at the premature age of thirty-five. These aspects notwithstanding, the Roman Catholic Church recognized the unique nature of Bernadette's visionary experience and established a bureau to authenticate **miracles** occurring on the site. Around two million visitors go to Lourdes each year, and thousands of pilgrims have been healed by their faith. See also **Faith-healing**.

Lovecraft, Howard Phillips (1890–1937) American occult and horror-fiction author who became a cult figure in underground literature in the 1960s. Lovecraft developed a mythology around "the dread Cthulhu", in which powers of **evil** and darkness threatened to break through to control the world, and he was obsessed with the theme of global threat (*The Colours out of Space, The Dunwich Horror, The Shadow over Innsmouth*). Lovecraft invented the concept of the "legendary" occult text *The Necronomicon*, and at least two versions of this text now exist, both purporting to be authentic. Lovecraft's supernatural tales have been collected into a number of volumes, including *The Tomb, At the Mountains of Madness, The Haunter of the Dark*, and *The Lurker at the Threshold*.

Love Potion In **witchcraft** and **herbalism**, an aphrodisiac said to cause a person to fall in love with someone else – often the next person who simply happens to appear. Some traditional herbal or "aphrodisiac" recipes draw on herbs or foods that appeared to resemble the human sexual organs – asparagus, oysters, cucumbers, bananas, and so on. Certain herbs, such as mint, **mandrake**, and **verbena**, have also been used in love potions. Very often an **incantation** is performed as part of the magical **conjuration**. American herbalist Jeanne Rose describes a traditional Egyptian love potion in her book *Herbal Guide to Inner Health*. The recipe calls for 1 pint of water, 1 ounce of mashed liquorice root, 1 ounce of mashed sesame seed, 1 ounce of bruised fennel seed, and some honey. The ingredients are boiled in a pot, allowed to simmer for five minutes and are then cooled, made into an infusion, and strained. The potion is taken twice a day with locks of the desirable person's hair entwined around the fingers, and a powerful **magical formula** of love and passion is recited at the same time.

Lovers, The In the **Tarot**, the card that depicts two naked figures standing in the Garden of Eden – personifying innocence regained. The **holy guardian angel** towers over them, bestowing grace. The card symbolizes the gradual fusion of sexual polarities and the mystical **transcendence** of duality. It is also reminiscent of the Greek myth of Castor and Polydeuces (Pollux) who were placed in the sky by **Zeus** as solar and lunar opposites with a common destiny. The pathway of *The Lovers* links **Tiphareth** and **Binah** on the **Tree of Life**, spheres which in themselves represent the divine son and the great mother, respectively. See also **Androgyne; Dual Signs.**

Lower Spirits Term used by **occultists** to describe **elementals**, lesser **devas, fairies,** and other low-ranking **supernatural** beings.

LSD General name for the potent **psychedelic** drug lysergic acid diethylamide, which was popularized in the 1960s by Michael Hollingshead, **Dr. Timothy Leary**, and Baba **Ram Dass**. LSD was first synthesized by the Swiss pharmacologist Albert Hofmann, who discovered its effects accidentally in 1943 while investigating **ergot**, from which it is derived. On a per-weight basis, LSD is the most potent psychedelic substance known. An intake of 250 micrograms causes a profound **altered state of consciousness**, characterized by visionary, symbolic experiences and heightened awareness of emotions, sounds, and colours. Leary advocated the use of LSD as a sacrament in conjunction with the initiatory book the ***Tibetan Book of the Dead***, which describes the passage of the soul from death to rebirth. See also **Eleusis; Hallucinations.**

Lucid Dream See **Dream, Lucid.**

Lucifer In **astrology** and astronomy, name given to **Venus** as the morning star.

Lucifer One of the many names for the **Devil**. Lucifer means "light bearer", and he was originally an **angel** of light; however, he has been classified among medieval **demons** and **devils** because he fell from grace by rebelling against the **Elohim**. In the theosophical tradition, Lucifer has been looked upon more kindly and is regarded as a personification of the independent and self-conscious mind, which desires to evolve through many lifetimes towards the **Light**.

Luck Good fortune. **Occultists** have traditionally believed that luck can be summoned through **rituals**, by heeding **omens** and portents, by using divinatory **oracles**, and by wearing or displaying **lucky charms** and **amulets**. See also **Divination; Fortune-teller; Horseshoe, Lucky.**

Lucky Charm Small object worn to bring good **luck**. For example, in Asia and many parts of Africa **turquoise** is prized as a "lucky stone" that can ward off the **evil-eye**, and it is worn in rings, necklaces, and bracelets as a protection. A lucky charm can also be an **incantation** or **spell** designed to summon the powers of good fortune.

Lughnassadh See **Lammas.**

Lully, Raymond (Ramon Lull) (c. 1235–1315) Spanish-born Christian **mystic** and prolific traveller, who originally spent much of his time in courtly life, pursuing the favours of aristocratic ladies. It is said that his conversion to mystical affairs stems from an affair involving Signora Ambrosia Eleoanora de Genes, to whom Lully was greatly attracted, despite the fact she was in love with, and married to, another man. The Signora, tiring of his amorous pursuits, called Lully to her in private and exposed her cancerous breast to him, at the same time urging him to transform his "useless and criminal passion into holy love" and direct his affections to the Creator. Ashamed of his blatant passion, Lully withdrew to his home, cast himself beneath a crucifix, and dedicated himself to Christ. In subsequent years Lully became a fervent evangelist and travelled widely – in Italy, France, Cyprus, and northern Africa – his main quest being to prove the "errors" of **Islam**. On two different visits Lully preached to the crowds in Tunis in an effort to convert them from **Mohammed** to Christ, and was imprisoned and stoned as a result. On the second occasion, Lully was so badly injured that he lay dazed on the seashore, given up for dead. He was rescued by Genoese merchants who took him away in their boat, but he died soon afterwards within sight of Majorca.

Lully has been described in occult tradition as a great alchemist as well as a noted mystic, and a legend prevails that he transformed a large quantity of quicksilver, tin, and lead into **gold** at the request of King Edward III. It is generally thought, however, that this tale was concocted by the English alchemist Sir George Ripley, who popularized the works of Raymond Lully. As far as is known, Lully never visited England.

Luminaries In **astrology**, the **sun** and **moon**.

Luminous Arc Theosophical term, synonymous with **ascending arc**.

Luminous Body Term sometimes used by **occultists** as a synonym for the **astral body**.

Luminous Paths In Western **magic**, a synonym for the twenty-two **Tarot** paths of the **Major Arcana**, when used for visionary **pathworkings**. See also **Tree of Life**.

Luna In ancient Rome, the goddess of the **moon**. She was identified with **Selene** and also with the Greek goddess **Artemis**. See also **Lunar Goddesses**.

Lunar Pertaining to the **moon**. See also **Luna**.

Lunar Goddesses Traditionally, the **sun** has been regarded as a masculine force and the **moon** as feminine. Consequently, the moon is often personified as a lunar goddess and is worshipped in this form. Many of the ancient **pantheons** featured lunar goddesses. They include: **Isis** and **Hathor** (Egypt); **Astarte** (Phoenicia); **Ishtar** (Babylonia); **Artemis**, **Hecate**, and **Selene** (Greece); **Diana** and **Luna** (Rome). In China the moon is the force behind all things that are **yin**, or feminine. See also **Feminine Principle**.

Lunar Pitris Theosophical expression meaning "lunar fathers" or "lunar ancestors", used to describe seven classes of beings, three of the incorporeal (arupa), the other four corporeal (rupa) in form, who are said to come from the "Moon-Chain" to the "Earth-Chain" as part of the process of spiritual evolution. See also **Theosophy**.

Lunation Term used in **astrology** to describe the exact moment of the **moon**'s conjunction with the **sun**. It is the time of new moon.

Lung Gom In Tibetan **mysticism**, the apparent ability of spiritual **adepts** and **Masters** to travel long distances across land without rest, and with very little effort.

Lung Wang In traditional Chinese folk-legends, the dragon-king who resided in all lakes, brought rain and storms, and ruled the oceans. He was also associated with water-sports.

Lupercalia In ancient Rome, a fertility festival sacred to **Lupercus** that was held annually on February 15. It included purification ceremonies, which were believed to aid the renewal of life and Nature, and also rites which were intended to protect domesticated animals from wolves.

Luperci The "wolf-warders" who in ancient Rome ran around the Palatine Hill during the festival known as the **Lupercalia**. They wore only goatskins and would strike women with goatskin thongs to enhance their fertility. See also **Lupercus**.

Lupercus Roman fertility god, sometimes identified with **Pan** and Faunus. Lupercus protected the flock from wild ravenous wolves.

Luria, Isaac (1534–1572) Influential Kabbalist and poet who grew up in Egypt and studied under David ben Solomon ibn Abi Zimra. Luria was well versed in rabbinical literature and the non-mystical study of Jewish law, but finally decided on a life of **esoteric** pursuits. He retired to an island on the Nile near Cairo and studied the kabbalistic writings of **Moses Cordovero** and the texts of the ***Zohar***. It was during this period that he wrote his commentary on the *Book of Concealment*. Luria continued to read the **Kabbalah** in earnest and after settling in Safed with his family in 1570, studied for a short while with Cordovero himself. After Cordovero died in 1570, Luria replaced him as a central figure and became the focal member of a group of distinguished Kabbalists, including Hayyim Vital. Luria soon acquired the status of a great spiritual teacher and Master – one in possession of the "Holy Spirit". He taught the Kabbalah orally to his disciples and instructed them in the techniques of **kavvanah** – **meditation** and **prayer** techniques based on the **sephiroth**.

Luria left no major writings, but it is known that he believed in the mystical concept that **God**'s "self-limitation" gave rise to **Light** and made the creation of the finite universe possible. This Light flowed from God and in due course would return to him. Luria believed, however, that some of this Light became diffused, giving rise to the "**evil**" of the lower worlds.

Lycanthropy From the Greek *lukos*, "a wolf", and *anthropos*, "a man", the belief among practitioners of **witchcraft** and **sorcery** that a man may transform himself into a wolf. In Europe the wolf was traditionally regarded as the most ferocious animal, and in this regard the **sorcerer** capable of such transformation personified bestial power and terror – hence the many legends of the **werewolf**. The term is also used generally to describe the magical act of changing into any wild animal, for example a hyena or tiger, and there are examples of "leopard-men" in Africa and "jackal-men" in the Congo particularly. Some legends relating to lycanthropy may have their origin in the **psychedelic** experience, since it is now considered that hallucinatory witchcraft potions are responsible for the legend of witches travelling through the air to the sabbat, riding on their broomsticks. Many **shamans** – some of whom use psychedelic sacraments – similarly believe themselves capable of self-transformation, and assume the form of their power animals. See also **Hallucination**; **Shamanism**.

Lyon-Poisson Heraldic monster, half-lion and half-fish.

Lytton, Sir Edward Bulwer (1803–1873) See **Bulwer-Lytton, Sir Edward**.

M

Maat In ancient Egyptian **mythology**, the goddess of truth, whose symbol was a **feather**. In the Osirian **Judgment Hall**, the heart of the deceased was weighed in the scales against a feather and the person's fate decided accordingly. Those who were judged to be *maa kheru* (true of voice) were allowed to enter the Kingdom of **Osiris** (the **Elysian Fields**).

Maban Among the **Aborigines** of South and Western Australia, a "live-giving" shell that is placed in the ears to enable a person to hear and speak to the spirits.

Mabinogion Collection of eleven Welsh tales translated and compiled by Lady Charlotte Guest, and first published in 1838. The stories include material from the Arthurian legends and represent a rich source of Celtic **folklore**, **magic**, and daily life.

McDougall, Professor William (1871–1938) Leading social psychologist whose interest in **parapsychology** was stimulated by the work of **William James** and the psychic medium **Mrs. Leonore Piper**. Despite his illustrious academic career as a reader at University College, London, and professor of psychology at Harvard University (1920–1927), McDougall was interested in researching the possibility of life after death and studied **telepathy** and **clairvoyance** as well as the evidence for post-mortem survival. He became head of the psychology department at Duke University in 1927 and encouraged **Dr. J. B. Rhine** to establish the Parapsychology Laboratory there.

Machen, Arthur (1863–1947) Welsh **mystic** and author whose novels and short stories often allude to a **supernatural**, **pagan** reality beneath the veneer of familiar appearances. Machen was born at Caerleon-on-Usk, and developed a profound fondness for the Welsh countryside which, for him, was imbued with Celtic mystery. In 1880, after his education at Hereford Cathedral School, he went to London. There he worked for a book publisher and also as a cataloguer and translator. In 1901 he joined Sir Frank Benson's Shakespearean Company and later worked with Sir George Alexander at the St James's Theatre. For a brief period Machen was a member of the **Hermetic Order of the Golden Dawn**, although he quickly came to prefer **mystics** to ritual **occultists**. Machen's most accomplished novel is *The Hill of Dreams* (1900), but many of his short stories, including "The Great Return", "The Happy Children", "A Fragment of Life", and "The White People", are equally impressive. His personal reminiscences, *Far Off Things*, *Things Near and Far*, and *The London Adventure* were published between 1915 and 1923.

McKenna, Terence (1946–2000)
Sometimes paired with Timothy Leary as a spiritual maverick of the American "new consciousness" movement, McKenna advocated a shamanic perspective which promoted the psilocybin experience as an important means of communicating with the World Soul. McKenna spent nearly thirty years studying **shamanism** and the "ethnopharmacology of spiritual transformation". For many years he travelled in Asia and the Amazon, studying shamanism and native healing and he later established Botanical Dimensions, a shamanically oriented research garden in Hawaii. His books include *Food of the Gods*, *True Hallucinations* and a collection of essays and interviews, *The Archaic Revival*.

McKenzie, James Hewat (1869–1929)
Scottish psychical researcher who founded the British College of Psychic Science in 1920. He was interested in studying **trance mediums** and investigated Frau Silbert, **Mrs. Eileen Garrett**, and **Mrs. Osborne Leonard**. He also developed the British College as a centre for demonstrating mediumistic abilities. McKenzie wrote the book *Spirit Intercourse: Its Theory and Practice* (1918).

Macrocosm and Microcosm From the Greek *makros kosmos*, "great world", and *mikros kosmos*, "little world", the concept that people and the world are a copy in miniature of **God**'s universe. This view was advocated by the theologian **Origen** and taken up by such Renaissance **occultists** as **Paracelsus** and **Henry Cornelius Agrippa**. Similarly, in the medieval **Kabbalah**, the primordial or archetypal man, **Adam Kadmon**, is regarded as reflecting the image of God the Father, and thereby provides the necessary link between humankind and the Creator of the universe.

Macroprosopus In the **Kabbalah**, the so-called Greater Countenance of **God**, which symbolizes the harmony in the universe following the act of Creation. The Greater Countenance is forever concealed, while the Lesser Countenance, or manifested God, reveals himself through the sacred name of the **Tetragrammaton**.

Macumba Magical religion, similar to **voodoo**, practised mainly in Brazil. Macumba combines Haitian folk-beliefs, African animism, Latin American **spiritualism**, and aspects of Christianity. Macumba is sometimes said to be a fusion of **superstitions** that survive among illiterate Brazilians as a remnant of the country's black slave religion (dating from the sixteenth through the nineteenth centuries). However, Macumba is not as easy to categorize as that. It is a force behind popular folk songs and Carnival sambas, and its holidays (January 1 and May 13) receive extensive television coverage. There are claimed to be 40,000 Macumba centres in Rio de Janeiro and the state of Guanabara alone, and 365 churches in San Salvador (one for each day of the year). Over a million devotees have been known to celebrate the festival of the goddess Iemanja in Rio. While Macumba may appeal to the more exuberant members of Brazilian society, it also counts among its devotees a number of intellectuals, who have embraced it as a more exhilarating and rewarding religion than orthodox Christianity.

Madhyamika In **Mahayana Buddhism**, the so-called **Middle Path** between existence and non-existence, which one follows in order to comprehend the Void (**Sunyata**). See also **Nagarjuna**.

Maenads Also known as **Bacchantes**, the female devotees of **Dionysus**, who roused themselves into a great frenzy and celebrated with ecstatic dance and song, killing live animals and devouring their flesh.

Magen David The "Star of David" in Judaism. Also known as the "Jewish Star", it is a **hexagram** made up of two intersecting triangles which, in the **Kabbalah**, symbolize the interrelatedness of Matter and Spirit.

Maggid In Jewish **mysticism**, a spiritual entity that communicates through an **adept** while the latter is in a state of **trance**. The term is also used to describe a person of high spiritual attainment.

Magi The legendary "wise men" of the East from whom the term **magic** is derived. The Magi were a priestly caste, and were one of the six tribes of Medes described by Herodotus. Skilled in interpreting dreams and divining the future by the stars, the Magi were regarded with great awe. Their beliefs intermingled with the doctrines of **Zoroastrianism** and may actually have preceded it. In due course the Magi penetrated into Greece and India, and possibly also China. They feature in the biblical narrative as the "three wise men" – Kasper, Melchior, and Balthasar – who brought gold, frankincense, and myrrh as gifts for the baby Jesus.

Magic Technique of harnessing the secret powers of Nature and seeking to influence events for one's own purpose. If the purpose is beneficial it is known as **white magic**, but if it is intended to bring harm to others, or to destroy property, it is regarded as **black magic**.

Magicians employ a variety of **ritual** procedures. Sometimes, as in **imitative magic**, they seek to imitate the end result desired by using models of real people or objects, or by dressing in ceremonial regalia in order to identify symbolically with a particular **deity**. In certain black magic procedures, it is believed that harm can be inflicted upon a person by burning a wax doll or sticking pins into it, as if it were the real person. Sometimes "positive" effects are sought by similar procedures. ***The Magus*** – a classical textbook of magic written by **Francis Barrett** – includes a "scapegoat" ritual for transferring illness and pain from a sick woman to an unsuspecting frog: "Take the eyes of a frog, which must be extricated before sunrise, and bind them to the breasts of a woman who be ill. Then let the frog go blind into the water again and as he goes so will the woman be rid of her pains..." Here, removing the eyes of the frog confirms the magician's mastery over the animal, who can no longer jump to freedom. The woman's breasts, with their life-giving milk, represent health, and the casting of the frog into water is a ritual act of cleansing. Taken overall, the frog literally carries the disease away.

Modern Western magic, especially as practised in groups that follow the tradition established by the **Hermetic Order of the Golden Dawn**, has as its main function the **self-initiation** of its members and must be regarded primarily as a form of white magic. However, there have been cases of alleged **magical attack** and ritual practices that summon bestial or demonic forces, which clearly are more related to black magic. White magicians seek to activate the spiritual **archetypes** in the unconscious mind by identifying with such life-sustaining deities as **Osiris**, **Thoth**, **Apollo**, **Ra**, and **Horus** (male), and **Isis**, **Aphrodite**, **Hathor**, **Demeter**, and **Persephone** (female). Black magicians worship such animal-human prototypes as the **Devil**, the **Horned God**, **Lilith**, and a variety of other personifications of darkness and **evil**.

Magic, Black Magic performed with evil intent. The "black magician" or **sorcerer** calls upon the supernatural powers of darkness – devils, demons, and evil spirits – and performs ceremonies invoking bestial or malevolent forces intended to harm another person. Black magic invariably involves **imitative magic**, in which there is said to be a link between a person or object and something sharing its resemblance (e.g. a wax figure or doll). Injuries ritually inflicted upon the figure with pins or nails are intended to have a harmful effect upon the person represented by the figurine. Some magicians claim that the technique is only effective when the sorcerer has enough willpower to use the ritual figure as a focus for inflicting negative **thought-forms** on the person under attack. See also **Grimoires**; **Spells**; **Talisman**.

Magic, Celestial Belief that the planets are ruled by **spirits** that influence people. For example, in kabbalistic **magic**, the planets are ruled by the following **archangels**: Tzaphkiel (**Saturn**); Tzadkiel (**Jupiter**); Kamael (**Mars**); **Raphael** (**Sun**); Haniel (**Venus**); **Michael** (**Mercury**); **Gabriel** (**Moon**); **Sandalphon** (**Earth**).

Magic, Ceremonial Magic that employs **rituals**, symbols, and ceremony as a means of representing the supernatural and mystical forces linking the universe and humanity. Ceremonial magic stimulates the senses – sight, hearing, smell, taste, and touch – by including in its rituals ceremonial costume, dramatic invocations to the **gods** or **spirits**, potent incense, and mystic sacraments. The aim of ceremonial magic in its "highest" sense is a transcendental experience, transporting the magician beyond the limitations of the mind towards mystical reality. However, as a term, it is also associated with medieval magical **grimoires**, which describe procedures for summoning spirits. These books, which are designed to confer power rather than transcendence on the magician, include the *Key of Solomon*, the *Grimoire of Honorius*, and the *Grand Grimoire*. In modern times the most complete system of ceremonial magic has been the body of rituals practised in the **Hermetic Order of the Golden Dawn**. See also **Key of Solomon**.

Magic, Contagious The belief that objects that have been in contact with each other still have a link, and that one can be harmed magically – for example, by a magical rite performed over one's fingernails, hair clippings, or possessions.

Magic, Defensive Magical **rituals** and **spells** used to defend oneself from harmful **sorcery** or evil influences. See also **Banishing Ritual**.

Magic, Destructive Virtually synonymous with **black magic**, any magical act intended to destroy people, property, or crops, or to affect people's lives in a harmful way.

Magic, Enochian System of **magic** derived from the work of Elizabethan occultists **Dr. John Dee** and **Edward Kelley**, who met in 1581. Dee and Kelley made use of wax tablets called **almadels** engraved with magic symbols; they also used magical squares, the largest consisting of 49 rows, filled with letters of the alphabet. Nearby, on his table, Kelley had a large crystal stone upon which he focused his concentration and entered a state of **trance** reverie. In due course, "angels" would appear, and they would point to various letters on the squares in turn. These were written down by Dee as Kelley called them out. When these invocations were completely transcribed, Kelley then reversed their order, for he believed that the angels communicated them backwards to avoid unleashing the magical power which they contained.

Dee and Kelley considered that the communications formed the basis of a new language known as Enochian. These magical **conjurations** were subsequently incorporated into magical practice by the ritual magicians of the **Hermetic Order of the Golden Dawn**, who used them to induce trance visions on the **astral plane**. See also **Pathworkings**.

Magic, High Magic intended to bring about the spiritual transformation of the person who practises it. This form of magic is designed to channel the magician's consciousness towards the sacred **light** within, which is often personified by the **high gods** of different **cosmologies**. The aim of high magic has been described as communication with one's **holy guardian angel**, or higher **self**. It is also known as **Theurgy**.

Magic, Image The use of a magical image – a doll made of wax, clay, etc. – in magical **spells**. In **black magic** harm may be inflicted upon a victim by forming the magical image and then pricking it with pins, breaking its limbs off, or consigning it to a fire. This practice is thought to originate in ancient Mesopotamia. See also **Magic, Imitative**.

Magic, Imitative Form of magical practice in which the anticipated result in real life is mimicked, or imitated, in ritual. The most common form is through **image magic**, in which an image of a real person may be subjected to hostile acts (pins, burning, etc.) in the hope that real injury and misfortune will befall the victim. The technique can also be applied to mental images. For example, a phobia could be visualized as a hostile creature (e.g. a spider, snake, or **dragon**) and "shrunk" in the imagination in the hope that the symptoms of fear would disappear with it. This technique is used in some forms of **psychotherapy** that involve techniques of "active imagination". For example, in **guided-imagery** techniques used in cancer treatment, the patient may be asked to visualize the cancerous growth as a "dragon" that is gradually overcome by the patient in the form of a "knight in armour". These treatments are often remarkably successful.

Magic, Low Magic intended to produce a utilitarian or domestic effect. Examples would include attracting an influx of sudden wealth, a new lover, a change of occupation, or a resurgence of good fortune.

Magic, Mortuary Magical rites and ceremonies performed in order to ensure that the deceased person will have an enjoyable life in the afterworld. Mortuary magic was highly developed in ancient Egypt.

Magic, Natural Magical **spells**, enchantments, and **conjurations** believed to have an effect on Nature (e.g. bringing much needed rain or thunderstorms, affecting the wind or other aspects of the weather, contacting **Nature-spirits**, or influencing cycles of fertility).

Magic, Protective Spells, rituals, and **enchantments** designed to counter the evil effects of **black magic**.

Magic, Sexual Magical rituals and ceremonies that invoke the principle of fertility, and which usually involve sexual acts that simulate the procreative union of the **gods**. See also **Ordo Templi Orientis**; **Tantra**.

Magic, Sympathetic Expression coined by the anthropologist Sir James Frazer (1854–1941), author of famous work on magical philosophy, *The Golden Bough*. For Frazer, the concept of "like affecting like" – a principle often found in magical ceremonies – owed its meaning to the concept of a magical "sympathy" between two objects, or beings, separated by distance. The act of mimicry through **ritual** served to produce a cause-and-effect relationship, thus making magical acts apparently "effective".

Magic, White Magic performed for a spiritual, healing, or generally positive purpose, as distinct from **black magic** which is performed for self-gain, to inflict harm or injury, or for other evil purposes. See also **Theurgy**.

Magical Ally See **Familiar; Power Animal.**

Magical Attack Alleged ability of **magicians** to harm each other, especially by adopting hostile animal **thought-forms** on the **astral plane**. Magical attack does not take place on a physical level, but depends on the assumption that all living beings share a common and universal **life-force** that can be summoned, guided, and directed by visualisation and ritual procedures.

There are two celebrated cases of magical attack in recent occult history. The first involved **Dion Fortune**, who in 1922, at the time of the incident, had recently established the **Fraternity of the Inner Light** and was drawing members away from the **Hermetic Order of the Golden Dawn** (specifically the Alpha and Omega Temple headed by **Mrs. Moina Mathers**). Dion Fortune believed that Mrs. Mathers (Soror Vestigia) launched a magical attack against her as a result of this rivalry. During the episode, which is described in Dion Fortune's *Psychic Self Defence*, she was subjected to a vision of a gigantic cat, "twice the size of a tiger. It appeared absolutely solid and tangible. I stared at it, petrified for a second, and then it vanished. I instantly realized that it was a simulacrum, or thought-form, that was being projected by someone with occult powers." Soon afterwards, Soror Vestigia began to appear to Dion Fortune in her dreams, and a nightmare attack followed in which she was "whirled through the air". Dion Fortune summoned the inner chiefs to protect her, and the visions ceased; but when she awoke she discovered that "from neck to waist I was scored with scratches as if I had been clawed by a gigantic cat".

The second case of magical attack involved two occult groups in the late nineteenth century in France, one headed by **Stanislaus de Guaita** and **Sar Peladan** and the other by **Joseph-Antoine Boullan**. See also **Mathers, Mrs. Moina.**

Magical Correspondences In modern Western **magic**, a system for comparing the **gods** and **goddesses** of different **pantheons** in terms of their symbolic roles and attributes. In 1909, a list of correspondences developed by **MacGregor Mathers** and later supplemented by **Aleister Crowley** was published under the title 777 (also included in *The Qabalah of Aleister Crowley*, New York, 1973). Using the kabbalistic **Tree of Life** as a matrix, for example, it becomes possible to compare **mother-goddesses** (**Demeter, Hathor, Sophia, Rhea**); warrior gods (**Mars, Horus**); solar gods/rebirth deities (**Apollo, Ra, Osiris**); and **lunar goddesses** (**Isis, Ishtar, Artemis, Hecate, Luna, Selene,** and **Diana**); as well as the precious stones, perfumes, sacred plants, and animals ascribed to them. See also **Archetypes; Kabbalah.**

Magical Formulae Conjurations, **invocations, spells,** or magical **prayers,** regarded by ceremonial magicians as powerful and effective for a given **ritual** purpose. One of the best sources for the formulae of Western **magic** is **Israel Regardie**'s four-volume work *The Golden Dawn*. Another is **A. E. Waite**'s *Book of Ceremonial Magic*. See also **Goetia; Hermetic Order of the Golden Dawn; Magic, Ceremonial.**

Magical Herb Any herb believed to possess magical properties. Several hallucinogenic herbs, including deadly nightshade,

mandrake, henbane, and thorn apple, have been used by **witches** in their **flying ointments,** and other herbs are used magically as sexual stimulants (damiana, yohimbe) or to induce vivid **dreams** (wild lettuce).

Magical Name Special name, usually in Latin, taken by a ritual **magician** to confirm membership in a particular magical order. The following are the magical names of some well-known occult figures who belonged to the **Hermetic Order of the Golden Dawn: Arthur Edward Waite** (*Sacramentum Regis*); **William Butler Yeats** (*Daemon Est Deus Inversus*); **Arthur Machen** (*Avallaunius*); **MacGregor Mathers** (*Deo Duce Comite Ferro*); **Aleister Crowley** (*Perdurabo*), and **Dion Fortune/Violet Firth** (*Deo Non Fortuna*). The last of these reveals how Violet Firth acquired her pen-name, by which she is much better known.

Magical Numbers In magical **cosmology,** certain gods have been ascribed numerical values. The **Gnostic** deity **Abraxas** was regarded by **Basilides** and his followers as a personification of Time; and in both Greek and Hebrew his name added to 365, the number of days in a year (Greek: Alpha-1, Beta-2, Rho-100, Alpha-1, Xi-60, Alpha-1, Sigma-200 = 365; Hebrew: Aleph-1, Beth-2, Resh-200, Aleph-1, Qoph-100, Aleph-1, Samekh-60 = 365). In the Book of Revelation, the number of the Beast or **Anti-Christ** was 666; and it was this name and number that the magician **Aleister Crowley** identified with after assuming the role of Lord of the **New Aeon** in 1904.

Magical Reality In **shamanism,** the magical dimension that becomes experientially real to the **shaman** while in an **altered state of consciousness.** The shaman may enter the magical reality by journeying to the upper or lower worlds through the **Tree of Life,** or by consuming a hallucinogenic sacrament. Drumming and chanting are also powerful techniques for entering this state.

Magic Circle Circle inscribed on the floor of a temple for magical ceremonial purposes. It is "activated", or rendered sacred, through various ritual procedures.

Magician One skilled in the arts of **magic.** The term is generally applied to ceremonial or **ritual** magicians who invoke **deities** or **spirits;** make use of such symbolic regalia as cloaks, swords, cups, daggers, and wands; and claim special powers and **supernatural** insights. The word is also used by non-occultists as a synonym for one skilled in conjuring, although strictly speaking this is "stage magic" and has nothing to do with ceremonial workings or the magical states of consciousness stimulated by ritual. See also **Magic, Ceremonial.**

Magician, The See *Magus, The.*

Magick **Aleister Crowley**'s special spelling of the word. Crowley defined magick as "the Science and Art of causing Change to occur in conformity with Will" (*Magick in Theory and Practice*, 1929). See also **Will.**

Magic Letter Square A square arranged so that the letters of the words may be read in either direction, both vertically and horizontally. Such squares are believed to have magical properties and may form the basis of an incantation. The most famous example is the so-called "Sator" square which has the following lines:

S A T O R
A R E P O
T E N E T
O P E R A
R O T A S

MacGregor Mathers, a leading figure in the **Hermetic Order of the Golden Dawn,** interpreted this to mean "The Creator (*sator*), slow-moving (*arepo*), maintains (*tenet*) His creations (*opera*) as vortices (*rotas*)," although this is only one of several possible meanings. See also **Abracadabra**.

Magic Number Square A square arranged so that the numbers in each row of the square have the same total when added in any direction. In **magic**, the number square appropriate to each planet is known as its **kamea**. The following are examples:

4	9	2
3	5	7
8	1	6

Saturn

4	14	15	1
9	7	6	12
5	11	10	8
16	2	3	13

Jupiter

11	24	7	20	3
4	12	25	8	16
17	5	13	21	9
10	18	1	14	22
23	6	19	2	15

Mars

Magic number squares are an important feature in the medieval **grimoire** *The Sacred Magic of Abra-melin the Mage*, the squares being regarded as sources of magical power. See also **Abraham the Jew**.

Magic Seal Magical motif is produced by drawing the **kamea** or **magic number square** of a planet and then connecting the numbers in the square by a sequence of lines. The following diagrams are the kamea and seal for the planet **Saturn**:

4	9	2
3	5	7
8	1	6

kamea

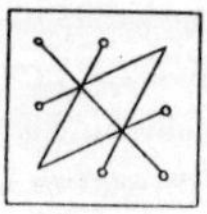

seal

Magic Square A square arranged to include words or numbers in such a way that the words may be read horizontally or vertically in both directions, and the numbers have the same total when added in any direction. The first of these is a **magic letter square**, the second a **magic number square**.

Magister Templi In modern Western **magic**, the third highest ritual grade attainable on the kabbalistic **Tree of Life**. It equates with the sphere of **Binah** and is represented symbolically as 8° = 3°. See also **Ipsissimus**.

Magna Mater Latin for "Great Mother", a term used in ancient Rome to describe the **mother-goddess**, especially with reference to **Rhea** and **Cybele**.

Magnetic Healing See **Mesmer, Friedrich Anton**.

Magnestism, Animal See **Animal Magnetism; Mesmer, Friedrich Anton**.

Magnetotherapy Controversial form of healing therapy proposed by Dr. Elisha Perkins (1741–1799) who maintained that the body could be freed from disease by touching it with different metals – especially copper, zinc, **iron**, and **silver**. Sometimes combinations of these metals, together with **gold** or platinum, were used in the treatments. Magnetotherapy is no longer regarded as credible.

Magnum Opus From the Latin, **Great Work**. An alchemical term referring to the task of the transformation of the base elements into **gold** and, by extension, spiritual **rebirth**. It is therefore a synonym for **self-realization** or **illumination**. See also **Alchemy**.

Magus In modern Western **magic**, the second highest ritual grade attainable on the kabbalistic **Tree of Life**. The grade of Magus equates with the sphere **Chokmah** and is represented symbolically as 9° = 2°. See **Ipsissimus**.

Magus, The Title of an occult work on kabbalistic **magic, numerology, alchemy**, and magical stones written by **Francis Barrett** and published in London in 1801. It included illustrations of such **devils** as Theulus and **Asmodeus**, and has been reissued in several facsimile editions.

MAGIC: Magic involves harnessing the powers of Nature for purposes of self-transformation. Here, witches are shown "drawing down the Moon" – invoking the Great Goddess of fertility and intuition. Drawing by Naomi Lewis.

Magus, The Also, *The Magician*. In the **Tarot**, the card which symbolizes the virginal, or "pure," male energy in the cosmos, and which is the direct counterpart of ***The High Priestess*** – the virgin goddess. Lying above the **Abyss** on the kabbalistic **Tree of Life**, the path of *The Magus* stands above Creation in an archetypal sense. The magician raises one hand aloft to draw down the creative energies of **Kether**, which may then be transmitted further down the Tree. Designs in some of the various Tarot packs show the magician standing in a paradise-garden, again symbolic of purity. *The Magus* is linked mythically to **Thoth**, the **logos** of the universe; and is a higher form of **Hermes/Mercury** associated mythologically with **Hod**, lower down the Tree. *The Magus* represents the path from **Binah** to **Kether** in the **Kabbalah**.

Maha Sanskrit term meaning "great". It has many applications. See also ***Mahabharata***; **Mahabhava**; **Maharishi**; **Mahasakti**; **Mahatma**; **Mahayana Buddhism**.

Mahabharata Sanskrit for "Great Bharata", an Indian epic poem, composed in its present form around 300 B.C. Written in Sanskrit, it consists of eighteen books, including the ***Bhagavad-Gita***, and is mainly concerned with the rivalry between the **Pandavas** – descendants of Bharata – and their cousins, the **Kauravas**. The ***Ramayana*** and the *Mahabharata* are the two great Hindu epics.

Mahabhava In **Hinduism**, the highest form of self-dedication to a divine **incarnation**. The followers of the cult of **Vishnu** practise devotion to **Krishna** – one of Vishnu's incarnations – and epitomize this approach.

Maharaj Ji, Guru (1957–) Spiritual leader of the **Divine Light Mission**. Guru Maharaj Ji was born Prem Pal Singh Rawat in Hardwar, India, and was declared to be a Perfect Master at the age of eight, succeeding his father, Shri Hans Ji Maharaj, who died in 1966, and who was also a **bhakti yogi**. The young Maharaj Ji attended St. Joseph's Academy in India until leaving India in 1971 to spread the "Knowledge of Inner Peace" around the world. He believes that the Truth is universal and therefore not confined to **Hinduism**, and has toured through Europe, South Africa, the United States, Japan, and Australia, opening branches of the Divine Light Mission and giving the Knowledge to those who wish to receive it. According to the Maharaj Ji, those who gain this Knowledge have a fourfold experience. They feel a vibration of cosmic energy (the Word of God) within them; they see a bright inner light; they taste a divine nectar within the mouth; and they hear faint but beautiful music. Those who receive this **initiation** are known as **premies**, and they are entitled to give **satsang** to new disciples. While the teachings of Maharaj Ji belong to a recognizable mystical tradition, the Guru's personal standing has receded in recent years.

Maharishi Sanskrit term meaning "Great Seer" or "Adept". See also **Maharishi Mahesh Yogi**.

Maharishi Mahesh Yogi Founder of the **Transcendental Meditation** (**TM**) movement. The Maharishi originally trained to be a physicist, but turned to mysticism and became a disciple of Guru Dev, who died in 1953. The Maharishi does not demand the devotion of his followers and is a **jnana** rather than **bhakti** guru. His approach to meditation is comparatively simple, focusing on the use of an individual **mantra** that is carefully taught to the **chela**, or disciple. The Maharishi believes that when the mind is attuned to the mantra it acquires a more profound and **transcendental power**, helping the person attain true self-knowledge. In due course, the mind is emptied of its contents and the experience of Pure Being remains. This is the true nature of the mind, and attaining this transcendental state enhances one's sense of happiness and unity with life.

Maharshi Sanskrit term meaning "Great Sage". See also **Maharshi, Ramana.**

Maharshi, Ramana (1879–1950) Indian mystic who as a schoolboy had an experience that resembled **death** and which showed him that there is a vital **spirit** within the body that **transcends** the physical dimension. From then on, Ramana was determined to find out more about what he later called the "I Am". He left home and travelled to Tiruvannamalai, a town located at the foot of Arunchala. Here he sat pondering the true nature of Being, sustained by offerings of food brought to him by passers-by. Ramana began to attract a following and many came to receive *darshan* (audience) with him. Much of this time was spent in meditative silence, but some questions and answers were recorded by such disciples as **Arthur Osborne** and various Indian writers. Ramana Maharshi believed that the true **self** and **God** are one, and that the **ego**, or false self, should be surrendered to the Higher Truth. One's actions then become expressions of God, not of one's own will or intention. Ramana Maharshi was one of the greatest exponents of the Hindu doctrine of non-dualism, known as **Advaita.**

Mahasakti Sanskrit term meaning "the greatest expression, or power, of Sakti". Sakti (or **Shakti**) is the Universal Energy, and is the force sustaining the Great Triad: **Shiva, Vishnu**, and **Brahma.**

Mahasunya In **Hinduism**, "the Great Void" – the space beyond finite manifestation; the vast emptiness that will remain after the dissolution of the universe. See also **Sunya.**

Mahat From the Sanskrit "Great One", the First Principle of the Universe. It is taken to mean Universal Mind, Supreme Intelligence. Compare with **Godhead.** See also **Manas.**

Mahatma Also *Mahatman.* Sanskrit term meaning "Great Spirit", "Great Soul", "Adept", or "Master". Although it means "one who has attained Universal Knowledge and Self-realization", this title is also used to describe outstanding social and political leaders, such as Mohandas K. Gandhi (1869–1948).

Mahavira (c. 540–468 B.C.) Influential spiritual figure among the **Jains** and sometimes – incorrectly – claimed to be their "founder". Mahavira, whose real name was Vardhamana, was a contemporary of **Gautama Buddha** and was said to be a perfectly realized being, even at his time of birth. He spent many years meditating and preaching, and helped structure the Jains into four groups: monks, nuns, laymen, and laywomen. The name Mahavira means "Great Hero", and he is still venerated by the Jains today.

Mahayana Buddhism The so-called "Great Vehicle" of **Buddhism**, as distinct from the **Hinayana** or "Small Vehicle" – these two schools being the major streams in Buddhist thought. Mahayana Buddhism emphasizes that all people may become **arahants** or **bodhisattvas** if they follow **Gautama Buddha**'s precepts and share their love with other people. This interpretation is potentially more far-ranging than **Hinayana Buddhism**, which focuses on withdrawal from the world and the attainment of individual enlightenment without stressing the need to share the fruits of one's spiritual knowledge with others. In general, Mahayana Buddhism is more **esoteric**, and Hinayana more fundamentalist.

Mahesh In **Hinduism**, one of the names for **Shiva.** It translates as "Great Lord".

Maimonides Dream Laboratory Laboratory formerly located in the Maimonides Medical Center in Brooklyn, New York, which was established to try to demonstrate scientifically that a person acting as an "agent" could transfer his or her thoughts through **mental telepathy** to the mind of a sleeping subject, thereby altering the subject's **dreams**. At Maimonides, the brainwave patterns of the sleeping subject were carefully monitored and the projected images and dream content correlated and strictly assessed. The major account of the work at the Maimonides Dream Laboratory is *Dream Telepathy* (1973), co-authored by **Dr. Montague Ullman** (Director of Psychiatry at Maimonides), **Dr. Stanley Krippner** (former Director of the Dream Laboratory), and psychic author Alan Vaughan.

Maithuna In **Tantra**, sexual intercourse, especially when performed with a ritual intent. When the female partner takes the active role it is known as *maithuna viparita* ("obverse intercourse"). There is a Tamil expression that translates as "dancing upon the lover", which connotes much the same thing.

Maitreya The name of the **Buddha** who is still to come. According to **Mahayana Buddhism**, Gautama was the fourth Buddha on earth and Maitreya will be the fifth and final Buddha in this succession.

Major Arcana In the **Tarot**, the twenty-two "mythological" cards, or trumps, which are assigned by **occultists** to paths on the kabbalistic **Tree of Life**. In sequence from **Malkuth** at the foot of the Tree to **Kether** at the crown, they are: ***The World, Judgment, The Moon, The Sun, The Star, The Tower, The Devil, Death, Temperance, The Hermit, Justice, The Hanged Man, The Wheel of Fortune, Strength, The Charioteer, The Lovers, The Hierophant, The Emperor, The Empress, The High Priestess, The Magus***, and ***The Fool***. For symbolic ascriptions, see individual listings.

Malefics In **astrology**, planets said to cause a negative or harmful influence – especially **Mars** and **Saturn**.

Male Principle In mystical cosmologies there is an interplay between masculine and feminine forces. Of these, the masculine principle is usually regarded as positive, outward going, dynamic, and solar. It is also intellectual rather than intuitive. See also **Chokmah**; **Yang**. Compare with **Binah**; **Feminine Principle**; **Lunar Goddesses**; **Yin**.

Malkuth The tenth emanation or **sephirah** on the kabbalistic **Tree of Life**. In Western **magic**, Malkuth is associated with **goddesses** of the earth, especially **Persephone** (Greece), **Proserpina** (Rome), and **Geb** (Egypt). Malkuth is the domain of the manifested universe, the immediate environment, the plane of physical reality. As a consequence, all "inner journeys of consciousness" begin symbolically in Malkuth; it is particularly appropriate, for example, that the myth of the rape of Persephone confirms her both as queen of the **Underworld** and as a lunar **goddess**. From an occult point of view, the Underworld equates with the lower unconscious mind, and the **moon**, represented by the sphere of **Yesod**, is the first sephirah reached on the mystic inner journey up the Tree of Life. Malkuth is closely linked to the **Tarot** card ***The World***.

Malleus Maleficarum Famous medieval book on **witchcraft** whose title translates as *The Hammer of the Witches*. First published in 1486, the *Malleus* was written by two Inquisitors, **Heinrich Kramer** and **Jacob Sprenger**, and includes details of the **spells** and enchantments of **witches** as well as an appalling section on the torture of witches, which is abbreviated in most modern editions. The most common edition of the *Malleus* in English is that translated by the **Reverend Montague Summers**, which first appeared as a limited edition in 1928 and has since been reprinted many times.

Malphas In medieval **demonology**, the grand president of **Hell** who appeared in the form of a crow as well as a human being. He was notorious for double-crossing his devotees and spoke with a hoarse voice. Malphas had forty legions of **devils** at his command.

Mama Cocha In the **cosmology** of the Incas, the great **mother-goddess** who ruled rain and water and was the wife of **Viracocha**. Mama Cocha presided over Lake Titicaca.

Mana In Melanesian religion and magical belief, **supernatural** power associated with the spirits of the dead. The word is also used in Polynesia to describe a generalized power or force that may be transmitted to a person by various sacred objects, including representations of the dead.

Manas Sanskrit term meaning "mind". It can refer to the mind at any stage or level. For example, buddhi-manas is the higher mind, or **self**, while kama-manas is the lower or personal mind. Because, in Hindu **mysticism**, there is in reality only one consciousness or Mind, which underlies all creation and manifestation, manas is sometimes equated with **mahat** – the First Principle, from which all else comes forth.

Mandala Sanskrit word meaning "a circle". In **Hinduism** and **Mahayana Buddhism**, the mandala is used as a motif symbolizing the universe and the power of the **gods**, and is a vehicle for **meditation**. Interpreted variously as symbols of wholeness and unity, or as examples of the solar disc, mandalas may be regarded as "doorways" to inner, sacred space. They have attracted the attention of several Western commentators on spiritual art and philosophy, including José and Miriam Arguelles, Giuseppe Tucci, and **Carl Gustav Jung**.

Mandeans Palestinian **Gnostic** sect, dating from the first or early second century A.D. Their **cosmology** included strong emphasis on the duality of light and darkness, and on the formation of the universe by creator gods which emanated from the **Godhead**. Like many Gnostic sects, the Mandeans regarded the physical world as the antithesis of the **spirit** and described the **soul**, or spirit of life, as being lost in an alien world. One Mandean tract includes the lines: "I am a Mana of the great life … who has thrown me into the body-stump? … My eyes, which were opened from the abode of light, now belong to the stump … How I must obey, how endure, how must I quiet my mind! How I must hear of the seven and twelve mysteries, how must I groan! How must my mild Father's Word dwell among the creatures of the dark!" The prophet **Mani** was originally raised in a Mandean community, but sought to reform many of its ideas. Nevertheless, Manicheism and Mandean beliefs share many points in common.

Mandira In **Hinduism**, the sanctuary of a **god** or **goddess**. Rites are performed in the sanctuary by **priests** and the **deity** is offered food, flowers, and incense.

Mandrake *Mandragora officinarum*, a plant with magical and **supernatural** associations. The mandrake is described in Genesis as an ingredient in **love potions**, and was similarly regarded by the Greek doctor Theophrastos (c. 370–328 B.C.) as both a soporific and an aphrodisiac. Always regarded as sinister because its roots resemble the form of a human being, it was associated in the Middle Ages with the bodies of executed criminals and was said to grow under the gallows and thrive on the dripping semen of men who had been hanged. When the mandrake was pulled from the ground the root would emit "wild shrieks" and send anyone who heard these piteous screams totally insane. Mandrake contains the so-called "deliriant" alkaloids, scopolamine and hyoscyamine, and was an ingredient in medieval witches' ointments, especially those prepared as love potions and **flying ointments**.

Manes In ancient Rome, the spirits of the dead, who resided in the **Underworld**. Festivals were held three times a year in their honour, and on these occasions the manes could come back to haunt the world of the living. These spirits were ruled in the Underworld by **Mania**, a goddess associated with **Persephone**.

Mani (c. A.D. 216–c. 276) Also Manichaeus. The son of a Babylonian prince of Persian descent, Mani grew up in a **Mandean** community in Mesopotamia where **Gnostic** ideas were common. Around the year 228, when he was twelve, he received a revelation from a celestial **angel** who appeared to him on behalf of "the King of the Paradise of Light". This angel urged him to forsake the Mandeans and pursue a new moral quest.

Mani was later shown "the mystery of the Deep and the High; the mystery of Light and Darkness". At this stage, Mani was not required to make a public stand; but in about 240 the angel advised him that the Lord had now selected him to be an apostle. He travelled to India, where he became interested in **Buddhism**, and later visited Babylonia and Persia. The Great King Shapur gave him three audiences and was favourably impressed by Mani's teachings on Light and Darkness, instructing his local authorities to protect the "new religion". However, Mani later attracted hostility from a **Zoroastrian** named Karter, who supervised the fire-temples; and he was opposed by the **Magi** in general, who were consolidating their place as the dominant religious form in Persia.

As Mani's missionary zeal continued, he began to refer to himself increasingly as "an apostle of Jesus Christ", further alienating himself from traditional Persian religion. Meanwhile, Shapur died in 273 and was succeeded by his son Hormizd I, who was favourably disposed to Mani. However, Hormizd died after only a year and was succeeded by his brother Bahram I, who reigned between 274 and 277. Bahram was a supporter of Karter and the Zoroastrian cause, and he asked Mani why relevations should have been given to him as a prophet rather than to himself as Great King. Mani replied that it was God's will. This was not well received and Mani was imprisoned, with heavy chains around his neck and ankles. After a month of fasting, Mani's strength was exhausted and he died. See also **Manicheism**.

Mania In ancient Rome, the goddess of the dead, sometimes referred to as "Mother of ghosts". She ruled over the **lares** and the **manes** in the **Underworld**.

Manicheism Doctrine of **Mani**, who believed in the absolute **dualism** of light and darkness and held that the world had been created by **Saklas** – ruler of darkness. Mani maintained that Adam and Eve were the offspring of two **demons**, Asqalun and Namrael, and that his role as a spiritual leader was to awaken light in humankind in the same way **Ohrmazd**-Jesus had done before him. Mani believed that true **Gnostic** Christianity had disappeared early on and that the Paraclete, or Spirit of Truth, had called on him to restore it. The orthodox church fathers differed from Mani on this point and suppressed his teachings around the year 600. The influence of Manicheism continued, however, and was a strong influence on the **Bogomils**, **Cathars**, and other medieval heretical sects. See also **Heresy**.

Manifestation From the Latin *manifestus*, "clear". Anything that becomes clearly visible, or apparent to the senses. The term is sometimes used in **spiritualism** and **occultism** as a synonym for a **materialization** – something that allegedly "manifests" from the inner planes.

Manipura In **Kundalini Yoga**, the **chakra** or energy centre located in the region of the solar plexus. The Manipura chakra is activated by using an appropriate **mantra**

while meditating on the **Tattva** symbol of **Fire, tejas.**

Manitou Among the Algonquins and other North American Indians, **supernatural** spirits said to reside everywhere in Nature, representing a great source of magical power. **Shamans** and **medicine-men** would contact the manitou in their rituals. Some American Indian tribes referred to the Great Manitou as the **supreme being.**

Manning, Matthew (1956–) English **psychic** and **spiritual healer** who, like **Uri Geller**, has demonstrated an apparently **paranormal** ability to bend metal objects by willpower alone. Manning first became aware of his **psi**-abilities when he was eleven. While he was on holiday with his family, furniture in his bedroom began moving without explanation and tables and chairs were upturned. Later, at his boarding-school, similar events occurred and several pupils were tipped from their two-tiered bunks. The headmaster of the school contemplated Manning's removal from the school, but the psychic phenomena ceased when he began to take up **automatic writing.** Matthew Manning has since undergone tests with several scientists, including a group convened by the Toronto Society for Psychical Research in 1973, who came to the view that his powers resembled a form of magnetism or electricity and were accompanied by a change in his brainwave state. Manning claims to be able to see **auras**, and has since developed the faculty of **psychokinesis.**

Mansions of the Moon In **astrology**, the twenty-eight divisions of the moon's journey through the 360-degree cycle of its orbit. Each mansion represents approximately one day's travel of the moon, the cycle commencing at zero degrees **Aries** (the first **house**).

Mantic From the Greek *mantis*, "a prophet", anything related to prophecy or **divination.**

Mantichora Also Manticore. Mythic beast that took its name from the Persian *mardkhora*, a man-eating tiger. The mantichora had a lion's body and the tail of a scorpion. Its head was human except that it had a triple row of teeth in both its upper and lower jaw. The mantichora could fire the spines in its tail as if they were arrows, and had a fondness for eating children.

Mantra In **Hinduism**, a sacred utterance or sound, often intoned silently as part of one's **meditation.** Because in many mystical traditions the essence of a god is its name, or vibrational quality, the mantra is a way of uniting oneself with the **deity.** Sometimes the **guru** gives his **chela** a personal mantra, which should be kept secret. Other mantras are chanted in ritual and are less **esoteric.** The mantra *Om Namah Shivaya*, which forms part of the Siddha Meditation practices developed by **Swami Muktananda**, means simply, "I honour the inner self." See also **Om.**

Manu Mythic figure described in the *Rig-Veda* as one of the fathers of humankind. The archetypal law-giver in **Hinduism**, he is said to be the originator of the code of laws *Manu Smrti*, which may date from the second century B.C. See also **Vedas.**

Maqam In **Islam**, a profound state of religious or mystical "grace" in which the devotee is continually aware of the close presence of **God.**

Mara Old English word meaning a female **demon** – especially with reference to elf-women who would appear to men during a nightmare or dream. See also **Elves.**

Mara In **Buddhism**, the name of a **demon** who, without success, attacked **Gautama Buddha** as he sat meditating beneath a tree. Mara is sometimes considered a form of **Kama**, god of desire.

Märchen A German **folktale**, or story, as distinct from an event that is supposed to have really occurred.

Marduk Originally a **deity** of fertility and agriculture, Marduk became the Babylonian **high god** after defeating **Tiamat**. Marduk was a solar deity and maintained the forces of order in the universe. He was popular in Assyria between the fourteenth and seventh centuries B.C., but was subsequently displaced by the tribal war god, Assur.

Marga Sanskrit term meaning "path". In Hindu **mysticism**, human evolution may be defined as a twofold cycle. The first phase is the Pravritta Marga (the outgoing path), and the second the Nivritti Marga (the path of return). In the first phase, one descends, or "falls", into the pattern of incarnations; in the second, one begins to return to the **God-head**. See also **Reincarnation**.

Marijuana See **Hashish**; **Hemp, Indian**.

Mark, Devil's See **Devil's Mark**.

Marrngit Among the Murngin Aborigines of Arnhem Land in Australia, a **medicine-man** who has powers of healing and psychic dissociation. The Marrngit can read other people's thoughts and "see" what is happening a long way away. He can also locate a **sorcerer** who has stolen someone else's **soul**. See **Aborigines, Australian**.

Mars In Roman **mythology**, the god of war. With **Jupiter**, **Mars** was one of the most notable gods in the Roman **pantheon**; and his cause was furthered by Emperor Augustus, who built two temples in his honour. March 15 (the month which derives its name from him) was a festival day, put aside to celebrate the marriage of Mars; and in the northern hemisphere this day represented the official beginning of spring.

Mars In **astrology**, a personification of violent or hostile acts, aggression, and strong willpower. Those with Mars strongly aspected in their chart are inclined to be pugnacious and single-minded in their actions and are said to be generally lacking in refinement. However, seen in a more positive light, the "Martian" person can differentiate truth from falsehood and may demonstrate great moral courage, being willing to take a stand against a tide of vacillating popular opinion. The sign of the **zodiac** most compatible with Mars is **Aries**, the Ram.

Martello, Leo Louis (1931–2000) American **hypnotist**, **occultist**, and **wiccan**, and founder of the Witches Anti-Defamation League, one of the first pagan civil rights organizations in the United States. He was also Director of Witches International Craft Association and a pastor of the Temple of Spiritual Guidance. His books include *It's in the Stars*, *It's in the Cards*, *Weird Ways of Witchcraft*, and *How to Prevent Psychic Blackmail*.

Martinism Esoteric teaching of **Martinez de Pasqually**, who drew on various mystical traditions, including **Gnosticism**, the **Kabbalah**, and the **Hermetica**. De Pasqually believed that one could only attain salvation by contacting the divine source of all Being and by participating in an initiatory ceremony invoking one's **holy guardian angel**. Once the latter had been achieved, one could go through life in a "reintegrated" way. There were Martinist Orders in Foix, Bordeaux, Paris, and Lyons; but the movement declined after the death of de Pasqually in 1774.

Martino, Ernesto de (1908–) Italian professor of the history of religions at Cagliari University. De Martino became interested in the links between **parapsychology** and anthropology, especially with regard to the claimed supernatural powers of **witch-doctors** and **shamans**. His books include

Death and Ritual Dirge in the Ancient World (1958), *South Italy and Magic* (1959), and *Magic: Primitive and Modern* (1967, republished 1999).

Masculine Planets In **astrology**, the **sun** (planet of light); **Mars** associated with war and destruction); **Jupiter** (wealth and abundance); **Saturn** (aloofness and solitude); and **Uranus** (spiritual intuition). Compare with **Feminine Planets**.

Masculine Principle See **Male Principle**.

Mask A facial covering, often used in magical and religious ceremonies to allow a practitioner to assume the role of the invoked **god** or **spirit**, or to frighten **demons** and hostile forces away.

Maslow, Abraham (1908–1970) American psychologist credited with establishing humanistic and **transpersonal psychology**. Maslow graduated with a PhD from the University of Wisconsin and became chairman of the psychology department at Brandeis University in 1951. Reacting against behaviourism, Maslow emphasized creativity, well-being and spirituality as important dimensions of human life and believed that we should all strive for self-actualization, fulfilling our individual potentials as completely as possible. His exploration of peak experiences moved humanistic psychology closer to the terrain associated with mysticism, and to this extent Maslow continued an approach pioneered by **Jung**. Maslow became one of the conceptual founders of the personal growth movement. Together with Anthony Sutich, he defined the transpersonal perspective which is central to an understanding of the New Spirituality.

Master In **occultism** and **mysticism**, a great **adept** or illuminated being. Masters are often said to be invisible or **discarnate**, influencing the world through the charismatic leaders of occult sects and groups. See also **Illuminati**; **Koot Hoomi**.

Master of the Divine Name In Jewish **mysticism**, the title given to those who possessed the knowledge of the sacred name of **God** and who knew how to use the sacred formulae for mystical or magical purposes. Such people were called **Ba'al Shem**, a term which predates the medieval **Kabbalah**.

Materialization In **spiritualization**, the alleged ability of **psychic mediums** to manifest the likeness of deceased persons so that they can be perceived by others present at the **seance**. Materializations are said to take form in **ectoplasm**, an etheric substance exuded by the medium while in **trance**. Some psychical researchers claimed to have photographed materializations using infra-red apparatus, athough the results are controversial. See also **Psychic Photography**.

Material Plane See **Matter**. Compare with **Astral Plane**.

Materia Prima In **Alchemy**, the "first substance" or Universal First Cause from which all other substances were said to have come forth. For base metals to be transmuted into **silver** or **gold**, they had to first be reduced to their *materia prima*, and then reconstituted as one of the "noble" metals that had an immediate link with **God**. See also **Transmutation**.

Mathers, Mrs. Moina (1865–1928) The sister of French philosopher **Henry Bergson**. Moina Bergson married the influential English occultist **Samuel MacGregor Mathers** in 1890 and spent most of her married life with him in Paris. After his death in 1918 she became head of the Alpha and Omega Temple of the **Hermetic Order of the Golden Dawn** and something of a rival to Dion Fortune. Mrs. Mathers is remembered, rightly or wrongly, primarily for the claims made against her by Dion Fortune, who maintained that Mrs. Mathers attacked her magically on the **astral plane** in the form of a huge cat. Dion Fortune also accused Mrs. Mathers of the "psychic murder" of Alpha-Omega member Netta Fornario, whose body was found naked on the island of Iona accompanied by a Golden Dawn cloak and a silver chain. See also **Magical Attack**.

Mathers, Samuel Liddell MacGregor (1854–1918) A key figure in the **Hermetic Order of the Golden Dawn**, Mathers developed the **rituals** that formed the basis of the order and also translated a number of medieval magical works into English, including Knorr Von Rosenroth's *Kabbalah Denudata* (*The Kabbalah Unveiled*); Solomon Trismosin's alchemical treatise *Splendor Solis*; and several **grimoires**, including *The Sacred Magic of Abra-melin the Mage*, the ***Key of Solomon***, and *The Grimoire of Armadel*. Mathers spent much of his time in the British Museum reading-room, studying and translating ancient texts.

As the Golden Dawn grew in importance, Mathers – who had taken a senior rank and began to claim inspiration from the **Secret Chiefs** – became increasingly autocratic. After moving to Paris with his wife, Moina Mathers, in 1892, he demanded financial support from Golden Dawn members while he translated occult texts at his leisure, and schisms soon began to appear in the Order. Mathers died in Paris in 1918. The probable cause was Spanish influenza, but according to Mather's wife, it resulted from a **transcendental** encounter with the Secret Chiefs which no mortal could survive.

Matrona In the **Kabbalah**, the female aspect of **God**. She is also known as **Shekhinah**.

Matter In many occult, theosophical, and **Gnostic** systems, the antithesis of **Spirit** and the grossest emanation of the **Godhead** in the process of Creation. **Occultists** believe generally that matter is animated by an inner, vibrant force that provides life and dynamism in the universe and that this energy is identical, in essence, to **God**. Matter is not regarded as "reality", but as the outer form of an inner, transcendent process. Among the Gnostics, matter was regarded as **evil** because of its "distance" from the Spirit. See also **Theosophy**.

Matthews, John (1948–) Currently based in Oxford, England, Matthews has spent more than thirty years researching **Celtic** mythology, the Grail legends and other aspects of the Western esoteric traditions. Well known on both sides of the Atlantic for his lectures and workshops, Matthews is the author or editor of over fifty books, among them *The Celtic Seers' Sourcebook*, *The Druid Sourcebook*, *The Elements of the Arthurian Tradition* and *The Western Way*, co-authored with his wife Caitlin.

Matutine In **astrology**, the situation where the **moon**, **Mercury**, or **Venus** rise in the morning before the **sun**. The planet is matutine until it reaches its first "station", the point in its orbit where it becomes retrograde.

Mau Mau A nationalist secret society among the Kikuyu tribesfoik of Kenya, the Mau Mau were active between 1952 and 1960, when they were suppressed. Stirred up by several prophets, the Mau Mau were bound by oaths and strict ritual practices, and inflicted terror both upon the white settlers and the black Kenyans who refused to become members.

Maya In **Buddhism**, the mother of **Gautama**. A chaste and virtuous woman, and queen of the Sakyas, she was prepared by the wives of the **gods** for his birth: Gautama entered her womb in the form of a white elephant. Maya died seven days after Gautama's birth, her role as mother of the **avatar** fulfilled.

Maya From a Sanskrit root *ma*, meaning "to form, or limit". The term "maya" is often used to describe the illusory nature of appearances. However, to the extent that maya represents phenomenal existence, it is a vital aspect of the creative process and is necessary if spiritual evolution is to occur. See also **Illusion.**

May Day Pagan festival of **rebirth** and renewal celebrated on the first day of May. Associated with the Celtic festival of **Beltane,** May Day includes among its ceremonies the election of a Queen of May who personifies the powers of fertility. Young people bring garlands of flowers to the ceremony and there is much merriment and dancing around the famous **maypole.** In England the Morris men also perform their colourful dances at this time.

Maypole Pole with streamers, central to the celebrations and dances performed on **May Day.** The maypole itself is a symbol of the phallus, an important motif in the May Day ceremonies, which honour fertility and the regeneration of Nature.

Mazdaism The worship of **Ahura Mazda.** See also **Zoroaster.**

Mazdayasni Din Term by which followers of **Zoroaster** refer to their own religion. It combines *Mazda* ("Omniscient Lord of Light"), *yasni* ("worshipping"), and *din* ("faith"). See also **Parsee.**

Maze Mythic symbol that characterizes the wandering path of life, with its seemingly never-ending dead-ends, false turns, obstructions, and multiple choices. The best-known example of a maze is the famous **labyrinth** at the Palace of Knossos.

MC In **astrology**, the standard abbreviation for *medium coeli*, or **Midheaven.**

Mead, G. R. S. (1863–1933) One-time secretary to **Madame Helena Blavatsky** in the London branch of the **Theosophical Society,** Mead was a scholar who specialized in studies of **Gnosticism** and the **Hermetica.** In 1909 he founded an **esoteric** group known as the Quest Society, which published the magazine *The Quest* and held meetings for those interested in aspects of the Western **mystery** tradition. Mead is best remembered for his editions of the *Pistis Sophia* (1896) and *Thrice Greatest Hermes* (1906). His other books include *Fragments of a Faith Forgotten* (1900), *Apollonius of Tyana* (1901), *Echoes of the Gnosis* (1907), and *The Subtle Body* (1919).

Mecca The most sacred city in **Islam** and the birthplace of **Mohammed.** Pilgrimage to Mecca at least once in their lifetime is a requirement for all devout Moslems and it is here that the famous **Ka'ba** temple is located.

Medea In Greek **mythology**, the **witch** who was in love with Jason, and used magic enchantments to enable him to steal the Golden Fleece. When Jason deserted her, she killed their two children – Mermerus and Pheres – and fled to Athens, where she married King Aegeus. Medea was a niece of **Circe,** another notorious witch and enchantress.

Medicine-man In primitive societies, the **witch-doctor**, **shaman**, or **priest** responsible for divining illness and preparing effective magical remedies. He protects the community from **witchcraft** and **black magic**; and, through **trance** and **incantations**, holds regular discourse with the **gods** and **spirits.**

Medina In **Islam**, the most sacred city after **Mecca.** It was to Medina (then known as Yathrib) that **Mohammed** travelled when escaping from his enemies in Mecca, and it is also the site of the prophet's tomb.

Meditation Technique of mind control that often leads to a feeling of inner calm and peacefulness and may result in profound experiences of **self-realization** and **transcendental** awareness. Meditation is a discipline found in many of the world's leading religions, including **Buddhism**, **Hinduism**, **Islam**, and Christianity.

There are two broad approaches to meditation. The first focuses on the powers of concentration and requires that one's attention be fixed on a meditative symbol (e.g. a **mandala**), a rhythmic sound or chant (e.g. a **mantra**), or on one's pattern of breathing. The concept here is to turn the processes of thought inward until the mind transcends itself.

The second approach focuses more on "detached awareness" and emphasizes the dispassionate observation of what is happening now, rather than on attaining a higher state of consciousness. This technique enables the meditator to understand the flux of life, and the ebb and flow of human experience.

In recent times, meditation techniques have been recognized for their vital role in health, and doctors who practise **holistic health** have recommended meditation as a treatment for the many forms of stress-related disease, including cancer.

Medium In **spiritualism**, one who acts as an intermediary between the world of **spirits** and **discarnate** entities and the everyday world of normal reality. Spirits are summoned during a **seance** and their influence may be perceived through **materializations**, through **ouija board** communications, through an agreed code of rappings and knocks, or through **automatic writing** or **automatic painting** and drawing. If a discarnate entity takes over the body of the medium during a seance, that entity is known as the **control**.

Medium Coeli See **Midheaven**.

Medmenham Abbey Abbey in Buckinghamshire where members of the notorious **Hell Fire Club** used to meet. See also **Dashwood, Sir Francis.**

Medusa See **Gorgons.**

Meher Baba (1894–1969) Self-proclaimed Indian **avatar** born in Poona of Persian parents. Meher Baba's original name was Merwan (Meher) Sheriar Irani and he was converted to the spiritual path while he was in his late teens. One evening he was cycling to his home from college when an old Moslem woman, Hazrat Babajan, called him to her side. She didn't speak to him, but they embraced and she kissed his forehead. Baba went to see her several times afterwards and then one evening, according to his account, "she made me realize in a flash the infinite bliss of Self-realization". After this spiritual breakthrough, Meher seemed to move around in a trance-like state, largely unaware of life around him. His parents thought he had become an imbecile, but Meher later explained that he was in a state of high **ecstasy** and that Babajan's kiss had cast aside the barrier between him and **God.**

Anxious to find a spiritual master, Meher went to visit **Sai Baba**. One of the disciples, Upashni, encountered Meher, throwing a stone at him which drew blood from his forehead. This had the effect of returning Meher to earth-consciousness, and also confirmed Upashni as his teacher. Later the roles were reversed and Upashni proclaimed Meher to be the Avatar, a true Spiritual Master. From this time on he was known as Meher Baba.

In 1922, Meher Baba opened an **ashram** in Bombay and accepted devotees from many different spiritual traditions, as well as Untouchables. Then, in 1925, he took a vow of silence "to save mankind from the monumental forces of ignorance". He continued to open ashrams, however, and later visited the United States and Europe. His charismatic personality had an enormous effect on many people and he still retains a large following, many years after his death.

Melampus According to the *Aeneid* and *The Odyssey*, a famous soothsayer from Argos, who was able to predict the future and understand the languages of all animals.

Melusine A water-spirit or **mermaid**. The melusine features in heraldry and is depicted on the arms of the House of Lusignan. Several other European families, among them the Houses of Luxembourg, Rohan, and Sassenaye, claim descent from such a mermaid, and have actually altered their pedigrees to this effect. Some heraldic motifs show the melusine with two tails.

Memory, Cosmic See **Akashic Records**.

Memory, Far See **Far Memory**.

Mendes, Goat of Form in which the **Devil** is said to manifest during the **witches' sabbath**. Here the Devil takes a form that is half-goat and half-human, and sits cross-legged upon the altar with an inverted **pentagram** inscribed upon his forehead and a blazing torch between his horns. The goat is male, but he also has female breasts. The Goat of Mendes takes its name from the sacred goat kept captive in the Egyptian city of the same name. Here, women were supposed to mate with the goat in the same way that medieval witches had ritual intercourse with the Devil. The Goat of Mendes features on the **Tarot** card ***The Devil***.

Menhir From the Breton *men* ("a stone"), and *hir* ("high"), a prehistoric stone monolith. See also **Celt**; **Dolmen**; **Druid**.

Men of High Degree Term used generally to describe Aboriginal **shamans** or **medicine-men**. See also **Aborigines, Australian**.

Mental Body Theosophical concept of an inner body, or aspect of the personality, consisting of thoughts and mental impressions. This body, which is said to possess its own degree of consciousness, may be projected onto the **astral plane**, where it brings consciousness to the imaginal world of the "subconscious" mind. The mental body is capable of both abstract and concrete conceptualization. See also **Theosophy**.

Mental Radio Expression coined by the Pulitzer Prize-winning American novelist Upton Sinclair, to describe an experiment involving the mental transfer of thought impressions between his wife Mary and himself. Sinclair's experiments took place over a three-year period and are described in his book *Mental Radio* (1930, republished 1963). See also **Telepathy, Mental**.

Mental Telepathy See **Telepathy, Mental**.

Mentiferous Having the ability to transfer mind or thought. One who is telepathic. See also **Telepathy, Mental**.

Mephistopheles From a Greek expression meaning "one who does not like light", the **demon** to whom **Faust** is said to have sold his **soul**. In Goethe's celebrated work, *Faust*, Mephistopheles is said to have been able to change his form into that of a dog, and he also appeared before Faust as the **Devil** himself.

Mercury The Roman counterpart of **Hermes**.

Mercury In **alchemy**, a name for quicksilver. The two primordial forces in alchemy were the **sun** and **moon**, represented by **sulphur** and **quicksilver**, respectively. Quicksilver was regarded by the alchemists as the "womb", or "mother", of all metals (including **gold**), and to this extent was associated with the **materia prima**.

Mercury In **astrology**, the planet that traditionally personifies logical or rational human qualities, together with scholarship and learning. It represents the ability to discriminate or observe objectively, and also refers to the acts of arranging, ordering, and purifying. In the same way that Mercury was the messenger of the **gods** in ancient Roman **mythology**, people with a well-aspected Mercury in their charts are said to make excellent communicators and could make their careers in one of the media professions, in trade, or in politics. The **zodiac** sign most compatible with Mercury is **Gemini**.

Meridian In **acupuncture**, the channels which carry **ch'i**, or life energy, to different parts of the body. There are twelve principal meridians and these are correlated with the following organs:

Arm Sunlight Yang	–	Large Intestine
Leg Sunlight Yang	–	Stomach
Arm Greater Yin	–	Lungs
Leg Greater Yin	–	Spleen
Arm Lesser Yang	–	"Triple Warmer"
Leg Lesser Yang	–	Gall bladder
Arm Absolute Yin	–	"Circulation Sex"
Leg Absolute Yin	–	Liver
Arm Greater Yang	–	Small Intestine
Leg Greater Yang	–	Bladder
Arm Lesser Yin	–	Heart
Leg Lesser Yin	–	Kidneys

See also **Yang**; **Yin**.

Merkabah Mystical tradition in the **Kabbalah** featuring the Merkabah, or Throne Chariot of **God**, which could ascend or descend through the different heavenly halls or palaces known as the **Hekhaloth** – the last of which revealed the divine Glory of God. During the period of the Second Temple, the Vision of Ezekiel was interpreted as a mystical flight to **heaven**, and the kabbalistic mystics evolved a technique of using the symbol of the chariot as a meditative focus. The **mystic** would make an inner journey to the seven palaces and use secret magic names to ensure safe passage through each of these palaces in turn. Until recently, these mystical procedures and formulae were little known except to kabbalistic scholars. However, the relevant texts from the ***Greater Hekhaloth*** – the key work of the Merkabah mystics – have been published in English in an important book titled *Meditation and Kabbalah* (1982) by **Aryeh Kaplan**.

Merlin **Wizard** and **Druid** who features prominently in the Arthurian legends. The persona of Merlin may derive from a bard and seer known as Myraddin, who assisted the British chieftain Ambrosius Aurelianius and lived near Solway Firth. His magical **spells** are said to have caused the Battle of Arderydd near Carlisle, but a vision from the heavens transformed him into a raving lunatic who thereafter lived a rambling existence in the forests of the Scottish lowlands.

The mythic Merlin was of fairy birth, born of a virgin – a "demon" child. While still only a child, Merlin became well known for his magical powers of **prophecy** and visited Vortigern's court when he was five years old. The King was puzzled by a **curse** that was affecting the construction of his fortress on Salisbury Plain. Astrologers had told the monarch that the blood of a young child was required to counteract the curse, but Merlin maintained that the trouble lay with two mighty **dragons** – one white and the other red – which were locked in ferocious combat beneath the earth. Merlin predicted that the white dragon would prove victorious and that the death of the red monster would herald the death of Vortigern himself. When these events came to pass, Merlin became famous as a wizard and served the next king, Uther Pendragon, assisting in the construction of the new castle at Carlisle, which housed the mystical Round Table. Merlin also tutored the young and future king, Arthur, who obtained the magical sword Excalibur from the Lady in the Lake and was protected by it in battle.

Merlin in due course found his match in the enchantress **Vivian**, with whom he fell in love. One day, while walking in the forest of Broceliande, Vivian entreated Merlin to tell her his most powerful spell – a spell which would enable a **witch** to trap any man and subject him to her command. Merlin was so infatuated by Vivian that he parted with his secret formula of enchantment and she in turn trapped him with the spell when he fell asleep in the forest.

Mermaids Legendary, bewitching creatures usually depicted as beautiful naked women with tails of fishes. Mermaids were said to dwell on craggy rocks, holding a comb and mirror, and singing alluring and enchanting songs that would draw sailors and their vessels to their doom.

Mermen The male counterparts of **mermaids**. See also **Elemental; Water-spirits**.

Meru, Mount In **Hinduism**, the mythic centre of the world where the cities of the **gods** are located. Situated in the Himalayas, Mount Meru is said to be the centre of the "world-lotus" and represents the Hindu equivalent of the Greek Mount Olympus. Some Theosophists identify it esoterically with the North Pole. See also **Axis Mundi; Olympus, Mount**.

Mescal Beans Unrelated to the **peyote**, mescal beans are the dark red seeds of the shrub *Sophors secundiflora*, and were used extensively by the Plains Indians to induce initiatory visions in the "Red Bean Dance". The Kiowa and Comanche Indians still make use of mescal beans in a ceremonial capacity.

Mescaline The psycho-active ingredient in the **peyote cactus**, a hallucinogenic plant which is used as a sacrament by the Huichol Indians in Mexico and among the Plains Indians of the south-west United States. Mescaline attracted widespread attention after the publication of **Aldous Huxley**'s two books on his visionary experiences with the **psychedelic**: *The Doctors of Perception* (1954) and *Heaven and Hell* (1956). In fact, it had been synthesized as early as 1919. The first scientific paper on peyote was earlier still – dating from 1888 – and had been written by Ludwig Lewin following his experiments with the effects of the drug on animals. Havelock Ellis and **Williams James** were early pioneers of mescaline experience and wrote personal accounts of the visionary effects of the drug. See also **Hallucination**.

Mesmer, Friedrich Anton (1733–1815) Austrian doctor and astrologer who developed the theory of **animal magnetism** and gave his name to **mesmerism**, an early form of **hypnosis**. Mesmer graduated in medicine from the University of Vienna in 1766 and began to use "magnetism" on his patients. His first client was Fraulein Oesterline, an epileptic. Mesmer attached magnets to her arms and legs and her convulsions disappeared within six hours. Mesmer later went to Paris and established a medical practice treating wealthy aristocrats. Mesmer himself wore a leather shirt to trap his own "magnetic fluid", but his patients were asked to sit around a tub filled with water and **iron** filings. A number of iron rod "conductors" protruded from the tub, and the patients held these rods while also being bound by a cord to make a circle and thereby close the "force". According to Mesmer, "magnetism" from the tub would transfer to each of the patients, eliminating their illnesses. According to the French scientist Jean Bailly, who investigated Mesmer's approach, patients were also "magnetized" by the doctor's finger, or wand, which he moved up and down in front of their faces or over their diseased organs. The effects were varied. According to Bailly, "some are tranquil and experience no effect. Others cough and spit, feel pains, heat or perspiration ..."

Mesmerism An early term for **hypnosis.** Originally, it was presumed that waves of magnetic force issued forth from the hypnotist's hands or eyes and were responsible for producing a **trance-state** in the subject. However, this view is no longer accepted. See also **Animal Magnetism; Mesmer, Friedrich Anton.**

Messenger In **Theosophy**, a spiritual intermediary who comes at the bidding of one of the **mahatmas**, or Masters of Wisdom.

Metagnomy Knowledge obtained from a source outside the five normal human senses.

Metals, Planetary In **alchemy** and **astrology**, symbolic correlations exist between the **planets** (which include the **sun** and **moon**) and certain metals. These correlations are as follows: **Saturn** (lead), **Jupiter** (tin), Mars (**iron**), the sun (**gold**), **Venus** (copper), Mercury (**quicksilver**), and the moon (**silver**).

Metaphysics The philosophical and scientific study of reality, existence, and knowledge. From a mystical viewpoint it is taken to mean the study of the Supreme Reality which lies beyond appearances; and to this extent, it encompasses such concepts as **God, cosmic consciousness,** and the nature of Truth.

Métapsychique Term proposed by the French psychical researcher **Professor Charles Richet** as an equivalent to **psychical research** or **parapsychology**. Richet maintained that psychic phenomena were essentially physiological in nature and not linked to an immortal **soul** or survival after **death**.

Metatron A heavenly **angel** who features prominently in the *Book of the Visions of Ezekiel* (fourth century) and various other visionary tracts and apocalypses in the **Hekhaloth** tradition of Jewish **mysticism.** In one Talmudic text he is referred to as the "lesser YHVH"; and in Genesis he is associated with Enoch, who "walked with God", ascended into **heaven**, and was later changed into the angel himself. **Occultists** regard Metatron as the **archangel** governing **Kether**, the supreme **sephirah** on the kabbalistic **Tree of Life**. See also **Kabbalah.**

Metempsychosis The doctrine that the **soul** may reincarnate into animal bodies after death. It is differentiated from other reincarnational doctrines, which hold that the soul may only pass into another human body. See also **Reincarnation.**

Metteya The **Pali** name for **Maitreya.**

Michael In Western **magic**, the **archangel** said to govern the southern quarter. He rules the element **Fire**, and is invoked during the **banishing ritual** of the Lesser Pentagram. Michael is regarded by **occultists** as the archangel governing **Hod** on the kabbalistic **Tree of Life.**

Microcosm See **Macrocosm and Microcosm.**

Microprosopus In the **Kabbalah**, the so-called Lesser Countenance of **God**. See also **Macroprosopus; Tetragrammaton.**

Middle Eye See **Third Eye.**

Middle Path Known in **Mahayana Buddhism** as Madhyamika, this is the path between existence and non-existence, which one follows in order to comprehend the **Void** (**sunyata**). See also **Nagarjuna.**

Middle Pillar In the **Kabbalah**, the central "pillar" on the **Tree of Life**. The Tree, which consists of ten **sephiroth**, or **emanations** of **God**, can be viewed as being aligned in three columns headed by **Kether, Chokmah,** and **Binah**, respectively. The Middle Pillar is the column headed by Kether and is regarded by occultists as the magical equivalent of the mystical "Middle Way". The sephiroth that lead to Kether on the Middle Pillar are, in order of ascent: **Malkuth**, **Yesod**, **Tiphareth**, and **Daath**.

Midgard Serpent In Scandinavian **mythology**, a huge serpent that was the offspring of **Loki** and Angerboda. **Odin** threw him into the sea and he lay in the depths, encircling the world. **Thor** tried to catch him without success, but **Ragnarok** finally killed him with his hammer. However, Thor himself perished in this contest – a victim of the serpent's venom.

Midheaven In **astrology**, the so-called South point, or **cusp** of the tenth **house**. It should not be equated with the tenth house as a whole, however, and is sometimes confused with the **zenith**, which is the point opposite the **nadir**.

Midpoint In **astrology**, an unoccupied, unaspected degree of the **horoscope** that lies between, and equidistant from, two other planets.

Midrash In Judaism, the rabbinical commentaries on the biblical texts which define the faith.

Milarepa, Jetsun (1052–1135) Tibetan **mystic**. As a young man he practised **black magic**; but, after meeting a **lama** named Marpa, he sought mystical **initiation**. He was sent to meditate in the mountains and achieved the **transcendental** vision of the Supreme Oneness that encompasses all. The major work on this mystic is *Tibet's Great Yogi, Milarepa*, by **W. Y. Evans-Wentz**.

Mind One's individual faculties of consciousness, awareness, and thought. **Occultists** regard the mind as a lower aspect of the **self** and maintain that in an **altered state of consciousness** – for example, in an **out-of-the-body experience** – the mind can be "projected" outside the body and experience a new range of perceptions. Occultists and **mystics** also believe that the mind may be altered to become more "sensitive", so that it is receptive to **psi** phenomena (the various manifestations of **extrasensory perception**).

Mind Over Matter Popular term for **psychokinesis**.

Mind Reading A popular term for mental telepathy. See also **Telepathy, Mental**.

Minggah Among the **Aborigines** of western New South Wales, a **spirit**-haunted tree. The **medicine-man** has, as his magical allies, friendly spirits who reside in the tree, and he is able to take refuge in the Minggah at a time of danger.

Minor Arcana In the **Tarot**, the fifty-six minor cards. These fall into four suits: **swords**, **wands**, **pentacles**, and **cups**. The Minor Arcana has no application as a meditative device, but plays an important role in Tarot **divination**. See also **Major Arcana**.

Minotaur In Greek **mythology**, a famous monster with a human body and the head of a bull. The minotaur was kept in the **labyrinth** at the Palace of Minos and was fed on the bodies of human victims – seven boys and seven girls selected each year in Athens as a ritual sacrifice.

Miracle From the Latin *mirari*, "to wonder", a **supernatural** or extraordinary event that has no rational explanation and which is often believed to result from divine intervention. Jesus Christ is said in the biblical narratives to have produced many miraculous cures, and his approach of **laying-on-of-hands** has been taken up by many Christian **faith-healers**. See also **Edwards, Harry**; **Lourdes**.

Miroku In Japanese **Buddhism**, the name of the **Buddha** who is still to come. See also Maitreya.

Mishnah In Judaism, the oral law of **God**. Traditionally the Mishnah was supposed to complement the written Law of Moses and to this extent may be regarded as a body of interpretations and notations of the **Torah**.

Mistletoe Plant with magical associations. **Druid** priests used to distribute mistletoe to the worshippers after a white bull had been sacrificed to the beneficent spirits, and this mistletoe was taken home and hung from the ceiling to frighten away **evil** forces. Among the Romans, mistletoe was similarly regarded as a protection against the **Devil** and enabled one to speak to **ghosts**. However, in Scandinavian **mythology**, mistletoe had a more unfortunate mythic association, for the sun-god **Balder** was slain by a branch of mistletoe gathered by the jealous **Loki**. Contemporary couples kiss beneath the mistletoe at Christmas to ensure fertility; but the plant is not allowed within the church because of its **pagan** associations.

Mithra Also Mithras. Persian **god** of light who, according to the **Avesta**, would appear before sunrise and watch over the earth and firmament while riding in a chariot drawn by four white horses. Mithra was regarded as the all-knowing god, and as a **deity** of fertility and abundance. He was also the untiring opponent of all things **evil**, and would ruthlessly destroy wickedness wherever he discovered it. Following the expedition of Alexander the Great and the fusion of religious beliefs that followed his conquests, Mithra became associated with Helios, the Greek god of light. The cult of Mithra was introduced into the Roman Empire when Pompey returned to Rome after capturing Jerusalem in 63 B.C., bringing captives with him who were devotees of the Persian religion. By the end of the first century, the cult of Mithra was well established, especially among the Roman soldiers, and by A.D. 250 it had become a major rival to Christianity.

Mithra was lord of the four **elements** – which are symbolized by his four horses – and came to be regarded as a mediator between the common people and the "unknowable" god who transcended existence. In this respect Mithra was like a **demiurge**. Always linked to **astrology**, Mithra was associated with the constellation of **Taurus**, which, as the **sun** entered it, heralded the beginning of spring. Mithra was often depicted overcoming the bull (Taurus), which had been the first animal created by **Ohrmazd**. In Mithraic **cosmology**, the useful herbs and plants of Nature were said to have sprung from the carcass of the bull slain by Mithra, thus identifying the bull as a source of fertility, new life, and abundant crops. The blood of the bull also represented the **life-force** which would nourish the earth and its people.

Mizraim An ancient name for Egypt, still used in **Freemasonry**.

Moed In Judaism, the division of the **Mishnah** which deals with the laws of the sabbath, high holy days, Passover sacrifices, and similar laws to do with feasts.

Mohammed (570–632) Also Mahomet, Muhammad. The founder of **Islam**. Mohammed was born in **Mecca** and, as a young man, tended his uncle's sheep in the desert. Later he went to Syria and is said to have met a Christian monk named Bahira, who predicted that Mohammed would become a prophet. While still in his twenties, he became a merchant and married a wealthy widow named Kahdijah – who was fifteen years older than him. The marriage lasted twenty years and produced six (or seven) children.

Around the age of forty, Mohammed began to feel that he was undergoing a spiritual trial; and he periodically retreated alone to a cave called Hira, in the hills near Mecca. Here he would meditate on **God** and the nature of the universe. One night, possibly in the year 612, Mohammed had a visionary dream in which the angel Jibril (**Gabriel**) appeared to him and commanded him to "read in the name of the Lord". Later Jibril appeared again and told Mohammed that he was "in truth, the Prophet of Allah"; and a series of revelations were given to him over the next twenty-three years. Included in these visionary communications were details of **heaven** and **hell**; the nature of human existence; insights into the principles of righteousness, love, and mercy; and, foremost, the greatest truth of all – the necessity of submission to **Allah**, the One True God.

Jibril instructed Mohammed to preach to the Meccans, but at first his efforts at conversion were in vain. He attacked the idolatry and self-interest of the ruling classes, but was regarded by many as a **magician**, possessed by **genii**.

In 620 Mohammed had another vision, again aided by Jibril, in which he was carried from the **Ka'ba** at Mecca to the Temple in Jerusalem, on a winged horse. In this vision, Mohammed ascended a ladder of light to the foot of God's heavenly throne. Meanwhile, there were moves to kill Mohammed. With a group of converts, he set off for Yathrib (later known as **Medina**). Here he was more successful in gaining conversions, although the Jews continued to resist him. Mohammed now began a series of "holy wars" and amassed huge armies to overcome any opposition. He returned to take Mecca and established the Ka'ba as the centre of the Islamic faith.

Mohammed divided the new religion into Iman ("faith") and Din (practices, **prayer**, alms, fasting, and the personal pilgrimage to Mecca). The tenets of his belief embrace belief in God, his **angels**, his scriptures, and his prophets, together with belief in the Resurrection and the Day of Judgment. While the **Qur'an** holds that Mohammed is the most illustrious of the prophets, Moslems also recognize Moses and Jesus as lesser, but nevertheless significant, prophets within the Islamic tradition.

Mohin Degadlus In **Hasidism**, the Hebrew expression for mystical **ecstasy**.

Moksha A synonym for **mukti**: freedom from **reincarnation** and **karma** as a result of gaining **cosmic consciousness**, or knowledge of the Supreme Reality.

Moleoscopy **Divination** by interpreting the moles on a person's skin to interpret aspects of character and to predict future events. Some astrologers believe that moles result from the influences of the planets in the **natal horoscope**. **Saturn** governs black moles: **Jupiter**, purple-brown; **Venus**, light brown; and the **moon**, blue-white. Moles assigned to **Mercury** are honey-coloured, while those influenced by the **sun** are yellow. The position of the mole on different parts of the body was traditionally believed to have divinatory or psychological significance. A mole located on the ankle, for example, indicated ambition; while one on the breast indicated an unpleasant nature. A mole on the toe indicated a love of art, while one on the knee was considered a sign of extravagance.

Monad From the Greek *monas*, "a single entity". A self-contained system of any size. A monad may be a single living cell, a human being, a planet, or a galaxy. Theosophists use the term to describe the one universal **life-force** which animates all matter at a sub-atomic level. See also **Theosophy**.

Mondo In **Zen Buddhism**, a method of question-and-answer teaching used by the Masters to instruct their disciples in the principles of Zen. From a rational viewpoint, the answer may appear not to relate to the question; but, as with the **koan**, which the mondo resembles, enlightenment may sometimes be found by transcending the nature of paradox, and by breaking down linear systems of thought.

Monism The mystical and religious belief that all is One, that a supreme and infinite Being encompasses all creation. In **Hinduism**, this belief is called **Advaita.** One of the greatest proponents of this doctrine in recent years was the Indian mystic **Ramana Maharshi.**

Monition In **occultism**, a warning that comes to a person through **extrasensory perception.** See also **Premonition.**

Monkshood *Aconitum napellus*, a poisonous herb said in Greek legend to have come forth from the saliva that dripped from the mouth of the monster **Cerberus.** Monkshood was used by medieval **witches** in **flying ointments** and "love philtres", but is one of the most poisonous and dangerous of all magical herbs, often causing death when consumed.

Monoceros Mythic creature described by Pliny as resembling a horse with a stag's head, elephant's feet, and the tail of a boar. It had a short black horn in the centre of its forehead, and to this extent resembled a **unicorn.**

Monotheism The belief in one **God.** Monotheism may be contrasted with **polythesim**, in which a **pantheon** of gods is acknowledged and worshipped. Christianity and **Islam** are examples of monotheistic religions.

Monroe, Robert A. (1915–1995) American businessman who, in 1958, began having **out-of-the-body experiences.** One afternoon, while resting on the couch in his living-room, Monroe felt a "warm light" upon his body and began to "vibrate" involuntarily. Over the next few months Monroe noticed that he could move his fingertips when the vibrations began, and "feel" things normally beyond his reach. Later he discovered that he could project his total consciousness outside his physical body, although his first experience of such dissolution was accompanied by a feeling of panic and the thought that perhaps he had died. Monroe later began to systemically explore the new faculty he had discovered, and subsequently identified three "locales" that could be "visited" in the dissociated state. In Locale One, according to Monroe, time seemed to cease, and past and future co-existed with the feeling of "now". In Locale Two, one's will and visual abilities seemed to be able to create **thought-forms**, which then became experientially real. In Monroe's terms, "to think something is to make it happen ..." Locale Three, meanwhile, had a time-warp dimension, which provided imagery inconsistent with modern science.

An account of Monroe's experiences, *Journeys Out of the Body*, was published with a foreword by the leading parapsychologist **Charles Tart.** It remains one of the classic contemporary accounts of **astral projection.** See also **Fox, Oliver; Muldoon, Sylvan.**

Moon Celestial body traditionally associated with **magic**, fertility, and the secret powers of Nature. As a reflector of **light**, the moon has been regarded as a "funnel" drawing on the light of the stars and constellations and transmitting their energies to the Earth. The earliest calendars measured the passage of time by the "moons", probably because the twenty-eight days of the lunar month are a convenient measure. Similarly, because the female menstrual cycle is monthly it has been traditionally symbolized as a lunar cycle and the moon has become a motif of fertility. The worship of **lunar goddesses** is a central feature of **witchcraft.**

Moon In **astrology**, perhaps the most important celestial body after the **sun**, since it moves through all the **signs** of the **zodiac** and therefore has a profound influence on one's **horoscope.** The moon is regarded by astrologers as a strong influence on one's emotions and moods, and people with the moon strongly aspected in their natal chart are regarded as sensitive and intuitive. However, they may also be impressionable and easily influenced. This interpretation of the moon's influence derives from the fact that the moon enters a new sign of the zodiac approximately every two-and-a-half days, whereas the **sun** changes signs only twelve times every year. See also **Lunar Goddesses**.

Moon, The In the **Tarot**, the card that symbolizes the processes of biological and spiritual evolution. A lobster, representing an early form of life, emerges from the waters; while on land we see two dogs – one an aggressive wolf, and the other a more domesticated and "evolved" form: both of these animals look upwards towards the **moon**, to which the dog is sacred. The element **Water** predominates in the symbolism of *The Moon*, and the card is affiliated with the lunar sphere **Yesod**, which is associated on the kabbalistic **Tree of Life** with sexuality and the cycles of fertility. *The Moon* represents the path from **Malkuth** to **Yesod** in the **Kabbalah**.

Moore, Old (1656–1715) Author of *Old Moore's Almanack* – a famous astrological reference work. Old Moore was Dr. Francis Moore, a teacher, physician, and astrologer who published his first *Almanack* in 1699 to advertise pills and medical potions. His second publication, issued a year later, included astrological predictions. The Almanack continued after Old Moore's death, and at one stage had a circulation of half a million copies. See also **Astrology**.

Morning Glory See **Ololiuhqui**.

Mortuary Magic See **Magic, Mortuary**.

Morya The name of one of the **mahatmas** that is alleged to have inspired the formation of the **Theosophical Society** in 1875. Morya was also **Madame Helena Blavatsky**'s personal **guru**.

Moses, the Reverend William Stainton (1839–1892) Anglican clergyman and teacher who became interested in **psychical research** after ill health forced his retirement from the Church. Moses began investigating **trance** phenomena, **levitation**, and **automatic writing** in 1872 and believed he was in touch with a group of **spirits** whose individual personalities revealed themselves through different scripts. He helped found the **Society for Psychical Research** in London in 1882, and also formed the **London Spiritualist Alliance** which became the **College of Psychic Studies**. Moses edited the spiritualist journal *Light*, and wrote several books, including *Spirit Identity* (1879), *Psychography* (1882), and *Spirit Teachings* (1883). After his death, Moses and his group of spirits allegedly communicated through the mediumship of **Mrs. Leonore Piper**.

Moslem Also Muslim. From the Arabic *aslama*, "submit to God". A devotee of **Islam**; a follower of the spiritual doctrines of the prophet **Mohammed**.

Mosque From the Arabic *masjid*, "a temple". A **Moslem** place of worship. The quadrangle court and fountain, and also the minaret, are features of the mosque. There are no seats inside: devotees kneel on carpets or mats and pray as members of a spiritual community. The central niche, or *mihrab*, of each mosque is aligned to face towards **Mecca**, irrespective of the country where it is located.

Moss, Dr. Thelma American parapsychologist, highly regarded for her work investigating the applications of **Kirlian photography**. Dr. Moss believes that the Kirlian light corona can provide clues to a subject's state of health and is potentially valuable in cancer research. She has also investigated the Kirlian "**auras**" of several **faith healers**, and was formerly a research scientist with the UCLA Neuropsychiatric Institute. Her books include *The Probability of the Impossible* (1974); *The Body Electric* (1979); and a pioneering book on **LSD**, *My Self and I* (1962), written under the pen-name Constance Newland.

Moss-folk In German and Scandinavian **folklore**, fairy creatures who lived in the forests and had occasional contact with people. They would sometimes borrow domestic goods or foods, but would always repay gifts many times over. On certain occasions the moss-folk would beg for human breast-milk to feed their sick children, but this aroused fear and superstition among the local mothers, who viewed the moss-folk with apprehension.

Mother-goddess A goddess who personifies the force of Nature and the cycles of fertility. Often the mother-goddess is considered to be the mother of the manifested universe: it is from her womb that Creation comes forth. The mother-goddess appears in every primitive religion in which fertility rites have an important role, and she is also important in the ancient Greek mysteries of **Eleusis**. In the **Tarot**, the archetype of the mother-goddess is presented as *The Empress*.

Mount Meru See **Meru, Mount**.

Mount Olympus See **Olympus, Mount**.

Mu See **Lemuria**.

Mudra In **Hinduism**, a ritual hand gesture made during worship. Different **deities** require different gestures: eighteen are involved in the worship of **Vishnu**, ten for **Shiva**, seven for **Ganesha**, and ten for **Shakti**. Mudras are regarded as having special **esoteric** significance. In Tantric Hinduism, the term mudra is also used to describe any cereal aphrodisiac used in ritual worships; and the female partner in sexual worship. See also **Tantra**.

Mukta In **Hinduism**, one who has attained **mukti** or **moksha**, mystical "liberation". Such a person has no further need to reincarnate. See also **Reincarnation**.

Muktananda, Swami (1908–1982) Indian **mystic** and practitioner of **Siddha Yoga**. A devotee of the late Swami Nityananda, Muktananda attracted an international reputation as a teacher of **Kundalini Yoga** and visited the United States and Australia on several occasions. Muktananda believed that the grace of the **guru** was essential to the spiritual awakening of the disciple. He maintained that the **kundalini** could be aroused in a person as a direct thought-transmission from the guru, through the guru's touch, or spontaneously through the pupil's spiritual devotion to the master. Muktananda produced several practical guides to Siddha Yoga. His other works include *Guru* and *Kundalini*. Muktananda's work now continues through the auspices of the Siddha Yoga Foundation, headed by Gurumayi Chidvilasananda.

Mukti Sanskrit term for "liberation". It is used by Hindus to refer to the freedom (i.e. from the endless cycles of **rebirth**) earned by one who is enlightened and has no further need to incarnate. It can be summarized as "liberation from **karma**". See also **Enlightenment**.

Muladhara In **Kundalini Yoga**, the **chakra** or energy centre at the base of the spine where the **kundalini** serpent energy lies "coiled", ready to be awakened. The Muladhara chakra is activated by using an appropriate **mantra** while meditating on the **Tattva** symbol of **Earth**, **prithivi**.

Mulaprakriti Sanskrit term meaning "the root of Nature". Theosophists and **occultists** identify it as the **feminine principle**, which underlies the manifested universe and is the cause of **maya**.

Muldoon, Sylvan American pioneer of research into **astral projection**. Muldoon began experiencing "psychic dissociation" at the age of twelve, and shared his mother's interest in **spiritualism**. It was while attending a spiritualist meeting in Clinton, Iowa, that he experienced his first astral projection. Muldoon, who was in ill health at the time, was resting on a bed when he became aware that he had two bodies – one of which had "projected" at an oblique angle to the other. Muldoon noticed the famous "cord", which is often said to characterize **out-of-the-body experience**: "My two identical bodies were joined by means of an elastic-like cable, one end of which was fastened to the medulla oblongata region of the astral counterpart, while the other end centred between the eyes." Muldoon's classical work, *The Projection of the Astral Body*, co-authored with **Hereward Carrington**, was first published in 1929 and has remained in print ever since.

Multilocation In **parapsychology**, a situation where the body (or body-image) seems to be present in three or more places simultaneously. See also **Astral Projection; Bilocation; Dissociation; Out-of-the-Body Experience.**

Mumford, Jonn (1937–) Born in Windsor, Ontario, and now based in Sydney, Australia, Dr. Mumford is widely regarded as one of the world's leading authorities on **tantric** magic. After training in chiropractic in Portland, Oregon, and later in Sydney, Dr. Mumford specialized for many years in the treatment of muscular and skeletal disorders. However he always had a deep interest in metaphysics and Eastern **mysticism**. In 1973 he was initiated by Paramahansa Swami Satyananda Saraswati of Bihar, India, and he now conducts international workshops and lectures on relaxation, sexuality, **tantra** and **yoga**. His best-known books include *Ecstasy Through Tantra*, *Karma Manual* and *Psychosomatic Yoga*.

Mummers Actors who take part in symbolic European folk-plays, often held during the winter. Mummers wear masks and colourful costumes, and preserve the ancient **pagan** themes of fertility and renewal in their dances and acting.

Mummification Ancient Egyptian practice of embalming human bodies and also the bodies of sacred animals. In ancient Egypt, the body was considered to be a vital part of the human identity and survival in the afterlife was not possible without it. When a person died, the intestines and other organs were removed and the body cavities filled with preserving incenses and bitumen. The organs that had been removed were separately bandaged and preserved in "canopic jars". These jars and the mummified body were then interred together. Mummification was well established at the time of the compilation of the Pyramid Texts (around 2400 B.C.) and continued until the fourth century A.D., when it was replaced by Christian burial practices.

Mundane Aspects In **astrology**, aspects in a **horoscope** that are indicated by **planets** occupying **cusps**.

Mundane Astrology See Astrology, Mundane.

Muni In **Hinduism** and **yoga**, a sage or wise man. **Gautama Buddha**, who was a member of the Sakya clan, is sometimes referred to as **Sakyamuni**.

Murphy, Bridey Famous case of claimed **reincarnation**. American businessman Morey Bernstein hypnotized a subject named Ruth Simmons, who then seemed able to recall a previous life as "Bridey Murphy" in Ireland. Under hypnosis, Simmons maintained that she had been born in Cork in 1798, died in 1864, and was reborn in the United States in 1923. Bridey spoke with an Irish accent and was able to provide details of obscure words and place-names, many of which were subsequently validated. The case remains controversial, although some critics believe that Simmons was drawing solely on subconscious memories and impressions arising from stories she had read as a child.

Murphy, Dr. Gardner (1895–1975) Distinguished psychologist who became president of the American **Society for Psychical Research** in 1962. His main research interests were **telepathy**, **clairvoyance**, **precognition**, and evidence relating to survival after death. A former professor of psychology at the City College of New York, Murphy was the author of the definitive *Historical Introduction to Modern Psychology* (1929; revised 1949) as well as several books on **parapsychology**, including *William James and Psychical Research* (1960) and *The Challenge of Psychical Research* (1961).

Murray, Dr. George Gilbert (1866–1957) Australian-born professor of Greek at Oxford University (1908–1936) who discovered that he possessed a remarkable telepathic faculty while playing guessing-games with his wife and children. He later submitted a detailed report on his experiments to the British **Society for Psychical Research** and became its president during 1915–1916. An authority on Greek literature and religion, Gilbert believed that the classical Greek notion of "sympathy" was remarkably similar to the modern notion of **telepathy**.

Murray, Margaret A. (1862–1963) English Egyptologist and anthropologist who maintained that **witchcraft** was a remnant of an ancient religion centred around the **mother-goddess** and the **Horned God**, and that this tradition had existed in secret through all ages, up to the present. Murray's book, *The Witch-Cult in Western Europe* (1921), "reconstructed" the Old Religion and put forward the view that the **witches** had been unfairly persecuted as a rival religion to Christianity. Most modern scholars reject the idea of a linear witchcraft tradition, but the concept has had a strong romantic appeal for contemporary practitioners of **Wicca**.

Muryans In Cornish folk-legend, **fairies** who were originally larger than human beings in size but who, year by year, grew smaller in size until they became ants and died.

Muscle-reading Phenomenon identified in **parapsychology** as a possible explanation for some cases of claimed **mental telepathy**. Here one person may respond to unconscious muscular movements made by a second person and often correctly identify the thought processes associated with those movements – even though no "psychic" communication has taken place.

Muses, The In Greek mythology, the personification of creative inspiration. The Muses were the nine daughters of **Zeus** and Mnemosyne, and each had a different specialization: Calliope (epic poetry); Clio (history); Erato (love poetry); Euterpe (music and lyric poetry); Melpomene (tragedy); Polyhymnia (hymns and sacred music); Terpsichore (dance); Thalia (comedy); and Urania (astronomy). Homer, Hesiod, and Virgil wrote invocations to the Muses, and many English poets, among them **William Blake**, Milton, Byron, and Spenser, believed that they were similarly inspired by them.

Mushroom, Sacred See ***Amanita muscaria***; **Psilocybe**; **Soma**.

Music of the Spheres Concept introduced by **Pythagoras**, who related the mathematical relationship between tones on the musical scale to the orbits of the planetary spheres. The symbolic links between celestial bodies and music also interested such Renaissance mystics as **Marsilio Ficino**, who sought to correlate the different stars and constellations with musical tones.

Muslim See **Moslem**.

Mutable Signs In **astrology**, the changeable **signs** of the **zodiac: Gemini, Sagittarius, Virgo**, and **Pisces**. These are distinguished from the **cardinal signs** and the **fixed signs**. See also **Double-bodied Signs**.

Mute Signs In **astrology**, those signs of the **zodiac** which have as their motif a creature that emits no sounds: **Cancer, Scorpio** and **Pisces**.

Myers, Frederic William Henry (1843–1901) Classical scholar, poet, and essayist who helped found the **Society for Psychical Research** (SPR) in London in 1882, and became its president in 1900. Myers was one of the investigators of the American **psychic medium Mrs. Leonore Piper**, and originated the term **telepathy**. He was regarded as one of the most active members of the SPR and devoted most of his time to psychical research. Myers believed that spiritualist phenomena had their origin in the "subliminal consciousness" and that many **psychic** abilities – such as **clairvoyance, telekinesis**, and **automatic writing** – derived from this neglected level of the mind. Myers collaborated with **Frank Podmore** and **Edmund Gurney** in producing *Phantasms of the Living* (1886), and was working on the monumental book *Human Personality and Its Survival of Bodily Death* (1903) at the time of his death. It was completed by **Richard Hodgson** and Alice Johnson, and published posthumously. Regarded as one of the major texts of psychical research, it summarized Myer's main theories and experimental findings.

Myomany In ancient Assyria, Rome, and Egypt, a form of **divination** involving rats and mice. Their cries or particular activities were often said to indicate the presence of **evil**. When King Sennacherib of Assyria (r. 705–681 B.C.) invaded Egypt, his soldiers were alarmed to discover that their quivers and bows had been gnawed by rats. The next morning, many of them fled unarmed and were slain by their enemies. In Egypt the rat was similarly regarded as a symbol of destruction.

Myrrh Transparent aromatic gum, yellow-brown in colour. Myrrh was one of the three gifts (with **gold** and frankincense) brought by the **Magi** to honour the infant Jesus. In ancient Egypt it was used both as a **ritual** offering to the **sun-god Ra**, and also to embalm corpses. In Western **magic** it is associated with the planet **Saturn**, symbolic of **death**.

Myrtle Evergreen plant symbolically associated with love and marriage. The ancient Egyptians consecrated it to **Hathor**, and in ancient Greece it was sacred to **Aphrodite** – both **goddesses** of love. Similarly, in ancient Rome, where the goddess **Venus** ruled love and fertility, brides wore wreaths of myrtle blossom on their wedding day.

Mystagogue One who, in the role of **adept**, initiates a **neophyte** into an **esoteric** or occult secret. See also **Initiation**.

Mysteria Mystica Maxima The British lodge of the **Ordo Templi Orientis**, founded by the ceremonial magician **Aleister Crowley** in 1912. Its principal member was **Victor Neuberg**. Crowley later amalgamated the M ∴ M ∴ M ∴ with his other occult order, the Argenteum Astrum, or A ∴ A ∴

Mystery From the Greek *myein*, "to keep one's mouth closed", a secret or occult truth not to be disclosed to the uninitiated.

Mystery Religion In ancient Greece and Rome, initiatory rites and ceremonies whose inner teachings and practices were secret. There were famous mystery cults at **Eleusis** and on the island of Samothrace. The deities honoured in the mystery religions included **Demeter** and **Persephone, Attis** and **Cybele, Dionysus, Isis, Serapis,** and **Mithra.**

Mystic One who through contemplation, **meditation,** or self-surrender seeks union with the **Godhead;** and who believes in the attainment of universal wisdom, **cosmic consciousness,** or spiritual **transcendence.** Mystics are generally differentiated from **occultists** as being less interested in **psychic** powers, mental abilities, or ceremonial activities. Occultists who practise Western **magic** and use the kabbalistic **Tree of Life** as their framework for spiritual growth sometimes maintain that the mystic path to the Godhead is more direct than the occult route. In the **Kabbalah** it is represented by the ascent of the **Middle Pillar** on the Tree (the "middle-way" through **Malkuth, Tiphareth,** and **Kether**), as distinct from the occult journey through each of the ten **sephiroth.**

Mysticism The act of seeking union with the **Godhead.** It has been defined by Thomas Aquinas as "the knowledge of God through experience"; and by Evelyn Underhill as "the art of union with Reality". **Mystics** believe that the Godhead or Supreme Being sustains the manifested universe and is responsible for all aspects of existence and consciousness. This Supreme Being is portrayed in different traditions as an anthropomorphic figure, as a **Spirit,** or as **Light,** or as an abstract infinite Reality. Despite these variations, all mystical techniques have as their final goal communication with, and knowledge of, that **transcendental** state of Being.

Mystic Union In **mysticism,** union with the **Godhead** through contemplation and **prayer.** Mystic union is sometimes regarded as a type of spiritual marriage with the Creator.

Myth A story or fable relating to a **god** or **supernatural** being. In popular usage the word also has the negative connotation of something illusory or false. Following the researches of **C. G. Jung** and other psychologists, it has become apparent that mythic images are present at a deep level of the unconscious mind and may be viewed as an expression of the **archetypes** of the **collective unconscious.** To this extent, the various **deities** of myth and legend personify common human attributes or universal principles in Nature and the cosmos. Myths often express the spiritual values of a culture and provide a framework of meaning within which members of a society live and function. Occultists sometimes adapt myths for ceremonial purposes and invoke different **gods** in ritual to enhance their spiritual awareness and personal growth.

Mythological Correspondences See **Magical Correspondences.**

Mythology The collective myths of a culture. See also **Myth.**

N

Nada In **Siddha Yoga**, divine music or sounds which can be heard in deep states of **meditation**.

Nadi In **Kundalini Yoga**, channel in the body through which the **life-force**, or **prana**, is said to flow. In a physical sense the blood vessels, nerves, and lymph ducts are regarded as nadis; but there are also "subtle" channels which, like the **chakras**, are not physiologically based. Different sources maintain that the nadis vary in number between 72,000 and 350,000; but the main three – which are central to the arousal of the **kundalini** – are **ida**, **pingala**, **sushumna**. See also **Yoga**.

Nadir In **astrology**, the point opposite the **zenith**: the lowest point below the earth. It should not be confused with the **immum coeli**.

Nadisuddhi In **yoga**, the purification of the **nadis**, or energy channels, by means of conjoined breathing and mental exercises.

Nagarjuna Indian Buddhist sage who lived in the second century A.D. and taught the doctrine of the so-called **Middle Path** between existence and non-existence. According to this teaching, "Nothing comes into existence, nor does anything disappear. Nothing is eternal, nor has anything an end. Nothing is identical, nor is anything differentiated. Nothing moves in one direction, nor in any other." By transcending such paradoxes, Nagarjuna taught, one could come to know the **Void** (**sunyata**). Nagarjuna is said to have received these teachings from the **nagas**, or serpents, who kept them in trust from **Gautama Buddha**. The doctrine of sunyata is followed by devotees of **Mahayana Buddhism**.

Nagas In Indian **mythology**, serpents who lived beneath the earth in magnificent temples and palaces. Ruled by the huge serpent **Vasuki**, the nagas sometimes appeared as humans or, alternatively, as monsters. However, the nagas also had an esoteric role; according to a Buddhist tradition, **Gautama** imparted some of his most profound teachings to them – especially the doctrine of the universal **Void** (**sunyata**), which was too abstract for most people to understand. Seven centuries later the great sage **Nagarjuna** ("Arjuna of the Nagas") was initiated by the nagas into the **esoteric** truth that "all is Void", and thereby brought forth the doctrine which distinguishes **Mahayana Buddhism** from its **Hinayana** counterpart. See also **Buddhism**.

Nag Hammadi Library A collection of **Gnostic** writings discovered in 1945 in a cemetery near Nag Hammadi, a town located south of Cairo on the Nile. The Nag Hammadi Library parallels the discovery of the **Dead Sea Scrolls** in importance and offers an illuminating perspective on religious beliefs current during the formative years of Christianity. The library includes such texts as *The Gospel of Truth*, *The Gospel of Thomas*, *The Sophia of Jesus Christ*, and several apocalypses. The texts are especially significant because the Gnostic philosophy had previously been known to scholars primarily through the writings of such Church spokesmen as Irenaeus, Clement, Hippolytus, and Tertullian, who were critical of Gnostic beliefs. The texts of the Nag Hammadi Library present Gnosticism on its own terms. The Nag Hammadi Library was first published in English in 1977.

Nagual Also Nawal. In central American **magic** and folk belief, a **witch** who is able to transform into an animal, often for a sinister or **evil** purpose. The term is sometimes used to mean a "companion spirit" or alter ego; and if harm befalls the nagual, this rebounds on the witch or **sorcerer** in question. See also **Lycanthropy; Shamanism; Sorcery.**

Naiads Also Naiades. In Greek **mythology, nymphs** of the rivers, streams and fountains.

Naljorpa In Tibetan **mysticism,** "one who has attained perfect serenity". It is usually interpreted to mean a **mystic** or **adept** who possesses magical powers, is skilled in entering **trance** states, and has divinatory **dreams.**

Namaskar In **Hinduism,** a salutation performed out of devotion to **God.** The palms are placed together and raised to touch that point on the forehead that is popularly known as the **third eye.** This salutation represents the meeting of the higher and lower aspects of one's nature.

Namaste See **Namaskar.**

Name, Divine In many religions, **God** has a sacred name and its pronunciation is jealously guarded as an **esoteric** teaching. Among the Jewish **mystics** the **Tetragrammaton,** or fourfold name of God, **YHVH,** was never vocalized and was replaced with **Adonai,** or "Lord". There was also a version known as the **Shem hameforash** consisting of 216 letters – later reduced to YHVH.

In **Hinduism,** divine names often form the basis of secret **mantras,** which are taught to the **chela** by the **guru,** and many upper-caste devotees of **Shiva** repeat his name 108 times a day. **Islam** also has a tradition of sacred names, of which the main seven are: La ilaha illa Llah (There is no God but God); **Allah** (God); Huwa (He); Al-Haqq (the Truth); Al-Hayy (the Living); Al-qayyum (Self-sufficient); and Al-Qahhar (the Irresistible). God is also described as the Compassionate and the Merciful One. See also **God-name.**

Name, Magical See **Magical Name.**

Names of Power Magical **conjurations** and ritual formulae, which include sacred **god-names,** deemed to have a strong magical effect. In ancient Egypt these formulae were called **hekau.** See also **Tetragrammaton; Words of Power.**

Namu Amida Butsu In Japanese **Shin Buddhism,** a sacred **mantra** or **prayer** recited by devotees as a means to salvation. It translates as "I take refuge in the Amida Buddha."

Nanak Among the **Sikhs,** a term applied collectively to the ten Sikh gurus, the first of whom was **Guru Nanak.** The Sikhs believe these gurus were one in spirit and form a collective unity.

Nanak, Guru (1469–1538) Founder of the **Sikhs** and the first of their ten gurus, Nanak was born at Talwandi near Lahore. When he was around the age of thirty he became an **ascetic** and travelled widely in India and western Asia meeting spiritual leaders from different religious traditions. His quest was to find the "inner light" he believed had disappeared from both **Islam** and **Hinduism.** Nanak came to believe in a **God** that was both **transcendent** and **immanent,** "everywhere present" in his creation. This God could be contacted in **meditation,** especially that based on the divine name. Nanak rejected the concept of the **avatar,** although in his own lifetime he came to be regarded as a saint, especially in the Punjab. See also **Name, Divine.**

Nandi The name of the milk-white bull ridden by the Hindu deity **Shiva,** god of destruction and disasters.

Nanna The Sumerian **moon**-god and counterpart of the Babylonian Sin.

Naraka In Hindu **mythology,** a **hell**-state depicted as a world of darkness where the wicked are attacked by serpents, venomous insects, noxious gases, flames, and burning oil. Naraka is said to cause the cleansing of evil souls prior to their next **incarnation**.

Narasinha In Indian **mythology**, the fourth **incarnation** of **Vishnu**. According to legend, a **demon** named Hiranya-Kasipu made the bold assertion that Vishnu was not omnipresent. Striking a particular palace column, he rashly asked whether Vishnu was inside it. Vishnu emerged from the column in the form of Narasinha, a lion-headed man, and tore the demon to shreds.

Narayana The most sacred name of **Vishnu** and one which serves in an initiatory **mantra** used by Vaishnavites. The name means "moving on the waters", and it refers to the origin of Narayana, who was born from the primordial **egg** which floated on the waters before the Creation. The whole universe flowed into existence as a result of his **will**.

Nastrond In Scandinavian **mythology**, a **hell**-region located in the depths of **Niflheim** (the cold North), which was said to be a dark abode, far from the sun, with walls formed of wreathing, venomous snakes. It was surrounded by the serpent monster **Nidhoggr**, who tormented the dead. It was in Nastrond that **Loki** was chained to a rock.

Nat In Burmese folk belief, **nature-spirits** who live in the forests and dwell in trees. The nats have a predominantly malign character, although sometimes they serve as house-guardians. The nats feature strongly in Burmese **animism**.

Natal Astrology See **Astrology, Natal**.

Natal Horoscope See **Horoscope, Natal**.

Nataraja The name for **Shiva** in his form as the **god** who dances the universe into existence and then destroys it in an insane act of frenzy.

Natema Among the Jivaro Indians of Ecuador, a sacramental, hallucinogenic beverage made from the leaves of the **banisteriopsis** vine. Jivaro **shamans** drink the brew in order to have initiatory visions. See also **Hallucination; Initiation; Tsentsak**.

Nativity See **Horoscope, Natal**.

Natural Magic See **Magic, Natural**.

Natura naturans Concept introduced by the Spanish-born Arabian philosopher Averroes (1126–1198), who described **God** as the active power behind Nature. Averroes wrote philosophical commentaries, which became known in the West through Latin translation. The expression *Natura naturans* was later used by the Dutch philosopher Baruch Spinoza (1632–1677), who taught that all mind and matter is a manifestation of the all-embracing substance that is God.

Nature-spirit Popular name for a **deva** or **elemental**. Occultists regard Nature-spirits as energy-beings who sustain Nature and personify the life processes in plants, flowers, and trees. **Dryads, fairies, elves**, and **pixies** belong in this category.

Nature-worship The worship of life-sustaining forces of Nature personified by the cycles of the seasons, which inevitably result in the rebirth of spring and new life. Nature-worship relates also to fertility and sexuality and is usually associated with deities of the **Earth** and **moon**. Nature-worship is practised in **modern witchcraft**, which draws heavily on the Celtic mystical tradition. See also **Celts; Eleusis**.

Nawal See **Nagual**.

Near-death Experience State of consciousness experienced by hospital patients who have been declared clinically dead, but who have subsequently revived.

The near-death experience is often characterized by the **out-of-the-body experience**, visions of spiritual beings, and the sensation of travelling through a tunnel towards a profound and serene **light**. There are certain parallels between this experience and **trance** techniques developed by native **shamans**. See also **Astral Projection; Death; Soul; Spirit.**

Nebulae Star-clusters. In **astrology**, they are often regarded as providing a negative **aspect** relating to the eyes, if they are rising at the moment of birth, or if they are found in **conjunction** with the **moon**. For example, the Pleiades of **Taurus** are associated with possible blindness. In general, the main nebulae (Praesepe, the Hyades, the Pleiades, Alderbaran-Antares, and the Aselli) are associated with defects of the eye that can arise naturally, from genetic defects (when afflicted by **Saturn**), or from an accident (when afflicted by **Mars**). See also **Malefic.**

Necessitas In Roman **mythology**, the goddess governing the **destiny** of humankind. She was the mother of the three **Fates** and the counterpart of the Greek goddess **Themis.**

Necromancy From the Greek *nekros*, "dead", and *manteia*, "divination", a form of **divination** in which the **spirits** of the dead are summoned to provide **omens** relating to future events. The biblical narrative describes how the Witch of Endor summoned the spirit of Samuel to answer Saul's questions; and Lucan, in his *Pharsalia*, describes a **ritual** of necromancy in which the **witch** Enrichtho used the body of a dead soldier and other hideous ingredients in her rites. In more recent times, the famous French occultist **Eliphas Lévi** endeavoured to summon the spirit of **Apollonius of Tyana** by calling on **Hermes, Asklepios**, and **Osiris**, and then Apollonius himself. An account of this bizarre conjuration is given in Lévi's *Dogme et Rituel de la Haute Magie*, which describes the results as follows: "Three times and with closed eyes I invoked Apollonius. When I again looked forth there was a man in front of me, wrapped from head to foot in a species of shroud… he was lean, melancholy and beardless." The ghostly figure disappeared as Lévi brandished his ritual sword in front of it, but it later reappeared. Lévi says that "the apparition did not speak to me, but it seemed that the questions I had designed to ask, answered themselves in my mind."

Necrophilia Sexual intercourse with the dead. This sometimes arises among psychopathic murderers who believe their victims to be still alive. Necrophilia is also a feature of the most debased forms of **black magic.**

Nectar In Greek **mythology**, the drink of the **gods**. It was poured by the cupbearers Ganymeda (Hebe) and Ganymede.

Nembutsu In Japanese **Shin Buddhism**, the act of chanting the sacred **mantra, Namu Amida Butsu.**

Nemesis In Greek **mythology**, the **goddess** of anger and vengeance who punished those who broke the moral code. It became her role to encourage moderation in society and she therefore sought to eliminate pride and arrogance. Nemesis was the daughter of Erebus and Nyx.

Neopaganism General term used to describe followers of **Wicca, Goddess** worship and contemporary forms of shamanism and Earth-based rituals. Neopagans venerate the life-force and the sacred cycles of Mother Nature and pay homage to Her through a variety of eclectic rituals, most of which derive from contemporary forms of **witchcraft.**

Neophyte One who is a candidate for **initiation**. In the **Hermetic Order of the**

Golden Dawn the probationary grade of Neophyte was not attributed to the **Tree of Life**, but nevertheless was intended to provide candidates with a glimpse of the **Light** that they would aspire to in subsequent ceremonial workings. Accordingly, the Neophyte grade was regarded by these occult practitioners as highly symbolic and extremely significant.

Neoplatonism School of philosophy that blended the ideas of **Plato** and various Eastern religions. Neoplatonism was developed in the third century by **Plotinus** and his successors **Iamblichus, Porphyry**, and Proclus. According to this philosophy, all material and spiritual existence emanated from the One – the transcendent **Godhead** – through the actions of the divine mind, or **logos**, and the **world soul**. Neoplatonism was banned by the Emperor Justinian I in 529, but was revived in the Renaissance by such **mystics** as **Pico della Mirandola** and **Marsilio Ficino**.

Nepenthe A magic drink that was said to relieve sorrow and grief. According to ***The Odyssey***, Polydama, the Queen of Egypt, entertained Helen of Troy and gave her the drink to banish her melancholy.

Nephelomancy **Divination** by interpreting the formation and direction of clouds.

Nephesch In the **Kabbalah**, the animal instincts. Some practitioners of Western **magic** ascribe Nephesch to the tenth **sephirah, Malkuth**, on the **Tree of Life**. However, it is more appropriately linked to the ninth sephirah, **Yesod**, which is the symbolic energy centre for sexuality, fertility, and the more primeval aspects of human consciousness. Yesod is also the sphere of the **moon**. It can be argued that **modern witchcraft** is a form of Nephesch-worship.

Nephthys In Egyptian **mythology**, a **goddess** associated with **death**. She was married to **Set**, but gave birth to **Anubis** as the result of an affair with **Osiris** in which she disguised herself as **Isis**. Nephthys had magical powers and was able to transform people into animals in order to defend them. She could also restore the dead to life. Nephthys protected the deceased in the Osirian **Judgment Hall**.

Neptune In **astrology**, the **planet** that symbolizes divine principles and which is equated with "the spirit of God that moved upon the waters". Neptune is the Infinite Ocean from which the universe came forth, and is therefore associated with spiritual consciousness and wisdom. Astrologers usually classify Neptune as a **feminine planet**, despite its male connotation in Roman mythology. In the Western occult tradition **Water** is regarded as a feminine **element**.

Neptune The Roman counterpart of the Greek god **Poseidon**, lord of the sea and brother of **Zeus**.

Nereid Alternative name for an **Oceanid** or ocean-nymph, the Nereids were the daughters of Nereus, son of **Oceanus**.

Neschamah In the **Kabbalah**, the spiritual part of the **soul**: one's higher spiritual self. It is identified with the three **supernals** on the **Tree of Life: Kether, Chokmah**, and **Binah**, which are the three "upper" **sephiroth** depicted on the body of **Adam Kadmon**.

Neti, Neti Hindu phrase meaning "not this, not that." It is used by practitioners of **Vedanta** to emphasize that the Supreme Reality cannot be understood by physical or mental attributes and that the nature of the **Godhead** is a transcendent, all-encompassing state in which the **self** is absorbed into **Brahman**. Compare with **Advaita**.

Netzach A Hebrew word meaning "victory" or "endurance", the seventh **emanation** or

sephirah on the kabbalistic **Tree of Life**. In Western **magic**, Netzach is regarded as the sphere of creativity, subjectivity, and the emotions – a very clear contrast to the sphere of **Hod**, which represents intellect and rational thought. Netzach is the sphere of love and spiritual passion and is therefore associated by **occultists** with such deities as **Aphrodite**, **Venus**, **Hathor**, and any other goddesses who personify these qualities.

Neuburg, Victor (1883–1940) Poet and **occultist**, who for a time was **Aleister Crowley**'s homosexual partner in rites of **sexual magic**. Neuberg shared Crowley's belief that the perfect symbolic human form was the heavenly **androgyne** – a figure containing both sexual polarities – and he became involved in Crowley's magical orders, the Argenteum Astrum and the **Mysteria Mystica Maxima**. Neuberg went with Crowley to the Algerian desert in 1909 and there they summoned the so-called **Thirty Aethyrs** of **Enochian magic**: powerful **conjurations** derived from the work of **Dr. John Dee** and **Edward Kelley**. Crowley focused meditatively on a large topaz while making the conjurations, and Neuberg transcribed his trance utterances. The results of this ceremonial working are included in Crowley's *Vision and the Voice* (1929) and in Jean Overton Fuller's biographical work *The Magical Dilemma of Victor Neuberg* (1965). Neuberg avoided Crowley later in his life and moved away from the occult altogether. In the literary world he is remembered as an inspirational force in the careers of Pamela Hansford Johnson and Dylan Thomas.

Neumann, Teresa (1898–1962) Famous stigmatic who was born at Konnersreuth in Germany and lived there all her life. After injuring her back on a farm in 1918, she became bedridden and suffered from a variety of complaints including paralysis of the legs, appendicitis, and temporary blindness. She began praying to St. Teresa of Lisieux in 1923 and regained her sight; two years later she overcame her other ailments in a similar way. In 1926 she began to exhibit signs of the **stigmata** on her hands, feet, and side, and had visions of Christ's Passion each week for several years. While she was in a **trance** state her wounds would bleed, and she was able to exist on very little food. During the 1920s and 1930s her village became a site of pilgrimage, although the Roman Catholic Church was cautious about her and finally disowned her in 1938. Towards the end of her life the stigmata seemed to diminish.

New Aeon Expression used by the magician **Aleister Crowley** and his devotees to describe the two-thousand-year cycle that commenced in 1904 following his illumination through the entity **Aiwaz**. Crowley claimed that his new magical cosmology replaced Christianity and he installed himself as the personification of the magical child, **Horus**. The New Aeon is thus referred to by Crowley's followers as the Aeon of Horus.

New Age Phrase connoting the post **psychedelic Aquarian Age** believed by some to herald a new era of mystical and spiritual enlightenment. It has become a popular label for the many alternative approaches to spirituality in contemporary Western culture.

Newbrough, Dr. John Ballou (1828–1891) American **spiritualist** and practitioner of **automatic writing**, who claimed to produce the remarkable Oahspe or **Kosmon Bible** through his **psychic** contact with the **angels**. Oahspe was originally published anonymously in 1882, but a letter to the Boston periodical *The Banner of Light* revealed that Dr. Newbrough had produced the book in the dark, using a typewriter which was guided by "some other intelligence". Newbrough took fifty weeks to finish the work and maintained that at times he could see the hands of the angels, fully materialized, above his head.

New Isis Lodge Magical order (1955–1962) established in England by the occultist **Kenneth Grant**. A lodge of the **Ordo Templi Orientis**, it combined the worship of **Nut** and **Isis** with sexual magic principles formulated by **Aleister Crowley**. See also **Magic, Sexual**.

New Thought Term given to the theories of **Phineas P. Quimby**, who was an important influence on **Mary Baker Eddy**. The New Thought Alliance has as its credo "To teach the Infinitude of the Supreme One; the Divinity of man and his infinite possibilities through the creative power of constructive thinking and obedience to the voice of the indwelling Presence, which is our source of Inspiration, Power, Health and Prosperity."

Ngathungi Technique of pointing the bone used by the **Aborigines** of the Lower Murray region in Australia. The **medicine-man** has a pointing bone, which is attached to an object that has been in contact with the victim. He takes this implement, says "Let the breath leave the body ...," and chants a song of hatred for an hour, directed at the victim. He then concentrates his mind until he can visualize this person in his mind's eye, and sends the instruction "Die!"

Niampar Jagpa In Tibetan **mysticism**, any technique for bringing the mind to a state of total stillness and preparing it for **meditation**. The term means "to make equal, or level" and refers to the act of eliminating the "waves" of agitation that roll through the mind in normal consciousness.

Nibbana Buddhist equivalent of the Hindu **nirvana**. Buddhists do not place as much emphasis on the annihilation of the **self**, however, and refer to nibbana as a state of consciousness in which greed, hatred, and delusion – the three evils – are overcome. The mystic who attains nibbana is liberated from illusion and therefore his work is complete. See also **Buddhism**; **Hinduism**.

Nibelungs In Scandinavian and Teutonic **mythology**, a band of **dwarfs** who lived below the earth in **Niflheim** and guarded precious treasure. In due course **Siegfried** overcame them.

Nictalopes People who can see clearly in the dark – a phenomenon which has been recorded only rarely in medical annals.

Nidhoggr In Scandinavian **mythology**, the serpent-monster who constantly gnawed at the roots of the world tree, **Yggdrasil**, attempting to destroy the earth's foundations. He dwelt near **Nastrond** in the icy depths of **Niflheim**.

Niflheim The Scandinavian **Underworld** ruled by the goddess **Hel**. An icy region, lying in the extreme north, it was the domain of the **souls** of the dead. The monstrous serpent **Nidhoggr** dwelt there.

Niggun In certain forms of **Hasidism**, a melody without words, used to induce meditative states of consciousness.

Night Houses In **astrology**, the first six houses, which lie below the horizon. See also **House**.

Nigromancy From the Latin *niger*, meaning "black", a term sometimes used erroneously to denote **black magic**. It is really a variant on **necromancy**, which derives from the Greek *nekros*, meaning "corpse".

Nimbus The **halo** of light sometimes depicted around the form of divine and saintly personages (e.g. Christ and the Christian saints). Some **occultists** believe that the nimbus may be a symbolic representation of the spiritual **aura**.

NOSTRADAMUS: Among seers and visionaries, Nostradamus (1503–1566) is perhaps the most controversial. He predicted the arrival of the King of Terror in July 1999, heralding the End of the World.

Nine In **numerology**, this number denotes **cosmic** significance (nine is the number of the spheres in medieval **cosmology**). As the "highest" of the numbers (**Ten** (1 + 0) equates with **one**), nine symbolizes spiritual achievement and is the number of **initiation**.

Nirang In **Zoroastrianism**, consecrated bull's urine. It is drunk by the **priest** and rubbed on his body during the purifactory **bareshnum** ceremony. The urine is believed to bestow spiritual and mystical power.

Nirmanakaya In **Hinduism**, a type of **nirvana** in which the spiritual master chooses not to enter into final union with **Brahman**, but chooses to help humanity instead – thereby still maintaining contact with the physical world. Nirmanakaya is the level of spiritual consciousness ascribed to a **bodhisattva**.

Nirvana In **Hinduism** and **yoga**, union with the supreme **Godhead** – **Brahman**. In nirvana the **ego** is transcended and the **self** merges with Brahman, thereby extinguishing one's individual nature. The mystic who attains nirvana has no further need of **rebirth** in the cycle of incarnations. See also **Nibbana**.

Nixie In Scandinavian folk belief, a water-spirit hostile to people. The female nixie was like a **siren** and would sometimes lure men to their death by drowning; the male was depicted either as an elderly **dwarf** or as a **centaur** with cloven feet.

Nixie Pae Among the Cashinahua Indians of Peru, spirit creatures with bows and arrows who appear to the **shaman** when he consumes the sacramental **banisteriopsis** beverage. The nixi pae are accompanied by coloured snakes, trumpeting armadillos, and singing frogs.

Niyamas In the system of **Patanjali**, practices based on the law of **karma**, which are regarded as appropriate for all students and practitioners of **yoga**. There are five niyamas: saucha, or purity of the physical body and the elimination of toxic waste products; santosha, the ability to live in the eternal "now"; **tapas**, indifference to extremes or changes in external conditions; svadhyaya, self-development and learning; and ishvarapranidhana, personal devotion to the philosophical way of life. See also **Yamas**.

Nodes of the Planets In **astrology**, the points at which the orbits of the planets intersect the ecliptic.

No-mind Zen doctrine ascribed to Hui-Neng (638–713), the father of Chinese **Buddhism**, who maintained that the object of Zen was to perceive one's inner **self**, which in turn meant "seeing into nothingness". In order to attain this, one had to learn to apply the principles of no-mind (i.e. transcend the processes of thought itself).

Non-attachment Phrase proposed by British writer and philosopher **Aldous Huxley** to characterize the **mystic** path. According to Huxley, the mystic is able to live without attachment to possessions, desires, wealth, fame, or emotions. The concept arises from the doctrine of **maya** in **Hinduism**, which states that the manifested world is essentially illusory.

Non-REM Period (NREM) In **parapsychology**, a period of sleep during which there are no eye movements. This is the non-dreaming phase of sleep. See also **REM Periods**.

Norns In Scandinavian **mythology**, the three goddesses who guarded the world tree, **Yggdrasil**, and ordained the **fate** of humankind. Their names were Verdandi (the present), Urd (the past), and Skuld (the future). They are the equivalent of the Roman **Fates**.

North In Western **ceremonial magic**, the direction associated with the element **Earth**. It is said to be ruled by the archangel **Uriel**. See also **Directions, Four**.

Northern Signs In **astrology**, the signs of the **zodiac** from **Aries** through to **Virgo**. See also **Commanding Signs**.

North Point In **astrology**, the **Immum coeli** or **cusp** of the fourth **house**. It is located at the bottom of the **horoscope**.

Norton, Rosaleen (1917–1979) Australian **witch** and **occult** artist, whose paintings and drawings resemble those of **Austin Osman Spare**. Norton had fantasy visions as a child and was expelled from high school for allegedly corrupting the other children with her "**pagan**" influence. Norton later became an art student and also studied the writings of **Carl Jung, Eliphas Lévi, Dion Fortune**, and **Aleister Crowley**. She began experimenting with **trance** techniques and came to believe that the ancient **gods** could be contacted on the inner planes. Several **deities** – including **Pan, Jupiter**, and **Hecate** – feature in her art, which was the subject of controversial obscenity charges in the Sydney courts during the 1950s. A book describing her philosophy and drawings, *The Art of Rosaleen Norton* (originally issued as a limited edition), was republished in 1982.

Nostradamus (1503–1566) The magical pseudonym of Michel de Nostre Dame, who became Catherine de Medici's favourite astrologer. A Provençal Jew, Nostradamus wrote in archaic French and Latin as well as in his regional tongue and published his famous predictive writings, *The Centuries*, in 1555. The book has been in print ever since. Nostradamus at times seems to have had a remarkable foresight into the events of the French Revolution, and some have discerned references in his writings to Mussolini and Hitler. According to Nostramus the King of Terror was scheduled to appear in July 1999, heralding the End of the World, but he failed to do so. The problem with Nostradamus is that his writings are often heavily symbolic and are presented in a jumbled sequence: the year 1999 was one of the few specific references in his writings. Personal interpretations of his predictive writings vary considerably.

Notarikon In the **Kabbalah**, a technique of abbreviating Hebrew words and **god-names** to disguise **esoteric** knowledge. There are two forms: in the first method a new word is formed by taking the first and final letters of another word or words; in the second, the letters in a word represent the first and final letters of each word in a sentence. The prayer-ending Amen derives via notarikon from a Hebrew phrase meaning "The Lord and Faithful King". See also **Gematria; Temura**.

No-thing That which is no particular thing and therefore encompasses everything. From this perspective one can formulate the concept which is found both in Christianity and Jewish **mysticism**, that the world was created out of nothing (i.e. from Infinity). In the **Kabbalah**, the name for the Infinite Light, or **Godhead**, is **Ain Soph Aur**.

Noumenon In ancient Greek philosophy, the true and essential nature of being, as distinct from the illusory perceptions of the senses.

Nous Greek word, used by Aristotle to describe the divine aspect of the mind or **soul**. It may be compared with the Sanskrit words **mahat** and **manas**.

November Eve In **witchcraft**, an alternative name for **All Hallows' Eve**, or Halloween.

Nox Roman **goddess** of night, and the counterpart of **Nyx**.

Nudity Regarded by some **occultists** as a sign of ritual equality and openness, nudity is also favoured by ceremonial **magicians** who wish to dispense with cumbersome robes. **Witches** who perform their ceremonies naked are described as being "sky-clad".

Numbers, Magical See **Magical Numbers.**

Numerology Occult system of thought that analyzes the symbolism of numbers and ascribes numerical values to the letters of the alphabet. The kabbalist **Cornelius Agrippa** provided an esoteric explanation of numbers in his work *Occult Philosophy* (1533), which in turn drew on the speculations of **Pythagoras.** According to Agrippa, the symbolism was as follows. **one:** the origin of all things, **God; two:** marriage and communion, but alternatively division and evil; **three:** the Trinity, wisdom; **four:** solidity, permanence, and foundation; **five:** justice; **six:** creation (the world being created in six days, God resting on the seventh), labour, and service; **seven:** life; **eight:** fullness and balance; **nine:** cosmic significance (the number of the spheres); **ten:** completeness. Numbers beyond ten can be "reduced" to a smaller number (e.g. 14 = 10 + 4 = 1 + 0 + 4 = 5).

Numerologists ascribe numerical values to the alphabet as follows:

1	2	3	4	5	6	7	8	9
A	B	C	D	E	F	G	H	I
J	K	L	M	N	O	P	Q	R
S	T	U	V	W	X	Y	Z	

One's full name can be "reduced" to its "ruling number" using the method described above. The date of birth can also be plotted to indicate intellectual, emotional, and physical aspects of one's character and personality:

Mind level	3	6	9
Emotional level	2	5	8
Physical level	1	4	7

The number 0 (zero) is not included.

As an example, July 25, 1948 (7/25/1948) would be diagrammatically represented as:

Mind level			9
Emotional level	2	5	8
Physical level	1	4	7

Numinous Word coined by **Rudolf Otto** to express the idea of the sacred and holy essence of the great religions.

Nut Also Nuit. In ancient Egypt, the sky-goddess. She and her brother Geb were the parents of **Osiris, Isis, Set,** and **Nephthys.** Nut was often represented as a woman with an elongated body that arched across the sky so that only her fingertips and toes touched the earth.

Nyame Ashanti sky-god and ruler of storms and lightning. Nyame created the **moon, sun,** and rain. See also **Ananse.**

Nymph In folk legends, the general name given to spirit creatures who were believed to reside in different locations. In ancient Greece these were known as follows: **Oceanides** (nymphs of the sea and ocean); **Dryads** (nymphs who lived in trees); **Oreads** (nymphs of the mountains); and **Naiads** (nymphs of the rivers and streams). Oceanides, Oreads, and Naiads were immortal; but Dryads would die with the death of their trees. See also **Hamadryad.**

Nyx The Greek goddess of Night, who was both the sister and wife of Erebus, god of darkness. Both were born of **Chaos.**

Nzambi Among the Bantu, the supreme god who created humankind. The first man created was evil and hostile, so Nzambi buried him and created another in his place. His wife was fashioned from wood, and this couple were the ancestors of the human race.

O

Oahspe See **Kosmon Bible; Newbrough, Dr. John Ballou.**

Oak Tree with ancient mythical and magical associations. It was sacred to the Jews because Abraham had encountered an **angel** of **Jehovah** beneath its branches; and the devotees of the Phoenician god **Baal** made sacrificial offerings "under every leafy oak" (Ezekiel 6:13). An **Oracle** to **Zeus** (in Dodona in north-eastern Greece) was located in a grove of oaks; and Socrates regarded the oak as the "oracle tree". The oak was also sacred to the Roman god **Jupiter**; while among the **Druids** no rite took place without the assistance of the oak and **mistletoe**. Among the Gaels, the oak was the sacred tree of the **high god Dagda**; and in Scandinavia, where it was considered the "thunder tree", it was dedicated to **Thor**.

Oannes Babylonian **deity**, part fish, part man, who became identified with **Ea**.

Oath A pronouncement made in the name of truth that also summons **supernatural** forces to invoke punishment should the utterance prove to be incorrect or unfaithful. Christians may make an oath on the Bible, invoking **Jehovah**; while a **Moslem** may make an oath in the name of **Allah**. In the occult tradition an oath of secrecy may form part of an **initiation** ceremony; and should this oath be broken and secret truths subsequently revealed, it is believed that a "psychic current" rebounds upon the practitioner in question by way of punishment.

Obeah Word used in the West Indies to denote **supernatural** and magical power. This power is also believed to reside in certain **ritual** objects, such as balls of graveyard earth mixed with feathers, hair, and human or animal remains. The **magicians**, known as obeah-men and obeah-women, use evil **spells** and enchantments to counteract the hostile world and develop prestige for themselves within their own community. See also **Voodoo**.

Obelisk A tall, four-sided monolith, tapered on the side and forming a pyramid-like point at its apex. In ancient Egyptian religion, the obelisk was generally associated with the worship of the sun-god **Ra**.

Object Reading The use of a personal object, like a watch, or pendant, to gain "psychic impressions" of the person to whom it belongs. See **Psychometry**.

Obsession See **Possession**.

Obsidian Vitreous lava or glassy volcanic rock, which in certain parts of the world has magical significance. Among the Aztecs it was sacred to the sky-god **Tezcatlipoca** and was fashioned into mirrors which were used by diviners for **skrying**. It was also used for the eyes of the **idols** in the Temple of **Quetzalcoatl**. Obsidian also had ceremonial and initiatory uses among the North American Indians.

Occultation In **astrology**, the situation when a **planet** or star is eclipsed by the **moon** or by some other celestial sphere.

Occult Hierarchy In **Theosophy**, the **Great White Lodge**. Many occult groups, especially those with ceremonial grades, have been inclined to believe in a hierarchy of occult **adepts** on the "inner planes". In the **Hermetic Order of the Golden Dawn**, these were known as the **Secret Chiefs**.

Occultism From the latin *occulere*, "to hide", a term originally used to suggest a secret and hidden tradition of **esoteric** knowledge. The word is now used generally to include the study of **magic, mysticism,**

Theosophy, and **spiritualism**. It may also be used with reference to secret societies like the **Rosicrucians** and **Freemasonry**.

Occultist A term used variously to describe a practitioner of any one of the "secret" mystic arts within the traditions of **magic**, **Theosophy**, **mysticism**, or **spiritualism**. See also **Occultism**.

Oceanides In ancient Greek **mythology**, the **nymphs** of the ocean. There were three thousand such nymphs, all of them the daughters of the Titan **Oceanus** and his wife Tethys.

Oceanus In Greek **mythology**, the oldest of the twelve **Titans** and the husband of Tethys. Oceanus was the father of the **Oceanides** and the grandfather of the **Nereides** – **nymphs** of the waters.

Och Acording to the *Arbatel of Magick* there are seven different **Olympic spirits**, appointed by **God** to rule the world. Och, the spirit of the **sun**, bestows good health and wisdom. He is able to "converteth all things into most pure gold and precious stones" and has 36,536 legions of lesser spirits at his command.

Octad In **numerology**, the number **eight**.

Octinomos From a Greek expression meaning "he who has an eight-lettered name". In occult tradition, the master **magician** has an eight-lettered name; thus **Aleister Crowley** took the magical name **Baphomet** when he assumed leadership of the **Ordo Templi Orientis** in 1922.

Odic Force Magnetic **life-force** which, according to **Baron Karl von Reichenbach**, permeated the universe and was especially noticeable in the rays of the **sun** and **moon**, in crystals and metals, and in the living human and animal form. Von Reichenbach associated this odic force with the **aura** perceived by **psychics**.

Odin In Scandinavian **mythology**, the supreme **god** and All-Father who lived in **Valhalla** with the spirits of fallen heroes. While he was the god of war and the dead, he was also believed to have set the **sun** and **moon** on their courses at the beginning of the world and had a positive role as god of inspiration, **ecstasy**, **magic**, and poetry. King of the **Aesir**, he was informed about events in the world by two ravens. He rode an eight-legged horse named Sleipnir and owned the magical ring **Draupnir**. Odin often travelled among the heroes in the form of an old man with one eye. It was said that he had sacrificed his other eye in return for sacred knowledge, and that this eye was hidden in the **Underworld** in the well of Mimir, god of inland waters and the springs of wisdom. Odin was finally overcome by the monstrous wolf **Fenris**, during the holocaust of **Ragnarok**.

Odysseus In Greek mythology, the son of Laertes and Anticlea and the main character in Homer's epic poem *The Odyssey*. Odysseus was the King of Ithaca and became one of the leading Greek heroes during the Trojan War. He was known to the Romans as **Ulysses**.

Odyssey, The Epic poem, attributed to Homer, which describes the wanderings of the classical Greek hero **Odysseus**. It is divided into twenty-four books, the first twelve of which describe Odysseus's travels on the sea, the second twelve on land. The adventures take place after the fall of Troy, as Odysseus journeys home.

Ogdoad Especially in ancient Egyptian religions, a **pantheon** consisting of eight **deities**. The **cosmogony** at Hermeopolis in Upper Egypt took this form and consisted of the following gods: Nun and his consort Naunet; Huh and Hauhet; Kuk and Kauket;

and **Amon** and Amaunet. In this system the second name in each pair is the feminine form of the first, masculine form. The names mean, respectively: water, unendingness, darkness, and air/spirit. The term Ogdoad was also used in the **Gnostic** system of **Valentinus**, which was based on eight mystical **emanations**. In the beginning was the **Abyss** (masculine), from which came forth Silence (feminine). These gave rise to Mind (masculine) and Truth (feminine), who then projected Word (masculine) and Life (feminine). From their union Man (masculine) and the Church (feminine) were born.

Oghams Celtic divinatory system featuring twenty-five characters associated with trees and shrubs. They are the birch, rowan, alder, willow, ash, hawthorn, **oak**, holly, hazel, apple, grape-vine, ivy, reed, blackthorn, elder, silver fir, furze, heather, white poplar, yew, spindle, honeysuckle, pine and beech. An additional character in the system is "grove", representing a collection of trees and "the totality of knowledge". Each tree character is represented by a stave and is associated with specific physical, mental and spiritual qualities. The ogham system is sometimes referred to as the "alphabet of the trees".

Ogre In medieval **folklore**, a hideous and frightening man-eating giant.

Ogum Also Ogun. Among the Yorubas and devotees of **Macumba**, the warrior god and Lord of Iron. His colour is red and he includes **Mars** among his subservient spirits. In some areas Ogum is associated with St. George and in others with St. Anthony (Santo Antonio).

Ohrmazd Name by which the **Zoroastrian** Lord of Wisdom **Ahura Mazda** was known in the Middle Period (c. A.D. 200–700).

Oimelc See **Imbolc**.

Oinomancy Divination by interpreting the different shapes and forms of spilt wine.

Ointments, Flying See **Flying Ointments**.

Olcott, Colonel Henry Steel (1832–1907) American Theosophist who, with **Madame Helena Blavatsky**, founded the **Theosophical Society** in 1875 and became its president. When the Society transferred its headquarters to Adyar, Madras, in 1878, Olcott became increasingly interested in **Buddhism** which, together with **Hinduism**, provided a major influence on the development of Theosophical doctrines. A well-educated and cultured man, Olcott was a member of the Royal Asiatic Society and the Bengal Academy of Music. His books include *People from the Other World* (1875), *Theosophy, Religion and Occult Languages* (1885), *A Buddhist Catechism* (1881), and the three-volume work *Old Diary Leaves* (1895–1904).

Old Religion Expression used by contemporary **Wiccan** devotees to describe **witchcraft**. The term has acquired special significance since the publication of **Margaret Murray**'s influential book *The Witch-Cult in Western Europe* (1921), which described witchcraft as an ancient fertility cult.

Old Soul In **Theosophy**, one who has incarnated many times previously on earth, and who has accumulated spiritual wisdom through the lessons of the different lifetimes. See also **Reincarnation**.

Olibanum Fragrant gum resin known in ancient times as **frankincense**.

Olive Tree sacred to the Greek goddess **Athena**, who was said to have caused it to first bear fruit. According to legend the olive tree on the Acropolis was burnt by Xerxes when he conquered Athens in 480 B.C., but the tree reappeared, as if through an act of **magic**.

The olive is also a Christian symbol of peace and divine blessings because a **dove** brought a sprig of olive to Noah, indicating that the Flood was subsiding and that it was safe for him to come out of the Ark.

Ololiuhqui Hallucinogenic variety of the plant species *Rivea corymbosa* (morning glory), whose seeds were used by the Aztecs as an intoxicant. It is also used as a shamanic sacrament by the Zapotec Indians of Mexico. Ololiuhqui causes vivid **hallucinations** characterized by bright colours and patterns, and was popular during the **psychedelic** era of the 1960s. See also **Trance, Shamanic.**

Olympians, Twelve Great The twelve great **deities** of classical Greek mythology: **Zeus, Hera, Poseidon, Demeter, Apollo,** Artemis, Hephaestus, Pallas **Athena**, Ares, **Aphrodite, Hermes,** and Hestia. Sometimes **Hades (Pluto)** is also added to the list.

Olympic Spirits In the medieval **grimoire** the ***Arbatel of Magick***, the seven planetary **spirits** of Olympus appointed by **God** to rule the world. They were **Aratron (Saturn)**; **Bether (Jupiter)**; **Phalec (Mars)**; **Och (sun)**; **Hagith (Venus)**; **Ophiel (Mercury)**; and **Phul (moon)**. With the exception of Saturn, who has no counterpart among the **Twelve Great Olympians**, the classical Greek deities who correlate with these spirits are **Zeus (Bether)**, Ares (**Phalec**), **Apollo (Och)**, **Aphrodite (Hagith)**, **Hermes (Ophiel)**, and **Artemis (Phul)**.

Olympus, Mount In ancient Greek **mythology**, the home of the **gods** and **goddesses.** Mount Olympus (elevation 9,794 feet) is the highest peak in the Greek peninsula and is located in Macedonia, close to the border of Thessaly. Compare with Meru, Mount.

Om In **yoga**, a mystical **mantra**, or sacred utterance, which symbolizes the essence of the entire universe and the spirit of **Brahman.** It is pronouneed A-U-M, thus characterizing the trinitarian principle of the "three-in-one" (**Brahma, Vishnu,** and **Shiva**) who rule the manifested universe. See also **Trimurti.**

Omen A sign relating to some future event. Omens may be favourable or unfavourable and can occur spontaneously or be sought as a result of the many different methods of **divination.** See also **Augur; Prophecy.**

Ometecuhtli In Aztec religion, the "Lord of Duality", one the major Creation gods in the Aztec pantheon. Ometecuhtli was an important **deity**, but ranked beneath the supreme and ineffable **Tloque Nahuaque**, who personified universal divine power.

Om Man-ni Pad-me Hum Tibetan Buddhist **mantra**, which translates literally as "Om – the jewel in the lotus – Hum." The symbolism of the central part of the mantra refers to the sexual union of the **lingam** within the **yoni.** See also **Om.**

Omnipotence Absolute power over all things: an attribute often ascribed in different religions to the **Supreme Being,** or **God.**

Omniscient One who is all-knowing. As with **omnipotence**, this attribute is often ascribed in different religions to the **Supreme Being,** or **God.**

One In **numerology** the symbol of unity, often associated with **God**, the **Supreme Being**, and the origin of everything in the universe. Those whose **ruling** number is **one** are said to be dominating, independent, jealous of rivals, and single-minded in their purpose. See also **Numerology.**

One God, The In religions based on **monotheism**, the **Supreme Being** who created the universe and represents **transcendental** Reality. Among the world's great religions,

Christianity, Judaism, and **Islam** are the most notable examples of monotheism. See also **Allah; God.**

Oneiromancy **Divination** by interpreting the symbolic or prophetic contents of **dreams**. In many ancient cultures, dreams have been viewed as portents of the **gods**, a perspective reformulated by the psychologist **Carl Jung**, who believed that dreams often reveal spiritual **archetypes** from the **collective unconscious**.

Oni In Japanese folk belief, **demons** with claws and horns that in many ways resemble the **devils** of medieval **sorcery**.

Onocentaur Medieval variant on the classical **centaur**, it was half-man, half-ass. Dedicated at all costs to preserving its liberty, it would starve itself to death if captured.

Onomancy Divination by means of interpreting the letters in a person's name, with particular reference to the numbers of vowels and the numerical total of the letters. See also **Numerology**.

Onychomancy Divination by interpreting fingernails. The practitioner would watch the shadows cast on the fingernails of a young boy and interpret future omens by assessing the shadow-shapes formed on the surface of the nails.

Ophidian Current From the Greek *ophis*, "a snake", sexual energies used in magical ceremonies, especially in the **Ordo Templi Orientis**. Here the symbolism of the snake parallels that of the **kundalini** serpent, which is aroused in the **chakra** at the base of the spine. See also **Tantra**.

Ophiel According to the *Arbatel of Magick*, there are seven different **Olympic spirits** appointed by **God** to rule the world. Ophiel is the spirit of **Mercury**, and is a teacher of all the magical arts. He can convert **quicksilver** into the **Philosopher's Stone.**

Ophiolatry From the Greek *ophis*, "a snake", serpent worship. The symbolism of the snake often has a sexual connotation. See also **Magic, Sexual; Ophidian Current; Tantra.**

Ophites **Gnostic** sect in Syria, members of which traced their descent from Seth and worshipped the serpent (*ophis*). The Ophites believed that the snake was really **Sophia**, personification of wisdom, and the enemy of **Ialdabaoth**. The Ophites are sometimes known as Sethian-Ophites. See also **Ophiolatry.**

Opposition In **astrology**, the situation that exists when two **planets** are separated by 180 degrees and are therefore opposite each other. Depending on the planets in question, an opposition could be deemed to be favourable or unfavourable.

Oracle A person serving as an intermediary between a supernatural being and those seeking counsel or **prophecy**. Often the oracle takes the role of a **medium** and becomes possessed by the **god** from whom the prophecy is sought. At Delphi, in ancient times, the Pythian oracle would enter a **trance**-state and make oracular pronouncements that were said to be communications from **Apollo**. These statements were then communicated to the gathering by the officiating priests. See **Delphic Oracle; Pythia.**

Orb In **astrology**, the space on a **horoscope** within which an **aspect** is deemed to be effective. Astrologers differentiate between "wide" or "exact" aspects.

Order of the Temple See **Knights Templar.**

Ordo Templi Orientis Sexual magic order formed by **Karl Kellner** around 1896. After Kellner died in 1905, leadership passed to **Theodor Reuss**, and then in 1922 to **Aleister Crowley**. There are now two organizations that bear the name OTO. The first of these is headed by the tantric **occultist** **Kenneth Grant** in England, and the second by the successors of Grady McMurtry in California. Members of the OTO arouse sexual energy during their magical ceremonies and identify with the **gods** and **goddesses** who personify this principle.

Oreads In Greek mythology, the mountain nymphs who attended **Artemis** on the hunt. The most famous of these was Echo. See **Nymph**.

Orenda Among the Iroquois Indians of North America, the term for the life-principle. Objects, animals, and human beings could possess it and **medicine-men** could draw upon it as a source of magical power. It can be compared with **mana** (Melanesia/Polynesia), **manitou** (Algonquin Indians, and **wakan** (Sioux Indians).

Orgy Sexual revelry and debauchery, associated in the occult tradition with such ceremonies as the medieval **witches' sabbath**, during which the **Horned God** was worshipped, and with the frenzied dancing and drunken rites held in classical Rome and Greece in honour of **Bacchus** and **Dionysus**.

Origen (c. 185–c. 284) One of the most influential theologians in the early Christian church, Origen fell from favour because he advocated the pre-existence of the **soul** and its **reincarnation** in subsequent lifetimes. Although St. Gregory of Nyssa called him "the prince of Christian learning in the third century", it is clear that Origen was strongly influenced by Platonic thought and inclined towards **Gnosticism**. His **theology** was condemned at the Fifth Ecumenical Council in 553, when the "Anathemas Against Pre-Existence" became part of Church doctrine.

Ornithomancy **Divination** by interpreting the songs or flight patterns of birds. In ancient Rome this form of divination was part of the national religion. See also **Augury**.

Orpheus Legendary singer in Greek **mythology**. The son of the **muse** Calliope, and the Olympian god **Apollo**, Orpheus is associated with the region of Thrace in northern Greece. He sang so beautifully and played his lyre so enchantingly that birds and animals came to listen to him. He is also famous in Greek mythology as one of the few living beings (like **Theseus**, **Heracles**, and **Odysseus**) who visited **Hades**. Orpheus descended to the **Underworld** to seek his wife Eurydice, who had been fatally bitten by a snake. His beautiful singing endeared him to Hades, who agreed to release Eurydice if Orpheus did not look at her before they reached their home. Orpheus failed in this task and his wife was compelled to return to the Underworld.

Orphic Cults Cults in Hellenistic Greece and in the Roman Empire which claimed affiliation with the legendary singer **Orpheus**. The so-called Orphic literature consists of numerous hymns, songs, and poems composed by various authors but attributed to Orpheus and incorporated into the mystery tradition. See also **Mystery Religion**.

Osiris In ancient Egypt, a major **deity** associated with vegetation and fertility, who personified the principle of spiritual **rebirth**. Osiris was the son of Geb and **Nut**, and husband of **Isis**, and the brother of **Set**. Set was jealous of Osiris and one day tricked him into climbing into a chest, which was later thrown into the Nile. Isis retrieved his dead body, but Set again discovered it and tore it into fourteen pieces, which he scattered around the kingdom. Isis again went in search of Osiris's body and found all the parts except the phallus, which had been swallowed by a crab in the Nile. Nevertheless, through her magical skills, Isis embalmed her husband and restored him to life. In so doing, she gave rise to the concept that the immortality of the **soul** was dependent on the preservation of the body. Osiris meanwhile became Lord of the **Underworld** and ruled in the **Judgment Hall**. See also **Mummification.**

Osis, Dr. Karlis (1917–1997) Latvian-born American parapyschologist who was best known for his research into the **out-of-the-body experience** and the **near-death experience**. Dr. Osis was a research associate at the Parapsychological Laboratory at Duke University between 1951 and 1957, and a colleague of well-known psychical researcher **Dr. J. B. Rhine**. He was subsequently appointed Director of Research at the American **Society for Psychical Research** in 1962. Dr. Osis's work, described in *At the Hour of Death* (1977), involved an extensive interview-survey of doctors and nurses present when patients experienced the near-death state and the visionary states of consciousness often associated with it. Dr. Osis was also the author of *Deathbed Observations by Physicians and Nurses* (1961). See also **Psychical Research**.

Osmond, Dr. Humphry (1917–) Canadian psychiatrist who has made a special study of hallucinatory chemicals and their effect on human consciousness. He coined the term **psychedelic**, meaning "mind-manifesting", and is regarded as one of the pioneers of the study of **altered states of consciousness**. Osmond met **Aldous Huxley** in 1953 and together they explored the mystical powers of **mescaline**. They later developed an extensive correspondence, which forms an important part of Huxley's posthumous publication *Moksha* (1977). Osmond has also studied **parapsychology**, **mediums**, and **telepathy**, and is interested in the potential application of psychedelics in these research areas.

OTO Initials of the **Ordo Templi Orientis.**

Otto, Rudolf (1869–1937) German theologian who was professor at the Universities of Breslau and Marburg. He introduced the term **numinous** to describe the essence of that which is sacred, and had a profound interest in **mysticism**. He also compared the concepts of **God** and the **soul** advocated by **Meister Eckhart** and the Indian mystical philosopher **Sankara**, and found many parallels in their thought. Otto's major works are *The Idea of the Holy* (1931) and *Mysticism East and West* (1932).

Otz Chiim In the **Kabbalah**, the Hebrew term for the **Tree of Life**.

Ouija Board In **spiritualism**, a device used to seek a message from the **spirits**. The board is usually heart-shaped and made of wood or plastic. It is mounted on wheels or castors to allow free movement, and includes the letters of the alphabet arranged in a circle, together with the numbers one to ten and the words "yes" and "no". During a **seance**, each member of the circle places a finger on the pointer in the centre of the ouija board and asks for a message from the spirits. The pointer then moves around the board spelling out answers to the questions – letter by letter.

Spiritualists believe that the communications obtained in this manner are provided by deceased spirit-beings anxious to maintain contact with the world of the living. To this extent the use of the ouija board can be regarded as a low-key form of **necromancy**. In **parapsychology**, however, the general explanation for such communications is that they originate in the subconscious minds of those attending the seance. See also **Myers, Frederic William Henry**.

Ouroboros Gnostic and alchemical symbol of the snake devouring its own tail. It symbolizes the cycles of life and Nature, the fusion of opposites, and the transcendence of duality. See also **Alchemy**.

Ousby, W. J. (1904–) English **hypnotist** who investigated **witchcraft** and **Juju** in Africa and later studied **yoga** and fire-walking. Ousby developed techniques of self-hypnosis based in part on his knowledge of **meditation** and ancient **trance** techniques. His books include *Self-Hypnosis and Scientific Self-Suggestion* and *The Theory and Practice of Hypnotism.*

Ouspensky, Peter Demianovich (1878–1947) Russian-born mathematician and philosopher who became interested in **Theosophy** and sought to combine mathematics, religion, and **mysticism** into a coherent system of thought. Ouspensky met **George Gurdjieff** in 1915 and began philosophical study groups in St. Petersburg, which Gurdjieff regularly attended. The two men remained closely associated for eight years, but later quarrelled and went their separate ways.

Although Ouspensky is often thought of as Gurdjieff's leading disciple, he was an original thinker in his own right and his important book *The Fourth Dimension* was published in 1909, before Ouspensky met Gurdjieff. Ouspensky's other works include *Tertium Organum* (1922), *A New Model of the Universe* (1934), and an account of his years with Gurdjieff, *In Search of the Miraculous*, published after his death, in 1948.

Out-of-the-body Experience (OBE) A dissociative experience characterized by the sensation that one's consciousness is separate and distinct from one's body, and at some distance removed. Numerous case histories exist of people who have claimed to float above their bodies or above rooftops, and even to pass through walls and other solid objects. The out-of-the-body experience is commonly referred to as **astral projection**, although the latter term is more correctly used when the OBE is produced under will. The OBE, on the other hand, may occur spontaneously as a result of illness or fasting, or during the **psychedelic** experience. See also **Crookall, Robert; Dreams, Lucid; Fox, Oliver; Green, Celia; Monroe, Robert; Muldoon, Sylvan.**

Overlooking Word used to describe the act of cursing a victim with the **evil-eye.**

Overself Hindu and Theosophical term for the Great Self, or **Atman** – the state of universal consciousness that unites human beings and the cosmos.

Oversoul Theosophical and mystical term for the **group soul.**

Owen, Dr. Alan R. G. (1919–) English mathematician at Cambridge University who has become a leading authority on **telepathy** and **poltergeists**. Dr. Owen has also studied the paranormal abilities of the English psychic **Matthew Manning**. His books include *Can We Explain the Poltergeist?*, *Hysteria, Hypnosis and Healing*, and *Science and the Spook.*

Owl Bird associated in many cultures with evil powers, **death**, and misfortune. The Romans regarded the owl as a sinister bird associated with omens of bad tidings, but also used it as a motif to combat the effects of the **evil-eye**. In folk belief, the owl is also thought of as the bird of wisdom, possibly as a result of its link with the ancient Greek goddess **Athena.**

Oxalis Mystic emblem among the **Druids**. See also **Clover.**

P

Pact An agreement. In medieval **magic**, it was often taken to mean a pact with the **Devil** in which one bartered one's **soul** for worldly pleasures and supernatural powers. See also **Faust**.

Padmasana In **yoga**, the **asana** popularly known as the lotus position. See also **Lotus, Full; Lotus, Half; Lotus Posture.**

Paean A song or chant of praise. The first paean was sung by **Apollo** after he had killed the giant serpent Python at Delphi.

Pagan One who is not a Christian, Jew, or **Moslem**. The term is used derogatorily to describe a **heathen** or "unbeliever", but has now assumed a new currency among practitioners of **witchcraft** and **magic**. The so-called New Pagans are dedicated to reviving the **Old Religion** and re-establishing the worship of Nature and the **lunar goddess**.

Pagoda A Buddhist memorial or shrine mound; a form of **stupa**. In the Orient, the pagoda may be very elaborate, taking the form of a profusely decorated temple or tower.

Pakht In ancient Egypt, a **goddess** who had the head of a lion and was sometimes identified with **Bast**.

Palee See **Pali**.

Pali The language in which the texts of Hinayana **Buddhism** are written. Pali was the language of the Indian Buddhists who took their religion into South-east Asia, and certain Sanskrit terms used in yoga differ in Pali (e.g. **nirvana** [Sanskrit]; **nibbana** [Pali]).

Palindrome A word that has the same spelling when read forward or in reverse order. Such words are sometimes used in **magic squares** and are believed to have considerable potency as **magical formulae**.

Palladino, Eusapia (1854–1918) Widely regarded as one of the most notable **physical mediums** in the history of **psychical research**, Eusapia was born in a small Italian village and orphaned as a child. She grew up in Naples with a family that dabbled in **spiritualism**, and soon took an active role in their **seances**. Her **paranormal** abilities came to the attention of occult student Ercole Chiaja, who arranged for her to demonstrate her powers of psychic **levitation** at a meeting in Paris. Eusapia also produced rappings and other "manifestations" at seances and claimed to be in contact with a spirit named John King who served as her **control**. She was investigated by a number of distinguished psychical researchers including **Professor Charles Richet, Sir Oliver Lodge, Richard Hodgson, Hereward Carrington**, and **Everard Feilding**; but the final verdict concerning her psychic abilities was mixed. Some believed her to be a fraud, others maintained that she combined genuine psychic ability with trickery only when her powers were "weak".

Palmistry The study of the hand and its interpretation for purposes of **divination**. Distinguishing features include the whorls and line patterns, and the colour and texture of the skin. Several modern palmists, including **Cyrus Abayakora, Mir Bashir, Cheiro**, and **Noel Jaquin**, have endeavoured to place palmistry on a scientific basis. See also **Chiromancy**.

Pan In ancient Greek **mythology**, the son of **Hermes** and Dryope. Pan was the god of flocks and shepherds, but also had a more far-reaching role as lord of Nature and all forms of wildlife. He was depicted as half-man, half-goat, and played a pipe with seven reeds. Ever lecherous, he had numerous love affairs with the **nymphs**, especially Echo, Syrinx, and

Pithys. Pan's name means "All", and among practitioners of **witchcraft** he is regarded as a **high god**. See also **Pantheism**.

Pandavas In Indian **mythology**, the family to which **Arjuna** belonged. The Pandavas were the rivals and enemies of their cousins the **Kauravas**, and the ***Mahabharata*** describes their struggles.

Panentheism Religious belief that all things are in **God**, but that God **transcends** the manifested world. God is the Supreme Reality and the highest Unity. See also **Pantheism**.

Pan-pipe The seven-reeded pipe played by the Greek god **Pan**. It was also known as a syrinx, because the nymph Syrinx had been transformed into the reed from which Pan fashioned his first pan-pipe.

Panpsychism Belief that **God** is **immanent** in the world in the form of a psychic force of spirit. See also **Psyche**.

Pansophy From the Greek *pansophos*, meaning "all-wise", universal knowledge.

Pantheism The religious and mystical doctrine that the whole universe is **God** and that every part of the universe is an aspect or manifestation of God. The term is also used to describe the worship of all the gods of a **pantheon**, and is sometimes applied generally to mean "Nature worship". See also **Pan**.

Pantheon A group of **gods** and **goddesses** who are worshipped collectively. Ancient Greece, Rome, and Egypt provide excellent examples of civilizations where a pantheon of deities has been worshipped. See also **Ennead; Ogdoad; Olympians, Twelve Great**.

Paphia In ancient Greek mythology, the name for **Aphrodite** in her role as **goddess** of sexual love. She was worshipped at Paphos.

Paphian Erotic, illicit love, sometimes used to describe acts of prostitution. The term derives from **Paphia**, which was one of the names for the **goddess** of love, **Aphrodite**.

Papus (1865–1916) Spanish-born physician who lived in Paris, published a number of occult works, and contributed significantly to the literature on the **Tarot**. Papus, whose real name was Gérard Encausse, was influenced by **Theosophy** and spent much of his time delving into hermetic, kabbalistic, and alchemical texts. A member of the kabbalistic Order of the Rose-Cross, Papus believed that **esoteric** knowledge was transmitted by a secret line of occult **adepts** and counted himself among their number. He acquired a reputation as a necromancer and, on one occasion in 1905, was summoned to the Russian Imperial Palace where he performed a ceremony to summon the **spirit** of Czar Alexander III.

Like **Eliphas Lévi**, Papus was best known for his writings on the Tarot and for connecting the cards of the **Major Arcana** to the Hebrew alphabet. His most significant work in English is *The Tarot of the Bohemians* (reissued 1970), but he published widely in French. His other books include *Traité Méthodique de Science Occulte* (1891), *La Kabbale* (1892), *Le Diable et L'occultisme* (1895), and *La Magie et L'Hypnose* (1897). See also **Alchemy; Hermetica; Kabbalah; Necromancy; Rosicrucians**.

Para Prefix meaning "beyond" or "beside". It may be joined to certain scientific words to suggest the study of that which is beyond the normal confines of that discipline (e.g. *parapsychology*, *paraphysics*). It is sometimes combined with the names of deities (e.g. **Parabrahm**).

Parabrahm That which is beyond **Brahma**; the Supreme, Infinite, and Absolute Reality.

Paracelsus (1493–1541) One of the most illustrious of the medieval alchemists,

Paracelsus was born Philippus Aureolus Theophrastus Bombastus von Hohenheim in Einsiedeln, Switzerland. He pursued medical studies under the direction of his father, who was a physician in Basle, but also studied **alchemy** and **occultism** with Trimethius of Spanheim. Paracelsus emphasized the hermetic doctrine of the **macrocosm and microcosm**, believing that human beings were mirrors of the universe. He regarded disease as a form of imbalance, and maintained that a healthy person combined the three alchemical elements of **sulphur** (male), **mercury** (female), and **salt** (neutral) in perfect harmony. For Paracelsus, the true nature of alchemy had to do with the inner person, and not with chemical processes in a laboratory. He is said to have received the secret of the **Philosopher's Stone** from Solomon of Trismosin in 1521. Paracelsus was not without his eccentricities, however, and maintained that he had successfully created an artificial human being, or **homunculus**. The main works of Paracelsus are contained in the two-volume edition *The Hermetic and Alchemical Writings of Paracelsus* (edited by **A. E. Waite**, 1894) and *The Archidoxes of Magic* (reissued 1975).

Paradise See **Heaven**.

Paramita Buddhist term meaning "perfection". There are six paramitas in all: *silaparamita* (observing the precepts); *ksantiparamita* (correct forbearance); *viryaparamita* (zeal); *dhyanaparamita* (concentration during **meditation**); *prajnaparamita* (wisdom); and *danaparamita* (the act of relinquishing). See also **Buddhism**.

Paramnesia Distortion or falsification of the memory so that one recalls things not previously seen or experienced. Compare with **Déjà Vu**.

Paranirvana Complete **nirvana** and liberation from the cycle of birth and **rebirth**.

Paranormal That which cannot be explained by the known scientific laws of Nature. See also **Parapsychology**.

Parapsychology The scientific study of **paranormal** phenomena. This includes **mental telepathy**, **precognition**, **extrasensory perception**, **psychokinesis**, and the **out-of-the-body experience**. See also **Rhine, Dr. J. B.**; **Tart, Dr. Charles**.

Parapsychology Foundation Organization established in 1951 by the Irish-born **psychic medium Eileen Garrett**. The function of the Foundation is to research the workings and potential of the human mind; and to this end the Foundation publishes a bimonthly journal, *Parapsychology Review*, and funds a specialized library that is open to the public.

Parcae The Latin name by which the three **Fates** were known.

Paroketh In the **Kabbalah**, the "veil" that separates **Tiphareth** from the lower spheres on the **Tree of Life**. The **mystic** has to pass through Paroketh to receive the solar rebirth – **initiation** of Tiphareth.

Paroptic Vision The ability to see without the use of the eyes, apparently by perception through the skin. See also **Eyeless Vision**.

Parsees Also Parsis. See **Zoroastrians**.

Parvati In Indian **mythology**, the beautiful and gentle wife of **Shiva** in her aspect as the **goddess** of the mountains. Parvati is regarded as the daughter of the Himalayas and the personification of **cosmic** energy. She is the leader of the **elves** and **nature-spirits** and the fierce opponent of the **demons**. Shiva's wife has other "aspects" or personas too, among them Devi, Sati, and **Kali**.

Pasqually, Martinez See **Martinism**.

Passing Over Spiritualist expression meaning "to die". Because spiritualists believe in an afterlife, **death** is regarded as a state of transition, and one "passes over" to the "other side". See also **Spiritualism**.

Past-life Regression Technique, used by some practitioners of **hypnosis**, in which subjects are regressed beyond their point of birth into alleged earlier **incarnations**. The technique remains highly controversial, but some hypnotists claim to have uncovered highly specific, factual data pertaining to past lives not available to the subject during waking consciousness. Among the best-known advocates of past-life regression are Dr. Helen Wambach and Dr. Morris Netherton in the United States, Joe Heeton and the late Arnall Bloxham in Britain, and Peter Ramster in Australia. See also **Murphy, Bridey; Reincarnation**.

Patanjali (c. A.D. 400) The compiler of the famous yoga Sutras, which provide a distinct way of looking at the world (*darsana*) and therefore enable the practitioner to gain a vision of Reality. The framework proposed by Patanjali has eight divisions: **yama, niyama, asana, pranyama**, pratyhara, **dharana, dhyana**, and **samadhi**, the last of these being the state of blissful union with **Brahman**. The Patanjali who compiled the Sutras should not be confused with another Patanjali (c. 200 B.C.), who wrote the commentary known as *Mahabhasya* on Panini's Grammar and was an authority on Sanskrit. See **Sutras; Yoga**.

Path, The Mystical term for the journey towards enlightenment and **self-realization**. It is variously known as the Path of Perfection, the Way of Salvation, the Path of Liberation, or the Spiritual path. See also **Mysticism**.

Pathworkings In modern Western **magic**, a **guided-imagery** technique in which the subject is led along "inner pathways" of consciousness in order to experience archetypal visions. Pathworkings often make use of the symbolism of the **Major Arcana** of the **Tarot**, and are designed to trigger a personal experience of the **gods** and **goddesses** of the magical **pantheon**. Pathworkings may be regarded as inner magical journeys that make use of active **imagination**. Among the most detailed descriptions of pathworkings in contemporary occult literature are **Dolores Ashcroft-Nowicki**'s *The Shining Paths* (1983) and Nevill Drury's *Sacred Encounters* (2002).

Peak Experiences Term used by the psychologist **Abraham Maslow** (1908–1970) to describe experiences of sudden and profound joy, **ecstasy**, and **illumination**. Maslow associated them with insights of perfection and wonderment. In his book *Motivation and Personality* (1970), he described the highest peaks as those "feelings of limitless horizons opening up to the vision, the feeling of being simultaneously more powerful and also more helpless than one ever was before, the feeling of great ecstasy and wonder and awe, the loss of placing in time and space ...." With the growth of literature in the **human potential movement** and the **transpersonal movement**, Maslow's term has become generally synonymous with "mystical experience". See also **Cosmic Consciousness**.

Pegasus In Greek mythology, the legendary winged horse which emerged from the blood of the gorgon **Medusa** when Perseus cut off her head. It was mounted on Pegasus that the Corinthian hero Bellerophon killed the monstrous **Chimera**.

Peji Inner sanctuary within a **Macumba** temple, where the ritual adornments of the **gods** and **goddesses** are kept and ceremonial offerings made.

Peladan, Sar Josephin (1858–1918) Astrologer, **magician**, and novelist who became a fashionable aesthete in the Rosicrucian salons in Paris during the 1890s. Peladan took the title "La Sar Merodack" after the Kings of Babylon, and wore a full, Assyrian-style beard for effect. Sar Peladan was a friend and occult colleague of **Stanislas de Guaita** and assisted him in the **magical attacks** against **Joseph-Antoine Boullan.** See also **Rosicrucians.**

Penates Roman household **deities,** related to the **lares.** The penates were literally the gods of the pantry, and every household had a shrine with figurines of these deities.

Pendulum Small metal weight, suspended on a thread, and used in **dowsing, psychometry,** and **radiesthesia** as a diagnostic implement. Dowsers believe that they can locate subterranean water, oil, and minerals using a pendulum; and radiesthetists hold a pendulum over a triangular chart and a drop of the patient's blood in order to diagnose that person's illness. See also **Psionic Medicine; Radionics.**

Pentacles Discs bearing the motif of the five-pointed star. In the **Tarot,** they are one of the **four suits** – the others being **cups, wands** and **swords** – and represent the feminine element **Earth.**

Pentagram A five-pointed star. The pentagram is an important symbol in Western **magic** and represents the four **elements** surmounted by the **Spirit.** It is regarded as a symbol of human spiritual aspirations when the point faces upwards; but is a symbol of bestiality and retrograde evolution when facing down. The pentagram is inscribed in the air at the four quarters during the **banishing ritual** of the Lesser Pentagram, a ceremonial purging of negative influences from the magical temple.

Perennial Philosophy Phrase coined by the German philosopher Gottfried Leibniz (1646–1716) and summarized by **Aldous Huxley** as "the metaphysic that recognizes a divine Reality substantial to the world of things and lives and minds; the psychology that finds in the soul something similar to, or even identical with, divine Reality; the ethic that places man's final end in the knowledge of the immanent and transcendent Ground of all being ... ." Huxley used this concept to explore the universal themes in comparative **mysticism,** believing that "rudiments of the Perennial Philosophy may be found among the traditionary lore of primitive peoples in every region of the world, and in its fully developed forms ... in every one of the higher religions." Huxley's book *The Perennial Philosophy* – one of his major works of non-fiction – was published in 1946.

Periapt From the Greek *periapton,* "an object fastened around", an **amulet** or **charm** worn as a protection against **spells** and the **evil-eye.**

Persea Species of wild laurel tree sacred to the ancient Egyptians and considered to be a symbol of eternal fame. **Thoth,** the Egyptian god of wisdom, and Safekh, goddess of knowledge, wrote the names of pharaohs and high priests on its leaves to ensure that they were remembered forever.

Persephone In Greek **mythology,** the goddess of spring. Persephone was the daughter of **Zeus** and **Demeter** and is the archetypal "Divine Maiden". Persephone was picking flowers on the Nysian plain when she was overwhelmed by the beauty of a narcissus. At this moment the earth opened and **Hades** rushed forth in his chariot, snatching Persephone down into the bowels of the earth. She became Queen of the **Underworld;** but after Demeter appealed to Zeus, she was able to spend two thirds of the year above the ground and only a third below. Persephone was the personification of the wheat grain, and symbolized the cyclic patterns of Nature. She was the central **deity** in the **Mysteries of Eleusis**. Persephone was also known as **Kore**, and her Roman counterpart was **Proserpina**.

Peyote Cactus Cactus used in shamanic ceremonies because of its **psychedelic** properties. The Huichol Indians conduct a ritual hunt for this sacred plant after the rainy season in the early spring, and subsequently consume around a dozen "buttons" each, during the night. After approximately an hour, exhilarating effects occur – colour and sound are intensified and subjects experience heightened awareness and perception. Peyote cactus contains eight isoquinoline alkaloids, one of which – **mescaline** – produces vivid **hallucinations**. See also **Huxley, Aldous; Shamanism.**

Phalec According to the *Arbatel of Magick*, there are seven different **spirits** of Olympus, appointed by God to rule the world. Phalec is the spirit of **Mars** and governs all activities relating to war.

Phallus The male sexual organ, known in **yoga** and Indian religion as the **lingam**. The paramount male symbol in all creeds and practices based on fertility and sexual worship, the phallus is represented by such diverse forms as the **maypole**, the **magician's wand**, and the snake. In **Tantric Yoga** the procreative sexual union of **Shiva** and **Shakti** gives rise to the entire universe.

Phantasmata Occult term for the **thought-forms** that arise in the **imagination** and which, in an **altered state of consciousness**, seem to have a separate existence. The ethnomycologist **R. Gordon Wasson** believed that the initiates of **Eleusis**, after consuming a **psychedelic ergot** beverage, had visionary encounters with **Persephone**, and that these hallucinatory experiences were part of the process of spiritual **rebirth**. See also **Pathworkings.**

Phantasms of the Living Expression used by the pioneering psychical researchers **Edmund Gurney** and **F. W. H. Myers** to describe **apparitions** of people who are still alive, as opposed to those who have died. The appearance of the **double**, however, is often a sign of impending disaster or **death**. See also **Astral Body; Doppelgänger.**

Phantom From the Latin *phantasma*, an **apparition** or **ghost** presumed to be the **spirit** of a deceased person.

Phenomena In **spiritualism**, **manifestations** from the **spirit** world that appear during **seances**. They may take the form of **ectoplasm**, automata, **materializations**, **levitation**, **rappings**, or they may be apprehended by **psychic photography**.

Philosopher's Stone In alchemy, the so-called **prima materia** or First Substance from which all other metals derived and which could therefore be used to transmute base metals into **gold** or **silver**. It was associated with the **Elixir of Life** and could only be recognized by initiates. While many medieval alchemists sought the Philosopher's Stone in their laboratories, it is clear that the essential idea behind it is a mystical one. It is a central symbol for the essence of life and the Oneness of Creation. The **hexagram** is also associated with the Philosopher's Stone, and characteristically it too represents the interrelatedness of **matter** and **spirit**.

Philosophus In the **Hermetic Order of the Golden Dawn**, the ritual grade associated with the magical initiation of **Netzach**, the seventh sphere on the kabbalistic **Tree of Life**.

Philtre A magical potion, intended to arouse love or sexual passion. See also **Love Potion.**

Phoenix Mythical bird resembling an eagle, which appears in the **mythology** of many countries. The Phoenix is traditionally associated with the **sun**, and in Arabian legend sits in a nest that is ignited by solar rays. In this account, the Phoenix is consumed in flame and reduced to ashes; but a worm emerges from the ashes and from it, in turn, arises a new Phoenix. In China, it was similarly associated with the sun and was regarded as an envoy from the heavens, appearing during times when the **gods** were benevolent. In medieval Europe, it featured both in Christian **cosmology** – as a symbol of resurrection and the triumph of life over **death** – and in **alchemy**, where it represented both the **Philosopher's Stone** and the **Elixir of Life**. The Phoenix also has a parallel in the **Bennu bird** of Egyptian mythology. See also **Rebirth**.

Photography, Psychic See Psychic Photography.

Phrenology The art and pseudo-science of interpreting a person's mental abilities by reading the "bumps" on the skull. Phrenology was pioneered by Dr. F. J. Gall (1756–1828), a Viennese physician, and his colleague Dr. J. G. Spurzheim. Together they produced a work titled *The Physiognomical System*, which endeavoured to put phrenology on a systematic basis.

Phrygian Mysteries See Cybele.

Phul According to the *Arbatel of Magick*, there are seven different **Olympic spirits**, appointed to **God** to rule the world. Phul is the spirit of the **moon** and governs the spirits of the element **Water**. He is able to change all metals into **silver** and can make people live to an age of three hundred years.

Phylacteries Small leather bags containing magical **words of power** or **spells**. They were worn or carried like an **amulet**.

Physical Medium In **spiritualism**, a **psychic medium** who is able to manifest physical phenomena, such as **ectoplasm**, during a **seance**.

Physical Plane See Earth Plane.

Physiognomy Technique for interpreting personal character on the basis of the features of the face. This system, which was developed by **Johann Kaspar Levater**, drew heavily on **astrology** and divided the main characteristics as follows: solar (round and jovial); venusian (classically beautiful and fair); martian (heavy, rough, and "war-like"); mercurial (classical but dark in colouring); lunar (cold and pale); jovian (noble and patriarchal); and saturnine (mournful-looking with dark colouring). All of the main features of the face – nose, teeth, eyes, cheeks, lips, forehead, chin, etc. – had particular significance, and could be interpreted symbolically. Levater's system is described in his four-volume treatise, *Physiognomical Fragments for the Promotion of the Knowledge and Love of Man* (1775–1778).

Picatrix Eleventh-century magical text, which drew heavily on the Greek **mystery** tradition and which was studied by such Renaissance **mystics** as **Marsilio Ficino** and **Cornelius Agrippa**. The *Picatrix* includes **cosmology**, **astrology**, and formulae for invoking planetary **spirits**. A German-language edition was published in 1962; it has not been translated into English. Compare with ***Arbatel of Magick***.

Pico della Mirandola, Giovanni (1463–1494) Renaissance philosopher and **mystic** who was well versed in the **Kabbalah** and understood Greek and Latin as well as Hebrew. A disciple of the Jewish teacher Jochanum, he arrived in Rome at the age of twenty-four, armed with nine hundred propositions relating to logic, mathematics, physics, and the Kabbalah, and proclaimed – somewhat surprisingly – that the Kabbalah could be employed to convert Jews to

Christianity. Pico advocated invocation of the **archangels** associated with the **Tree of Life**, and also believed in the alchemical transmutation of base metals into **gold** and **silver**, which he claimed to have witnessed firsthand. Pico was imprisoned by the **Inquisition** on the grounds of **heresy**, although many of his beliefs were theologically sound. He once wrote: "We may more easily love God than comprehend Him or speak of Him", and he considered religion, rather than philosophy, to be the path to **enlightenment**. His kabbalistic and Neoplatonic inclinations, however, always made him suspect with the authorities. See also **Neoplatonism**.

Pietism Any religious approach that emphasizes emotional feelings and devotion as being more important than intellect and the formation of creeds and doctrines. The term is originally Lutheran. Compare with **Bhakti**.

Pike, James (1913–1969) Californian Episcopalian bishop who became involved in the occult after his son committed suicide. Pike sought to contact the **spirit** of his son through various **psychic mediums** and believed he finally achieved this goal through **Arthur Ford**. Pike was subsequently accused of **heresy** and was forced to resign his office. An account of Pike's spiritual and psychic quest is contained in his book *The Other Side.*

Pineal Gland Small vascular, conical body situated behind the third ventricle of the brain. It has no known anatomical function, but is often described by **mystics** and **occultists** as the gland of **extrasensory perception**: the so-called **third eye**.

Pingala In **Kundalini Yoga**, the positively charged solar current that circles around the central axis of the nervous system, **sushumna**. It counterbalances the negatively charged lunar current known as **ida**. See also **Nadi**.

Piper, Mrs. Leonore (1859–1950) Remarkable American **psychic medium** who discovered her paranormal powers while consulting a **psychic healer** about a tumour. On her second visit she fell into a **trance** state and obtained a spirit-message for one of the other people present. Mrs. Piper began to give regular psychic "readings" and in 1887, following an earlier meeting with **William James**, she attracted the attention of **Richard Hodgson** – the psychical researcher who had exposed **Madame Helena Blavatsky**'s mediumistic frauds in India. Hodgson was impressed by Mrs. Piper's facility for producing detailed information about deceased relatives, and used extensive methods of analytical detection before concluding that she possessed remarkable and authentic powers. Both Hodgson and James accepted the reality of the afterlife on the basis of their contact with Mrs. Piper, but it is possible that she obtained her information by using **mental telepathy**. Whatever the explanation, Mrs. Piper remains one of the most notable and trustworthy psychic mediums in the history of **spiritualism**.

Pisces In **astrology**, the **sign** of the **zodiac** for those born between February 20 and March 20. A **Water** sign, ruled by **Jupiter** (or, according to some astrologers, by **Neptune**), Pisces is symbolized by the motif of two fish, facing in opposite directions. People born under the sign of Pisces are said to be patient and sensitive, but often lack personal direction. They may be artistic, but are often impractical and worry a lot. Charity work, nursing, art, and archaeology are careers association with Pisces.

Pitris In **Hinduism** and **Theosophy**, ancestor-beings associated with the **moon** who were the forerunners of present humanity. They were said to be either incorporeal (arupa) or corporeal (rupa) in nature.

PK In **parapsychology**, shorthand for **psychokinesis**.

Planchette A variant on a **ouija board**, used by spiritualists to communicate with the spirits of the dead. The board has castors and a mounted pencil, which allows messages to flow from the "other side" without conscious involvement from the **medium**.

Planes In mystical and occult **cosmology**, the universe is often described as consisting of different planes of **manifestation**. It is common in mystical literature to find references to the spiritual, etheric, mental, astral, and physical planes, which are said to be characterized by increasing "density". The psychical or **earth plane** equates with the material, tangible world of waking consciousness; and the **astral plane** can be compared to the domain of the lower unconscious. The mental plane is characterized by archetypal images; while the etheric and spiritual planes reflect the universal **life-force** and people's inherent divinity. See also **Emanations**.

Planetary Ages of Man Ancient ascription of **planets** to different phases of human life: **moon** – personal growth (ages up to 4 years); **Mercury** – education (5–14); **Venus** – the emotions (15–22); **sun** – virility (23–42); **Mars** – ambition (43–57); **Jupiter** – reflection (58–69); **Saturn** – resignation (70+).

Planetary Metals Metals linked symbolically to the **planets** in medieval **cosmology** and **alchemy**. The correlations were: **sun** (**gold**); **moon** (**silver**); **Mercury** (**quicksilver**); **Venus** (copper); **Mars** (**iron**); **Jupiter** (tin); and **Saturn** (lead).

Planetary Spirits See ***Arbatel of Magick***.

Planet of Death The so-called Eighth Sphere – regarded as a physical location by some Theosophists – where very evil beings or **lost souls** cease to exist.

Planets, Seven In traditional **astrology**, the following planets: **Saturn**, **Jupiter**, **Mars**, the **sun**, **Venus**, **Mercury**, and the **moon**.

Plato (c. 427–347 B.C.) One of the most important of the classical Greek philosophers and a thinker who has profoundly influenced the development of mystical and **esoteric** thought. Plato, a disciple of **Socrates**, founded his famous Academy in Athens for the study of philosophy. Plato developed his theory of ideal forms, which differentiated the realm of the senses from Reality itself. According to Plato, impressions received by the senses were impermanent and ever changing; whereas the world of Forms (or Ideals) was eternal and changeless and the source of true knowledge. Plato's **cosmology** is described in his major book *The Republic*, and provides a model of the universe as a spherical structure encompassing the fixed stars and the **seven planets**. The three **Fates** (Clotho, Lachesis, and Atropos) guide human destiny, but allow freedom of choice; thus people are ultimately responsible for the good and evil in their own lives. Plato was initiated in the temple at **Eleusis** and may have been influenced by his visionary experiences in formulating his theory of ideal Forms, or **archetypes**.

Pleroma From a Greek word meaning "fullness," a term used by the **Gnostics** to signify the world of light – the Universal Soul. It was also the abode of the heavenly **aeons**.

Plotinus (205–270) Egyptian-born Greek philosopher who was the founding figure of **Neoplatonism**. He studied in Alexandria, became a pupil of Ammonius, and finally settled in Rome in 244, establishing a school of philosophy. Plotinus believed that the ultimate goal was to discover the One-ness underlying manifested existence and that this task involved transcending philosophy itself.

According to **Porphyry**, a close friend and disciple, Plotinus attained the mystical vision of Unity at least four times in his life.

Pluto The Roman Lord of the **Underworld** and the counterpart of **Hades** in Greek **mythology**. He was also identified with **Dis**.

Pluto The most distant of the known **planets** within the solar system. Pluto was discovered in 1930 and consequently has played no role in traditional **astrology**. Some contemporary occultists believe, however, that Pluto should be recognized as the **ruler** of **Scorpio**.

Pneuma Greek word for "air", "breath", and "spirit", closely associated with Life itself. Compare with **Prana**.

P'o In **Taoism**, the "earthly" part of the **soul**. Characterized as passive and negative, it may compare to the **hun** part of the soul, which is the "heavenly" counterpart.

Podmore, Frank (1856–1910) English psychical researcher who worked with many other notable investigators of **spiritualism**, including **F. W. H. Myers** and **Edmund Gurney**. Although he converted to spiritualism while studying at Pembroke College, Oxford, he became increasingly sceptical and spent much of his time investigating haunted houses and **poltergeist** activity, with a view to discover fraud. Towards the end of his life Podmore again became more sympathetic, and felt that he had received **psychic** communications from his deceased colleagues, Myers and **Richard Hodgson**. Podmore is best known as the co-author (with Myers and Gurney) of *Phantasms of the Living* (1886); but he wrote several other books, including *Apparitions and Thought Transference* (1892), *Studies in Psychical Research* (1897), and *Modern Spiritualism: a History and a Criticism* (1902). See also **Psychical Research**.

Poimandres *Shepherd of Men*, the title of the main tractate in the **Hermetica**. It is usually referred to as *The Divine Pymander of Hermes Trismegistus* (English-language edition 1923).

Point of Love In **astrology**, the position of **Venus** in the solar **horoscope**. The point of love is always located in the first, second, eleventh, or twelfth **houses**.

Poltergeist From the German *polter*, "a noise", and *geist*, "a spirit", a **ghost** or **discarnate** entity who makes a variety of sounds – whisperings, raps, singing – and is mischievously given to breaking such household items as vases and cups, starting fires, or moving objects from one side of a room to the other. Poltergeists have been reported in many countries, and detailed accounts have been compiled by such occult writers as **A. R. G. Owen** and **Colin Wilson**. The parapsychologist **Dr. Hereward Carrington** believed that poltergeist activity was connected with juveniles achieving puberty, and that somehow the combination of sexual maturity and psychological tension produced an energy-effect in the home environment. Dr. Owen believes that this idea contains "the germ of a correct theory," and that many poltergeist outbreaks are attributable to the release of emotional tension.

Polytheism The belief in, and worship of, more than one **god**. Polytheism may be compared to **monotheism**, which is the belief in one god. See also **Pantheism**; **Pantheon**.

Ponto Riscado In **Macumba**, a magical diagram used ceremonially to summon a **god** or **goddess**.

Popul Vuh The sacred book of the Quiche-Maya Indians of Guatemala. The book draws on the oral tradition of the ancient Maya, and includes many myths and legends relating to the creation of the world and the nature of existence.

Porphyry (c. 232–305) Disciple and friend of **Plotinus** and a leading figure in the philosophical school of **Neoplatonism.** Porphyry studied **demonology** and the magical incantations and formulae for overcoming evil **spirits.** However, he was also an important philosopher and produced a handbook of logic, *Isagoge*, which was very influential in the Middle Ages. He edited and compiled Plotinus's writings under the title *The Enneads.*

Portent An **omen** from the **gods**, relating to future events. See also **Divination.**

Poseidon In Greek **mythology**, the god of the sea, and one of the **Twelve Great Olympians.** In classical Greek **cosmology**, the universe was divided among the three sons of **Cronus** and **Rhea**, with **Zeus** being given rulership of the sky; **Hades** the **Underworld**; and Poseidon the sea. The earth was common to all three. Poseidon's Roman counterpart is **Neptune.**

Possession Emotional and mental state in which a subject feels "possessed" by a **spirit** or **discarnate** entity, which takes over aspects of the personality totally or in part, and appears to operate independently of the person concerned. Spirit-possession is a feature of **voodoo** and **spiritualism**, and also resembles some forms of schizophrenia. See also **Control; Exorcism.**

Post-hypnotic Suggestion A suggestion given by the practitioner during **hypnosis**, which has its effect after the subject returns to waking consciousness.

Poughkeepsie Seer See **Davis, Andrew Jackson.**

Power Animal In **shamanism**, a creature which appears on the **spirit journey** of the **soul** while the **shaman** is in a state of **trance.** The power animal usually resembles an actual species but may sometimes be a mythical or imaginary creature. It is invariably regarded as a personification of magical power and may be summoned in **rituals** and ceremonies. See also **Familiar.**

Practicus In the **Hermetic Order of the Golden Dawn**, the **ritual** grade associated with the magical initiation of **Hod**, the eighth sphere on the kabbalistic **Tree of Life.**

Prajna Buddhist term meaning **transcendental** wisdom and intuition. It is attained by mastery of the six perfections or **paramitas**, and leads to the attainment of **sunyata** (the **Void**).

Prakriti Sanskrit word denoting Nature, or physical reality. It consists of the three **gunas: sattva** (harmony); **rajas** (motion); and **tamas** (heaviness). It is the direct opposite of **purusha** or **Spirit.**

Pralaya Sanskrit term for the dissolution of the universe at the end of a **kalpa** or "Day of Brahma". During this phase the universe is quiescent.

Prana Sanskrit word usually translated as **life-force.** It can be used to describe specific vital fluids and energy in the body, and can also be used in a more general and all-encompassing way to denote the principle underlying Life itself.

Prana Pratistha In **Hinduism**, the act of consecrating an image or **idol** for worship. The ceremony includes **prayers** and **mantras** during which the **deity** is summoned to occupy the idol being consecrated.

Pranayama In **yoga**, the science of breathing. The exercises of pranayama, which involve cycles of rhythmic breathing, may be used to raise the **kundalini** energy, or to stabilize the **prana** or life-energy in the body. See also **Siddha Yoga.**

Prapatti Marga In **Hinduism**, the path of total and complete surrender to the **Godhead.**

Prasad In **Hinduism**, sweets and fruit or other food which are offered to a **deity** or **saint** and later partaken of by the followers themselves as a religious blessing.

Prayer The act of addressing a **deity** or **spirit**, often in praise, to make a request, or to acknowledge a personal failing. Praying usually takes a ceremonial form (e.g. with head inclined downwards and the hands held together).

Prayer Wheel Revolving metal drum, containing written **prayers**, used by the Buddhists of Tibet during their religious ceremonies. See also **Buddhism; Mahayana Buddhism.**

Precession of the Equinoxes In **astrology**, a situation that refers to the slow revolution of the Earth's pole around the elliptic once every 26,000 years – which in turn changes the relationship of the **signs** of the **zodiac** to the constellations. Approximately two thousand years are spent by the vernal point of the equinox in each constellation. The present era is the Age of Pisces, and it will be followed by the **Aquarian Age.**

Precognition Type of **extrasensory perception** in which one has apparent awareness of future events.

Predestination The belief that one's **fate** and **destiny** are predetermined at birth and that the events of one's life unfold accordingly. Belief in predestination is the direct opposite of belief in free will.

Prediction See **Divination; Prophecy.**

Predictive Astrology See **Astrology, Predictive.**

Pre-existence of the Soul Religious doctrine, associated with the theologian and **mystic Origen**, according to which the **soul** existed prior to its present **incarnation.** It is logically associated with belief in **reincarnation.** Belief in pre-existence became a Christian **heresy** following a decree passed at the Fifth Ecumenical Council in A.D. 553.

Premies Term used by followers of **Guru Maharaj Ji** to describe those who have "taken the Knowledge", and who conduct **satsang** at the numerous branches of the **Divine Light Mission.**

Premonition An intuitive **paranormal** awareness of something about to happen. When premonitions occur they are often warnings of imminent disasters, danger, or **death.** They are sometimes described as belonging to the borderline between **dreams** and **sleep**, and on occasions manifest in dreams as a presentiment of things soon to happen in the waking world. See also **Dream, Lucid; Monition; Precognition.**

Prenatal Regression See **Past-life Regression.**

Prescience Knowledge of future events. See also **Precognition; Presentiment; Prophecy.**

Presentiment From the Latin *praesentire*, "to perceive beforehand", a foreboding, or knowledge of that which is about to occur. See also **Prescience.**

Pretas In **Hinduism**, discarnate beings and **apparitions** of the dead that haunt cemeteries and are regarded as malevolent. See also **Ghosts.**

Priapus In Greek **mythology**, the son of **Dionysus** and **Aphrodite**. Like **Pan**, Priapus was a god of fertility and vegetation and protected farmers and shepherds.

Price, Henry (1881–1948) British researcher who became legendary for his efforts in detecting psychic frauds. Price investigated many leading British and European spirit **mediums**, including Stella C, **Eileen Garrett** – whom he believed to be genuine – and Mrs. Helen Duncan and **William Hope**, who he was convinced were fakes. Price became well known for his famous investigation of **Borley Rectory** – said to be the "most haunted house in England" – and was a member of both the British and American **Society for Psychical Research**. He established the National Laboratory of Psychical Research in 1925 and amassed a personal collection of twenty-thousand books on **psychical research**, which became the Harry Price Library of Magical Literature at the University of London. Price's many publications include *Revelations of a Spirit Medium* (1922), *Leaves from a Psychist's Case-Book* (1933), *Confessions of a Ghost Hunter* (1936), *Fifty Years of Psychical Research* (1939), and his autobiography, *Search for Truth* (1942).

Priest, Priestess In organized religions, the officially recognized mediator or "channel of inspiration" between the **deity** and the devotees of the faith. The priest performs acts of ceremonial sacrifice, makes offerings, gives **prayers**, and provides spiritual guidance to the worshippers. The priest may be differentiated from the **shaman**, whose role is individual communication with the **god** or gods, often in a state of **trance**, and who is associated more with hunter-gatherer societies than cultures with formalized religious expression.

Primum Mobile In kabbalistic **cosmology**, the "first swirlings" of the Infinite Light as it moved through the darkness of **Chaos**, manifesting in **Kether** on the **Tree of Life**. The traditional Hebrew term is *Rashith ha Galgalim*.

Prince of Darkness In **demonology** and **occultism**, the **Devil** – known variously as **Satan**, **Lucifer**, **Beelzebub**, and **Mephistopheles**.

Prithivi In **Hinduism** and Western **magic**, the element **Earth**, symbolized by a yellow square.

Profane That which is not **sacred** or religious in nature. It may also be used to describe the act of being disrespectful or irreverent in a sacred place or debasing sacred objects in a blasphemous way. The **Black Mass** performed by **satanists** involves profane ceremonies which parody the Christian church service and the partaking of the **host**.

Prognosis In **predictive astrology**, the likely outcome that can be discerned following evaluation of the **horoscope** and its major **aspects**.

Progressed Horoscope See **Horoscope, Progressed**.

Prophecy From the Greek *prophetes*, "one who speaks before", a prediction made as the result of divine guidance or intervention. In the Bible, prophecies have become part of Christian doctrine. See also **Divination**; **Eschatology**.

Proserpina, Proserpine See **Persephone**.

Protean Soul In **occultism** and **magic**, the **astral body**, which can be shaped by the **imagination** to form a vehicle for journeys on the **astral plane**. It is this body which can be used in sorcery for **magical attack**. See also **Nagual**.

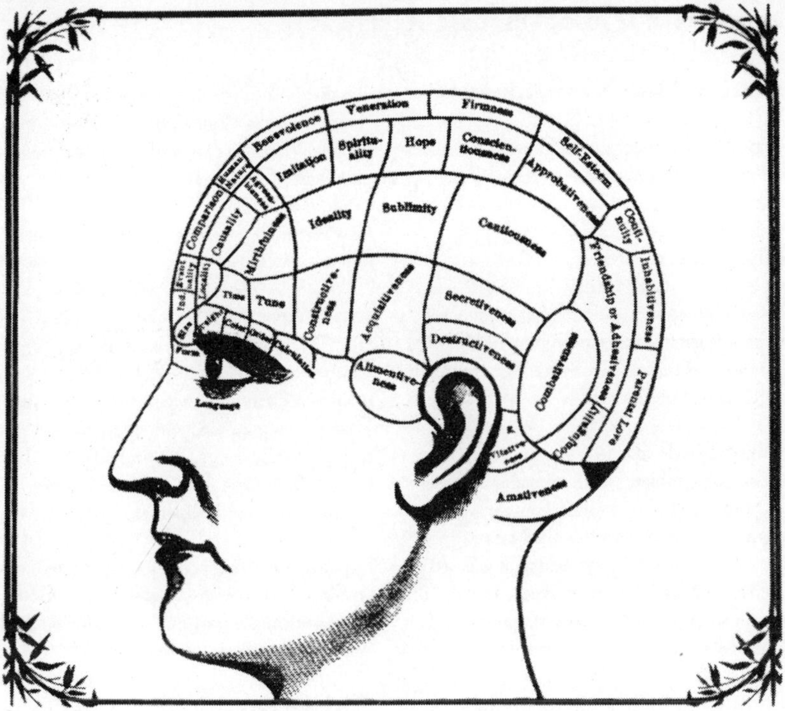

PHRENOLOGY: Traditionally, the art of reading the "bumps" on a person's skull in order to show that conformations of the skull correspond with characteristics of the mind and body. Despite the fact that phrenology for most people has been dismissed as a superstition or pseudo-science, modern-day phrenologists claim that their art has been misrepresented. In the same way that a tennis player might develop strengthened wrists and forearms, and an athlete specific muscles in the legs and torso, phrenologists claim that a similar relationship exists between aspects of the mind that a person chooses to develop, and external areas of the skull above specific regions of the brain. Contemporary practitioners spend many years studying charts of these correlations, taking into account different skull structures, hair growth and other variables. Phrenologists believe strongly that balanced development of the mind is essential and to this extent their views parallel those made by some contemporary psychologists that our technological society has been drawing too heavily on left-hemisphere activities of the brain (associated with analytical thought, logic, sequence and order), and undervaluing right-hemisphere functions of consciousness (artistic endeavour, holistic thought, orientation in space).

Protective Magic See Magic, Protective.

Providence Supernatural power that guides the course of events to a positive outcome. It may be distinguished from **fate** and **destiny**, which may be either favourable or unfavourable.

Psi Greek letter of the alphabet, often used to denote **extrasensory perception** and **paranormal** powers, which are then regarded as **psi phenomena**.

Psilocybin Psychedelic synthesized by Dr. Albert Hofmann from the hallucinatory mushroom *Psilocycbe mexicana*, which is regarded as a sacrament by the Mazatec Indians of Mexico. The mushroom is used by both healers and sorcerers because of its intoxicating properties. See also **Sabina, Maria**; **Shamanism**.

Psionic Medicine A development from medical **radiesthesia**, in which **pendulum dowsing** and **homeopathy** are combined with the so-called W. O. Wood chart – a triangular diagram that indicates degrees on a plus and minus scale. A sample of blood from the patient is placed in the right-hand corner of the triangle and the "diagnostic witness" (a group of tissues and diseases in homeopathic potency) on the left. Homeopathic remedies are placed at the apex of the triangle. According to practitioners, when the forces in the three corners are "in balance," indicating that the correct remedy has been found, the **dowser**'s pendulum maintains an even trajectory above the zero degree marker.

Psi Phenomena Paranormal powers. See also **Psi**.

Psychagogues Necromancers, who invoke the spirits of the dead. See also **Lévi, Eliphas**; **Necromancy**; **Peladan, Sar Josephin**.

Psyche Greek word for "mind", "consciousness", "spirit", and "soul" – originally used to denote the state of being alive, and the **life-force** itself. It is used in modern psychology to mean the mental faculties, encompassing both the conscious and unconscious mind.

Psychedelic From the Greek words *psyche*, "soul" or "mind", and *delos*, "evident", a substance that stimulates the contents of the unconscious mind to become manifest. The word is generally used with reference to hallucinogenic drugs **LSD**, and related chemicals. It was coined by **Dr. Humphry Osmond**. See also **Hallucination**.

Psychic One who possesses paranormal powers of **extrasensory perception**: **precognition**, **clairvoyance**, **mental telepathy**, ability to see and diagnose the **aura**.

Psychical Research Research into **paranormal** phenomena, the "latent" extrasensory powers of human beings, and all forms of psychic ability, including **mediums**, **trance** states, **dissociation** states, and events that suggest the existence of life after death.

Psychic Attack See **Magical Attack**.

Psychic Cord Term sometimes used by psychical researchers and parapsychologists to describe the **silver** cord that is said to connect the physical and astral bodies. It is sometimes reported during the **out-of-the-body experience**. See **Astral Projection**; **Green, Celia**.

Psychic Healing Healing techniques that use **psychic** or spiritual power. Often the healer is regarded as a channel for **cosmic** power that enters the body of the diseased person through **laying-on-of-hands** or through the **aura**. Psychic healing effected at a distance is known as **absent healing**. See also **Faith Healing**.

Psychic Medium In **spiritualism** and **parapsychology**, a person who is able to act as a channel for psychic communications with the spirit-world or who can receive clairvoyant or telepathic messages from other people at a distance. See also **Clairvoyance; Medium; Telepathy, Mental.**

Psychic Photography Photography that claims to depict the presence of **spirits, ghosts**, or other **discarnate** beings. One of the best-known practitioners of this form of photography was **William Hope**, whom psychical researcher **Harry Price** denounced as a fraud. The contemporary American psychic **Ted Serios** claims that he can transfer **thought-forms** onto a film through **mental telepathy**, a rather different faculty from that claimed by Hope. See also **Cottingley Fairies.**

Psychic Surgery Healing technique, practised in the Philippines and Brazil, in which the healer claims to make incisions in the body of his patient and perform surgical procedures, without the use of instruments. According to these practitioners, the force of **God** opens the bodies of the patients and allows the healer to locate diseased organs and remove malignant body tissue. There are currently approximately thirty psychic surgeons in the Philippines, and their claims have generated international controversy. In 1974 the American Judge Daniel H. Hanscom found, after a detailed inquiry, that the Filipino healers used sleight-of-hand techniques, concealed blood sacs, and substituted animal and vegetable matter to simulate surgery. Despite fierce press criticism and the hostility of the orthodox medical authorities, psychic surgeons continue to practise in several cities in the Philippines, the majority of practitioners operating from hotel foyers in conjunction with international travel agencies. There is no doubt that extraordinary and sometimes "miraculous" cures have occurred from time to time, but the question of whether these are in fact placebo cures remains the main issue in the debate.

Psychism Outmoded word, used in **Theosophy** and early spiritualist literature, meaning **extrasensory perception.**

Psychogram In **spiritualism**, a message from a **spirit** or **discarnate** entity.

Psychography See **Direct Writing.**

Psychokinesis In **parapsychology**, the **paranormal** ability to move physical objects through the powers of the mind. Several experiments have been held in parapsychology laboratories to try to demonstrate scientifically whether psychic subjects can influence the fall of dice. Psychokinesis is frequently abbreviated **PK.**

Psychometry Diagnostic technique of determining the characteristics of people who are not present, by means of objects that have been in their possession. The practitioner might use a personal object such as a watch, a ring, or other jewellery, and hold the object with the eyes closed, in order to receive psychic impressions of its owner. The term "psychometry" was coined by the psychical researcher Dr. J. R. Buchanan.

Psychoplasm In **spiritualism**, an alternative name for **ectoplasm**, the mysterious substance that sometimes emanates from **physical mediums** during a **seance.**

Psychosomatic That which relates to mind (*psyche*) and body (*soma*). The term is often used to describe stress-related diseases in which physical symptoms are produced by emotional traumas. Psychosomatic complaints can often be effectively treated by **hypnosis, meditation**, or **guided imagery.**

Ptah In ancient Egyptian religion, the creator of the universe. Ptah's cult had its centre at Memphis, where he was worshipped along with his wife **Sekhmet**, the lion goddess.

Puck Half-human, half-fairy, Puck was a **hobgoblin** who, in Shakespeare's *A Midsummer Night's Dream*, served as jester and attendant to King Oberon. He was a mischievous character, and could change the appearance of familiar objects as well as his own shape, and would mislead mortals with his tricks.

Puck-led To be inexplicably led astray, as if misguided by the hobgoblin **Puck**.

Puharich, Henry (Andrija) Karl (1918–) American parapsychologist best known for his close association with Israeli psychic **Uri Geller**. Puharich has had a distinguished career as a scientific researcher in the field of **mental telepathy**, and was also one of the first writers to draw attention to the sacramental properties of **psychedelic** mushrooms. His works include *The Sacred Mushroom* (1959), *Beyond Telepathy* (1962), and *Uri* (1974).

Pure Land Buddhism Sect of **Mahayana Buddhism** that emphasizes faith in the **Amida Buddha**, or Buddha of Infinite Light. For members of this sect, this Buddha is more exalted than **Gautama Buddha**. Pure Land Buddhism was introduced to China around A.D. 402 by Hui Yuan, and was established in Japan (where it is known as Jodo) by Honen during the twelfth century.

Purusha Sanskrit word used to denote the Spirit and also the idea of Heavenly or Archetypal Man. It is sometimes used interchangeably with **Brahma** and may be compared to the kabbalistic concept of **Adam Kadmon**. See also **Macrocosm and Microcosm**.

Pymander See **Poimandres**.

Pyramid, Great One of the largest (but not the highest) buildings in the world, with a base of fourteen acres and including 90 million cubic feet of stone, the Great Pyramid is located at Giza in Egypt and dates from the fifth millennium B.C. The Great Pyramid is aligned exactly to magnetic north, and its position is at the exact centre of the Earth's land mass. In ancient times the Great Pyramid had a polished limestone face that could reflect light like a beacon: the word "pyramid" itself translates as "glorious light" (from the Greek *pyros*, "fire").

Pyromancy Form of **divination** involving fire. The practitioner seeks prophetic guidance while throwing leaves, twigs, or incense into the flames of a fire. Changes in the colour of the flames, and their shape and intensity, are interpreted as an omen of things to come.

Pythagoras (c. 572–479 B.C.) Greek philosopher, mathematician, and **mystic**, born in Samos. He travelled in Egypt and then settled in Croton, southern Italy, where he established a religious brotherhood. Pythagoras taught several mystical doctrines, including the immortality of the **soul** and its **transmigration**, and the value of the contemplative life. A gifted mathematician, he related the orbits of the planets to the musical scale and originated the concept of the "music of the spheres".

Pythia See **Delphic Oracle**.

Q

Qabalah See Kabbalah.

QBL Hebrew word meaning "from mouth to ear" and thereby signifying a secret oral tradition. It provides the core meaning for the Qabalah or **Kabbalah**, the secret tradition of Jewish **mysticism**.

Qlippoth Also Kelipoth. In the **Kabbalah**, the negative or "impure" shells of existence, which formed during Creation. In modern Western **magic**, they are taken to be the spheres of the Tree of Evil, the obverse image of the **Tree of Life**.

Quadrants In **astrology**, the four quarters of the **horoscope** or **zodiac**. The quadrants of the horoscope are the **houses** one to three; four to six; seven to nine; and ten to twelve. In the zodiac, they are the **signs Aries** to **Gemini**; **Cancer** to **Virgo**; **Libra** to **Sagittarius**; and **Capricorn** to **Pisces**.

Quadrupedal In **astrology**, the **signs** of the **zodiac** represented by four-footed creatures: **Aries, Taurus, Leo, Sagittarius**, and **Capricorn**.

Quadruplicities In **astrology**, the division of the **signs** of the **zodiac** into threefold classification of **cardinal signs, fixed signs**, and **mutable signs**. The quadruplicities are **Aries, Cancer, Libra**, and **Capricorn** (cardinal); **Taurus, Leo, Scorpio**, and **Aquarius** (fixed); and **Gemini, Virgo, Sagittarius**, and **Pisces** (mutable).

Qualifications, Four In **Hinduism**, there are four "qualifications" for the person seeking spiritual liberation. They are vairagya (indifference, or objectivity); viveka (discrimination); mumukshutwa (the desire to awaken spiritual consciousness); and shatsampatti (the six accomplishments of self-control).

Quaternity In **Theosophy** and **numerology**, a union of four intrinsic components. Theosophists divide a person into four bodies (physical, etheric, astral, and the self); and **astrology** includes many combinations of four; including the four **signs** of the **zodiac**, which make up each of the three "crosses": the so-called mutable, fixed, and cardinal signs.

Querent In **astrology** or **divination**, one who asks questions of the **seer** or **fortune-teller**.

Quest Society Esoteric group established in 1909 by the Theosophical scholar **G. R. S. Mead** to study the Western **mystery** tradition.

Quetzalcoatl Toltec **deity** who featured prominently in the Aztec **pantheon** as **god** of the wind, fertility, and wisdom. Personified as a feathered serpent, he was said to have invented the science of agriculture and also the calendar, and was associated with the Morning Star. Quetzalcoatl ruled during a **golden age** and then disappeared. When Cortez landed in Mexico with his conquistadors, the Aztecs at first thought Quetzalcoatl had returned to them.

Quicksilver In **alchemy**, the metal associated with the planet **Mercury**. Quicksilver was regarded by some alchemists as a symbol of the **soul**.

Quimbanda In **Macumba**, a term used to denote **black magic** or **sorcery**.

Quimby, Phineas Parkhurst (1802–1866) American founder of **New Thought**, a system of mental healing in which the mind was considered the source for curing physical symptoms of disease. Quimby attended a lecture on **mesmerism** when he was thirty-six, and thereafter practised as a "magnetic healer". Quimby had a profound influence on **Mary Baker Eddy**, founder of **Christian Science**.

Quinary In **numerology**, **astrology**, and **mysticism**, a combination of five within a system. In astrology there are five planets beyond the orbit of the Earth around the **sun**; and in **Kundalini Yoga**, there are five "elemental" **chakras** (**Muladhara: Earth**; **Swadisthana: Water**; **Manipura: Fire**; **Anahata: Air**; and **Akasha: Spirit**). In modern Western **magic**, human beings are symbolized by the five-pointed star, or **pentagram**, See also **Elements**; **Tattvas**.

Quincunx In **astrology**, an **aspect** characterized by an angle of 150 degrees between the **planets**.

Quintessence In Pythagorean **mysticism**, the "fifth element" of **Spirit** that fills the universe and gives it life and vitality (the other **four elements** being **Earth**, **Water**, **Fire**, and **Air**). In **Hinduism**, the fifth element is **Akasha**; and in medieval **alchemy** it is the transcendental **Philosopher's Stone**. The quintessence is the "pure essence".

Qum In Iran, the holy city of the Shi'ite **Moslems**. It is located in central Iran, south of Tehran.

Qumran Site of the foothills on the north-western shores of the Dead Sea where the famous Dead Sea Scrolls were discovered. The **Essenes** established a monastic community there during the second century. Excavations began at Qumran in 1951.

Qur'an Also Koran. The sacred scripture of the **Moslems**. The text of the Qur'an was first revealed to **Mohammed** in a cave near **Mecca** by the **archangel** Jibril (**Gabriel**), who brought the texts in bundles bound in silk and embossed with precious stones from Paradise. Subsequent revelations occurred over a period of twenty-three years. Mohammed memorized the 114 suras, or chapters, as they were given to him, and wrote them down soon afterwards. They were arranged in their present order by a committee of followers who came together after Mohammed's death. Moslems interpret the Qur'an as the Word of God; and some maintain that while Mohammed served as a channel for these divine revelations, the original Qur'an is still in **Heaven**.

R

Ra In ancient Egyptian religion, the **sun**-god. The sky-goddess **Nut** carried Ra on her back to the heavens and he became lord and creator of the world. He subsequently became identified as a god of birth and **rebirth** because he would be reborn with the new dawn each day. The centre for the worship of Ra was at Heliopolis, and he was regarded as the main **deity** in the **Ennead.**

Rackham, Arthur (1867–1939) English book illustrator, internationally renowned for his pictures of **fairies, elves, goblins,** and water **nymphs.** Many of his best fairy-tale illustrations are included in his editions of *Rip Van Winkle* (1905), *A Midsummer Night's Dream* (1908), *The Rheingold and the Valkyrie* (1910), and *Peter Pan in Kensington Gardens* (1912).

Radical In **astrology**, that which pertains to the **radix.**

Radical Position In **astrology**, the position of a **planet** in a birth chart. See **Horoscope, Natal.**

Radiesthesia Technique of "medical dowsing", using a **pendulum.** In modern radiesthesia there are four basic movements of the pendulum over the body which provide an indication of disease: clockwise, counter-clockwise, left to right across the body, and away and towards the body at right-angles to it. Radiesthetists interpret the motions of the pendulum to indicate the presence or absence of **life-force**, or vitality, and regard disease as a form of inner imbalance.

Radionics System of alternative medicine developed by **Dr. Albert Abrams**, who believed that diseased body tissue affected the nervous system and gave forth dull "emanations". Abrams believed that electronic phenomena were possibly involved with this, and he invented a variable-resistance instrument called a "black box" to measure the ohm resistance and "electronic reactions" of different diseases. He found, for example, that cancer produced a 50-ohm resistance, while syphilis had a 55-ohm resistance. Abrams later modified his technique so he could take readings from a drop of blood. In 1924 a committee established by the Royal Society of Medicine investigated Abrams's techniques and were favourably impressed. However, radionics did not fare so well after Abrams's death. **Dr. Ruth Drown** in the United States and **George de la Warr** in England both developed new variants on the black boxes and made various claims concerning the diagnoses of disease, none of them scientific. Both Dr. Drown and George de la Warr, in their respective countries, were taken to court for fraud.

Radix In **astrology**, the **horoscope** drawn up for the moment of birth. See also **Solar Revolution Horoscope.**

Ragnarok In Scandinavian **mythology**, the time when nearly all of the **gods**, the universe, and all living things were destroyed. After the death of **Baler**, the great god **Odin** led an army forth from **Valhalla** to fight the **giants** and the forces of **evil.** Finally, the heavens fell and the world was totally destroyed. However, it was believed that the holocaust of Ragnarok would in turn give rise to a new breed of people and gods. Odin's son, **Vidar**, was among the survivors who would lead the resurgence and herald the Golden Age.

Ra-Horakte Also Ra Harakhte. In ancient Egyptian religion, the title of **Ra**, the **sun**-god, in his form as a falcon bearing the solar disc. The designation "Horakte" means "Horus of the Horizon". See also **Horus.**

Rais, Gilles de (1404–1440) French marshal who fought alongside Joan of Arc at

Orleans. He is remembered primarily, however, as the murderer of at least 140 children whose hearts, hands, eyes, and blood he used in appalling demonic **rituals**. After a trial before the Bishop of Nantes, he was sentenced to death and hanged.

Rajas In Hindu **cosmology**, one of the three **gunas**, or characteristics of primordial matter. Rajas has the quality of motion. The other two gunas are **sattva** (harmony) and **tamas** (inertia).

Raja Yoga System of "royal" **yoga** based on the Sutras of **Patanjali**. Raja Yoga has eight branches, each of which is referred to as an anga, or "limb". Together the eight limbs create a unity of thought and purpose and allow the practitioner to find union with **Brahman**. The eight angas are: **yama** (ethical restraints), **niyama** (moral observances); **asana** (**meditation** posture); **pranayama** (control of the breath); pratyahara (mastery of the senses); **dharana** (mental concentration); **dhyana** (meditation); and **samadhi** (attainment of **cosmic consciousness**).

Rajneesh, Bhagwan Shree (1931–1990) Indian spiritual teacher and **mystic** who, at one time, headed large communities in Poona in India and Oregon in the United States. A former university academic, Rajneesh was recognized by some as an important spiritual philosopher whose discourses paralleled those of **Krishnamurti**. Rajneesh had particular appeal to a Western audience, and created controversy for encouraging his followers, or **sannyasins**, to free themselves from constricting moral codes. While he was typecast as the "sex guru" by the popular media, this description undervalues his achievements. The teachings of Rajneesh in fact encompass many religions, but he is not defined by any of them. He was an illuminating speaker on **Zen**, **Taoism**, Tibetan **Buddhism**, Christianity, and ancient Greek philosophy; and was also an advocate of bioenergy and modern bodywork therapies. Rajneesh, known later in his life as Osho, was a prolific author and his many books include *The Book of Secrets*, *The Empty Boat*, *The Hidden Harmony*, *Meditation: The Art of Ecstasy*, *Only One Sky*, *Returning to the Source*, *Roots and Wings*, *The Supreme Doctrine*, *My Way: The Way of the White Clouds*, and *The Orange Book*.

Rakshasas In Indian **mythology**, **evil** and violent beings who could transform their appearance through their magical powers. Their king was **Ravana**.

Rama In Indian **mythology**, an **avatar** of **Vishnu** who incarnated as **Ramachandra**, Parasu-Rama, and Balarama.

Ramachandra In **Hinduism**, the seventh **incarnation** of **Vishnu**. He was depicted as the ideal hero: charming, virtuous, and courageous – the embodiment of righteousness. He plays an important role in the ***Ramayana***, an epic work describing his travels and challenges; and he was the enemy of the demon **Ravana**, who snatched his beautiful wife **Sita** away, but was finally overcome. Ramachandra is often known simply as Rama, although this can lead to confusion since Rama also incarnated as Parasu-Rama in his sixth incarnation of Vishnu.

Ramakrishna, Paramahamsa (1836–1886) Indian **mystic**, born in Bengal. Ramakrishna had religious experiences as a child and once, while enacting the role of **Shiva** in a play, fell into a **trance** state for three days. At the age of twenty Ramakrishna became chief **priest** in a temple dedicated to **Kali**, and her worship became dominant in his life. After an unsuccessful marriage to a child bride, Ramakrishna came to believe that sexuality was an obstacle to mystical consciousness and he remained celibate for the rest of his life. One of his most famous disciples was Swami Vivekananda, who popularized his cause. Ramakrishna is best known for his view that "many paths lead to the same God." He was also convinced that the true essence of religion lay in experience, not in doctrine.

Ramayana Indian epic poem consisting of 24,000 couplets. The poem, which is earlier than the ***Mahabharata***, describes the challenges of Rama (i.e. **Ramachandra**), including his quest to save his lovely wife **Sita** from the clutches of the demon-king **Ravana**. Ravana imprisoned Sita in his island kingdom of Lanka; but Rama constructed a bridge to the island, assisted by Nala, and invaded Lanka with an army of monkeys. Finally, the contest resolved itself when Rama pierced Ravana's chest with an arrow. Five of the seven books in the *Ramayana* are ascribed to the fourth-century writer Valmiki; the other two are by unknown poets.

Ram Dass, Baba (1931–) Spiritual name of former Harvard psychologist Richard Alpert, who became a colleague and friend of **Timothy Leary** and a key figure in the **LSD** controversy of the 1960s. Alpert's spiritual direction changed when he went to India to show LSD to the holy men. A Californian named Bhagwan Dass took Alpert to a **sadhu** known as the Maharaji, who lived in the foothills of the Himalayas, and Alpert offered the guru his sacrament. The holy man then proceeded to consume over 900 micrograms of LSD – around four times the normal dose – and was apparently totally unaffected.

Convinced that he had found a guru whose consciousness transcended biophysical stimulation, Alpert became a convert to **Raja Yoga** and took the name Baba Ram Dass. Ram Dass now lectures widely on the Indian spiritual tradition, relating it in a popular but insightful way to aspects of modern Western life. He also provides help and support to the dying.

Ram Dass is the author of several books, including *Be Here Now* (1971), *Doing your Own Being* (1973), and *Grist for the Mill* (co-authored with Stephen Levine, 1979). While still Richard Alpert, he had co-authored a guide to LSD exploration based on the ***Tibetan Book of the Dead***, entitled *The Psychedelic Experience* (written with Timothy Leary and Ralph Metzner, 1964).

Randolph, Pascal Beverley (1825–1871) American Rosicrucian, Freemason, and medium who founded several groups. Randolph was a member of the Societas Rosicruciana in Anglia – an important predecessor to the **Hermetic Order of the Golden Dawn**. He became interested in sexual magic and is believed to have taught **Karl Kellner** a number of techniques which subsequently emerged as teachings within the **Ordo Templi Orientis**.

Raphael The astrological pseudonym of Robert Cross Smith (1795–1832), who gave his name to the original *Raphael's Astronomical Ephemeris*. This publication is still issued annually and gives listings of planetary positions at noon and midnight for each day of the year, as well as other information useful for astrologers. There have been many "Raphaels" since Smith, ensuring the continuity of the ***Ephemeris***. See also **Astrology**.

Raphael One of the seven **archangels**, or messengers, of **God**. Raphael features prominently in the apocryphal *Book of Tobit*, and also plays an important role in modern Western **magic** where he is invoked in the East as the archangel of **Air**. He is associated with the sphere of **Tiphareth** on the kabbalistic **Tree of Life**.

Rappings In **spiritualism**, noises produced by **spirits** as a means of communicating with the living. See also **Poltergeists**.

Rapport In **parapsychology**, the **paranormal** bond of mystical connection between two individuals, which seems to be related to such extrasensory powers as **mental telepathy**.

Rapture A sudden state of joyous **ecstasy** associated with some types of devotional **mysticism**. St. Teresa de Jesus is said to have compared it to a state of drunkenness.

Rasputin, Grigori Efimovich (1872–1916) Siberian **mystic** credited with clairvoyant and healing powers. After deserting his family he became a member of the Khylsty sect, whose members practised flagellation and sexual rites, believing – like the **Gnostics** – that the human body was **evil** and the **spirit** pure. However, the Khylsts were also dedicated to Christ and believed in the healing power of **prayer**. Rasputin was presented to Czar Nicholas II in November 1905, and soon became a close associate of the royal family. He enhanced his reputation as a healer by touching the bleeding leg of the infant Alexis – who suffered from haemophilia – and announced that he would overcome the dreaded complaint. Later, Rasputin warned the Czar that war would ensue in Europe, but this prophecy was ignored. After a series of political intrigues and changes in the balance of power in Russia, Rasputin was finally poisoned and shot by Prince Felix Yusupov.

Raudive, Dr. Konstantin See **Electronic Voice Phenomenon**.

Rav Hebrew word meaning a "master". The expression *Rav Ha-Hasid* means "a master of devotion".

Ravana In Indian **mythology**, the demon king of the **Rakshasas**, who lived in the kingdom of Lanka (Sri Lanka, the former Ceylon). He incarnated as **Vishnu**'s enemy three times, the second as the deadly foe of Rama (i.e. **Ramachandra**). He was finally slain in combat by an arrow from Rama's bow.

Raymond Son of noted psychical researcher **Sir Oliver Lodge**. Lodge believed he obtained spirit-communication from his son at **seances**, and published a book on that subject, *Raymond*, in 1916.

Rays, Seven Theosophical teaching which maintains that the universe evolves along seven paths, or "rays", and that every living creature is developing along one of these paths.

Re See **Ra**.

Rebirth Mystical term, which can refer either to **reincarnation** or the act of spiritual awakening. See also **Enlightenment**; **Initiation**; **Metempsychosis**; **Transmigration**.

Rectification In **astrology**, the process of clarifying an uncertain birth-time by evaluating known personal characteristics or events in one's life, and relating them back to characteristics of a **natal horoscope** that matches these factors.

Redcap In Scottish **folklore**, an evil **spirit** who took the form of an old man with long nails and a red cap stained with blood. Often found lurking in the peel-towers located on the Scottish border, he could be driven away by the sign of the cross or by reciting verses from the Bible.

Regardie, Dr. Francis Israel (1907–1985) English-born authority on ritual magic who lived most of his life in the United States. Regardie was at one time **Aleister Crowley**'s personal secretary and became a member of the Stella Matutina, a magical group descended from the **Hermetic Order of the Golden Dawn**. Regardie attracted considerable controversy in occult circles when he published the complete rituals of the order (1937–1940), but this four-volume source work, *The Golden Dawn*, is now regarded as the bible of practising ceremonial **occultists**. Regardie is widely considered to have been the foremost authority on modern Western magic. His most important books include *The Tree of Life* (1932; republished 1969), *The Philosopher's Stone* (1938; republished 1970), *The Art of True Healing* (1964), and *Ceremonial Magic* (1982). His biography of Aleister Crowley, *The Eye in the Triangle* (1970), is one of the major works on the celebrated ceremonial magician.

Reichenbach, Baron Karl von (1788–1869) German physicist whose place in occult history is somewhat akin to that of **Anton Mesmer**. Reichenbach claimed to have discovered an **emanation** or radiation present in animals, plants, magnets, and crystals, as well as human beings, and believed it could be perceived by **psychics** as a type of luminosity. Reichenbach experimented with **sensitives** who could see this force clearly in a darkened room. His term for it was the **odic force**.

Reincarnation The belief that one's identity survives physical **death** and may be reborn in different physical bodies, in a succession of future lives. Belief in reincarnation is commonly associated with the concept of spiritual evolution. In **Hinduism**, the **karma** earned in the present lifetime has a direct bearing on the subsequent incarnation. Reincarnation is an important part of Hindu and Buddhist belief, and has also been central in the Western **mystery** tradition. Many influential thinkers, including **Pythagoras**, **Plato**, **Plotinus**, Hegel, Emerson, and **William James** have embraced it; and it is an accepted teaching among most adherents of modern **Theosophy**, **spiritualism**, and **occultism**. The most impressive evidence for the reality of reincarnation is contained in *Twenty Cases Suggestive of Reincarnation* (1995) by **Dr. Ian Stevenson**, of the School of Medicine at the University of Virginia. Dr. Stevenson specialises in cases involving verifiable reincarnational memories in young children. See also **Metempsychosis**; **Rebirth**; **Transmigration**.

Relic Object venerated because of its connection with an important spiritual figure or saint.

Religion A system of beliefs and practices relating to the worship of **supernatural** beings, **deities**, **spirits** or **God**. Religions can be of two sorts: **monotheism**, which entails belief in one god; or **polytheism**, in which more than one **deity** is worshipped.

REM Periods In psychology, periods of rapid eye movements (REMs), which are accompanied by dreaming. See also **Dreams**; **Non-REM Period**.

Rescue Circles In **spiritualism**, meetings specially convened to advise **discarnate** beings that they are actually dead and to offer prayers releasing them from their ties with the living. Rescue circles are believed to assist those who have experienced sudden **death** and are unaccustomed to their newly discovered discarnate condition.

Resurrection The religious belief that one may rise again from the dead. Although this doctrine is most commonly associated with Jesus Christ, followers of **Osiris** in ancient Egypt and **Attis** in Phrygia similarly believed in a resurrected god. According to leading authority on comparative religion **Mircea Eliade**, belief in resurrection is characteristic of a culture with a linear **cosmology** (creation-life-death-final judgment); whereas **reincarnation** – a related, but distinctly different doctrine – is more characteristic of "cyclic" cosmologies, which place less emphasis on the origin of the world and the concept of a final judgment.

Retreat A place where mystical practitioners can withdraw for the purpose of spiritual contemplation, often under the guidance of a teacher or **guru**.

Retrocognition In **parapsychology**, knowledge of past events obtained by

paranormal means. It is the exact opposite of **precognition**.

Retrograde In **astrology**, a term applied to the apparent backward motion of a **planet** in relation to the **zodiac**. Retrograde movements occur when planets decrease in longitude viewed from the Earth.

Reuss, Theodor (1855–1923) German **occultist** who succeeded **Karl Kellner** as head of the **Ordo Templi Orientis**. Reuss dispensed charters of membership to several prominent occultists, including **Papus** and **Rudolph Steiner**. In 1922 he resigned from the order, appointing **Aleister Crowley** his successor.

Revelation From the Latin *revelare*, something that has been revealed. In **mysticism**, this is often a sacred or **esoteric** truth revealed by a divine being, or **god**. See also **Apocalypse**.

Revenant From the French *revenir*, "to return", a **ghost** or **discarnate** being who has returned from the dead, often for a specific purpose: to avenge a wrongdoing, or to make contact with a loved one. See also **Necromancy**.

Rhabdic Force Force that **dowsers** maintain is active when the **divining rod** is being used to detect subterranean water.

Rhabdomancy The art of **divination** by using a rod. The term is generally associated with **dowsing**, but also applies to divination by interpreting the flight of arrows. See also **Dowsers; Hazel**.

Rhapsodomancy Form of **divination** in which one opens a sacred book and interprets as prophetic the first line that comes to view.

Rhea In Greek **mythology**, the sister and wife of **Kronos** and the mother of the **gods**. Her children included **Demeter, Hades, Poseidon**, and **Zeus**.

Rhiannon Celtic fertility **goddess**. In Wales she was regarded as the "Great Queen", and was depicted as a mare-goddess.

Rhine, Dr. Joseph Banks (1895–1980) Distinguished American psychical researcher who co-founded the Parapsychology Laboratory at Duke University in 1935 with **Dr. William McDougall**. Rhine was its Director until 1965, when he retired. He is often referred to as the father of **parapsychology** – a term he invented – for he put research into **mental telepathy, clairvoyance, precognition**, and **psychokinesis** onto a systematic, scientific basis. He made use of **Zener cards** in his **extrasensory perception** (**ESP**) tests, and over many years performed a number of experiments that seemed to indicate the presence of **psi phenomena** at a level greater than could be expected through chance. After his retirement, Dr. Rhine continued to research ESP and held summer schools dealing with the subject. He was the author of many books in the field, including *Extra-Sensory Perception* (1935), *The Reach of the Mind* (1947), *New World of the Mind* (1953), and *Parapsychology, Frontier Science of the Mind* (1957). See also **Psychical Research**.

Richet, Professor Charles Robert (1850–1935) Nobel Prize-winning physiologist who was also a prominent psychical researcher and investigated the **trance medium Eusapia Palladino**. He became president of the **Society of Psychical Research** in London in 1905, and in 1918 became honorary president of the Institut Métapsychique International in Paris. Richet was fascinated by **extrasensory perception**, which he believed to be a natural, latent function of human consciousness. He coined the term *métapsychique* as the French equivalent of **psychical research**.

Right-hand Path In **mysticism** and **occultism**, the **esoteric** path associated with spiritual **illumination**, virtue, and positive aspirations. It is the path of **Light**, as distinct from the so-called **left-hand path** of darkness, which runs counter to spiritual evolution and equates with **evil**, bestiality, and **black magic**. See also **Magic, White**.

Rig-Veda See **Vedas**.

Ring, Kenneth (1935–) American psychologist and researcher who is internationally regarded as one of the leading authorities on the **near-death experience**. Ring received his PhD from the University of Minnesota and has served as an editorial advisor for *ReVision*, a leading journal in transpersonal psychology. His main contribution to consciousness research has been in the field of near-death studies, and he is credited with producing the first scientific investigation of this phenomenon, the results of which were published in his first book *Life at Death* (1980). Since then he has produced several other important publications on this topic, including *Heading Toward Omega*, *The Omega Project*, *Lessons from the Light* and a co-authored book titled *Mindsight* which describes the near-death experiences of blind people.

Ring-pass-not Mystical expression relating to the "circle of bounds", which limits the consciousness of **occultists** who have not yet attained higher states of spiritual unity.

Rinpoche Honorific term among Tibetan **Buddhists**, used in addressing a **lama**. It translates as "precious one".

Rishi An Indian holy man or **seer**, especially one who has the mystical ability to interpret divine law.

Rishis In Indian **cosmology**, seven mythic beings who preserved and handed down the sacred knowledge contained in the **Vedas**. The seven Rishis were the stars in the constellation of the Great Bear. The term rishi now has general usage, meaning a **seer**.

Rising Sign In **astrology**, the **sign** rising on the eastern horizon at the moment of birth. It is usually referred to as the **ascendant**.

Rites of Passage Rites of **initiation** in which a **neophyte** undergoes a symbolic ceremony that leads from one status to another. Rites of passage are often associated with major life changes (birth, puberty, marriage, death).

Ritod In Tibet, a house or dwelling used for **meditation**. It is usually in a secluded location, in a mountain valley or near a lake.

Ritual A prescribed form of religious or magical ceremony, often designed to invoke or placate a **deity**. Rituals are characterized by symbolic attire and formalized behaviour, and may involve imitating the deity in a ceremonial context in order to obtain **supernatural** power, spiritual **illumination**, or other specific blessings from the god who is worshipped.

Ritual Magic See **Magic, Ceremonial**.

Robes Ceremonial costumes worn by the **priests** of religious denominations and also by ritual **magicians**. They usually have symbolic significance, their colour and design indicating a season, a **god**, or motifs of cosmological importance.

Robin Goodfellow In British **folklore**, a name for the **hobgoblin Puck**, who was noted for his mischievous tricks and his habit of misleading travellers. He was also able to change shape.

Roc Also Rukh. Enormous mythic bird, which was believed to feed on young elephants and serpents and resembled an eagle. It is described in the *Arabian Nights*. On one occasion, Sinbad the Sailor climbed onto its huge foot and was carried away by it. However, he alighted safely and discovered the Valley of Diamonds. The Roc bears some resemblance to both the **Griffin** and the **Garuda** bird.

Rods See **Wands**.

Rolle, Richard (c. 1300–1349) Yorkshire-born poet who is regarded as the first mystical writer in the English language. Rolle was a devotional **mystic** and expressed his longing for **God** in terms of love and joy. The holy name of Jesu formed part of his **meditation** and, by his own account, rescued him from the **Devil**'s temptations.

Rompo Mythic creature, found in India and Africa, which was a composite animal that combined the features of a hare, a badger, and a bear. It had human ears and fed on dead people. Some researchers believe that it derives in part from a hyena.

Root Races Theosophical teaching that humankind has evolved through different phases of spiritual growth and intellectual development, each of these being known as a root race. The present state of humanity is broadly identified as the fifth root race. It was preceded by the Atlantean (fourth) and Lemurian (third) root races, both of which were engulfed in cataclysms.

Rosae Rubeae et Aureae Cruci The Red Rose and the Cross of Gold: the name of the inner or Second Order of the **Hermetic Order of the Golden Dawn**. Its grades included Adeptus Minor, Adeptus Major, and Adeptus Exemptus, and it embraced the spheres of **Tiphareth**, **Geburah**, and **Chesed** on the kabbalistic **Tree of Life**. See also **Adept**; **Kabbalah**.

Rose Cross A golden cross with a rose at its centre: the emblem of the **esoteric** order of the **Rosicrucians**.

Rosemary A plant with mythic and magical associations. It was believed to ward off evil **spirits**, **witches**, and **fairies**, and was also a protection against storms. At funerals, sprigs of rosemary symbolize remembrance.

Rosenkreuz, Christian See **Rosicrucians**.

Rosenroth, Christian Knorr von (1636–1689) German baron who travelled widely in western Europe, acquiring a strong interest in both Christian and kabbalistic **mysticism**. He is best known for translating the main books of the ***Zohar*** into Latin, under the title *Kabbala Denudata* ("The Kabbalah Unveiled"). This work, published in two volumes (1677–1684), gave many readers access to the *Zohar* for the first time, and until the late nineteenth century it remained the major non-Jewish source-work for the Kabbalah. Rosenroth's translation was rendered into English by **MacGregor Mathers** in 1887.

Roshi In **Zen Buddhism**, a Master of exalted rank.

Rosicrucians Name used by many occult groups who have claimed inspiration from Christian Rosenkreuz. The origin of the Rosicrucians ("Rosy Cross") dates from the publication around 1614–1616 of three books purporting to emanate from an occult brotherhood. (It is likely that all three were written by Johann Valentin Andreae.) The first of these publications, *Fama Fraternitatis*, described Christian Rosenkreuz's meeting with the Wise Men of Damcar and how he translated the mystical book *Liber M* into Latin. The second, *Confessio Fraternitatis R.C.*, provided more details of Christian Rosenkreuz and invited members of the public to join the Order. The third, *Chymische Hochzeit Christiani Rosenkreutz*, was a hermetic allegory in which the central figure witnesses a Royal Marriage and later discovers the King's "secret books of wisdom".

The Rosicrucian **myth** has been a strong influence on several mystical groups, including the **Hermetic Order of the Golden Dawn** (who incorporated Rosicrucian elements into their Second Order **initiations**). Similarly, **Dr. Franz Hartmann** started a Rosicrucian order in Germany; and **Sar Josephin Peladan** ran a fashionable Rosicrucian salon in Paris. Competing Rosicrucian orders of questionable authenticity now market the **esoteric** wisdom of Christian Rosenkreuz in the United States.

Roszák, Theodore American historian and philosopher who has written widely on alternative approaches to spirituality. A recipient of a Guggenheim Fellowship, Roszak teaches at California State University. Roszak coined the term "counterculture" and was among the first observers to discern a new spiritual force amidst the eclecticism and diverse metaphysical perspectives embraced by American youth. His most influential books include *The Making of a Counter Culture, Where the Wasteland Ends, Unfinished Animal* and *The Voice of the Earth.*

Rowan Tree with mythic and magical associations. The rowan, or mountain ash, was sacred among the **Druids** and was regarded in the Middle Ages as protection against **witchcraft** and the forces of **evil**. Rowan-Tree Witch Day was celebrated at the Celtic festival of **Beltane**.

Ruach In the **Kabbalah**, that part of the **soul** that lies between the **Neschamah** and the **Nephesch**. Referred to by **magicians** as the "higher astral soul", the Ruach corresponds to the spiritual realm between, and including, **Chesed** and **Hod** on the **Tree of Life**.

Rudra Indian **demon**-god of storms and fierce winds, also associated with the forces of **death**. A skilful archer, he would bring disease with his arrows.

Rudras In Hindu **cosmology**, **supernatural** beings who dwell between the earth and sky and assist **Rudra**, the god of storms and disease.

Ruler In **astrology**, planets that are said to rule the different **signs** of the **zodiac**. The modern astrological ascriptions (including Pluto) are as follows: **Mars** (**Aries**); **Venus** (**Taurus** and **Libra**); **Mercury** (**Gemini**); **moon** (**Cancer**); **sun** (**Leo**); **Mercury** (**Virgo**); **Pluto** (**Scorpio**); **Jupiter** (**Sagittarius**); **Saturn** (**Capricorn**); **Uranus** (**Aquarius**); and **Neptune** (**Pisces**).

Ruler In **numerology**, the number one arrives at after totalling the numbers in the birth-date and "reducing" the total to a number between 2 and 11 (a "double 11" is also possible). According to numerologists, the ruling number provides insights for the "basic guidance" of our lives.

Rumi, Jalal'al-Din (1207–1273) Persian mystical poet, born in Balkh (northern Afghanistan). He is best known for his extraordinary book *Mathnawi*, which captures the essence of Sufi thought and consists of 25,000 rhyming couplets. Rumi describes the sacred "One-ness" of **God** and the **transcendental** rapture of those who have attained the vision of his divine mystery. Rumi's **mysticism** is never puritanical. He became a **whirling dervish** and was exuberant and passionate in his approach to mystical **ecstasy**. "I was a grave man of formal praying," he wrote, acknowledging his dervish teacher **Shams of Tabriz**. "You made me the sport of the children in the street." He also wrote many poems about love and wine – which for him were symbolic of mystical experience – and believed that people and God could find each other in many mysterious ways. In so doing, Rumi believed, people mirrored the **Godhead**: "We are the flute, the music you; The mountain we, which echoes you …"

Rumi's literary outpouring was enormous. In addition to the *Mathnawi*, he also wrote over two thousand mystical odes, which are contained in the *Diwani Shamsi Tabriz*; as well as the *Rubaiyat*, which contains at least 1600 quatrains that can be ascribed to his authorship. Rumi is generally regarded as the greatest mystical poet in the Persian language. See also **Sufism**.

Runes From the German *raunen*, meaning "a secret" or "mystery", occult symbols that are known in many areas of northern Europe. According to one tradition the Scandinavian god **Odin** hung for nine days and nights on the **World Tree** and paid with one of his eyes for his knowledge of the runes. However, the runes that feature in **modern witchcraft** may be of more modern origin. They are sometimes known as the "Alphabet of Honorius".

Rusalki In Slavonic folk belief, the **spirits** of girls whose deaths were the result of drowning. The Rusalki were mischievous spirits and were regarded as the divinities of streams, rivers, and forests.

Russell, George William (1867–1935) Better known by his pen-name, "A.E.", Russell was born in Northern Ireland and later met **William Butler Yeats** at Dublin Art School. They became good friends and shared many mystical and cultural interests. Both had affiliations with the **Theosophical Society**, and both became important figures in the so-called Irish literary renaissance. A natural **mystic**, Russell knew both the ascent of the **soul** towards light and also its plunge into despair and doubt. A superbly lyrical writer he is best known for his classical book *The Candle of Vision* (1918). His other books include *Song and its Fountains*, *Homeward Songs by the Way*, and *The Avatars*. Russell was also a talented artist and produced mystical paintings comparable in style to those of Odilon Redon.

S

Sabazius Phrygian **deity** sometimes identified with **Dionysus, Zeus,** and **Jupiter** and worshipped in Athens in the late fifth century B.C. Symbolized by a snake, he was often portrayed bearing the thunderbolt of Zeus.

Sabbaths, Greater In **Wicca**, the celebrations of **Candlemas** (February 2), **May Eve** (April 30), **Lammas** (August 1) and **Halloween** (October 31). The traditional Druidic names for these celebrations are **Imbolc** or Oimelc, **Beltane, Lughnassadh** and **Samhain** respectively.

Sabbaths, Lesser In **Wicca**, the celebrations held at the time of the midsummer and midwinter solstices, and the equinoxes in spring and autumn.

Sabbatic Goat A term applied to **Baphomet**.

Sabbats, Witches' See **Sabbaths, Greater; Sabbaths, Lesser**.

Sacrament A **ritual** or object that has special ceremonial significance and is regarded as the outward, visible sign of inner spiritual grace. In Christianity, the **host** and wine taken in communion are sacraments because for the devotee they are the body and blood of Christ. In certain pre-literate societies, especially those involving **shamanism**, the **god** may be identified with a mushroom or sacred plant that is eaten to provide communion with the spirit-world.

Sacred That which is holy, or dedicated to a **god**. The opposite of **profane**.

Sacrifice An offering made to a **deity**, often upon an altar. Sacrifices are performed ritually to placate the **god** and to offer blood

– which is symbolic of the **life-force** and invariably associated with fertility. Some **magicians** believe that the **ritual** slaughter of a sacrificial animal releases life energy, which can be tapped magically and used to attune the magician to the god invoked in ritual (e.g. **doves** are symbolic of the goddess **Venus**). In many pre-literate societies, the sacrificed animal may become the "scapegoat" for infringements of taboos by members of that group. Here the act of sacrificing the creature ceremonially has a purgative effect, eliminating potential harm and **evil**.

Saddha Hindu term for one who possesses the **supernatural** powers or **siddhis**, which arise in advanced forms of **yoga**.

Sadhana In **Hinduism**, a general term for exercises that are believed to lead to **self-realization**, or spiritual **illumination**. They often involve supervision by a **guru**.

Sadhu Hindu term for a holy man or **ascetic** who has renounced the world in order to seek spiritual liberation.

Sagittarius In **astrology**, the **sign** of the **zodiac** for those born between November 23 and December 21. A **Fire** sign, ruled by **Jupiter, Sagittarius** is symbolized by the **centaur** – half-horse, half-man – which represents the conflict between the intellect and the animal instincts. Those born under the sign of Sagittarius are said to be often rebellious and strong-willed, but honest and trustworthy. They are generous, artistic, and musical and make excellent organizers. For this reason they are ideally suited to professional administrative roles, provided they can curb their naturally independent instincts.

Sahasrara In **yoga**, the supreme **chakra** or psychic centre, often identified with the pineal gland, and referred to as the "thousand-petalled lotus". It is the dwelling place of **Shiva**, the **god** who drives away ignorance.

Sahu In ancient Egyptian **magic** and religion, the "highest" of the five human bodies, sometimes known as the "spiritual body". It is through the sahu that the **magician** or **priest** perceives the **transcendental** gods and undergoes spiritual transformation. The names of the other four "bodies" in Egyptian religious belief are **Aufu, Ka, Haidit**, and **Khu**.

Sai Baba (1856–1918) Indian **Bhakti** mystic from Hisderabad who lived for most of his life in a rundown **mosque** in the village of Shirdi. He began to acquire a reputation for **miracles** and was known for his ability to **astral travel** and predict the future. A sacred fire, which he lit and tended through his lifetime, has been maintained to this day by his supporters; and the ashes of the fire are believed to have healing properties. Consequently, the mosque where Sai Baba lived has now become a shrine for pilgrims.

Saint One who is holy or possessed of **God**. The term is often used to refer to Christian men and women who have been canonized by the Roman Catholic Church, but it also has general application and is sometimes used to denote spiritual leaders and **mystics** in the Hindu and Buddhist traditions.

Saint Germain, Comte de (1710–1780) Famous **Rosicrucian adept** who claimed to be immortal. Said to be the son of Prince Rakoczy of Transylvania, the Comte was educated at the University of Siena and later visited several European courts, where he masqueraded under many grandiose titles. He was known variously as Comte Bellamarre, Marquis de Montserrat, and Chevalier Schoening, and could speak several languages. The Comte enticed his audience with his extravagant claims, including the tale that he had received the magical **wand** of Moses from

King Cyrus in Babylon, thereby maintaining that he was one of the **Illuminati**. The Comte de Saint Germain was said to have derived his wealth from his knowledge of **alchemy** and his discovery of the secret of the **Philosopher's Stone**. Despite his flamboyant claims, he is certainly among the most remarkable of all occult writers and his initiatory book *The Most Holy Trinosophia* is a significant contribution to the Western mystical tradition.

Sakta See **Shakta**.

Sakti See **Shakti**.

Sakyamuni Name by which **Gautama Buddha** is known. It translates as "the sage of the Sakyas", a reference to the clan to which Gautama belonged. See also **Muni**.

Salam Word used as a greeting among **Moslems**, it means "peace".

Salamander In medieval **alchemy** and **magic**, the spirit of the element **Fire**. The mythic salamander is a lizard that was believed to dwell within the flames and was nourished by fire. It bears no resemblance to the order of amphibians known as Caudara, which are a factual species.

Salem Witches Salem, Massachusetts (now renamed Danvers), became notorious in 1692 as the result of a **witch-hunt** that culminated in a dramatic trial. Two young girls, Elizabeth Parris and Abigail Williams, accused a Carib Indian house slave named Tituba, and two other women – **Sarah Good** and Sarah Osburn – of being **witches** and harassing them with magic **spells**. Tituba "confessed" to these crimes, and a feeling of hysteria and fear quickly spread among the local Puritan inhabitants. Many others were accused of being witches, and people became frightened of venturing out at night in case **Satan** or evil forces ensnared them. In due course, two hundred people were arrested in New England and thirty-four – including Sara Good – went to the gallows. The Salem witchcraft incident bears comparison with the Loudon and **Aix-en-Provence** demonic hysteria cases although it is now thought to have been caused by ergot poisoning, which induces vivid hallucinations. See also **Grandier, Urbain; Hysteria; Witchcraft.**

Salt In **alchemy**, the symbol of Earth and the body, personified as female. Salt was regarded by the alchemists as one of the three vital ingredients of Nature, the other two constituents being **sulphur** and **mercury**, representing the **spirit** and **soul** respectively.

Samadhi Hindu term, also used in **Jainism** and **Buddhism**, referring to the highest stage of yogic **meditation**. Samadhi is the eighth limb, or **anga**, in the Sutras of **Patanjali** – which form the basis of **Raja Yoga**. This stage of yogic consciousness leads to **self-realization**; it is referred to in the *Bhagavad-Gita* as "seeing the self in all things and all things in the self."

Samadhi Tank A sensory deprivation tank that totally eliminates all visual and auditory stimuli. The subject enters the tank, which contains saline water slightly above body temperature, and floats naked in total darkness for extended periods of time. Sessions in a samadhi tank can produce profound mystical experiences. See also **Lilly, Dr. John**.

Samhain A major **Wiccan** sabbath, also known as Halloween and celebrated on October 31, Samhain is a celebration to honour the dead. *Samhain* means "summer's end" and it is a time of grieving, as the dying sun passes into the nether world. However Samhain is regarded as both an ending and a beginning – for the sun-god will be reborn with the passage of the seasons. Samhain is said to be the time of the year when the thin veil between the everyday and nether worlds is most transparent – allowing Wiccans to communicate more readily with the spirits of the departed. Samhain is also a time to reflect on one's own mortality. Mythologically, this is the season during which the dying God sleeps in the underworld awaiting rebirth. At the same time the seed of new life gestates within the womb of the Great Mother – who in this cycle is regarded as the Queen of Darkness. See also **Halloween, All Hallows Eve.**

Samhita Hindu term meaning a collection of **hymns, mantras,** or **magic formulae.** It is also the collective name for the four **Vedas:** the ***Rig-Veda***, the *Sama-Veda*, the *Yajur-Veda*, and the *Atharva-Veda*.

Samkhya Ancient system of Indian thought, regarded by some as the oldest darshana, or doctrine. The main aim of samkhya is to differentiate the **soul** or **spirit** (**purusha**) from matter (**prakriti**). Samkhya differs from **yoga** in placing more emphasis on metaphysical knowledge and "proof" than on **meditation.** Salvation results from knowledge of the omniscient Spirit, which is differentiated clearly from external reality (**tattva**). Samkhya (which translates as "discernment") can be summarized as "liberation through knowledge".

Samsara In **Hinduism,** the cycle of birth, death, and **rebirth,** which arises as a result of **karma.** When one attains **self-realization,** or spiritual liberation (**moksha**), there is no further need to reincarnate. See also **Wheel of Life and Death.**

Samvitti Nadi In **Siddha Yoga,** "the channel of consciousness" – a term applied to the energy channel **sushumna,** through which the **kundalini** is raised.

Sandalphon In modern Western **magic,** the **archangel** ascribed to the sphere of **Malkuth** on the kabbalistic **Tree of Life.** Sandalphon is thus the archangel who protects the physical world.

Sanders, Alex (1916–1988) Contemporary English **witch** who, with **Gerald Gardner,** is acknowledged as a central figure in the **modern witchcraft** revival. Sanders maintained that he came from a family in which witchcraft has been practised for generations, and that he was initiated into the "craft" by his grandmother. Sanders became highly visible in the media during the 1970s – especially with his high priestess, Maxine – and has been the subject of several books and a film. In his later years he combined magical ritual with spirit possession and claimed to be a **trance** medium. His tradition of witchcraft is often referred to as "Alexandrian", an ingenious play on the words of his name, which suggests a certain antiquity in his rituals.

Sankara (c. 788–820) Indian philosopher and **mystic** who taught the doctrine of **Advaita,** or non-dualism. According to Sankara, **Brahman** was the Supreme Reality, and the world perceived by the senses was thus neither real nor unreal. For Sankara, Brahman was the one Truth – beyond description, omnipresent, and eternal. See also **Vedanta.**

Sannyasa In **Hinduism,** the act of renunciation – in which one leaves former social preoccupations and attachments in search of divine **self-realization.**

Sannyasin In **Hinduism,** one who renounces their former life in society in order to obtain spiritual liberation. In India, the sannyasin becomes dependent on others for physical livelihood, but in turn bestows spiritual grace upon those who offer sustenance. The term has also been used to describe followers of **Bhagwan Shree Rajneesh.**

SHAMAN: This illustration of a Siberian shaman with his drum comes from Noord en Oost Tartatye, *and dates from 1705.*

Sanskrit The classical language of the Indian Brahmins, and the parent-language of modern Hindi. In traditional Sanskrit dramas, the high-caste characters spoke in Sanskrit and the low-caste in Prakrita – a simplified and degenerated form. Sanskrit is now spoken mainly among Brahmin priests and is the language in which many of the Mahayana Buddhist texts were written. See also **Mahayana Buddhism**.

Sarasvati In Indian **mythology**, the beautiful wife of **Brahma** and the **goddess** of wisdom and music. She is sometimes depicted with four arms, seated on a **lotus**.

Saros In Chaldean and Babylonian **astrology**, the concept of the lunar cycle in which a cycle of sixty days was interpreted as sixty years. After a period of 223 **lunations**, the **sun** and **moon** would once again be in comparable positions and the eclipses would follow a similar sequence as before. The concept of the saros thus enabled eclipses to be predicted accurately.

Sat In **Hinduism**, that which is real: the pure essence of being.

Satan The personification of **evil**, known variously as the **Prince of Darkness**, **Lucifer**, and the **Devil**. Satan takes his name from the Hebrew word *satan*, "an enemy", and in the Bible is depicted as the great adversary of **God** and the tempter of humankind. In John 8:44, Jesus describes the god worshipped by the Jews as the Devil; and in 2 Corinthians 4:4, Paul identifies the Devil, or Satan, as "the god of this world … who has blinded the minds of them which believe not."

In the Middle Ages the **Knights Templar** were accused of worshipping Satan in the form of **Baphomet**; and **witchcraft** and various heretical sects – including the Cathars and Waldenses – were also charged with Satanic practices. While these accusations were clearly misguided, there have existed from time to time various sects and groups whose purpose has been to mimic and profane the Christian mass and the spiritual principles it represents. The best-known contemporary example is provided by **Anton La Vey's** former **Church of Satan** in San Francisco, California.

Satanic Mass In **satanism**, a blasphemous **ritual** that parodies the Christian mass, invokes the powers of darkness, and sometimes employs the use of a naked woman as an altar. See **Black Mass**.

Satanism The worship of **Satan**. See also **Satanist**.

Satanist A worshipper of **Satan**. To the extent that Satan is a personification of **evil** and the powers of darkness, satanists can be regarded as practitioners of **black magic**, although the two terms are not synonymous. See also **Left-hand Path**.

Satchitananda Sanskrit term for Absolute Reality. It is a combination of three words: **sat** ("pure being"), chit ("pure thought"), and **ananda** ("bliss").

Satguru In **Hinduism**, one who is proclaimed to be the "Highest Master" and who is regarded by his devotees as an **avatar**, or **incarnation** of a **deity**.

Satori In **Zen Buddhism**, a sudden **enlightenment**. This state of mind is often attained when paradoxes and contradictions – as presented in Zen **koans** – are understood, and one's "inner Buddha-nature" is realized.

Satsang In **Hinduism**, a religious gathering of devotees seeking spiritual truth and **enlightenment**. Satsang often takes place in an **ashram**.

Sattva In **Hinduism**, one of the three **gunas** or qualities of primordial matter. Sattva represents harmony, balance, and luminosity, and is the most **transcendental** of the gunas. It is sometimes correlated with **Brahma**.

Saturn In Roman **mythology**, the **god** of agriculture and the harvest. The husband of Ops, he is the Roman counterpart of the Greek god **Cronus**. His famous harvest festival, the **Saturnalia**, was held annually in mid-December.

Saturn In **astrology**, a **planet** that casts an inhibiting or limiting **aspect** on one's life and career. Saturn inclines towards solitude rather than friendship and social conviviality, and is regarded as a generally negative planet. In fact, with **Mars** it is one of the two **malefics**.

Saturnalia Famous festival held in ancient Rome during harvest time, to honour **Saturn**, **god** of agriculture. The Saturnalia was characterized by freedom and equality: slaves were allowed to ridicule their masters, gifts were exchanged, war could not be declared, and rejoicing and debauchery were the accepted fashion.

Saturnine In **astrology**, one who has a dour, gloomy, or morose temperament as a result of the influence of **Saturn**. Saturn is regarded by astrologers as one of the two **malefics**, the other being **Mars**.

Satyrs Also Satyri. In Greek and Roman **mythology**, woodland **deities**. They resembled men, but had the bodies of goats, and short horns on their heads. The attendants of **Dionysus**, **Bacchus**, and **Pan**, they were renowned for their sexual orgies and lasciviousness.

Scales, The See **Libra**.

Scarab In ancient Egyptian **mythology**, the symbol of **Khepera** – the sun-god in his **aspect** as lord of **rebirth** and **immortality**. The female scarab beetle rolls a ball of excrement with her hind legs and encloses her larvae in it. In Egyptian religion, the scarab became identified with the **sun** because it flew during the hottest part of the day and was said to roll its dung-ball from east to west. Khepera rolled the sun across the sky in much the same fashion.

Sceptres See **Wands**.

Schneider Brothers Willy (1903–1971) and Rudi (1908–1957) Schneider, famous **physical mediums** who were able to produce **materializations** and other "phenomena" in the presence of psychical researchers and under strictly supervised conditions. Born in Braunau, Austria, the brothers discovered their mediumistic abilities while engaging in a family **seance**. The Schneiders later gave sittings under the auspices of the British **Society for Psychical Research**, and were carefully investigated by **Baron Schrenck-Notzing**, Dr. Eugene Osty, and **Harry Price**. Osty demonstrated that Rudi Schneider was able to produce "an invisible substance", which was capable of absorbing infrared rays and setting off photographic flashlights, but which did not appear on film negatives. The Schneider brothers are regarded as among the most impressive mediums in the history of **psychical research** and are considered by most authorities to be genuine.

Schrenck-Notzing, Baron Albert von (1862–1929) Distinguished German physician who became one of the leading psychical researchers of his day and studied **trance mediums** over a forty-year period. Schrenk-Notzing investigated **Eusapia Palladino** and the Austrian **Schneider brothers** and collaborated with several other prominent psychical researchers, including **Professor Charles Richet**, **F. W. H. Myers**, and **Sir Oliver Lodge**. Schrenk-Notzing came to believe that **psychic** phenomena were mental rather than "other worldly" in origin, and wrote extensively on the subject. His books include *The Battle Over the Phenomena of Materialisation* (1914), *The Physical Phenomena of the Great Mediums* (1926), and *The Phenomena of the Medium Rudi Schneider* (1933).

Schure, Edouard (1841–1929) French Theosophist and **mystic** whom **Rudolph Steiner** considered to be "one of the best guides for finding the path to the spirit in our day". Schure believed that divinely illuminated beings have appeared in each epoch to guide mankind towards higher spiritual knowledge. These include **Rama, Krishna, Hermes, Moses, Orpheus, Pythagoras,** and **Pluto.** Schure's approach to the mystery tradition is romantic rather than scholarly, and the once fashionable occult concept of an ancient lineage of mystical **adepts** holds less sway today. Nevertheless, Schure's writings are of continuing interest. His main books are *The Great Initiates* and *From Sphinx to Christ.* See also **Illuminati.**

Scientology Modern quasi-scientific cult that in some countries has acquired the status of a religion. Founded by **L. Ron Hubbard,** Scientology is a combination of psychology, **occultism,** and science fiction. Scientology endeavours to uncover information of one's past **incarnations** and to apply this knowledge for ongoing spiritual evolution. The supreme goal of Scientology is "the urge toward existence as Infinity" and is known as the "God Dynamic".

Scorpio In **astrology,** the **sign** of the **zodiac** for those born between October 23 and November 22. A **Water** sign, ruled by **Mars,** Scorpio is symbolized by the scorpion or asp. Those born under the sign of Scorpio are said to have great strength of character, and to be watchful and naturally cautious. They are resourceful and make excellent friends, although the "sting" in the scorpion's tail indicates that passionate friendships and love affairs can sometimes turn bitter and become tragic or violent. Careers in science, medicine, and diplomacy are associated with Scorpio; and many **occultists** – especially those who thrive on secrecy – are found under this sign.

Scrofula See **King's Evil.**

Scrying See **Skrying.**

Scylla In Greek **mythology,** a squid-like monster with six heads, eighteen rows of teeth, and twelve feet. Scylla was originally a water-nymph, but she was transformed by **Circe** into a fearsome creature. Thereafter, she turned her attention to devouring seamen as they passed by in their sailing vessels.

Seal of Solomon A **hexagram** consisting of two interlocking triangles, one facing up, the other down.

Seance In **spiritualism,** a "sitting" or meeting convened for the purpose of summoning and communicating with **spirits** or **discarnate** beings. The **psychic medium** serves as the channel for the communications. See also **Automatic Writing; Control; Ouija Board.**

Secondary Personality In **parapsychology** and **spiritualism,** an ancillary personality that presents itself during a **trance,** and which has different personality traits from the trance subject.

Second Sight Popular term for the **paranormal** faculty of **clairvoyance.** The person possessing "second sight" is able to witness events not seen through the normal senses, and sometimes receives "impressions" of future events. See also **Precognition.**

Secret Chiefs In modern Western **magic,** especially with reference to the **Hermetic Order of the Golden Dawn,** high-ranking spiritual beings who were believed to provide guidance and inspiration to the leaders of the

Inner Order. In the Golden Dawn, the Secret Chiefs were said to reside above the **Abyss**, in the transcendental regions of the **Tree of Life**. They were the magical equivalent of the Theosophical **Masters** or **mahatmas**.

Secret Doctrine Body of **esoteric** mystical knowledge which, according to **Madame Helena Blavatsky** – who compiled a six-volume work with this title – represented the cumulative occult wisdom of the "great Adepts of the Aryan Race". For Madame Blavatsky, the "secret doctrine" belonged not to one religion, but to all of the great spiritual traditions; and it represented the essence of **Hinduism**, **Buddhism**, Christianity, **Islam**, Judaism, and **Zoroastrianism**.

Secret Tradition Occult concept of a line of mystical and magical **adepts** who have passed their **esoteric** knowledge from generation to generation since earliest times. At all times this knowledge has been jealously guarded by **initiates**.

Secret Wisdom General term for traditional occult knowledge, especially that associated with the Western **mystery** tradition, which many believe to have passed down through **adepts** and **initiates** of different secret orders (e.g. the **Rosicrucians**, **Freemasonry**, and the **Illuminati**). The existence of an unbroken lineage of occult adepts was challenged by **A. E. Waite**, the great occult scholar, and remains a matter of controversy.

Sedna Eskimo sea-goddess who ruled over the sea animals and determined how many could be slain as food or used for fuel or clothing. The Eskimo **shamans** would journey to the bottom of the sea to determine how prosperous the future hunt would be and to see whether Sedna required placation. The goddess would advise the shamans whether breaches of **taboos** had occurred.

Seed-syllable Expression used to describe the most significant **mantra** in Hindu **mysticism**: the single-syllable **Om**.

Seer One who prophesies the future or who is gifted with **second sight**. See also **Clairvoyance**; **Divination**; **Oracle**.

Sekhmet Also Sekhet. In Egyptian **mythology**, the wife of **Ptah**. Sekhmet was depicted with the head of a lioness. She is regarded by the tantric occultist **Kenneth Grant** as the personification of "solar-phallic or sexual heat ... considered by the ancients as the divine inspirer or breather, the spirit of creation..." To this extent she is the Egyptian counterpart of the Hindu **Shakti**.

Selene Also Selena. In Greek **mythology**, the name for the **lunar goddess** in her waxing-moon aspect, as distinct from her waning-moon personification as **Hecate**.

Self In **mysticism** and occult philosophy, the divine essence of one's being. It may be contrasted to the **ego** which mystics regard as a transitory identity which disappears at **death**. The self, on the other hand, contains the spark of **Godhead** and is the source of pure consciousness.

Self-Realization Knowledge of one's true, inner **self**: spiritual **enlightenment**. See also **Ego**.

Semi-sextile In **astrology**, an **aspect** characterized by an angle of 30 degrees between two planets.

Sensation Body Term used by **occultists** to describe the **etheric body**, which they believe provides awareness through the senses when united with the physical body.

Senses, Significance of the In **astrology**, the **significators** of the different human faculties, or senses, are: **Mercury** (sight);

Venus (touch); **Mars** (taste); **Jupiter** (smell); and **Saturn** (hearing).

Sensitive In **spiritualism** and **parapsychology**, one who possesses powers of **extrasensory perception**..The term is sometimes used synonymously with **psychic medium**, but a sensitive need not necessarily enter a state of **trance**.

Sensory Deprivation State in which external stimuli are removed from consciousness. Sensory deprivation conditions such as experienced in a **samadhi tank** may produce profound mystical experiences as **archetypes** from the unconscious present themselves in religious visions. See **Lilly, Dr. John**.

Sepher Yetzirah The kabbalistic work known as *The Book of Creation*. The *Sepher Yetzirah* is the earliest metaphysical text in the Hebrew language, and describes **God**'s revelations to Abraham. The visionary tract – which was originally passed down orally – describes the ten **sephiroth** of the **Tree of Life**, and the "twenty-two letters and sounds which comprise the Foundation of all things". The *Sepher Yetzirah* is one of the most important books of the **Kabbalah**; but it does not represent the complete tradition, for it does not describe the **Ain Soph Aur**, **Adam Kadmon**, or the **Shekhinah**.

Sephirah In the **Kabbalah**, one of the ten **emanations** on the **Tree of Life**. See also **Sephiroth**.

Sephiroth The ten spheres or **emanations** on the kabbalistic **Tree of Life**, a symbol which depicts the divine energy of Creation proceeding like a "lightning flash" through ten different stages, culminating in physical manifestation. The sephiroth represent levels of spiritual reality both in the cosmos and in people because the Tree, metaphorically, is the "Body of God", and people are created in his image. The Tree is sometimes shown superimposed on the body of **Adam Kadmon** – the Archetypal Man. The ten sephiroth, in descending order, are **Kether** (the Crown); **Chokmah** (Wisdom); **Binah** (Understanding); **Chesed** (Mercy); **Geburah** (Power); **Tiphareth** (Beauty and Harmony); **Netzach** (Victory); **Hod** (Splendour); **Yesod** (Foundation); and **Malkuth** (the Kingdom). See also **Kabbalah**.

Seraphim In Hebrew **cosmology**, the highest of the nine orders of **angels**. The seraphim are guardians of **God**'s throne and have three pairs of wings.

Serapis Greek name for the sacred bull of Memphis. His worshippers believed he was an **incarnation** of **Osiris**. Serapis became the chief **deity** in Alexandria and a large temple called the Serapeum was built in his honour. Serapis was a **god** of the **Underworld** and was later worshipped in Greece and Rome alongside **Zeus**, **Jupiter**, and **Dionysus**.

Serialism Theory proposed by **J. W. Dunne**, according to which an infinite series of dimensions exists within the nature of Time so that elements of the past, the present, and the future can co-exist at a given moment. Those who are gifted with **extrasensory perception** may have access to other dimensions of the serial universe. See Dunne's book *The Serial Universe* (1934).

Serios, Ted (1918–) American **psychic** who is apparently able to transmit mental images onto photographic film – usually using a Polaroid camera, which develops prints almost instantaneously. Serios has been investigated by **Dr. Jule Eisenbud** at the University of Denver, and **Dr. Ian Stevenson** and J. Gaither Pratt at the University of Virginia. In all experiments, Serios demonstrated an uncanny ability to project **thought-forms** onto film. See also **Psychic Photography**.

Serpent Power Term popularized by the orientalist **Sir John Woodroffe.** It is used as a synonym for the **kundalini,** which can be aroused from the base of the spine through techniques of **yoga** and **Tantra.** See also **Chakras; Ida; Pingala; Sushumna.**

Servants of the Light International magical organization currently headed by **Dolores Ashcroft-Nowicki.** Based on magical techniques developed by **Dion Fortune** and her fellow practitioners in the **Fraternity of the Inner Light,** the SOL currently has lodges in Australia, Canada, Mexico, the Netherlands, Sweden, Britain and the United States and around 2,600 students scattered across twenty-three countries. Dolores Ashcroft-Nowicki periodically visits her SOL members in these different countries and is able to manage the growth of the SOL and its core magical procedures by utilizing the resources of the Internet and by frequently updating her website. The SOL remains one of the most prominent contemporary organizations dedicated to the exploration of visionary magic in the world today.

Set In Egyptian **mythology,** the brother of **Osiris** and **Isis.** Set was jealous of his brother and tricked Osiris into climbing into a beautiful chest; Set and a group of conspirators then sealed and weighted it heavily, and cast it into the Nile. Isis recovered the body of Osiris and became pregnant by him through an act of magical conception. However, Set discovered Osiris once again and tore his body into fourteen pieces, which he scattered around the kingdom. In the Egyptian **pantheon,** as the adversary of Osiris – who symbolizes the renewal of life – Set is the dark God and the personification of **evil.** He was identified by the Greeks with **Typhon.**

Seth See **Set.**

Setian A member of the **Temple of Set.**

Seven In **mythology** and **numerology,** a number with mystic and **supernatural** connotations. There were seven **planets** in ancient astronomy; the world (according to Genesis) had been created in seven days; Joshua and the Israelites marched around Jericho for seven days; and each of the four phases of the **moon** lasts for seven days. There are seven notes on the musical scale and seven colours in the rainbow. Accordingly, seven is the number of completeness, wisdom, spiritual truth, and cosmic harmony. The seventh son of a seventh son is traditionally said to possess supernatural powers.

Seven Stewards of Heaven One of the names by which the seven **Olympic Spirits** are known. See also ***Arbatel of Magick.***

Sextile In **astrology,** an **aspect** characterized by an angle of 60 degrees between two planets.

Sexual Magic See **Magic, Sexual.**

Shaddai Hebrew word meaning "almighty". It is a common **god-name** in Jewish mystical writing, and is used as a formula of invocation in modern Western **magic.**

Shade Victorian spiritualist term, now rarely used, for an **apparition** or **ghost.**

Shadow Reading Form of **divination,** practised in India, in which a person's full shadow, palm, and fingers are measured. Ancient scripts written on palm leaves in various languages are then consulted, and finally the **seer** offers specific predictions to the client.

Shadows, Book of In **witchcraft,** the personal book of **spells, rituals,** and **folklore** a **witch** compiles after being initiated into the **coven.** The *Book of Shadows* is kept secret and, traditionally, is destroyed when the witch dies.

Shadowy Arc See **Descending Arc**.

Shaivites Devotees of the Hindu god **Shiva**.

Shakta In Hinduism, a devotee of the goddess **Shakti**, personification of **cosmic** energy. See also **Tantra**.

Shakti In Hindu **cosmology**, the personification of the creative principle and the consort of **Shiva**. Between them, these two **gods** give rise to the manifested world. The term is used to describe a female partner in tantric rituals. See also **Tantra**.

Shaktipat Diksha Term used by the late **Swami Muktananda** to describe the yogic initiation in which the **guru** transmits spiritual energy to the **chela**, thereby awakening the **kundalini** in that person. According to Muktananda, shaktipat could be received by the chela in one of four ways: *sparsha diksha*, through the guru's touch; *mantra diksha*, through his words; *drik diksha*, through his gaze; and *manasa diksha*, through his power of thought. See also **Yoga**.

Shakuru Among the Pawnee Indians, the sun-god – honoured annually with colourful religious ritual and dances.

Shaman, Shamaness A **sorcerer**, magician or **spirit-healer** who is able to enter a **trance** state under will and who serves as an intermediary between people and the realm of **gods** and **spirits**. Shamans make use of drums, ritual objects, and ceremonial costume in identifying with the gods; and they often enter a state of trance in order to undertake a **journey of the soul**. The purpose of this spirit-journey is to recover stolen spirits or to seek information from the **deities** relating to the availability of food and the likely outcome of the hunt. Associated with hunter-gatherer societies, the shaman may be distinguished from the **spirit-medium**, who is possessed in trance but does not control the experience; and also from the **priest**, who conducts rituals but does not necessarily enter a state of trance.

Shamanic visualization Contemporary application of traditional shamanic practice in which a person undertakes a "spirit-journey" in the mind's eye, usually to the accompaniment of a monotonous and regular drum-beat. During this spirit-journey the meditator may make contact with power animals, spirit-helpers or inner guides – all of whom may assist in processes of healing or self-renewal, or in some form of magical activity. See **Shaman**.

Shamanism Pre-literate technique of gaining **trance** consciousness, in which the **medicine-man**, healer, or **sorcerer** undertakes a **journey of the soul** in order to encounter the **gods** or **spirits**. The shaman may use the monotonous sound of a drum-beat to "ride" into this trance state, and usually performs his ceremonies in darkness. **Psychedelics** are sometimes used to enhance the states of visionary consciousness. Shamanism is found in Siberia, North and South America, and Indonesia, and is characterized by trance states in which the shaman retains control of his experience – unlike states of spirit-possession, where the gods or spirits dominate proceedings.

Shamash Mesopotamian sun-god and brother of the fertility-goddess **Ishtar**. Shamash was the personification of light and righteousness and had the power to deliver **oracles** or **prophecy**. Compare with **Apollo**.

Shambhala According to Tibetan Buddhist tradition, a mystical kingdom hidden beyond the snow peaks of the Himalayas. According to the sacred texts of the Tibetan Canon, a line of enlightened kings has dwelt in Shambhala, guarding the secret doctrines of **Buddhism**. It is said that, when the world has declined amidst war, greed, and power to such a state that truth has been lost in the world, a King of Shambhala will emerge from the secret city with a huge army to conquer **evil** and herald the **Golden Age**.

Shams of Tabriz (?–1247) The Sufi teacher of **Jalal'al-Din Rumi**, the noted Persian poet. Shams is credited with attuning Rumi to the Path of Love. He also encouraged Rumi to abandon his academic role as a religious professor at Konya, in order to pursue the ecstatic quest for divine **enlightenment**. It is thought that Shams was murdered by some of Rumi's former pupils, who were jealous of his influence. See also **Sufism**.

Shape-shifting The **supernatural** ability to transform one's shape into that of an animal, bird, or mythic creature. Shape-shifting is sometimes ascribed to **witches**, **shamans**, and **sorcerers**. See also **Lycanthropy**.

Shaykh In **Sufism**, a spiritual master whose role it is to guide devotees in the path of true faith and away from deception and ignorance. The shaykh is the Sufi equivalent of the Hindu **guru**.

Shedim In the **Kabbalah**, demonic beings who confuse the mind of the **mystic** while the latter is engaged in **meditation**.

Shekhinah In the Jewish mystical tradition, **God**'s female aspect and **immanent** presence, which is said to "dwell in exile" in the physical universe. Shekhinah is associated with the **sephirah Malkuth** on the kabbalistic **Tree of Life**.

Shem ha-meforash In Judaism, the seventy-two-syllable name of God, which consists of 216 letters. According to Jewish tradition, the source of this name may be found in Exodus 14:19–21, which contains three verses containing seventy-two Hebrew letters. At a later stage, the Shem ha-meforash was simplified to the form **YHVH**, known as the **Tetragrammaton**.

Sheol From the Hebrew *she'ol*, "a cave", the dark **Underworld** where departed **spirits** are thought to dwell after **death**. The word is sometimes used generally to mean **hell**, although Sheol is closer to **Hades**, and **Gehenna** is more akin to the Western notion of hell.

Shesha In Indian **mythology**, the king of the **naga** serpents. The nagas played an important role in the formation of **Mahayana Buddhism**. See also **Vasuki**.

Shin Buddhism Japanese name for **Pure Land Buddhism**, which is based on devotion to **Amida Buddha** (as distinct from **Gautama Buddha**).

Shinto Japanese religion also known as Kami-no-Michi, the "Way of the Gods". Shinto was originally a form of **nature-worship**, but later merged with **Buddhism**. During the Tokugawa period, Shinto emerged in a new light in league with Confucianism: the Emperor was said to be the divine leader of the nation and claimed lineal descent from the sun-goddess Amaterasu Omikami. From 1868 onwards, the Emperor was confirmed as the absolute religious and political leader and was worshipped accordingly; Shinto thus became the official religion of Japan. Emperor Hirohito, however, renounced his "divinity" in 1946. The most sacred site of Shinto is at Ise, where a temple of the sun-goddess houses a mirror that she is said to have given to Jimmu, the first Emperor (seventh century B.C.).

Shi Tenno In traditional Japanese **cosmology**, the guardians of the four cardinal **directions**. Their names were Jikoku (East); Zocho (West); Bishamon (North); and Komoku (South). The Shi Tenno were powerful protectors against **demons** and **evil spirits**.

Shiva In Indian **mythology**, one of the three gods of the **Trimurti**, the other two being **Brahma** and **Vishnu**. Shiva has many aspects. In his identification with the Vedic god **Rudra**, Shiva is a god of destruction and storms. However, as Pashupati, Lord of the Animals, he is a gentle **deity** – the Hindu equivalent of Christ, the Good Shepherd. Shiva's horned headdress has led him to be identified with Mhasoba, a southern buffalo god, and it is certain that he is to some extent a totemic deity. Shiva is famous for his dance, which again has two aspects. In its peaceful form, *lasya*, Shiva's dance personifies love and tenderness; but its hostile or wrathful form, *tandeva*, characterizes explosive and destructive energy in the universe. Shiva is often depicted with three eyes and four arms, wearing living snakes as ornaments, and with a necklace of human skulls. Despite his frightening appearance, however, Shiva is "the Beneficent, the Gracious, the Blessed One". He is one of the major Hindu deities.

Shrine A sacred location or object. Temples, chapels, tombs, and sacred groves often have special significance because of their historic connection with a holy personage and are venerated for this reason.

Sibyls In ancient Greece and Rome, women who lived in caves and who were renowned for their gifts of **prophecy**. The most famous of the sibyls lived at Cumae near Naples, and guarded the Temple of **Apollo**, near the entrance to the **Underworld**. According to Varro, there were ten sibyls in all, the others residing in Persia, Libya, Delphi, Samos, Cimmeria, Erythrae, Tibur, Marpessa, and Phrygia.

Siddha In **yoga**, one who has attained an advanced state of self-knowledge and who can claim to be a "perfect master".

Siddhartha One of the names by which **Gautama Buddha** is known.

Siddha Yoga The "**yoga** of perfection" – a school of yoga formulated and developed by the late **Swami Muktananda**. In Siddha Yoga, according to Muktananda, the **kundalini** energy can be aroused in a devotee through the intervention of the **guru**. See also **Shaktipat Diksha**.

Siddhis In **yoga**, magical or mystical powers that arise in the practitioner who is advanced in the technique of **self-realization**, and has become a **siddha** (perfect master). Siddhis include **levitation**, the ability to increase in height, and the faculty of passing through solid objects unimpeded.

Sidereal Gods and Goddesses From the Latin *sidus*, "a star", Greek and Roman **deities** of the sky. They include **Zeus**, **Artemis**, **Apollo**, Helios, **Selene**, **Luna**, and **Diana**.

Sidgwick, Henry (1838–1900)
A distinguished academic, Sidgwick was professor of moral philosophy at Cambridge University and the first president of the **Society for Psychical Research**. He collaborated closely with **Sir William Barrett** and **Edmund Gurney** in investigating the **paranormal** and interviewed **Madame Helena Blavatsky** when she visited London. As a result, **Richard Hodgson** was asked to go to India to study her claimed mediumistic and extrasensory powers more closely. Sidgwick spent five years working on the **Census of Hallucinations** – a study that analyzed over 17,000 questionnaires dealing with experiences of hauntings and apparitions. He was also involved in evaluating the psychic mediums **Mrs. Leonore Piper** and **Eusapia Palladino**. A prolific author in the fields of ethical philosophy and politics, Sidgwick produced numerous articles for the Society for Psychical Research, and was responsible for the publication of the Census of Hallucinations report in 1894.

Sidhe Also Side. The fairy folk of ancient Ireland. See also **Tuatha de Danaan.**

Sigil An occult symbol that represents a specific **supernatural** being or entity. In medieval **magic**, sigils were used to summon **spirits** and **angels**. In recent times, the trance occultist **Austin Osman Spare** developed his own alphabet or magical sigils to release atavistic images from his unconscious mind.

Sign In **astrology**, one of the twelve divisions of the **zodiac**. The twelve signs, in their usual order, are: **Aries, Taurus, Gemini, Cancer, Leo, Virgo, Libra, Scorpio, Sagittarius, Capricorn, Aquarius,** and **Pisces.** The signs are each ascribed to the four **elements**, and are classified as **cardinal, fixed,** and **mutable**, as follows:

	Cardinal	*Fixed*	*Mutable*
Fire	Aries	Leo	Sagittarius
Water	Cancer	Scorpio	Pisces
Air	Libra	Aquarius	Gemini
Earth	Capricorn	Taurus	Virgo

Signatures Mystical concept which holds that since plants were created by **God** for people to use, their shape reflects their function or character. In medieval **herbalism**, yellow flowers or roots were used to treat jaundice; while **mandrakes**, whose roots have a human shape, were said to "scream" and to grow from the semen of men sent to the gallows to die.

Significator In **astrology**, the significator of a **natal horoscope** is the planet which is most strongly aspected: it is usually held to be the **ruler** of the **ascendant**. Significators can also be identified for the different astrological **houses.**

Sikhs Devotees of a religion with approximately 10 million followers, mostly located in the Punjab region of India. Sikhism derives from the teachings of **Guru Nanak**, and emphasizes the Unity of God and the Brotherhood of Man. Nanak was influenced by, and sympathetic to, both **Hinduism** and **Islam**; and his religious views, to some extent, combined both. His concept of **God**, however, was more akin to Hinduism. Nanak taught that God was the One Truth, formless, omnipotent, and impossible to define. In Sikhism faith alone leads to salvation.

Sileni In Greek **mythology**, mythic creatures that resembled **satyrs**, except that they had the bodies of horses instead of goats. See also **Silenus.**

Silenus In Greek **mythology**, the oldest of the **satyrs**. In the region of Phrygia, Silenus was a **deity** in his own right, but was later identified as the son of **Pan** or **Hermes.**

Silvanus Also Sylvanus. Roman god of fields, gardens, and woods, who was half-man, half-goat. He is often confused with **Silenus**, but was in fact one of the numina – the protective spirits of home and garden.

Silver Metal associated with the element Water and the **moon**. In Western **magic** and the **Tattvas**, the symbol of the moon is a silver crescent.

Silver Cord See **Cord, Silver.**

Simon Magus Sorcerer mentioned in Acts 8 who gathered a following among the Samaritans; many believed he had divine and magical powers and worshipped him as if he were a **god**. Simon Magus is said to have learned the magical arts in Egypt and became an **initiate** in the sect of Dositheus. Simon Magus was an antagonist of Peter in Rome, and at different times Emperor Nero challenged Peter to prove that Jesus had superior abilities. A particular test proved conclusive: Nero ordered that a tower be raised in the Campus Martius, from which Simon Magus claimed he would "ascend into

Heaven". Simon Magus, according to tradition, stretched forth his hands and began to fly, and Nero asked Peter whether this meant Jesus and his followers were deceivers. At this point Peter is said to have called on Christ to banish the **angels** of **Satan** supporting Simon Magus in the air, whereupon the magician fell to earth in the Sacra Via, his body broken into four pieces.

Simulacrum That which is a copy of a likeness or copy of an original. The word is used to describe acts of **imitative magic**, where a simulacrum may be injured with the intent of harming a person at a distance; and it is also used to describe the body-image an **occultist** visualizes in attempting to project his or her consciousness onto the **astral plane**. See also **Magic, Black**.

Sin In Mesopotamian religion, the **moon** god who personified goodness and kept a vigil against the forces of **evil**. Sin was a wise **deity** and advised the other gods on appropriate courses of action. He also marked the passage of time through each month. Sin was identified by the Sumerians with Nanna.

Sinclair, Upton See **Mental Radio**.

Sinister From the Latin word meaning "left", that which is on the left-hand side. It has come to mean something undesirable or unfortunate; in **occultism** the **left-hand path** is associated with **black magic** and **sorcery**. Compare with **Right-hand Path**.

Sirens In Greek **mythology**, three notorious sea-**nymphs** – part-bird, part-women – who lured sailors to their **death** on treacherous rocks by singing enchanting songs. Their names were Leucosia, Ligeia, and Parthenope. **Circe** warned **Odysseus** of their seductive powers, and he in turn instructed his companions to stuff their ears with wax. When the charms of the Sirens failed to have an effect on the crew, the three sea-nymphs hurled themselves into the sea and perished.

Sirius From the Greek *seirios*, "scorching", the brightest star in the constellation Canis Major. Regarded by the ancients as the most vivid star in the heavens, Sirius has attracted renewed interest in recent years among cosmologists and **ufologists** interested in the origins of alien intelligence. See also **Dogons**.

Sistrum A metal rattle used as a musical instrument by the ancient Egyptians in their worship of **Isis**. Used generally to describe a rattle used in dancing, the sistrum (plural, sistra) has its place in South American **shamanism**, where it often accompanies the drum as a sacred instrument. It also featured in the religious traditions of the Aztecs and Romans.

Sitter In a spiritualist **seance**, an alternative name for the **querent**.

Siva See **Shiva**.

Six In **numerology**, a number indicative of love, domesticity, family affairs, and loyalty. Six consists of the first masculine number (three) multiplied by the first feminine number (two) and therefore characterizes productive and harmonious union.

Sixth Sense Popular term for **extrasensory perception**. It derives from the idea that the faculties of **paranormal** perception lie beyond the familiar five physical senses. See also **Presentiment**.

Skinner, Stephen (1948–) Australian-born **occultist**, resident in London. Skinner, an authority on medieval **magic**, **geomancy** and feng-shui, established the Askin publishing house in 1972 to produce facsimile editions of magical writings by **Dr. John Dee**, Cornelius Agrippa, and **Paracelsus**. Skinner is the co-author with the late **Francis King** of

Techniques of High Magic (London, 1974), one of the most coherent books on practical techniques of modern magic ever written. His other books include *The Oracle of Geomancy* (1977), *Terrestrial Astrology* (1980), and *The Living Earth Manual of Feng-Shui* (1982), as well as editions of magical writings by **Aleister Crowley**.

Skrying Form of **divination** in which the practitioner gazes at a shiny or polished surface to induce a **trance**-state in which scenes, people, words, or images appear as part of a **psychic** communication. The familiar **crystal ball** of the gypsy **fortune-teller** provides the best example; but mirrors, polished metal, coal or bone, and even cups of clear liquid, have also been used for skrying.

Slate-writing In **spiritualism**, a popular form of **automatic writing** in which the **sitter** and the **psychic medium** hold a slate beneath a table to which a fragment of slate-pencil has been affixed. During the **seance**, the **spirit** indicates its presence with the scratching sound of writing, and withdraws on the sign of three raps. When the slate is withdrawn from beneath the table it is seen to be covered with "spirit-messages". A leading practitioner of this form of spirit-communication was **William Eglinton**.

Sleep State in which the body is at rest, the muscles are relaxed, the pulse is slow, and the breathing gentle. Sleep is usually characterized by unconsciousness, and the typical person sleeps for around seven hours a day. Occultists have long believed that in the sleeping state some faculties of consciousness transfer to the **astral body**, and that it is through this vehicle that **dreams** and nightmares become experientially real. The degree to which consciousness is transferred is crucial. If transference is extensive, the dream is known as a **lucid dream**, a state of consciousness closely resembling an **out-of-the-body experience**.

Smith, Hélène See **Flournoy, Théodore**.

Snake Worship See **Ophiolatry**.

Soal, Dr. Samuel George (1889–1975) The holder of the first doctorate awarded in England for the study of **parapsychology**, Dr. Soal became president of the **Society for Psychical Research** in 1949. He is best known for his extensive statistical experiments with **Zener cards** in the 1930s, and made a special study of **telepathy**, **clairvoyance**, **automatic writing**, and **psychic mediums**. Dr. Soal lectured on telepathy at many universities, and was co-author of *Modern Experiments in Telepathy* (1954) and *The Mind Readers* (1959).

Society for Psychical Research (SPR) Organization formed in 1882, largely as an offshoot of the Ghost Society at Cambridge University. Th aim of the SPR was and is to study the **paranormal** functions of the mind, **hypnotism**, **clairvoyance**, **apparitions**, spiritualist **phenomena**, and evidence for life after death. The SPR has attracted many distinguished thinkers among its membership, including **Professor Henry Sidgwick**, **Sir William Crookes**, **Sir Oliver Lodge**, and **Sir William Barrett**. The Archbishop of Canterbury, E. W. Benson, was one of its members; and two British Prime Ministers – William Ewart Gladstone and Arthur Balfour – were honorary associates. The SPR still exists and has a fine library in its London headquarters.

Sol The Roman name for the sun-god. His Greek counterpart was known variously as **Apollo**, Helios, Hyperion, and Phoebus. Sol is one of the traditional "planets" in astrology.

Solar Gods Traditionally, the **sun** has been regarded as a masculine force and the **moon** as feminine. Consequently, the sun is often personified as a solar god and is worshipped in this form. Many of the ancient **pantheons**

featured solar gods. They include **Ra** (Egypt); **Mithra** (Persia); Hyperion, Helios, and **Apollo** (Greece); and **Sol** (Rome). In China, the sun is the force behind all things that are **yang**, or masculine.

Solar Plexus A large network of nerves found behind the stomach. The solar plexus is regarded in **yoga** as the seat of the **chakra** or energy centre known as **Manipura**. According to **Carlos Castaneda**, it is also the source of the magical power of the **shaman**.

Solar Revolution Horoscope See **Horoscope, Solar Revolution.**

Solistry Divination by interpreting the lines and markings on the soles of the feet. This mystical art was practised in ancient times in China, India and Persia. Compare with **Palmistry**.

Solomon Legendary King of Israel (r. 974–937 B.C.). Solomon was the son of David and Bathsheba and was famed for his wisdom. He acquired considerable wealth through trade and built his legendary temple in Jerusalem. Many works have been attributed to him, including the biblical books Proverbs, Ecclesiastes and The Song of Songs; and in the Middle Ages he was claimed to be the author of several magical **grimoires** including *The Lesser Key of Solomon* and *The Greater Key of Solomon*. See also ***Key of Solomon***.

Soma Sacred plant that was used to make a narcotic drink, consumed in Vedic sacrificial rites held in honour of the warrior god **Indra**. Soma was said to be the drink of the **gods** and to bestow divinity upon mortals. Soma has been identified by some writers as the leafless plant *Sarcostemma acidum*, but the ethnomycologist **R. Gordon Wasson** has produced impressive evidence that soma was in fact ***Amanita muscaria***, the hallucinogenic mushroom with a red cap and white spots known as fly agaric. See also **Hallucination**.

Soma In Vedic India, the personification of the sacred soma juice. Soma was originally regarded as an Earth-god, and later as a lunar deity – for the **moon** was said to provide semen, or life-essence.

Son of Light Occult term for a practitioner of **white magic**.

Soothsayer From the Old English *soth*, "the truth", one who has the **supernatural** ability to divine future events. See also **Divination**.

Sophia In **Gnosticism**, the female personification of Divine Wisdom. In the Gnosis of **Valentinus**, she is an **archetype** of the Great Mother; and in some Gnostic **cosmologies** bears resemblance to the Virgin Mary. Sophia is sometimes referred to as the female **logos**.

Sophic Hydrolith Traditional alchemical term for the **Philosopher's Stone**. It is also the title of an anonymous seventeenth-century book that describes how to manufacture the secret stone – which bestowed immortality and wisdom.

Sorcerer, Sorceress A **magician**, **wizard**, or **shaman** who uses magical **spells** and **incantations** to summon **spirits** for **evil** purposes or to gain personal power.

Sorcery The act of summoning **supernatural** powers or **spirits** through **spells** and **incantations**. The word is generally applied to **black magic**. See also **Goetia; Magic**.

Sortilege Divination by casting or drawing lots. It can take various forms: drawing straws from a cluster or a card from a pack; opening a book at random and taking the first passage one notices as an oracle; or simply throwing dice.

Soul The eternal, immaterial, spiritual dimension of an organism, which animates its physical form and gives it life. In some mystical traditions animals, plants, and even inanimate objects such as rocks can have souls. The Greek philosopher **Plato** believed that the soul could exist independently of the body, although it was still part of **God**; and in many traditions the projection of the soul beyond the body (as in the **spirit-journey** of the **shaman**) is taken as proof of immortality and the transitional nature of **death**. In **Hinduism** and most branches of **occultism**, the soul is believed capable of **reincarnation** or **transmigration** into other human or animal forms. Sometimes the soul is regarded as a unified entity (as in Platonic thought), while at other times it is divided into different parts. In the **Kabbalah**, for example, the soul has three divisions: the **Neschamah**, the **Ruach**, and the **Nephesch**. Of these the first, or "higher soul", shares the spiritual qualities of the Trinity (the **sephiroth** above the **Abyss**), while the other divisions of the soul are less elevated. See also **self**; **Spirit**.

Soul, Old See **Old Soul**.

Soul Body See **Astral Body**.

South In Western **ceremonial magic**, the direction associated with the element **Fire**. It is said to be ruled by the **archangel Michael**. See also **Directions, Four**.

Sovereign Grand Architect of the Universe, The In **Freemasonry**, the name by which the **Supreme Being** is known. Belief in **God** is a condition of membership for those seeking to be initiated as Freemasons. It is normal in Freemasonry to refer to God by an acronym made up of the initials of this title: T.·.S.·.G.·.A.·.O.·.T.·.U.·.

Spagyric Art A term used to describe **alchemy**. It is thought to have been coined by **Paracelsus**.

Spangler, David (1945–) American mystic and author who, during the early 1970s, was co-director of the **Findhorn Community** in Scotland. Spangler had several mystical experiences as a child and for a period in his twenties also channelled a **discarnate** being as a healing guide and inspirational source. He is now regarded as a leading spokesperson for the **New Age** movement. While his personal orientation is towards Christian mysticism, his perspective is essentially global and transcends denominational differences. His books include *Emergence: Rebirth of the Sacred* and *Towards a Planetary Vision.*

Spare, Austin Osman (1886–1956) English **trance** artist and occultist who won a scholarship to the Royal College of Art when he was only sixteen. Spare came into contact with Egyptian **mythology**, **witchcraft**, and the magician **Aleister Crowley**, and began to incorporate his occult beliefs into his art. Spare believed in **reincarnation** and claimed that his former lives – whether as a human or as an animal – were deeply imbedded in his unconscious mind and could be rediscovered in trance. Spare developed his own alphabet of **sigils**, which could be used magically to unleash atavistic imagery. Spare was one of England's finest illustrators, although his work is less well known than that of Aubrey Beardsley, **Arthur Rackham**, or Edmund J. Sullivan. Spare's best work is contained in his *Book of Pleasure*, first published in 1913 (reissued Montreal, 1975).

Speaking in Tongues See **Xenoglossy**.

Spectre In **spiritualism**, an **apparition** or **ghost**.

Speculum Any object used in **skrying** to focus one's gaze in entering a state of trance-consciousness. Examples include the **crystal ball**, or any objects with shiny, reflective surfaces that are used for this purpose.

Spell An **incantation** or **invocation**, performed by a **witch**, **wizard**, or **magician**, which is believed to have a tangible outcome – for either good or evil. Spells can be a form of **absent healing**, or can be used to inflict harm to person or property. See also **Evil-eye**; **Magic**.

Spence, James Lewis (1874–1955) Scottish poet and politician best known for his interest in magic, mythology and the occult. Spence became sub-editor with *The Scotsman* and was later one of the founder members of the National Party of Scotland. But it is his writings on mythology and occultism that have secured his reputation. Spence was generally sympathetic to occult groups and societies while maintaining a sense of distance from their more extravagant claims. He had difficulty with such concepts as "the church existing before the foundations of the world" and the "inner sanctuary of Christianity", but nevertheless believed strongly in the value of authentic **mysticism**. Spence was a prolific author and wrote on a variety of occult subjects. His *Encyclopaedia of Occultism* (London 1920) remains a standard reference on the subject. His other books include *The History of Atlantis*, *The Magic Arts in Celtic Britain*, and *The Fairy Tradition in Britain*.

Spheres In mystical **cosmology**, levels of spiritual awareness or specific celestial objects in the heavens (e.g. planetary spheres). See also **Music of the Spheres**. Compare with **Aeons**; **Emanations**; **Sephiroth**.

Sphinx Composite mythic creature consisting of a human head and breast, the body, feet, and tail of a lion, and the wings of a bird. The most famous example is the **Great Sphinx** at Giza, which represents **Horus** and has a king's head. The Greek Sphinx had a woman's head and breasts and was said to be the offspring of **Typhon** and **Echidna**. Travellers who came near her were devoured if they could not answer her question: "What creature goes on four legs in the morning, on two at noonday, and on three in the evening?" The answer to the riddle of the sphinx was: "man", who crawls as a baby while young, walks erect in manhood, and requires the use of a staff when bent over with old age. **Oedipus** successfully answered the sphinx, who then threw herself off a cliff to her death.

Spindle of Fate In classical Greek **mythology**, the spindle turned by the three **Fates** – Atropos, Clotho, and Lachesis – in unfolding **destiny**.

Spirit The divine spark or "essence" within each person which, in mystical belief, unites that person with the **Godhead**. It is the vital ingredient in life. See also **Life-force**; **Prana**.

Spirit-Beings See Spirits.

Spirit Doctors In **spiritualism** and **faith healing**, doctors who have died and who assist the living through a **psychic medium**, who serves as a healer. A famous example in recent times is provided by faith-healer **Harry Edwards**, who believed he was aided in his **laying-on-of-hands** by the **discarnate** spirits of Louis Pasteur and Lord Lister.

Spirit Helper In **shamanism**, **spiritualism**, and **witchcraft**, a spirit being that acts as a guide, guardian, or **familiar**.

Spiritism French form of **spiritualism** associated with the teachings of **Allan Kardec**. Kardec combined techniques of contacting the spirits of the dead with a strong belief in **reincarnation**.

Spirit-journey See **Journey of the Soul**.

Spirit Photography See **Psychic Photography**.

Spirits **Discarnate** entities, often the spirits of ancestors, who are believed to influence the world of the living. In hunter-gatherer societies, placating the spirits is necessary if life is to continue harmoniously, and if abundant crops and favourable hunting or harvesting conditions are to be guaranteed. In modern **spiritualism**, spirits are summoned during a **seance** for information relating to life in the afterworld and to provide reassurance that one's deceased relatives are still interested in temporal matters and can provide guidance to the living.

Spirits of the Elements See **Elements**.

Spiritual Healing See **Faith Healing**.

Spiritualism The belief that the **spirits** of the dead can communicate with the living through a **psychic medium**. **Seances** are conducted to summon a particular spirit, and the medium enters a state of trance. The deceased spirit subsequently "possesses" the medium and either addresses the gathering directly or communicates through **automatic writing** or **automatic painting or drawing.** Spiritualists regard the phenomena occurring at seances as proof of life after **death**.

Spirit Voice Recordings An alternative term for the **electronic voice phenomenon** discovered by **Dr. Konstantin Raudive**. The expression is used by those who hold the view that the voices on the Raudive recordings are those of **discarnate spirits** of deceased people.

Spodomancy Form of **divination** in which the cinders taken from sacrificial fires are interpreted for **omens**.

Spontaneous Psi Experience Expression used in **parapsychology** to describe an involuntary psychic or paranormal experience. See also **Psi**.

SPR Initials of the **Society for Psychical Research**.

Sprenger, Jacob (c. 1436–1495) Swiss-born Dominican Inquisitor who, with **Heinrich Kramer**, compiled the notorious medieval source-work on **witchcraft**, ***Malleus Maleficarum***. Sprenger became prior of the Convent of Cologne, and founded the Fraternity of the Rosary after being inspired by a religious vision. He rose in power and status and in 1481 became Inquisitor for the provinces of Cologne, Treves, and Mainz. It is generally considered that Sprenger was the more scholarly of the two authors, although Kramer did most of the compilation work on the *Malleus*. See also **Inquisition**.

Sprite A nature-spirit. See also **Elves; Fairies; Nymphs; Pixies**.

Square In **astrology**, an **aspect** characterized by an angle of 90 degrees between two **planets**.

Star, Five-pointed See **Pentagram**.

Star, The In the **Tarot**, the card of the **Major Arcana** that depicts a beautiful naked woman kneeling by a pool and pouring water from flasks held in both hands. Regarded as a personification of the "white goddess" in her various forms – **Isis, Hathor**, or **Aphrodite** – she is considered to be a receptacle for the waters of the **Spirit** which flow down upon the earth. In Western **magic**, which combines the Tarot paths of the Major Arcana with the ten **sephiroth** on the **Tree of Life**, the path of *The Star* connects **Yesod** and **Netzach**.

Starhawk (1951–) The magical name of Miriam Simos, an influential contemporary **witch** who founded two **covens** in San Francisco, California, and produced a definitive volume on contemporary neo-**pagan** practice: *The Spiral Dance* (1979). According to Starhawk, "For women, the Goddess is an image of personal strength and creative power; for men, she is the nurturing source within." **Modern witchcraft** has attracted a strong feminist following because of its appeal to the **lunar goddess** in her various forms, and Starhawk is currently engaged in exploring the political implications of witchcraft and neo-paganism.

Stars, Divination by the See **Astrology**.

Station In **astrology**, the point in a **planet**'s orbit where it becomes direct or retrograde. See also **Matutine**.

Steinbrecher, Edwin American metaphysician who developed the so-called "Guide Meditation" for contacting "the inner gods" and who founded the D.O.M.E. Foundation, now based in Los Angeles. The initials of Steinbrecher's organization derive from the latin expression *Dei Omnes Munda Edunt:* "All the Gods/Goddesses bring forth the Worlds". The Guide Meditation incorporates **Tarot** symbols – which "correspond to reality creating images within all of us" – and astrology which "provides a map of the inner and outer worlds". However, the essence of the D.O.M.E. Foundation system involves inner contact with a "Guide" similar to the magical ally called by a traditional **shaman**.

The D.O.M.E. Meditation technique utilizes a relaxed body posture with the back straight and both feet flat on the floor. The hands rest on the thighs, the palms face upwards and the eyes are closed. The meditator imagines himself entering a cave and tries through an act of will to enhance the sense of its being moist or dry, dark or light. Steinbrecher believes that the meditator should retain the sense of being consciously within the body rather than watching an external body image, and in this respect the D.O.M.E method resembles identically the shamanic and magical concepts of transferring perceptual consciousness to the inner planes. Like the shaman, Steinbrecher has found it valuable to call for an animal ally who will in turn lead the meditator to the appropriate Guide. On various occasions such animals as deer, lions, dogs and cats have appeared and have led the way to the Guide who, in Steinbrecher's experience, has initially always taken a male form.

The D.O.M.E. method advocates focusing on and summoning the transcendent inner sun, which is the "archetype of the self" – "the inner life-centre". The basic intent is to "place spiritual authority back within the individual ... its true and holy place." In the Guide Meditation system, **astrology** is combined with the Tarot in order to identify dominating and conflicting archetypes within the self, so that the encounter process becomes a form of therapy. For example, **Aries** equates with the **Emperor** and **Mercury** with the **Magician**, **Venus** with the **Empress**, **Gemini** with the **Lovers** and **Aquarius** with the **Star**. According to Steinbrecher, we are able to analyze the horoscope in order to identify the "high energy" areas via squares, oppositions and opposing zodiacal fields; "unions", or harmonizing forces, via the conjunctions, **sextiles**, parallels and **quincunxes**, and basic archetypes via the **sun sign** and **ruler** of the **ascendant**. The horoscope is thus a chart and symbolic guide to the individual cosmos of each meditator.

In the final analysis, the aim of the Guide Meditation is self-integration, individuation, and a broader spiritual perspective. As Steinbrecher writes: "Outer world perceptions become acute, and the world literally becomes *new*. The creative energy wells up from within and a knowledge of a *oneness with all* becomes a fact of being." See also **Tarot**; **Inner Guide**; **Shamanic Visualization**.

Steiner, Rudolph (1861–1925) German **occultist**, Theosophist, and scholar who founded the Anthroposophical Society after breaking away from **Theosophy**. Steiner was an authority on the German author Goethe, and his theories on education are still pursued in the many Steiner Schools throughout the world. However, he was also a **clairvoyant** and a highly knowledgeable occultist who investigated the myths of **Atlantis** and **Lemuria** and the development of occult faculties of consciousness. He was connected with several occult movements, including the **Ordo Templi Orientis** and Engel's Order of the **Illuminati**, and wrote prolifically on **esoteric** subjects. His works include *Occult Science*, *Christianity as Mystical Fact*, and *The Knowledge of Higher Worlds and Its Attainment*.

Stevenson, Professor Ian (1918–) Arguably the world's leading authority on cases of claimed **reincarnation**, Professor Stevenson is Chairman of the Department of Neurology and Psychiatry at the University of Virginia School of Medicine. Stevenson has spent many years investigating instances of "reincarnation memory patterns" in young children, where conscious or unconscious fraud would appear to be out of the question. Stevenson's research data is international in scope and includes the cases of Shanti Devi and Prabhu Khairti in India; Eduardo Esplusus-Cabrera in Cuba; and Alexandrina Samona in Sicily. Some of the results of Professor Stevenson's exhaustive research are contained in *Twenty Cases Suggestive of Reincarnation* (first published 1966, third edition 1995).

Stichomancy **Divination** by interpreting a passage picked at random in a book – often a sacred text. It is more commonly known as **bibliomancy**.

Stigmata Wounds or markings that sometimes bleed and which resemble those on the body of Christ as he suffered on the cross. Stigmata sometimes appear on the bodies of Christian **mystics** who are profoundly devoted to Jesus. St. Francis of Assisi experienced stigmata, and in recent times they appeared on the body of the German woman **Teresa Neumann** after she prayed to St. Teresa of Lisieux and had visions of Christ's Passion.

St. John's Wort Medium-sized herbaceous perennial that grows in the grasslands and woods of Britain, Europe, and Asia, and which is traditionally regarded as an excellent source of healing oil for wounds and abrasions. In the Middle Ages, people would hang St. John's Wort in doors and windows on St. John's Day to keep away the **Devil** and **evil** spirits. The herb was also used in magic **charms** and **talismans**.

Stolistes In the Neophyte grade of the **Hermetic Order of the Golden Dawn**, the bearer of the "Cup of Lustral Water". In this ceremonial working the **magician** representing the role of Stolistes stands in the northern quarter of the temple.

Strength In the **Tarot**, the card of the **Major Arcana** that depicts a woman prying open the jaws of a **lion**. Symbolic of the triumph of intuition over brute animal strength, this card indicates the "victory" of the higher aspects of the **soul** (**Neschamah** and **Ruach**) over the lower or animal soul (**Nephesch**). In Western **magic**, which combines the Tarot paths of the Major Arcana with the ten **sephiroth** on the **Tree of Life**, the path of *Strength* connects **Geburah** and **Chesed**. Very much a stabilizing force in the psyche, *Strength* is also associated with the spiritual consolidation required prior to the inner journey across the **Abyss**.

Stupa An important sacred symbol in **Buddhism**, the stupa is a mound which may take many different forms, from a simple burial mound to an elaborate **pagoda**. Symbolically, the stupa relates to **Gautama Buddha**'s topknot, and therefore his spiritual attainment of **nirvana**. In its own way, each stupa is also a form of **Mount Meru**, the mystical centre of the world.

Styx In Greek mythology, one of the five rivers of **Hades**. The Styx circled Hades nine times and **Charon** was responsible for ferrying the souls of the dead across to the infernal regions.

Subconscious In modern analytic psychology, that part of the mind which lies below the threshold of consciousness. It can be tapped using the techniques of **guided imagery**, **hypnosis**, **automatic writing**, **automatic painting and drawing**, and random association, and may be the origin of many of the phenomena reported in spiritualistic **seances**.

Subliminal That which is below the threshold of consciousness.

Subtle Body In **occultism**, the etheric body, or "subtle" counterpart of the physical body.

Subtle Planes In **Theosophy**, **mysticism**, and **occultism**, the "inner" or "higher" planes of being, which are regarded as more "subtle" than the plane of physical reality. In many **cosmologies**, the subtle planes are expressed as **emanations** from the **Godhead** (the "grossest" and the furthest removed from the **Spirit**, being the level of the everyday world).

Succubus A **demon** or **discarnate spirit**-entity that takes the form of a woman and has sexual intercourse with a man. See also **Incubus**.

Sufism The mystical tradition within **Islam**. Sufism, according to **Abu Hamid Ghazali**, "aims at detaching the heart from all that is not Allah, and at giving to it the sole occupation of the meditation of the Divine Being". In Sufism, total submission to **Allah** and love for him leads to the attainment of spiritual truth. Accordingly, although Sufism is Islamic, at heart it is universal; "There is no Reality but Reality."

The Sufi son of the Mogul Emperor Shah Jahan affirmed that there was no real difference between Sufism and **Advaita** Vedantism – both being expressions of the great One-ness or Unity of God. Sufism also has parallels in other religions, and may not be purely Islamic in origin. Henry Corbin, a noted scholar of comparative religion, believes that Sufism may derive from **Zoroastrianism**, in particular from the devotees in the province of Pars who did not flee when the **Moslems** conquered Persia. Whether this is so or not, Sufis maintain that **Mohammed** himself was the first Sufi and his cousin Ali, the fourth caliph, a Sufi also. To this extent, the spiritual tradition of Sufism is at least as old as Islam itself.

The word *sufi* means "a wearer of wool" and contrasts the humble clothes worn by Sufis and the luxurious clothes worn by those in positions of worldly authority. Sufis live a simple life, do not accumulate possessions, and dedicate themselves to the Way (**Tariqah**). As the receptacles of Allah, they open themselves to his grace; and while observing all the traditional practices of exoteric Islam, also seek inner communion with God: "I am the hearing wherewith he heareth and the sight wherewith he seeth." The Sufi thus experiences his own divinity as an expression of the One God who encompasses All. See also **Jalal'al-Din Rumi**; **Shams of Tabriz**; **Vedanta**.

Suggestion Technique used in **hypnosis** and **guided imagery**. Hypnosis is an **altered state of consciousness** in which the subject intensifies personal concentration and attentiveness. In this state, the subject responds to suggestions or cues from the hypnotist and is capable of bringing into conscious awareness memories and images that were formerly **subliminal**.

Sulphur In **alchemy**, the symbol of **fire** and the **spirit**, personified as male. Sulphur was regarded by the alchemists as one of the three vital ingredients of Nature, the other two constituents being **quicksilver** and **salt**, representing the soul and body respectively.

Summers, Montague (1880–1948) English author who wrote prolifically on **satanism**, **demonology**, **black magic**, and **werewolves**. Summers took the title "Reverend", although it is not known what religious orders he had been admitted to, and was a firm believer in the reality of the powers of **evil**. While obsessed with the dangers of black magic and satanism, and an advocate of the death penalty for the practice of **witchcraft**, he spent most of his life documenting these subjects and thereby stimulating interest in them. His books include *The History of Witchcraft and Demonology*, *The Vampire in Europe*, and *The Geography of Witchcraft*. He also translated the notorious medieval sourcebook of witchcraft, ***Malleus Maleficarum***, into English.

Sun The symbol of Life and **Light**, personified universally as a **deity** of goodness, spiritual **illumination**, and **rebirth**. As the symbolic centre of our immediate universe and the most dominant celestial orb, the sun has great mythological significance, being regarded variously as the eye of **Ahura Mazda**, **Zeus**, **Ra**, **Allah**, and **Varuna**. As a giver of life, the sun is usually regarded as masculine – in contrast to the **moon**, which symbolizes reflected light and is traditionally regarded as female. Among the most important sun-gods in the occult **mystery** tradition are Ra, **Osiris**, **Horus**, and **Khepera** (ancient Egypt); Helios and **Apollo** (ancient Greece); **Mithra** (ancient Persia); and **Sol** (ancient Rome).

Sun In **astrology**, the most important of the celestial bodies, and one of the most significant factors in a **horoscope**. The sun is associated with **Leo**, and considerable attention is paid by astrologers to both the **sign** and the **house** occupied by the sun at a given moment. The sun is said to define the basic temperament of a person, and to be the source of a person's vitality (i.e. "inner light").

Sun, The In the **Tarot**, the card of the **Major Arcana** that depicts a young boy and girl dancing in a magical ring and holding hands. They represent innocence and the synthesis of opposite polarities, a common theme in the Tarot. However, they are usually shown with a barrier (e.g. a wall) between themselves and the light, indicating that they have not yet attained spiritual maturity. In Western **magic**, which combines the Tarot paths of the Major Arcana with the ten **sephiroth** on the **Tree of Life**, the path of *The Sun* connects **Yesod** and **Hod**.

Sun Sign In **astrology**, the **sign** of the **zodiac** through which the sun is passing at the moment of one's birth. The sun sign is identical with one's birth sign.

Sunya In **Hinduism**, the **Void**, or zero. This number represents both Everything and Nothing, and equates with **Nirvana**. See also **Sunyata**.

Sunyata The term for the Universal **Void** in the **Mahayana Buddhist** texts. Sunyata is the Supreme Reality. See also **Sunya**.

Superconscious Term coined by the pioneering psychical researcher **F. W. H. Myers** to describe "higher" aspects of consciousness, which sometimes manifested as psychic phenomena.

Superior Planets In **astrology**, those planets which lie outside Earth's orbit: **Mars**, **Jupiter**, **Saturn**, **Uranus**, **Neptune**, and **Pluto**.

Supernals In the **Kabbalah**, the three **sephiroth** (**Kether**, **Chokmah**, and **Binah**) that lie above the **Abyss**. The supernals represent the most sacred domains of mystical consciousness symbolized by the **Tree of Life**, and are the kabbalistic equivalent of the **Trinity**.

Supernatural From the Latin *super*, "above" or "beyond," that which is beyond normal physical reality. The term is used as a synonym for the **paranormal**; but the latter is preferred by parapsychologists because **extrasensory perception** is now regarded by many researchers as a latent but natural human faculty, not as something "beyond" the world as we know it.

Superstition An irrational belief, often based on fear, which is accompanied by a strong belief in **supernatural** forces and powers affecting one's life. People who are superstitious often look for **omens** and have a special reverence for magic **charms** and **amulets**, which are believed to ward off **evil** influence. See also **Evil-eye.**

Supreme Being In **mysticism** and **occultism**, the personification of ultimate reality: **God**. Not all mystical traditions believe in a being as such – in the **Kabbalah** and **Mahayana Buddhism**, Infinite Light and the **Void**, respectively, are considered the supreme and absolute state of being.

Supreme Spirit In **spiritualism**, a term for **God**.

Survival In **spiritualism**, the continuity of the personality or **ego** after **death**. In spiritualist belief, the evidence for survival is obtained at **seances**, where communications from the dead are channelled through a **psychic medium.**

Sushumna In **yoga**, the primary **nadi** or energy channel in the body, corresponding with the spinal column. It is the only nadi that connects all the **chakras**, and is therefore regarded as the channel through which the **kundalini** is raised. Sushumna culminates in the supreme chakra, **Sahasrara.**

Suster, Gerald (1951–2001) A well-known British writer whose work focused primarily on the magic of **Aleister Crowley** and related subjects, Suster was educated at Trinity Hall, Cambridge. During his life Suster produced over thirty books, including nine novels, a book on the magical legacy of Aleister Crowley and a study of the occult ideas of Adolph Hitler. However he is best known for his book *Crowley's Apprentice*, an overview of the life and ideas of the influential magical practitioner, **Israel Regardie**, who was a close friend. An obituary by fellow Thelemite G. M. Kelly published shortly after Suster's death described him as "a gentleman, and in today's occult community that made him stand out like a glowing star in an often otherwise dark universe". See also **Regardie, Israel; Crowley, Aleister; Thelema.**

Sutra In **Hinduism** and **Buddhism**, an aphorism that provides spiritual or philosophical guidance. In the Hindu tradition, the Sutras of **Patanjali** represent the practical basis of **Raja Yoga**. The Sutras is also the name given to the second part of the **Tripitaka**, which contains the teachings of **Gautama Buddha**.

Suzuki, Daisetz T. (1870–1966) Internationally famous authority on **Zen Buddhism**. Suzuki claimed that he had himself attained **satori**, and he spent much of his professional academic life lecturing on Zen and writing books on it. For Suzuki, **enlightenment** was sudden, not gradual. He once said, "We must leap from finity to infinity and then we shall know what we are." Suzuki's many books include *Introduction to Zen Buddhism* (1934), *Training of the Zen Buddhist Monk* (1934), *Manual of Zen Buddhism* (1935), *The Essence of Buddhism* (1947), *The Zen Doctrine of No-Mind* (1949), and *Essays in Zen Buddhism* (three volumes, 1949–1951).

Svadhisthana In **yoga**, the **chakra** located below the navel in the sacral region.

Swami A Hindu holy man, spiritual teacher, or **adept**. See also **Rishi**.

Swastika Universal mythic symbol consisting of an equal-armed cross with four "arms", which appear to rotate in the same direction. Regarded by many as a type of "sun-wheel", the swastika represents eternal movement and spiritual renewal. The counterclockwise swastika adopted by the Nazis is regarded as symbolizing movement "away from the **Godhead**", and has become a contemporary motif of **evil**; while the clockwise swastika represents movement towards **God** and suggests a **cosmic** rhythm in tune with the universe.

Swedenborg, Emanuel (1688–1772) Often described as the "scientist who became a visionary", Emanuel Swedenborg showed considerable promise as a scientific student and later met the astronomer Sir Edmund Halley in England. He evolved his own "nebular hypothesis" to explain the birth of the planets, and also had a flair for scientific inventions – including a special airgun and a proposal for a submarine. However, Swedenborg is best known for his religious and mystical beliefs, which began to take a clear direction when he was in his fifties. Swedenborg claimed that he was able to communicate with heavenly beings, and his religious writings provide a clear account of what he regarded as direct messages from **spirits** and **angels**. His book *Heaven and Hell*, for example, is based on his personal visionary experiences and confirms his view that all aspects of life have their source in the **Godhead**. Swedenborg's teachings represent the doctrines of the so-called New Church (formerly known as the Swedenborgian Church), established in 1788 by Robert Hindmarsh.

Swords One of the four suits of the **Minor Arcana** of the **Tarot**. Swords are one of the two masculine suits (the other being **wands**), and are ascribed to the element **Fire**.

Sycamore Tree with mythic associations. Regarded in ancient Egypt as the **Tree of Life**, it was sacred to **Hathor**, **goddess** of love, and **Nut**, the sky-goddess and protectoress of the dead.

Sylph An **element**, or **spirit** of the element **Air**. See also **Elements**.

Symbol A representation of an abstract quality. **Mysticism** and **occultism** abound with symbols that often point to a **transcendental** reality beyond conscious understanding (e.g. the Great Mother as the womb of the universe; the infinite ocean of the **Spirit**; the **Holy Grail** as a symbol of divine inspiration and spiritual renewal; and the personification of the **sun** as a symbol of **illumination** [discovery of the inner light] and mystical **initiation**).

Symonds, John English occult author and novelist who is best known for his illuminating study of the magician **Aleister Crowley**, *The Great Beast* (1971). Symonds was appointed literary executor to Crowley's estate and, with **Kenneth Grant**, has edited a number of his more important magical writings, including *The Confessions of Aleister Crowley*, *The Magical Record of the Beast 666*, *Magick*, and *White Stains*. Symonds has also written a lucid account of the life of **Madame Helena Blavatsky**, titled *In the Astral Light* (1965).

Sympathetic Magic See **Magic, Sympathetic**.

Synastry In **astrology**, a technique of comparing the **horoscopes** of two or more people in order to determine the degree of personal compatibility and the likely outcome of the relationship between them. The technique can also be used to compare the destinies of political parties and national leaders, and even trends in international affairs. See also **Astrology, Mundane**.

Synchronicity Term used by the Swiss psychoanalyst **Carl Jung** to describe "meaningful coincidences". In Jung's view, it was not uncommon for symbols of the unconscious mind to coincide in **dreams** or mystical experiences with events occurring in the waking world of physical reality. Jung believed that synchronicity provided a rationale for **astrology** and some forms of **divination**, such as the *I Ching*.

Syncretism The merging of religious ideas and traditions. Examples include the Greek-Egyptian deity **Serapis**, who is a Hellenistic form of **Osiris**; and the Roman and **Gnostic** deities **Mithra** and **Abraxas**, both of whom have Persian antecedents.

Syzygy In **astrology**, the "yoking together" of two celestial bodies, whether in **opposition** or **conjunction**. The term is often used to describe such a relationship between a **planet** and the **sun**.

T

Tables of Houses In **astrology**, tables which show the degrees of the **signs** which occupy the **cusps** of all the **houses**, including details of **midheaven** and **ascendant**. The tables need to show the different latitudes for every degree of right ascension or for every four minutes of sidereal time.

Table-turning In **spiritualism**, a technique of communicating with the spirits of the dead. During a **seance**, a group of people assemble around a small wooden table and lightly place their hands on the table-top, palms down. At the same time, their fingers are outstretched to touch and make an unbroken circle. The table begins to "quiver" beneath the circle of hands and one of the **sitters** then proposes that the **spirit** communicate by making the table tilt or "rap" systematically (e.g. one rap indicating "yes", two raps "no"). According to some accounts, tables have levitated during such seances. See also **Levitation; Poltergeist; Psychic Medium.**

Taboo An activity forbidden by the accepted conventions or code of behaviour in a given society. In some pre-literate societies broken taboos have to be atoned for and may necessitate a **shaman** undertaking a special "spirit-journey" to seek guidance from the ruling **deity** or deities. Alternatively, special offerings and **prayers** of propitiation may be made.

Tabula Smaragdina The Latin name for the legendary **Emerald Tablet**. This tablet is said to have contained the essential wisdom-teaching of the Hermetic and alchemical traditions. See **Alchemy; Hermes Trismegistus; Hermetica.**

T'ai Chi Ch'uan Literally, "supreme ultimate fist". T'ai Chi Ch'uan is a form of self-expression, resembling dance, in which the practitioner surrenders to the natural flows of energy in the universe. It explores the processes of mind and body through creative movement, and reflects the view in the *I Ching* that "Nature is always in motion." The person learning the basic movements of T'ai Chi Ch'uan begins to experience transformations – inward and outward polarities – and the flow of **Ch'i** or life-energy, within the body. In recent years, the practice of T'ai Chi Ch'uan has become very popular in Western countries.

Talisman A magical object, like a **charm**, which is worn to attract good fortune. The talisman is often inscribed with the **god-name** or image of a **supernatural** power believed to bring luck to the person wearing it. See also **Abraxas; Amulet; Luck.**

Talmud In Judaism, the term given to the Mishnah and Gemara regarded together. The Mishnah is a textbook of opinions on the "oral Law" compiled by Rabbi Judah ha-Nasi in the second century. The Gemara is a series of discourses on the Mishnah in a question and answer style and includes anecdotes and non-legal material.

Tamas In **Hinduism**, one of the three **gunas**, or qualities of matter, the others being **sattva** and **rajas**. Tamas is negative and represents heaviness, delusion, and inertia.

Tammuz Babylonian god of vegetation who died each winter and was reborn the following spring. Tammuz was the husband of **Ishtar**, goddess of love and fertility.

Tane In Polynesia, the sky-god and lord of fertility, who protected the birds and forests and created the first man out of red clay. Tane also protected those who worked in wood, and the popular **tiki amulet** symbolizes his creative power.

Tantra Form of **Kundalini Yoga** in which the divine female energy, or **Shakti**, is aroused through ceremonial sexual union. The orgasm is resisted by self-control, however, so that the energy generated may stimulate the arousal of the **kundalini** from the **Muladhara chakra**. Tantrics regard the universe as the divine play of **Shakti** and **Shiva**, and believe that liberation may be attained by enjoyment. In the Western magical tradition, Tantra has had a profound influence on the development of rites of **sexual magic**, as practised in the **Ordo Templi Orientis.**

Taoism Ancient mystical tradition, said to have been founded by the Chinese sage **Lao Tzu**. According to Taoism, each human being is a reflection of the entire universe – a microcosm within the macrocosm. Both the universe and its inhabitants are subject to the same divine law, the Law of the Tao. To live according to the Tao is to live in harmony with Nature, heeding the flow of **yin** and **yang** energies, which are the very basis of life. See also **Macrocosm and Microcosm.**

Tao Te Ching The classic work of **Taoism**, often ascribed to **Lao Tzu**. The book is essentially a treatise on "the Way" – a method of attaining the supreme Truth in the universe. The person who accepts the teaching of the Tao practises **Wu Wei**, the path of non-action; understands the constant ebb and flow of change in life; and performs all actions in harmony with the universe.

Tapas Sanskrit word meaning "abstraction", "contemplation", or "meditation". The act of performing tapas is regarded by Hindus as a spiritual discipline, and is sometimes used to describe the ritual purifications of the body. Tapas is the practical aspect of **darshan**. See also **Asanas; Yoga.**

Target In **parapsychology**, and especially in experiments testing for **extrasensory perception**, the specific mental image or data which the subject is endeavouring to transmit. In **psychokinesis**, the word refers to the object which the subject endeavours to influence by willpower.

Tariqah In Islamic mysticism, "the Way", or spiritual path. See also **Sufism**.

Taroc See **Tarot**.

Tarot A pack of seventy-eight cards, often regarded as the precursor of modern playing cards, and commonly used in **divination**. The Tarot pack is divided into the **Major Arcana** (twenty-two cards) and the **Minor Arcana** (fifty-six cards). The latter consists of four suits – **wands**, **swords**, **cups**, and **pentacles** – and approximates the four suits of the modern pack. The Major Arcana, on the other hand, has archetypal significance, and the cards are regarded by **occultists** as symbolic meditative pathways that can be correlated with the kabbalistic **Tree of Life**. The Major Arcana includes the following cards: ***The World***; ***Judgment***; ***The Moon***; ***The Sun***; ***The Star***; ***The Tower***; ***The Devil***; ***Death***; ***Temperance***; ***The Hermit***; ***Justice***; ***The Hanged Man***; ***The Wheel of Fortune***; ***Strength***; ***The Charioteer***; ***The Lovers***; ***The Hierophant***; ***The Emperor***; ***The Empress***; ***The High Priestess***; ***The Magus***; and ***The Fool*** (see individual listings). Tarot card divination is a form of **cartomancy**.

Tart, Professor Charles (1937–) Internationally respected for his scientific research into **trance**, **dreams**, **out-of-the-body experience**, and **extrasensory perception**, Professor Tart is one of the number of contemporary scientists (others include **Dr. Stanislav Grof** and **Dr. John Lilly**), who have sought to close the gulf between science and **mysticism**. Tart has investigated the apparent **astral projection** faculties of Ingò Swann and **Robert Monroe** and has called for the recognition of "state-specific sciences" (i.e. scientific systems that recognize the existence of different states of consciousness, each with their distinct types of "reality"). Tart has written and compiled several important books, including *Altered States of Consciousness* (1969), *States of Consciousness* (1975), and *Transpersonal Psychologies* (1975).

Tartarus In Greek **mythology**, the lowest region of **Hades**, where the wicked were punished. Darker than the darkest night, it was surrounded – according to Virgil – by a river of fire.

Tashi Lama In Tibetan **Buddhism**, the **lama** who is regarded as second in importance only to the ruling **Dalai Lama**. The Tashi Lama is regarded as an incarnation of the **bodhisattva** known as Wodmagmed. Politically, he has enjoyed support from the Chinese, while the Dalai Lama has traditionally been supported by the British.

Tasseography **Divination** by reading tea leaves. The dregs of a cup of tea are swirled round three times inside the cup, and the cup is then inverted on its saucer. The **seer** then takes the cup and interprets the patterns of leaves inside it. The leaves closer to the rim are said to relate to events about to pass, while those at the bottom represent the distant future. The following patterns are taken as **omens**: stars (success); triangles (good fortune); squares (protection); bird-like shapes (an important message); and dagger shapes (personal misfortune).

Tathagata A term used by **Gautama Buddha** to describe himself. It translates as "he who has thus attained" or "he who has become enlightened".

Tattvas In **Hinduism**, the different qualities of Nature – often identified with the four elements. The Tattvas are **prithivi** (a yellow square symbolic of **Earth**); **apas** (a silver crescent symbolic of **Water**); **tejas** (a red triangle symbolic of **Fire**); and **vayu** (a blue hexagram symbolic of **Air**). Sometimes the **fifth element Akasha** (a black **egg** symbolic of **spirit**) is also included among the Tattvas. See also **Elements.**

Taurobolium Ritual associated with the cults of **Cybele** and **Mithra** in the Roman Empire. The ritual was essentially a **rebirth** ceremony in which neophytes would be baptized in the blood of the sacred bull. The blood – in itself regarded as a symbol of **life-force** – bestowed special powers of mystical renewal.

Taurus In **astrology**, the **sign** of the **zodiac** for those born between April 21 and May 20. An **Earth** sign, ruled by **Venus**, **Taurus** is symbolized by the bull. This animal was associated by the Babylonians with the beginning of spring, and by the Greeks with the transformation of **Zeus**. Apis (or **Serapis**) was also venerated as an incarnation of **Osiris** in the form of a bull. While those born under the sign of Taurus are often considered to be obstinate, practical, and even lazy, they are also said to make excellent friends, are fond of music, and are generous with money. Taureans make faithful lovers and reliable, patient companions. They often gravitate towards careers in handicrafts, building, or music.

Tea Leaf Reading See **Tasseography.**

Tejas In **Hinduism** and Western **magic**, one of the **Tattvas** or symbols of the **elements.** Tejas is symbolized by a red triangle and represents the element **Fire**. It is associated with the **Manipura chakra.**

Telekinesis In **parapsychology**, the movement of physical objects without a physical cause. The term telekinesis is used when this **paranormal** phenomenon manifests spontaneously; where it is consciously willed to occur it is referred to as **psychokinesis**. See also **Levitation; Poltergeist.**

Telepathy See **Telepathy, Mental.**

Telepathy, Dream Technique developed by parapsychologists at the **Maimonides Dream Laboratory** in New York, for testing whether a conscious subject can influence the **dreams** of a sleeping person through controlled **mental telepathy**. Because the scientific monitoring of **REM periods** eliminates conscious or unconscious fraud on the part of the dreaming subject (the recipient of "telepathic" messages), the technique has been hailed as an important breakthrough in parapsychological research. See also **Kripper, Dr. Stanley.**

Telepathy, Mental In **parapsychology**, the apparent ability of two people to communicate on a mind-to-mind basis, without recourse to speech or other normal channels of communication. Mental telepathy is one of the best-known and most widely accepted faculties of **extrasensory perception.** See also **Mental Radio.**

Teleplasm An outmoded and little-used term for **ectoplasm**. See also **Physical Medium; Spiritualism.**

Teleportation In **spiritualism**, the apparent ability to transport human beings or physical objects through space without physical or mechanical means.

Telesthesia In **parapsychology**, "the perception of the senses from afar". **Occultists** sometimes use the expression as a synonym for travelling **clairvoyance.**

Temperance In the **Tarot**, the card of the **Major Arcana** that shows the **archangel Raphael** standing with one leg in a stream (symbol of **Water**), the other on dry land (symbol of **Earth**). With him, and at his command, are an **eagle** (symbol of **Air**), and a **lion** (symbol of **Fire**) – so in this capacity the archangel unites the four **elements** in harmony. Above Raphael in the sky shines a rainbow-representative of God's covenant with mankind – and the light of new day can be seen rising in the distance over a mountain peak. *Temperance* personifies the process of spiritual **illumination** and **initiation**, for it reveals the inner light that may potentially develop within each person. The tempering, or balancing, qualities of the path are in accord with **Carl Jung**'s principle of **individuation** – the process of acquiring harmony and "wholeness" within the inner self. In Western **magic**, which combines the Tarot paths of the Major Arcana with the ten **sephiroth** on the **Tree of Life**, the path of *Temperance* connects **Yesod** and **Tiphareth** and is an intregral part of the mystic journey up the **Middle Pillar**.

Templars See **Knights Templar**.

Temple A building erected and dedicated to the worship of a god or **gods**, and often thought to be the dwelling place of the **deity** to whom it is consecrated. In Western **magic**, the temple is a sacred location (often a room within a house) in which ceremonial rites and magical **invocations** are performed. It usually has a **magic circle** inscribed upon the floor and is adorned to reflect the symbolism of the invoked deity.

Temple of Set Organization founded to replace Anton La Vey's Church of Satan. In early 1975, La Vey sent out advice in his newsletter advising that all higher degrees of initiation issued through the Church of Satan would be available in return for contributions in cash, property or valuable objects of art. This had a major impact among his followers and in June 1975 an act of mass desertion took place. Headed by leading defector Michael Aquino, key members of the priesthood resigned from the Church of Satan, at the same time making it clear that they were not leaving the priesthood, but taking it with them. In a subsequent magical ceremony, Aquino summoned the Prince of Darkness, "To tell us what we may do to continue our Quest". The result, acording to Aquino, was an act of automatic writing … "a communication from a god to a human being". In a document known as *The Book of Coming Forth by Night*, Satan revealed himself as the ancient Egyptian god **Set**, and named Michael Aquino as La Vey's replacement. Aquino was also described in the script as the successor to **Aleister Crowley**, and Magus, fifth degree, of the new **Aeon** of Set. Set also announced in this communication that the sacred magical word for the new era would be "xeper", meaning "to become". Aquino retired from the high priesthood of the Temple of Set in 1996 and Don Webb assumed the role of Magus, fifth degree. See also **Xeper; Crowley, Aleister; La Vey, Anton; Church of Satan.**

Temple of the Flesh An occult and mystical term for the physical body.

Temurah Also Temura. Kabbalistic technique of modifying the sequence of letters to achieve a particular effect. The first half of the Hebrew alphabet is written in reverse order and located above the remaining section so that the letters form vertical pairs:

k	y	th	ch	z	v	h	d	g	b	a
l	m	n	s	o	p	th	q	r	sh	t

In this code, k = l, y = m, th = n, and so on. A given word is disguised in temurah by substituting the code letter in each case, so that completely new words are formed. Compare with **Gematria; Notarikon.** See also **Kabbalah.**

Teonanacatl Name given by the Nahuatl Indians of Mexico to a variety of mushrooms used in religious worship prior to the arrival of the Spaniards. Used to describe a number of agaric mushrooms, including *psilocybe*, the word "teonanacatl" translates as "flesh of the gods" – a reference to the sacred visions arising from the hallucinatory qualities of the mushrooms. See also **Hallucination**; **Psilocybin**.

Terreiro In **Macumba**, the **temple** where ceremonial worship takes place and offerings are made to the **gods**.

Tetrad In **numerology**, the number **four**.

Tetragrammaton In the Jewish mystical tradition, the sacred four-lettered name of **God**, rendered variously as IHVH, JHVH, or YHVH. The name has been transcribed as **Jehovah**, and more recently as **Yahweh**; but it was never written down by devout Jews because it was considered too sacred for general use. It was often replaced by the word **Adonai**, meaning "Lord."

Tezcatlipoca Aztec **god** of life and air who ruled as the **sun** of the first universe. He is often depicted struggling with the serpent-god **Quetzalcoatl**. Tezcatlipoca was, paradoxically, a god of darkness; and was represented by a dark **obsidian** mirror that was believed to reflect the future of humankind.

Thanatology The study of **death** and the **near-death experience**.

Thanatos In Greek **mythology**, the god of **death**. His Roman counterpart is Mors.

Thaumaturge From the Greek *thaumatourgos*, "one who works wonders", a miracle-worker or **magician**.

Thaumaturgy **Magic**, or the working of wonders or **miracles** by calling on **supernatural** powers. See also **Thaumaturge**.

Theism From the Greek *theos*, "a god", the belief in **gods** or a **God**. The belief in a single God who **transcends** the universe, but is also **immanent** within it, is known as **monotheism**; belief in a plurality of gods is known as **polytheism**. The distinction between monotheism and polytheism is less marked in **cosmologies** where individual gods are regarded as an **emanation** of the transcendent **Godhead**, as in some forms of Egyptian and **Gnostic** religion.

Thelema Greek word for **will**, which the ceremonial **magician Aleister Crowley** used to define one's true, occult purpose. Crowley formulated the magical axiom "Do what thou wilt shall be the whole of the Law." However, he did not interpret this to mean self-indulgence, believing as he did that the magician was obliged to discover his true will, or inner purpose in life, and to have communion with the **holy guardian angel**. As Crowley's disciple **Kenneth Grant** has written, "The purpose of **magick** is to unveil the True Will and reveal the Hidden Light."

Themis In Greek **mythology**, the daughter of **Uranus** and **Gaea**, the mother of the **Three Fates**. Themis was one of the twelve **Titans** and was the first Greek **goddess** to have a temple erected in her honour.

Theocracy The uniting, or "mingling," of several **gods** or divine attributes within one composite personality. The word is also used to describe the mystical union with **God**.

Theogony From the Greek *theos*, "a god," the study of the origin and genealogy of **gods** in a **pantheon** (e.g. the **Twelve Great Olympians**).

Theology The study of religion and sacred doctrines. This includes the relationship of the divine and physical worlds, the study of the nature and will of **God**, and religious teachings relating to the creation of the universe.

TEMPERANCE: An important Tarot card in the Major Arcana, symbolizing the reconciliation of opposites. From the Rider Tarot deck.

Theomachy A combat with, or among, the **gods**; opposition to divine will. The biblical account of **Lucifer**'s fall from grace provides an example of a contest of this sort.

Theopathy Literally, "the suffering of God", the religious and mystical emotions aroused by meditating on **God**: religious **ecstasy**.

Theophagy The practice of "eating the god" during a sacred or sacrificial ceremony. The animal- or food-offering personifies the **god**, and the act of partaking of the sacrifice confers supernatural power upon the devotees.

Theophany The manifestation or appearance of a **deity** or **god** before humankind.

Theosophical Society Mystical and occult organization founded in New York in 1875 by **Madame Helena Blavatsky**, **Colonel H. S. Olcott**, **William Q. Judge**, and a small group of other interested people. The society had three basic aims: (1) the brotherhood of man, without distinction of race, colour, religion, or social position; (2) the serious study of the ancient world religions for purposes of comparison and the selection therefrom of universal ethics; and (3) the study and development of the latent **divine** powers in people.

The Theosophical Society has been influential in cultural and political affairs ever since, attracting such members as **Sir William Crookes**, Thomas Alva Edison, **William Butler Yeats**, and **Rudolf Steiner**. (Steiner in due course broke away, founding the Anthroposophical Society.) Mahatma Gandhi first studied the ***Bhagavad-Gita*** with Theosophists; and the influential **Dr. Annie Besant**, who became the second president of the Theosophical Society in 1891, worked tirelessly in favour of Indian home rule, believing it to be the will of the supernatural powers formulating the "Great Plan".

While the Theosophical Society has drawn primarily on **Buddhism** and **Hinduism** for its religious teachings, its members generally believe in a universal wisdom-teaching or **esoteric** tradition which has been available in all cultures and which draws on perennial and universal Truth. See also **Arundale, George; Krishnamurti, Jiddu; Leadbeater, Charles.**

Theosophy The teaching and doctrines of the **Theosophical Society**.

Theosophy From the Greek, *theos*, "a god", *sophos* "wise", divine wisdom. The term is used to describe a number of **esoteric** and mystical systems that describe the relationship of human beings to the universe and the **Godhead** (e.g. **Gnosticism**, **Neoplatonism**, **Kabbalah**). Usually, these belief systems describe **emanations** from the **Infinite God**, or **Supreme Being**, who reveals different aspects of **transcendent** reality through various intermediary **deities**, **spirits**, "intelligences", and levels of **manifestation**. See also **Aeons; Archons; Subtle Planes.**

Theravada Buddhism See **Hinayana Buddhism.**

Theurgy From the Greek *theourgos*, "a divine worker", the working of **miracles** through supernatural aid. Among the **Neoplatonists** miraculous effects were believed to result from magical **invocations** to **gods** and **spirits**, and the word theurgy has come to mean "divine magic" or **white magic**. This interpretation of magic has been succinctly defined by **Israel Regardie** in his major work *The Tree of Life* (1932), where he writes: "the object of magic … is the return of man to the gods."

Third Eye Expression made popular by the mystical author **Lobsang Rampa**, whose book *The Third Eye* was an international bestseller. The third eye is the sixth of the seven **chakras**

in **Kundalini Yoga**, and is located between and slightly above the eyebrows, at the centre of the forehead. It is sometimes linked to the **pineal gland**, which is regarded by **occultists** as the seat of **psychic** and **paranormal** powers.

Thirteen A number widely regarded as unlucky. For the superstitious, Friday the thirteenth is a day to beware of, and it is an ill **omen** for thirteen people to sit down at a table together; the first and last people to rise from it are likely to die or suffer grievous misfortune before a year has passed. The origins of the superstition are unknown, but the fact that thirteen guests sat down with Jesus at the Last Supper – the first to rise being the traitor Judas – may have contributed to it.

Thirty Aethyrs The magical **invocations** employed by the **occultists Aleister Crowley** and **Victor Neuburg** during their remarkable ceremonial workings in Algeria in 1909. The invocations were based on the **Enochian** magic system of **Dr. John Dee** and **Edward Kelley**, and included the conjuration of the Demon of Chaos, **Choronzon**. Crowley also invoked two of the Aethyrs in Mexico in 1900.

Thor In Scandinavian **mythology**, the **god** of the sky and thunder. The son of **Odin**, Thor was depicted as a strong but friendly man with a red beard, who aided farmers and sailors. However, he was the sworn enemy of the **giants** and **demons** who threatened to overturn the forces of order in the world. Thor possessed a famous hammer, which he used to break the winter ice and make possible the arrival of spring. At **Ragnarok**, Thor and the **Midgard Serpent** destroyed each other.

Thoth In ancient Egyptian **mythology**, the **god** of wisdom and **magic**. Thoth was the scribe of the **gods**, invented numbers, and measured time. He was also a **moon**-god. Together with his consort **Maat**, Thoth was present in the **Judgment Hall**, where the hearts of the deceased were weighed against the **feather** of truth. Thoth recorded the judgments of the dead, and the first month of the Egyptian year was named after him. He was depicted either as an ibis or as an ibis-headed man, and was identified by the Greeks with **Hermes**, messenger of the gods.

Thought-form A mental image that forms on the **astral plane** as a result of willed intent. The ability to "hold pictures in the imagination" has a magical application, because **occultists** believe it is possible to transfer consciousness to thought-forms and use them as "magical bodies" on the inner or **subtle planes**. Thought-forms can also personify the collective will of a magical group. See also **Astral Projection; Egrigor; Shape-shifting; Simulacrum.**

Thought Photography The apparent ability of some psychics to transmit mental images onto photographic film. See also **Psychic Photography; Serios, Ted.**

Thought-reading A popular term for **mental telepathy**.

Thought-transference See **Mental Telepathy**. The American novelist Upton Sinclair engaged in "thought transference" experiments with his wife Mary, and coined the expression "**mental radio**" to describe the apparent transfer of thoughts and impressions.

Thouless, Dr. Robert H. Distinguished English psychologist who made an extensive study of **extrasensory perception** (**ESP**). With a colleague, Dr. B. P. Wiesner, Thouless formulated the view that ESP could be "incoming and cognitive" (the familiar term ESP was applicable for this), or "motor-related and outgoing" (in which case the term **PK**, or **psychokinesis**, was more applicable). In Dr. Thouless's view, extrasensory perception bypassed the normal range of human senses. Thouless was president of the **Society for Psychical Research** between 1942 and 1944 and wrote several books, including *Psychology of Religion* (1923), *Straight and Crooked Thinking* and *Authority and Freedom* (1954). He was also the author of numerous scientific papers on extrasensory perception.

Three A number widely regarded as spiritual and creative. In Christianity it is the number of the Trinity; and in the **Kabbalah**, three **sephiroth** (**Kether**, **Chokmah**, and **Binah**) lie above the **Abyss**. In **Hinduism**, a triad of gods – the **trimurti** of **Brahma**, **Vishna**, and **Shiva** – are the vital aspects of creation; and among the Pythagoreans three was considered a perfect number because it had a beginning, a middle, and an end. On the level of popular **numerology**, three symbolizes intelligence, vitality, artistic ability, and ambition. It is also a lucky number and is regarded as a popular choice on love **charms**.

Throne In **astrology**, a planet is described as being "on its throne" when it is located in the **sign** of which it is the **ruler** (e.g. **sun** in **Leo**).

Throne Mysticism See **Merkabah**.

Thundering Rod In **ceremonial magic**, the magical **wand** of the **sorcerer**. The wand is one of several "magical weapons" used in Western **magic** and is ascribed to the sephirah **Hod** on the kabbalistic **Tree of Life**. It is associated with **Mercury** and the element **Air**.

Thurible A shallow dish mounted on three legs and used in **witchcraft**. The thurible is placed on the altar and used to mix herbs and burn incense.

Tiamat Babylonian **goddess** of the sea; the personification of chaos and **evil**. Tiamat was depicted as a monstrous **dragon**. The warrior-god **Marduk** finally slew her, and the two halves of her body formed heaven and earth.

Tibetan Book of the Dead See **Bardo**; **Book of the Dead**.

T'ien In **Taoism**, the term for **heaven**. Related to the Chinese word *ti*, which originally meant a "tribal lord" and then came to denote "the Lord over all", T'ien represents the omnipresent Lord: the supreme spiritual reality.

Tiki Polynesian **amulet**, usually worn around the neck. The tiki is a human figure and is usually made of wood and mother-of-pearl. It depicts the first man created by the sky god **Tane**.

Tiphareth In the **Kabbalah**, the sixth mystical **emanation** on the **Tree of Life**. In the traditional Kabbalah it is the sphere of Beauty, harmonizing the forces of Mercy (**Chesed**) and Judgment (**Geburah**), higher on the Tree.

Occultists identify Tiphareth as the sphere of spiritual **rebirth**, and ascribe to it the solar **deities** of different **pantheons** – including **Ra**, **Apollo**, and **Mithra** – as well as the resurrected gods **Osiris** and Jesus Christ. In modern Western **magic**, the **Tarot** path of *Temperance* identifies the direct mystical ascent to Tiphareth from **Malkuth**, the physical world. See also **Solar Gods**.

Tisiphone In Greek and Roman **mythology**, one of the three **Erinyes** or **Furies** – the avenging spirits. The other two were Alecto and Megaera.

Titans, The Twelve In Greek **mythology**, the twelve children of **Uranus** and **Gaea** who ruled the earth before the reign of the **Twelve Great Olympians**. The Titans were the "first race" on earth and personified the violent side of Nature. After their defeat they were sent to **Tartarus**. The Titans were both male and female. Their names were **Oceanus**, Hyperion, Crius, Coeus, **Kronos**, and Iapetus (male personifications of the sea, **sun**, memory, **moon**, harvests, and justice, respectively); and Tethys, Thia, Eurybia (or Mnemosyne), Phoebe, **Rhea**, and **Themis** (their female counterparts).

Tloque Nahuaque Among the Aztecs, the supreme and ineffable **god** who created the world during the so-called "first era" of the Water Sun. After 1716 years the world was ravaged by floods and lightning and in the second era – that of the Earth Sun – was populated by giants. In Aztec **cosmology**, life developed through five suns, or eras, in all. The cult of Tloque Nahuaque was centred in Texcoco. See also **Ometecuhtli**.

TM See **Transcendental Meditation.**

Tobioscope Russian device, developed from apparatus used in **Kirlian photography**, which is claimed to identify the exact location of **acupuncture** points on the body by electronic means. See also **Meridians**.

Toning See **Fransisters and Brothers.**

Torah Hebrew word meaning "teaching". It refers specifically to the first five books of the Old Testament, known as the Pentateuch, which were said to have been dictated to Moses by God on Mount Sinai. In Judaism there is also said to be an "oral Law", and this consists of learned opinions and discussions related to the written Torah.

Totem An animal, object, or mythic creature that symbolizes the unity of a clan or family group and is regarded as sacred. Native American totem poles depict totem animals, carved and painted in bright colours.

Tower, The In the **Tarot**, the card of the **Major Arcana** that depicts the arrogant attempt by people to scale the heights of **heaven**. The tower shown on this card reaches to lofty heights, but is fragmented by a blast of lightning from the **Godhead**, dislodging the crown (i.e. **Kether**), which is its turret. Two human figures are also shown plummeting to the Earth. Regarded by **occultists** as a symbolic warning against pride on the mystic journey, the symbolism of *The Tower* is sometimes compared to the Tower of Babel. Associated with the sexual sphere of the **Tree of Life**, *The Tower* is also in some degree a phallic symbol and the energy of the thunderbolt is the magical equivalent of the **kundalini**. There is a clear implication that the **magicians** should balance personality and ambitions, and proceed on the inner journey with a "solid foundation" of humility and systematic endeavour. In Western **magic**, which combines the Tarot paths of the Major Arcana with the ten **sephiroth** of the **Tree of Life**, the path of *The Tower* connects **Hod** and **Netzach**.

Trance See **Trance, Hypnotic.**

Trance, Hypnotic An **altered state of consciousness** in which a subject's powers of concentration are mobilized, and subconscious memories and perceptions brought to the surface. Hypnotherapists relax their subjects progressively, often by using a countdown of numbers or by progressively relaxing the body limb by limb from the feet to the head. The pioneering European hypnotherapists recognized the value of the **imagination** for therapeutic purposes, and combined relaxation techniques with **guided imagery**. For example, Alfred Binet encouraged his patients to "talk" to the visual images that arose in what he called "provoked introspection", and Wolfgang Kretschmer described the process in 1922 as *bilderstreifendenken* – "thinking in the form of a movie". For Kretschmer, hypnotic trance could be used to "expose internal psychic problems" that presented themselves in the consciousness of the subject. See also **Hypnosis**.

Trance, Mediumistic In **spiritualism** and some forms of pre-literate religion, a type of trance state characterized by the withdrawal from the familiar behavioural patterns of the normal conscious personality and its replacement by a **secondary personality**, which acts as if it is another personality "possessing" the body of the **medium**. This secondary personality is referred to in spiritualism as the **control** and in pre-literate societies is often interpreted as a **deity** or ancestral spirit. Mediums often have no recollection of their psychic "transformation" while in the trance state, and are usually unaware of specific utterances or pronouncements that have been made.

Trance, Shamanic In pre-literate religion, a type of **trance** state characterized by the **journey of the soul**. The **shaman** undertakes this journey in order to obtain information, and sometimes visionary insights, from the **gods** of creation whose rules and **taboos** govern society. The shaman enters the magical dimension in a state of sensory deprivation (usually total darkness) and often uses percussive instruments to establish a rhythm that is used to propel him on his vision-quest. Shamanic trance differs from **mediumistic trance** to the extent that the shaman returns with full knowledge of his visionary journey and is able to report on his encounter with the gods. The **deities** do not "possess" the shaman as they do in mediumism, although in some shamanic initiations the body of the shaman is transformed by the gods in order to bestow supernatural powers. See also **Shamanism**.

Trance Medium A **psychic medium** who is able to enter a state of trance, usually to communicate with the **spirits** of the dead. In modern **spiritualism**, the possessing entity is called a **control**.

Trance Personality See **Control**.

Transcendent, Transcendental That which exceeds the bounds of possible human experience and knowledge. It is often applied to the "unknowable" **God** who lies far beyond human comprehension. The concept of a transcendent **Supreme Being** may be compared with the idea of an **immanent** God who is omnipresent in Nature and accessible to the senses.

Transcendental Meditation (TM) Form of **meditation** advocated by the **Maharishi Mahesh Yogi**. TM requires that the person meditating relax totally and concentrate on repeating an individual secret **mantra**. Essentially, this form of meditation is said to heighten the powers of self-awareness, allows deep tranquillity, and represents a journey to the inner **self**. TM has several million adherents in the United States and is also popular in Britain, Europe, and Australia.

Transfiguration Medium A **psychic medium** who, while entering a state of trance **possession**, takes on the facial characteristics and mannerisms of the communicating spirit as he or she was known while alive on earth. See also **Control**.

Transit In **astrology**, the movement of a **planet** through a **sign** or **house**. The angles between planets on a **horoscope** are interpreted for their different **aspects**.

Transitional Rites See **Rites of Passage**.

Transmigration The belief that, after **death**, the **soul** can pass into another physical body – either human or animal. Transmigration is synonymous with **metempsychosis**, but differs from the doctrine of **reincarnation**, according to which the human soul is capable only of future human incarnations and does not devolve into an animal form.

Transpersonal Psychology Name given to the so-called "fourth force" in psychology.

Transpersonal psychology follows on from "first force" classical psychoanalytical theory; "second force" behaviourist psychology; and "third force" humanistic psychology. It deals with such areas of human consciousness as self-transcendence, **peak experience**, mystical transformation, and ultimate values. The term "transpersonal" itself refers to that which transcends the **ego**, and thus implies a sympathy for mystical and **paranormal** topics and ideas. The term was first used in a lecture in 1967 by the psychiatrist **Dr. Stanislav Grof**, and became the title of the new psychological movement following a proposal by Abraham Maslow and Anthony Sutich.

The Transpersonal Movement is closely associated with **Esalen Institute.**

Trapas A Tibetan Buddhist monk of lower rank than a **lama.**

Tree of Life In the **Kabbalah**, the multiple symbol known in Hebrew as the **Otz Chiim**. The Tree consists of ten spheres, or **sephiroth**, through which – according to mystical tradition – the creation of the world came about. The sephiroth are aligned in three columns headed by the **supernals** (**Kether**, **Chokmah**, and **Binah**) and together symbolize the process by which the Infinite Light **Ain Soph Aur** becomes manifest in the universe. Beneath the supernals are the "seven days of creation": **Chesed**, **Geburah**, **Tiphareth**, **Netzach**, **Hod**, **Yesod**, and **Malkuth**. Taken as a whole, the Tree of Life is also a symbol of the archetypal man **Adam Kadmon**, and the sephiroth have a role resembling that of the **chakras** in **yoga**. The mystical path of self-knowledge entails the rediscovery of all of the levels of one's being, ranging from Malkuth (physical reality) to the infinite Source. With this in mind, the medieval Kabbalists divided the Tree of Life into three sections of the soul: **Nephesch** (the animal soul) corresponding to the sephirah Yesod; **Ruach** (the middle soul) corresponding to the sephiroth from Hod to Chesed; and **Neschamah** (the spiritual soul) corresponding to the supernals – especially Binah.

Practitioners of Western **magic**, who use the Tree of Life as a glyph for the unconscious mind, sometimes distinguished the "magical" path (which embraces all ten sephiroth) from the "mystical" path of the **Middle Pillar**, which is an ascent from Malkuth through Yesod and Tiphareth to Kether on the central pillar of the Tree. **Occultists** also identify the twenty-two cards of the **Major Arcana** of the **Tarot** with the paths connecting the ten sephiroth, although this view is not accepted by traditional scholars of the Kabbalah.

Triangle In Western **magic**, a symbol of finite **manifestation**. In **rituals**, it is used for the purpose of evoking **spirits**. A **talisman** is placed in the centre of the triangle, together with the **seal** or **sign** of the entity to be summoned. Ceremonial **magicians** take considerable care to mentally reinforce the confines of the triangle in order to contain the evoked spirit. The triangle may be compared with the **magic circle**, which is a symbol of **invocation**. In this case, by contrast, the magician stands within the circle and summons **supernatural** forces, which may lead to his own spiritual transformation.

Triloka In Hindu **cosmology**, the three worlds of *svarga* (**heaven**); *bhumi* (**Earth**); and *patala* (**hell**).

Trimurti In **Hinduism**, the triad of gods **Brahma**, **Vishnu**, and **Shiva**, who are believed to be three aspects of the supreme and infinite **Brahman**. According to the *Vishnu Purana*, "The Lord God, though one without a second, assumes the three forms respectively of Brahma, Vishnu and Shiva for creation, preservation and dissolution of the world." Some writers have discerned a parallel between the trimurti and the Christian Trinity.

Trine In **astrology**, an **aspect** characterized by an angle of 120 degrees between two **planets**.

Trip Colloquial expression for the **psychedelic** experience. The hallucinogenic "journey" is sometimes characterized as a "good trip" (beneficial, enjoyable, enlightening) or a "bad trip" (frightening, paranoic, evil, or alarming). See also **Flying Ointments; Hallucination.**

Tripitaka Also known as the "Three Baskets," the Tripitaka is the Buddhist Canon which, according to some authorities, was compiled within a century of **Gautama Buddha**'s death. It consists of (1) doctrine; (2) the rules and laws for priests and ascetics; and (3) philosophical dissertations. The most complete version of the Tripitaka has been preserved by the **Theravada** Buddhists and is written in **Pali**.

Trolls In Scandinavian **mythology**, elemental spirits who lived in caves in the mountains and emerged after nightfall to steal women and substitute **changelings** for human offspring. Trolls took two forms – they were either **giants** or **dwarfs** – and they were regarded by country folk with extreme caution. They could be kept away by sprigs of **mistletoe**, large bonfires, or the sound of church bells.

Trump In the **Tarot**, a general term for each of the twenty-two cards of the **Major Arcana**.

Tuat In ancient Egyptian **mythology**, the netherworld of darkness, which corresponded with the twelve hours (or dungeons) of Night. The Egyptians conceived of the land of the living as being surrounded by a chain of mountains. The sun rose by emerging through a hole in the East and sank through a hole in the West. Fairly close to these mountains, and beyond them, lay the Tuat. According to **Sir Wallis Budge**, the Tuat was located not underground, but parallel with the mountains and on the same plane as the earth and sky. The sun-god passed through the Tuat each day, safely protected from the forces of **evil** by **magical formulae** or **hekau** which enabled him to pass from one dungeon to the next. See also ***Am Tuat*; Khepera.**

Tuatha De Danaan In the Celtic tradition of Ireland, the **gods** who became the rulers of the country after defeating the Fomorians. These **deities** – the people of **Dana** – took their name from the **mother-goddess** Dana. The male leader of the Tuatha De Danaan was **Dagda**.

Tulasi In **Hinduism**, a sacred plant (*Ocynum sanctum*) that features in the **mythology** of **Vishnu** and his wife **Lakshmi**. Vishnu, the sun- and sky-god who is part of the **trimurti**, had many lovers and one of these was Tulasi, an earth-goddess. In an act of jealousy, Lakshmi turned Tulasi into a plant. Today the plant is venerated in Hindu temples and is used by the superstitious to avert misfortune.

Tulku Tibetan Buddhist term meaning "one who is divinely incarnated". It is often used with reference to the **Dalai Lama**.

Tumo The Tibetan Buddhist technique of keeping warm in spite of snow, ice, and freezing winds. The Tumo technique is a specific **meditation** that channels mystical heat through the veins, arteries, and nerve channels and enables the **adept** to remain warm without a fire and with only minimal clothing. The French author **Alexandra David-Neel** has described how she learned tumo by bathing in an icy mountain stream and then, without drying or dressing, meditated through the night. In due course she was able to become immune to cold weather conditions and no longer needed a fire to keep warm. Tibetan Buddhists believe that knowledge of tumo sharpens the mental faculties of perception and intuition.

Tunraq Among the Netsilik Eskimos, the protector-spirit given to the **shaman** during his **initiation**. According to traditional Eskimo belief, it was possible for the shaman to acquire further tunraqs, either as gifts from other shamans or following the spirits' own volition. Tunraqs generally had an animal form or were ancestors of the dead. The famous Netsilik shaman Iksivalitaq, who died in 1940, was said to have had seven tunraqs – including the spirit of a dog with no ears, the spirit of a killer whale, and the ghost of his grandfather.

Tun Wu Among the Ch'an Buddhists, the Chinese term for **satori**.

Turiya Sanskrit term for the state of consciousness that transcends the three "ordinary states" of waking, sleep, and dreamless sleep (**jagrat**, svapna, and sushupti, respectively). Turiya is defined as the One Reality of undifferentiated consciousness which transcends all aspects of thought.

Twelve A number widely regarded as a symbol of completion and totality. There are twelve months in a year and twelve tribes of Israel; twelve labours of **Heracles** and **Twelve Great Olympians**. Jesus had twelve apostles, and there are traditionally "twelve days of Christmas". Twelve is related to the number **seven** – another number of mystical significance – because seven consists of 4 + 3 and twelve is 4 x 3. See also **Numerology**.

Twigg, Ena (1914–) English-born **psychic medium** who maintained that at the age of seven she was able to speak to the "misty people". After her marriage to Harry Twigg she became seriously ill, but was assured by three **spirit** beings that she would regain her health. She recovered, joined the organization that has now become the Spiritualist Association of Great Britain, and has become one of the foremost psychic mediums of her time. Her autobiography, titled *Ena Twigg – Medium*, was written in collaboration with Ruth Hagy Brod.

Twitchell, Paul (1908–1971) American-born founder of the contemporary **Eckankar** (ECK) movement. Twitchell claimed that at an early age he was sent by his grandmother to Paris, where he met the Indian **guru** Sudar Singh – however, this was not substantiated by his family. It is known, however, that in 1950 Twitchell and his wife Camille joined Swami Premananda's Self Revelation Church of Absolute Monism, although Camille deserted him and Twitchell was asked to leave because of misconduct. He was later initiated by the Hindu mystic Kirpal Singh into the "divine science of the soul".

Twitchell formed Eckankar in 1964, describing it as the "cosmic current" through which **God** could be realized. Many spiritual teachers of the past, including St. Paul and Jesus, were ECK masters, according to Twitchell. He regarded himself as the 971st such master and, after a fatal heart attack, was succeeded by the 972nd ECK master, Darwin Gross. Twitchell achieved fame as a result of developing various techniques of **astral travel**, and many of his disciples claimed to see him while his physical body was elsewhere. His books include *The Far Country* and *Introduction to Eckankar*. Brad Steiger's biography of Twitchell, *In My Soul I Am Free*, was published in 1968.

Two A number associated with division and lack of harmony. As the opposite of **one**, it stands apart from **God** and is therefore considered by many to be **evil**. However, on the level of popular **numerology**, two is considered to be a number associated with the person who follows rather than leads; therefore, it has the attributes of gentleness and tact, although these qualities are often combined with indecision and hesitation.

Typhon In Greek **mythology**, a monstrous, fire-breathing giant with a hundred **dragon** heads and a body covered with serpents. The youngest son of **Gaea**, Typhon was the father of many monsters in turn – including the **Hydra** of Lerna, the **Chimera**, and **Cerberus**. Typhon was finally struck by a thunderbolt from **Zeus** and despatched to **Tartarus**, the lowest region of **Hades**.

Typtology In **spiritualism**, the term given to the act of receiving **psychic** messages through **table-turning**.

Tyrrell, George Nugent Merle (1879–1952) English parapsychologist who was a student of Guglielmo Marconi and a pioneer in the development of radio. Tyrrell joined the **Society for Psychical Research** in 1908, and undertook extensive experiments in **mental telepathy** and **precognition** during the 1920s. He became increasingly interested in **spiritualism**, the question of survival after **death**, and the nature of human consciousness. For example, Tyrrell believed that **ghosts** were "subjective" and telepathic, and existed in regions of the human personality outside the field of normal consciousness. He was one of the first scientific investigators to incorporate topics that had been previously regarded as **supernatural** within the realm of mainstream psychological theory. Tyrrell was also a prolific author. His many books include *Science and Psychical Phenomena* (1938), *The Personality of Man* (1946), and *Apparitions* (1953). He became president of the Society for Psychical Research in 1945.

U

UFO See **Unidentified Flying Objects**.

Ufology The study of **unidentified flying objects**. Research and investigation groups have existed in most Western countries since sightings of **flying saucers** became prevalent after 1947, following Kenneth Arnold's report of aerial discs. Ufology ranges in content from official air force investigations of unidentified flying objects (which are usually classified as weather balloons, optical illusions, or meteorological phenomena), through to claimed "contact" cases involving alleged meetings with aliens.

Ullman, Dr. Montague (1916–) American psychiatrist who became interested in **parapsychology** and worked with **Dr. Stanley Krippner** in establishing the **Maimonides Dream Laboratory** in New York. For many years, Dr. Ullman has been involved in the clinical investigation of telepathic dreams and the interpretation of **dreams** in psychotherapy. His books include *Behavioral Changes in Patients Following Strokes* and *Dream Telepathy* (1973), co-authored with Dr. Krippner and **Alan Vaughan**.

Ulysses The Roman name for the Greek hero **Odysseus**.

Umbral Eclipse In **astrology**, an eclipse of the **moon**, which occurs when the moon enters the Earth's shadow (from the Latin *umbra*, "a shadow"). The term is also used to describe an eclipse of the **sun** where the disc of the moon is fully contained within that of the sun.

Unconscious In psychoanalysis, that part of the **psyche** which is not within the range of waking consciousness. The unconscious aspects of the mind lie below the threshold of consciousness, but can be brought into the field of conscious awareness by such techniques as **hypnosis** and **guided imagery**. Carl Jung identified the archetypal areas of the psyche as the **collective unconscious**. The term **subconscious** is often used as a synonym.

Unconscious, Collective See **Collective Unconscious**.

Unction Ceremonial anointing with oil, either as an act of consecration or in special rites to heal the sick. In magical ceremonies, practitioners may be anointed with "holy oil" to personify the sacred quest of **theurgy**. For example, ceremonial **magicians** following the tradition of the **Hermetic Order of the Golden Dawn** anoint the four points of the microcosm (**Kether, Chesed, Geburah**, and **Malkuth**, from the kabbalistic **Tree of Life**) upon the forehead, left and right shoulders, and solar plexus, respectively. The ointment consists of the oils of olive, myrrh, cinnamon, and galangal.

Underhill, Evelyn (1875–1941) English poet, novelist, and **mystic**. Raised in an Anglican family, she had a religious visionary experience in 1906 that convinced her of the universal truth of the Church of Rome. She later taught philosophy of religion at Manchester College, Oxford, and gained an honorary doctorate in divinity from Aberdeen University. Notwithstanding her orthodox religious background, she was fascinated by the occult tradition and joined the **Hermetic Order of the Golden Dawn** in 1904. Her best-known work is the classic *Mysticism*, first published in 1911.

Underwood, Peter British occult author who for many years has been president of the famous **Ghost Club**, an organization originally founded in 1862. Underwood has been engaged in scientific **psychical research** for over thirty years, specializing in the study of **extrasensory perception, mental telepathy**, and **hauntings**. In *Beyond the Senses*, a work on **parapsychology** by Paul Tabori and Phyllis Raphael, he was described as a "veteran psychical researcher ... representing the middle-ground attitude between extreme scepticism and uncritical belief" – an assessment Underwood himself accepts. He is the author of several books on the occult, including *Haunted London, Ghosts of North West England, The Ghost Hunter's Companion*, and *Inside the Occult*.

Underworld In many ancient **mythologies**, a domain beneath the earth where the **souls** of the deceased went after **death**. In Greek mythology, **Hades** was located in the West, on the edge of the Earth. There were said to be five rivers in the Underworld: **Acheron** (woe); Cocytus (waiting); Lethe (forgetfulness); Phlegethon (fire); and the **Styx** (by which the **gods** sealed their **oaths**). **Charon** ferried the souls of the dead to the entrance of the Underworld, which was guarded by **Cerberus**. The deceased were subsequently judged and either allowed entrance to the blessed **Elysian Fields** or condemned to a world of torment in **Tartarus**. In Scandinavian mythology, **Niflheim** was located in the icy North.

Undine A female **elemental** or **sprite** associated with **water**. See also **Nereides; Nymphs; Oceanides**.

Unfortunate Signs In **astrology**, the so-called negative signs of the **zodiac**: **Taurus, Cancer, Virgo, Scorpio, Capricorn**, and **Aquarius**.

Unguent An ointment or salve. In the Middle Ages, hallucinatory unguents were prepared by **witches** to produce the visionary sensation of flight to the sabbath. See also **Flying Ointments**.

Unicorn A mythic creature in folk legend and heraldry, which usually takes the form of a horse with a single horn extending from its forehead. However, unicorns in various parts of the world are also depicted with the body of a goat, rhinoceros, ram, or serpent. In the Middle Ages, the unicorn had Christian associations – its horn symbolizing the unity of God the Father and God the Son – but it also featured in the tradition of courtly love, for only a virgin holding a mirror was able to tame it. The unicorn was usually regarded as a symbol of purity and spiritual unity, its horn being considered masculine and its body feminine. In **alchemy**, the unicorn was associated with the male-female or androgynous **Mercury**: a motif indicating attainment of the Great Work.

Unidentified Flying Object (UFO) Flying object that is not identified as a man-made aircraft or missile and which does not conform with natural meteorological or astronomical phenomena. UFOs have been subject to official investigation through such channels as the US Air Force's Project Blue Book and the Condon Committee Investigation at the University of Colorado. While many UFO reports have been categorized as misinterpretations of natural phenomena (e.g. cloud formations, meteors), the Condon Committee was shown to be biased in favour of weak reports at the expense of well-documented ones and failed to account for sightings by observers skilled in night-time identification (e.g. astronomers, policemen, patrol officers). Consequently, the scientific study of UFOs remains unresolved, and no convincing explanation has been forthcoming. UFOs are regarded variously as of extraterrestrial origin or as secret machines under development by the major powers and spotted while on test flights. The psychoanalyst **Carl Jung** regarded UFOs as a projection of the **unconscious**, but was puzzled by reports of waste products (e.g. filament threads) emitted by some UFOs.

Unio Mystica See **Mystic Union**.

Union of Opposites Mystical concept found in Indian **yoga** and also in the **Kabbalah**, Western **magic**, and **alchemy**. In many traditions, the attainment of **self-realization** necessitates the transcendence of duality, and this includes the harmony of sexual opposites within a person. In **Kundalini Yoga**, the energy channels **ida** and **pingala** – representing the female and male polarities respectively – are united in the supreme **chakra**, **Sahasrara**. Similarly, in alchemy the heavenly **androgyne** personifies the harmony of opposites. In the Kabbalah, the supreme and "neutral" **sephirah Kether** transcends **Chokmah** (the Great Father) and **Binah** (the Great Mother).

Unity consciousness The experience of Oneness with God. According to the mystical traditions this is all that really exists.

Universal Mind In **Theosophy**, **mysticism**, and **occultism**, the mind of the **Supreme Being**, or **God**, which pervades the universe and gives order and meaning to all aspects of Creation. See also **Cosmic Consciousness**.

Universal Solvent In **alchemy**, the universal substance from which all other specific constituents evolved; a name for the **life-force**. See also **Elixir of Life**.

Upanishads A collection of 108 spiritual treatises from the Vedic scriptures, concerned primarily with the nature of reality and the supreme state of the **soul**. The *Upanishads* focus collectively on the transcendent and immanent **Brahman** and the attainment of knowledge of the **self** through **meditation**. The word *upanishad* translates as "sitting at the Master's Feet", and also has the connotation of a secret teaching. The *Upanishads* are central to the Indian spiritual tradition.

Uraeus In ancient Egyptian **mythology**, the fire-breathing viper or asp that protected the sun-god **Ra** by destroying his enemies. The solar disc upon his head was often shown surrounded by the uraeus, which symbolized royal dominion and authority.

Urania In Greek **mythology**, one of nine **Muses**. Urania governed astronomy and **astrology**, and was regarded by John Milton as the muse of poetry. She was also identified with **Aphrodite** in her role as **goddess** of spiritual love.

Uranus Also Ouranos. In Greek **mythology**, the most ancient of the **gods** and father of the **Titans**. Uranus was the husband of **Gaea** and personified the sky and heavens. He was sometimes known as Father Sky.

Uranus In **astrology**, a planet associated with change and revolution – a reference to Uranus's overthrow by his son **Kronos** in classical Greek **mythology**. Uranus represents rebellion, independence, impatience, and new inventions and discoveries.

Uriel In modern Western **magic**, an **archangel** invoked in the **banishing ritual** of the Lesser Pentagram. Uriel is summoned in the northern quarter and is ascribed to the element **Earth**. His counterparts are **Raphael** (East: **Air**); **Michael** (South: **Fire**); and **Gabriel** (West: **Water**).

Urim and Thummim Among the ancient Hebrews, two objects – possibly flat discs – attached to the breastplate of the **high priest**. The Urim and Thummim were consulted in **divination** to enable the high priest to learn the will of **God**. See also **Sortilege**.

Uroboros See **Ouroboros**.

Ursuline Convent Possession See **Aix-en-Provence Nuns**.

V

Vaikuntha In Indian **mythology**, the city of splendid golden palaces where **Vishnu** ruled as Lord of Light. It was located, according to some accounts, at the mystical centre of the world: **Mount Meru**.

Vaisnavism Also Vaishnavism. In **Hinduism**, devotional sect whose followers worship **Vishnu**, primarily in his incarnations as **Krishna** and **Rama**. Devotees are known as Vaisnavites.

Valentinus (110–175) Leading teacher and poet among the **Gnostics**. Born in Egypt, Valentinus was possibly a disciple of **Basilides** and claimed to have access to St. Paul's **esoteric** teachings through Theodas, one of Paul's followers. According to Valentinus, the **Godhead** encompassed thirty **aeons**, including four major groupings: Abyss and Silence, Mind and Truth, Word and Life, Man and Church. The thirtieth aeon, **Sophia**, gave rise to matter and also produced as her offspring **Ialdaboath** (a **deity** mistaken by the Jews for the creator **Yahweh**). According to Valentinus, the role of Jesus was to restore Sophia (Wisdom) to her status as part of the **pleroma**, or Godhead.

Valentinian Gnosticism was not without its controversial features. According to its founder, the pairs of aeons were extremely sexual, and it was appropriate for sect members to imitate this. The Valentinian sex celebrations were held just prior to the Roman **Lupercalia** and led to fierce condemnation from Clement of Alexandria, Irenaeus, and other critics of the Gnostic sects.

Valhalla In Scandinavian **mythology**, the hall of **Odin** where warriors and heroes killed in battle resided in the afterworld. Here Odin and his comrades drank and feasted, awaiting **Ragnarok** – the final encounter with the **giants** and forces of **evil**.

Valiente, Doreen (1922–1999) One of the leading figures in the international **Wiccan** community and sometimes referred to as the "mother of modern paganism", Valiente was born Doreen Dominy in London, in 1922. Brought up as a Christian she escaped from the convent school to which she had been sent and never returned. Dominy worked as a secretary but also practised as a clairvoyant. In 1944 she married Casimiro Valiente, a refugee from the Spanish Civil War. Valiente was initiated into witchcraft in 1953 by **Gerald Gardner** and became High Priestess of his coven. However she broke with Gardner in 1957 when he ignored the coven's vows of secrecy by seeking publicity. Valiente was a gifted writer as well as a gifted ritualist and her text "The Charge of the Goddess" is now a central component in contemporary Wiccan ceremonies around the world. She also produced several influential books, including *Witchcraft for Tomorrow* and *The Rebirth of Witchcraft*, which have become standard references for neopagan practitioners.

Valkyries In Scandinavian **mythology**, the battle-maidens of **Odin** who dwelt with him in **Valhalla**. At Odin's bidding, the Valkyries rode into the fray to carry the fallen heroes to the paradise of Valhalla, where they made them welcome with pork and mead.

Vamana See **Bali**.

Vampire A bloodsucking **demon** who was believed to be a corpse that had returned to life. Vampires were usually of pale complexion and ice-cold to touch. They had gleaming eyes, pointed ears, and long fingernails, and were able to transform themselves into animals. The most famous vampire in folk legend was Count **Dracula**. See also **Lycanthropy**; **Werewolf**; **Zombie**.

Vanir In Scandinavian **mythology**, the peaceful **gods** who protected the crops and Nature, and all living things. The Vanir **deities** feuded with the **Aesir** gods headed by **Odin**, until they were admitted to the citadel in the sky known as **Asgard**.

Van Pelt, Dr. S. J. (1908–) British psychiatrist and hypnotherapist. Dr. Van Pelt has been president of the British Society of Medical Hypnotists and editor of the *British Journal of Medical Hypnotism*. He helped pioneer the use of **hypnosis** for treating such complaints as insomnia, migraine, asthma, and alcoholism; and has been instrumental in placing hypnosis on a scientific level, away from the taint of pseudo-occult **mesmerism**. Van Pelt's best-known book is *Hypnotism and the Power Within*.

Varengan In Persian **mythology**, a magical bird whose feathers were regarded as a protection against **curses** and **spells**. Capable of flying as swiftly as an arrow, it was the fastest of all birds.

Varuna Vedic sky-god who was regarded as an omniscient lord of wisdom and was later associated with the **moon** and the dead. It is thought that the Persian deity **Zurvan** and the Gnostic deity **Abraxas** derive at least in part from Varuna.

Vasilyev, Professor Leonid Leonidovich Russian physiologist who worked at the Bekhterev Brain Institute in Leningrad between 1921 and 1938, and was appointed professor of physiology at Leningrad University in 1943. Vasilyev became interested in **parapsychology** and, after a number of experiments on **hypnosis** and **mental telepathy**, came to the conclusion that telepathic communications are not "**electromagnetic**" but are based on a natural form of communication not unlike that found among migratory animal species. Man, according to Professor Vasilyev, retains his "telepathic gift" as a legacy from his "zoological ancestors". See also **Psi**; **Telepathy**.

Vasuki In Indian **cosmology**, one of the rulers of the **nagas** who play an important role in esoteric **Mahayana Buddhism**. Vasuki, a giant serpent, was used by the **gods** as a rope to stir the waves.

Vaughan, Thomas (1622–1665) Noted Welsh hermeticist, alchemist, and **mystic** who wrote under the pseudonym of Eugenius Philalethes. Vaughan believed in the kabbalistic principle that "the spirit of man is itself the spirit of the Living God" – accepting the concept of the **macrocosm and microcosm**. Vaughan's principal works include *Anthroposophia Theomagica*, a discourse on the nature of man and his state after death; *Magia Adamica*, a treatise on the antiquity of **magic**; *Coelum Terrae*, a work of **heaven** and **chaos**; *Lumen de Lumine*, a tract on **theurgy**; and *Euphrates*, a work on **alchemy**. His writings were compiled by **A. E. Waite** and published as *The Works of Thomas Vaughan* (London, 1919; reissued New York, 1968). See also **Hermetica**.

Vaulderie French expression used by members of the French **Inquisition** to describe the act of forming a satanic pact. Named after the hermit Robinet de Vaulse, who was accused of this crime, it became a familiar charge against **witches**. It was linked to the witches' **flying ointments** – which, according to the Inquisition, enabled devil-worshippers to "fly wherever they wished to go … the devil [carrying] them to the place where they should hold their assembly". See also **Witches' Sabbath**.

Vayu In **Hinduism**, one of the **Tattvas**, or **elements**. Vayu is the symbol of **Air**, and is represented by a blue hexagon. It is associated with the **chakra Anahata** located near the thymus gland. See also **Kundalini Yoga**.

Vedanta Hindu spiritual tradition and philosophy based primarily on the four **Vedas**. Vedanta has as its central proposition that **Brahman** – the Supreme Reality – is unchanging and represents absolute existence and absolute bliss. Brahman is also the source of human consciousness. According to Vedanta, one can discover the **immanent** aspects of Brahman within one's own being. It follows that one's true purpose can be defined as the quest for self-knowledge. Vedantins believe that the ***Bhagavad-Gita***, the Sutras of **Patanjali**, Shankara's *Crest-Jewel of Discrimination*, and the *Gospel of Sri Ramakrishna* are important contributions to spiritual knowledge; and they advocate the techniques of **yoga** as a means of uniting with the **Godhead**. It is through union with Brahman that the Vedantin finds release from **rebirth**.

Vedantin A devotee or practitioner of **Vedanta**.

Vedas Hindu sacred texts, dating from around 1200–1800 B.C., and written in the Vedic language (a form of Sanskrit). The principal texts are the four works known collectively as the Samhitas: the ***Rig-Veda***, a collection of 1028 **hymns**; the *Sama-Veda*, a body of chants and **mantras**; the *Yajur-Veda*, which consists of sacrificial **rituals** and **prayers**; and the *Atharva-Veda*, a collection of mystical formulae, mantras, and magic **spells**. The word *veda* means "knowledge".

Vehicle of Vitality An occult term for the **etheric body**, which channels vitality and consciousness to the physical body during life, but passes onto the "inner planes" after **death**. According to occult belief, the etheric body has only a transient existence and may appear, after death, as an **apparition** or **ghost**.

Velada Among the Mazatec Indians of Mexico, a healing ceremony involving the use of *psilocybe* mushrooms. Both the patient and the female **shaman** take the **psychedelic**

mushroom so both may hear the healing words which are revealed from the spirit-world. The shamaness, meanwhile, goes on a **spirit-journey** to discover the cause of sickness and to seek the healing power from the **gods**. Among the Mazatecs, folk belief and Christianity have fused so that cures are attributed both to the sacred mushroom and also to "God the Father and God the Son". See also **Psilocybin**.

Venus In Roman **mythology**, the counterpart of the Greek **goddess** of love, **Aphrodite**. Venus personified sexuality, fertility, prosperity, and good luck. The Romans venerated her in late April and early May – the season for promiscuity.

Venus In **astrology**, a **planet** associated with sexual love and desire, and relationships in general. Astrologers regard Venus as a beneficent planet, attracting harmony, affection, and love. Its particular location in the **horoscope** indicates sympathy and friendship and often a degree of sentimentality. According to some astrologers, a man with the **sun** and Venus closely aspected is likely to be effeminate, while Venus in conjunction with **Saturn** or **Mercury** may indicate female domination.

Verbena See Vervain.

Vernal Equinox The **equinox** that occurs on March 21, the first day of spring. It equates with the entry of the **sun** into **Aries**, the first **sign** of the **zodiac**.

Vervain *Verbena officinalis*, sacred plant among the ancient Romans, who believed that vervain was able to repel the enemy in war. Accordingly, vervain was associated with **Mars** and was worn by ambassadors and heralds in their missions to other nations. Vervain was also sacred among the **Druids**, who used it in **spells** of enchantment.

Vestal Virgins In ancient Rome, **priestesses** who dedicated themselves to serving Vesta, goddess of the hearth. The vestales were between six and ten years of age as they entered training – a process taking ten years. They then remained in service for another ten years: tending the sacred fire on the altar of Vesta so that it never went out, carrying water from the fountain known as Egeria, and serving as custodians of the Palladium from Troy. The Vestal Virgins later spent another ten years instructing novices, and were then free to renounce their vow of celibacy, and marry if they wished. The Vestal Virgins were held in high regard in Rome, and it was said that the tradition was as old as Aeneas, who was believed to have selected the first vestales. Rhea Silvia, the mother of Rome's legendary founders, Romulus and Remus, was herself a Vestal Virgin.

Vevers In **voodoo**, symbolic signs, resembling magical **sigils**, which are drawn on the ground to invoke the **loa**, or **gods**, in ritual ceremonies.

Via Mystica Latin for "mystic way" or "mystic path" – a reference to the spiritual path that leads to union with **God**. See also **Mystic Union**.

Vibrations In many occult and mystical traditions, the underlying energy matrix of the universe and a major "cause" of occult phenomena. In many **cosmologies**, the universe is believed to have been created through an utterance of **God**, the power of sound bringing the various worlds into being. In modern times, **mental telepathy** and other psychic communications have often been compared to radio waves and other forms of vibration, and the pseudo-healing science of **radionics** is based on the premise that different diseases resonate to different "frequencies". See also **Mental Radio**.

Vidar In Scandinavian **mythology**, the son of **Odin**, who slew the **Fenris Wolf** and survived **Ragnarok** – becoming the **deity** who would herald the **Golden Age**.

Vidya From the Sanskrit *vid*, "to know or understand", spiritual or mystical knowledge. See also **Vedas**.

Vihara In **Buddhism**, a monastery or nunnery, or any place inhabited by **ascetics** or **priests**. The dwellings where **Gautama Buddha** resided are also called *viharas*. The term is sometimes used generally to describe a resting place.

Violent Signs In **astrology**, the signs **Aries**, **Libra**, **Scorpio**, **Capricorn**, and **Aquarius**.

Viracocha Among the Incas, the personification of Life and the creator of the universe. Viracocha was the lord of thunder and brought the **sun**, **moon**, and stars into existence. He was said to dwell in the depths of Lake Titicaca and received sacrificial offerings of children and animals. See also **Mamacocha**.

Virginity In **mysticism** and **magic**, a condition that symbolizes purity, innocence, and spirituality. In medieval folk legend only a virgin could tame the **unicorn**, itself a symbol of male and female polarity; and in the **Tarot**, the supreme male and female archetypes are the virgin male (***The Magician***) and the virgin female (***The High Priestess***). Among the great religions, both Jesus Christ and **Gautama Buddha** were said to have been born of a virgin – symbolic of their "pure" spiritual being.

Virgo In **astrology**, the **sign** of the **zodiac** for those born between August 23 and September 22. An **Earth** sign, ruled by **Mercury**, **Virgo** is represented by the figure of the virgin. Those born under the sign of Virgo are often analytical and methodical in their day-to-day lives and can appear reserved and cool in manner. They have an excellent grasp of complex details and often choose careers in business. In their personal relationships they are usually intensely loyal, but often nervous and lacking in self-confidence. They are also inclined to be self-centred and critical of others. Virgos are traditionally associated with an interest in food or drugs, and are often found in careers linked to nutrition, analytical chemistry, or pharmacy.

Virgula Furcata Latin for "forked rod", a reference to the **divining rod** used by a **dowser**. The sixteenth-century writer Agricola used the expression to refer to the traditional forked rod of hazel, but contemporary dowsers sometimes use rods made of stainless steel.

Vishnu In **Hinduism**, one of the three major **gods** of the **trimurti**, the other two being **Brahma** and **Shiva**. Vishnu was originally a Vedic god who acquired prominence as the peaceful sky-god, protector of the universe. As a guide and friend of humankind, Vishnu was believed to have incarnated on several occasions (the number of incarnations varies from ten to thirty-nine) in order to save the world in times of crisis. Among Vishnu's most famous incarnations were **Rama** (described in the ***Ramayana***) and **Krishna** (described in the ***Bhagavad-Gita***). Many devotees also consider **Gautama Buddha** as an incarnation. Vishnu's final appearance as **Kalki**, at the end of the world, is still to come.

Vishudda In **Kundalini Yoga**, the **chakra** associated with the **Tattva Akasha** (a black oval **egg**), representing the element **Spirit**. The Vishudda chakra is located in the region of the thyroid gland.

Vision In **mysticism**, an **altered state of consciousness** or **peak experience**, in which sacred images dominate one's perception and are accompanied by feelings of awe, mystery, and **transcendence**. On a less profound level, mental images and visions may appear during a state of reverie, during **skrying**, or in sessions of **guided imagery**. Mystical visions usually have archetypal content and arise from the spiritual areas of the **psyche**. See also **Archetype; Collective Unconscious; Cosmic Consciousness; Hallucinations.**

Vision, Clairvoyant See **Clairvoyance; Second Sight.**

Vision, Crystal See **Crystal-gazing; Crystalomancy.**

Visionary One who has the capacity to see beyond. While for many this implies a person who is idealistic and impractical, it can also be used to describe one who is gifted with **paranormal** vision or who has profound and universal insights into the human condition. See also **Adept; Avatar; Guru; Master.**

Vital Field In **Theosophy**, the field of life-energies or **pranas** which sustain the physical body and unite it to a spiritual source. It is closely identified with the **etheric body**.

Vital Force The **life-force**, which resides in all living things and which, in mystical and occult traditions, is presumed to be the source of health and vitality. If the life-force is blocked from the organism, disease results and eventually death ensues. The life-force is known variously as **ch'i (Taoism)**; **ki** (Japanese **Buddhism**); and **prana** (Hinduism).

Vitalism The belief that living organisms may be distinguished from inorganic matter by virtue of the presence of a **vital force**. This force, sometimes known as *élan vital*, is capable of existing independently of physical form. See also **Life-force; Nous.**

Vivian In Arthurian folk legend, the enchantress who finally ensnared the **wizard Merlin** by trapping him with his own magical **spell**.

Voices from the Dead Term used in **parapsychology** to describe the mysterious voices – believed by some to be those of **discarnate** beings – heard on the electronic recordings of **Dr. Konstantin Raudive**. The expression is also used by spiritualists to describe **direct voice communication**, where the **psychic medium** speaks with all the vocal mannerisms of a deceased person. See also **Electronic Voice Phenomenon.**

Void, The The supreme, **transcendent** Reality which lies beyond form and **manifestation**. Often regarded as the **First Cause**, and sometimes identified with the **Godhead**, the Void is also characterized in some **cosmologies** as **chaos** and formlessness. **Ain Soph Aur** is the "limitless Light" of the **Kabbalah**; and **sunyata** is the supreme Void in **Mahayana Buddhism**.

Volatile In **alchemy**, the quality ascribed to the supreme and androgynous substance **quicksilver**, personified by **Mercury**.

Voodoo Also Vodoun, Vaudoux, Vondou. Haitian magical practices involving chanting, drumming, singing, and dancing, and which lead to states of **dissociation**, **trance**, and spirit **possession**. The word voodoo derives from the West African word *vodun*, meaning "a god" or "spirit": the rites of voodoo were imported into Haiti and other parts of the Caribbean during the period of the slave trade, when Africans were brought across to work on the plantations. Voodoo rites include sexual sacrifices; snake dances; the ritual use of corpses; the evocation of **spirits**, **monsters**, and **zombies**; and occasional **cannibalism**. In some voodoo ceremonies, practitioners are possessed by the **loa**, or gods. Among the principal **deities** are Ogoun, the warrior god;

Baron Samedi, the god of cemeteries; and his other evil counterparts, Baron Cimitiere, Baron Piquant, and Ghede, who with him rule the forces of **evil**.

Voyance In **parapsychology**, paranormal vision or perception; **psi** ability. See also **Clairvoyance**; **Psychometry**.

Vyantaras In **Jainism**, wood **spirits** regarded with apprehension because of their mischievous deeds.

W

Waite, Arthur Edward (1857–1942) Noted occult historian and **mystic**. Born in Brooklyn, New York, Waite came with his mother to England when very young and spent most of his life in his adopted country. Influenced by the writings of **Madame Helena Blavatsky** and the French **occultist Eliphas Lévi**, Waite began to explore the Western occult tradition in earnest and in due course became the leading occult scholar of his time. Waite rejected the notion of the **Mahatmas** and left **Theosophy** to join the **Hermetic Order of the Golden Dawn**, later (around 1916) becoming leader of a 'inter-faction.

Waite had been raised in a Roman Catholic environment and believed that the Western occult tradition provided an esoteric **mystery** tradition that the orthodox Christian Church had either forgotten or never possessed. He attracted Christian figures like **Evelyn Underhill** and writer Charles Williams to the Golden Dawn, and was decidedly more a mystic than an occultist. Nevertheless, with artist Pamela Colman-Smith, he created the most popular **Tarot** deck – the so-called Rider Pack – and authored several books on Western **magic**, including *Devil Worship in France* and *The Book of Ceremonial Magic*. His other books include *The Brotherhood of the Rosy Cross*, *The Real History of the Rosicrucians*, *The Holy Kabbalah*, *The Holy Grail*, *The Secret Tradition in Freemasonry*, and perhaps his most eloquent work on mysticism, *Azoth*. Waite also compiled and translated many of the **esoteric** writings of **Paracelsus** and Eliphas Lévi, as well as anthologizing the important works of alchemist **Thomas Vaughan**.

Wakan Also Wakanda. Among the traditional Sioux Indians, the universal **life-force** that permeates all aspects of Nature and is a source of spiritual power.

Wallace, Alfred Russel (1823–1913) Welsh naturalist who, with Charles Darwin, proposed the "natural selection" theory of evolution. Russel became interested in **hypnotism** and psychical research and was an honorary member of the **Society of Psychical Research** from 1882 onward. He was also a founding member of the **London Spiritualist Alliance**. His metaphysical books include *On Miracles and Modern Spiritualism* (1875) and *A Defence of Modern Spiritualism* (1894).

Walpurgis Night Also Walpurgisnacht. **May Day** eve, April 30, which has traditionally been regarded as a night when dark forces are afoot. In Germany, Walpurgis Night is associated with Mount Brocken in the Herz mountain range, for it was here that the **witches** were said to gather and hold their sabbath. See also **All Hallows' Eve; Witches' Sabbath.**

Wand In modern **ceremonial magic**, one of the four traditional implements, the others being the dagger or **sword**, the **cup**, and the **pentacle**. The wand is fashioned from ash or hazel and inscribed with the god-name YHVH and the **archangel** name **Raphael**. It represents the element **Air** in ceremonial workings. See also **Magic, Ceremonial.**

Wands Also Rods. One of the four suits of the **Minor Arcana** of the **Tarot**, wands is one of the two masculine suits (the other being **swords**) and is ascribed to the element **Air**.

Warlock The male counterpart of a female **witch**. The term is also used to describe a **sorcerer** who is skilled in summoning **supernatural** evil forces and practising **black magic**. See **Satanism**.

Wasson, R. Gordon (1898–1986) American private researcher and ethnomycologist who, with his wife Valentina, began in the early 1950s to explore the impact of psychoactive mushrooms on different cultures in Siberia, India, Europe, and North and South America. Wasson believed that visionary experiences associated with the use of **psychedelic** mushrooms have played a profound role in shaping religious beliefs. Wasson is best known for his suggestion – now seriously considered by academic specialists – that the legendary planet **soma** in Indian mythology was in fact ***Amanita muscaria***. In his book *The Road to Eleusis* (1978), Wasson explored initiation in classical Greece and provided an analysis of *The Homeric Hymn to Demeter*. He suggested that the visions of the **neophytes** in the **Mysteries of Eleusis** were caused by the presence of **ergot** in the sacred ceremonial drink. Ergot is the parasitic fungus from which the psychedelic **LSD** was later synthesized. Wasson's other books include *Soma: The Divine Mushroom of Immortality* (1969), *Maria Sabina and her Mazatec Mushroom Velada* (1974), and *The Wondrous Mushroom* (1980).

Water One of the four alchemical **elements**, the others being **Earth**, **Fire**, and **Air**. The **spirits** of water are known as **undines** and **mermaids**, or **mermen**. The three astrological **signs** linked to water are **Cancer**, **Scorpio**, and **Pisces**. See also **Water Signs**.

Water-bearer, The In **astrology**, a popular name for **Aquarius**, the eleventh **sign** of the **zodiac**.

Water Divining See **Dowser**.

Water Signs In **astrology**, **Cancer**, **Scorpio**, and **Pisces**, which characterize the element **Water** in its **cardinal**, **fixed**, and **mutable** aspects respectively.

Water-sprite A nature-spirit or **elemental** of **Water**. In Greek **mythology**, these sprites were the **oceanides** or **nereids**. In medieval folklore they are the **mermaids**, **undines**, and **mermen**.

Watts, Alan (1915–1973) British philosopher and lecturer on **Zen Buddhism** who became a leading figure in the American counterculture. Watts emigrated to the United States in 1936, embraced Christianity, and was ordained as an Anglican priest in 1944. He served as the Episcopal chaplain at Northwestern University for six years but then left the Church to pursue an alternative lifestyle. Always interested in Zen Buddhism and **Taoism**, Watts sought to reconcile these Eastern perspectives within a Western context, while also experimenting with psychedelics like **LSD**. He became friendly with such figures as **Timothy Leary**, Allen Ginsberg and Jack Kerouac and was a familiar figure on the campus lecture circuit. Watts believed that "all doctrines of God are ultimately false and idolatrous, because doctrines are forms of words which can never be more than pointers to mystical vision." He was, nevertheless, a prolific author himself. His books include *The Way of Zen*, *The Wisdom of Insecurity*, *The Joyous Cosmology* and *Two Hands of God*.

Weighing of the Soul In ancient Egyptian **mythology** the weighing of the heart of a deceased person against the **feather** of truth. This ceremony took place in the **Judgment Hall** and was overviewed by **Osiris**, **Maat**, and **Thoth** – who recorded the verdict.

Weishaupt, Adam (1748–1830) Bavarian founder of the Order of the Illuminati. See also **Illuminati**.

Weretiger In traditional Malaysian folk belief, a man who is capable of transforming himself into a tiger. The local expression for this manifestation of **lycanthropy** is *jadi-jadian*.

Werewolf In occult folk belief, a person who is believed to be capable of transforming into the form of a wolf and eating human flesh. See also **Lycanthropy**. Compare with **Vampire**.

West In Western **ceremonial magic**, the direction associated with the element **Water**. It is said to be ruled by the **archangel Gabriel**. See also **Directions, Four**.

Westcott, Dr. William Wynn (1848–1925) Influential English **occultist** and **Freemason**. Westcott obtained a series of Masonic writings, which he asked **MacGregor Mathers** to develop into a series of graded magical **rituals**. In due course, these became the basis of the ceremonial practices of the **Hermetic Order of the Golden Dawn**, and both Westcott and Mathers held senior grades within the new order. Westcott produced a number of occult writings including *An Introduction to the Qabalah* (1910) and translations of the *Sepher Yetzirah* (1911) and **Eliphas Lévi**'s *The Magical Ritual of the Sanctum Regnum* (1896). He was also the editor of an important occult series of monographs known as *Collectanea Hermetica*, published by the Theosophical Publishing House in London, in the 1890s. See also **Freemasonry**.

Wheatley, Dennis (1897–1977) English adventure writer who wrote a number of novels dealing with **satanism** and **black magic**. Wheatley maintained that he had never taken part in magical ceremonies, although he knew many leading figures in the occult world. His best-known books include *The Devil and All His Works* (a study of magic and the occult), *The Devil Rides Out*, *The Gates of Hell*, *To the Devil – a Daughter*, *They Used Dark Powers*, and *The Haunting of Toby Jugg*.

Wheel of Fortune, The In the **Tarot**, the card of the **Major Arcana** that symbolizes the forces of **fate** and **destiny**. In the **Kabbalah**, words composed of similar letters (and therefore having the same numerical total) are believed to have related meanings, and the words *Taro*, *Rota*, and *Ator* are similarly regarded by some **occultists** as being linked.

According to American occultist **Paul Foster Case**, *The Wheel of Fortune* can be summarized by the pronouncement that "The Wheel (rota) of Tarot speaks the Law of Hathor (ator)" – an interpretation that reflects Case's personal belief that the Tarot had an Egyptian origin. Other occultists see this card as a magical **mandala**, a symbol reflecting the mastery of opposite polarities within the psyche. On the kabbalistic **Tree of Life**, the path of *The Wheel of Fortune* links **Netzach** and **Chesed**, the first of these being a feminine sphere, the second masculine. See also **Gematria.**

Wheel of Life and Death Hindu concept, incorporating belief in **karma** and **reincarnation**, in which one undergoes a succession of births, **deaths**, and **rebirths** until the spiritual lessons of life have been learned to such a degree that liberation (**moksha**) is attained. The person who experiences the transcendence of moksha has no further need to reincarnate. See also **Samsara.**

Wheel of the Year In **Wicca**, the cycle of the seasons, or more specifically the cycle of Nature's fertility. Wiccans celebrate both the lunar and the solar cycles of Nature. **Esbats** are monthly meetings of the coven held at the time of full moon, while the solar cycle is marked by eight **sabbaths** referred to collectively as the Wheel of the Year: these are the solstices, equinoxes and the four points between. As American Wiccan author Margot Adler has observed, these meetings and festivals renew a sense of living communion with natural cycles, and with the changes in the seasons and the land. See **Sabbaths, Greater; Sabbaths, Lesser;** and **Esbats.**

Whirling Dervishes See **Dervishes, Whirling.**

White Brotherhood, Great See **Great White Lodge.**

White Magic See **Magic, White.**

Wicca An alternative name for witchcraft. Practitioners of **modern witchcraft** continue to debate the origin of the word, which may derive from the Old English root *wit*, meaning "wisdom", or the Indo-European root *wic*, meaning "to bend." According to the contemporary witch Margot Adler, the latter definition characterizes the wiccan as a person "skilled in the craft of shaping, bending, and changing reality".

Wiccan A male or female practitioner of **modern witchcraft**. See also **Wicca.**

Widdershins In **witchcraft**, a ceremonial direction associated with negative **magic**; the exact opposite of **deosil**. If a practitioner faces the **circle** and moves to the left, that direction is described as negative (left equates with **sinister**). Widdershins is therefore clockwise, although in many books describing occult traditions it is incorrectly given as counterclockwise. Taking a clockface and regarding twelve o'clock as North, it can be seen that the hands move from West to East – contrary to the movement of the **sun**. The term widdershins derives from the Anglo-Saxon *wither sith*, "to talk against", and in witchcraft refers to the direction "against the sun".

Wier, Johannes (1515–1588) Also called Wierius, a sixteenth-century demonologist who chronicled the hierarchy of **hell** in his extraordinary work *Pseudomonarchia Daemonum*. Among the most prominent **demons** in Wier's compilation are **Beelzebub**, **Satan**, Euronymous, Moloch, **Pluto**, and **Baalberith**. Wier also listed **Proserpine** and **Astaroth** as arch-demonesses. Wier was a pupil and friend of the legendary **occultist Cornelius Agrippa**, and like him had a profound regard for magical **cosmology**.

Wierius See **Wier, Johannes.**

Wilber, Ken (1949–) A practitioner of Buddhist **meditation**, American author and philosopher Ken Wilber is a leading transpersonal theorist and has been acclaimed by many as "the long-sought Einstein of consciousness research". A prolific author and former editor-in-chief of *ReVision*, Wilber has sought to develop a unified field theory of consciousness, encompassing the world's great psychological, philosophical and spiritual traditions. His many books include *The Spectrum of Consciousness*; *No Boundary*; *The Holographic Paradigm*; *Sex, Ecology and Spirituality*, and *A Brief History of Everything*.

Wilby, Basil See **Knight, Gareth.**

Will In Western **magic**, an important factor in the attainment of spiritual knowledge. Unlike Eastern schools of devotional **mysticism**, which advocate the surrender of the **ego** to a higher spiritual reality, Western magic emphasizes the will of the **magician** as the means of maintaining control over psychic and spiritual events. Acts of **invocation** and **evocation** are performed in such a way as to ensure the magician has control over the **supernatural** forces summoned.

Will-o'-the-wisp Popular name for the flickering, ethereal light sometimes observed over graveyards, and traditionally associated with the **spirits** of the dead. See also **Ignis Fatuus.**

Wilson, Colin (1931–) English writer who attracted widespread acclaim in 1956 for his first book, *The Outsider*, which discussed the existential "loneliness" of visionaries, artists, and creators. Wilson became interested in the **transcendental** aspects of the **psyche** as a source of powerful positive energy, and in some of his writings contrasts this type of perception with the negative energy tapped by murderers and criminals. In subsequent works Wilson advanced the view that people have an innate **paranormal** faculty – which he calls **Faculty X** – a human potential that underlies **extrasensory perception** and many other so-called "occult" phenomena. Wilson believes that people need to awaken Faculty X as part of the next phase of evolution. He is a prolific author and has written widely in the fields of metaphysics, psychology, and the occult, as well as popular fiction. His major occult books include *The Philosopher's Stone*, *The Mind Parasites*, *The Occult*, and *Mysteries*.

Wilson, Jack See **Ghost Dance, Great.**

Wireenun Among the **Aborigines** of western New South Wales, a **medicine-man** or **shaman**, who derives his magical powers from his contact with the great god **Baiame.**

Wiringin Among the Weilwan and Kamilaroi **Aborigines**, a **shaman** or **medicine-man**, sometimes referred to simply as a "clever man". See also **Men of High Degree.**

Wise Men, Three See **Magi.**

Wishing Well A well where one makes an unspoken wish while dropping a coin into the well as a token offering. The **superstition** derives from the traditional folk belief that **spirit-beings** resided in wells and could make wishes come true through their **magic** powers.

Witch A practitioner of **witchcraft**; one who has been initiated as a member of a **coven.** The term is more commonly used to describe female practitioners, but can also be used for males. A male witch is also known as a **warlock.**

Witch Balls Glass balls hung in the home to avert harmful influences, especially those attributed to the **evil-eye**. See **Magic, Protective; Spells.**

Witch-coven See **Coven.**

WIZARD: In occult tradition, the wizard or magus is a figure of veneration. The magician is a master of the Elements, represented here by the Sword (Fire), the Wand (Air), the Cup (Water) and the Disc or Pentacle (Earth). Line drawing by Nevill Drury (1973).

Witchcraft See **Witchcraft, Modern; Witchcraft, Traditional.**

Witchcraft, Modern Neo-pagan movement strongly influenced by such figures as **Gerald Gardner, Alex Sanders, Doreen Valiente, Z. Budapest** and **Starhawk.** Witchcraft is the worship of the **Old Religion**, and focuses primarily on the **Great Goddess** in her many forms: **Artemis, Astarte, Aphrodite, Diana, Hecate.** As such, it draws on many of the ancient **pantheons**, differing from modern Western **magic** primarily in its emphasis on **lunar goddesses** rather than **solar gods.** In modern witchcraft, the women rather than the men play the paramount role; and members of the **coven** regularly meet at **sabbaths** to perform seasonal **rituals.** Witches perform rituals dressed in ceremonial regalia or naked (**sky-clad**). These rituals invariably involve the invocation of the Goddess in one of her forms: and the ceremony of "drawing down the moon", in which the lunar energy is drawn into the body of the High Priestess within the magic circle.

Witchcraft, Traditional Medieval religious movement often – incorrectly – identified with **devil-worship, satanism**, and **black magic.** Today, traditional witchcraft is regarded by most authorities as a folk religion that blended **superstitions, fortune-telling, folklore**, and **herbalism** with remnants of various pre-Christian religious beliefs (e.g. the **Celts** and the **Druids**). Witchcraft actually has more in common with the many forms of **Nature-worship** and **fertility rituals** found in pre-industrial societies, than with the diabolical and satanic practices of black magicians whose main antagonist is the Christian Church. Nevertheless, in the Middle Ages most categories of **heathens, pagans**, and **heretics** were combined and uniformly persecuted by the officers of the **Inquisition.** The notorious book ***Malleus Maleficarum*** describes the persecutions meted out to medieval **witches**; and such figures as **Matthew Hopkins** and the officials engaged in the **Salem** witch trials characterize the ferocity of witchcraft persecutions prior to the modern era.

Witch-doctor In pre-literate societies, a practitioner of **magic** and **witchcraft** who uses his knowledge of **spells, enchantments**, and **evocations** to cure disease and ward off evil influences. Witch-doctors are found in many primitive cultures in Africa, Australia, Melanesia, Polynesia, South and Central America, and Haiti. See also **Medicine-man; Shaman; Soul-loss.**

Witches, Aberdeen See **Aberdeen Witches.**

Witches, Salem See **Salem Witches.**

Witches' Sabbath Meeting of a witches' **coven**, held in order to perform magical rites and ceremonies. The traditional witches' sabbath – which belongs more to the imagination than to history – brought together a large number of **witches** and **warlocks** who would gather around a bonfire or **cauldron**, light black candles, and perform sacrifices. The goat-headed **god** (**Cernunnos**) would be present, seated on a throne, and the Sabbath would culminate in a sexual orgy. It now seems that these fantasies derive in part from the visionary episodes brought on by **flying ointments, psychedelic** mixtures that cause sensations of flying and vivid sexual **hallucinations.**

The modern witches' sabbath is held at specific times of the year that mark transitions in the seasons. This is an important point to remember, because **witchcraft** is today regarded more correctly as a form of **Nature-worship.** The main sabbaths are **All Hallows' Eve** or **Halloween** (October 31), which represents the end of autumn and the beginning of winter; **Imbolc** (February 1), the first signs of spring; **Beltane**

(May 1), an important celebration of fertility; and **Lammas** (August 1), the beginning of the harvest.

Witch-finder See Hopkins, Matthew.

Witch-hunt The relentless persecution of **witches** was a charateristic of the **Inquisition**, and is described in the infamous treatise *Malleus Maleficarum* (*The Hammer of the Witches*). Witch-hunts were also conducted in East Anglia by self-styled witch-finder **Matthew Hopkins** in the 1640s; and at Salem, Massachusetts, in 1692 among the Puritan community. See also **Salem Witches**.

Witch's Cup A chalice used in **witchcraft** during the preparation of special philtres, and also to drink consecrated wine. It usually takes the form of a goblet made of polished metal or horn.

Witch's Mark Additional protuberances, breasts, or nipples upon the body of an accused **witch**, regarded by persecutors and inquisitors as evidence that the witch was suckling **familiars**.

Withershins See Widdershins.

Wizard From the Old English *wis*, meaning "wise", a sage, **adept**, or **magician** skilled in summoning **supernatural** powers. The most famous wizard in occult tradition is the legendary **Merlin**. See also **Sorcerer**; **Warlock**.

Wolf-boy See Grenier, Jean.

Woodman, Dr. William Robert (1828–1891) English Freemason and Rosicrucian who, with **Dr. Wynn Westcott** and **MacGregor Mathers**, founded the influential magical group, the **Hermetic Order of the Golden Dawn**. Woodman was apparently a knowledgeable Hebrew scholar and an accomplished Kabbalist, and many of his writings were said to be in the secret archive of the Second Order. However, none of these works has ever been published and Woodman remains something of an enigmatic figure in occult history. See also **Freemasonry**; **Rosicrucians**.

Woodroffe, Sir John George (1865–1936) English barrister and authority on **Tantra**, who wrote under the pen name of Arthur Avalon. Woodroffe went to Calcutta in 1890 and later served as officiating chief high justice of Bengal. However, like his counterpart **W. Y. Evans-Wentz**, he was fascinated by obscure **esoteric** texts and spent much of his time researching and translating texts on **Kundalini Yoga**. His books include *The Serpent Power*, *Shakti and Shakta*, and *Tantra of the Great Liberation*.

Words of Power Magical **conjurations** and **invocations** used in **rituals** and ceremonies for a specific result: to confer power upon the **magician**, to banish **evil** and darkness, or – in the case of the Egyptian sun-god – to ensure safe passage through the dungeons of the **Tuat**. In Western **magic**, words of power are usually Jewish **god-names**, deriving in the main from the **Kabbalah**. See also **Hekau**; **Magical Formulae**. Compare with **Mantra**.

World, The In the **Tarot**, the card of the **Major Arcana** that shows a maiden dancing in a wreath of wheat grains. The card is reminiscent of the mythology of the Greek goddess **Persephone**, and represents the descent into the **Underworld** of the unconscious **psyche**. Persephone symbolized the wheat grain; but after her abduction by **Hades**, she also became Queen of the Underworld. She thus came to represent both life and death and was an important figure in the **Mysteries of Eleusis**. The figure on *The World* appears feminine, but her genitals are hidden: she is in fact androgynous – reflecting the harmonizing or uniting aspects of the **Middle Pillar** on the kabbalistic **Tree of Life**. She is the personification of the Jewish

Shekhinah, and the first "path" into the unconscious. In Western **magic**, *The World* is regarded as a major initiatory path linking **Malkuth** and **Yesod** and also representing **Kether** on a lower plane: "as above, so below." See **Kabbalah; Macrocosm and Microcosm.**

Worlds, Four In the **Kabbalah**, the four planes of creative manifestation. The highest plane is **Atziluth**, the world of **archetypes**. In **Briah**, the world of creation, these archetypes begin to crystallize into specific ideas; while in **Yetzirah**, the world of formation, images become tangible. They achieve physical form in the fourth world, **Assiah**. The four worlds can be correlated with the **sephiroth Kether, Tiphareth, Yesod**, and **Malkuth**, respectively. See also **Emanations; Kabbalah; Tree of Life.**

World Soul Theosophical concept of the immanent **Godhead**, which structures and organizes the universe and provides it with vitality and purpose.

World Tree In **shamanism**, the axis which unites the upper and lower worlds with "middle Earth". The **shaman** makes a trance-journey to its upper branches, or ventures down through its roots to the lower world, in order to contact the **gods** and ancestor spirits. The symbol of the Tree occurs in several **cosmologies**. Notable examples include **Yggdrasil** in Scandinavian **mythology** and the **Tree of Life** in the Jewish **Kabbalah**. See also **Axis Mundi; Journey of the Soul.**

Wotan The Teutonic counterpart of the Scandinavian god **Odin**. He was also known as Woden by the Anglo-Saxons, and Wednesday is named after him.

Wovoka See **Ghost Dance, Great.**

Wraith An **apparition**, of either a person who has recently died or one who is about to do so. See also **Doppelgänger; Ghost; Spectre.**

Writing, Automatic See **Automatic Writing.**

Wu In **Taoism**, "eternal non-being", the essence of Tao. The realization of Wu confers **enlightenment**. To this extent, the term Wu is used as the Chinese equivalent of the Japanese **satori**.

Wu Wei In **Taoism**, the path of non-action. Those who heed Wu Wei recognize the need to flow with the energies of the universe, accepting the ever changing vortexes of **yin** and **yang**, which represent the essence of life.

Wyvern Also Wivern. In folk legend and heraldry, a flying serpent, resembling a **dragon**, with **eagle's legs** and a barbed and knotted tail.

X

X, Faculty See **Faculty X**.

Xango Also Sango. In **Macumba**, the **god** of thunder. Many practitioners of Macumba in Brazil identify Xango with St. Jerome, and he also bears resemblance to **Thor** and **Jupiter**. Devotees worship Xango on Wednesday and offer him dishes made from tortoise, goat, and cockerel.

Xenoglossy Also Xenoglossis, Xenoglossisia. In **parapsychology** and **spiritualism**, the act of **speaking-in-tongues** in a language of which one has no conscious knowledge. The phenomenon sometimes arises in spiritualist seances when the **psychic medium** enters a **trance** state. It is also a characteristic of Pentacostal Christianity. From a psychological viewpoint, xenoglossy sometimes draws on subconscious memory and presents words and phrases from languages with which one has come into contact at an earlier time. According to academic studies, Pentacostal xenoglossy does not exhibit any linguistic consistency, and has been described by some researchers, perhaps unkindly, as "gibberish".

Xenology The study of the frontier areas of **parapsychology** and **psychical research**, which remain scientifically unproven and require further investigation. See also **paranormal**; **psi**.

Xeper In the **Temple of Set**, the magical word of the New Aeon. Pronounced *khefer* and translated as "I have come into being", its associated symbols were the scarab beetle and the dawning sun. In a recent statement exploring the significance of *xeper*, Temple Magus Don Webb has written that this word "generates the Aeon of Set, and is the current form of the Eternal Word of the Prince of Darkness". Webb describes *xeper* as "the experience of an individual psyche becoming aware of its own existence and deciding to expand and evolve that existence through its own actions".

Xibalba Among the Quiche Indians of Central America, the **Underworld** and counterpart of **Hades**.

Xiuhtecutli Aztec **god** of **fire** and ruler of the **sun**. In Aztec rituals, live sacrificial victims were cast into flames as an offering to him.

Xolotl In the Aztec **pantheon**, the twin of **Quetzalcoatl** and the patron **god** of **magicians**. He personified the planet **Venus** as the Evening Star, and Quetzalcoatl personified Venus as the Morning Star.

X-ray Vision The alleged ability of some **psychic healers** to "see" into the body to diagnose illness. The term is also used in **spiritualism** to describe the faculty of psychics who are able to read messages inside sealed envelopes.

Xudam Etruscan **god**, subsequently identified with the Roman **deity** **Mercury**.

Xylomancy A form of **divination**, practised by the Slavs. The position and shape of dry pieces of wood found in one's path are interpreted for **omens**.

Y

Yahweh The **God** of Israel whose name, YHVH, was regarded as too sacred to be pronounced. Yahweh guided Moses, and the Jews believed he had made a special covenant with them, elevating them to the status of an elect people. Yahweh was considered the Creator of the World and became identified among the Christians with the Divine Father who had given his only son, Jesus Christ, as a redeemer to the world.

Yajur-Veda See **Vedas**.

Yaksha In **Hinduism**, a nature spirit often thought to reside inside a tree. The yaksha is worshipped in a sacred grove and is usually regarded as female.

Yama In the **Raja Yoga** of **Patanjali**, one of the so-called "eight limbs" of spiritual attainment. Yama can be translated as "ethical restraints", and includes such factors as: truthfulness; honesty; self-restraint of passions and desires; and non-injury in thought, word, and action.

Yama In Vedic **cosmology**, the immortal sun-god who chose to become mortal and in so doing became the first ancestor, together with his consort, Yami. After their death, Yama and Yami became King and Queen of the **Underworld**, Yama assuming the role of judging the dead and determining their destiny. His palace was guarded by two four-eyed dogs and he was capable of instilling great fear and dread, but for the righteous Yama was able to offer bliss and **paradise** in the afterworld.

Yami See **Yama**.

Yang In **Taoism**, the aspect of the universal life-force – **ch'i** – which is active, positive, and "masculine." It is outward looking in emphasis and radiates light in all directions. As such, it is the dynamic opposite of **yin**. Yang includes **heaven**, **fire**, and **summer**.

Yantra In **Hinduism**, a mystical diagram that portrays in a visual manner what a **mantra** indicates with sound. Used in **meditation**, the yantra has a focal point and multiple, enclosed triangles that symbolize different levels of form and divine energy. Practitioners of **Tantra** regard the human body as "the best of yantras".

Yasna In **Zoroastrianism**, one of the three divisions of the sacred text known as the **Avesta**. It consists of seventy-two chapters and includes the hymns and songs known collectively as the **Gathas**.

Yeats, William Butler (1865–1939) Noted Irish poet who, in his early twenties, became attracted to **Theosophy** and **esoteric** thought. He was a friend of mystical writer **George Russell** (better known as "A.E."), became a member of the Dublin Hermetic Society, and later made contact with **Madame Helena Blavatsky**, **G. R. S. Mead**, and **MacGregor Mathers** in London. Yeats became a member of the Isis-Urania Lodge of the **Hermetic Order of the Golden Dawn** in 1890, taking the magical name *Daemon est Deus Inversus* – "the Devil is the reverse side of God". When Mathers retired to Paris to translate occult manuscripts, Yeats became head of the order and soon afterwards had to ward off an attempt to challenge his authority from **Aleister Crowley**, who was keen to attain high magical office.

In 1905, Yeats resigned from the Order, together with his friend **Arthur Machen** and founder member **Wynn Westcott**. Yeats's experience of ceremonial magic and the visionary symbols of the **Tarot** nevertheless continued to influence his creative writing and he often incorporated Tarot images into his verse. As Kenneth and Steffi Grant wrote in their Carfax Monographs, "It was the

Golden Dawn that taught Yeats to consolidate his visions and to create a magical vehicle that would carry his ambition towards name and fame." Yeats's international reputation as a poet was acknowledged when he was awarded the Nobel Prize for Literature in 1923.

Yesod The ninth emanation or **sephirah** on the kabbalistic **Tree of Life**. In Western **magic**, Yesod is associated with the **moon** and the element **Water**. Regarded as a female sphere, it is the seat of the sexual instinct and corresponds to the genital **chakra** on the archetypal man, **Adam Kadmon**. On the Tree of Life, Yesod has the function of channelling the energies of the higher planes down to the earth below (**Malkuth**). Occultists associated Yesod with the **astral plane**, because if the sephiroth above Malkuth are collectively regarded as a map of the unconscious **psyche**, Yesod is the most accessible area of the mind. There is no doubt that it was the aspect of the psyche first explored in psychoanalysis and it remains the key energy-nexus in Freudian thought. Because Yesod is the sphere of fertility and lunar imagery, it is identified with **witchcraft** and **goddess** worship. It is also the seat of the so-called "animal soul" known by the Kabbalists as **Nephesch**. See also **Kabbalah**.

Yeti See **Abominable Snowman**.

Yetzirah In the **Kabbalah**, the third of the four worlds – the world of formation. Yetzirah is identified with the sphere of **Yesod** on the **Tree of Life**. In kabbalistic **cosmology**, Yetzirah is also the domain of ten divisions of **angels**, who are collectively ruled by the archangel **Metatron**. The orders of angels are as follows: Malachim, Arelim, Chajoth, Ophanim, Chashmalim, Elim, Elohim, Benei, Ishim, and **Seraphim**. See also **Assiah**; **Atziluth**; **Briah**; **Worlds, Four**.

Yfrit In **Islam**, a fallen **angel** or one of the **genii**. See **Efreet**.

Yggdrasil In Scandinavian mythology, a sacred ash tree which overshadowed the entire universe; its roots, branches, and trunk united heaven, Earth, and the nether-regions. The roots of Yggdrasil lay in **Hel**, while the trunk ascended through **Midgard** – the Earth. Rising through the mountain known as **Asgard**, it branched into the sky – its leaves were the clouds in the sky, and its fruit were the stars.

YHVH One of the spellings of **Yahweh** in Judaism. This sacred name was not pronounced and was often substituted by such lesser **god-names** as **Adonai** or **Shaddai**. YHVH is a form of the **Tetragrammaton**. It is also written as **JHVH** and **IHVH**.

Yi King See *I Ching*.

Yin In **Taoism**, that aspect of the universal life-force – **ch'i** – which is passive, negative, and "feminine". It is inward looking in emphasis and dark rather than bright. As such, it is the dynamic opposite of **Yang**. Yin includes **earth**, **moon**, **water**, and winter.

Ymir In Scandinavian **mythology**, a giant whose body formed in the mists of **Niflheim** when the universe was born, and who subsequently became the ancestor of the other giants. The Earth, heavens, and sea formed his body; and after his defeat at the hands of **Odin**, the world tree **Yggdrasil** emerged from his body.

Yoga From the Sanskrit *yuj*, "to bind together", Hindu spiritual teachings and techniques related to the attainment of **self-realization** and union with **Brahman**, the supreme reality. The four main concepts underlying the Hindu spiritual tradition are **karma**, the law of causality which links people to the universe; **maya**, the illusion of the manifested world; **nirvana**, absolute reality beyond illusion; and yoga, as the means of gaining liberation from the senses. Because people tend to confuse feelings and thoughts with "spirit", a means has to be found to overcome these sensory limitations. Yoga is thus a means of training to see things as they *are*, rather than as they seem. One of the basic techniques in yoga is therefore **meditation**, since this turns one's consciousness towards the inner reality and finally towards transcendence in **samadhi**.

In order for the mind to be calmed, a certain number of tensions or obstacles (**klesas**) have to be overcome. Basically, these are ignorance; the sense of **ego** and identification with the body; attention to pleasure; repulsion from pain; and the desire for life. From the yogic viewpoint, people are trapped in a world clouded by impure perceptions and preconceived ideas. It is this false reality that has to be transcended. According to the important yogic philosopher **Patanjali**, there are four basic processes: (1) withdrawal of attention from the external world (pratyahara); (2) concentration of energy in a definite direction (**dharana**); (3) the subsequent spontaneous flow of consciousness (**dhyana**); (4) unity of consciousness (**samadhi**).

In **Kundalini Yoga**, psychic energy is raised through the channel **sushumna**, which corresponds to the spinal cord; and **ida** and **pingala**, which are coiled within it, corresponding to the sympathetic nerve ganglion on either side of the spine. The **kundalini** energy is aroused from the base of the spine and passes through the seven **chakras**: (1) **Muladhara**, located near the coccyx; (2) **Swadhisthana**, below the navel in the sacral region; (3) **Manipura**, above the navel in the lumbar region; (4) **Anahata**, located near the heart; (5) **Vishudda**, associated with the cervical region and the throat; (6) **Ajna**, located between, and just slightly above, the eyes; (7) **Sahasrara**, located on the crown of the head and associated with the attainment of **cosmic consciousness**.

As a **yogi** (male) or **yogini** (female) practitioner of yoga finds unity of mind and body, he or she merges with the object of perceptions and loses all sense of duality, finally perceiving the Supreme Reality beyond the limitations of the senses.

Yogi A male practitioner of **yoga**.

Yogini A female practitioner of **yoga**.

Yoni Hindu name for the vulva. In **Tantra**, the **lingam** and yoni symbolize the divine creative and generative powers and the fusion of male and female polarities in the universe. The yoni is often portrayed in art and sculpture as a stone circle, sometimes with the lingam rising from it.

Yuga In **Hinduism**, a measurement of time which is one thousandth part of a **kalpa** or **Day of Brahma**. See also **Kali Yuga**.

Z

Zain, C. C. (1882–1951) Pseudonym of Elbert Benjamin, who founded the First Temple of Astrology in the United States. This later became the Church of Light, an organization that offers courses on different aspects of the occult tradition. Zain maintained that he was contacted by "The Brotherhood of Light" in 1909 and was instructed by secret **adepts** to prepare a complete occult system for teaching the religion of **astrology**. Zain also wrote a large book on the **Tarot**, which linked the symbolism to both the **Kabbalah** and ancient Egyptian symbolism (*The Sacred Tarot*, reissued, Los Angeles, 1969).

Zarathustra (c. 600 B.C.) Greek, **Zoroaster**. Persian prophet who at the age of fifteen retreated to a mountain cave and had a vision of **Ahura Mazda** – the **Supreme Being**. Thereafter, he endeavoured to preach the gospel of the one god who overcomes **evil**. After a period of wandering through Persia and Afghanistan and experiencing many mystical visions, Zarathustra gained only one convert, his cousin. However, he was given an audience with King Vishtaspa who requested a miracle as proof of his spiritual teachings. Zarathustra produced heavenly fire that could not be extinguished, but which nevertheless burned those who came near; and the King agreed to let the prophet stay at his court. Zarathustra subsequently earned considerable influence with the royal family and the King began to spread the faith, building fire **temples** for the worship of Ahura Mazda.

Zarathustra divided the world into the Followers of Truth (Asha) and the Followers of the Lie (Druj). Although Ahura Mazda transcended this division, the seeds were thereby sown for the dualistic thought that characterized later **Zoroastrianism**. Unlike the **Gnostics**, who held that the world was evil, Zarathustra believed that the world was intrinsically good, because it had been created by Ahura Mazda (**Ohrmazd**), but had since been corrupted by the Devil (**Ahriman**). People essentially had a choice of serving the two masters; fate in the afterworld was determined accordingly.

Zarathustra is said to have written the **Gathas** – teachings which form part of the **Avesta**. The religion of Zoroastrianism still survives among the Parsees.

Zazen Meditation posture used by practitioners of **Zen Buddhism**. According to Dogen, a thirteenth-century Japanese Zen master, zazen had two forms; one with the right foot on the left thigh and the left foot on the right thigh, the other with the left foot on the right thigh and the right foot crossed underneath. The right hand rests on the left foot while the back of the left hand rests in the palm of the right hand. The thumbs are then placed in juxtaposition. Meanwhile, the body is kept vertical, the mouth is closed, and the eyes are open. The practitioner then proceeds to regulate breathing and learns to overcome sensory attachments.

Zelator In the **Hermetic Order of the Golden Dawn**, the initiatory grade of ceremonial **magic** associated with the sphere of **Malkuth** on the kabbalistic **Tree of Life**.

Zen Buddhism School of meditative **Mahayana Buddhism** introduced into China around 520 by the Indian monk **Bodhidharma**. Japanese Zen in turn derives from Chinese **Ch'an Buddhism** and was introduced by **Eisai** (1141–1215). Zen draws on two main techniques. The first derives from the Soto school and makes use of **zazen** meditation. The second derives from the Rinzai school and employs **koans**, or paradoxical question and answer dialogue. This may lead to sudden, intuitive **enlightenment** as the split between rational and irrational is transcended and the "Buddha within" is discovered. Some questions in Zen dialogue are answered with silence, others by repeating the question. Whatever the technique, Zen leads its practitioners towards the attainment of sudden, and instantaneous, self-realization, or **satori**.

The paradox of Zen can be glimpsed in the following poem:

> *When one looks at it, one cannot see it;*
> *When one listens for it, one cannot hear it;*
> *However, when one uses it, it is inexhaustible.*

Zend-Avesta The sacred writings of the **Zoroastrians**. Strictly, the **Avesta** is the body of texts, and the Zend is its translation and interpretation in Pahlavi.

Zener Cards Cards used in experimental tests for **extrasensory perception**. Developed by **Dr. J. B. Rhine** in consultation with psychologist Dr. Karl Zener, they were used in pioneering research at Duke University and continue to be popular with parapsychologists. Zener cards include five symbols, each of which is clearly depicted: a star, a circle, a cross, a square, and a motif consisting of three wavy lines. A Zener pack consists of twenty-five cards, five of each symbol, and in ESP tests a subject has to guess the sequence of symbols for each of the cards in turn so that the percentage of correct scores can be evaluated against "chance". A subject consistently scoring in excess of the five correct "hits" per run is regarded as exhibiting **psi** ability. See also **Mental Telepathy**.

Zenith In **astrology**, the "pole of the horizontal", or the point directly overhead. The closer a **planet** is to the zenith of a given position, the stronger is its influence.

Zeus In Greek **mythology**, the most powerful of the **gods** and ruler of heaven and earth. The son of **Kronos** and **Rhea**, Zeus had seven wives and numerous romances. He was capable of changing into different forms – a satyr, a white bull, a swan, a shower of gold – and became known as "the Father of Gods and Men". Zeus hurled the thunderbolts that cause storms and **death**, and was therefore also called "the Cloud-Gatherer". The **oak** tree and **eagle** were sacred to him. See also **Jove**; **Jupiter**.

Zoanthropy From the Greek *zoion*, "an animal", the belief that a human being can transform into an animal, acquiring its characteristics. See also **Lycanthropy**; **Shape-shifting**; **Werewolf**.

Zodiac In **astrology**, the twelvefold division of the sky into **signs**. Zodiac means "circle of animals" and refers to the symbols of the twelve constellations. The so-called "northern" signs are the first six signs of the zodiac: **Aries**, **Taurus**, **Gemini**, **Cancer**, **Leo**, and **Virgo**; the "southern" signs are the remaining six: **Libra**, **Scorpio**, **Sagittarius**, **Capricorn**, **Aquarius**, and **Pisces**. The positions of each of the planets at birth is mapped in the chart of the heavens or **horoscope**, and significant **aspects** evaluated. The sign of the zodiac under which one is born is known as the **sun** sign, and it is regarded as a dominant factor in determining one's character and personal make-up.

Zodiacal Man In **astrology**, the concept that the twelve **signs** of the **zodiac** rule different parts of the body. See **Astrology, Medical**.

Zohar, Danah American author who has explored **parapsychology** and the relationship of quantum physics to personal growth and identity. Zohar graduated in physics and philosophy from Massachusetts Institute of Technology in 1966 and undertook further research in philosophy and religion at Harvard. She is now based in Britain and is the author of several influential books including *Through the Time Barrier* and *The Quantum Self*.

Zohar, The More exactly, *Sepher Ha-Zohar*, "The Book of Splendour" – the principal work of the **Kabbalah**. It is thought to have been written by the Spanish mystic **Moses de León** and first circulated from his home in Guadalajara, between 1280 and 1290. It includes commentaries on the **Torah**; a work titled *The Book of Concealment*; an account of the seven Heavenly Halls of God's chariot-throne (**Merkabah**); and a commentary on the Song of Songs.

Zombie Among **voodoo** practitioners, especially in Haiti, a corpse that has allegedly been brought back to life through magical **spells** of enchantment. The zombie is said to act like a robot, and can be employed by its master in menial tasks of labour, having only negligible intelligence and no will of its own. According to folk belief, if zombies eat salt they are awakened from their condition of being "living dead" and hasten back to their graveyards to bury themselves in the earth. Belief in zombies is also found in the Caribbean and parts of West Africa.

Zoroaster The Greek name for the Persian prophet and teacher **Zarathustra**.

Zoroastrianism The doctrines and teachings of **Zarathustra**, the Persian prophet known to the Greeks as Zoroaster.

Zoroastrians Followers of the prophet **Zarathustra** (**Zoroaster**). When Persia was conquered by the Arabs in 650, the majority of Zoroastrians fled to India and their descendants are now found mainly in the State of Bombay, where they number around 100,000. The Zoroastrians are now known as Parsees and they continue their practice of praying to the **sun** as a symbol of life, commencing each day with a fire-worshipping ceremony.

Zurvan Also Zervan. Persian god of time who was the father of both **Ahura Mazda** and **Angra Mainyu** – personifications of good and evil, respectively. In Persian **cosmology**, time was measured by the path of the **sun**, and this was symbolized on statues of Zurvan by a snake coiled around his body. Zurvan may derive from the Indian sky-god **Varuna**; he in turn contributed to the symbolism of the Basilidean high god **Abraxas**, who had serpentine coils instead of legs. Zurvan was known as Aion by the **Neoplatonists**. See also **Basilides; Gnostics.**

FURTHER READING

Abraham, L., *A Dictionary of Alchemical Imagery*, Cambridge University Press, Cambridge 1998

Achterberg, J. *Imagery in Healing*, Shambhala Publications, Boston 1985

Adler, M., *Drawing Down the Moon*, Beacon Press, Boston 1988

Alvarado, L., *Psychology, Astrology and Western Magic: Image and Myth in Self-Discovery*, Llewellyn, St. Paul, Minnesota 1991

Anderson, W.T., *The Upstart Spring: Esalen and the American Awakening*, Addison Wesley, Reading, Mass. 1983

Anthony, D., Ecker, B., and Wilber, K., *Spiritual Choices*, Paragon House, New York 1987

Argüelles, J. and M., *Mandala*, Shambhala Publications, Berkeley 1972

Ashcroft-Nowicki, D., *First Steps in Ritual*, Aquarian Press, Wellingborough 1982

Highways of the Mind: The Art and History of Pathworking, Aquarian Press, Wellingborough 1987

The Shining Paths: An Experiential Journey Through the Tree of Life, Aquarian Press, Wellingborough 1983

Barbour, I.G., *Myths, Models and Paradigms*, Harper & Row, New York 1976

Bardon, F., *The Practice of Magical Evocation*, Rudolph Pravica, Graz-Puntigam, Austria 1967

Bayless, R., *Apparitions and Survival of Death*, University Books, New York 1973

Bharati, A., *Light at the Center*, Ross-Erikson, Santa Barbara 1976

Blackmore, S., *Dying to Live: Science and the Near-Death Experience*, Grafton, London 1993

Bliss, S. (ed.), *The New Holistic Health Workbook*, Viking Penguin, New York 1985

Bolen, J.S., *Goddesses in Everywoman*, Harper & Row, New York 1985

Budapest, Z., *The Holy Book of Women's Mysteries*, Wingbow Press, Oakland, California 1989

Budge, E.A.Wallis, *The Egyptian Heaven and Hell*, Hopkinson, London 1925

Burckhardt, T., *Alchemy*, Penguin Books, Baltimore 1971

Campbell. J., *The Hero with a Thousand Faces*, Pantheon, New York 1949

The Inner Reaches of Outer Space: Metaphor as Myth and as Religion, Harper & Row, New York 1988

Myths to Live By, Viking Press, New York 1972; Souvenir Press, London, 1973

Capra, F., *The Tao of Physics*, Shambhala Publications, Boulder, Colorado 1975

The Turning Point, Wildwood House, London 1982

Uncommon Wisdom, Simon & Schuster, New York 1988

Castaneda, C., *The Teachings of Don Juan*, University of California Press, Berkeley 1968

Cavendish, R., *The Tarot*, Michael Joseph, London 1973

Christie-Murray, David, *Reincarnation: Ancient Beliefs and Modern Evidence*, Prism Press, Dorset 1985

Cranston, Sylvia, *Reincarnation: The Phoenix Fire Mystery*, Theosophical University Press, Pasadena, California 1994

Crowley, A., *Magick in Theory and Practice*, privately published, Paris 1929 (republished by Dover and Castle Books, New York, various editions)

Crowley, V., *Wicca: the Old Religion in the New Millennium*, Thorsons, London 1996

Dalai Lama, H.H., *My Land and My People*, Warner Books, New York 1997

Dalai Lama, H.H., with Jean-Claude Carrière, *Violence and Compassion*, Doubleday, New York 2001

Doore, G. (ed.), *What Survives? Contemporary Explorations of Life After Death*, Tarcher, Los Angeles 1990

Drury, N., *The Elements of Shamanism*, Element Books, Dorset 1989

Exploring the Labyrinth: Making Sense of the New Spirituality, Continuum, New York 1999

The Healing Power, Muller, London 1981

The History of Magic in the Modern Age, Constable, London 2000

Sacred Encounters, Watkins Publishing, London 2002

The Visionary Human, Element Books, Dorset 1991

Edinger, E., *Ego and Archetype*, Penguin, London 1973

Eliade, M., *Cosmos and History*, Harper & Row, New York 1959

The Sacred and The Profane, Harper & Row, New York 1961

Shamanism, Princeton University Press, New Jersey 1972

Yoga, Immortality and Freedom, Princeton University Press, New Jersey 1969

Ellison, A., *The Reality of the Paranormal*, Harrap, London 1988

Evans-Wentz, W.Y. (ed.), *The Tibetan Book of the Dead*, Oxford University Press, New York 1960

Farrar, J. and S., *Eight Sabbats for Witches*, Hale, London 1981

The Witches' Bible, Magickal Childe, New York 1985

The Witches' Goddess, Hale, London 1987

The Witches' Way, Hale, London 1984

Feinstein, D., and Krippner, S., *Personal Mythology*, Tarcher, Los Angeles 1988

Ferguson, D.S. (ed.), *New Age Spirituality*, Westminster/John Knox Press, Louisville, Kentucky 1993

Fortune, D., *The Mystical Qabalah*, Ernest Benn, London 1957

Furst, P.T. (ed.), *Flesh of the Gods*, Allen & Unwin, London 1972

Gettings, F., *Dictionary of Astrology*, Routledge & Kegan Paul, London 1985

Goldwag, E. (ed.), *Inner Balance*, Prentice-Hall, Englewood Cliffs, New Jersey 1979

Goleman, D. (ed.), *Consciousness: Brain, States of Awareness and Mysticism*, Harper & Row, New York 1979

The Meditative Mind, Tarcher, Los Angeles 1988

Gottlieb, R.S., *A New Creation: America's Contemporary Spiritual Voices*, Crossroad, New York 1990

Green, C., *Out-of-the-Body Experiences*, Ballantine, New York 1973

Greer, M.K., *Women of the Golden Dawn*, Park Street Press, Rochester, Vermont 1995

Grey, M., *Return from Death: An Exploration of the Near-Death Experience*, Arkana, London 1985

Grof, S. (ed.), *The Adventure of Self-Discovery*, State University of New York Press, Albany 1988

Ancient Wisdom, Modern Science, State University of New York Press, Albany 1984

Beyond the Brain, State University of New York Press, Albany 1985

Grof S., and Halifax J., *The Human Encounter with Death*, Dutton, New York 1979

Guiley, R.E., *Encyclopedia of Mystical and Paranormal Experience*, HarperCollins, New York 1991

Guirdham, Arthur, *The Cathars and Reincarnation*, Spearman, London 1970

Hagon, Z., *Channelling*, Prism Press, Dorset 1989

Halifax, J. (ed.), *Shamanic Voices*, Arkana, New York 1991

Harner, M., *The Jivaro*, University of California Press, Berkeley 1984

The Way of the Shaman, Harper & Row, San Francisco 1980

Heelas, P., *The New Age Movement*, Blackwell, Oxford 1996

Houston, J., *The Hero and the Goddess*, Ballantine, New York 1992

Howe, E., *The Magicians of the Golden Dawn*, Routledge & Kegan Paul, London 1972

Huxley, A., *The Doors of Perception / Heaven and Hell*, Penguin, London 1963

Moksha: Writings on Psychedelics and the Visionary Experience, Stonehill, New York 1977

The Perennial Philosophy, Chatto & Windus, London 1946

Inglis, Brian, *Natural and Supernatural*, Prism Press, Dorset 1992

The Paranormal, Granada, London 1985

Jordan, M., *Witches: An Encyclopedia of Paganism and Magic*, Kyle Cathie, London 1996

Jung, C.G., *Man and his Symbols*, Dell, New York 1968

Memories, Dreams, Reflections, Random House, New York 1961

Symbols of Transformation, Bollingen Foundation, New Jersey 1956

Kalweit, H., *Dreamtime and Inner Space*, Shambhala Publications, Boston 1988

Kaplan, A., *Meditation and Kabbalah*, Samuel Weiser Inc., New York 1982

Kaufmann, W., *Religions in Four Dimensions*, Readers Digest Press / T.Y. Crowell, New York 1976

Kelly, A., *Crafting the Art of Magic*, Llewellyn, St. Paul, Minnesota 1991

King, F. (ed.), *Astral Projection, Magic and Alchemy*, Spearman, London 1971

Tantra: The Way of Action, Destiny Books, Rochester, Vermont 1990

King, F., and Skinner, S., *Techniques of High Magic: A Manual of Self-Initiation*, C. W. Daniel, London 1976

Krishna, G., *Kundalini*, Robinson & Watkins, London 1971

Kübler-Ross, E., *Death: The Final Stage of Growth*, Prentice-Hall, Englewood Cliffs, New Jersey, 1975

On Life After Death, Celestial Arts, Berkeley, California 1991

Kuhn, T., *The Structure of Scientific Revolutions*, second edition, University of Chicago Press, Chicago 1970

Further Reading

Lehrman, F. (ed.), *The Sacred Landscape*, Celestial Arts, Berkeley, California 1988

Lewis, J.R. (ed.), *Magical Religion and Modern Witchcraft*, State University of New York Press, Albany, 1996

Lewis, J.R., and Melton, J.G., *Perspectives on the New Age*, State University Press of New York, Allbany 1992

Lilly, J., *The Centre of the Cyclone*, Calder & Boyars, London 1973

Simulations of God, Simon & Schuster, New York 1975

Lings, M., *Muhammad*, Allen & Unwin, London 1983

Lovelock, J., *Gaia: A New Look at Life on Earth*, Oxford University Press, London and New York 1979

Mackenzie, A., *Hauntings and Apparitions*, Paladin, London 1983

Mann, A.T. (ed.), *The Future of Astrology*, Unwin Hyman, London 1988

Maslow, A., *The Farther Reaches of Human Nature*, Viking, New York 1971

Masters, R., and Houston J., *The Varieties of Psychedelic Experience*, Holt Rinehart & Winston, New York 1966

Matt, D.C., *The Essential Kabbalah*, HarperCollins, New York 1995

Matthews, C. and J., *The Western Way*, Arkana, London 1994

May, R., *Cosmic Consciousness Revisited*, Element Books, Dorset 1993

Physicians of the Soul, Amity Press, Warwick, New York 1988

McDermot, V., *The Cult of the Seer in the Ancient Middle East*, University of California Press, Berkeley 1971

McKenna, T., *The Archaic Revival*, HarperCollins, San Francisco 1991

Metzner, R., *Maps of Consciousness*, Collier Macmillan, New York 1971

The Unfolding Self: Varieties of Transformative Experience, Origin Press, Novato, California 1998

Miller, S., *After Death: Mapping the Journey*, Simon & Schuster, New York 1997

Moody, R. *Life After Life*, Bantam Books, New York 1978

Mumford, J., *Ecstasy Through Tantra*, Llewellyn, St. Paul, Minnesota 1988

Murti, T.R.V., *The Central Philosophy of Buddhism*, Allen & Unwin, London 1972

Neihardt, J.G., *Black Elk Speaks*, Pocket Books, New York 1972

Oesterreich, T.K., *Possession: Demoniacal and Other*, University Books, New York 1966

Ornstein, R., *The Psychology of Consciousness*, Cape, London 1975

Radha, S., *Kundalini Yoga for the West*, Shambhala Publications, Boulder, Colorado 1981

Redgrove, H.S., *Alchemy: Ancient and Modern*, Rider, London 1922

Regardie, I. (ed.), *The Golden Dawn*, vols 1–4, Aries Press, Chicago 1937–40

The Middle Pillar, Aries Press, Chicago 1945

The Philosopher's Stone, Llewellyn, St. Paul, Minnesota 1970

The Tree of Life: A Study in Magic, Rider, London 1932

Rice, E., *Eastern Definitions*, Doubleday, New York 1978

Ring, K., *Heading Towards Omega*, Morrow, New York 1984

Life at Death: A Scientific Investigation of the Near-Death Experience, Coward McCann & Geoghegan, New York 1980

Rogo, D.S., *The Return from Silence: A Study of the Near-Death Experience*, Aquarian Press, Wellingborough 1989

The Search for Yesterday, Prentice-Hall, Englewood Cliffs, New Jersey 1985

Roszak, T., *Unfinished Animal*, Harper & Row, New York 1975

The Voice of the Earth, Simon & Schuster, New York 1992

Russell, P., *The Awakening Earth*, Routledge & Kegan Paul, London 1982

Scholem, G., *Major Trends in Jewish Mysticism*, Schocken, New York 1961

On the Mystical Shape of the Godhead, Schocken, New York 1997

Origins of the Kabbalah, Princeton University Press, New Jersey 1990

Schultes, R.E., Hofmann, A., and Ratsch, C., *Plants of the Gods* (revised edition), Inner Traditions International, Rochester, Vermont 2001

Seligmann, K., *Magic, Supernaturalism and Religion*, Pantheon, New York 1971

Shapiro, M., and Hendricks, R.A., *A Dictionary of Mythologies*, Granada, London 1981

Singer, J., *Seeing Through the Visible World*, HarperCollins, San Francisco 1990

Spangler, D, *Emergence: Rebirth of the Sacred*, Dell, New York 1984

Spence, L., *An Encyclopedia of Occultism*, Routledge, London 1920

Starhawk, *The Spiral Dance*, Harper & Row, New York 1979

Dreaming the Dark, Beacon Press, Boston 1982

Stevenson, I., *Twenty Cases Suggestive of Reincarnation*, University of Virginia Press, Charlottesville, Virginia 1995

Sutherland, C., *Transformed by the Light: Life After Near-Death Experiences*, Bantam Books, Sydney and New York 1992

Tart, C. (ed.), *Altered States of Consciousness*, Wiley, New York 1969

(ed.), *Transpersonal Psychologies*, Harper & Row, New York 1975

Valiente, D., *An ABC of Witchcraft, Past and Present*, Hale, London 1973

Witchcraft for Tomorrow, Hale, London 1978

Valle, R.S., and von Eckartsberg, R. (eds.), *The Metaphors of Consciousness*, Plenum Press, New York 1981

Voigt, A., and Drury, N., *Wisdom from the Earth: The Living Legacy of the Aboriginal Dreamtime*, Shambhala Publications, Boston 1998

Waite, A.E., *The Holy Kabbalah*, University Books, New York 1960

The Pictorial Key to the Tarot, Samuel Weiser Inc., New York 1973

Walsh, R.N., and Vaughan, F. (eds.) *Beyond Ego*, Tarcher, Los Angeles 1980

Wasson, R.G., *The Wondrous Mushroom*, McGraw-Hill, New York 1980

Watts, A., *The Joyous Cosmology*, Vintage Books, New York 1962

This is It and Other Essays on Zen and Spiritual Experience, Pantheon, New York 1960

Webb, J., *The Occult Establishment*, Richard Drew Publishing, Glasgow 1981

White, J. (ed.), *The Highest State of Consciousness*, Doubleday Anchor, New York 1972

Wilber, K., *A Brief History of Everything*, Gill & Macmillan, Dublin 1996

The Spectrum of Consciousness, Quest Books, Wheaton, Illinois 1977

Up from Eden, Doubleday Anchor, New York 1981

Woods, R. (ed.), *Understanding Mysticism*, Image Books / Doubleday, New York 1980

Zaleski, C., *Otherworld Journeys*, Oxford University Press, New York 1987

Zimmer, H., *Myths and Symbols of Indian Art and Civilization*, Harper & Row, New York 1962

Zohar, D., *The Quantum Self*, Flamingo / HarperCollins, London 1991

Zukav, G., *The Dancing Wu Li Masters: An Overview of the New Physics*, Morrow, New York 1979